Mission, Ministry, Order

MISSION, MINISTRY, ORDER

Reading the Tradition in the Present Context

David Noel Power, OMI

continuum

NEW YORK • LONDON

2008

The Continuum International Publishing Group Inc.
80 Maiden Lane, New York, NY 10038

The Continuum International Publishing Group Ltd
The Tower Building, 11 York Road, London SE1 7NX

www.continuumbooks.com

Copyright © 2008 by David Noel Power

Except as otherwise identified, the Scripture text is from the *New Revised Standard Version Bible,* copyright 1989, by the Division of Christian Education of the National Council of the Churches of Christ in the USA, and is used by permission. Quotes marked RSV are from the *Revised Standard Version Bible,* copyright 1946, 1952, 1971 by the Division of Christian Education of the National Council of the Churches of Christ in the USA; used by permission.

Printed in the United States of America

Library of Congress Cataloging-in-Publication Data

Power, David Noel.

Mission, ministry, order : reading the tradition in the present context / David Noel Power.
    p. cm.
Includes bibliographical references and index.
ISBN-13: 978-0-8264-2852-3 (hardcover : alk. paper)
ISBN-10: 0-8264-2852-5 (hardcover : alk. paper)
ISBN-13: 978-0-8264-2853-0 (pbk. : alk. paper)
ISBN-10: 0-8264-2853-3 (pbk. : alk. paper) 1. Mission of the church. 2. Catholic Church—Doctrines. 3. Church. 4. Theology, Doctrinal. I. Title.

BX1746.P63 2008
262'.02—dc22

2008017475

Contents

Acknowledgments

During my years of teaching first in Ireland and then in Rome, and since coming to the USA in 1977, I have had contact with students from many parts of the world and had occasion over the years to visit different and culturally diverse communities. Since 2000, I have spent time teaching in Tahiti, in Canada, in South Africa, and in San Antonio, Texas. This has helped to shape the perspective on the theology of ministry on which I began to work in doing doctoral studies at the time of the Second Vatican Council. In the meantime, interaction with members and scholars of several Christian Churches has been important. It is impossible to express sufficient gratitude to all those persons and communities that have influenced my research and thought. I would like to mention in particular the students at St. Joseph Theological Institute, Cedara, South Africa, whose liveliness was an inspiration during a period when I was working on the book and sojourned among them.

There are a few particular acknowledgments that I would like to make. I thank Bishop Fritz Lobinger, bishop emeritus of Aliwal, South Africa, for giving me time to speak with him and for telling me of some of his own research. I also thank Susan Rakoczy, Elizabeth Johnson, and Andrew Small, who looked at parts of the manuscript and offered comments.

I thank Frank Oveis, who took an early interest in the work and was instrumental in having it accepted by Continuum Publishing Company, as well as Gabriella Page-Fort, who guided it through the process of production.

I trust that the publisher's transposition from the U.K./Irish English in which I write into U.S. English will not disturb the reader. Regrettably, costs have made it impossible to include the listing of the selected bibliography (twenty-two pages in typescript) of the works cited in the course of the book. All bibliographical information however is available in the notes, and the index should be of help in locating the names of authors cited.

David N. Power, OMI
Washington, D.C.
March 31, 2008

Introduction

One Baptism, Many Gifts for Mission and Ministry

It hardly needs repeating that churches around the world have witnessed a growth in services and ministries of different sorts since the Second Vatican Council (1962–65), a growth marked by diversity in the ways in which local churches have embraced their mission. In giving shape and order to ministry, the life of the Church is now at a critical moment in the reception of the Council and in developing ecumenical communion. Since it was convened for pastoral purposes, its reception is to be gauged at the level of pastoral consequences. Theological insight can only assist this process, and both ministry itself and the theology of ministry are works in progress. What is apparent at this stage is that the theology of the sacrament of order cannot be treated apart from a comprehensive theology of ministry within ecclesial communities. This affects not only the inner life of the Catholic Church but also the ecumenical efforts and hopes that all the baptized, enriched by their diverse traditions, may be the one people of God, the one body of Christ. Questions about mission and ministry belong within conversation and cooperation between churches and ecclesial communities.

Literature on the topic exists in many languages and comes from many countries. European and North American churches may no longer impose their ideas and solutions across the world. While many ministries flourish, most churches report the insufficiency of ordained priests to assure a regular eucharistic celebration for all local communities. Dealing properly with this issue would mean recognizing that communities are themselves responsible for their mission and for the ministries this needs. Eucharist is, properly speaking, a living reality at the heart of a life from which it cannot be divorced by counting it primarily as ritual. If the life of a community is to find a center in the Eucharist, then each community needs its ordained minister. The encouragement of local responsibility for life and mission cannot be properly given without providing the possibility for the just Sunday celebration of the Eucharist through ministers who belong to the local church. In this regard, a noteworthy contribution is that of Bishop Fritz Lobinger of South Africa in his work entitled *Like His Sisters and Brothers*, which is rooted in the experience of pastoral leadership and is about ordaining those whom he calls *Viri Probati*.[1] What his book tells us is that many churches out of long experience already have good candidates, whose baptismal ministry and leadership have shown their readiness and competency. Only a prolongation, and indeed a rehabilitation, of medieval clerical culture prevents recognizing and affirming charisms already at work.

Ministries and other services have to be considered in the light of the Church's mission and how it is evolving. Although this book is about ministries and their ordering, it looks at them in terms of their service of the Church's mission. In that sense, the book titled *Love without Calculation: A Theological Reflection on Divine Kenosis* is prelude to this one, and especially part 2 of that work, "The Kenosis of the Church and Its Mission." At the heart of the matter is how the Christian community follows Christ and speaks his name before the world, in witness and in word.

The title of the book, *Mission, Ministry, Order*, reflects its perspective. The Church is given a mission and develops its ministry to correspond with how this mission is perceived. Ministries are charismatic in origin, arising from gifts of the Spirit, within the life of particular communities. As they take shape, the life of the Church needs to be given some order, for the sake of the particular church and for the sake of communion between churches. The sacrament of order has a history showing that its location is within the larger development of ecclesial life, which it serves, and that it is not an inflexible structure to be imposed nor itself the origin of ministries.

In relating ministry to mission, the distinction made by the Vatican Council in its Constitution on the Church (*Lumen gentium*, 1964) between responsibility for the sacred and responsibility for the secular helped up to a point in highlighting the charge of all the baptized to testify to and to promote the reign of God in all things. However, it cannot be pressed too far nor made an overarching theological principle. There is no visible separation between the two domains in this world. It is the believing community—in its entire membership and in all its works, liturgy included—that is sent on mission, sharing in the consecration of Jesus Christ. The testimony to God's grace and kingdom is that of a community that lives by the gospel of Christ and that corporately takes on the services of the needy and the promotion of the wisdom of the gospel in all things human and earthly.

While questions of Church order seemed to be often determined by the distinction between the ordained and the rest of the baptized under the papacy of John Paul II, he nevertheless articulated a number of factors about the Church's mission that are important in all considerations of ministry. In testifying to the gospel of Jesus Christ, Christians have to be attentive to what he liked to call the *areopagi* of evangelization, in relation to which the mission and ministries of the Church are being refocused (*Redemptoris missio* 37 [1990]). These he named as the world of communications, the world of scientific research, the world of culture, the field of international relations and dialogue, politics, and economics. In all of these fields, Christians have to learn to communicate and work with those who are not of the Christian faith, but at the same time they are inspired by Christ in the service they render. It is clear that in these areopagi, the laity are to the fore and have the most competence, but ordained and laity have to ponder together what promotes God's reign, following the wisdom of Christ to discern what is important for promoting a peaceful and genuine human community that embodies justice.

The subject of ministry is one that this author has visited a number of times, beginning with doctoral studies while Vatican II was in progress. The purpose here is to work within the horizon enunciated in an earlier book, *Gifts That Differ*, first published in 1980, and in a revised edition in 1985:

> Ministeriality is a quality of the church community as a unit or body, before it is a predicate of any of its members. The fundamental principle for an understanding and structuring of ministry is that the church is the sacrament of God's kingdom in the world, a living presence which must deal with temporal questions. How the church sees itself in relation to these questions determines the ministeriality of the community. . . . Today we have to look at the community's experience of Christ and of the kingdom in order to discern the charisms and ministries of the church.[2]

The relation to the Church's communion with Christ in his self-emptying, or kenosis, as key to its presence in the world has to be to the fore:

> Because of the Son's communion with the Father, the divinity itself is known in the self-emptying of Christ, in this commitment of the Son to the poor and oppressed. The church's communion with the Son, the Son's union with his Father and the mission which he receives from the Father are revealed in the church's commitment to the poor. It is this dedication to the service of the poor, and the church's identity as the household of the poor, which serve as the criteria for the discernment of ministries.[3]

Given the key role of symbolic expression recovering the primary symbols of ministry would mean recovering their creative possibility. In face of the continued cleavage between the ordained and the rest of the baptized, a reading of the symbols of *diakonia, exousia, charis, basileia,* and *kenōsis* affords a way of speaking of the Church itself in its witness to faith in Christ and Spirit, which is inclusive of all services. The life of the Church requires the sacrament of order, but it belongs within a harmonious working of all God's saving and renewing gifts of Word and Spirit. In fostering communion and mission, the community itself has priority rather than the exercise of power of the some over the many, something that cannot be camouflaged by calling it a service to the priesthood of all the faithful. Efforts to retrieve a distinctive clerical culture are not appropriate. The present moment is one of opportunity, a moment of *kairos*, which allows a more profound renewal of communal responsibility and mission.

In renewing the ministry of the Church today, we are not just engaged in looking for what have been traditional ministries or in looking for guarantees in the past for what is newly emerging.[4] We are more deeply engaged in a process of interpretation, not just theoretical but concrete. We need to be more conscious of just how we read and reason when we claim the sanction of Scripture, tradition, and magisterial teaching. Practical decision is inherent, not subsequent to, understanding. New solidarities are being built in face of suppression, disorder, exploitation, and victimization, whether these derive from the actions of social, cultural, and political forces, or from actions taken within ecclesial communities themselves. These solidarities are the place where mission and ministry are formed.

The philosopher Hans-Georg Gadamer pointed out that language is not purely descriptive of the apparent and tangible but that it shows or makes manifest our way of being as persons who live together, people who live in the world of creation, communally, and according to accepted social forms. There is a close association between what is said in the language traditions of a people or a culture, what they are, and what they have the power to do within the world or worlds in which they live. Language traditions—their composite of narrative, poetry, law, wisdom, drama, ritual, and the visual arts—are not static. They continually develop through their connection with action, through their encounter with other cultures, through their changing modes of seeing the universe, drawing on what went before and also showing new possibilities for being and action. Because of the centrality of the practical to human life, Gadamer pointed out that all interpretation and appropriation of a tradition comes to relief in practice, in what are taken as the conclusions about how to live, about what is right and wrong and responsible. After his great work *Truth and Method*, reflecting on the present conditions of the world, on what some have called its civil and cultural decay, and on what is often talked of as globalization—he noted the need for a renewed sense of solidarity. This now provides the context in which to grasp our fundamental being, to receive traditions and ponder right action. It is worth citing one paragraph of his book *Reason in the Age of Science* because it is so pertinent to a core sense of being that is necessary to reflection on the Church, its mission, and its ministries:

> Just as we, in our over stimulated process of progress of our technological civilization, are blind to stable, unchanging elements of our social life together, so it could be with the reawakening consciousness of solidarity of a humanity that slowly begins to know itself as humanity, for that means knowing that it belongs together for better or for worse and that it has to solve the problem of its life on this planet. And for that reason I believe in the rediscovery of solidarities that could enter into the future society of humanity.[5]

Some of the philosopher's reflections were prompted by the criticism that his view of language traditions and their power to develop through connections with reality and action was too optimistic. Language traditions and cultures can in fact be quite oppressive. Words and symbols are used to foster and protect ideologies and to maintain inequalities of order in society and community; they may also spell out false ideas of how humanity relates to earth and creation. Hence a whole range of literature has developed treating of the ideological uses of language, symbol, and ritual, whether in liberation philosophies and theologies, in postcolonial critiques of the development of power relations between peoples, in the works of feminism, or in writings about ecology. In the face of such critique, Gadamer's own intuition is precisely the need to develop a sensitivity to fundamental solidarities with those who suffer from the domination of others and with the things that suffer from a human technological domination. These are also matters that constantly surface in theological inquiry into the mission and ministry of the Church, especially in developing solidarity with the poor.

In face of the demands for being and action, there are inventive ways of speaking that are allied to renewal. This is important to Christian believers, who continue to look to the salvific event of Christ and hence to the language in which its meaning is expressed as their lodestone. Is it possible to formulate faith in Christ and the revelation of the Trinity in such a way as to inspire change in the mission and ministries of churches? It should be clear that we cannot hope to renew ministry by a simple or isolated appeal to what was done at any time or what has been said about order and the baptized priesthood of the holy people of Christ's body. It is the language of faith itself and the solidarities to which hope calls us that need to be at the heart of all considerations about what it is to serve and about what structures need to be socially formed in order for people to continue to live.

When ministries are treated one by one—whether this be episcopacy, deaconate, music ministry, justice ministry, ecclesial lay ministry, or something else—it is not always obvious how much structural change is needed for a true renewal of the Church's mission and ministries. Testimony of the life of a community, exercise of charisms in ministerial service, institutional or social structures, interact and change together. In the reception of Vatican II, what is at stake is not a matter of adding ministries, of changing the style of particular ministries, nor of improving cooperation and interchange. It is a matter of total renewal, involving how communities and Church government are structurally changed, even as the role of mission is given new shape, both practical and theological.

In the light of the above, this book has been planned to allow for the fact that theological reflection follows practical developments. First, there is an overview of how ministries have taken shape over the last fifty years, with particular attention to the ways in which ministry is affected by how churches see their mission and their presence in society. With this is related a treatment of how the theology of ministry developed to include the role of the laity, before, during, and after the Second Vatican Council. The second part of the book examines the tradition of the Church on ministry from the New Testament onward, seeing this in the light of current concerns. The third part of the book is in the nature of a theological reflection on the mission and ministry of our own time, in the process revisiting ideas about priesthood and representation. All of this is related more explicitly to how ministry today serves the life and mission of the kingdom, as in the light of the Spirit this is now understood, allowing also for how this may be hindered by residual or new ideologies.[6] There may be some overlapping and some repetitions in following the order outlined, but it seemed an appropriate way of getting at the issues involved.

The amount of writing on the topic is intimidating. There is no pretense in this book to being exhaustive nor to list all pertinent bibliography. Given the lapse of time between submission of the manuscript and publication, some may note certain unavoidable omissions. What is cited or listed is simply whatever has actually been consulted and found profitable. Some may find that important books or articles have not been noted. If so, they will know how to complement or correct what I have written.

PART 1

Church Mission and Ministry in Present Context

Introduction

This work is concerned with the relation between the Church's ministry and its mission and with the ordering of ministries within communities. It is the present state of the Church, with its many questions about mission and about ministry, that gives the context within which tradition is read. While some works focus more directly on changing concepts of mission, this one focuses on how ministry is seen in the light of mission. Doing contextual theology usually means the relation of theological thought to social and cultural realities, but it must include historical contexts and even the particular context of ecclesial life within which research and reflection take place. The first part of the book is intended to present the current historical context. Theology has developed in the light of practice, and a variety of ecclesial situations challenge churches to a creative reading of Scripture and ecclesiastical writings, as well as of the history of mission, ministry, and order in different epochs.

Since the Second Vatican Council, the situation has continued to change through a process of reception. Though the Council itself is key to later changes, the book opens with a survey of developments around the world since then in the conception of mission, in the emergence of ministries, and in community ordering. One might speak of what comes to light as a varied reception and implementation of the Council, in different parts of the world. A readily accessible way in which to get a picture of the situation is to trace the story of individual churches or regional communions through reading official documents of episcopal bodies. These do not give the full story, but they are a good indicator. Both the Council and these implementations have their antecedents over a period of time, antecedents that help to explain it and its aftermath. It is helpful then to see what was developing in the decades immediately preceding the Council, or what created the living and theological milieu in which the Council was convened. In all of this, I intend to keep in mind the relation between ministry and mission, for it is in a recovery and adaptation of a sense of mission that ministries develop and are ordered. Chapters 1 and 2 trace developments in mission and ministry since Vatican II. Chapter 3 looks at the period immediately preceding the Council in the interest of showing how the Council and the process of change that followed it were incited by issues that had already been raised before it was convoked. Chapter 4 is a reading of some of the conciliar documents in the light of their reception.

If one were to follow another logic, one would put the first chapter in the third place; putting it first gives us a living context from which to look back, showing how the historical event and the documents of Vatican II are now read and implemented. It is always possible for a reader to reverse the order if this seems desirable. Reading the chapters in the sequence written is not really necessary. Whichever sequence is followed, the three periods intersect.

1

Mission and Ministry since Vatican II (A)

Latin America, Asia, Africa

A theology of ministry has to be developed in relation to the life of the Church today around the globe. Changes are taking place in the ways of ministry and in relations between the ordained and the communities to which they belong. The resources of tradition are read in this context, discerning signs in the present that point to the movement of the Spirit and fidelity to the gospel, with a new awareness of diversity. Though each local church develops it own particular characteristics, due to what is called globalization what is happening in one church affects others. An overarching vision of mission and ministry derives from the communion that exists, in theory and in practice, between churches around the world, in all countries and in all confessions. Communities of faith look at the world in which they live and conceive and carry out the mission that comes to them from Jesus Christ and his Spirit. It is in relation to this sense of mission that changes are coming about, not only in how things are done but also in the structures of liturgy, government, and administration, however hesitant these may be. With recognition of differences in the relation of Church to history, culture, and society, the development and theology of mission and ministry might well become more local, more centered in churches around the world and not in Rome, whose role too has to change even as churches seek to realize a universal ecclesial communion.

In an article in the journal *Cristianesimo nella storia*, Giuseppe Alberigo, editor of the five-volume history of the Second Vatican Council, asks why the great promise of this Council does not seem to have been fulfilled and may indeed be jeopardized for any foreseeable future.[1] He answers that with the doctrinal and spiritual flowering that was crystallized in the event of the Council, there came no parallel structural change in the way the Church is governed. There was no cross-fertilization between ecclesiological and spiritual movements on the one hand, and modernization of canonical structures on the other. His immediate interest is in the relation between Rome and local churches, but his diagnosis applies to all that has to do with developments in ecclesial mission and ministry. Much that is important has occurred, but some still often think and act in terms of an institutional model of Church and ministry.

Others[2] also opine that the Council's teaching on the Church has not been translated into the corresponding canonical provisions. When canonical rigidity dominates practice, this can occasion theological regression, thought justifying the status quo rather than inspiring new action and new ways of being Church. Admitting the importance of structural change, attention needs to be given to the ways in which an understanding of mission and ministry is being articulated through liturgy, catechesis, and theology. This articulation has to be inclusive and organic rather than built on polarities, such as sacred/secular, clergy/laity, ordained/baptized, women/men. It draws on all ecclesial traditions, east and west, north and south. If the thinking is not done and the reading of traditions does not become more critical, ecclesial development is hindered since it is left only with the paradigms that prevailed in the centuries following the Protestant and Catholic Reformations of the sixteenth century.

In the Catholic Church in these early years of the third millennium, a particular way of seeing the principle of continuity at times dominates the reception of Vatican II. Positions are pursued that try to retrieve the immediate past, the life of the Church between Trent and Vatican II, giving this a somewhat normative role and guiding the return to sources along these lines. Other possibilities and aspirations are still alive. To retrieve them, more attention to the catholic diversity of local churches is advisable, for this allows us to see the Church of Christ as a communion of local churches rather than as a universal Church, of which local communities are a "portion."[3] With this in view, this chapter presents a survey of some telling developments in local churches around the world. Noteworthy is how the sense of mission and the understanding of ministry work hand in hand. Structural changes are at least inaugurated if not fully developed. The survey is not exhaustive,[4] but with some cautions it is sufficient to show how living context is important in shaping mission and ministry, the connection between these two, and what new theological questions are raised about ministry, priesthood, and order.

It is easier to trace orientations and developments in official episcopal documents than it is to know what is happening in practice. There usually seems to be a gap between episcopal policies and exhortations and the realities of Church action. Nonetheless, these official statements give enough evidence to show what is involved in trying to renew the reality and the thinking about Church, mission, and ministry, and they provide most of the material in this chapter and the next.

Paul VI and Ministries

As preface to any discussion of developments around the world, a word needs to be said about the positions taken and decreed by Paul VI in the postconciliar (1972) document titled *Ministeria quaedam* (1972).[5] Whatever its presently perceived shortcomings, it gave an impetus to discussion and change in different countries.

As part of the renewal of ecclesial life begun at Vatican II, a commission had been appointed to look into the question of the minor orders, which for centuries were given as steps on the way to priestly ordination but had their origins in ministries assigned to members of the faithful. When Pope Paul VI eventually made official pronouncement on these offices, along with *Ministeria quaedam (MQ)* he issued a document on the permanent deaconate: *Ad pascendum* (1972),[6] which promulgated regulations to cover the restoration of the deaconate as a permanent order, to which married men could be admitted as well as single. These two documents signal an initial movement toward a restructuring of office and ministry in the Catholic Church.

In *MQ*, Paul VI suppressed all use of the word "order" in connection with the ministries formerly designated as minor orders. Of these ministries, he decreed that those of exorcist and porter should be suppressed, at least as general ministries for the whole Church, while those of lector and acolyte should be retained. In keeping these two ministries, he did not wish them to be in any way reserved to clerics or connected with the clerical state. Nor did he wish them to be viewed as offices conferring a special status on those inducted into them. These two ministries, the Pope suggests, are important liturgical functions in the life of a Christian community. They are not a share in the priesthood of order, but are exercised by lay people in virtue of their share in Christ's priesthood through baptism. Because of their importance, they need to be exercised by chosen persons and merit a special installation or institution. This, however, is not to be confused with ordination, which is a name to be reserved for the conferring of episcopacy, presbyterate, and deaconate. All of this, the Pope states, is closer to the truth and more in keeping with the contemporary mind than were the former canonical and liturgical prescriptions on minor orders. He does, however, maintain one restriction from an earlier tradition: the exclusion of women from these offices.

The office of lector and that of acolyte are henceforth the only two liturgical offices outside the sacrament of order that have a canonical status and a rite of installation common to all parts of the Latin Church. This does not mean that they are the only liturgical offices to which people can be named and into which they can be inducted by an official blessing. The Pope states, "Besides the offices common to the Latin Church, there is nothing to prevent episcopal conferences from requesting others of the Apostolic See, if they judge the establishment of such offices in their region to be necessary or very useful." Among such possible offices, he mentions those of porters, exorcists, catechists, and the promotion of works of charity.

With the document in its hands, the Roman Congregation for Divine Worship published the rites of blessing for installation into the ministries of acolyte and lector. The position on lay ministries, however, did not remain stable for long. For reasons known only to those sufficiently acquainted with the intricacies of Vatican administration, another Sacred Congregation had to have its stake in the matter. In January 1973, the Congregation for the Discipline of Sacraments issued the instruction *Immensae caritatis* on facilitating the distribution and reception of the sacrament of the Eucharist.[7] This instruction was in fact a follow-up on a decree, *Fidei custos*,[8] which had been sent to local bishops in 1969, about matters related to Holy communion. Among other things, this instruction touched on the question of eucharistic ministry. It laid down that local ordinaries may designate, or permit pastors to designate, some men and women as extraordinary ministers of communion within the confines of their own jurisdiction. These persons are to exercise their ministry by way of complement to that of priests, deacons, acolytes, and lectors. The provision for extraordinary ministers is intended to make the distribution of communion easier in large assemblies, to make communion to the sick more common, and to make it possible for all the faithful to receive communion even when ordinary ministers are not available. The persons designated for this ministry may be commissioned by a special blessing, if the bishops see fit.

Prescriptions about the functions of the laity in the liturgy are supported by some doctrinal or theological reasons. Paul VI invokes two principles of the Council's constitution on the liturgy. The first is the general principle that calls for full and active participation of all the faithful in the Church's worship. The second requires an apt distribution of functions and ministries in the assembly. In changing the rules about minor orders and in describing the roles of the acolyte and the lector, the Pope intends to implement these principles. Theologically, therefore, the two ministries are rooted in that priesthood of which the first letter of Peter speaks when it names the Christian people "a chosen race, a royal priesthood, a consecrated nation, a people set apart" (1 Pet 2:9). In other words, these ministries are a way of realizing the share in Christ's priestly office that the people receive through the sacraments of initiation. They also imply responsibilities outside the assembly, more specifically in relation to scriptural instruction, liturgical instruction, and care of the sick.

It is evident that Paul VI did not think of lay ministry uniquely in terms of liturgy. For example, in his postsynodal exhortation *Evangelii nuntiandi* of 1975 there is a broad vision of lay participation in the Church's ministries. The whole Church is missionary, and the laity share in its mission in virtue of the sacraments of initiation. The point the Pope emphasizes above all else is the special importance of the Christian laity's presence in the evolution of temporal affairs, for in this way the gospel can become a leaven in society. The practice of forming basic Christian communities on some continents showed that mission and formation of a greater sense of community go together, and this results in a greater diversification of ministries in the building up of the Christian people. In face of such developments, Paul VI offers the following reflection:

> These ministries, apparently new but closely tied up with the church's living experience down the centuries—such as catechists, directors of prayer and chant, Christians devoted to the service of God's Word or to assisting their brethren in need, the heads of small communities, or other persons charged with the responsibility of apostolic movements—these ministries are valuable for the

establishment, life and growth of the church, and for her capacity to influence her surroundings and to reach those who are remote from her.[9]

The revised Code of Canon Law, issued in 1983, states some norms about lay participation in liturgical ministry.[10] Recalling the possibility of promoting men to the offices of acolyte and reader, it allows for the temporary deputation of any lay person to fulfill the role of reader, commentator, cantor, or other minister necessary to the liturgy as foreseen by law. It also allows that any lay person, when the necessary ministers are wanting and where the needs of the Church demand it, may be called upon to exercise the ministry of the Word, preside over liturgical worship, confer baptism, and distribute holy communion. This but gives formal recognition to the established practice whereby in many countries Sunday services had begun to be conducted under the presidency of a lay person, and whereby baptisms were celebrated likewise by lay persons. In the appropriate place, the code also mentions that where ordained ministers are unavailable, lay persons may be delegated to officiate at marriages, but no mention is made of having lay persons preside at funeral liturgies. There is no exclusion of women from the services mentioned in these canons.

Against this background of positions taken by the Pope and the central government of the Catholic Church, developments in ministries around the world can be examined. The space for laity in ministry and in general the restructuring of Church order are largely prompted by a developing vision of the Church's mission and of its witness to the gospel.

Latin America: CELAM and the Church in Brazil

In this part of the chapter, we first take notice of the proceedings that engaged the whole Latin American continent. Because of its important role and distinctive perceptions, specific attention is then given to the church of Brazil.

At the CELAM (conference of Latin American bishops)[11] conferences held in Medellín and Puebla, the churches of Latin America had as principal task to redefine the mission of the Church in the light of the documents of the Second Vatican Council. It was at Medellín that CELAM made explicit its fundamental option for the poor and saw its mission in the service of the gospel and of God's kingdom in this light.

In its final report,[12] the meeting of the churches at Puebla spoke of the continued mission of the Church to preach the gospel or to evangelize. It took as its leitmotif the "evangelization of culture." Culture embraces the whole life of a people. It is the "whole web of values that inspire them and of disvalues that debilitate them; insofar as they are shared in common by all the members, they bring them together on the basis of a 'collective consciousness.'"[13] Since these values do not exist in the abstract, culture embodies all public forms of expression, inclusive of customs, languages, societal institutions, and structures. In a particular way, Puebla acknowledged popular religiosity as a religious and cultural phenomenon by which people themselves, often the poor and underesteemed, express their lives, their hopes, their faith. Influenced in this by the postsynodal exhortation of Paul VI,

Evangelii nuntiandi, the assembly inserted the promotion of justice and human development into the promotion of God's reign on earth, which is served by the mission of the Church. This cannot be done, however, without attending to the quality and practice of religion and all that is afoot in the modern changes of life in society and to the increasing influence of secularism.

Since evangelization means pervading culture at every level and in every form of expression, this meant working out the role of the laity in the life and mission of the Church, in collaboration with bishops and priests. At Puebla, both *Evangelii nuntiandi* (*EN*) and *Ministeria quaedam* were mentioned as pertinent texts to be considered in incorporating all the baptized into the mission and into the ministry of the Church. *EN* was of more basic importance since it included the development of peoples in the missionary purpose of the Church and was sensitive to the forms and meaning of popular religious practices.

The bishops at all three CELAM conferences of Medellín, Puebla, and Santo Domingo gave special place to the laity's mission in evangelizing the temporal order. It is primarily by acting out their mission in the secular sphere that the laity realize their baptismal dignity and their communion in the threefold office of Christ. Underlining this point, the Puebla report deplored the almost total absence of Christian influence in the public sector, whether in social development, politics, education, or cultural expression. At the same time, it noted that the baptized could not assume this role unless they were grounded in the faith and participated in a vibrant ecclesial life. For this reason, in conjunction with the promotion of the mission of the laity, the text acknowledged the importance of existing basic ecclesial communities.[14] On their part, therefore, bishops and priests needed to learn how to work with the laity and with these communities in the exercise of their own calling.

The emergence of basic ecclesial communities provides a key to understanding developments of ministry in the Latin American historical context. These were small communities of committed Christians who learned how to read the signs of the times, listen to the gospel in the context of their human reality, and work out together how to develop a life in a communion of faith, but also in a communion of apostolic commitment. Calling for a new evangelization that was overdue on the Latin American continent, Medellín looked to them as the "basic cell of the Church," in keeping with the ecclesial metaphor of the body of Christ. By the time of the Puebla conference, controversy had grown up around these communities and the theological expression given them in theologies of liberation. Some, especially in urban areas, seemed to a number of Church leaders to have been caught up into ideological movements that owed too much to Marxism and left-wing politics. In developing this orientation, they appeared to be in contestation of episcopal authority. The Puebla conference[15] on the whole wanted to continue to take a positive attitude to this communitarian development in the Church, but nonetheless desired to safeguard the reality from so-called popular churches and from ideologies. Hence the final report was careful to define what it meant by this phenomenon and spoke of how the inner life of communities should be developed and how they were to relate to priestly and episcopal leaders. It also gave some precise rulings about appointment to office and ministry, which it saw as a step beyond engagement in mission and evangelization proper to all Christians because of their role as believers in the secular world.

The Puebla report shows that the emergence and recognition of small ecclesial communities is in line with the preferential option for the poor, since they are largely made up of the poor and through them the poor themselves take their life in Church and in society in hand. Their members receive varied charisms to serve the life of the Church, its reflection on the Word, its education of its young, its incorporation of new members, its leadership in prayer, its leadership in social action in helping the poor in society (641). Precisely because they represent a lay movement, they are described as a valid and worthwhile point of departure for building up a new society, the "civilization of love" (642).

What are called lay ministries (804–5), which it is stressed have to include women, occur in an organized form both within basic communities and in the movements of the lay apostolate. Given a profusion of charisms or gifts for the service of the Church, an activity is called a ministry in a more precise sense when it is given in some official form, through some kind of conferral. The ministries that may be conferred on lay persons in a stable way are named as "those services that relate to truly important aspects of ecclesial life," and that deal with the Word of God, the liturgy, and the direction of the community. All of these are, however, marked by the reality of lay involvement in bettering and serving the presence of God's kingdom and the evangelization of secular reality. They bring a special contribution to the mission of the Church precisely because they carry the insights and engagements of lay people that are peculiar to them. These ministries are not a substitution for the absence of the ordained, nor do they take on any of the characteristics of the life and ministry of the ordained. Those holding such ministries work with the ordained, alongside them and sharing in their own way a common responsibility.

By the time of the Santo Domingo conference,[16] the controversy over communities at the base had grown, and the desire of many bishops and of Roman authorities to include them in Church structures and to exercise more control over them was greater. Hence, while their human dimensions were affirmed and their role in Church life acknowledged, they were described as "cells of the parish," making it clear that they were to be integrated into parish and diocesan structures.[17]

Alongside this role of small communities in relation to the whole, developments in Latin American also saw the emergence of organized, nonterritorial, lay movements. On the one hand, these were often praised because they were clearly related to the place of the laity in the secular sphere, because of their ability to organize action on a supradiocesan level, and because of their care in giving a proper apostolic formation to their members. On the other hand, at times they too seemed to escape diocesan and parish control, and hence in the eyes of the episcopal conferences of Puebla and Santo Domingo, they needed to be more carefully related to episcopal leadership and to the life of parishes. Among other counsels, their members were admonished not to see their own activities outside the context of parish life and commitment.

Aparecida

CELAM held a fifth general assembly at Aparecida, Brazil, in 2007. The title for the conference and the preparatory document, published in March 2007, was "Discípulos y misioneros de Jesucristo, para que nuestros pueblos en Él tengan vida."[18] A critique of this preparatory document indicates some withdrawal from the positions taken by previous conferences.[19] It is rightly concerned with the quality of ecclesial community, with its witness, missionary orientation, and its attachment to Jesus Christ as the Son of God, sent into the world for its redemption. However, it is written largely without reference to Medellín, Puebla, and Santo Domingo, or without the attempt to relate its concerns to theirs. Most noteworthy is the absence of the imagery and concept of the kingdom of God at work in the world and of the Church's service in promoting this reign. There is no mention of the poor and of the nature of the Church as the Church of the Poor, except in the sense that the poor are to be the beneficiaries of the Church's option to struggle for justice for them and for their human as well as spiritual development.

There is little offered by way of a reading of the signs of the times in a biblical sense, signs that include the continuing deterioration of the world of the poor, the "laicity" of Latin American states, and the process of globalization. These are simply taken to be negative indicators, viewed as out of harmony with the transcendental and with a gospel that points primarily to this. The document treats of the relationship to Jesus Christ as though it were direct and immediate, or one fostered by Scripture, sacrament, and devotion, to the neglect of the human context and of the historical and cultural mediations of this encounter with Christ.

A November 2006 notification of the Congregation for the Doctrine of the Faith (CDF) on the works of Jon Sobrino[20] is connected with the preparation of this conference. Though it is professedly about the errors and dangers of what he says about the divinity of Christ, the prelude to the document shows a concern with how the Church relates to the world of the poor, as the Church of the Poor. In commenting on the preparation for Aparecida, Sobrino and others had expressed the hope that the conference would follow in the line of Medellín, Puebla, and San Domingo in its commitment to the poor and its engagement with them in their suffering and in their hopes. He called for an interpretation of the image of the Church of the Poor which would proclaim that "the poor are the inspiring principle of the Church and not only the beneficiaries of its option for the poor."[21] A true configuration to Christ means a sharing with the poor in their real poverty, in diverse and analogous ways, for only thus do we know what we can know of him, what we are permitted to hope for, what we can do, and what we can celebrate.

In its comment on the way Sobrino sees the option for the poor, the CDF accuses him of adopting a false principle for the interpretation of the gospel. Affirming its admiration for his commitment to the poor, it states that the poor have no special status when it comes to the transmission of the faith. This can be known only through fidelity to the transmission of the one apostolic tradition. In this the Congregation seems to cut off any such debate at Aparecida—but to appeal to the apostolic tradition is to beg the question. It is an understanding of this tradition that Sobrino is seeking. He believes that Christ is known through the knowledge we have of his presence among the poor, in solidarity with their suffering and their hopes.

The concluding document of the conference was published quite soon after the end of the meeting and was approved for publication by the Holy See.[22] In line with the preparatory document and following on the orientation given by Pope Benedict XVI in his opening address, the text adopts a largely doctrinal approach.[23] In face of the ills of society and the reduced influence of the Church over matters of poverty, justice, marriage, and social life, as well as in face of the movement of many Catholics to evangelical communities, the assembly chose to reinforce the institutional image of the Church and the continuity of dogmatic teaching concerning Jesus Christ.

Considering the primary work of the Church to be that of evangelization, making known Jesus Christ and his gospel, the concluding document, as does the preparatory one, stresses that to be missionaries Christians need to be disciples. Opting for the formula that Jesus Christ is the way, the truth, and the life, CELAM teaches that in him humanity is offered the true freedom of the children of God, and that it is within that optic that the option for the poor is to be pursued. There is no clear christological doctrine in either document, that is to say no clear presentation of the figure of Jesus Christ other than in traditional formulas and other than to say how he shows his disciples the way of loving service. Recalling how the people of the continent have always followed Christ, the prelude to the final document evokes the practices of popular piety that show the people's love for the suffering Christ and the God of compassion, who offers pardon and reconciliation. In this context it mentions the figure of the Virgin of Guadalupe (7). Later, in speaking of Christ as the way, the truth, and the life (136–42), it puts forward his commandment and example of love and service as the way to follow.

Opting anew for the mission to the poor, the bishops stressed their own teaching role in speaking to society and in guiding the faithful in the work and witness of their mission in the secular and temporal order. Structurally, the accent is placed on the diocese and on the parish, which is defined as a community of communities, in order to make place for the work of small Christian communities and of the new lay movements that have taken on new vigor in recent decades. It is said that in such communities it is possible to build a sense of communion and to foster the hearing of the Word of God.

In tension, however, with the more formal and doctrinal approach of the document as a whole, there are the elements of continuity with Medellín and Puebla. The bishops still espouse the work of base communities and the pastoral method of "see, judge, act," whereby hearing the gospel is wed with reading the signs of the times and the concrete reality of people's lives. They also address the "structures of sin" within society and reinforce the need to find ways for encouraging the participation of all in the life and mission of the Church, though this does have to be within the basic diocesan and parochial ecclesial structure. Even though the teaching on Christ is traditionally doctrinal, room is made for looking to him for the inspiration of the option for the poor.

The Church in Brazil

To have a more concrete and specific idea of how ministries developed, we will give special attention to the life of the church in Brazil up to the convocation of Aparecida.[24] In the church of Brazil, as in other Latin American churches, the formation and organization of *comunidades ecclesiais de base* (CEB), or basic ecclesial communities (BEC), has played a significant role in determining a sense of Church, a sense of mission, and a development of ministries. The term is not without some fluidity, since it may mean a group of no more than ten, but a document of the permanent council of the Conference of Brazilian Bishops, issued in 1982,[25] uses CEB to speak of a grouping of small groups, intended to give human dimensions to the experience of being Church. The document says that a CEB is formed by families, adults, and youth, in a tight interpersonal relationship of faith. These people enjoy solidarity and a common commitment, and together they listen to the Word of God, organize their apostolate and community endeavors, and celebrate the Eucharist. In this way, they can be seen as cells of the greater community, which is the parish or diocese. Education is addressed to the needs and capacities of the people concerned. This involves what is called conscientization to their situation as a people politically, economically, and even religiously exploited, along with development of the ability to organize internally, and a pondering of the address of the gospel to the poor. In the words used by some theologians, the people were enabled to form a sense of themselves as agents of their own history, and indeed as being themselves agents in the Church and in the mission of the Church in society.

The document noted that this phenomenon is a practical implementation of what the Vatican Council projected when it spoke of the Church as the people of God, as a communion in which "to each is given the manifestation of the Spirit for the common good" (1 Cor 12:7). It is a concrete endeavor to live the life of the Church as a sacrament, sign, and instrument of profound union with God and of the unity of the human race. The assumption of an active role of all the baptized is a key characteristic. This is rooted in the sacraments of baptism and confirmation and entails an active collaboration with the ministry of the ordained. The ordained in turn have to find their true place at the heart of such common life and to see the mission of the Church as a work of collaboration, grasping their own role in relation to this reality. The bishops observe that progress in this style of living as Church has been possible because these communities possess an integral vision of history and of God's action in the world, whereby the story of humanity and the story of salvation are interconnected. It is this integral vision that has led base communities, and indeed the whole church of Brazil, to commit themselves to the quest for justice and the liberation of the poor.

As to the inner force of these cells of the greater Church, the document points first to their cultural integration into the traditions and the past of the Brazilian people, in its very heterogeneity and variety of origins and cultures, and then to the way in which their entire life is centered in prayer and especially in the common reading of the Word of God. Indeed, common prayer is fundamentally a listening to this Word and a discernment of the movements of the grace of the Spirit in daily life, especially in the midst of human vulnerability and weakness, where hope is shared. It is a common prayer, where every voice is heard, unhindered by class distinctions, whether social or ecclesiastical. It is a prayer in which the poor are present and active, with their own tradition formed by popular religiosity and native religious expression. It is a prayer which lifts the common people out of a sense of subjection and powerlessness, seeing themselves as one with Christ, children of the Father, and bearers of the gifts of the Spirit.

Within this ecclesial growth, new ministries took shape and old ministries were redefined. Initiation of candidates for baptism, or a more simple initiation of those already baptized wishing to be aggregated to the community, was important both to the activation of the life of faith and to the emergence of ministries. Decisions affecting the life of the community and its apostolate are rooted in the community's shared life and sense of shared responsibility and personal initiatives occur in this context. It is in this communion that charisms and ministries have their roots. Choice, discernment and training, are seen as the responsibility of the whole. A whole new range of ministries thus came to take shape and to be named. These include leadership in the tasks needed to guide the study of the Word, assemblies of prayer, community welfare, social action, health care and the struggle for justice. Solidarity with the poor, the suffering, and the weak of society has to be formed in prayer and expressed in action. The interests of those who are more engaged in ministries of Word and prayer are in no way different from the interests of those engaged in community and social action. An integrated view of Christian life, of prayer, of worship, of mission, and of social apostolate is vital and is the responsibility of the community as a whole. Within this ecclesial movement, the ordained are called upon to reshape their relation to communities, their own sense of ministry, and indeed their own communion with Father, Son, and Spirit. Even such terms as representing Christ, or acting in the person of Christ, though traditional, have to be rethought in relation to the active and common life of all the baptized forming together one community and one communion.

Subsequent to the publication of this document, which takes stock of development in the life of the Church, the churches of Latin America passed through the travail of Rome's criticism and at times harsh action against bishops, theologians, and people. The movement did not however die, being of the Spirit, but it did mature through the process of this trial. To give further guidance, in 1999 the CNBB (Conference of Brazilian Bishops) in its 37th General Assembly approved and promulgated a document on the mission and ministries of lay Christians, men and women, entitled *Missão e ministérios dos cristãos leigos e leigas.*[26] This document looks back on the experience of the previous decades and gives a careful theological and pastoral formulation of this mission and its ministries. Its preamble points out that new things have come to light and need to be taken into account.

First, there are developments and changes in the involvement of lay Christians, women and men, in the service of God's kingdom in the world and in society. There is the contribution that Christian communities, and in particular basic communities, have made to promoting the Church's mission to the care of the poor and suffering, to the promotion of justice and peace in society. In this service of small communities, however, it has been necessary to guard against a tendency to clericalize lay ministry, treating it perhaps as a delegation of responsibilities of the ordained or highlighting distinctions between lay persons in a local church. Alongside this, there has been the growth of lay movements that have a more universal outreach and membership, as well as the increase of parish services and involvement. There is now a need to coordinate these activities.

Second, there is a more-ample vision of the mission of the Church that embraces attention to culture and inculturation of the gospel, inclusive of attention to the significance of popular religiosity and to traditional religions. There is a need for dialogue with other churches and with religious movements among the people. What the document suggests is that these new interests ought not to be seen alongside the concern with social, political, and economic issues. The Church, through all its members and its ministries, has to develop its mission in a way that allows all these factors to belong together in the life of a people.

In face of practical realities and of magisterial and theological theories and distinctions, the document adopts an approach to mission and ministries that is rooted in the reality of the Church as a living communion and community. For both the inner life of the Church and for its role in the world, the fundamental idea is that the Church in its entirety and being is ministerial and missionary. When the mission of the Church is defined as service to the kingdom of God in the world, and when this is seen as the responsibility of the community as such and so the responsibility of all, then it is possible to use some distinctions that have become common in a way that pursues relationality rather than separation or division.

Though *Lumen gentium* (1964) distinguished the participation of Christians in the threefold office of Christ as priest, prophet, and king, this does not mean that there is a division of members based on the proportion of their share in one or other of these offices. Rather, it means that the community as such, and then each of its members, shares in a complete and integrated way in each of these offices. Being a priestly people, living by Christ's own mission and in the power of the Spirit, has to mean being a prophetic witness to the gospel in the world. It likewise means acting by the truth of this kingship, serving the needs of humanity, in a special solidarity with the suffering, so as to dominate the forces of evil in God's name and integrate the whole of created reality into the economy of Christ's redemptive action. Being a prophetic and royal priesthood means worshipping God in Christ's liturgy, not as an action apart but as one that includes the concerns of the total mission. For that reason, discernment of actions and judgments in the light of God's Word has to be a part of the worship of communities, however this is to be regulated.

The document addresses the distinction between the sacred function of the ordained and the secular function of the baptized laity in a comparable manner. It is because they function in the secular world, but in a prophetic, priestly, and royal, or in an evangelical way that they may be said to have a mission of a secular order. Secularity does not define the mission but rather the field of witness and service. The distinction between service *ad intra* and service *ad extra* employed by the Vatican Council has to be seen in the same way. The Church as people and as a community has to envisage both its building up as a communion of faith and evangelical life and its service of bringing the gospel to society. There is no need for a sharp distinction between liturgical and other ministries, since all ministries find their place in a people that is sacerdotal, royal, and prophetic. All three qualities find their proper symbolic and living expression and resource in the Church's worship. Functions may differ, but not concerns and interests, which have to be shared in a communion of life.

This approach qualifies and sets in context the distinction between hierarchy and laity (2.3), which is deemed insufficient to the reality of the Church and its shared responsibility. Ordained ministry is service to the community but is situated within the community and acts in harmony with other members of the community. It is within the reality of a living Church and of a shared mission, animated by the Spirit, that ordained ministry finds its due place, both theologically and practically. If the ordained ministers are to serve the unity of the Church and fidelity in life and mission to its apostolic foundation, then their call has to flow from the reality of a lived communion and has to be charismatic to its roots, as well as sacramentally affirmed and conferred.

Section 2.2 of the document tries to sort out some terms in the light of this integral vision of the Church's life and mission, not simply in a theological but also in a practical fashion. Thus it distinguishes between charism, services, and ministries. All the baptized are endowed with charisms of the Spirit for the good of the whole, and while these come from the Spirit, they have a human side and include the concern with things human. What is distinct about ministry in a tighter sense of the term is that it is a service which receives some kind of ecclesial recognition, a recognition given in the light of its usefulness to the Church and its mission.

In distinguishing among ministries, all of which are "a gift from on high," it is possible to employ a certain typology or variation of types. There are ministries that are recognized but without any formal procedure, factual ministries to which a community gives a place and a name, and recognizes persons so endowed. Then there are ministries that are formally recognized in some canonical way or by some simple liturgical gesture. Then there are those which have been "instituted", either by universal law as with the service of acolyte or reader, or by particular or local law, as Paul VI suggested might be the case for catechists. Finally, there are the ministries which are given recognition and into which persons are installed through the sacrament of order. For each, a discernment of the charism of service has to be the proper grounding and this discernment belongs not simply to authorities but to communities, since it is communities that they are supposed to serve.

In treating of the ministries that emerge in the present circumstances of ecclesial life, the CNBB gives priority to how it sees the life, mission, and ministry of the laity as these fit with their baptismal call and consecration. It also, however, mentions ministries of *suppléance*, which of their nature belong to the ordained but are in fact confided to members of the laity. These are such matters as being charged with the leadership of parishes or providing liturgical ministries in the absence of a priest. They require a special delegation, as a share in a role that is properly of the ordained. While these ministries are important at present, of their nature they ought to disappear. The solution to the dilemma of the present provisional nature of ecclesial organization is tied up with choice of candidates for ordination and with the discernment of charisms. The document does not go into what changes might come about, but some need is intimated.

The document also has much to say about how to formulate the mission of the Church in relation to social, cultural, and religious realities, themselves always in flux. Likewise, it has much to say about the proper education and formation for mission. None of these necessities, however, are to be addressed in such a way as to derogate from the integral vision of Church and mission, which is the foundation of the document.[27]

In 2002, the CNBB issued its directives for the life and mission of the Church for the years 2003 to 2006.[28] There is nothing specifically about the mission and ministry of the laity, but the document builds its concept of Church and its pastoral plan on an understanding of mission. The Church is to continue to be the Church of the Poor, and it is to see itself as a missionary presence in society. The mission is certainly to make Christ known, but one with this is the building up within society of a kingdom of justice, peace, and reconciliation. In such a mission all must participate, and hence the statement gives considerable attention to what is required for the fitting formation of all members of the Church.

In the collective response of the church of Brazil to the preparatory document of CELAM for Aparecida put together under the auspices of the Bishops' Conference,[29] clear note was taken of the situation of the people to whom the gospel is directed. This is not a formal episcopal document but a summary of responses received from communities in the region. However, it is noteworthy in as much as it shows what is being done and how people are thinking about mission and ministry. In keeping with its options for the poor, the Church at all levels needs to address those conditions that allow so many people to be kept in extreme poverty. It has to take note of violations of human rights, the effects of globalization, ecological problems affecting living conditions, urbanization, and social threats to family life. It also needs to be conscious of the reality of religious syncretism and of the transfer of many Catholics to Pentecostal communities. This last fact is a serious challenge to the ministeriality of ecclesial communities, and especially the lack of enough qualified ministers (3.5). Though ordained ministry remains central to the life of a Church community, other ministries are needed for pastoral work, and the document takes special note of the contribution made by women. Apparently some of the respondents wanted the question of women's ordination to be brought into open discussion. Although then there is emphasis on the need for an adequate biblical, theological, spiritual, and pastoral formation for such work, this is in the context of the abundance of the charisms of the Spirit found among the laity and of the service they are in fact rendering to the Church (4). The document points out that all activities and ministries must be related to the organic structure of parish communities. However, to allow for the presence of both basic Christian communities and new movements in the lives of the faithful, it speaks of the parish as a community of communities, or as a network of communities (5.2).[30] In other words, parishes cannot work properly if they do not recognize the vital role played by small communities within their boundaries.

Conclusions on Latin America

While defining their mission in terms of the evangelical option for the poor, throughout Latin America and the Caribbean, churches have to consider their life, their mission, and their ministries in the light of what has been learned through the experience of base Christian communities. This is a rather diversified experience and includes an effort in a number of churches to resituate these communities, theologically, pastorally, and canonically, overcoming the difficulties that they experienced in conjunction with the critique of liberation theology. In Latin America, and in a special way in Brazil, these small communities were in a specific sense "from the base." They were genuinely movements of lay persons, who were given educational or pedagogical opportunities that accommodate themselves to life in small rural or urban groups, where people learned such fundamentals as reading and writing. In the process they were helped to take cognizance of their economic and political situation, while seeking to become more engaged in the living of their Christian faith. From such roots, there emerged new units in the Church, not devoid of help from bishops, priests, and religious, but with much lay community and charismatic, as well as institutionally recognized, involvement.

The Brazilian and other episcopal conferences embraced and promoted such community life and activity, which intentionally or otherwise created structures that were not parish or traditional but centered on life and life-worlds as people lived them. Not only did the engagement of the laity in the life and mission of the Church take shape under such circumstances, but the clergy-laity relation also changed, and ideas about the role of the ordained, their relation to communities, and even the choice of candidates.

A number of things contributed to issues raised about these communities. Sometimes, they seemed to become too politically involved and to lose their moorings in true Christian faith, and too contestatory of ecclesiastical authority and structures. On the other hand, Roman authorities and some local authorities were simply fearful of significant changes in structure and of the challenges to bishops or priests that they felt were excessive. Political situations changed with the disappearance of military regimes, affecting the issues facing people but not greatly alleviating the suffering of the poor. On a whole, however, the experience was positive since it helped to engage the baptized in what their Christian role in society truly is and to rethink clergy-laity relations accordingly. On the other hand, there is some attempt to curb or control them in the ways that community life is made to center on parish organisms and to turn in the direction of new lay movements.[31]

The question of Church order is articulated specifically in two ways. First this happens in discussing the meaning of the word *ministry*, which in some cases is restricted in its use to formally given appointments. Second, it is asked how communities and lay movements that have vitality are to be related to parish and diocese. The key to the matter is the vitality of community developments that give the context within which these questions are raised. Canonically and liturgically, some special recognition may need to be given to roles and offices that appear most necessary to maintaining the life of a community, so that there is some differentiation between charisms and their service to life and mission. Canonical statutes can also serve to integrate movements and communities into the larger communion of the Church. The risk, however, is that of a rebirth of the bureaucratic and the autocratic.

The ecclesial and missionary situation is becoming ever more complex. As they move forward, the churches in Latin America are now faced with a number of new factors that will influence the relation between community, mission, and ministry. These factors are the success of the Pentecostal movement and the creation of sects among the poor, renewed interest to integrate popular religiosity into the expression of faith, attention to indigenous peoples, globalization of markets and communication, and the call of the postsynodal exhortation *Ecclesia in America* (1999)[32] for the churches both South and North to work together in solidarity in facing the concerns of culture, human community, justice, and poverty.

Ecclesia in America[33] lists all the fortunes of globalization, with its negative effects on human community and human society, which churches North and South need to address together in solidarity and in a communion of faith, love, and hope, as is revealed even by perusing the table of contents. Christian agents well skilled in the field of politics, trade, economics, and the like are clearly needed so that they can bring the conversation into those fields where the future is being constructed. While never neglecting the fact that faith, community, and identity are forged at the local level, some will have to be able to assume apostolates that are exercised on national and international planes.

The assimilation of the communion ecclesiology of Vatican II in this document, however, decidedly follows the hierarchical model. The nature of the diocese and of the parish as primary ecclesial organism is highlighted, with no mention of small communities. While there is enough mention of the role of the laity in the secular sphere, the role of bishop as pastor is put in high relief, as is that of the parish priest. While the Church is a sacrament of communion (§33), the Bishop is its chief architect builder and guarantor (§36). In the parish, the priest is the sign and center of unity, bringing all together in the celebration of the Eucharist and the sacraments (§39). He is to encourage the laity in their own vocation, but it is even said that it is the priest who "discerns" the charisms of the faithful. When in this exhortation the laity are said to be coresponsible in the life of the Church and its mission, this is by way of sharing in the responsibility of bishop and priest. For the future of the churches of Latin America, one sees, on reading this document against the background of the ecclesial movement of recent decades, that much depends on how well a meeting point may be found between a synodal and a hierarchical model of Church life and mission.

A number of factors seem to account for signs of a return to a firmer episcopal control over the life of communities. One is that the move away from Catholicism to Pentecostal churches is a feature of life in Central and South America. It is sometimes thought that a response to this is to strengthen the sense of Catholic identity and that traditional structures do this best. Another factor is the breakdown of family structures and new attitudes to sexual mores. In face of this, it is said that the move to Pentecostal churches is at least in part the result of individualism and postmodern ethos, since these new churches leave more personal freedom in such matters and do not challenge the right to belong of persons in irregular unions. A third factor mentioned is that they promote a type of religion that promises material prosperity if one recognizes Jesus as Savior, whereas Catholics are given more rigorous sacramental demands if they are to be members and are dissuaded from believing in a link between religion and material well-being. A fourth factor lies in a way of looking at the Church's option for the poor and the desire to help people out of aggravated situations of poverty. This is thought to be better promoted by a strong institutional Church, which can make its voice heard in the public sector, than by the promotion of the BCCs formed among the poor and in which the poor themselves are agents.

Another analysis of the situation[34] would still leave the option for vital BCCs as the more evangelical one to follow. This locates the success of Pentecostal churches in their response to an abandonment of the poor, which is threefold: social, existential, and pastoral. Social abandonment is the name for the situation of those who have been little helped by current political and economic policies and who are left in situations of dire poverty. They often feel that they are helped more by these new-style communities than in the traditional Catholic or Protestant churches. Existential abandonment is a reality experienced quite widely and not only in Latin America by persons who have lost their cultural, social, spiritual, and moral bearings. Whether it be the Church's way of promoting family values, sexual values, social values, or political values, they find little that responds to their deep hunger and desire or that aids them in negotiating the realities of contemporary life and the apparent dissolution of ideals in modern life, which forms part of their experience. Urbanization, the globalization of economies, the move away from traditional holdings and relationships, the breakup of the extended family form of belonging leave people disoriented. The rather rigorous sexual and social ethic preached by the Catholic Church does not seem to address what they have to pass through in search of a meaningful life. If this is the case, then along with the sense of social and experiential abandonment goes the feeling of pastoral abandonment, of being deserted by their pastors, who do not speak directly and personally to their dilemmas but offer only a "high ethic," to which they are expected to conform. This is exacerbated when no moves are made to address the lack of pastors, and people are left even without that which is supposed to be the core of Catholic life and meaning: namely, the sacraments.

When this threefold sense of abandonment is squarely faced, it is argued that encouraging base Christian communities is still the better pastoral policy, granted that they too have to consider and remedy their own defects or deficiencies. One can say that the tension and even conflict experienced in the churches of Latin America gravitates around the option for the poor. All may agree on this priority, as does the Vatican notification on the work of Jon Sobrino, but there are two differing responses as to how this mission is to be undertaken and how ministry relates to it.

Churches of Asia

In the churches of Asia, there was a comparable evolution of ministries in conjunction also with a redefinition of mission and an accentuation of participatory community life, through the medium of small community formation. In this case, the creation of these base local communities resulted, to a considerable extent, from the initiative of the bishops. Their creation, formation, and service were woven into pastoral planning, designed to involve the laity in the life of the Church as a community of faith, in its evangelization, its liturgy, and its mission. In face of the very submissive attitude expected of Catholics during the period of the implantation of the Church, creating such groupings seemed a way to involve all the baptized. The situation on the ground was rather different from that in Latin America. Though issues of economic and political exploitation certainly existed, Asian peoples were more conscious of cultural alienation and deprivation, and of the need to find their place in what is an intensely religious milieu, marked by the existence of the traditional religions of Hinduism and Buddhism, and more recently also of Islam. Inculturation, relating the Christian faith to the strong points of an ancient religious culture, a dialogue and cooperation with peoples of living faith—all were key factors in the life of Asian Churches and of their communities.[35]

What has been going on across Asia, with its internal differences in mind, is quite well known from the activities of the Federation of Asian Bishops' Conferences (FABC) and its auxiliary bodies.[36] Even before forming this federation, the Asian bishops had met in Manila in 1970, to take stock of the position of the Church in Asia in the wake of the Second Vatican Council. They called for a new evangelization that befitted a postcolonial world and a Church that had attained its own maturity and was no longer living as the outgrowth of European missionary endeavors. This evangelization needed to take into account the changing face of Asia, with its teeming masses, but also with its long-standing cultures and religious traditions. If anything marked the Asian world, it was its deeply religious sense. Preaching the gospel could not ignore this nor condemn the great religious traditions of the continent. Taking a cue from the Vatican Council, the bishops spoke of a response of service, in solidarity with peoples of other religions, engaged in a common task of building a truly human community, with central attention to the lot of the poor and suffering. Two concrete tasks spelled out for the Church in its life and mission were that of becoming truly a Church of the Poor and that of inculturation of the gospel and of Church life. Recognizing that all the baptized needed to be engaged in the work of evangelization, one of the resolutions of the assembly called for the "clarification of the roles of priests, religious, and laity," a clarification that needed to be both theological and pastoral.[37]

The first meeting of the FABC after its formation, held in Taipei in 1974, issued a statement on the local church.[38] At that time the primary focus of evangelization was to build up a truly local church on each part of the continent, one that would be in dialogue with peoples of all living traditions, cultures, and religions, and in a special way with the poor. The local church should engage priests, religious, and laity together in this construction and in all its missionary works.

Meeting at Bangkok in 1982, the third assembly of the FABC[39] spelled out theologically the reality of local church. The assembled bishops saw it as a community of graced communion rooted in the life of the Trinity, one whose life is nourished by prayer, contemplation, and sacramental celebration. It is to be a community "for others," living out the paschal mystery in faithful discipleship of Jesus. Living under the constant guidance of the Spirit, an essential feature of the Church needed to be one of genuine participation on the part of all, and one of coresponsibility of all its members in the promotion of the kingdom of God in society, "sensitively attuned to the work of the Spirit in the resounding symphony of Asian communion."[40]

In its syllabus of immediate concerns, this assembly noted the role played in the development of the Church by small Christian communities and the need to foster the manifold participation of the laity in the life and mission of local churches and of the communion of churches. The bishops advocated "that small Christian communities at all levels of Church life be more widely and intensively fostered, characterized by their openness and outreach to society through evangelization, social service, dialogue, ecumenical, and interreligious cooperation with peoples of all faiths and by their close union with their priests and bishops."[41] Hence the assembly saw the need for the laity's initiatives and the importance of including them. First, they have roles in the life of prayer and community building. Beyond that, they have their proper responsibilities in such things as social work, education, and charitable actions, and in these areas it is they who should often be in charge, rather than acting solely under clerical supervision. Consequently, the assembly asked that churches work out the proper structure of coresponsibility.

The fourth assembly of the FABC, held in Tokyo in 1986, took as its specific concern the vocation and mission of the laity in the Church and in the world of Asia.[42] Its statement was based on the teaching of Vatican II about the role of the lay baptized in the secular order, but the bishops treated this in such a way as to make their evangelizing presence integral to their lives and their participation in the lives of their own Christian communities. They looked at the part the laity have in the activities of a small community or network of communities, and in the less locally restricted works of the organized lay apostolate. This latter, they thought, needed to be more "kingdom oriented," less focused on inner ecclesial concerns, and more engaged with the life of society and of the poor in society.

The assembly spoke a word of caution to the ordained who are too preoccupied with juridical problems and norms, whereas they need to avow and work with lay leadership in many fields. "The renewal of inner ecclesial structures, it is said, does not consist only in strengthening and multiplying the existing parochial and diocesan organizations, nor in creating new ones." What is more deeply called for is to create the right atmosphere of communion, collegiality, and coresponsibility, which allows ordained and laity to work together for a common purpose.

Meeting again at Bangkok in 1990 for its fifth plenary assembly,[43] the FABC looked ahead to the new millennium and its missionary demands. Speaking of a new way of being Church, the report of the meeting said that the Church in Asia needed to be a communion of communities, in which laity, clergy, and religious would have to work together and recognize each other as sisters and brothers, and where the roles of women and men would be equally included. The bishops looked for moves toward the building of true community, which would include fostering leadership of various types of small communities, such as neighborhood, basic ecclesial communities, and "covenant" communities. In this there is some recognition of voluntary association as well as geographically determined togetherness. The report echoes the description of the early church in Acts 2:42, seeing all of these communities as being of one mind and heart, constantly sharing their lives and their work together on the basis of prayer and the reading of the Gospel of Jesus. To support and nourish this common life, it is necessary to discern and recognize all gifts, thus being led at all stages by the Spirit of God, from whom the gifts come, and not always according to what is foreplanned.

The final statement of the sixth plenary assembly,[44] held at Manila in 1995, is an elaboration of the particularities of the mission of the church in Asia. It indicates that since the inception of the FABC, the Church has been engaged in a threefold dialogue: with the different faiths of Asia, with the cultures of Asia, and with the poor multitudes of Asia. In this it has pursued a vision of life rooted in the gospel and fostered by the discipleship of Jesus Christ and by the desire to promote the kingdom of God. One with the religious sentiments of Asian peoples, the church in Asia should have a holistic vision of life that knows no discrimination of gender, creed, culture, class, or color. To work for peace and justice and the fullness of life for all, it is necessary to work against the evils that affect the peoples of the continent, particularly warfare, hunger, poverty, injustice, and deeply ingrained enmities. The life of the Church itself must be a life of communion, which in its witness testifies to the life that it promotes for all peoples.

The statement lists five concerns that demand immediate pastoral focus. These are the Asian family, the complex issue of women and the girl child, the struggles and life-giving movements of youth, ecological problems, and the needs of displaced persons. Though the statement does not go into the particulars of relations between the ordained and the rest of the baptized, it takes it for granted that such a complex mission has to engage all the members of the Church, who need to live together and work together, respecting one another's gifts and contributions in a spirit of coresponsibility.

The Asian bishops' theological ground for dialogue with other religions and with cultures is the action of the Spirit that takes place outside the boundaries of the Church. To spell this out and to relate it to the mission of the Church, the documents of other organisms of the Federation, such as the Bishops' Institute for Interreligious Affairs (BIRA), use the biblical and theological term *kingdom of God*. This expresses both the sense of the pervasive presence of God's Spirit and the final eschatological goal of salvation, already in some way being worked out as reconciliation, peace, and justice are established as worldly realities through the cooperation of people of many faiths and cultures.[45] In working with others, the Church is an instrument of salvation and of the spread of God's kingdom, emptying itself out in its service, after the manner of Jesus himself (Phil 2:7).

Following on the 1995 plenary meeting in Manila, the member conferences were taken up by the preparation for the special Synod on Asia convoked by the Pope, and thereafter with its implementation.[46] The work of this synod was quite controlled by Roman authorities, but nonetheless the bishops gave voice to their own Asian concerns in a somewhat free exchange. The interventions, the propositions voted, and the final apostolic exhortation exhibit concerns about what is proper to Asia, where living amid peoples of other living faiths, working for the poor, and resolving racial, religious, and political conflicts form part of daily life. In formulating a sense of mission in this context, much attention was given to what the Church does and says by way of witness to Christ and the gospel of Christ. It is primarily by witness as a living communion of discipleship that the Church carries out its mission, even if calling others to share this faith is not excluded.

Not much explicit attention was given to the laity at the synod, and indeed it is even said that the synod was rather hierarchical and paternalistic in that regard, speaking of the lack of preparation on the part of lay people and of the need for their preparation and ongoing formation if they are to take due part in the Church's mission, and do so in proper communion with the hierarchy. The final message did, however, affirm the work of the Spirit in empowering all the baptized and in preparing what it called the "age of the laity" in the coming millennium. The message mentions life in small Christian communities as a result of the Spirit's work. Proposition 30 also names small communities as a new way of being Church, to be included in any comprehensive pastoral plan, though proposition 29 on the participation of the laity in the work of evangelization is weak in spelling out the terms of coresponsibility. All in all, what came out of this synod is less affirmative than the statements of the FABC over the years, so that it has to be read as part of an ongoing story of a church that still lives the élan of the event of the Second Vatican Council, even if some hesitations have been introduced due to concerns with a Rome-centered, hierarchical communion.

Other FABC meetings that followed the synod[47] have continued to develop an Asian vision of the Church. This work is no longer concerned with the patterns of lay involvement, of common responsibility, of relations between the ordained and the baptized laity in the life of communities and in the work of evangelization. What was said in earlier documents and the fruit of experience are taken for granted, given that matters of ecclesial action and organization need ongoing attention and development. The threefold dialogue—with different religions, with the cultures of Asia, and with the poor—remains the context within which the churches of Asia spell out their mission in the name of Christ, and in which the lives, services, and ministries of communities take shape.[48] What becomes always clearer is the need to address charism, service, and ministry in the light of what is spelled out as the mission of the Church and the kind of discipleship that this postulates. There is a new focus on the family as the basic unit of the Church, and small communities are seen as the result or fruit of families coming together in an active ecclesial life. This has to have implications for the need and formation of services and ministries, for the manner of sharing the Word, and for the manner of celebrating the liturgy, inclusive of the Eucharist. Within such a community, it also has consequences for the relation of ordained ministers to the rest of the baptized. In face of this ecclesiological FABC perspective, one thinks naturally of the household churches of early Christianity and the story of how they were ordered.

Mission Congresses

Several missionary congresses or colloquia held under the auspices of the FABC complete the Asian picture on ministry. In the reports of a colloquium held in Hong Kong in 1977 there are two listings of ministries or services in the communities.[49] The first reads as follows: "Leadership roles in the Christian communities are slowly emerging. Among the more important services and functions that are developing are community leaders, ministers of the Eucharist, prayer leader, catechist, treasurer, social worker, youth leader, educator, facilitator of harmonizer of differences, etc." The second listing includes evangelist, catechist, ministers for liturgy, ministry of family apostolate, ministry of healing, ministry of interreligious dialogue, ministry of social concern, ministry to youth, ministry to workers, ministry of education, community builders, ministry of communication, and ministry of pastoral community leadership. Neither list is intended to be exhaustive. Both try to enumerate what the participants in the congress saw emerging among their peoples and saw as important to their life and to their mission in a religiously pluralistic society.

While the Hong Kong meeting spoke of small communities, a congress held in Manila in 1979[50] suggested that it is helpful to see the emergence of basic Christian communities as something that comes "from the bottom," in order to gauge their full dynamic potential.[51] Talking of ministries, the Manila congress followed the distinctions made at Hong Kong, but it had a special word to say on how ordained ministry belongs in and to the Church community. The forms of this ministry need to be determined by community development and the ecclesial awareness of all. Seeing a resistance to lay participation on the part of some clergy, the congress members advocated that they learn to be free from the trammels of hierarchical status and to learn to live as part of the communities that they are called to serve, seeing the laity as equal partners in responsibility, albeit in different roles.

How seriously the stories of the poor are being told and heard is a question prompted by the work and presence of churches across Asia; this was the topic treated at an Asian Mission Congress in Bangkok in 2006,[52] sponsored by the FABC. In a keynote address, Bishop Luis Antonio Tagle of Imus, Philippines, developed the theme of story. Stories forge identity. The stories of Christ forge the Christian identity. The stories of Christ as received and told by the people of Asia forge the Christian Asian identity.

The Congress was organized as a celebration of life and faith. It focused on telling the stories of the Church across the Asian Continent. Marked in these stories was the relation of Christian churches to the peoples, languages, cultures, and religions of Asia. In speaking to this topic in the keynote address, the bishop-theologian developed the importance of the poor in the stories of Jesus and how they have been received among the poor peoples of Asia. However, he went on to say that the stories have to be told by those "who are with the poor." He says nothing of the need to listen to the stories of Jesus told by the poor, or of how they tell the story of how they have lived through suffering and hope, as communities, by following the story of Jesus. It remains to be seen how stories and community and even mission begin among the poor and with Christ's and the Church's preferential option for the poor. The danger is that even in focusing on the poor, the structural format of the Church and the ministry among such communities remains traditional and untouched.

Thailand

Not all the churches of Asia implement the policies of the FABC in the same way, given the great diversity between countries of that continent. Some particular examples will help to illustrate this. At the cusp of the millennium, the episcopal conference of Thailand issued its master plan for the first decade, 2000 to 2010.[53] Christians there are a minority, a minority indeed that has struggled long for its right to exist. Now they find themselves, with all the peoples of the country, forced to deal with economic globalization, with all that this brings along by way of a threat to traditional communities and culture. In this situation, the bishops of Thailand, in addressing the Church, wish to serve the spiritual needs of all by keeping alive the message of the gospel in their midst. They speak of Christians as being the "seed of the kingdom of God," called and sent to uphold religious values over against the dominant interests of the new social and temporal order. To realize this evangelical goal, the Church needs to strengthen its own bonds of community. Hence the episcopacy asks for a strong and reliable cooperation between clergy, religious, and laity, with a sense of solidarity built on principles of the equality of all, and yet with rich diversity, realizing among themselves a harmonious blending between pastoral ministry and the work of evangelization. The bishops believe that a strong point of communion comes from the effort to uphold the family. Family is the first unit, the "domestic Church," and wider communities are formed through different families coming together for worship, service, and mutual bonding. It is thus that the Church can be a witness in society to truth and love and reconciliation, planting indeed a veritable "seed of the kingdom."

Philippines

The church of the Philippines, while it wholeheartedly participates in the work of the FABC, is in a somewhat unique position in Asia, since it is a largely Catholic country, with a church that was brought into being by the efforts of Spanish missionaries in the early years of colonizing the East. In the southern islands, the dialogue with Islam is part of the context of evangelization, but on the other islands the new evangelization is a matter of rejuvenating a traditional Catholicism. This has to be done in dialogue with the cultures of their peoples and in dialogue with the poor, who suffer under socioeconomic and political injustice.

In all of this, there is a great resemblance to the situations in Latin American countries. The bishops' conference has enunciated its pastoral plans quite consistently, but some special note may be taken of a 1999 pastoral letter.[54] In this letter the bishops express their intention to develop a dialogue with cultures and with the world of the poor, as well as to take a stance in face of the secularization, which is making its presence felt across the country due to influences from the West. To complete the vocabulary of incarnation introduced by *Ad gentes* (1965, par. 10), as well as that of inculturation, the letter endorses the language of contextualization used by a number of Filipino theologians.[55] In the pastoral strategies that it adopts to work through these dialogues and to develop a sense of mission to which all the baptized feel party, the Filipino Church embraces the ideal of developing small Christian communities and allowing services and ministries to develop within and from them, integral to the coresponsibility in mission of the whole community.

Sometimes observers question how successful or how grassroots these basic ecclesial communities are. To some, these groups often seem to be quite controlled by the hierarchy and priests and to be rather inward-looking groups of people who focus on worship, or even on charismatic prayer, and uphold the hierarchical paradigm of Church government. Finding a mission and goal is a great part of the challenge. Under the Marcos regime, the small communities, especially on islands such as Mindanao and Negros, and the Sulu Archipelago,[56] had a clear idea of what they wished to protest and to change, even if they were also accused of being too political or too contestatory of priests and bishops. Now, when there is some semblance of democracy in the country but also the advent of economic globalization, they find it difficult to come up with an alternate prophetic charism to exercise toward the transformation of the temporal order, in favor of the poor and of spiritual horizons.[57]

Conclusions about Churches of Asia

Since gaining their independence from European domination, the churches in Asia are finding their own voice and their own physiognomy. As in other parts of the world, leadership and ministry address the conditions of poverty under which millions live. This serves a mission not only to Christian believers but to all the peoples of the continent. It is a mission that is undertaken in dialogue and in cooperation with members of other great religions, and is related to a continental spiritual heritage that is older than Christianity. As this mission is advanced, two factors are important. First is a way of expressing the faith in terms appropriate to peoples and cultures and to a spiritual experience that is larger than that of Christian churches. Second is the concern to develop communities that allow for exchange on a more human level, and that fit the social and community structures of cultural heritage. The interest in fostering small communities corresponds to this second concern and necessarily leads to new types of ministry and to new forms of ecclesial structure. The collaborative relation between the laity and the ordained is worked out in this context and is not readily fitted into the distinction between responsibilities for the sacred and responsibilities for the secular.

Churches of Africa

Given the consequences of English, French, Belgian, Portuguese, and German colonialism, finding a true African voice and a true ecclesial autonomy were vital considerations for African identity. Moving away from colonial domination brought fresh kinds of suffering and oppression, and for the Church this meant living by the preferential option for the poor in face of new realities. Several regions, such as those incorporated into the Association of Member Episcopal Conferences in Eastern Africa (AMECEA)[58] and the Church of Zaire (now the Democratic

Republic of the Congo) opted for the pastoral priority of building up the Church and revitalizing its life and its mission through small communities, which would serve to invigorate the people in the immediacy of their own lives and also give rise to new charisms and new ministries. Inculturation—the relation of a life of faith to African cultural, tribal, and religious traditions—was a key factor in the life of these groups. Episcopal bodies consistently formulated the life and mission of the Church in ways that include the dynamism of small Christian communities, built to dimensions that are human and interpersonal, rather than dominantly social and institutional.

Given some necessary cautions about what in fact went on, we can follow the path of these communities to some degree by looking at the statements of plenary assemblies of the AMECEA[59] and SECAM (see below), with some specific attention to the Church in Zaire/Democratic Republic of the Congo, given the particular initiatives taken in the time of Cardinal Malula.

AMECEA

In 1973 and 1976, AMECEA had treated the importance of local communities in the Church's life, making a pastoral option for small Christian communities.[60] In an article in 1976, Bishop John N. Jenga of Kenya wrote that "the Church has failed miserably to recognise the importance of these basic natural community units in the life of the Church." The preparatory work for the plenary assembly of 1976 had defined them as "those basic and manageable social groupings whose members can have real inter-personal relationships and feel a sense of communal belonging, both in living and working," thus having an influence on their environment.[61]

The most extensive treatment of such communities is found in the message issued after a plenary assembly in Zomba, Malawi, in 1979.[62] In that message, the bishops spoke of the small Christian community as the most basic local unit of the Church, within which a vision of the Church as a mystery of communion is fostered. Together, groups of these small communities make up the parish, which is to be a community of communities and whose organization, service, and ministry are to be centered on this reality. The size of the small community may vary, but one of its chief purposes is to restore the human dimension to life and exchange among the baptized. It is described as a body in which the members reflect together on the Word of God and make decisions about life and mission in this light, under the guidance of the Spirit. A variety of gifts or charisms are given to members through the Spirit, for the building up of the community and for undertaking its mission in society, principally in the option for the poor and in the work of the inculturation of the gospel.

These communities, constituted at the grassroots among people struggling with poverty, will have their own internal lay leaders for all aspects of ecclesial life, inclusive of worship, education, and apostolate, but this is not to take away from the distinctive character of the baptized laity, which is to transform the world in Christ's name, this being their right and duty as "apostles." Rather than see leadership in worship or catechesis as opposed to the lay state, in fact it is the very intensity of common life in worship, education, and the assimilation of new members that allows it and its members to fulfill their apostolic role. The reflection on the Word and common prayer are done in the light of the mission and incorporates acts of discernment respecting apostolic works. In training priests for work in parishes, it was to be clear that their ministry would be marked by working through these groups and that they would work with lay leaders as true collaborators in the service of the one mission.

This vision of the Church and the pastoral option for small communities is a constant of all the AMECEA messages, whatever the specific topic of the plenary sessions. Before the African Synod in 1994 and looking forward to the new millennium, the 1992 meeting (Lusaka, Zambia) took up the question of inculturation and pointed to it as the normal process of evangelization in Africa. Making a renewed option for the building and activity of small communities, the bishops emphasized that these should include women as well as men in roles of leadership. In face of some lack in the lives and in the knowledge of the faith in these bodies, however, the assembly asked for better training for the work of evangelization for priests, religious, and laity.

After the Synod for Africa, at the 1999 assembly in Nairobi, Kenya, the AMECEA followed two theological options for the enunciation of the Church's mission and the work of evangelization, options for the family and for the poor. In speaking of the Church as the family of God, the bishops follow the model of the African family, with its extended membership and its care for others, its solidarity, its warm human relations, its acceptance and trust of all, its readiness for dialogue and "palaver." With this ecclesiology, the option for small communities as the basic local unit of the Church was renewed, with all that this implies about an evolution of services and ministries and for a cooperative spirit between ordained and laity, where all are "true partners in evangelization."

Especially when it comes to structures and procedures of government, the adoption of this model for Church communities does not go without dispute. Some critics from within Africa itself affirm that African-style government, in Church and society, is quite autocratic and male dominated. Others, however, think that African traditions do provide models for government that give a voice to the community and they point to what could be called consensus models. Even a chief, although he comes from the lineage of former chiefs, is not necessarily the eldest son but the one presented by the elders and accepted by the people. Though decisions about life are formulated by the chief, the process is such that it involves the council of elders and through them all the people. If women are included in this process of consensus making, some think that the model would work in ecclesial communities and even in dioceses. This would obviously mean changing the process by which bishops are now named and the process for approving candidates for ordination to priesthood and deaconate, or nomination to other leadership ministries.

The second theological option of the assembly is comparable to that of the FABC. It is to speak of mission in terms of promoting God's kingdom and serving integral human development. The work of the Church has its foundation in the reconciling mission of Christ, serving a reality greater than itself in promoting harmony, peace, and justice, and in taking the service of poor as core to its being. This implies recognizing the work of the Spirit in African customs and traditions, moving toward an eschatological goal, which is that of the fullness of God's kingdom.

The orientations of the Synod for Africa and of the 1999 assembly were carried through in the 2002 meeting on Church witness, held at Dar es Salaam, Tanzania, with the title of its final message reading, "You Shall Be My Witnesses."[63] The assembly proposed two theological foundations for the mission of the Church in this region. One is the notion of a deep evangelization, the other the preferential option of the Church for the poor.

To talk of a deeper evangelization is to say that genuine witness to the gospel has to have deep roots. It means to convert the personal and collective consciences of people, to infuse all their activities with the spirit of the gospel, and to convert what the session called the "milieus" in which people live. These are the social, cultural, economic, and political realities by which lives and activities are informed. Of the things that the assembly saw as pertinent to this evangelization, two are worthy of mention here, having to do with ecclesial structures and activities.[64] The first is the need to continue, guide, and encourage the role of small communities in the African church. The other is the resolution to "empower the laity" to take their full part in the life and mission of the Church, something that is indeed quite obviously necessary if the "milieus" are to be transformed. On the second theological foundation enunciated by the assembly, the assembly stated that "a deeper evangelization cannot be conceived without having as spiritual foundation the preferential option for the poor of our own African land."

After this 1994 synod, AMECEA had rewritten its vision and mission statement[65] to spell out more clearly what the work of evangelization in Eastern Africa needs to be. The vision is that of being "A Holy Spirit filled family of God, committed to holistic evangelization and integral development." The mission is to include the preferential option for the poor, with the work of inculturation, ecumenism, and interreligious dialogue as necessary components. The emphasis on small Christian communities as agents of evangelization is to be revitalized, with what this implies for the education and empowerment of the laity and of religious men and women.[66]

IMBISA

For its part, the Interregional Meeting of Bishops of Southern Africa (IMBISA)[67] has also addressed the meaning of evangelization in the current situation of peoples in that part of the world. The bishops prepared and held a plenary assembly in 2001, with a focus on poverty and economic justice.[68] The aim of this meeting was "to involve the whole Family of God in Southern Africa in solving problems of poverty and economic injustice in a spirit of freedom and coresponsibility in order to build a better world on the solid foundation of sound ethical and spiritual principles." Rather than jump straight to biblical and theological principles, however, the assembly proposed two initial steps. The first would be insertion of Church members and communities into the living situation of those who suffer poverty and injustice. The second would be a social analysis that would uncover the reasons or root causes of this impoverishment. This says much about how mission and ministry need to evolve in such a field of work.

Democratic Republic of the Congo/Zaire

Though more could be said about other churches, given the documentation in considering ministerial developments in Francophone Africa, the easiest example to follow is that of the Church of Zaire, now known as the Democratic Republic of the Congo.[69] With initiatives taken by Cardinal Malula of Kinshasa, shortly after the Vatican Council, Zaire adopted the pastoral policy of creating small Christian communities as the basic unit of the Church, giving them the ministers that they needed to flourish. The parish, served by ordained ministers, would then be seen as a community of communities, and priests would need to develop the skills of working with leaders of the small communities in a spirit of collaboration. Malula and some of his fellow bishops saw the need for a new evangelization in the era of postcolonialism that would be more centered on human communities and not on ecclesiastical structures. Like the bishops of East Africa, the bishops of Zaire wanted to restore the human dimension to activating Christian life together. Malula himself has said that he first gave formally instituted ministries to lay persons because there were not enough priests to achieve this goal, but that later he thought of them and tried to develop them as properly lay ministries, by which the baptized realized their participation in the threefold office of Christ. For the episcopal body itself, the church of Zaire wanted to foster a great sense of collegiality in the exercise of their pastoral office, one that was in keeping with the image of the Church as a mystery of communion flowing from the life of the Trinity, and one that would allow them to tackle the issues of inculturation, the option for the poor, and the integration of serving human development into the mission of the Church.

In laying a theological foundation for the service and ministries of all the baptized, the diocese of Bukavu, for example, describes the communion of the Church itself as ministerial, within which specific ministries are located,[70] in virtue of the baptismal foundation of the community and of the charisms of the Spirit given to its members. For a church to achieve its proper organization and at the same time retain the sense of shared mission, formally chosen and instituted ministers ought to belong to the humanly dimensioned community in a full human as well as ecclesial sense of the Word. So as to remain within the communion of the wider Church, ministries of formal leadership need to be canonically recognized, and candidates approved by the Bishop and installed through appropriate liturgical rites. These rites, however, ought to reflect the discernment, choice, and approval of the communities that the leaders are to serve. Ministries instituted and formally conferred include lay presidency of many liturgical actions, pastoral leadership of communities, responsibility for catechesis and for the catechumenate, healing ministries, marriage counseling and preparation. At times too, lay persons are given diocesan pastoral responsibilities, in which they serve in closer collaboration with the bishop and find their structural place within diocesan pastoral councils, along-side presbyteral councils.

In the canonical language of the pastoral directives of Bukavu,[71] one finds in places the language of cooperation in and with the office of the bishop. This may change the perspective but also reveals the dilemma of increasingly giving to lay persons offices, duties, and ministries for which ordination would ordinarily be required. In practice, many communities do practically everything pastoral and liturgical with lay leadership but remain without the regular celebration of the Eucharist since this is reserved to the ordained, both canonically and theologically.

SECAM

Communiqués from meetings since the African Synod of the Symposium of Episcopal Conferences of Africa and Madagascar (SECAM) express a certain pessimism about the African continent and about the life and mission of the Church. The bishops or their spokespersons state that they wish to build on the model of the "Church as Family of God," adopted at the African Synod.[72] The pessimism arises from the state of the African continent and from what the bishops see as inner failures of the Church in living the faith. Though a communication of January 2007 reiterates the decision to deepen the identity of the Church as the family of God, it sees immense hurdles before it in fulfilling its mission, hurdles that it lists as "wars, conflicts of all sorts, chronic economic mismanagement of resources, the HIV/AIDS pandemic, hatred, negative self-image, tribalism, ethnocentrism, corruption, embezzlement, bad governance, etc." To meet these challenges, in 2002 a working paper on the restructuring of the conference was proposed. This had a twofold purpose: first, to serve the grass roots in communities across the continent; second, a greater continental collaboration and cohesion of churches. With regard to grass-roots realities, the symposium remarks a lack of deep faith and an inadequate conversion to a Christian way of life. Hence it stresses the need for instruction and inner evangelization. The language of small communities and their contribution to life and mission is absent from these SECAM communications.

African Synods

What the bishops took home from the African Synod of 1994 emerges from the survey of their documents in its aftermath, and indeed these questions and orientations appear in the postsynodal exhortation *Ecclesia in Africa*.[73] There is still one element of reflection that merits special mention, even though it is not much elaborated upon. This is the christological option made during the synod or in the exhortation. This is fundamental since the life of the Church is to make Christ known, through witness and Word. Hence mission and ministry are given shape by how peoples see the relation of Christ and his work to their lives and histories.

Given the perils facing African peoples at this time, the first orientation to making Christ known is to announce his Incarnation and his resurrection as a message of hope, a hope embodied in human history. It is the power of the resurrection and the meaning of the Incarnation that are given primacy, and the sense of both is related to the gift of the Spirit and to God's trinitarian communion, which is the source and origin of the life given to the world. The Incarnation is presented as the paradigm of Christ's entry into history and for the rooting of the gospel in cultures. This is woven into a sense of the long-standing presence of Christ and the Spirit in the history of African peoples, something indeed that has to be spelled out in greater detail than is done in the postsynodal exhortation. While the synod gave most attention to the reality of the Church and the need to address the issues of current reality, these christological orientations are a necessary foundation to show how the life of the Church, its mission, and its ministry are seen in Africa.

In the *lineamenta* (preparatory document) for the second African Synod, announced to take place within the next few years, this pneumatological Christology is not revisited but undoubtedly is at work. The major concern is with the problems of injustice and illness facing the African continent, with all those problems enunciated by SECAM.[74] More than ten years after the first synod and the promulgation of the postsynodal apostolic exhortation *Ecclesia in Africa*, there is a feeling of malaise in churches on the continent as they ask, What did the synod achieve?[75] Many African countries are still beset by poverty and warfare, governments are corrupt, and the HIV/AIDS pandemic continues to make inroads, with all its consequences for families and children. While the relation of the gospel to culture and matters of inculturation are not set aside, it is felt that the gospel has still not penetrated in depth into the way of life of newly developing societies and nations. The questions of reconciliation, justice, and peace appear to be the most urgent and need attention. The relation between the synods and the special focus of the one now convoked is set out in the *lineamenta* (§4):

> The two assemblies have in common an urgent need, at an historic moment, of an on-going, in-depth evangelisation. Furthermore, in proclaiming the coming of the Kingdom of God in Jesus Christ, a commitment to reconciliation, justice and peace appears to be where this Kingdom of Love is to be realised: ". . . the kingdom of God . . . means righteousness and peace and joy brought by the Holy Spirit" (Rom 14:17ff.). In Africa's current historical, social, political, cultural, and religious circumstances, the Church-Family of God draws her energy from Christ, the ever-living Word of God, so that she can overcome weariness and thoughts of surrender and free herself from all forms of oppression. In fact, Christ invites her to bear the yoke of his love and find refreshment in him for a new life, and to receive the enthusiasm and light to dispel the many dark clouds which hang over the peoples of Africa in these times.

In keeping with these concerns, there is a chapter on the role of the laity in trans-forming the world, with emphasis on the secular character of their mission. In many respects this is quite positive, as can be seen from what is said in paragraphs 61 and 62: In light of the major issues facing the church in Africa, "the time has come for lay Christians in Africa to make a large-scale, resolute commitment to Church and the State." This service to the public good belongs to the nature of the Church's mission but is the particular role of the lay faithful. The document says:

> To understand better the current meaning and need for the laity's mission in the single mission of the Church, we have to return to the idea of the Church as a family, a place "where help is given and received, and at the same time, a place where people are also prepared to serve those who are in need of help." The family is a community of life in which there is a diversity of talents, charisms, ministries, functions, duties and services, all of which contribute, each in its own way, to fulfilling the shared task. The Church is comprised of many members, but she is united; she is the Body of Christ, the People of God.

What is said about the service of the laity is related to the teaching of Vatican II on the secular character of their share in the work of Christ and of the Church (§62):

> The laity's secular character determines the specificity of their mission. They exercise their Christian mission in the midst of the world, in the ordinary con-ditions of family life and society. Each is a Christian in the world. Certainly, clerics and consecrated persons are also in the world, but their Christian mis-sion does not directly affect the building up of earthly realities. The laity, on the other hand, have earthly life as their specific mission. The role of the laity, there-fore, is to bring about the Kingdom of God in the administration and organi-sation of earthly realities according to the divine plan. Guided by the spirit of the Gospel, they must be in the world like leaven in the dough, salt and light (cf. Mt 5:13, 14).

Given the accent on the laity's secular character, however, there is not much room left for thinking about structural changes within the Church itself, in order to realize the participation of all in the work of evangelization and promotion of justice. There is no mention of small communities that had figured prominently in some pastoral plans on the continent. While the language of the Church as family of God is used, the focus is on the diocese and on the role of the bishop. Of the laity, it is pointed out that their mission has to be grounded in solid doctrine, devotion, and sacra-mental participation. Much is therefore said about their proper formation and preparation. The supposition seems to be that it is the bishops who are to say what a Christian presence in society is and to decide how peoples are to be formed to undertake their Christian tasks. Not enough is said of the contribution that the faithful themselves can make to understanding issues, to seeing things in the light of faith, or in taking apostolic initiatives. The change that came about after Vatican II in formulating ecclesiology and in describing mission, with a focus on issues of social justice and reconciliation, remains. The Church needs to come to grips with the troubles that infect civic, social, economic, and political life. However, in speaking of the life of the Church and of its organization, what has come back to the fore is a strong hierarchical and clerical model, occasioned possibly by the concern that the Church as a community has not had enough impact on social, economic, and political development.

Quite importantly, effective work in these areas is related to the process of inculturation and to dialogue with African traditional religions. The relation of peoples to their land, the tension between belonging to family, the autonomy needed by those who wish to contribute to the common good of all, and the need to act against forms of discrimination against women are all matters to consider in the light of the gospel and of Jesus Christ.

Small Christian Communities

In practice, during this period after Vatican II the growth and inner realization of small Christian communities (SCC) does not seem to have been spectacular, partly because of the resistance of large numbers of clergy or religious, who saw it as a pastoral option handed down from the top, rather than one worked out with the body of the faithful, inclusive of priests, religious, and laity.[76] In some or many cases, too, groups calling themselves SCCs did not realize the holistic model of the AMECEA directives. Some were little more than groups that gathered for some specific purpose, such as Bible study or catechesis, and indeed a frequent emphasis appears to have been on the inner life of the community itself, without sufficient attention to its place in society and to the role to be played in transforming this society.

In a study of one region, one writer may have highlighted and summarized the reasons why these small or base communities have not always had much impact, either in the Church or in society.[77] He finds that often these SCCs have not found a genuinely African voice because of the persistence in leadership of a "missionary mentality." He also reports the difficulties they have in relating to social and political developments, running the risk of becoming instruments of some political ambition. Last, he notes the ambiguity in the attitudes of the hierarchy. Even as bishops espouse the promotion of these communities, they try to keep tight control over them and express the desire to see them "come to maturity," which can mean nothing more than making them manageable means of catechization rather than communities that are granted some autonomy and initiative in developing Church life and integration into society.

Where the SCCs did come into being, however, they included three vital elements.[78] First, the groups gathered for prayer, Bible reading, and catechesis, in a process of self-evangelization. Second, with the choices made by the community as such, some members took on pastoral and liturgical services, such as preparing catechumens for baptism, preparing couples for marriage, preparing children for communion and confirmation, officiating at marriages and funerals, visiting the sick, and even leading Sunday communion services as need demanded. With such a setting, some ministries with a traditional African color took shape, such as healing and reconciliation of feuding persons or families. A third factor, related to both of these, was the assumption by the community and its charismatically gifted members of evangelical work and of work for bettering society, which follows the option for the poor, sometimes undertaken in ecumenical cooperation. Within this multiple activity, charisms appeared and lay persons assumed ministerial roles, some of which appeared as new to this time.

Judging from accounts given, these configurations of ecclesial community helped people to grasp concretely what it means to evangelize the culture and let the culture color the gospel's reception. The forms of catechumenate adopted enabled people to integrate and relate to traditional African society, to traditional religions, and to political and social issues. The relation between the ordained and the baptized laity was spelled out in new ways, leading to a greater sense of how all are involved in the life of the Church, even having a part as of right in processes of decision making.

Concluding Remarks on Churches in Africa

Some words need to be added to what this documentation reports as being done in African countries, given that the policy of centering Church life and mission in small communities is not everywhere well accepted or successful. If small communities are to become even more vital to the Church and its mission, and if new services and ministries are to take shape in this context, including a reshaping of ordained ministry, some things need to come into open discussion. On a human and cultural level, there needs to be some critique of traditional family and social structures, especially with regard to the place of women in family, society, and Church, so as not to let the patriarchal elements in African life dominate. Then the dialogue with the poor and with cultures needs to work along lines that allow for dialogue with the Independent Churches, which in many respects are more indigenous than the mainline churches and often more accessible to the poor.[79] It may sometimes be said that these churches encourage a dependence on spirits and ancestors that is not in keeping with the gospel or that they foster false hopes, but it still needs to be taken into account that they do draw people from socially abandoned segments of society, people for whom the gospel is surely intended and who have to be the concern of mainline churches.

Their success is in part accredited to the facts that the founding prophets truly addressed the very poor and that they allow people to find strong elements of living in community. In the midst of poverty, they give an experience of the empowering Spirit that speaks powerfully to traditional African cultural feelings. In hymns, preaching, and worship, they embody a language that would now be called "inculturated" in ways that the worship of mainline churches does not. One might add that at a time when traditional Catholic ritual is often lacking in helping people to find their social belonging in a changing world, the kind of ritual practiced in these communities is more pertinent to the reality of those who have little social and economic power.

In the work of inculturation, it is not enough for Catholic churches to advocate a renewal that is rightly concerned with tradition and universal communion. An internal dialogue with the people, and especially the poor, is necessary. Looking to the past of local churches, it is apparent that addressing culture has to include the appeal of what is called popular religiosity, that is the form in which the poor express their faith and their sense of God, of Christ, of Mary, of the saints, incorporating much of their relations to ancestors and the spirits at work in their lives. If the ordained ministry is to truly relate to cultural mores and perceptions, some reform of the choice of candidates and of their preparation is needed. Relating everything to the threefold office of Christ and representation of Christ is one paradigm, but forms of leadership that are more truly African and more truly communitarian cannot be readily compressed into it.

A sad observation is that many communities across Africa are not fully eucharistic, not having the ministries needed to assure regular Sunday celebration of the Mass. For the communion of the Church in Christ and the Spirit, for the inner life of the Church, and for the reinvigoration of missionary endeavor, the eucharistic action and communion in Christ's body and blood at each community's table is vital. Moves have been made to prepare African candidates for the priesthood and for the deaconate, but these do not respond to the need on the ground, and their training perpetuates the traditional outlook inherited with early evangelization. In effect, hierarchically and clerically conceived models of ministry, fostered even by the continued emphasis on the work of the laity in the field of the secular, are a constraint on new developments in discerning and preparing ministers for a community leadership that includes presiding locally and "in family" at the celebration of the Eucharist.

2

Mission and Ministry since Vatican II (B)

Europe, USA, General Reflections

The survey begun in the previous chapter continues here, attending to Europe and the USA. It ends with some general reflections on what has emerged across the world since the end of the Second Vatican Council.

Churches in Europe

The position of Christianity in Europe is quite different from its place in African, Asian, and Latin American society. Churches in Europe are faced with the reality that traditional Christianity is no longer the dominant factor in determining the vision and moral values of peoples or the organization of social life. Called the laicization or secularization of society, the situation is growing ever more complex, with the phenomenon of a growing religious pluralism among those who want to give purpose to life through a commitment to religious purpose. Churches are trying to generate a deeper faith among their remaining members and are compelled to ask how they may have some impact on the aims and goals of common life. They are not in a position to question some major values and achievements of secularization or laicization, recognizing how in the past Christianity has at times played a negative part in public life. Nor can they impose Christian beliefs on persons of other religious convictions. They are also constantly challenged to take account of the imperatives of ecumenical cooperation among churches.

After the close of the Second Vatican Council, bishops first found it necessary to acknowledge that faith was often not deeply ingrained and that religion was lived to a great extent as a private affair. On the other hand, in some countries, especially in France, Belgium, and Italy, organized Catholic Action in one form or another had brought lay persons into play as agents of an evangelizing influence in society. Bishops' conferences therefore turned their attention to a couple of questions. The first was how to lead the numbers who received sacraments as a matter of course into a conscious and active participation in the life and mission of the Church as a community. The second was to so change the institutional framework of the

Church that it would include the active participation, contribution, and rights of all the baptized. In considering these developments, we will look in turn at France, Italy, and Spain, selecting these from among other countries for special inquiry.

France

In the decades since Vatican II, the French episcopacy and Catholic community have gone more and more into the question of how to be a living presence in a country that ideologically and institutionally espouses *laïcité*. Given the negative factors in the history of Christian churches, one can explain historically why this social evolution occurred. Even if, however, memories need to be purified, as called for by the 2000 Jubilee Year, communities of Christian faith wish, in the name of Christ, to live in hope and work positively with others. These may be persons of other living faiths or those who are consciously humanitarian. With all of these, Christians seek the common good and the common unity of the human race. The first actions and documents of the episcopal conference were intended to reinforce the life of faith and to create a true sense of community and shared responsibility. In later years, the concern has turned more toward the kind of presence that the Church can guarantee in a laicized society, even as France is faced with a growing religious pluralism, due especially to immigration from other continents.[1] For this kind of engagement in public life, the Catholic Church has had to refine and redefine its members' attitudes toward society, toward other Christians, toward persons of other religions.

Beginnings of Response to Vatican II

The far-ranging pastoral and theological challenge to include lay persons, women and men, in the work and ministry of the Church was taken up shortly after the Council, beginning indeed with some small matters. When the Vatican document *Fidei custos* (1969) was sent to local bishops on some matters concerning Holy communion, the French bishops set up norms for the selection of extraordinary ministers of the Eucharist.[2] The French response to the Vatican documents on revising the ministries of acolyte and lector, and on extraordinary ministers, was rather crisp, pointing out that France already had extraordinary eucharistic ministers and querying the distinction between these and the ones who were to be installed as acolytes. The French bishops were actually trying to address the much-larger issue of lay ministries in the Church, in a variety of areas of ecclesial life, while at the same time holding to the singularity of the presbyteral ministry and office.

The 1971 plenary assembly of bishops at Lourdes was given a report written by Msgr. Robert Coffy, entitled *Eglise signe de salut au milieu des hommes*.[3] The immediate concern in asking for this report seems to have been to take stock of the implementation of liturgical renewal. Nevertheless, Msgr. Coffy went to the heart of the matter in identifying a lack of engagement in sacramental life on the part of many, even when they went through the rote of using Catholic liturgy in satisfying the need for rites of human passage. He linked this with the general de-Christianization and secularization of French society and so asked what it truly meant for the Church to be a presence in such a world. No serious renewal of sacramental life could take place without evangelization, beginning with the ranks of the baptized who come looking for infant baptism, the blessing of marriage, and funeral rites. This could not take place without a renewed vision of the Church itself, however, which Coffy proposed in terms taken from the documents of the Council. The Church in her being and in her life is a sacrament of salvation in the midst of the world, a community of faith that in its life and even in its social action witnesses to the salvation offered by God in Jesus Christ.

This certainly changes the position of bishops and priests in society, who are not simply the administrators and ministers of ecclesiastical work and liturgy, but also leaders of a community that witnesses and speaks to society about its vision and its values. With regard to the laity, it is imperative that they all be fully engaged in the life of the Church and in its program of evangelization. Even with decreasing numbers, a revised adult catechumenate was playing a role in rejuvenating communities, not only for the candidates but also for the parishes and other communities, which took this as a common concern of all the faithful. It is into such a context that the matter of specific lay ministries needed to be addressed. Therefore as ingredient in a much larger picture, the bishops could approve of formalizing such lay ministries as presiding at Sunday worship in the absence of priests, reading the Scriptures in the assembly, bringing communion to the sick, acting as catechists, and exercising already existing positions of leadership in Catholic Action, which as elsewhere, however, needed to look outside the Church and to engagement in a milieu where Christians need to cooperate with others.

In 1972, the Assembly of Bishops at Lourdes received a report, which they sanctioned for publication, adopting a certain number of conclusions.[4] This was a document on the preparation of candidates for the presbyteral ministry. The primary aim was to situate this ministry and its preparation in a new context, marked by three significant factors. First was the reality of being a priest in a secularized society, this meaning that it is not possible to administer parishes and preach the Word without reference to this social context. Second is the truth that the Church is now marked and enriched by the emergence of ministries exercised by laity, requiring a readiness for collaborative work on the part of the ordained. Third is the effort required to create truly apostolic communities that give an apostolic witness in this secularized society and from within which candidates for all ministries might emerge. On this last point, the report cited the constitution *Lumen gentium* 16 and the decree *Ad gentes* 3.

A section of this report dealt specifically with the ministries of the laity, pointing to the situation opened up by Paul VI in *Ministeria quaedam* (1972).[5] The report noted that in the teaching of the Second Vatican Council, the whole community is deemed responsible for building up the Church, drawing on the particular charisms of each and all. In addition to this, however, there are those who, according to provisions foreseen in *MQ*, devote themselves to a service of the Church that is relatively stable and in works that are officially recognized by the Church authorities because of the responsibility conferred.

At their plenary assembly in Lourdes in 1973, the bishops published another document on the question, this time with a title that asked how the presbyteral ministry retains its place when all are considered responsible and the whole Church is ministerial.[6] The booklet contains descriptions of what was actually taking place in the French church and some theological essays, including one by Yves Congar. Broadly speaking, the position taken was that in a de-Christianized society, the whole question of mission and ministry needs rethinking and that what is at stake is a new understanding of the relation between the ordained and the rest of the baptized, and a restructuring of ministry. In effect, more and more lay persons had assumed positions of responsibility, whether in line with the history of Catholic Action in the decades before the Council or in assuming what are normally considered pastoral charges. In this latter, one clear influence was the dearth of ordained priests, but the matter went deeper, indicating a new sense of community and lay responsibility. For some priests, this meant a crisis of priestly identity, but this had to be faced not by reactionary behavior but by pastorally and theologically spelling out the full nature of ecclesial ministry, in such a manner as to allow for a varied participation. The tone of the text was that it was necessary to continue along the lines already being traced out, for the sake of the inner life of the Church and for the sake of the work of evangelization.

Later Developments

In the years following, with the continued decrease in the number of priests and in the effort to revitalize smaller ecclesiastic units, lay persons assumed more roles in liturgical and pastoral leadership, even to the extent of being in effect administrators of parishes or quasi-parishes. Some communities themselves took on the task of choosing and appointing ministers. In this kind of situation, some feared a confusion between lay and ordained and indeed an intrusion of the laity into what is properly the ministry of the ordained. Others, however, saw the situation as one in which communities themselves take responsibility for ministries and even raise the question of proper procedures in candidacy for ordination.[7] Another reality was the emergence of communities constituted by associations or societies of clergy and faithful, such as one called Emmanuel, which seemed to set up their own structures of authority, being almost parallel to the parochial and diocesan administration of the church of France. Quite often the ideal of these quasi-parishes, or indeed parishes confided to such associations, is rooted in a strong distinction between Church and world, between clergy and laity.

Two documents emanating from the episcopal assembly of 1996 give a good idea of what had come into being over a little more than two decades and how the ministry of the Church had come to be seen. One is about the collaboration in pastoral work between ordained and lay in what pertains to liturgical and sacramental life.[8] The other is about the diaconate.[9]

In the first, which is called a press notice, the bishops wished to place the issue of lay collaboration in sacramental life into the wider perspective of the life and mission of the Church, and to see it alongside what needed to be said about the formation of deacons and priests. Since sacraments lead to a rediscovery of faith and its place in life, they are themselves moments of evangelization and commitment to mission. In baptism, marriage, and funerals, priests remain the principal officially appointed ministers and must not neglect this pastoral role, but it is important that in various ways the whole assembly assumes its part and responsibility and that trained lay persons take their place in the actual celebration, in its preparation, and in its aftermath. The press notice indicated that this was already being done to a great extent, but that the bishops wanted to avoid situations wherein lay persons seemed to substitute for priests or to take on new roles simply because of the penury of the ordained, or indeed situations that called the need for ordained ministers into question.

The principal document of the 1996 assembly was a report on its deliberations, prepared by Msgr. Claude Dagens, on how to present the faith in the France of today.[10] The report speaks to all the situations of public life in which the Church has to find a place and which it has to address, in what is formally and constitutionally a lay state and where the Christian faith is not followed by many of the citizens. As far as participation in mission and ministry is concerned, it is pertinent to note the title given to part 2 of the letter: "Forming the Church as Sacrament of Christ in Our Society."

As the title of the document itself (How to Present the Faith in Present-Day Society) indicates, the conference has retained the general perspective of the 1971 report but elaborates further upon it. The letter avows that the bishops do not want to be caught up in debate on the rights of the Church in a lay society, nor in debate about positive and negative factors in the emancipation of society from the Church. The important thing is to see how the Church fits into the life of the people and how it may continue to contribute to the general good and keep some hopes and perspective alive, not only for its own members but for all. Affirming the Church as sacrament of salvation and of Christ, in the particular reality of a historical moment, is the right theological perspective and one in which the work of evangelization may be incorporated, as is explicitly done in part 1, section 5.[11] There it is recalled that mission has to involve all—priests, deacons, lay—not in a purely functional sense but in ways that respect the sacramental placement of each within the sacrament of the Church itself. Hence new distribution of roles and ministries has taken place, and important structural changes allow for common and shared responsibility. The roles given to laity include liturgical, catechetical, apostolic, administrative, and financial ones. Structural changes provide for setting up presbyteral councils, diocesan pastoral councils, and pastoral councils for parishes and sectors of a diocese or parish. All of this is intended to enliven the inner life of the Church in all its aspects, and to enable it to engage fully in its service to society and in making known the person and gospel of Jesus Christ.

In general, we see that the French church, while not oblivious of global poverty, is most concerned with the practice of the Christian faith in a secular society. In this situation the Church has to establish its sense of mission and evangelization, and within this context it needs to develop a variety of services and ministries. At the same time, it is also clear that some particular issues about the cooperation between lay and ordained, and about the distinction between them, have arisen because of the growth of communities with lay members, men and women, in pastoral positions.

Church in Italy

In the years after the Vatican Council, the Italian church made some moves toward an expansion of ministries that would affirm the part of all the baptized in its life and mission. In 1973, after *Ministeria quaedam*, the episcopal assembly expressed its intention to make provisions for the installation of lay persons as acolytes and lectors, and also for the designation of extraordinary ministers of the Eucharist. The bishops likewise thought to look into the possibility of instituting ministries that would be peculiar to the Italian church, suggesting such offices as cantor, catechist, sacristan, administrator of works of charity. It was noted that this could not be addressed without due consideration of the place and role of women in the Church. Theologically and canonically, the bishops opined that with more lay ministries, it would be possible to accomplish cooperation between the ordained and the baptized in the threefold office of Christ, as augured by Vatican II.

The major preoccupation of the Italian bishops, however, was the distance between sacramental practice, often a matter of rote, and the depth of Christian faith. This issue was addressed in 1973 in a report entitled *Evangelizzazione e Sacramenti*,[12] in which questions of catechesis, instruction in the faith, and sacramental preparation were addressed. Preparation for the baptism of children, for first communion, for confirmation, and for marriage needed to be programmed and well executed, and this could not be done without the collaboration of competent lay persons. Such preparation, however, needed to have the orientations of the Second Vatican Council in mind and a comprehensive vision of the Church as a community of faith. What is asked for, in effect, is what is called "a new evangelization." People cannot see themselves as simple beneficiaries of a sacramental dispensation. They need to grasp what it is to live faith in Christ in an increasingly secularized society and to have a responsible role in maintaining or spreading the faith. The report puts all of this into the theological context of the reality of the Church as sacrament of Christ in the world.

The Italian church thought to complement, or even complete, this report by holding an ecclesial convention in 1975, in which ordained and lay took part, on the theme of "Evangelization and Human Development," subsequently publishing the acts of the congress.[13] In this meeting, the intention was to build up a greater sense of the life and mission of the Church, integrating the insights of *Lumen gentium, Gaudium et spes* (1965), and Paul VI's postsynodal exhortation *Evangelii nuntiandi* (1975), which included a just promotion of human development in the Church's mission. All of this had to be done in face of the growing secularization of the Italian people. While on one hand secularization is nothing other than the rightful deliverance of public life from ecclesiastical tutelage, it can also lead to a serious mutation of outlook and values that leave out matters of the spirit and all religious sense.

The meeting's final document notes the dependence of the Church on the laity for all forms of transmission of a living faith and for an effective presence in the various areas of common life in society. This recognition has to mean changes in the inner life of the Church. Liturgies should engage the active participation of the whole community, integrating and manifesting its variety of ministries and charisms, in a way that shows the link between liturgy and life. In all of this, building up and sustaining the role and importance of the local Church is of vital importance.

Keeping pace with the desire to include all the baptized in the mission of the Church, in 1998 the secretariat of the conference sent around a schema for parochial and diocesan evaluation of pastoral orientations, requiring the response of communities meeting as one.[14] To show how cooperation in serving the life and mission of the Church was then viewed, two questions of this instrument for evaluation are interesting. One (*scheda* I.2 [d]) asks whether parishes and dioceses promote a variety of qualified pastoral agents who are spiritually and theologically prepared and who have the competencies necessary for the particular work of evangelization asked of them. More to the point of full collaboration within communities, another (*scheda* I.2 [e]) asks whether pastoral councils are sufficiently used in working out pastoral and evangelizing programs.

An important step was taken at the general assembly of the conference in 2000, when the bishops produced a document which on the one hand they called a pastoral project and on the other a cultural project. By this dual appellation, they indicated the need to newly relate the life of the Church to a rapidly changing cultural milieu. The title of their document was "Communicating the Gospel in a Changing World."[15] The text projects a vision of a Church that is effectively a minority community in a secularized world. Sunday Mass attendance is dwindling, and though many Italians are still baptized and have some links with the Church as an institution, true and committed discipleship is practiced by the few. The missionary call of this community is to make Christ known in society and in every sector of society, in all the ways possible.

The first section of the episcopal document is a prolonged meditation on the mystery of Jesus Christ, as it is to be known and as it is to be lived. In the second section, the view that is projected of the Church is that of a vibrant parish eucharistic community, with its many and varied activities centered around its Sunday celebration. At one point the text treats pastoral workers, beginning with priests and including religious and members of the baptized faithful more directly involved in pastoral ministry, who collaborate with bishops and priests in this domain. More broadly, a parish will have many active ministries in which various members have some part. Special focus is placed on family and youth, given the need to pass on the faith within the community. Interchange on matters affecting pastoral ministry and the mission of the Church in society is an operative norm, and the document even speaks of initiating "community discernment" as a practical way of recognizing all the gifts of the Spirit present among the people.[16]

With this vision of the Church in place, the document speaks of ministries that result from the gifts of the Spirit, including the "new forms of ministry" that are needed to make Christ known in every sector of social and cultural life; here the task is seen as largely that of the baptized laity. While the focus is still that of the parish community and its collective discernment exercised in communion with ordained ministers, something is added about special activities. Such are those of Catholic Action in its new shape and the new ecclesial movements, which have a marked effect on Italian Catholic life.

The advantage of this project is the centrality of its sense of community, inclusive of its inner life and its missionary call. The Church appears as a community in mission, with a strong faith in Christ, and with the challenge of developing forms of life and of ministry that foster the presence of Christ in the world around it. Rather than talk only of particular ministries and services, ordained and lay, it produces a collaborative vision and relates all activities to the eucharistic community as such. In light of this, one may ask, What has happened in the Italian Church since 2000?

Other Bodies

To prepare a convention of the Italian church in Verona in 2006, the Episcopal Commission for the Laity in May 2005 sent out a letter inviting the readers to make Christ the heart of the world.[17] It spelled out how it understood the vocation of the laity and their cooperation within a harmonious ecclesial communion with the ordained. Basing its view of Christian mission on the foundation of witness to Christ and the gospel, the commission highlighted the call of the laity to change society through their place in the secular or temporal order of things.

A noteworthy preoccupation of this document is to see that the celebration of the Eucharist be at the heart of community life and mission. Hence in the absence of sufficient priests and the foreseeable future of an even-greater scarcity, the commission exhorts the laity to foster priestly vocations within their midst and seems to guard against situations in which lay members assume responsible pastoral and liturgical roles that are more properly those of the ordained. To make its case, the commission makes large use of the distinctions between laity and hierarchy, between the sacred and the secular, and between the ministerial priesthood and the royal priesthood of all the faithful, which it says points them primarily in the direction of evangelizing the world around them through their Christian testimony. Here we see that the old polarities are revived. More compromisingly, ministerial priesthood and royal priesthood are set apart, attributing the former to the clergy and the latter to the laity. This is to fall into the danger of putting two priesthoods in the Church, instead of different ways of sharing the one royal priesthood, not of individual members but of the Church, that is of the body and community of the Church, one with Christ in his royal priesthood.

There is some contrast between the bishops' letter of 2005 and proposals coming, first from a meeting held under the auspices of the CEI (Conferenza Episcopole Italiana) Commission on the Laity in 2000,[18] and then from a convention of the church of Sicily in 2001.[19]

In the document for the close of the 2000 convention on the identity and mission of the laity, the participants addressed a statement to the Church, bishops, priests, religious, and laity. Expressing disappointment over the fruits of the hopes generated by a Roman synod held in 1987, they suggest the need for a new vision of the Church. This ecclesial vision should be modeled on Jesus himself and on how he interacted with people. With simplicity and humility, he showed solidarity with all, and especially with the marginalized. Like Christ, the Church needs to empty itself (Phil 2:6–7) and to be ready to suffer poverty and persecution (*Lumen gentium* 8). To realize this vision, it is not enough to look to organizations. More fundamentally, the life of the Church has to be rooted in people's daily lives since it is from there that the Church has to build up itself and its mission. In effect, this is where the Christian laity live out their lives with others and where they exercise their mission, sometimes constructing associations to enable them to work together.

The members of the assembly asked for this fresh ecclesial vision and a deepening of the sense of the lay vocation in face of certain phenomena marking the life of the Italian church. As such phenomena, the document numbers the abstention of Catholics from political life, the diminution in the number of priests and religious serving the Church, the crisis provoked by the rigid adherence to the interests of particular associations, and the emergence of new ecclesial movements,[20] as well as a new sense of the need for a social and cultural project inspired by Christian faith. With the new consciousness generated amid such eventualities, many Catholic laity feel a distance between the realities of Christian community and what is said in Church documents. They believe that the laity need to be given a larger role in determining the modalities by which the Church lives its mission. This does not in any way represent a desire to trespass on the province of bishops and of the ordained, but it is a desire for a simple recognition of the fact that, given the essential importance of the mission of the laity, they need more say in giving it shape. A clerical Church, the document says, cannot find a due presence in the social and cultural life of the nation. From what Vatican II says of the laity, it should be clear that they do not simply carry out a mission mandated to them. Men and women, they must have an active part in discerning their role and in giving it shape within the life of the Christian community.[21]

In the meeting of the Church in Sicily in 2001, voting a number of propositions that were presented to the bishops at the end of the convention, the assembly asked for steps to be taken that in the spirit of Vatican II would overcome the clerical and sacral lens through which the Church is often seen. This would also mean to overcome the conflictual dualism between world and Church, so that the lay faithful could be true resources to the ecclesial community and true collaborators. In another proposition, it was asked that steps be taken to overcome clergy-lay dualism, showing that all share in the one baptismal priesthood, but according to different vocations and ministries, something that can be realized in communion with pastors when they themselves see the Church and its mission this way. The ideal for Church life proposed at this convention was characterized by the word *synodality*, meaning a harmonious collaboration, likened to a symphony, in which all gifts are recognized and valued in their diversity and all are coresponsible for the life and mission of the Church. The convention pointed out that what blocks the structural changes needed to revitalize the ecclesial communion is the self-image of the Church suggested in the dualisms that need to be overcome but which hang on quite obdurately.

Over all, in the Italian Church the position on ministries and on the respective roles of the ordained and the rest of the baptized has been influenced by two factors. The first is the secularization of culture and the new missionary position of the Church in society and culture. The second is the accent given to the primordiality of the community as such and to the shared and collaborative responsibility of all its members. However, the distinction between ordained and lay remains a preoccupation, and the old polarizations have not yet been laid to rest.[22]

Church in Spain

Three significant documents from plenary assemblies of the episcopal conference of Spain on the Church's mission and ministry merit attention. Two are pastoral plans to cover a period of some years: one, published in 1994, was for the years 1994–97; another, published in 2002, was for the years 2002–5. The third document, dated 1991, is on the place of the Christian laity in the mission and ministry of the communion of the Church.[23]

Harking back to previous statements, as far back as 1972, the first plan enunciates the missionary character of the Church and the need for a new evangelization, given the changes in social and cultural milieu that have taken place, and especially the absence of a Christian perspective in the social, political, and economic regulation of the European and Spanish world today. In other words, Church communities find themselves in a new missionary situation, where their witness to Christ and the gospel and their capacity to influence society for the better is put to the test. This same perspective on the life and mission of the Church is carried forward in the 2002 pastoral plan.

What the Spanish bishops point out is that the Church is, as Church and in its entirety, missionary, and that mission is grounded in communion, or in community life and common responsibility. This has to be shared by all, in harmonious collaboration. In the missionary situation of the day, the role and action of the laity has taken on new and primary significance, since it is in large measure through them that Church, gospel, and finally Christ are present in society and in the cultures of peoples. Roles and ministries are differentiated, and at times there is considerable stress on the hierarchical nature of ecclesial communion, but the basic picture is of a community in which all share responsibility. While this responsibility includes a differentiation of various kinds of activity, it means a common or shared discernment on what communities need for their own life and on how the Church may address contemporary social and cultural questions in the milieu to which it belongs.

Faith in Christ, a sound knowledge of the gospel, and eucharistic liturgy are at the heart of ecclesial communion, and it is on them that discernment of the call to mission and to service is grounded. The three documents are intended to reinvigorate parish life and locate local ecclesial communion chiefly in the parish. The text on the laity of 1991, however, is sensitive to the other forms of lay association that actually exist or are needed to help all the faithful to live and fulfill their Christian and missionary vocation. Hence the bishops wish to promote movements that reach beyond parish boundaries, such as Catholic Action and the new movements that have emerged since the Second Vatican Council. All of these, however, are expected to respect the ecclesial communion to which they belong and are in part to be judged on how they contribute to local parish life, rather than derogate from it.

All three documents provide considerable elaboration on how the baptized laity may influence the worlds of education, commerce, politics, social services, and international ventures. There are also guidelines on how this requires an ongoing discussion and discernment within communities. As far as ecclesial structures are concerned, it is pointed out that working together on parish and pastoral councils, or in other ecclesiastical organisms, is necessary for the collaboration of ordained, religious, and laity in the life and mission of the Church. Although there certainly are canonical provisions on the exercise of authority within these councils, the Spanish bishops highlight the values of common discernment, common planning, and the promotion of common action.

Conclusions on the Churches of Europe

The situation in other European Churches, such as Austria, Germany, Switzerland, England, or Ireland, could also be examined, but what is here presented seems sufficient to raise the pertinent pastoral and theological questions regarding ministry and the formulation of mission by the Church community. In all of what has been recounted of the situation of ministry and the vision of mission, one sees the continuing tensions in the life of the Italian, Spanish, and French Churches as they work out a sense of mission and the participation of diverse charisms and ministries within them. To begin with, there is a genuine development of lay charisms, lay ministries, lay mission; that of itself diversifies the question about Church and order, affecting also the place of the sacrament of order. At the same time, there is the continuous tension between a community-based Church in which all, including ordained, find their place; and a continuing clerical or hierarchical model of

Church, which continues to be given its justification in certain ways of appealing to polarizations accredited to the documents of Vatican II. Alongside this tension, there is the reality of some kind of split within the life of the Church and its administration engendered by the emergence of new ecclesial movements with an alternate organization and even an assumption of control in parish life. How the spiritual wealth of these realities, sometimes at odds with each other, may be integrated in giving vitality to the life and mission of the Church is an issue facing the Catholic Church in these European countries. One senses that none of these tensions can be resolved if there are not new approaches to choosing candidates for ordination and designing structures allowing for a more community-based or synodal governance of parishes and dioceses. These are not provisions that would automatically resolve tensions, but they would provide better structures within which they could be addressed, in line with the thoughts of Giuseppe Alberigo, cited above.

Church in the USA

Talking of churches in the USA, it must be remembered that to a great extent the period of ethnic parishes that were of European origin has in recent years been followed by an emergence of new ethnicities, primarily Hispanic, Asian (Vietnamese, Korean, Laotian, Filipino), and Haitian. These are host to peoples newly immigrated and often seeking refuge from their countries of origin, on account of poverty or on account of political persecution. There is also a burgeoning of African American communities, now at last given the possibility within the Catholic Church of finding their own voice. Naturally, this gives rise to considerable ecclesial diversity. However, certain trends can be put in evidence as pertinent to the development of charism, mission, community, and ministry.

As far as the episcopal conference (USCCB: US Conference of Catholic Bishops) is concerned, it has in many ways tried to monitor developments by keeping to the fore the typological distinction of *Lumen gentium*, stressing the role of Christian laity in transforming the secular order. However, because of the fact that many lay persons assume pastoral and liturgical responsibilities and are even appointed to this by bishops where there is a need, they have also sought to theologize and legislate what they have called Lay Ecclesial Ministry.[24] Their position is that lay persons belong properly to the temporal order, though they may normally exercise some liturgical functions, such as reader, cantor, parish director of liturgy, or educational services, such as that of catechist or director of religious education. When they take on pastoral leadership, especially in parishes where there is not a resident priest, they need a special delegation from the bishop, who must also see to their proper education and preparation. They see this as a ministry that is an extension of the baptismal priesthood and fits with the idea expressed by Yves Congar before the Vatican II, that in virtue of their royal priesthood, lay persons may be properly delegated to assist the hierarchy in their pastoral duties.[25]

Something that has clearly marked the American church and given life to many a parish is the experience of the Adult Catechumenate, with its implementation of what is rather badly called the RCIA (Rite [instead of Order] for the Christian Initiation of Adults), as well as of the initiation of baptized persons seeking aggregation to the Roman Catholic communion. The entire parish is asked to take responsibility for this, and it generates quite a number of special ministries, such as those of sponsor, catechist, director, and so forth. Not only are the candidates well prepared and gradually initiated, but all those who follow their journey learn more of their faith, of their mission, and of the nature of ecclesial community and communion.

Among the laity themselves, a certain amount is going on that has an impact on how the American church sees mission and ministry, though this is not the same among all the cultural communities mentioned. Among Hispanics, with the encouragement of some bishops and the bishops' office for Hispanics, there has been an effort to apply the Latin American model of base ecclesial communities.[26] Among others, there has been some move to make use of small groups, composed mostly of those of the middle-class on the social level. While they were at one time a lay initiative of lay persons, they are now officially sponsored in a number of dioceses as a means of evangelization and religious adult education or Bible reflection. A survey done a short time ago[27] suggested that there are about 37,000 such groups across the states and that the prime reason for their appearance and continuation is the desire for more spiritual nourishment than parishes and Sunday liturgy often provide, as well as a greater sense of being able to live a community of human dimensions within the faith. Whatever the name, these small communities are not to be confused with what is sought in the pastoral option of the Latin American, Asian, or African Bishops. They are not in themselves holistic groups from which leaders emerge to take on ministries of ecclesial responsibility, nor are they communities of the poor who seek to find their place and mission in Church and society, in view of their call to discipleship and discernment of the Spirit working among them.

In an effort to spell out the mission of the Church for the US community, in the light of the teachings of Vatican II and the option for the poor, the USCCB, working through its committees, issued two pastoral letters in the 1980s. One was on how Catholics relate to the economy when they have this vision before them, and the other on the service of peace. There were hearings around the country to garner the views of the whole body of believers, in all the pertinent areas of society. In this sense, the letters were the fruit of the Church at work, ordained and lay working together to create a vision of Church mission and service. There was also an effort to produce a document on women's place in Church and society, but the polarizations were so great that no fruit was borne. Since then, the episcopacy has been hesitant as a body to bring the Catholic communion to focus together on issues of the temporal order, and the community is left with sterile debates about the admission to communion of politicians who make the political option to vote pro-choice. Some initiatives have been taken to converse with civil leaders and to draw together in solidarity churches of North, South, and Central America. These, however, do not engage the Church as a whole and do not bring up questions about Church ordering and how to act as a body, endowed with many charisms and gifts.

Another important factor in the American church, not at all sponsored by the episcopacy, is the emergence of woman-church and the conscientization to the discipleship of Jesus that it brings. Last, there are presently the reactions to the loss of credibility by bishops and priests due to sex scandals and the obvious misman-agement of many bishops. While this incident is tragic and painful, in some way it seems to be leading some of the laity to a deeper realization of their responsibility for the Church and a call on the bishops to include them in decision-making pro-cesses.[28] At the same time an increasing polarization is generated in part by the efforts, through seminary training of a particular type, to bolster the self-identity of priests, which sets them apart from the laity and accentuates the sacred character of their calling.

In North America (Canada and the USA) many lay persons exercise ministries with professional preparation and professional salaries. There is also a tremendous theological output on the subject of ministry, and numerous courses are organized at college and university level. However, there is not a great feel of growth or of readiness to address the kind of structural change that would truly foster core-sponsibility of all the baptized in the affairs of the Church. The American churches may need to learn from other continents what is necessary to live the mission of Christ as a community through the option for the poor.[29]

General Reflections on Mission and Ministry since Vatican II

On questions of ministry, there is a notable interplay in the reception of Vatican II between the issues raised by *Lumen gentium* and those raised by *Gaudium et spes*. The latter, with its ideal of dialogue with society in all its realms and of integral human development, has served most to prompt churches to elaborate their vision and their sense of mission. This in turn has greatly affected movement in Church structuring and in attention to the charisms of ministry.

The most fundamental question for most churches in recent decades in pursuing the aspiration to Christian witness and mission has been how to live out the fun-damental option for the poor advocated by Pope John XXIII and the Second Vatican Council, and how to do this not simply by way of service to the impoverished but by being the Church of the Poor, one that lives a solidarity of all with the poor and in which the poor themselves are agents in forming Christian life and in mission.

Since the early postconciliar years when steps were being taken to acknowledge the existence of many and diversified types of ministry exercised by lay members, the tenor of the discussion has in important circles changed on several counts. Churches in the South were concerned about being living human communities of faith, witnessing to Christ in a diversified society that called out for an integral human development. To realize this, these churches acknowledged many charisms and diversified their ministries, truly seeking to activate the role of all the baptized in common life and in mission. In the North, churches saw themselves faced with the mission to witness to Christ in an increasingly secularized society, but also in solidarity with all the peoples of the world in the quest for development, peace, and justice. This led to much thought about mission, which gave vigor to the role of the laity, but the situation was complicated by the fact that many communities were without priests, so that lay persons took on more and more pastoral and liturgical ministries. Whatever the differences between North and South, it can be said in a general way that the call of the Spirit felt by churches across the world is that of living out the preferential option for the poor, with a fully participating member- ship, and facing situations where the very existence of local communities depends on lay leadership by women and men assuming responsibilities usually associated with those initiated into the sacrament of order. One of the most crucial factors in developments has been the role of women, both in initiating efforts at common life and evangelization, and in taking leadership positions, including officially ap- pointed ones. With all of this, however, Church teaching keeps to its position on the question of excluding them from ordination, as in another way it continues to employ the distinction between the role of the laity in the secular arena and that of the ordained in the sacred.

In the churches of the South, we have noted the importance given in living the Christian life and in the work of evangelization to small communities, by whatever name they go. Along with this, in Africa and Asia we have found special attention given to the role of families in forming communities, while indeed working within the larger concept of family proper to these peoples. This does not simply mean, as it may mean commonly enough in Church teaching, that family is the primary place of education and that the Church must guard the sanctity and rights of family life. On those continents it means attending to a constructive role that families have in forming, building, and serving the family of the Church. In this regard, one thinks of the influence of households in the so-called household churches of early Chris- tianity, and of the influence of their inner structure on Church structure. Is there a comparable, if certainly not identical, move today with attention to how families form communities?

One reaction to new situations is to try to think out the realities of community, charism, ministry, and order in fresh ways, not depending solely on traditional formulas into which new movements have to fit. Some of this fresh thinking is found not only among scholars but even in the episcopal texts considered above, where they try to go beyond a slavish adherence to the formulations of the docu- ments of the Second Vatican Council. They show that the Church needs diversifi- cation and difference in ordering ministries and indeed in talking of ordained ministry.

The matter of order is posed in new ways, prompted by the vitality that comes from communities and movements of the baptized. Communities are forming in ways more closely related to cultural forms and energies, and more connected with specific local issues, whether these are social, cultural, or economic. In this situation, order is not best established by relying overmuch on known categories or institutional forms. It has to take on new shapes that allow for the life and initiatives shown in communities and movements of the baptized. Rather than attending only to parishes and dioceses, churches need to ask what kind of autonomy may be given to congregations that have roots in other human environments. What roles deserve formal recognition, what kind of liturgical and canonical recognition is to be given, what synodal bodies need to be constituted, and what integration of newly forming bodies into a larger ecclesial communion may be effected? In the midst of such changes it has also to be worked out how dialogue with other Christian churches and with other living faiths can be fostered and made an integral part of ecclesial life.

It is not simple to have an overview of how matters are being dealt with on the ground, but there is a helpful survey provided by Bishop Fritz Lobinger of Aliwal, South Africa.[30] He gives information about specific communities and settings in different parts of the world, inclusive of Africa, Asia, North America, Brazil, and Europe. Much of the time, the effort seems to be to work with a reduced number of priests, while giving more responsibility in the general running of communities and noneucharistic liturgies to appointed lay members of these congregations. From the survey, however, what emerges most distinctly—and this is corroborated from other sources and from what has been said above—is the need for differentiation and pluralism in Church ordering. The magisterium works too narrowly with defined notions of bishops, priests, and deacons within a defined notion of the sacrament of order. It often seems to have only one ideal of priest, someone who is seminary trained, celibate, and at the disposal of a bishop (or religious superior) for assignment "anywhere." Within order, however, is it not possible to see community leaders, in a leadership that includes eucharistic presidency, as persons who work in teams and who are named from within a community for a specific place, rather than for general assignment, and who receive a different sort of training? If such a policy were worked out, one could think of different types of ministry within the ranks of sacramental order, not seeing one as superior to another but seeing people with diverse charisms and diverse responsibilities working together. This might mean that the teaching role of some presbyters who need to help local communities would be more important than the sacramental, while others would have a more localized ministry, working within particular congregations, together with the other charismatically gifted ministers among the people.

Over against this possibility or projection of diversification and differentiation, however, precisely because of the increasing role of the laity and the diversification of services and ministries, there have been efforts, always on the increase, it seems, to protect the formally established distinction between lay and ordained and to preserve a traditional tripartite distinction of bishop, presbyter, and deacon.

In some places major attention has been brought to bear on the choice, the preparation, and the canonical status of lay persons exercising what are dubbed pastoral roles or responsibilities, more traditionally associated with clerical persons. Even here there is a difference. Some churches accentuate the episcopal delegation and the professional preparation of candidates, thus sticking more closely to traditional doctrinal and canonical provisions. Others move a little away from this and see these developments as the opportunity for communities to express their own sense of identity and ownership, having considerable say in the choice of candidates. The bishop or his delegate may preside over the installation and needs to assure ongoing formation, but the people have an active voice in selecting their ministers. The parallel made is with the role of the community in the choice of bishops, presbyters, and deacons, which is known to us from tradition.

As churches continue to define their sense of mission in and to the world,[31] there is a need for a better theological, practical, and canonical integration of all the baptized into this mission, while still keeping alive the sacramental and liturgical character of the Church, with its specific but now more diversified ordering. This is marked in the South by the continuing urgency of a mission to the poor, a mission for justice, peace, and reconciliation, and a mission of dialogue with persons of other living faiths. In this, the liturgical synaxis is more clearly related to the mission and vice versa, placing ordained ministry in that context. In the North, especially in Europe, it is a matter of spelling out the presence and mission of the Church in secularized cultures, with the realization that ecclesial presence in the development of society is guaranteed by the laity.

Across continents and cultures, there are some common factors in the growth of small ecclesial communities, which show how Christian communion has to retrieve the human dimensions of being Church. This has to be rooted among the people and within the environment of their daily lives and aspirations, so that a new relation between communities and pastoral leaders and ministers is essential. The new paradigms and styles of leadership, and the activities of lay persons as ministers, always have some relation to the lack of an adequate number of ordained persons. In France, Germany, and North America, at first the experience of lay-led communities had more to do with the penury of clergy, but the issue readily translated into the issue of the nature and participation of all in Church life and mission. Nonetheless, especially in the churches of the South, it was clear from the beginning that there were deeper reasons for calling on laity to share mission, ministry, and pastoral leadership and for a new formation of ecclesial communities. There is, however, a difference between the story of small communities in Latin America (BCCs) and those in Africa and Asia. In the case of Latin America, they emerged to a great extent from lay initiative. Over time, they have been incorporated into pastoral plans and even made secondary to parish organization. While there is an effort to keep their effectiveness as ecclesial units that aid the presence of the Church in society and address societal issues, lay initiatives have received less recognition even though lay action is called for. In Africa and Asia, the formation of small Christian communities was from the beginning an episcopal initiative, seen as a necessary pastoral strategy in developing a new evangelization.

The European and North American experience of small communities is much more directly related to the falling number of ordinations to the priesthood and the need to find pastoral solutions in face of this. In a broad way, there is talk of the lay vocation and apostolic work, but the focus is often on those given pastoral and liturgical responsibilities. It is never enough to think that lay leaders are simply delegates and substitutes, which sometimes has been the major preoccupation in more affluent societies. The experience even then, however, has been enough to raise new issues about how clergy and laity relate in leading and in ministry, and about who should be ordained, with more active role given to the community in the choice, the approval, and the liturgical installation of ministers. Even in Europe, where these small communities became truly active and participatory, they served as a way of being conscious of what it is to live as a Christian in a secularized society, and thus to spell out the nature of the Church's mission in these times.

The overall conclusion that one may draw from the way in which smaller units and lay involvement developed together is that churches around the world are faced with the need to find new models and modes of living Christian community. What hinders this, however, is the rigidity of long-existing structures and a continued accentuation of the status difference between the ordained and the rest of the baptized. A key question is how the choice, preparation, ordination, and activity of the ordained may be truly a community reality. With new formation of ecclesial units, there has to be a new approach to what is done by ordination.

As the life of the Church has developed since Vatican II, everywhere catechumenal experiences and their integral part in the life of a Church have considerable influence. In Asia and Africa, when a community as a whole is responsible for the catechumenate or other forms of initiation, it is the opportunity to relate Christian discipleship to traditional culture and to religions. In Latin America, Asia, and Africa, the procedures of incorporating new members are a life-giving way of relating to the whole environment and background, incorporating relations to cultural traditions, to religious traditions and milieu, or to the world of poverty and suffering in which many people live, as well as to ecological concerns. The very self-identity of a Christian community changes, and in tandem with this, questions of mission, charism, and ministry develop into dynamic factors in the life of a Church. In Churches of the North, the catechumenate also has a role to play in forming communities that are synodal in mission, making the whole Church conscious of being Christian in a diversified, and often indeed corrupt, society, where the poor are left out. When they take cognizance of their mission, communities also take cognizance of the integral place of all the baptized, with the charisms, services, and ministries that all contribute.

Returning to an earlier point, something that becomes evident from this survey is that in spelling out the mission of the Church today and its ministry, there needs to be discussion on the usefulness and the limits of the distinction between the sacred role of priests on one hand, and the secular character of the laity's mission and participation in the threefold office of Christ on the other hand. In looking for foundations for this mission, both theological and pastoral, the Church needs to pay more attention to the joint responsibility of all the baptized as a community of living faith, inclusive of the ordained in their distinctive role. With that, there is a call for canonical provisions that affirm and foster this responsibility. We see signs of this, for example, in documents from Brazil and Italy.

Everywhere, there is a fresh insistence on the need for proper formation, for priests, religious, and laity, if they are to take a due role in the mission of the Church and the work of evangelization. Sometimes this means less attention to small communities and more focus on the parish as key structure, but the matter of small communities is not totally forgotten or neglected. As the life of churches takes new shape, it is more apparent that liturgical celebration and service to the world cannot be separated but that they coalesce in a living communion of Christ and Spirit. One cannot talk of lay participation in liturgical ministries without looking at their participation in mission. Vice versa, one cannot talk of mission and service to the kingdom without allying this to participation in liturgical action and ministry.

In the last few decades, some other factors have emerged that affect the issue of Church ordering, mission, lay involvement, and ecclesiastical structure. Many countries have witnessed the emergence of lay movements that are internationally organized, sometimes with specific ecclesiastical approval. Some then ask how these may redefine the nature of the Church's mission, the laity's role, and the relation to pastoral and canonical provisions. Another rather unhappy factor is that, almost as a response to increased lay involvement and even presented as a way of encouraging it but within theological and canonical limits, there is a move among some clergy, and even by Rome, to emphasize anew, theologically and practically, the ontological, ecclesiastical, sacramental, and cultural distinction between the ordained and the baptized. Without forging a new optic, it is almost inevitable that this perspective will prevail, thus jeopardizing many postconciliar fruits in the lives of local churches.

In light of all of the above, one can point to two key issues for developing ministry in different parts of the world. These are the needed social impact of Church community and ministry in witnessing to the advent of God's reign in human realities, and the need to provide communities with ministers to celebrate the Eucharist. The two may be discussed as interrelated or at times as though they have little connection. The connection between the two exists in the truth that, in Catholic perspective, a community that witnesses and evangelizes is a eucharistic community; in reality Church polity has not moved toward affording the possibility of regular eucharistic celebration to a host of congregations across the world. They are prevented from finding roots for their witness and their mission in constant communion at the Lord's table.

Despite the tendency to look backward, under the Spirit's guidance a new consciousness is being shaped, however slowly and hesitantly, which has great relevance for the matter of Church ordering and ministry. It is the sense of all the baptized being Church, an apostolic and missionary body of believers, a royal priesthood by reason of God's covenant through Christ. It is also a consciousness of how pervasive in the world is the action of God's Spirit, and of the need to discern the Spirit's action in the hopes, aspirations, traditions, and religions of the entire human race, in all its richness and diversity. As such, it is a consciousness that is beginning to set the Church free of many crippling dualisms. Once freed of the dualisms of matter and spirit, of male and female, of self and alien other, of clergy and laity, it is possible for a Church, beginning at the local level, to imagine an alternative humanity and an alternative ecclesial communion. How may readings of tradition assist this?

A final word has to be said on the christological foundations of mission. A formally doctrinal Christology, emphasizing the play of Christ's divinity in the work of his humanity, can give rise to a more institutionally oriented ecclesiology, attributing given and lasting structures of the Church to him as founder. On the other hand, the faith given expression in a number of churches, especially those where peoples are seeking a way out of colonial domination, has a clearer relation to their own history. For them, Christ is related to the history of peoples as the living presence of the living Christ. Belief in the presence and action of God's kingdom on one hand, and the gift of the Spirit on the other gives a shape to what people see of Christ and to the hope they have in him as God's Son and Savior.

3

Events and Theologies before Vatican II

The ferment of the decades before the Second Vatican Council may not be ignored if the Council's own place in history is to be understood. The antecedents are found both in Europe and to some degree in what were seen as missionary countries. Developments in lay participation and developments in the theology of the sacrament of order are included in this overview.

A New Situation

The clash between the Catholic Church as embodied in the papacy and the new states and democracies from the time of the French Revolution is well known. Not only was there the political challenge, but the forces of the Enlightenment brought a new, more experiential and more rational way of viewing reality, which sat uneasily with appeals to faith and divinely established teaching authority. In its teaching and in much of the approved theology, the Church did not accommodate well to this change, even though the First Vatican Council issued a decree on the relation between faith and reason. The notion of faith spelled out, as well as that of revelation, was dominantly doctrinal, a compilation of truths given to the world through Christ and taught by the magisterium.

Over time, to this sense of being faced by alien forces was added the perception that many people no longer adhered to Catholic faith and practice. In one well-known phrase, France in particular was called a *pays de mission*, missionary territory. Some observed that this challenge to the role of the Christian faith in contemporary life could not be met by stern reproof or by a simple insistence on possessing the truth by which countries and citizens should live. The Church needed to find a new place in a new society, and this was fostered by the growth among the faithful of what was called Catholic Action.

Some theologians engaged with cultural and popular experience in elucidating the faith. To a great extent they were responding to things happening in practice, breaking away from the ecclesiology commonly taught in seminaries at the time, where the Church was described as a perfect society, in which ordained ministers were endowed with all the powers needed to sanctify and to govern the faithful.

With a growing participation of lay persons in liturgy and in the apostolate, writers undertook the task of forging an ecclesiology that took this into account and that explained the relation of the Church to a newly developed order of temporal realities.

French theology probably had the largest practical impact because it specifically addressed engagement with the world, the need for theology to be pastoral, and the relation of faith to experience, as well as the particular demands of the de-Christianization of society. Both the lay apostolate and the priest-worker experiment are associated with developments in theological thought about mission and presence in society. The Dominican school of Le Saulchoir (near Paris), under the leadership of Marie-Dominique Chenu, espoused a theology related to the experiential, which it saw to be in continuity with the thinking of Thomas Aquinas. In doing this it moved back behind the sterile theology of schools and seminaries to one more rooted in biblical and patristic sources. In this effort to draw on sources for the revitalization of theology, the Dominicans joined forces with the Jesuit school of Fourvière (Lyon). Among French scholars special mention is made of Yves Congar because of his influence on a developing doctrine of the Church and because of the large part he played in opening Catholic communities to the exigencies and richness of ecumenical dialogue and exchange.

German theology was able to draw on the inspiration of the nineteenth-century Tübingen School in developing a theology in line with early church teachings and more ready to engage the question of the relation of faith and reason. Karl Rahner in particular showed the impact of historical consciousness in drawing on resources for a knowledge of revelation and a developing faith. He also pointed to human experience as a locus of divine presence to be pondered. Because of their impact on the practicalities of ecclesial life and the position of the hierarchy, these theologians were frowned upon and in one way or another silenced. Their work, however, was to be recovered in the course of the sessions of the Second Vatican Council.

Though in their own way they are pertinent, since they had an influence on the Church's sense of Catholic identity, this is not the place to enter into a discussion of movements of mind and organization that marked the life of the Church in the 1940s and 1950s and raised questions as to its inner life and its relations with others.[1] These are the biblical movement, the liturgical movement, the catechetical movement, and the Marian movement. Rather than seeing them as currents moving in a clear and unique direction, one could say that they provoked a certain turbulence of spirit resulting from the contrast between a sense of a need for change and opposition to all indicators of impending change. Here, however, we shall focus on what directly affected ministry and the active participation of the laity in the life of the Church, or what is often spoken of as Catholic Action.

Laity before the Council

While some developments in the theology of the sacrament of order were a challenge to the exercise of ministry, the greater challenge came from what was said about the call and role of the laity in the service of the Church's life and mission. With roots in such works as Émile Mersch's *Theology of the Mystical Body*,[2] and with some measured encouragement as well as caution from the encyclical *Mystici corporis*(1943), some theologians in the aftermath of World War II began to work on an ecclesiology that took the laity's mission into account. This ecclesiology had the advantage that it took practical truth into consideration as well as doctrinal tradition. It related to the liturgical movement's success in developing a greater lay participation in divine worship, and to the role of Christians in society as encouraged by the Catholic Action movement. The laity, long left out of treatises on the Church except under the title of passive and obedient subjects, were acknowledged in practice to have an active part in worship as well as in apostolate in the temporal world. How could a theology of the Church, it was asked, account for this active role?

Writings on the liturgy had already offered some explanation of lay participation in worship. This was done by speaking of the baptized person's relation to the priesthood of Jesus Christ. Through baptism and confirmation, the Christian is given the grace to live in obedience to the Gospel and in the service of others and is endowed with the gift of the Spirit. All are empowered to offer a spiritual sacrifice pleasing to God. Though this is the principal way in which the baptized Christian shares in the priesthood of Jesus Christ, these two sacraments confer a sacramental character that relates their recipients to the public order of the Church. In virtue of the character of baptism, the Christian actively shares in the public worship of the Church, thereby joining the offering of a holy life to the offering of Jesus Christ, which is represented in the Eucharist and in other parts of the liturgy. In this way the theology of worship had expanded on the teaching of Aquinas about the sacramental character, with its assertion of the part of all the baptized in Christ's priesthood, but modified its distinction between active and passive power to differentiate between the faithful and the ordained. On the other hand, what Thomas Aquinas said in explaining the character given at confirmation as source of an active duty in the Church, a duty to profess the faith publicly outside worship,[3] gave modern theologians a challenge and some kind of foundation.

The principal task was to develop a theology of the sacramental character, which writers were not satisfied to explain as a passive power related only to the reception of sacraments. On the contrary, since it was indeed a configuration to Christ the Priest, it could be explained as the root of an active participation in the offering of the eucharistic sacrifice and in all the other actions of the Church's public worship. This explanation was, in the main, accepted by Pope Pius XII in his encyclical *Mediator Dei* (1947).[4] Here he taught that the laity offer the Mass in union with the priest by reason of their own particular share in Christ's priesthood that comes to them through baptism. Despite an admonitory tone cautioning against too wide an application of this principle, which would undermine the ministerial priesthood, the document as a whole was looked upon as a moment of gain for the liturgical movement. Today, there may seem nothing remarkable in the teaching, but after centuries of lay passivity in the liturgy it was no mean advance.

Given their broader activity, it was apparent that it was not enough for ecclesiology to speak of lay participation in worship. One of the great liturgical writers of the twentieth century, Lambert Beauduin,[5] pointed out that liturgy could not be understood apart from the Church's mission and that liturgical practice and theology needed to be pastoral. Along with others, he saw that the considerable apostolic work of the members of Catholic Action in its various forms had to be taken into account. The Church's mission to make Christ's gospel known and effective in the world could not be achieved without the commitment and action of the laity, for which they needed to be nourished from the mystery of Christ. But if one ascribes this to the call that comes with baptism, what has to be said about all those who seek to live good lives but do not engage in any formal apostolate? Or what has to be said about the then standard theology of the Church, which attributed mission and apostolate in principle to the hierarchy? To a great extent, developing new trends in ecclesiology meant working out an answer to the questions that arose from Catholic Action and from a pastoral understanding of the liturgy. On the one hand, how could Catholic Action be related to the common vocation of the lay person; on the other, how could it be related to the mission given by Christ to the hierarchy?

Catholic Action was militantly apostolic, with its branches for workers and for students, and with its particular focus on youth in both cases. One cannot generalize too much about its composition and orientation. Comparing countries such as Belgium, France, and Italy, it is clear that in each of these Catholic Action had its own particular physiognomy. However, it can be said that its greatest concern was the loss of the world (primarily Europe) to the Church, whether among the working masses, in the field of education, or in the affairs of political and secular institutions. It was the perception that the laity who were motivated by faith were in effect involved in a work of re-Christianization, which provoked theologians to revise their theories and examine Christian tradition in a new light.

One may contrast the European scene with that in the United States in order to better understand the theological currents that influenced the teaching of Vatican II. Certainly in America there were lay persons deeply involved in living out their Christian vocation in the service of others, but they did not face the question of de-Christianization since America remained a highly religious and even in some ways Christian country, whatever hostility Catholics sometimes encountered. In its new developments, the laity's apostolate was largely the social apostolate, the care of the needy and distressed of society. Their social concern rendered workers in the field naked to the accusation of "going communist," but they could not easily be accused of taking over the Church's teaching office. In Europe, on the other hand, it was the loss of Christian influence in all sectors of public life that moved lay persons to take on a task of evangelization, a task not merely of implementing the gospel on the social scene but one of making the GOSPEL known.

Theological Writings

Yves de Montcheuil was one of the first theologians to address this question of a mission in a de-Christianized society.[6] He worked out a theology of vocation that-stated that every Christian had an apostolic calling by the very fact of being a member of the Church. He defined this as the call to give witness to Christ in the midst of the world. Catholic Action has to be founded on this, but it is not the only way of living out one's call and is not necessary for all. This was to state the general principle of the apostolic nature of the Christian call and to provide the context within which Catholic Action could be further explained. It remained to be asked how Catholic Action and its type of evangelization could be described as a distinctively lay apostolate, without violating the principle that Christ's mission had been confided through the Twelve to the hierarchy.

The principal author to deal with this question was Yves Congar, in his justly famous *Jalons pour une théologie du Laïcat*.[7] This was a comprehensive treatment of the lay person's call, within which special attention was given to the questions raised by Catholic Action. As Congar then explained it, the most fundamental thing about being a Christian is to share in the sacrifice of Jesus Christ through the spiritual sacrifice of a holy life and through every good deed that leads to communion with God. This is how we are called to live in the time between the sacrifice of Christ on the cross and the consummation of this mystery in his second coming. All are called to share actively in cult by the sacramental character, whether that of order or that of baptism and confirmation, but of course in different ways. All are likewise called to the apostolate through the sacraments of order and of initiation, but again in different ways.

To explain how Catholic Action in its own particular way is a share in the apostolate, Congar appealed to the double source or origin of the Church's mission, the sending of the apostles and the sending of the Holy Spirit, both having their origin in Christ. As an institution possessing a mission and the powers to execute it, the Church relates back to the twelve apostles. As a community of life, giving witness to Christ in the world and serving others in charity, it originates in the Holy Spirit. The apostolate of the laity has its source in the mission of the Spirit, not in that of the apostles, and its general character is to bring about the consecration of the world through involvement in secular affairs in a Christian spirit and following Christian principles. In Catholic Action, the mission that the laity receive from the Spirit is taken up under the direction of the hierarchy and ordered toward a specific objective: evangelization. In this way, it becomes a share in the mission of the hierarchy, even while remaining rooted in the sacraments of initiation and being a way of carrying out the distinctively lay calling of the *consecratio mundi* (consecration of the world). Laity do not need any new consecration in order to undertake this apostolate, since they are fitted to it by baptism and the grace of the Spirit. All that is needed to make it formally a share in the Church's mission is a mandate from the hierarchy.

At the time Congar strongly objected to the idea that lay persons need a special liturgical consecration in order to take on a specific or permanent apostolic task, which does not of its nature belong to the sacrament of order. By baptism, he contends, they are already fitted to serving by their lives, and all that they need beyond this in order to assume a specific apostolate of teaching or evangelization, even in a permanent way, is a mandate from the hierarchy. To require a liturgical blessing for this apostolate would be to deny its lay status and clericalize its service.

At that time he continued to look upon liturgical ministries of the type associated with the minor orders as properly clerical and not lay. Therefore he thought that it was quite fitting that laity, who permanently replaced clerics in the functions of acolyte, reader, or porter, should receive the minor orders.

There were some things about Congar's position in those preconciliar days (before 1962) to which Congar himself later pointed as he revised his thinking. In the first place, the way that he then thought of all liturgical blessing over persons as a kind of special consecration that smacked of clericalism contrasts with the vision of baptismal consecration that allows the laity to take even some ministerial role in worship. Whereas at that early stage Congar had said that because of baptismal consecration a hierarchical mandate is all that is necessary to allow laity to take part in the apostolate, today it may be said that insisting on a hierarchical mandate, rather than simply supervision, for every kind of liturgical or apostolic work puts limits on the laity's part in the church's mission.

Congar's book clearly did not, once and for all, solve the question about the distinction of cleric and lay person, since with others he emphasized the laity's secular involvement, and used the epithet "secular" as the key to the distinction between hierarchy and laity. Anything that could be seen as a direct way of making Christ present in the secular arena could be considered a lay function. When put to use later, this was a kind of two-edged sword, which in some cases put more limits on the laity's role than did Congar, even while accounting, in a positive way, for the ground of their apostolic mission.

Karl Rahner, in his writings on the lay apostolate,[8] stressed the role of all the baptized in sanctifying the world by fulfilling their duties as Christians in the midst of ordinary tasks. In this, they have a mission from baptism that requires no further mandate from a bishop. Because of the concern not to clericalize the laity, similar to Congar's, Rahner suggested that whenever lay persons exercise either an ecclesial teaching office or perform a liturgical function, they step outside their lay identity and take on what is properly a clerical function. One should not confuse order and jurisdiction. If someone, by dint of special mandate, performs liturgical activities proper to the ordained, that person ceases to act as a lay person.

The Christian philosophy of integral humanism espoused by Jacques Maritain likewise played a role in developing a sense of the missionary vocation of the laity rooted in Christian baptism. Maritain believed that it was the role of Catholics to serve the spiritual purpose of social and political action, using their personal gifts and working within the Church's *sensus fidei*. Rather than support organized forms of Catholic Action, he thought that the laity met their call better when supported by smaller associations of a more voluntary nature.[9]

Another who was influential in developing a theology of the laity's action in the temporal order was Hans Urs von Balthasar. Given the de-Christianization of the Western world, which he noted, the baptized are on the front lines of evangelization, bringing the gospel to bear on the whole of human life, to the glory of God. In line with this concern, he promoted secular institutes.[10] Though the Church institutionally is made up of clergy and lay, von Balthasar stresses that the aim of all mediation and sacrament is the communion of all in the mystery of Christ, without distinction. The ordained are to serve this purpose as an act of humble service. At the same time, he points out that the baptized laity have a share in the universal, kingly, and prophetic priesthood of Jesus Christ, and for this reason they exercise a ministeriality that is proper to themselves by reason of their baptism. He gives a couple of examples that have been known for a long time in history, to show that saying this is not a novelty. The first is the fact that, in the sacrament of marriage, it has always been held in the Western church that the couple themselves are the ministers. The second example is the practice of confession to lay persons, recognized in medieval times as a "quasi-sacrament." Von Balthasar pointed out that lay persons have long practiced the special call of the evangelical counsels in following Christ, but that in the past this was usually done by linking themselves in some way with monasteries or mendicant orders.

In the situation of the Church today, with its own particular concerns, one has to see what is distinctive of the role of the laity in the sphere of life that is proper to them, being careful not to reduce all lay activity to the participation in the mission of the hierarchy, as practiced in mobilizing the faithful through Catholic Action. To build up the Church in the world, to show the pleroma (*plērōma*, fullness) of Christ, by which he is present in all things created, the service of the laity is essential. It is they who bring the gospel to the world and give it a living form in their many secular occupations. One of the implications of this, as formulated by von Balthasar, is the need for bishops and priests to consult the laity in teaching about, or making decisions about, the relation of Christ and of the gospel to secular matters, since they also must recognize the different charisms of the Spirit given to the laity and the many services they render.

For von Balthasar, the finest realization of the lay vocation and of their share in the kingly and prophetic priesthood of Christ is through the practice of the evangelical counsels, in ways that fit with their state of life, single or married, and with their work in different spheres of life. He sees this as something new to our age and a form in which the very life of the Spirit and of the disciple in following Christ informs the world and society. It is because lay persons are immersed in the world, rather than withdrawn from it, that their practice of the evangelical counsels has particular meaning and effect. In line with this perception of the call of the baptized to follow Christ, von Balthasar sponsored the institution and life of secular institutes as something pertinent to the life and mission of the Church in this era.

World Congresses

In some ways, comparing the World Congresses on the Lay Apostolate in 1951 and 1957 demarcates progress in the laity's integration into the mission and theology of the Church. During the 1950s there were four forms of lay activity (as evidenced in the organization of the two congresses), which in practice and in theology prepare Vatican II:[11] (1) The Catholic Action of Belgium and France was aimed at re-Christianization of a growingly secularized society. (2) The Italian Catholic Action, which emerged out of opposition to the fascist regime after the war took on the form of involvement in politics in order to impede the advance of communism. (3) Movements like the Legion of Mary, founded in Ireland and spreading rapidly to Africa and China, were ordered to a direct apostolate of a spiritual nature, intended to increase the devotion of the lay faithful, to help them in the difficulties encountered in mission territory, or to convert some, such as the prostitutes of the city of Dublin. (4) Secular Institutes were recognized in 1947 through the Apostolic Constitution *Provida mater ecclesia*.

The World Congress of 1951 on the lay apostolate focused on the two forms of European Catholic Action among workers and students, risking setting these off against the generality of baptized persons. What was still lacking was a theology that could include all committed Catholics as active members of the Church and charged with its mission. In his address to the Congress, Pius XII broadened the notion from that of direct involvement in the affairs of the world, to bring it back to Christ, and gave it a more inclusive tenor, which could incorporate all the trends mentioned above and indeed include every person who acted out of Christian faith, whatever one's work. Notwithstanding this expansion, the fundamental notion or image that he put forward to define the mission of the laity was still that of the *consecratio mundi*, the consecration of the world to God's glory.

Speaking to the congress on the lay apostolate in 1957, Pius XII gave what was considered by many to be an answer to Rahner, by employing and justifying the Scholastic distinction between order and jurisdiction.[12] The essence of the clerical status, he said, is to be found in order or priesthood, not in jurisdiction or in teaching. When, therefore, a lay person is called upon to teach religion or give catechesis, this is a form of collaboration with the hierarchy that is quite appropriate to lay status and vocation. While this gave a more positive view of the laity's share in the teaching mission of the Church, it did not address itself to their liturgical ministry, but left the position as stated in *Mediator Dei*. Nor did it address Rahner's problem about separating and then confusing order and jurisdiction.

Even with these developments, the clergy/laity distinction was in practice strongly upheld. It was fortified through the sad history of the priest worker movement. Priests who had taken to the factory floors in an effort to bring Christ to the world of the workers learned to develop close collaboration with their lay colleagues. However, the intervention of the Holy See stopped this movement in its tracks, with the insistence that priests did not belong in this milieu and should leave such direct evangelization to the laity's call. Along with this went the silencing of Congar and the other Dominican, Marie-Dominique Chenu, who had stoutly upheld the vision of the world's consecration by the baptized or by priests working with them. The distinction between dedication to the world of the sacred and dedication to the world of the secular was given a key role in the documents of the Second Vatican Council, was not yet played out.

The Sacrament of Order from Trent to Vatican II

As these views on the laity's role in the Church were being worked out, some took fresh approaches to the theology of the sacrament of order. During the decades immediately preceding the Second Vatican Council,[13] the theological debate about the sacramentality of the episcopacy and the distinction between episcopate and presbyterate was put into a new perspective due to an effort to go beyond the habitual distinction between order and jurisdiction. This allowed that the fullness of episcopacy might be seen in its responsibilities for worship, mission, and Word, and not only as a power to rule, as Scholastic theology was wont to see it.

Two facts, brought to light by historical research, contributed much to the discussion. First, a number of bulls were discovered in which popes granted the authority to simple priests, abbots of monasteries, to ordain deacons and priests, and this required more thought on the exact powers of the episcopacy. Second, historical research showed that a number of the bishops of Rome had been promoted from diaconate to episcopate without passing through the order of presbyter, thus showing that ordination to the presbyterate, and the conferring of the priesthood by this ordination, was not considered a necessary prerequisite for episcopal consecration.

These two realities seemed to lead in different directions. The first fact was used to support the opinion that the power to ordain and confirm is already radically conferred in the presbyterate. This supports the opinion that the episcopate adds only power of jurisdiction to the power of orders conferred on presbyters. The second fact, however, was invoked to show that the episcopal consecration is in itself a sacrament that confers the priesthood, not only in the degree in which it is received through ordination to the presbyterate, but in its fullness. This would indicate that the episcopacy and not the presbyterate should be at the center of all discussion of the sacrament of order.

The second perspective gained some ascendancy. It was obvious to some that what was at stake could not be adequately considered while remaining within the perspective of a priesthood of ritual cult alone, and while connecting only the power to administer the sacraments with the sacrament of order. Fortunately, a widening of horizons was achieved by such theologians as Dom Bernard Botte, Yves Congar, and Joseph Lécuyer.[14] A heightening appreciation of liturgical and patristic tradition led them to a new appraisal of the bishop's role in the Church and of the sacrament of order in general. They suggested looking to the bishop rather than to the presbyter as the basic realization of the New Testament priesthood. It seemed to these authors that since the fullness of the priesthood is conferred through ordination to the episcopacy, the theology of orders ought to center around it and the priesthood of the presbytery ought to be understood in its vital relation to the episcopacy. The New Testament priesthood is not to be understood only in terms of cult, but is as much a priesthood of preaching the gospel and a pastoral leadership as a priesthood of cult. This meant a definite connection between the sacrament of order and the threefold ministry of Word, sacrament, and government. However, these writers refrained from affirming that jurisdiction was conferred through consecration or ordination and confined themselves to asserting that consecration gave a potentiality to receive jurisdiction and a grace of headship. This hesitation was caused, at least in part, by the assertion of Pope Pius XII in his encyclical on the Mystical Body, *Mystici Corporis*,[15] that jurisdiction comes to bishops through the intervention of the Roman Pontiff. Hence the question of what ministry and responsibility comes with ordination was opened but not resolved.

To understand these debates on the theology of the sacrament of order preceding the Second Vatican Council, one has to begin with some remarks on the Council of Trent (1545–63) and its aftermath. Theologians interested in a longer history had to put it in context and salvage it from the narrow and very dogmatic interpretations that had prevailed since the sixteenth century. The exclusion of the episcopate from the sacrament of order and its listing as a jurisdiction exercised in Christ's name were generally accepted in the centuries immediately preceding the Reformation and the Council of Trent. It always proved difficult, however, to reconcile this view of the episcopate with the bishop's special powers, such as administering the sacraments of order and confirmation, and with the acknowledged superiority of the bishop over presbyters and the importance given to the teaching magisterium. Thus while episcopal superiority was normally seen as having to do with jurisdiction, there were occasional theologians who affirmed that the episcopate is both an order and a sacrament and in this regard is higher than priesthood.

The debates at the Council of Trent favored neither view in explicit fashion, but they left room to consider the episcopate as a sacrament. The reception of the Council of Trent[16] is rightly credited with helping to perpetuate a view of the priesthood that focuses on the power to offer sacrifice and consecrate the body and blood of Christ. It also seemed to give firmer basis to the distinction between the power of order and the power of jurisdiction, and the dissociation of jurisdiction from the sacrament of order. However, the imbalance in theology that resulted is not to be attributed solely to the Council of Trent but rather to the failure of theologians to see Tridentine definitions in proper historical perspective and recognize the limited purpose which the fathers of the Council had set themselves. It was this historical consciousness that enabled some theologians before Vatican II to free themselves from a supposed Tridentine straight-jacket.

The history of the Council of Trent shows that in actual fact the issues appearing in the conciliar debates were quite broad. From the earliest sessions, the fathers of the Council showed great concern with the preaching office of bishops and priests, which was described in the June 17, 1546, decree for reform as the principal office of bishops. Some of the bishops present would have liked to see order defined in terms of the pastoral and ruling function, and not exclusively in those of the power to celebrate the Eucharist and forgive sins, but this was not done. The problems that had been those of the Schoolmen in their efforts at scientific synthesis recurred. The bishops needed to ask whether the episcopate is of divine institution. How is its superiority over the presbyterate to be defined? Is it to be considered as a distinct order and episcopal consecration a sacrament? Is the concept of priesthood grounded in the episcopacy or in the presbyterate/priesthood?

In the event, the final decree on the sacrament of order avoided taking a position on these issues and concentrated on defining points of Catholic doctrine and practice that they saw as being challenged by the Reformers. A catalog of errors gleaned from Luther, Calvin, Zwingli, and others was submitted to the Council by its theologians in 1562. This was not the product of a careful and unbiased study, but it had a marked influence on the Council. The debate on order was defined by listing the following assertions as teachings of the Reformers: (1) Order is not a sacrament but a simple rite designating the ministers of Word and sacrament. (2) There is no ecclesiastical hierarchy, and all the faithful are equally priests, so that the exercise of the ministry requires the consent of the people, and one who has been appointed priest can return to the lay state. (3) The only office recorded in the New Testament is the preaching office, and there is no question of a power to consecrate the body and blood of Christ or to offer sacrifice or to absolve sins. (4) Consequently, those who do not preach the gospel are not really priests. (5) Bishops are not superior to presbyters, and have no special power to ordain, and an ordination without the consent of the people is invalid.

In light of these articles proposed as errors, two principal points were affirmed in the Council's doctrinal decrees. In the first place, Trent defined that the distinction between ministerial priesthood and priesthood of the faithful is of divine origin, since the sacrament of order was instituted by Christ. It also defined that this priesthood means the power to consecrate and offer the body and blood of Christ and that the power of retaining and forgiving sins is associated with it. Hence the priesthood cannot be reduced to the ministry of the Word, nor can it be said that one who does not exercise this ministry no longer possesses the priestly role. In the Decree on the Eucharist (1551), Trent had stated that through the words "Do this in commemoration of me," Christ instituted the apostles as priests and gave them and their successors the power to offer his body and blood.[17] By way of contrast, the Decree on the Sacrament of Order (1563) says nothing about the manner or time of the ministerial priesthood's institution. It does state, however, that in the hierarchy, which is instituted by divine ordinance, there is a threefold division of bishop, presbyter, and deacon. Bishops are superior to presbyters because they have the power to ordain and confirm and because, in the power of governing, they are successors of the apostles. In affirming this superiority of bishop over presbyter, it was not the Council's intention to define dogmatically that this distinction between the two was of divine origin. It merely affirmed a de facto superiority of bishop over presbyter within a divinely instituted priesthood and hierarchy. Without touching on the dogmatic question of its origin, the Council decreed that the teaching on this distinction is to be respected for the good of the Church.

In the post-Tridentine period, the theology of priesthood and of order was developed largely upon the basis of these definitions. Because it was not in any way the Tridentine fathers' intention to give a complete and adequate treatment of priesthood and order, this meant that a theology based almost exclusively upon its doctrinal decrees and condemnations was incomplete and inadequate. For one thing, it meant that priesthood was defined in terms of cult and the offering of the Eucharist. It also meant that the presbyterate was taken as the starting point in a treatment of the sacrament of order and that the episcopate was inevitably considered as some kind of an addition to the priesthood of the presbyter. Though relying on this definition of priesthood, the majority of theologians between the Council of Trent and the twentieth century affirmed that the episcopate is an order distinct from the presbyterate and that episcopal consecration is a sacrament. They thought that this was warranted by Trent, but they then tried to relate the bishop's sacramental powers to the priesthood given in ordination to the presbyterate. Because of this difficulty, some theologians hesitated over the distinction between the two orders and preferred to speak of an inadequate distinction, allowing that the episcopate is an extension of a power already received by a presbyter.

The terms within which this debate was carried on were confined to a consideration of the power of order, to the exclusion of jurisdiction and the teaching office. This can be seen from the very arguments adduced to prove that episcopal consecration is a sacrament. In the first place, many authors prove from Scripture (1 Tim 4:14; 2 Tim 1:6) that all the elements necessary to constitute a sacrament are present in episcopal consecration, namely, the visible rite, the conferring of grace and of a spiritual power. This is also demonstrated from the rites of ordination. The principal theological argument is that the episcopate confers powers—of ordaining and confirming—that are not given to the presbyter, and to these powers must correspond the grace to exercise them, as well as a special character, or at least an extension of the priestly character. There were two consequences to this kind of theology. First, it meant that it was taken for granted that one needed to be ordained to the priesthood before acceding to the episcopacy. Second, it meant that most of the treatment about episcopacy and succession to the apostles had to do with the power of jurisdiction, judged to be inclusive of the power to teach with authority. At the advent of the Second Vatican Council, these were live issues, as were those affecting the place of all the baptized in the Church.

Both the theology of the laity and the theology of the sacrament of order could be placed within a widening vision of the sacramental economy. Karl Rahner and Edward Schillebeeckx led the way in modifying the Scholastic and catechetical definition of sacraments as signs instituted by Christ to give grace.[18] They both attended more to the reality of sacraments as celebrations of the Church and to the relations that this expressed and embraced. They spoke of the sacraments of the Church as sacraments of Christ, signifying the event remembered and the presence in the Church assembly of the Risen Christ and of his Spirit. In turn, this was related to the origin of salvation in God by speaking of Christ himself as the sacrament of God or the sacrament of encounter with God. With this sense of sacraments as living celebrations, there also went a sense of their place in history and of their own on-going historical trajectory. When Schillebeeckx wrote of the sacramental characters of baptism, confirmation, and order as expressive of relational reality, this provided a context within which to assimilate the findings on the laity and on the ordained already surveyed.

Missions

These can only be quite summary remarks, but note has to be taken of some open-ings to a worldwide Christianity rather than to a European Christianity spread throughout the world. Although they came into their own only in the course of or indeed after Vatican II, some developments in the Church's life in preceding years, in what were seen as mission countries, are important to how the Council proceeded and to how it has been received.

Some missionaries, for example Daniel Comboni (1831–81), gave a direction to Christian presence by way of focusing on community life. Following in some way the inspiration of the Jesuit or Franciscan reductions—or villages organized as Christian abodes—in earlier times, he found that the Christian faith could have a greater impact on culture and society if Christians lived together and gave the wit-ness of a strong common life that found its inspiration in Christ.[19] For him, this meant a way of transforming peoples, their vision of reality, and their way of life without associating missionaries with strong and even violent colonial powers. Even though he and others dissociated themselves from colonial authorities, the mis-sionary vision was still Eurocentric and did not find the ways of relating faith and culture.

The desire to be more indigenous in the way of being Christian, to be authen-tically African as well as Christian, found a landmark in a 1957 book published by a group of priests studying in Europe: *Des prêtres noirs s'interrogent*.[20] Simple though this may seem to us now, this expressed the desire to put leadership in the Church into the hands of those native to the countries where the gospel was taking root. The writers asked why the gospel often did not seem to have penetrated deeply into the lives of African peoples but was often mixed with ancestral practices and beliefs, thus raising the question about the relation of belief in Christ to people's traditions. These priests demonstrated a sensitivity both to the newness brought to their peo-ples by faith in Jesus Christ, and to the need to speak of him in African modes and in relation to African realities.

Developments in various countries also indicated a recognition of the impor-tance that lay catechists had had on the promulgation and sustenance of the faith from the very beginning, and of the need for more adapted ways of catechumenal preparation. Similarly, sentiments of the time raised the question of a more-in-digenous liturgy, even if then this meant little more than hymn singing in local languages and some liberty for body movement, even as the question of celebrating liturgy in the vernacular continued to be raised.

Background in Christology

How the sense of the Church's mission and hence of its ministry was developing related to what was being said about Jesus Christ and about salvation through him. The matter cannot be developed here at length, but a few points are worth identifying. With the advent of the historical-critical method in scriptural studies, nineteenth-century liberal theology made a sharp distinction between the Christ of faith and the Christ of history, and at times seemed to reduce Jesus to his human dimensions as an example and a teacher of wisdom or as a prophet speaking in God's name. By the 1950s, mainstream Christology was beginning to integrate the study of the New Testament through the tools of the historical-critical method. In their different ways, Rudolf Bultmann and Karl Barth had brought to the fore the primacy of a faith stance in reading the Scriptures as the Word of God. By appealing to hermeneutics, Bultmann tried to separate out an existential appeal to faith from the mythical elements of the New Testament presentation.

Catholic scholars also took note of the need to attend to the results of historical-critical method in order to grasp more of the humanity of Jesus and of his teaching on the kingdom of God, without in the process imperiling faith in Christ as God's revelation. One of the results of this was considerable discussion of the consciousness of Jesus, or as some put it, of the "I" of Jesus. This meant spelling out the manner of his human relation to the Father, Son though he was, how he related to his own Jewish background, and how his teachings on the kingdom of God were to be interpreted. Karl Adam may be taken as illustrative of a frequent resolution of the questions involved. In a book published in German in 1954 and in English translation in 1957,[21] he devoted several chapters to the consciousness of Jesus as it can be studied through the Gospels. However, relying on the methods of medieval Scholastic theology, he related all of this to the christological dogmas of early centuries, with accentuation of his divinity and the need to relate even human sayings and deeds to the divine self of Christ.

At the same time, however, in 1951 the centenary of the fifteen-hundredth anniversary of the Council of Chalcedon (451) was an occasion to place dogmatic teaching in turn into its historical setting. With the historical-critical approach to both Scripture and dogma in mind, such scholars as Karl Rahner and Bernard Lonergan showed more interest in relating these findings and the meaning of Christ to an understanding of the human. They asked how the revelation given in Christ, with its full human dimensions taken into account, could be related to human experience and to human history. Connecting the theology of the Spirit to the theology of Christ was an important factor in working out these orientations, since it gave a perspective on how Christ himself, in his risen life and in his teaching, is present and active in the Church as a historical community. Since the mission of the Church is that of Christ, it too can be related to ongoing human experience, and to history, so that the Church's own historically related life and structures are brought to reflection. In the power of the Spirit and in the light of history, the mission, ministry, and structures of the Church could thus be examined in their continuity, but also in the process of their periodic change. Furthermore, the relation of Christ's mystery and of his teaching to the kingdom of God present in the world could be further explored, a question that, as is known was developed in writing the documents of Vatican II on the Church, on the Church in the World, on the mission *ad gentes*, and on religious dialogue.

Conclusion

In brief, developments on ministry and order in the years preceding the Second Vatican Council are allied with the action of the laity and with a sensed need to move from a more cultic to a more pastoral view of ordained ministry. How theologians began to deal with the sources for theology is important to this. The appeal to historical consciousness in knowing Christ through the Scriptures and in studying history had an influence yet to be fully explored. At the same time the need for a global Church, for a Church culturally differentiated, was innate to what was felt to be necessary in a postcolonial era when the power of Christian churches could and should no longer be allied with colonial rule. One might not have expected the orientations chosen by the Vatican Council on the one hand, but on the other the seeds for fresh perspectives had been sown. Continuity has many forms.

4

Remarks on the Vatican Council and Its Reception

This chapter does not provide an analysis of the documents of the Second Vatican Council since there are already enough commentaries in existence.[1] It is rather a comment on their reception. The teachings and decisions of Councils are gradually received into the life of the Church over a period of time, and this in the long run determines what they mean for tradition and the mission of Christian communities. Forty years or so after Vatican II, some assessment of its reception is opportune. While the question is first about reception within the Catholic Church, this has to be related to how it is engaging in ecumenical dialogues.

Principles of Interpretation
In the light of actual developments in the Church, there is not a little debate over the way in which the conciliar documents are to be interpreted and put into effect. Recognizing that it is an ongoing task, Pope Benedict XVI asks for a more serene interpretation of the Council and its documents.[2] He sees a conflict between two currents in the Church, one which presses for a rupture with much that went before Vatican II, and another looking for a continuity that is both doctrinal and institutional. He likens the struggle over its meaning to the quarrels in the aftermath of the Council of Nicaea, as described by Basil of Caeserea in his work on the Holy Spirit.[3] Benedict asks for a "hermeneutic of reform" that is rooted in a sense of continuity rather than a "hermeneutic of discontinuity and rupture." Though the Pope does not explicitly say this, his remarks highlight the fact that in interpreting Vatican II, we are dealing not only with texts but with a historical event of lasting significance.

To dismiss the idea of some necessary discontinuity with the past of the post-Tridentine Church, the Pope may not have given an accurate account of this position. Though different hermeneutical principles are invoked,[4] discussion between their proponents is needed. There are those who look to the Council primarily as an assembly that gave the Church a set of teachings to be put into practice, teachings that require explanation and implementation. Since teaching authority is given primacy in this way of approaching the Council, continuity with the recent past is more easily affirmed. To establish this continuity, even as some changes are made, is the path to renewal. Others underline the fact that Vatican II has to be seen as a historical event subject to the rule of historical recall and interpretation. In this view, while the texts are of vital importance, they have to be set within their historical context in order to be understood and interpreted. Looking at the Council and its texts in this way, one deciphers currents of thought, the formulation of questions and issues, and the continuing ambiguities present within the apparent convergence of minds and votes. This means that interpretation has to unearth these issues, see how far the Council took them in the documents promulgated, and see how much they remain part of an ongoing and living ecclesial life, within a diversity of cultural and historical settings around the world. A third approach, maybe not well integrated into the conciliar documents but pertaining to the Council's significance, is to see how it points to a reading of the signs of the times as signs of the advent of God's kingdom. In doing this, one might also integrate the particular perspective of those who look for inspiration from the group calling itself "the Church of the Poor," in order to express what its members saw as the primary concern in advancing the mission and renewal of the Church.[5]

Speaking more formally of principles of interpretation, some—notably Giuseppe Alberigo and Christoph Theobald—underline that in the intention of Pope John XXIII, this was intended to be a pastoral council.[6] The major principle of interpretation is to see the pastoral implications, whether practical or catechetical, of what the Council teaches. In some way joining forces with this, others such as Peter Hünermann espouse a type of legal hermeneutics that assesses what was taught in terms of its practical and legal effects.[7]

Given the particular focus of this present work, major attention is given to how the reception of the Council affects mission and ministry. Some priority is given to the pastoral and legal forms of interpretation. Without repeating surveys of the teaching of the Second Vatican Council on the sacrament of order and on the laity in the Church, the remarks made here are intended to highlight issues that the Church inherits from the conciliar era, pointing out questions to which the event and its documents gave rise. Much has been seen in the overview of what has been taking place in various churches during the period since the Council. The questions now are, How is this to be related to Vatican II? What are the implications for the ecumenical context, marked by ecumenical agreements and reports?[8]

Documents of specific importance in setting the stage for the renewal of the Church's life, its mission, and its ministries are the Dogmatic Constitutions on Revelation (*Dei Verbum*, 1965) and on the Church (*Lumen gentium*, 1964), the Pastoral Constitution on the Church in the Modern World (*Gaudium et spes*, 1965), and the decrees on bishops, presbyters, lay apostolate, religious , mission, ecumenism, and relations with other religions. Fundamental to all that happened at the Council and in subsequent decades is the tension inherent in the Constitution on the Church between on the one side chapters 1 and 2, and on the other chapter 3. Both parts of *Lumen gentium* have to be taken into account, but they focus on different aspects of the Church, and it is not always apparent that chapter 2 in fact serves as foundation to chapter 3. *Gaudium et spes* was more ambitious in its scope and purpose but suffered from the fact that many of the issues that it addressed had not been the object of doctrinal and theological reflection in a Church that took a suspicious and defensive stance on economic and political events that came in the wake of the Enlightenment, as it had also failed to reflect on the cultural and social implications of preaching Christ in non-Western civilizations. Once some orientation was taken on the place of the Church in the world, not as defender of the faith but as a partner in a multifaceted dialogue, it was inevitable that it should be asked what relation exists between the positions taken in this document and the visage of the Church presented in *Lumen gentium*. Given the existence of these two major documents, in examining the reception of Vatican II, whatever about its inherent limitations, one can follow the distinction made at the Synod between *ecclesia ad intra* and *ecclesia ad extra* to see and understand the ongoing questions about mission and ministry. In many respects it is the issues regarding the Church's place in the world and its dialogue with "others" that has had major influence in the way the Council has been received. However, in this presentation the order followed in the sessions of the Council itself will be respected.

Inner Life of a Missionary Church

The two principal documents that directly affect the inner life of the Church are the Constitutions on Revelation and on the Church. There are also some secondary texts to be taken into account.

Dei Verbum

The Constitution on Revelation, *Dei Verbum*, is vital to the renewal of the Church and of its mission, since it places the hearing of the Word at the heart of revelation through history and at the heart of the life of the Church itself.[9] Though the document did not fully settle the relation between Scripture and tradition, it abandoned the language that speaks of "two sources of revelation." Rather than use this idea, which raises questions about the "deposit of faith," the orientation taken is that the Word is never heard once and for all but needs to be continually listened to and appropriated, within the historical, social, and cultural circumstances of a living community. After the Council, in 1994, with a preface by Cardinal Ratzinger, the Pontifical Biblical Commission issued a paper on *The Interpretation of the Bible and the Church*,[10] tracing the development of methods used in the reading of the Scriptures. Of particular note is part 4, on interpretation of the Bible in the life of the Church. There it is said that "actualization" of God's Word is constantly necessary because it is proclaimed and heard in a variety of life situations and circumstances, and needs interpretation in relation to these. According to the document, the living tradition of the community stimulates the task of actualization. Attention has to be given to the cultural context and culture heritage of peoples in various parts of the Church. In practice, it often comes to the surface that a community's own reflection and prayer, stimulated by the hearing of the Word, plays a vital role. This is tied up with the importance of small communities or faith-sharing groups.

An even more explicit attention to the historical implications of the Word in history, and of the relation of texts to an eschatological horizon, is espoused by the same commission in a document entitled *The Jewish People and Their Sacred Scriptures in the Christian Bible*.[11] On the one hand this paper shows that it is difficult for Christians to grasp the implications for itself of recognizing Judaism as a living religion of a people favored by God and of reading the Jewish Scriptures as a living book. On the other hand and in a more general way, it shows that all scriptural texts are actualized when their import for a lived history is grasped. The place of the Scriptures and their interpretation in the life of the Church is to be further addressed in a synod convoked for deliberation on the Word of God, for which the *lineamenta* (preparatory documents) have already appeared.

With the attention given to the place that the Scriptures have in the life of the Church today, there arises the need to relate the doctrinal formulations of centuries to their place in formulating the faith of the apostolic Church. The basic appeal to Scriptures, beneath and beyond doctrines, has become a point of reference in entering into ecumenical dialogue. Though it may not have been immediately apparent to all the participants in the Council, it has subsequently emerged that the teaching on revelation and on the place of the Scriptures in the light of the Church is the fundamental position that has to dominate relations between separated churches, as also the dialogue of Christians with Jews.

Lumen Gentium

In the development of a conciliar consciousness, it became clear that it is only when the Scriptures are assured their place in the life of the Church that it is possible to do a theology of the Church. The first part of *Lumen gentium* (*LG* cc. 1–2) focuses on the Church as people of God, body of Christ, and communion. It treats of the Church in the entirety of its composition, comprehensive of all the baptized. It relates the reality of the Church to the history of redemption and to its mission in the world through using the notions of sacrament and of reign of God. As people of God and body of Christ, all living in one communion in the Spirit, the Church is the sacrament of the unity of the human race and exhibits the communion to which in Christ all humanity is called. This is a communion visibly realized in the Church, which then serves as sign of a larger unity and has a mission to promote it. Another way of saying this in chapter 2 is that the Church is at the service of God's reign in the whole of humanity and the whole of creation. Church and kingdom are not identified, for the kingdom is more widespread through God's own presence and activity, but they are related inasmuch as the Church ministers to this presence.

This allows for improving relations between churches that split apart over the course of history. Though Christian churches still remain divided and have to work toward a visible ecclesial communion, the Church as people, body, and communion embraces all the baptized. The chapter also spells out the relation of the Church to peoples of other living faiths by seeing God at work in them and by seeing how all peoples of the earth are oriented to the same end of communion in God. The Church's mission is to spread the gospel of Christ, but this has to include the promotion of justice, peace, reconciliation (and one would now add, the care of the earth). Within this broad vision, the Catholic Church itself has to give primacy to membership in the Church through baptism and to the vocation of all the faithful. Ordained ministry is ordered to the service of this basic royal priesthood.

While seeing the Church in this broad vision, the fathers of the Council were nonetheless anxious to state the particular place of the Roman Catholic Church, or churches in communion with the See of Rome, in the divine dispensation of salvation. Hence, to both affirm the ecclesiality of other confessions and communities, and to uphold the role of the Catholic Church, they chose to say that the Church "subsists" in the Roman Catholic Church. This is a rather deliberately ambiguous phrase but one that has given much ground for debate within the Roman communion itself and in ecumenical dialogue between churches. It appears to refer primarily not to the faith and charity of the people but to the structures that the Council saw as essential to divine institution. Thus, without adjudicating the faith and the devotion and the Christian life of any communion, it could say that in the Catholic Church there are all the substantial elements that God intends the Church on earth to have. This could then be a guide in ecumenical circles when it comes to maintaining, even within a much-developed communion, what the Roman Catholic Church sees as necessary in obedience to God's will. However, in subsequent decades it has been difficult to state the relation between a primacy in love and a primacy in jurisdiction, and some wooden Roman interpretations of the phrase have given rise to either anger or sorrow. One might well ask whether the ancient role of patriarchates could teach us something: is it not possible to maintain communion between local churches in matters of teaching and discipline through a loving and fraternal mediation, without excessive resort to an appeal to canonical authority?

Baptized and Ordained

In *LG* 11 the relation between the baptized and the ordained is taken up in terms that repeat what had become standard formulations. No direct link is made to *LG* 9, and the identification of the Church as people of God, or as kingly and priestly people, citing 1 Pet 2.[12] What *LG* 9 says is that to be a royal priesthood means to be chosen by God to be a means and a sign, or sacrament, or the body chosen to be a visible means of salvation. It is a people who knows the true spiritual worship inaugurated in Christ and is a sign of Christ's dominion over sin and death.

In the following paragraphs, the chapter takes up the question of offices and ministries within this people. In comparing the priesthood of all the baptized and that of ordained ministers, *LG* 11 says that the distinction between the two is not only in degree but "in essence." However, they are "interrelated," each in its own way being a share in the one priesthood of Christ. The rest of the chapter is given over to illustrating how all the faithful therefore contribute to the building up of the body of Christ and to its mission, and in this way it goes beyond the formulation of difference quoted above. Since in many respects a functional differentiation is never far off the scene, in accentuating the difference between the ordained and the baptized, and in dividing up responsibilities, there is a continual risk of paying less attention to the communion as one royal priesthood in the one priesthood of Christ.

In chapter 3 (*LG* 18–29) the focus has been put on the hierarchy of ministries and offices, with much more emphasis given to the distinction between order and baptism, so that the Church is described in hierarchical terms. This was the place where the sacramentality of the episcopacy was incorporated into teaching, and where Vatican II could complement the teaching of Vatican I on the papacy, with teaching on the bishops and their collegiality as a body. Adopting the notion of the one royal priesthood and of the threefold office of Christ as priest, prophet, and king, the document explains how ordained and baptized all participate in these offices, but in different ways, which are not simply differences in degree but differences in kind. This difference is underlined by the vocabulary used. In writing of the ordained, the text uses *ministerium/ministeria* but when writing of the laity's participation, it uses *munus/munera*. Though the participation of the baptized faithful and the ordained are presented as complementary, the stress is on the hierarchy and on the ministerial priesthood. Communion in the visible Church thus appears as a communion of all with bishops and Pope, the accent being put on hierarchical structures. How chapters 2 and 3 are to be coordinated remains an issue of ongoing inquiry, as is the question of how ordained and baptized are to relate to each other in community through their respective parts in the threefold office of Christ and in the mission of serving the reign of God in the world.

Looking back to the chapter on the hierarchy, one has to say that living with the consequences of collegiality has proved to be a difficult path. In many theological and practical respects, the collegiality of bishops and their episcopal responsibility have been played down in the intervening years, with an ever-increasing emphasis on the central role of the Pope and the exercise of authority by the Roman Curia.[13] It is significant that Pope John Paul II at times gave the impression that he relied more on the College of Cardinals, a body made up of his own appointees, than on episcopal synods or episcopal conferences. In short, the idea of a centrally located universal Church prevails over that of a communion of local churches, and even the idea of ecclesial communion is interpreted in that way.[14]

Chapter 4 (*LG* 30–38) returns to the vocation of the laity and in section 31 makes distinctions in the Church's population, which have been much used in later magisterial teaching and theology and perhaps also abused in some theological writing. Ordained ministers are placed in an area of ecclesial life where they have responsibility for the sacred or the holy. Lay persons are said to be given responsibility for bringing Christ to the secular and consecrating it, to use the formulas of the 1950s. Religious are singled out for their living witnesses to the priority of God's kingdom in the mind and heart of a Christian. Positively, these descriptions show how the

Church as a body, composed of many members, relates to the holy as manifested in faith and sacrament, how it renders a living witness to the reign of God in the world, and how it seeks to bring about this reign in every sphere of human life and in the world.

The distinction has limitations that can prove worrisome. Edward Schillebeeckx wrote of this demarcation of responsibilities as a descriptive rather than an essential distinction.[15] To consider it in this way is useful. In the earlier chapters of *LG*, once the bishops had made room for all in the participation in Christ's priesthood and in the exercise of services in the Church, they found themselves faced with the dilemma of how to ground distinctions within God's people. What is given in chapter 4 is a way of describing what they saw happening in the Church, with appeal to traditional categories and conceptions. With subsequent developments and attention to communities and their responsibilities as such rather than to individuals or categories, the distinctions are less and less serviceable and appear to be grounded in almost quaint notions of the sacred and the secular. It is unfortunate, then, that the distinction returned time and time again in the subsequent teachings of the Council and that it has been given such moment in postconciliar magisterial teaching and in theological works. The distinction is better seen for what it is worth when the Council is understood as an event where the formulation proved helpful in taking all states and charisms into account. Instead of offering a settled response, it leaves room for further thought in the light of ecclesial reception.

It is in the light of these questions raised by the Constitution on the Church, and also by the decrees on ecumenism and on mission, that we see the full import of Alberigo's remark that the advance of conciliar thinking has effectively been stalled by the lack of corresponding change in ecclesiastical structures. In effect, conciliar thinking would require more decentralization, more autonomy for local churches, and more juridical inclusion of the laity in administrative and decision-making processes in communities and organisms at every level. However, the Code of Canon Law (revised 1983) and other decisions made, for example regarding liturgy, continue to embrace a centralized and clerical vision of the Christian life and ecclesial action.

Some doctrinal and theological factors involving ministry and ecclesial structure continue to create problems for collaborative ministry within the Roman Catholic Church or between all the churches and communities belonging within the one people of God. These include debates over the place of the episcopacy in tradition, the relation between local churches and their bishops and the Petrine apostolic authority, and the ordination of women. On the other hand, relations to other living faiths have proved to be of immense importance for the churches of Africa and Asia in determining their own sense of mission and the forms of dialogue to be pursued with others, in pursuing the goals of a common humanity and an order of justice, peace, reconciliation, and mutual respect.

Decrees on Bishops and Priests

The decrees on bishops and on presbyters (or priests) have had lasting effect in magisterial teaching, in the lives of churches, and in theologies of Church and order, because of their attempts to balance the relation of the ordained to Christ and to the people. While using the distinction between the offices of Christ to spell out the offices of the ordained, these two documents also looked for a way to relate personally to Christ, a way that would not divorce the ordained from the other baptized. The decree on priests starts by clearly placing the minister among the baptized, seeing the call to ministry as itself a baptismal grace rooted in one's call to follow Christ. Evoking the Scholastic theology, which saw the priest as a representative of Christ acting in the person of Christ, this decree coined the term that described the priest as representative of the person of Christ the Head. This was intended to follow the metaphor of Colossians (1:15–20; 2:9–10, 19), which makes the distinction between Head and members, not to separate them but precisely to unite them in the grace that flows from Christ. Thus what the priest would represent is the grace flowing from Christ into the body, but active in various ways and services within it. The role of the presbyter is not restricted to sacramental action but as one with this includes preaching and pastoral governance.

For all its clarity, the decree on presbyters (*presbyterorum ordinis*) has had mixed fortunes in its reception into the life of churches around the world.[16] There is a sense in which it is anachronistic inasmuch as it takes for granted a community in which there is an ample supply of ordained priests. While priests are called upon to be apostolic and not simply cult figures, and are asked to respect the charisms and roles of the lay faithful, the vast reduction in vocations to the priesthood in parts of the world was not foreseen. Nor therefore was it foreseen how the structures that supposed a clear differentiation between ordained and baptized would no longer satisfy. In the event, some call for a canonical revision of Church order and others prefer to revert to Tridentine formulas and retrieve those aspects of the sacrament of order that set priests apart.

The phrase *in persona Christi Capitis* (in the person of Christ the Head) has been given varied use in subsequent magisterial teaching. It is still used to some extent but is in some tension with the more Scholastic term *in persona Christi*. In his exhortation on the lay faithful, John Paul II twice refers to the priest's relation to Christ.[17] In the first instance, he uses the phrase of *Presbyterorum ordinis, in persona Christi Capitis*, saying that priests are called to prolong the presence of Christ, the one high priest, embodying his way of life and making him visible in the midst of the flock entrusted to their care. On the other hand they are "a sacramental representation of Jesus Christ—the Head and Shepherd—authoritatively proclaiming his Word, repeating his acts of forgiveness and his offer of salvation" (*Christifideles laici* 27 [1988]). At a later stage in the same letter, he excludes women from ordination on the basis of the sacramental representation of Christ in the Eucharist (§51), saying that *in persona Christi* means a distinction in function, not in dignity and holiness, and has to do with the sacramental representation of Christ as

Bridegroom. What this means for a theology of the Church and of order will be examined later in this work. Whatever the distinctions, theology has to show the reciprocal relation between the ministry of the ordained and that of other members within the one community and congregation.[18]

Another area of discussion that remains unresolved in these documents is that of the relation between bishop and priests. With use of the ancient term *presbyterium*, the conciliar texts allowed for theological developments that speak of the collegial and synodal government of a diocese, with the priests associated with the bishop in this role. Some have latched on to another phrase, however, namely, that the bishop possesses the fullness of the priesthood: in presbyters/priests they see collaborators, who in their own ministry share in that of the bishop. This pushes to extremes the biblical imagery of Moses and the elders, or of Aaron and his sons. What is opened up here is the need to draw on the entire tradition of the role of presbyters in the Church in all its diversity. From this we may see what new possibilities of development are opened up for churches around the world today. How some Protestant churches, inspired especially by John Calvin, have integrated presbyters or elders into the life of their communities is pertinent to this discussion, as is the question of the role of deacons.

Implementing what *LG* 29 said about restoring the permanent deaconate has reached an impasse. It does not seem clear what place deacons had in tradition or exactly what the Council intended. In general, writers pursue the link to charitable service and the relation to serving at the Eucharist, which is found in history, but without being able to pinpoint the diaconate's exact meaning, or the deacon's relation to the ministry of the bishop, or the diaconate's precise sacramental significance. This appears in the document on the deaconate issued by the International Theological Commission.[19] In practice, sometimes deacons are given responsibility for the charitable works of a local or regional church, but more commonly they are ordained to serve as auxiliary priests, preaching, baptizing, officiating at marriages, and presiding at Sunday liturgies in the absence of a priest. If the diaconal order is historically thought to be related to charitable services, it may well be asked whether present ecclesiastical structures leave this to lay members who do not need a special ordination, given their baptismal call. If the diaconate is made primarily ordination to preaching and to liturgy and to parochial leadership, it stands to reason that the candidates are in fact candidates for ordination to the presbyterate. In any case there can be no discussion of the sacramental symbolism of the diaconate without seeing it in relation to some specific ministry.

One telling point, a kind of litmus test for what development has taken place, is how the role of women in liturgy, mission, and ministry is integrated into structures. The decree on the apostolate of the laity complemented what had already been said in *LG*. It made some advances on women's place in the Church's life and on their contribution to its work and mission. Pope John Paul II took this up a number of times in his letters on the Lay Faithful (1988) and on Women (1995). The possibility of ordaining women is consistently ruled out, but there are quite strong statements on their equality with men in all other areas of Church activity and even government. At the beginning of Lent 2006, Pope Benedict XVI, in talking to the priests of the diocese of Rome, mentioned that the Church had to find ways of giving women a more significant place in its ministry, at various levels.[20] If Church authority were to act on these principles and appoint women to leading positions in the Roman Curia (ordination is not truly needed for roles of prefects and secretaries of Roman congregations, since they are administrative), in the offices of bishops' conferences, and in diocesan and parochial bodies, the Church would begin to change in practice and not only in theory. Then the context for discussion on ordination would be different.

Secular Character of the Laity's Role

As the model of priest as one set apart is retrieved, so prevails the accent on the secular characteristic of the life and mission of the baptized. Recently Pope Benedict has returned to the definition of the laity's vocation as a presence and a mission that belongs in the secular sphere of human activity. On the February 3, 2007, he gave an address to mark the sixtieth anniversary of the promulgation of the Apostolic Constitution *Provida mater ecclesia* on secular institutes. He spells out his understanding of the call of the laity to take their part in the mission of the Church. It is the call of the baptized, he says, to reflect the mystery of the Incarnation as an insertion into the midst of human affairs. In light of this, human affairs become themselves a *locus theologicus*, and Benedict spells out the secular quality of the lay vocation:

> Your call to holiness is to be described as an adherence in self-offering to the salvific design made manifest in the revealed Word; it is solidarity with history, the search for the Lord's will inscribed in human affairs as they are guided by divine providence. . . . The character of the secular mission is the witness given by the practice of human virtues, such as justice, peace, joy (Rom 14:17); the "good conduct of life" (1 Pet 2:12) . . . to show one's light before all people . . . (Matt 5:16), . . . a commitment to the construction of a society in which are recognized the dignity of the person and the values for its full realization, which can never be renounced.[21]

The Pope goes on to say that fulfilling such a mission implies much human effort but depends on the grace of the Spirit, which Christians receive to discern and work with the "signs of the times." While he exhorts them to a knowledge of the Scriptures, a life within the community of the Church, and a strong sacramental life, he goes no further in saying what is involved in the discernment of the signs of the times. Suffice it to note that it is the baptized themselves who are said to grasp these and live in conformity with them. Their part in thus shaping community life and the Church's mission, however, is not developed, but clearly the question is laid open.

Missions and the Life of Local Churches

The Decree on the Missionary Activity of the Church (*Ad gentes*, 1965) still speaks of implanting the gospel and sowing the seed of the Word, or even of implanting the Church (§6). Nonetheless it has moved away from the missiological paradigm of bringing peoples a church with all its ecclesiastical structures inherited from Europe. Instead, it offers a paradigm of how a local church grows through the hearing of the gospel and through the action of the Spirit among the people. It espouses the basic principles of respecting peoples and cultures in preaching the gospel and in the Church's life, likening the birth of Christianity among new peoples to the birth of the Incarnate Word from the womb of Mary, among the Jewish people of his own time (§§6–8). It also describes the young churches as themselves missionary, with the first believers the primary witnesses and proclaimers of the gospel. In the life, theologies, and magisterial teachings of churches after the Council, these principles were given an important application and development, giving rise to the Church structures, liturgies, and theologies proper to various continents, countries, and peoples around the world.[22]

At the Council the reality of the Church as a global body, one in its manifold diversity, was only beginning to emerge. The participation of bishops and experts from Africa and Asia was quantitatively small, both in terms of the number of indigenous rather than foreign-born bishops, and in terms of their interventions in the preparatory phase and in the course of the Synod itself.[23] The political situation of countries on these continents was marked by the slow and difficult process toward independence, a process that especially in Africa reached maturation only during the 1960s, when the Council was in progress. Ecclesiastically, churches were still under the tutelage of the Congregation for the Propagation of the Faith, and the number of local bishops and priests was relatively small. By some reports, there was also a reluctance to speak on the part of these bishops before the assembly, especially in one's own name. By their own local traditions, it would have been more opportune to let regional churches work out their consensus in their own way and then address themselves collectively to the bishops of other churches. At the beginning of the Council, these bishops had not had the possibility, or indeed the economic security, to organize themselves as a body. It was in part being together in Rome that gave them a chance to develop their own conciliar structures and to carry this élan toward internal continental exchange with them back to their churches.

The interventions that have been noted in studies focus on a few topics. One is the plea for a vernacular and more missionary oriented liturgy.[24] Another is concern for the regional autonomy of bishops; a third is the promotion of lay persons in taking responsibility within and for their churches. The documents of the Council do not bear the mark of a great attention to the Latin American, African, and Asian continents, the plight of their peoples, and their search to come out from under political and ecclesiastical colonialism. Not even when, in *Gaudium et spes*, the bishops turned their attention to the presence of the Church in society, did they go beyond generalities to deal with the reality of a globally differentiated and emerging community of peoples.

On the other hand, the leaders of these churches seem to have found an incentive in the event of the Council to take up their own issues with a more independent voice. After the Council the churches of the Southern Hemisphere found it desirable and possible to take up the issues of the Council and transpose them into the language and movements of their own people. This transfer of the ecclesial center of gravity from Europe to the South is indeed one of the most striking factors in the reception of Vatican II. If only from this point of view, one has to say that for a global Church, the process of reception cannot be simply an interpretation and application of texts. It must be one of a translation and transposition of what is in these documents into the lives of churches that were not the main authors of these texts but carried concerns that emerged at the Council or around it back into their own communities. Maybe a term suitable to the process that has been going on since 1965 is *creative reception.*

Inscribed in the conciliar document on missions (*Ad gentes*) is the need to balance the sense in which the gospel and the Church, as the community of Christ and Spirit, transcend limitations on one hand, and on the other hand the sense of the need to relate missionary activity to localities and cultures. This had to be worked out more fully after the Council, in doctrinal teaching, in theology, and in practice, with all churches participating, each within its own environment. When proclaiming Cyril and Methodius patrons of Europe in 1985 because of their missionary work among Slav peoples, John Paul II enunciated a fundamental principle, to which constant appeal has since been made: the work of evangelization is "the incarnation of the Gospel in autonomous cultures and at the same time the introduction of these cultures into the life of the Church."[25] That this principle may be implemented in a generous or in a rather restrictive way is apparent, for example, in the tension between local efforts at relating liturgy to cultures, and the efforts of the Roman Congregation for Worship and Sacraments to pull liturgies more into line with what it sees as "the substance" of the Roman liturgical tradition.[26] What happens in liturgical development mirrors what happens to the work of ordering the community and ministries of local churches.

This is a reminder that at the core of all Christian life, at the heart of the reality of Church, is the eucharistic community. The Constitution on the Liturgy emphasized this point but equated the ideal form of celebration with that of the diocese, the Bishop celebrating with priests, deacons, and people in one assembly, and this is repeated in the most recent General Instruction on the Roman Missal. Certainly ancient writers such as Ignatius of Antioch or Justin Martyr may be cited on this point, but what is neglected is that they are writing of small churches and assemblies, where indeed all could reasonably gather each Sunday for the exercise of *diakonia,* for the hearing of the Word, and for communion together at the table of the Lord's body and blood. Today we have to think about the needs and realities of diverse communities, even of many small communities within the one local or diocesan Church. The reality of assembly starts, not with a priest performing the prescribed ritual, but with the people who, living as a community in faith, come together for the twofold table of Word and sacrament. To this they bring not only the goods that they wish to share with each other and with the poor, but their own living faith and hope in the many ways in which these are nourished.

Unhappily, in these times many living communities, on small islands, in remote rural areas, even in great cities, are left without the possibility of a eucharistic celebration for want of properly ordained ministers. Nonetheless they gather, to share faith, hope, charity, Word, and prayer, under the guidance of women and men, in whom they find their leaders, to whom often enough bishops have given approval. Liturgists are known to argue that this is all they should do, since they cannot celebrate the Eucharist in its full ritual form. However, communities often know better. They have grasped that at the heart of their lives is the donation that the Lord makes, the gift of his body and blood, just as indeed the most perfect celebration finds its true meaning therein. They devise their own ritual performance to make sure that they can receive at least the bread of Christ's body, or even develop their communal prayer around the reserved sacrament, in which they know the symbolic reality of Christ's sacramentally offered love.

This matter has to be considered first and foremost from the side of those who are left without Eucharist but who nonetheless live in the faith of the gospel, with their leaders, and with the sorts of ritual performance that allow them to identify as Christian communities, living in the hope of Christ. It is useless to employ the language of rights when talking of this situation. The question is how a community forms itself as a community of discipleship in the Spirit and how it must in Christ's name be recognized by the greater Church. We await some action from ecclesiastical authorities which will show that they have gone beyond the illusion that they can multiply seminary trained priests to meet all needs in a realistic way. We know that this perception is lacking when directives multiply that hinder the gift of body *and* blood, or divide the assembly even spatially into clergy and people. When it is argued that it is better not to give the cup than to have lay persons clean the vessels wherefrom many have supped, we know that the Church has wandered far from the Lord and from true faith in his sacrament. In developing a sense of mission, in recognizing the ministries that will serve mission, churches have to respect the fact that the heart of the Church is to allow all communities, wherever they are, to be eucharistic communities. Not only will this affect the inner life of the Church, but by that very fact it will serve the mission of the Church to be ambassador of Christ in the world, a living presence for all of Christ and Spirit.

Church in the World: *Gaudium et Spes*
A great debating point in receiving Vatican II into the life of the Church is how to work with the rather controverted Pastoral Constitution on the Church in the Modern World, *Gaudium et spes* (GS). In the lead up to this document, the Council had to come to grips with the Church's relation to the world and with describing

how from a stance of faith Christians might consider the secular realm. Some who were pleased with *Lumen gentium* found *GS* hard to approve or to stomach. Nonetheless, for all the ambiguities that remain in the text because of its difficult gestation, it fosters an openness to the world that was not to be found in the era between Vatican I and Vatican II.

Its more dialogical attitude to modernity and its attention to cultural plurality, its discussion of temporal affairs such as the economy and war and peace, its new insights into marriage and sexuality, and its espousal of dialogue with multiple others have all proved to be of great moment, but also the object of much debate and disagreement. At root is an attempt to understand the human person, not just as an individual but in social and communal terms. Even more than in relation to other texts, churches have to come to grips with the issues raised rather than seeing the constitution as a finished piece. Many of the matters affecting the inner life of the Church are intimately related with what is seen as its presence and its mission in the world. In *GS*, so important is the opening to the world, to societies, and to culture that the positions taken on the inner life of the Church have to be revisited in the light of what it sought to initiate. Even more than the decree on missions, *GS* spells out the issues facing Christian churches in their mission in the world of today. The questions and concerns raised by the pastoral constitution come to light more clearly through the study of its redaction at the Council.[27] These can be looked at under several headings.

Church and World

The question of the Church's relation to the world was broached in a way that showed concern over the limitations of the European church, inclusive of the Papacy, in its dealings with the Enlightenment and the human developments that were guided by reason since that time. For many of the fathers and their assistant theologians, it was time to break with Vatican I and its aftermath, as symbolized by the papacy of Pius X, as much as it was time to complete the treatment of the Roman primacy by a treatment of the episcopacy. Even in its positive teaching, such as is found in the papal encyclicals on social doctrine, the Church presented itself as the *magistra*, formulating doctrines that governed the areas of work and social being. What some members of the Council wanted to generate was a dialogue with those responsible in the various fields of human endeavor and development. No doubt the Church would bring its own perspective on these matters in the light of the gospel, but it needed to be open to the fact that it was to receive new insight from an examination of matters of common concern together with others. The Church does not exist outside the world or adjacent to it. The world in its contingent and historical complexity is the theological place for hearing the gospel and for disci-pleship.[28] Its own understanding of revelation depends on its immersion in the world and on its readiness to see itself in solidarity with all, in good and in evil. Being pastoral in the name of Christ means working with an analysis of human realities and with a capacity to make judgments about the good related to experience, rather than starting with doctrinal principles to be applied.

Instead of following a deductive method in presenting the social teaching of the Church, the Church would do better to develop an inductive method, one that shows how pastors and faithful learn from practice, dialogue, and discernment. It cannot be claimed that GS worked with a clear methodology, but it did enough to show that some fresh approach had to be developed. Signs of this are still found in the work of the Pontifical Council on Justice and Peace and in several encyclicals, such as *Sollicitudo rei socialis* (1987) and *Laborem exercens* (1981). There is still an uneasy relation between a readiness to listen and a desire to teach.

In coming to grips with the relation between faith and secular reality, it is not sufficiently kept in mind that much of the insight into God's Word and presence in this process needs to come from the faithful. As persons of Christian allegiance, they are the ones engaged in public service and in the workplace. This belies the attempt to overplay the distinction between sacred and secular roles. There are not two realms of human and cosmic reality, the one the profane and the other the sacred. There is rather the divine or the holy present in the entire order of creation, and the need to be in touch with this in working toward the common good of humanity.

Church's Presence in the World

Some conciliar participants believed that the Church as a community and an institution needed to see itself as a significant presence in the world, among all those concerned with the future of humanity. Their intent was to engage in a reading of the signs of the times that marked the present moment of human history. To broaden the dialogue and give it a theological foundation, however, others advanced an approach grounded in the mystery of the Incarnation. In all human good and in all action for the good, it is possible to speak of a presence of Christ, finding him therefore present in other realities and communities, even as history may be related to him. The text eventually said: "The Word of God, through whom all things were made, became human and dwelt among us. . . . He entered world history, taking that history into himself and recapitulating it" (GS 38).

The prevailing thought of theologians and bishops was that this incarnationist approach, seeing Christ ever at work in the world, actually gave a foundation to a respect for the natural order and for what is achieved through human reasoning. This did not mean full agreement on what this meant. A residue of the medieval debates over the approach to reason can be found in discussions over various proposals made by commissions or groups. Some would have thought that new experience and dialogue with reason opened up new insights and a new challenge for the Church to learn more fully the meaning of the Incarnation and of the Spirit's presence. Some seemed to consider that a reason well formed by faith would cast some prescient light on what is new in the contemporary world, and that the Church needed to uphold perennial principles governing many of the issues under debate. This has long-range consequences greatly affecting the role that the laity may have in the understanding and transmission of the faith. They may be seen either as people who implement what the Church teaches in their secular occupations, or as people who because of their involvement in the world can enlighten the magisterium.

Different viewpoints among those who wished for greater engagement with the world means that the text does not lend itself to smooth reading. In continuing to pursue the matter, it may be helpful to look anew to the thought of Marie-Dominique Chenu, since this helped to spark the debate.[29] Though not a *peritus* (officially appointed expert), he exercised considerable influence, beginning with the adoption of this issue on the conciliar agenda. On a whole he was optimistic about developments in the modern world, finding in them and in the attention to justice that he observed in many places an openness to the Word of God, what he called "des pierres d'attente." According to Chenu, while the Church has and needs its doctrines, living the faith is living within an economy of salvation, an economy brought into being by the gifts of the Word and the Spirit, for which there is a readiness in much human endeavor. By these gifts God has entered history, and we cannot preach the good news of love and salvation without discerning this presence. The key term is *incarnation* because it is always amid fleshly realities that God is present and active. This does not confine God to the life of the Church, but the divine is found everywhere that the good of humanity is pursued. Chenu indeed brought together the two words *incarnation* and *consecration*. God, he believed, is sanctifying or consecrating the whole cosmos, and the Church is party to this design. Engagement with the world means being attentive to the signs of the times as signs of the presence of Word and Spirit.

Among the bishops and theologians at the Council, particularly the Germans, were those who criticized the presence of Chenu's theology in the text that preceded the constitution, which is dubbed Schema 13.[30] Chenu was considered to be too optimistic about modernity, and some thought that his reading of the signs of the times lacked a theological criterion. Human sinfulness cannot be set aside, and principles are needed for discerning right and wrong. The world has to be seen from the perspective not just of Word made flesh but of the cross, of the gospel of the two Adams, the contest between sin and grace. Forty years and more later, it remains part of the mission of the Church to work out the balance, even as it is moved by faith in the presence of Word and Spirit in all things human.

All this has deep implications for the mission of the Church in the world, for the lives of Christian communities, and so for the upsurge and structuring of ministries. Learning more about the meaning of looking for the signs of the times is crucial. Some at the Council, and in a particular way those grouped together as "The Church of the Poor," saw the danger of an evangelical compromise and the abdication of the Christian community's prophetic role in the conversation with the modern world. This role, in the name of the gospel, would give primacy to the world of the poor and the needs of the poor. In other words, the preferential option for the poor would have to mean immersion in the life of the poor, and it would mean interpreting the gospel through their eyes. This applies to the life of the Church itself and to its contribution to the future of a world order. The problem with the phrase "reading the signs of the times," as will be explained, highlights the tension that surrounds the dialogue of the Church with the world.

Church and a Worldwide Humanity

Chapter 2 of GS (23–32) is entitled "Proper Development of Culture" and represents an effort to see humanity in its full dimensions, not reducing societies to their economic and political concerns. Culture is inclusive of values and the expression of values, which is colored by diverse ethnographical and historical realities, and includes all the areas of symbolic and indeed artistic expression. This certainly gives a larger view of the human than what comes from social and economic analysis and gives a better idea of what is addressed in the proclamation of the gospel. However, the discussion at the Council was dominated by a dialogue with the cultures of Europe and North America and the desire to go beyond the negative assessment of the Enlightenment. The broad reality of cultural plurality in a global humanity and a global Church, and the need to find an ecclesial presence within this diversity, was only adumbrated and remained a task to be pursued beyond and after the Council. The position taken in *Nostra aetate* (1965) on religions or living faiths complements the openness to dialogue of *GS*. When working toward the common good and in taking a religious position on human development and on moral questions, the Christian churches are not alone. They are one with other living faiths in wishing to pursue a common purpose, in serving the good of the human person, and in attending to the holy present in the midst of the temporal. What at times is called the independence of the temporal order does not mean that the divine or that grace is absent from it. It means that the Catholic Church, or Christian churches, cannot assume to dictate how this order is to be pursued. While ever attentive to the gospel of Jesus Christ in their attention to what is called the secular and the common good, Christians are invited to work in dialogue with communities of other living faiths and with persons enlightened by a reason that itself is ordained to a common good. This is not simply in order to offer Christian beliefs but in order to be challenged and enlightened.

Humans and Creation

In referring to the relation between gospel and human activity, *Gaudium et spes* (33–39) focuses on human work and humanity's role in exercising dominion over the universe (§34). A limit to the extent and nature of this activity is affirmed inasmuch as humans are expected to respect the will of God as creator in what they do. However, there is no deeper consideration of the affinity between human being and all created being in its splendid richness, and of how this affects human work and invention. John Paul II in his encyclical *Sollicitudo rei socialis*[31] takes much the same approach in writing of human work and authentic human development. He does introduce a clause about humanity's "affinity with other creatures" (29.3), but without pursuing the thought further. In the Vatican's follow-up on relations with the Jewish people and on interreligious dialogue, much that is common in interests for human development is related to beliefs on creation. On this basis there is talk of sharing together in social action in the interests of a worldwide human community. This has to be developed to include shared interests in respect for creation in its totality. In the light of the ecological problems that have been put so clearly into light in recent decades, much more thought has to be given to this aspect of the Church's mission in the world.[32]

Signs of the Times

The symptom of an unresolved problematic of the Church's presence in the world is found within *Gaudium et spes* when it comes to the expression "reading the signs of the times." One of the important notions and phrases used in GS was indeed that of reading the signs of the times, but it had a history behind it. It had been used by Pope John XXIII in his encyclical *Pacem in terris* (1963) as a way of speaking about the Church's mission in relating to the world of our day, and it became quite common after that, owing much of its development, as has been said, to Marie-Dominique Chenu. The term is still used from time to time in magisterial teaching, but the question of its meaning and its implications for the mission of the Church remains and emerges even more forcefully in face of multiple changes.

To begin with, using the phrase meant taking note of the differences between the contemporary world and the ancient and medieval world. Progress in human development and on questions such as human rights in the aftermath of the Enlightenment could not be ignored. What is implied in the invitation to read the signs of the times is that the Church had never fully attuned itself to this "world" in its doctrines and in its pastoral work. It needed to do so to speak an efficacious word. This work was called *aggiornamento* in relaying the Christian faith, being able to distinguish its essence from its modes of expression, so as to address the world of today.

In its initial proposal the schema for the constitution talked of the signs of the times as the features of the contemporary world that were most indicative of its reality and toward which the Church needed to take a more positive approach.[33] In the words of the intervention in the debate of Cardinal Rugmabwa of Uganda, the term meant all those elements in the world through which God draws humans to himself.[34] A comparable sense of the meaning which the Council gave this expression is found in the memoirs of Archbishop Denis Hurley of Durban. He writes that for the fathers of the Council, the signs of the times "may be identified as happenings and developments of urgent significance for the Church in her work of illuminating and sanctifying the human family."[35] Then Hurley goes on to list things that the bishops and their consultants saw as signs: "the universalization of culture, the rapid growth of science and technology, the intense socialization of the human family, the emancipation of women, atheistic communism."

Taken in this sense, reading "the signs of the times" simply, though importantly, means being attentive to those features of contemporary life that are the most indicative of the present and future of humanity. This use of the expression was already criticized during the Council by two of the observers, Lukas Vischer (WCC) and Vilmos Vajta (Hungarian Lutheran). They thought that such use neglected the biblical and eschatological sense of the term and subdued the necessarily prophetic voice of the Church. After much work on the part of the Subcommission on the Signs of the Times, however, the Constitution held to the sense in which the words were used by Pope John XXIII, to mean all the indicators, positive and negative, of that which shapes the contemporary world and which the Church has the office of interpreting (*officium perscrutandi*).[36]

Pope John Paul II expanded on this idea of dialogue with the world in his encyclical *Redemptoris missio* (1990) by minting another expression, the *areopagi* of evangelization (cf. Acts 17:16–34). He pointed to those areas of public life where the human future is played out and where various forces, positive and negative, come together, and asked that the Church, in its varied members and with the light of the gospel, be present in such places. Developing the sense of dialogue espoused by Pope Paul VI,[37] he spoke of how the Church should find its place in this world and how it should understand it by developing a theology of God's presence through Word and Spirit. He was later to say that dialogue of its nature means conversion on the part of the Church, a conversion of both mind and attitude.[38] Naturally this idea of reading the signs of the times, or locating the areopagi of evangelization, has considerable consequences for how the Church understands its mission and develops its ministries. It also points to a diversity in the pastoral work of the Church in different places around the world.

Rightly, however, some have pointed out that the Council and the Popes mentioned have rather neglected the eschatological sense of reading the signs of the kingdom found in the Gospels, and especially in Matt 16:4.[39] In this text, the specific sign of the times that the Pharisees and Sadducees have failed to read is Jesus' feeding of the crowds, a deed done out of compassion. Along with this go the signs of healing and forgiving sins narrated by Matthew. When his critics therefore ask for a sign from heaven, like unto the theophany of Sinai, Jesus promises them only the sign of Jonah, that is his own death and resurrection. The signs to which Jesus therefore points are eschatological signs indicative of the advent of God's kingdom, or as Matthew puts it, the kingdom from above (Matt 4:17; 13:44, 45, 47). These are not signs of what is going on around the people in the form of what earthly powers do, but signs that are peculiar to divine advent.

Hence it has to be seen that beyond the general notion that God is in the world and ordering human activities through Word and Spirit, there is the meaning that the kingdom's advent calls some human initiatives into question, in the light of the gospel of Jesus Christ. An eschatological sign is a word of judgment, hope, and promise. However much Christians may be affirmative of human developments, preaching the gospel retains a critical edge and seeks out the true signs of the kingdom, which are not of the mainstream of these developments.[40]

It was the group called the Church of the Poor that was most attentive to the biblical sense of signs and located them especially in the world of the poor and in all that promised them true liberation or freedom. This freedom is not only a promise of eternal life, but includes a quest for authentic improvement of their human life in all its dimensions. Commitment to this kind of justice is evident in the writings of both Pope Paul VI and Pope John Paul II, so much so that toward the end of his life, the latter wrote on the eschatological commitment to those who suffer poverty and injustice expressed in the Eucharist. The teaching might be given a keener edge by being more deliberately related to the Scriptures. The Church does not only aid the poor but has an obligation in mission and in conscience to listen to the poor, who are specially chosen interpreters of the kingdom of God, promised in the covenant with the Jewish people and in the gospel.

Somewhere between reading the situation of the times through the signs most indicative of change and heeding the signs of the advent of God's reign among the poor, there has to come an analysis of reasons for poverty, for economic, social, political, and cultural depression. This is grounded in working with and attending to the voices of all who might be considered poor in one of the many forms of poverty that the world imposes upon its victims. It is in the midst of these that Christians have to attend to the signs of the times in the biblical sense. Indeed, this is one path along which it is possible to integrate cultural impoverishment with social and economic. A deep reason why peoples are often unable to find their place on a national or in a global situation is that they have lost the resources of their cultural heritage, and thus their identity on a modern world scene. In those who on a continent or in a country suffer most from poverty and injustice, one finds a sense of themselves as social misfits. Their living conditions make it impossible for them to fit into current trends of development and communication. Whatever in their bones and ways they retain of a traditional culture does not help them make the passage to the present, or when they act or are acted upon, they do not find clear personal and communal identity, being torn between several worlds. African, Asian, and Latin American churches are aware of this and hence write their mission and foster their ministries in accordance with these perceptions, though sometimes they retreat into a magisterial approach that offers the principles without the analysis and without the restructuring and resituating of ministries that the scene requires. Latin American churches have been chided for relying too heavily on a politically motivated social analysis, associated with encouragement of base Christian communities. African churches are sometimes thought to attend too much to a retrieval of a cultural heritage and not enough to other reasons for poverty, while Asian Churches suffer the criticism of being attached to the wisdom of Eastern religions and a culture that they inspire. Clearly these churches are on the way and are trying to better know and understand the world in which they witness to Christ and gospel, and to find therein the signs of God's gracious advent and presence.

Their necessarily complex approach is the way in which to appropriate the orientations of *Gaudium et spes*, not slavishly but creatively.[41]

Papal Views on Sundry Issues

This is not the place to rehearse all the positions taken by Popes Paul VI and John Paul II on various questions emanating from Vatican II. In light, however, of how ecclesial ministry is to develop, it is worth noting the importance they gave to the pastoral constitution, *Gaudium et spes*. The (potentially fruitful) tension in implementing the Council's double concern with an adequate presentation of Christian teaching and with following up on the concerns expressed in that constitution appeared quite soon after its close. In 1970, to mark the fifth anniversary of the closing of Vatican II, Paul VI issued an *adhortatio apostolica* (apostolic exhortation) called *Quinque iam anni*.[42] The conciliar document to which he made primary reference was *GS*. Calling it the *magna carta* of the Church's presence in the world, he took up the notion of the need to understand this world by reading the signs of the times. Along with this, he allied the search to find an adequate presentation of the gospel and the teaching of the Church to the world, using the distinction made by Pope John XXIII between the substance of this teaching and its more fluid form. For Paul VI, this meant attention to the world's distress and hunger and fidelity to Revelation. He admitted that the Church would have to submit herself to criticism because of her failings, saying, however, that the only true response to this is the Church's own inner conversion.

In his social encyclical *Laborem exercens* (1981), Pope John Paul II linked *Gaudium et spes* with the social teaching of popes from *Rerum novarum* (1891) to *Populorum progressio* (1967, no. 2).[43] This teaching, he says, is related to the true state of affairs in the world, in which there is a disproportionate distribution of wealth and poverty among the peoples of the world. This is today's "world question," which the Church has to address in its teaching and in its pastoral work in order to "build justice on earth." In the next social encyclical, *Sollicitudo rei socialis* (1987)[44] he wrote of the necessity of "theological reading of modern problems," which would bring to light the fundamental reasons for injustice (no. 35). It is not enough to do an economic and political analysis of the reasons for the underdevelopment of many. The moral causes have to be sought out and addressed. They are tied up with the "structure of sin" that reflects a prevailing greed and selfishness in the whole fabric of international society and the way in which it is organized. As a sign of hope, the Pope points to an ever increasing sense of solidarity among peoples that is built upon true respect for the human person (nos. 38-40). As a particular indication of hope for the future, he points to the "solidarity of the poor among themselves" (no. 39) as they seek together to present and defend their rights before the world. The Church needs to be present in a special way in this struggle.

The teaching of Benedict XVI on different matters is now of more immediate interest as we reflect on directions taken on mission and ministry. That churches must both proclaim their faith in Jesus Christ and yet dialogue with others remains a concern. Benedict XVI continues to remind bishops and faithful. Typical of how he usually speaks on the issue is a 2007 address to the bishops of Cambodia and Laos on their *ad limina* visit.[45] He adverted to their task of announcing "the Christian faith within a particular culture." While they do this, they are to be mindful that the Church may never cease to proclaim Jesus Christ but "does not wish to impose herself but to bear witness to her respect for human beings and for the society in which she lives." Hence, while Christians can be clear about their own identity and be nourished in faith and spirit by the Word of God and the sacraments, they can also show respect for other religious traditions and cultures. Among the activities that point to Christian identity and presence, the pope underlines their care for the poor of society since in doing so "they eloquently highlight God's love for all human beings without distinction."

On some occasions, however, Benedict has given his own perspective on the dialogue with cultures and religions, seeing it as something that continues to need refinement. In marking the fortieth anniversary of the promulgation of the decree *Ad gentes*, Benedict XVI related the theme of mission with that of the encounter between the gospel and cultures, between the Church and other religions. He first noted the distinctive starting point of Christian revelation and mission, which is the love of God for the world, originating in the divine communion of the Trinity and showing itself to the world in Jesus Christ. He then related mission to a consideration of changes in the anthropological, cultural, social, and religious ambience of peoples:

> From the beginning, the Christian People attended with clarity of mind to the importance of bringing participation in the richness of Christ's love to those who did not yet know Christ, by way of an unceasing missionary activity. . . . In these recent years the Church has felt the need to intensify this charge . . . in face of a slowing down of mission to peoples [mission *ad gentes*] brought about by the difficulties in changes effected in the anthropological, cultural, social, and religious conditions of humanity. The Church today is called upon to confront this challenge and enter into dialogue with diverse cultures and religions, seeking to work together with all persons of goodwill to bring about a peaceful sharing in life together of peoples. Hence the mission to peoples has been notably amplified; . . . the work of mission is not only to peoples and distant territories but is destined to affect the sociocultural ambience and see these as the destinaries of the missionary activity of the people of God.[46]

In the ill-fated address given at Regensburg on September 12, 2006, Pope Benedict sees a providential and irrevocable alliance between revelation, faith, and Greek thought. This puts stronger limits on the dialogue between Christianity and peoples of other cultures.[47] The following statement from this speech is certainly a harsh affirmation, if not indeed a crude dismissal, of inculturation of the gospel outside a European context:

[They are said to have] the right to return to the simple message of the New Testament prior to that inculturation, in order to inculturate it anew in their own particular milieux. This thesis is not simply false, but it is coarse and lacking in precision. The New Testament was written in Greek and bears the imprint of the Greek spirit, which had already come to maturity as the Old Testament developed. True, there are elements in the evolution of the early Church which do not have to be integrated into all cultures. Nonetheless, the fundamental decisions made about the relationship between faith and the use of human reason are part of the faith itself; they are developments consonant with the nature of faith itself.

This was an academic address, however, not a formal magisterial allocution, and it should not be allowed to call the earlier statement into question. But in his address in December 2005 to the Roman Curia, speaking of the proper interpretation of Vatican II, he affirmed the necessary and historical alliance between the Word of God and Greek thought. In the same discourse, on the other hand, he underlined what is to be gained by openness to world religions. Obviously a reader is left with the question as to how these two things are to be brought together.

Further queries have been raised by reason of a point made in Pope Benedict's address to the assembly of bishops of Latin America and the Caribbean (CELAM) when he opened their assembly at Aparecida in May 2007.[48] Referring to the religions practiced by the peoples of these countries prior to the advent of Christianity, he claims that the Christian faith brought their aspirations to fulfillment. In making this claim, he also said that trying to revive these early religious practices today would be a mistake.[49] These remarks were made without reference to the sometimes cruel imposition of the Christian faith imposed by colonization or to the suppression and demonization of indigenous cultures and religions. They were also made without reference to the fact that there are still communities practicing traditional religions on the continent, a matter that surely has to be taken into account in interreligious dialogue. Since then, in a Wednesday General Audience, the Pope has tried to modify his remarks in view of protests made, but as with his speech at Regensburg, the words stand and the message has not been revoked.

In 2007, in his encyclical letter on hope, *Spe salvi*,[50] Pope Benedict returns to the topic of dialogue with modernity, to spell out the true nature of hope. In number 22, he says that modernity in its quest for progress needs dialogue with Christianity, but he says as well that Christianity needs to dialogue with modernity in order to come to know for itself what hope means in today's world. Because of the enduring background of the Enlightenment, he goes on in number 23 to speak of the relation between reason and faith, suggesting that reason needs faith to provide it with the true criterion for distinguishing between good and evil and for formulating the goals that it pursues. Throughout the letter, the Pope emphasizes that true Christian hope has to do with eternal life. He adds that this may not be pursued in freedom here on Earth unless it is accompanied by a common quest for justice and peace and reconciliation among peoples. It is noteworthy that the entire discussion of the hope needed today refers to the European scene and its history, and that the encyclical is silent on what is happening on other continents and on the possibility of other dialogues around the world.

In the words of these documents, there is some caution and even restriction on the role of intercultural and interreligious dialogue and a more classical definition of its purpose. This does not negate the work that was intensely pursued in the aftermath of the Council in various regions and under the auspices of the Pontifical Council for Interreligious Dialogue, and that must still form a part of the Church's action in the world.

Communion of Churches: Ecumenical Considerations

The decrees of the Council on Christian Unity and on the relation to other religions continue to be invoked for matters of concern for the action and the mission of the Church among peoples. While ecumenical dialogue has helped communities to sort out both doctrinal and practical relations among constituent members of the one body of Christ, it has not often led to intense sharing of mission together in the preaching of the gospel and in Christian service to the kingdom of God in the world. Some further reflection on Christian ecumenism is therefore pertinent to the reception of Vatican II.

Discussions about the future of ministry and order have to be ecumenical, and all Christian churches have some particular insights to contribute to the future. It was only a beginning, but much hostility between the Roman Church and other Christian Churches and Confessions was set aside in chapter 2 of *Lumen gentium* and in the decree on ecumenism of the Second Vatican Council, though it can also be said that the full implications of the position taken have not been worked out and in ways have even been put to severe test.

Given the weak but in retrospect nonetheless heartening efforts in the decades before Vatican II to spell out in rather technical terms how baptized persons not of the Roman Church belonged to Christ's body, the statement of principle that all baptized in the faith of Christ belong to the body of Christ and to the people of God is even startling. What this implies for relations between churches in the common life of faith, in worship, in government, in forming Christian perspectives on secular matters, and in mission is still obscure and unrealized in practice.

Officially approved dialogues between the Catholic Church and other bodies have worked hard to spell out common doctrines and theologies, but these often do not have a corresponding effect in practice. For example, even though agreements between Catholics and Anglican, Catholics and Lutherans, Catholics and Reformed have stated common doctrines on the nature of the Eucharist, it still seems hard for Catholics to fully recognize the eucharistic order of these churches. This ranges from questions about their validity to questions about the need for full doctrinal agreement on all matters before sharing the common eucharistic table. The decree on ecumenism had said that it affirmed the action of Christ and the Spirit in the celebration of the Lord's Supper in other Churches, but the implications of this for a fuller recognition have not been thrashed out. Indeed, in its preparatory *lineamenta*, the October 2005 Synod on the Eucharist spoke of having to defend the authentic Catholic faith in the Eucharist against the opinions of "separated brethren." Fortunately, this disappeared from the working paper (*instrumentum laboris*) and did not show up in synodal propositions—but that it should be said at all tells much about current vacillations.[51]

The Decree on Ecumenism (*Unitatis redintegratio*, 1964) offered a recognition of the ecclesial character of other Church communities and also of the action of Christ and the Spirit in their celebration of the Lord's Supper. Hence, in the bilateral and multilateral dialogues that followed Vatican II, this recognition seemed to be an opening toward the possible mutual recognition of ministries. The question was raised, for example, in a 1972 report of an officially appointed joint Lutheran-Roman Catholic study commission, taking this statement of Vatican II as an explicit starting point.[52] The study reported that the discussion was helped by reconsideration of the meaning of apostolic succession and by reflection on the continuing exercise of ministries of charismatic origin. Making it quite clear that it is not only a matter of Catholic recognition of Lutheran ministry but of Lutheran recognition of Catholic ministry, the report remarked on the affirmation at the Council of the importance of the ministry of the Word.

A more formally theological report of this commission in 1981, on "The Ministry in the Church," places the issue of mutual recognition in the context of some convergence in the understanding and structuring of the Church's ministry.[53] This report noted how both Churches found it important to relate the question of ministry to its christological, pneumatological, and ecclesial foundations. It also reported that both Churches believed ordination by a laying on of hands to be necessary to appointment to office since it is a divine call to the ministry of Word and sacrament, with a promise of the Spirit.[54] With regard to the sacramentality of order, even the difference could to some degree be overcome by a wider recognition of a sacramental principle on the part of Lutherans and the Catholic readiness to make a clear difference between the major sacraments of baptism and Eucharist (or Lord's Supper) and other sacraments in the sevenfold list of the Catholic Church, which are all related ultimately to the Eucharist. However, the Catholic attention to defects in the ministry of other churches was noted, though it was said that this did not mean refusing to affirm the action of the Spirit in and through them.

In the intervening years, this matter of some lack in the ministries of other Churches and communities of the West has received some critical attention on the part of the Roman Church, which marks a more-hesitant approach to mutual recognition. Without talking of such statements as *Dominus Iesus* (2000), one may note what is said in the 1995 encyclical of Pope John Paul II, *Ut unum sint*. Repeating what was stated in *Unitatis redintegratio*, the Pope chose to underline "the lack of the Sacrament of Order," which prevents the fullness of unity that should flow from baptism and a full recognition of the celebration of the eucharistic mystery in those Churches and communities.[55]

Nonetheless, within the bilateral and multilateral discussions on church order, some advance has been made. There is a growing acceptance of the existence of the episcopacy as a sign that comes from the tradition of apostolic and ecclesial communion, but even then opinions of its place in the Church differ. To put it simply, Protestant Churches may well say that in times of crisis the existence of the episcopacy has to give way to the right preaching of the gospel and the right celebration of the sacraments of baptism and Lord's Supper, while the Catholic magisterium holds that none of this is possible without the inherited and divinely instituted episcopacy. Some Churches, such as the Methodist and the Presbyterian, hold that what is essential to episcopacy can be exercised in ways other than through a local monoepiscopacy, an idea that seems taboo to Orthodox and Catholic. Even as this is written, Catholic bishops are heard to say that the ordination of women is a great obstacle to ecumenical exchange and communion, while other Churches think it to be a postulate of genuine fidelity to the gospel to make this move. To discuss this matter together as an open issue seems well-nigh impossible in present circumstances. In parishes and dioceses of the Catholic Church there is the common recognition that the life of the Church could not exist without the ministry of women in all areas of Christian life, including worship. Why then the attempt to stem discussion of their ordination and the quasi-dogmatic affirmations of leading "churchmen" that it is an obstacle to church unity? Is it not time for an unbiased assessment of tradition on this matter in both practice and theological reasoning?[56]

It is not possible to do justice to all the statements and accords, which are quite numerous, but something may usefully be noted about Lutheran–Roman Catholic dialogue. According to the 1978 statement on *Eucharist*, some elements have been retrieved that can form a common basis for the theology and implementation of ministry in the Church in its necessary responsibility for the Eucharist.[57] These include the importance of the royal priesthood of all believers, which both describes what ministry has to serve and is a basis for the nurturing of ministry, through the work of the Spirit. Second is the primacy of Word and faith in conversion to Christ and the life of the Church, including its sacramental action. Third is a focus on the local church in describing and debating issues of ministry.

It is in such a context that questions about the continuity of apostolic tradition and about apostolic succession have to be placed. Traditionally, Lutheranism has not been much inclined to speak of apostolic succession, since to its adherents this means what Rome has in mind about the unbroken succession of bishops through ordination. This sounds like appealing to the importance of Church structures rather than to the power of Word and sacrament. However, the statement sees the possibility of a common retrieval of this language of succession, given the right context and a fuller way of speaking. First and foremost, there is the fidelity of the Church, by the work of the Spirit, to the apostolic witness about Christ. It is in service of this that one may talk of succession in apostolic ministry. Where episcopacy fits in is seen in two different ways, even as both Churches wish to maintain episcopal structure. For Catholics, the apostolic succession in ministry of the episcopacy is absolutely necessary. For Lutherans, ordination to the ministry of Word and sacrament is a gospel mandate, and within the action of this ministry the historical episcopacy is an important sign of fidelity and continuity. However, for them fidelity to the Word has priority and may at times be served by suffering a break in episcopal continuity. For Reformation Churches generally, the Church is defined primarily in terms of assembly for right worship, whereas Catholic doctrine relates the Church to the structures necessary for right worship and continuity of doctrine.

There is an admission on the part of Western Churches that placing ministry in the living context of koinonia and eucharistic fellowship is an advance on customary Western debates. It is through the dialogue of Western Churches with those of the East, and especially with Orthodox Churches, that this has come to the fore. To cite but the 1988 statement on the sacrament of order of the international joint theological commission of the Orthodox Church and the Roman Catholic Secretariat for Christian unity, one can see the importance of this perspective.[58]

This statement first signals the unique ministry of Christ and the apostles, asking how this may continue to be active in the life and ministry of the Church, which is to serve fidelity to it. Such fidelity in the transmission of a common heritage of teaching and doctrine is the concern of the whole community of the faithful and of all local churches, and not simply the affair of the ordained. Succession in ministry, and specifically in episcopacy, is indeed a succession of persons, but within a succession of Church community. This is most importantly a succession in giving authentic witness by word and deed. It is only in relation to this that one may place a continuous transmission of the powers needed to guide the community in its common concern and task. There is an abiding relation to the Twelve as those from whom the apostolic witness comes, and who received a mandate from the Lord, so that bishops, while claiming such an origin for their ministry, must also show themselves faithful to it. In this sense a bishop is a successor of the apostles, but his ministry has to be a response to a special charism of the Spirit given to him personally, lest it be seen as simply a transmission of office. The statement also retrieves the eschatological characteristic of the Church and its ministry, which comes from looking for an origin in the group of the Twelve. It was to them as the sign of the new people of the new covenant, in both reality and hope for the future, that Christ gave his mandate and the promise of the Spirit. Fidelity to origins means fidelity in hope as well as in belief.[59]

Following up the Baptism, Eucharist, and Ministry (BEM) document of 1982,[60] the Faith and Order Commission of the World Council of Churches published a statement in 2005 titled *Nature and Mission of the Church*, and this was adopted as an instrument for discussion at the WCC General Assembly in Porte Alegre, Brazil, in 2006.[61] Describing the Church in relation to the mystery and the work of the Trinity, this document presents the Church's mission as the service of "God's design to gather all creation under the lordship of Christ and to bring humanity and all creation into communion" (§34). Carrying out this mission includes proclaiming Christ, witnessing to Christ, and "sharing the suffering of all by advocacy and care of the poor, the needy, and the marginalized" (§40). This must include the healing of broken human relationships, as well as the relationships between humanity and creation. With all of this in mind, the statement describes the Church itself as sign and instrument of God's intention and plan for the world.

Toward the beginning of this document, and in relation to what was said in BEM, the Faith and Order Commission takes note of several enduring questions between Churches about institutional ecclesial elements in their structure (§13). First, it asks whether preaching and sacraments are to be seen as a means or simply as a witness to the activity of Word and Spirit in the hearts of believers. Second, with regard to ordained ministry, and in particular the episcopacy, it raises the issue whether such is to be seen as effective means and guarantee of the presence of Word and Spirit, or whether there may be times when the "sovereignty of Word and Spirit" prevails despite the errors and sins of the institution. Last, it flags the theological question of institutional continuity, especially of the episcopacy, as servant of the transmission of the apostolic faith. While some see this as essential to guarantee truth, others hold that there are times when the apostolic faith prevails in spite of, or even through, a break in continuity.

When the statement treats of ministry (§§82–89), it seeks a balance between the ministry of all the faithful, in virtue of the royal priesthood of all believers, and the ministry of the ordained. This has to be worked out in relation to the nature of the Church as people of God, the body of Christ, and as a communion. The primary question is not institutional, that is, the safeguarding of institutional distinctions, but the service to inner life and mission, through Word and sacrament.

Relation to Orthodox Ecclesiology

There can be some hope of arriving at an ecumenical consensus and cooperation that achieves unity while allowing for diversity. In dialogue, the Catholic Church has to situate itself in relation to the ecclesiologies of other Churches. A word on this seems pertinent since it affects attitudes to mission and ministry.

As Nicholas Lossky points out,[62] the final break between the Orthodox Church and the Roman Catholic Church is crystallized in the points that proved beyond resolution at the Council of Florence (ending 1445). These are the way of professing faith in the Holy Spirit in the Creed, and the question of the jurisdiction of the Bishop of Rome within the communion of Churches. Apart from these, however, the doctrine on the Church is differently presented in East and West. Because of the jurisdiction of the Pope, the West has tended to give priority to the universal aspect of Church communion as it centers around the Pope, whereas Orthodox ecclesiology attends to the communion expressed through the eucharistic action of each local church. John Meyendorff makes it clear that for Byzantine theology the eucharistic community cannot be seen as "part of" the Church, for in each Eucharist the "fullness of the Kingdom" is eschatologically expressed. Consequently, because it manifests the unity and wholeness of the Church, the Eucharist is the "ultimate theological norm for ecclesiastical structure."[63]

According to Orthodox theology, the hierarchy, ministry, discipline, and organization of the Church are all manifestations of the deeper nature of the Church as a eucharistic communion with Christ in the Spirit. All authority and ministry in the Church are charismatic. The gift of Christ and the Spirit, the two hands of the Father, as said by Irenaeus of Lyons, find their due place in eucharistic celebration. When the liturgy is celebrated, it expresses the call of all humans to holiness through the Incarnation of the Word, and it includes the whole of creation in the offering made in memorial and thanksgiving to the Father. What is done in the Eucharist irrigates the entire life of the faithful and through them the entire creation. While Western theologians sometimes make use of a distinction between vertical and horizontal directions in Church life and worship, or between visible and invisible, Greek discourse on the apophatic, liturgical, and eschatological orientation of ecclesial mystery and celebration cannot readily accommodate such language.

Orthodox ecclesiology hence is a theology of eucharistic communion, beginning with the local church, in its fidelity to the faith of the apostles, shared in catholic communion with other churches. While the foremost duties of the bishop are the preaching of the faith and the celebration of the liturgy, this is in practice shared with presbyters who work at the parish level, in communion with the bishop. The local church is in communion with other churches, and there is a fellowship of churches in one communion, wherein patriarchates have an important role, but Orthodox ecclesiology does not veer from the primacy of the local eucharistic community. For them, it is wrong to see this community as part of the Church universal, for in itself the local church is the eschatological expression of the fullness of the body of Christ. There is room for patriarchates and even primacy within the fellowship of churches, but this cannot suppress the relative fullness and autonomy of the local church.

When they speak of conciliarity or of *sobornost*, Orthodox Churches mean the communion in the unity of the faith and of participation in the divine of all churches adhere to the apostolic tradition. This communion is expressed and given life in the eucharistic celebration of local churches. In episcopal ordination, such conciliarity is further expressed by the participation of bishops of neighboring churches.

Having retained the tripartite hierarchy of bishop, presbyter, and deacon not only in theory but in practice, Orthodox theology also includes a treatment of the role of the laity. This has considerable importance especially in teaching so that the Orthodox Churches have never ceased to recognize the position of the lay theologian in their midst. All the baptized, however, are transformed through the sacraments; they belong within the kingdom of God and are witnesses to this kingdom in all that they do. The presence in society and culture of the kingdom of God is assured by the baptized faithful.

A great contribution to the Catholic Church of dialogue with Orthodox Churches has been the use of the image of communion, or *koinōnia*, to relate the mystery of the Church, its Eucharist, and its ministry to the mystery of the Trinity.[64] On the question of ministry and order, though the office of bishop is clearly presented, apostolic succession is placed within the fidelity of the whole Church to the teaching of the apostles and the apostolic tradition of the faith. The continuity in faith and tradition promised by God is a gift to the Church, and of this the ordained are the servants.

Relation to Protestant Theologies on Church

When Protestant doctrine and theologies recognize a divine call in ministry, its biblical origins as a divine ordinance, or even the importance to be given to a retention or a restoration of the episcopacy, they still find the Roman Catholic emphasis on structures and their continuity difficult to accept. The doctrine of justification by faith in Christ and the primacy of the Word are to the fore. Some would say that though organisms and structures have their continuity and their permanence outside of the assembly, it is in the gathering for the preaching of the Word and the celebration of the Lord's Supper that the Church truly exists. In some respects Catholic teaching is close to this when it professes that liturgy is the source and summit of the life of the Church, but differences remain. The concern is that the importance given to structures risks giving officeholders superiority over others and a control over the Word that they do not rightly possess. The churches of the Reformation traditionally associated this position with the doctrine and theology of the sacramental character, and with the Tridentine definition of the permanence of character. Ministers may be allowed sway over the Word and Eucharist, whereas they are themselves under the judgment of the Word. Hence, in present ecumenical efforts to restore the traditional episcopacy as an important sign in the life of the apostolic church, those of Reformation Churches do not let go of the provision for extraordinary ministry when the established Church appears to fail in its fidelity to Christ.

Important for Lutherans is that while Martin Luther upheld as gospel ordinance the call by God, and not by the congregation, to the pastoral ministry of Word and Sacrament, his teaching on the royal priesthood influenced his ideas of ordering the ministry. The normal way through which the call to preach and administer the Lord's Supper is handed on is through ordination within a line of succession going back to apostolic times. To safeguard the primacy of the priesthood of all believers, endowed by faith with the grace of justification and the Spirit and with the dignity and freedom of being believers, this strict temporal succession in ordering may have to be broken in times of crisis. This is precisely to safeguard the Word and the equal dignity of all believers, for which the service of pastoral ministry is ordained, and hence by implication to safeguard the fidelity of the ministry itself.

Reformed Churches find in John Calvin's writings the teaching about the "priesthood of all Christians." Although it belongs to those who are members of the body of Christ, for Calvin its meaning is seen in terms of serving of the kingdom of God in the world. The purpose of the Church is then Christ's exercise of authority through Christian living and through the Church's ministry for the "establishment and extension of his kingdom." This is done primarily through the action of every Christian who offers to God all that he or she has and is, in joining one's life to Christ and his once-and-for-all sacrifice. The liberating salvation enables them to do this and confers on the faithful the role of "priest," in accordance with its New Testament foundations. In Calvin, readers find the desire to return to evangelical forms of ministry in his comparison of governance by presbyters and elders with the ecclesiastical orders of the Roman Church, particularly its office of "priest." Calvin appealed especially to Eph 4:11–16, where he found the distinction between the offices that served the founding of the Church and those that endure as permanent offices, namely pastors and teachers. To these he added the ministry of government by elders, as ordained by Rom 12:7–8, and the ministry of the diaconate in caring for the poor, especially as evidenced in Acts 6. In the wake of Calvin, Reformed Churches have given special importance in the government of the Church to elders or presbyters, seeing this office as distinct from that of pastor and teacher.

A Catholic reader today will be responsive to the elements that Orthodox, Protestant, and Catholic have in common and to the common effort to relate to apostolic foundations, even though earlier such a reader might have been consciously and unconsciously dismissive of these other Churches. Nonetheless, there seem to be great difficulties in pursuing further the possibilities opened by the World Council of Churches and the Second Vatican Council. It seems hard to realize what Walter Kasper said of the interplay between the reality of the Church as an institution and as "an ever-new charismatic event."[65]

An ever-thorny issue is the ministry exercised by the Bishop of Rome within the communion of the Church. In his encyclical on ecumenism, *Ut unum sint*, Pope John Paul II invited reflection and dialogue on this, describing papal ministry as a service in love rather than primarily in jurisdictional terms. However, his own exercise of this ministry gave it a universal role that overshadowed the ministry of local churches, even as he seemed to recognize them by multiple visits around the world. One of the historical features of his years in Rome is in fact the emergence of ever more centralized authority. The power exercised by the Roman Curia and the papal preference for his personally appointed College of Cardinals over episcopal synods and episcopal conferences are hard to put together with his expressed ecumenical intent. When Pope Benedict XVI highlights the role of Papal Nuncios as that of being Papal Representatives, who are intended to make him and his pastoral solicitude present in the various churches of the world, the centralization of Church governance takes on considerable prominence, even if it is spoken of in pastoral rather than in jurisdictional terms.[66] For Reformed Churches, who highlight the gathering for Word and sacrament as the place where the Church truly exists as God's people; and for Orthodox Christians, who see the Eucharist as norm for all ecclesiastical structure, this has to be perplexing. It also is puzzling for Catholics who look to local church communities for the mission of rendering

Christ, gospel, and Spirit present in society, granted that this is done within wider ecclesial communion.

Going back to the fundamental importance of *Dei Verbum* (1965) in the teaching of Vatican II, one might give more attention to what is called spiritual ecumenism, a point reiterated more recently by Cardinal Kasper in a survey of progress and regress in ecumenical communion. Whatever the forms this may be given, the optic is that of discerning the Spirit's movements in diverse ecclesial communities, in light of the Scriptures, and discerning likewise where these converge in shaping the lives of churches and their sense of mission. It is a return to the Scriptures from within Christian living and viewing divisions in light of the Scriptures that has made the partial resolution of ancient disputes possible. The disputes on the procession of the Holy Spirit, on the two natures of Christ, and on the doctrine of justification are all seen differently when considered in light of the Word of God and with trust in the workings of the Spirit in the diversity of gifts. What is asked in the texts cited is whether churches today, given attention to their presence in the world, find some convergence in the ways in which they see and formulate a mission, which has to be a shared enterprise. Knowing that mission gives shape to ministry, we can well see what this might mean to dialogue on Church order.[67]

Beyond Impasse through New Focus on Mission?

A recent statement of the USA Lutheran–Roman Catholic dialogue shows well enough where we now stand on matters of this Church order.[68] After some attempt to summarize what is known from early Church history, the document evolves into a juxtaposition of Catholic and Lutheran positions. What is possibly most helpful is the way of stating the issue of apostolic succession. In this placement of ministry within the mystery of *koinōnia*, it is noted (§78) that Lutherans have in the past given little attention to the question of apostolic succession because of their focus on the authenticity of the ministry of Word and sacrament and their faith in the power of God's Word when it is proclaimed. In more recent times, however, in various dialogues they have acknowledged that the episcopacy and in each church the bishop may be sign and instrument of the apostolic succession, that is, the fidelity of the Church to the gospel throughout the ages. For Catholics, the same statement says (§81), the matter is more one of essential and divinely instituted Church structures; their claim is to have maintained the apostolic succession of bishops without interruption through episcopal consecration. At the same time, it is recognized that assessment of ministry and its efficacy cannot be "made exclusively on the basis of the presence or absence of a succession of episcopal consecrations." This is no doubt an acknowledgment on the part of Catholics that in apostolic succession, however maintained, it is the faithful transmission of God's Word and sacrament that is at stake.

It is possible that the sense of being missionary in the service of the reign of God in the world may give a common focus even to questions of Church ministry and order. Statements of the Orthodox Church, the World Council of Churches, several Protestant Churches, and the Roman Catholic Church show them particularly sensitive to the need to eradicate, in Christ's name, all discrimination, injustice, and war; to create one human family in this our global society, standing for the rights of the poor and oppressed.[69] While not all churches see the relation to building up the reign of God in the world in quite the same way, all are sensitive to this need and to shaping their preaching of the Word and their other ecclesial services to this need. There is also a danger in Church life of not allowing the right hand know what the left is doing, and consequently statements on order do not always dovetail with positions on mission. If the convergence were made, this could serve as a common focus when today Churches reconsider what changes in orientation and even what structural changes have to be given to order and ministry, to be inclusive of all their members' roles in making Christ and the Spirit known in today's society and world. At all periods of history, the ministry and structures of the Church have undergone some change in face of its way of spelling out and concretizing its mission. Historically, the truly characteristic note of these present times is the new consciousness of mission within the world as it is now taking shape. As the mission finds new meaning and impetus, so the ministry and ministerial structures of the Church will undergo change, either wittingly or unwittingly. Obedience to the Spirit and discernment of spirits is vital to this process, and this requires historical consciousness in doctrinal, canonical, and practical formulations and endeavors. Listening to the Word of God as it speaks to us in today's world, developing a stronger sense of mission to peoples of our time in fostering integral human development and the interests of the poor, and accommodating ecclesial ministries and structures all work together. This is an avenue along which Churches might come to a better resolution of the relation between particular and universal, given the great role that local communities play in bringing Christ and God's reign to their own people, within their own history, with their own cultural heritage.

Conclusion

In the reception in the Catholic Church of the work of the Council, the document on the Church in the World (*GS*) plays a key role, even though it came at the end of the Council and was finished in rather hurried fashion. One might do well to revisit the previous constitutions and decrees in the light of *Gaudium et spes*. Questions treated in them are seen in a new light when the Church's mission takes on a new relation to the world and to cultures on and when Churches and religions in working toward the common good of humanity or what is called the discernment and promotion of the reign of God in the world. All the questions about Church order need to be reconsidered in light of this constitution (*GS*) since order relates to ministry, and ministry to mission. Present issues in the Catholic community need to be worked out in dialogue with other Christian Churches. In ecumenical relations likewise, a sense of the urgency of mission in today's world helps to put the issues of ecclesial ministry and institution into perspective.

Part 2

Reading the Tradition

Introduction

The reading of the Christian tradition, starting with the Scriptures, is done in a variety of contexts and is interpreted accordingly. All interpretation has been done in the living context of a Church, and current interpretation is affected by some use of a historical-critical method even as it is done in relation to present realities. Sometimes this means attending to factors that were obscured or left out of the reckoning in maintaining a social and symbolic order. We need to be open to orientations and models of community that emerge from the consciousness of the faithful as they live a communion of faith that relates to their lives and aspirations. This may seem to be a large and complex agenda, but at its simplest it is a matter of knowing that people are influenced by their context and their suppositions in how they read the Scriptures or texts found in ecclesial tradition, even as in faith all look back to the salvific event of Jesus Christ. A plurality of readings may exist within a common appeal to the once and for all Christ event.

In teaching about ministry, its origins, and development, too much is at times sought in the Scriptures and the life of early Christian centuries, as though they presented a plan and an unchangeable constitution for ministerial structures. In fact, the exercise, structure, and theology of ministry and mission in the Church have a long history, marked by changes and differences. Scripture and early history serve as a necessary reference but do not provide definitive patterns of ministry. While comparable forms are found in different places and epochs, the tradition is not homogeneous but is related to diverse historical situations and shows the constant creative force of the Spirit.

Divine Institution

Since it is a recurring term and a recurring question, a word needs to be said at the outset on the claim to find a divine origin or institution in key developments of order. This way of speaking is still sometimes used, but when taken too literally, it is a misrepresentation of tradition. There are many institutional factors in the life and organization of the Church, and not all could in any sense be said to be of divine origin, but this depends on applying criteria of discernment. Seeing how institutions serve or do not serve fidelity to the gospel and the apostolic tradition is inherent to a theologically oriented historical investigation. The exact meaning of saying that something is of divine right or divine institution has to be clarified.

In a contribution to Lutheran–Roman Catholic dialogue in the United States of America and taking her cue from Avery Dulles, Margaret O'Gara has summarized positions within Catholic circles on what it means to speak of divine institution. Her principal point is that many now think of past forms of ministry with historical consciousness rather than considering them from a purely legal and institutional perspective.[1]

Karl Rahner

Claiming that something is of divine order, or *ius divinum*, has to be done with the nuances that Karl Rahner introduced into the debate on the episcopate.[2] The de facto existence of the monoepiscopate does not have to mean that it is *de iure divino* unless there are persuasive reasons to see that it is of necessity to the continuity of the Church with the gospel and with Christ. This requires taking into account what historical studies reveal about the ambiguities in our knowledge of the forms of Church order in early centuries.

Although Ignatius of Antioch argues for the position of the bishop in a Church, some places seem to have been ruled for a while by a college of presbyters. Several reasons made this give way to monepiscopacy, with its distinctive ministries of government, penitential discipline, teaching, and eucharistic unity. Only about the middle of the third century does the rule of one bishop for one place appear to have been universal or at least widespread. Rahner argues that though it took time to emerge, this development may be said to be of divine origin because in fact it was not purely arbitrary. Though it is not a feature of communities of the New Testament period, it served the purpose of fidelity to the gospel. It owes much to historical contingency, but it appears to have been well established as necessary to the apostolic existence of the Church and to have been received as such by the faithful. One can say that the Church was guided by the power of the Spirit to find forms of life that served fidelity to apostolic tradition and the gospel, and primary among those was the episcopacy.[3]

Rahner's position is corroborated by the work of Francis Sullivan, who has recently undertaken a minute study of how the ordering of the Church through episcopacy, presbyterate, and deaconate developed.[4] On the basis of textual and historical evidence, he shows that before this triple division was consolidated, various types of ecclesial organization existed. He distinguishes a twofold relation to apostolic origins that came together in the form of monoepiscopacy. On the one hand there was the mandate to proclaim and spread the gospel, and in early days this was done primarily through an itinerant mission of apostles. On the other hand there was the need for local churches to assure their leadership and their doctrinal legitimacy. In time, bishops received responsibility and authority for keeping fidelity to teaching as well as local leadership. Sullivan, in much the same way as Rahner, sees this as coming about through providential disposition, and it is its fidelity to apostolic origins that allows one to say that it is of divine institution. This does not mean that this form of ministry can be found in scriptural evidence. It does mean that through the guidance of the Spirit, it emerged as the appropriate and even necessary way to keep fidelity to apostolic witness and teaching, in a living community of persons.

Understanding divine institution in this way avoids legal suppositions about Christ's actions. It also allows for some flexibility in how matters may continue to develop. For Rahner, it does not absolutely exclude that under other, different historical conditions, Church order could take a different shape, ruled by the same fidelity and under the guidance of the same Spirit. It is possible that episcopal supervision in a local Church could, for example, take the form of a collegiate ministry that would better serve fidelity in another set of circumstances. One does not know how this would work unless it has been tried, and in this the appeal to what is learned from some Protestant traditions has to be taken into account.

In sundry articles, Rahner extended his consideration of historically conditioned realities in the life of the Church beyond the episcopate. These include the composition of the New Testament in Greek, the use of wheaten bread and grape wine in the Eucharist, and the exclusion of women from ordination to episcopacy and presbyterate. The basic question always remains the same: given that these are historically conditioned facts, do they nonetheless embody provisions to be maintained in the transmission of revelation and of the life of grace? The composition of the New Testament, which records the first-generation testimony to Christ, obviously cannot be changed, and the Greek text has to remain a constant point of reference, even while historically conditioned translations are also a necessity. How the books of the New Testament are read as testimony to the truth does change. The use of bread and wine is not of a nature to be so stringent and ought to be opened to further discussion, in which cultures have to be harmonized with the fact of historical remembrance of the time of Christian beginnings. The exclusion of women presents the most difficult case. Though that exclusion is often said to be of divine origin and law, it is not read from New Testament evidence alone, and over the centuries the rule has been upheld largely on the basis of ideas of woman's inferiority to man. Rahner rejects the validity of such argument but still asks whether the practice may be said to be of divine law. Supporting this idea would have to go along with a clear rejection of the validity of myths, philosophies, and practices of woman's subordination in the life of the Church. One has to ask whether it is possible to give women equal status in the Church and an equal exercise of responsibility on a par with that of men, while developing a set of arguments that would show good reason for ordaining only males.

Hans Urs von Balthasar

Hans Urs von Balthasar represents another approach. He too has reflected on the fluidity in the forms of ministry found in early centuries, noting that institutional and sacramental characteristics, inclusive of the presidency of the eucharistic gathering, had not crystallized for some time, perhaps not before 200 CE.[5] However, he opines that the sacramental form of episcopacy and Church governance that then emerged have become essential forms that are to be maintained, inclusive of the restriction of order to men. Unlike Rahner, he does not discuss any further structural change but with remarkable clarity shows how authority was diversely conceived and exercised in different contexts throughout the ages. In arguing thus, he illustrates how institution and order are intended to serve the proclamation of the Word and the celebration of the Eucharist and how, properly speaking, candidates for ordination are persons who embody the form of Christ in service to the community. In other words, personal discipleship, charism, and an authority exercised in service ideally merge. In following this trajectory through time, von Balthasar highlights the ideal of holiness that affected the exercise of episcopacy. The episcopacy in the West was marked by ideals taken from such as Benedict or Francis, but it was also influenced by cultural perception and social ambience in the time of the Carolingian Empire. This amounts to saying that while organisms may be of divine institution, how they serve the Church depends on the quality of officeholders and, over time, even on different ideals of holiness. Whatever the case, personal witness and office necessarily go together, and the exercise of authority without the personal witness is vain.

The work of these writers illustrates the complications and implications of narrating, reading, and interpreting the realities of the mission and the ministry of the Church over time. They remind us that this is not primarily a story of developing institutions but of how mission and ministry shaped Church ordering and Church life, inclusive of its institutional and sacramental structures and enactments. It is a mistake to look for simple homogeneity in the story of order, for only by taking differences into account is it possible to perceive the meaning of this story for ministry today and in the future. "Divine origin" may be a better term to use. If it is not given a strictly chronological meaning, it conveys a sense of trust in a guiding divine providence that is conveyed through Word and Spirit. It can serve to avoid implications associated with the term "divine institution," implications that the Church was given a firm constitutional basis in apostolic times or that we may attribute legalities of order to the mind of Christ.

Bearing this continuous movement and growth in mind, rather than depending on a master narrative of institutional development, there is need to attend to local and time-constricted stories, to grasp diversity in development of the sense of mission, of the Church's presence in society, and concomitantly diversity in the perception and exercise of authority. The urgency felt in shaping the mission of the Church in today's varied experience affects how traditions are appropriated. This entails a prophetic and critical reading of history, one that sees the limits, inspirations, and possibilities embodied in the stories. In converse with them, churches around the world may be moved by the Spirit to live the Christian mission anew, as the signs of the times indicate.[6]

Bibliography on the topic of Church order and ministry, on the roles of clergy and of laity, is so vast that its study seems overwhelming. No attempt is made here to consider all the available studies. Some overview has to be risked, and notes to each chapter indicate works that have proved valuable to the author and may lead readers to other titles. Many hands have contributed to the task of historical studies, and in effect there are enough materials to allow for insight, interpretation, and reflection about the development of Church ministry and order. For readers of English, they are gathered together and made readily available in the works of such as Alexandre Faivre, Bernard Cooke, and Kenan Osborne,[7] to say nothing of monographs on specific persons, local churches, or particular topics. These studies do not merely contribute history in a narrow sense of enlisting facts and citations, but embody considerable theological interpretation, which is quite valuable. Some works are available in English translation, and when it comes to reflection on the living mystery of the Church, one is inevitably drawn to the unreplaced, and possibly irreplaceable, work of Edward Schillebeeckx.[8]

Ecumenical concerns are always at work. It is interpretation that is the crux of the matter. The not inconsiderable literature drawn upon and quoted in the notes for the already cited recent common statement of the US Lutheran–Roman Catholic Dialogue, *The Church as Koinonia of Salvation: Its Structure and Ministries*, is revealing. It shows the differences of interpretation associated with sorting out how churches were ordered in the early centuries of the common era. It is not the time to support contradicting views but to consider matters together. How common historical materials may be theologically and critically considered in the light of present developments and needs is what is at stake and is in itself a difficult enterprise. Churches are still in the process of opening the way to further discussion within and between churches and confessions.

Developments involve communities, persons, particular eras, and places. They constitute a series of stories. One has to look at the development of Church life as a story, with its meanings, interactions, and determination of traditions.[9] In this way, one can see from the optic of the present what was taking place at any time, what connections were being made, what was being put into practice and why, what personalities contributed, and what theological and pastoral significance was attached to procedures and happenings. It is a process that reveals both convergences and dissimilarities. This is a theological interpretation "on the way," leaving open the question of what, out of all this, is to be considered necessary and unchangeable. In the present state of things, the need for such an approach is inescapable because we are too tied in to some fixed historical assumptions and to established symbolic orders, specifically hierarchical ones. Local churches and the communion of churches need some freedom in respect to these stabilities in order to let themselves be guided by a discernment of spirits working in their lives and a reading of the signs of the times, helped in their assessment of past and present by some critical thinking.

This part of the book opens with a presentation of New Testament books that exercise a role in present developments of mission and ministry. The next two chapters are concerned with ministries in the first millennium of ecclesiastical history. Chapter 6 gives an overview of what is generally known about church order in a diversity of regions or local churches. Chapter 7 draws insight from those who are dubbed significant figures or writers who have influenced history. Chapter 8 brings the reader into the second millennium.

5

The Scripture

The purpose here is not to survey all that has been written about ministries and authority in the canonical writings of the New Testament but to focus on what is pertinent to a revision of mission and a restructuring of community in looking to the future of churches today. A working principle is that this has to be an effort of ecumenical and global collaboration, garnering insights from various Christian traditions, only now overcoming conflicts in the hope of mutual enrichment.

First of all, the reading of Scripture alerts readers to the relationship between ecclesial vision and ecclesial mission. Elements that have proved important for this are the retrieval of the symbolism of the reign of God, with its connection between discipleship and mission, and of the symbolism of the people of God. Added to these is attention to what is meant in the New Testament by the exercise of authority.

The process of ordering early Christian communities insofar as this may be read from canonical literature is also considered from new vantage points. Critical consideration shows the historical circumstances and the cultural limits of New Testament writings and the picture of the Church they give. Some kinds of interpretation, especially postcolonial and feminist, open up new possibilities for ministry and order.

Hence the chapter is divided as follows: (1) what is said of the kingdom of God; (2) what comes from an understanding of the Church as the people of God; (3) what is said in different books about discipleship and its mission, and about authority within the discipleship; (4) what is known about the relation between charisms of the Spirit, ministries, authority, and ecclesial ordering, especially within local communities; (5) what contribution is made by certain forms of a critical hermeneutic of texts adopted in the contemporary interpretations mentioned above.

Kingdom of God

In current readings of the symbolism of the reign of God the universal aspects of the biblical texts are stretched and expanded in a way that is pertinent to the contemporary setting of the Church across continents and peoples.[1] Writers point out that the mission of Israel and of its king was to serve all the nations and that the presence of Israel among the nations meant something for the whole of God's creation. The texts in the Gospels that show Jesus turning his eyes to those not of the people are given importance, inclusive of his praise of the faith of non-Jews. From the letters of Paul, attention is drawn to how he sees the ministry of Jesus, and so of his apostle, as a universal and reconciling mission that is to bring all peoples together, breaking down barriers that divide and enmities that oppose.

In this way interpreters observe that the demands of the kingdom pertain not only to "personal and ecclesial affairs," but also to "social and institutional issues."[2] The dialogue with religions and public leaders likewise leads churches to look for a working of divine inspiration outside Christian communities in the setting up of God's reign. Thus, for example, the text about the disciples being a light to the world and the salt of the earth (Matt 5:13–14) is given a social reading and Paul's call to live by a new order (e.g., Rom 12:1–2; Col 2:15) is read to encompass a change in the way peoples live and organize public life. The contention with principalities and powers is thought to refer to the powers of this world and not only to a world of spirits. A this-worldly anticipation of the kingdom in the order of things is likewise taken from the promises about the kingdom spelled out in the book of Revelation (e.g., 11:15).

The recorded teaching of Jesus in the Gospels about the advent of the kingdom of God[3] takes over this image from books of the Old Testament and from apocalyptic expectations of Jesus' time and the time of early Christian discipleship. In the Old Testament the evolution of divine kingship is complex. As a way of expressing the lordship of Yahweh, the notion came into play with the first demands of the Israelite people to be given kings, affected by what they saw among other peoples. The initial reaction of the prophet Samuel to the request for a king (1 Sam 8:10–18) was to warn them about the evils that royalty brought with it, a prophecy indeed fulfilled over time in the rather tragic history of the Davidic dynasty and the kings of Israel.

A way of keeping the king and his power within the boundaries of covenant was to represent him as God's emissary and God's son, one who as pastor respected the role of Yahweh as the only true Lord, King, and Pastor. Another measure was to keep alive the offices of priesthood and prophecy, quite distinct from the royal court, and not dependent upon it. The purpose of all three offices was to serve the covenant and the law, to keep alive the memory of the Passover Exodus, God's choice of the people, and the expectation of a future that only God would assure. The three roles interacted with the prophets voicing the nature of true justice, true worship, and the hope of the future that kept current kingly and priestly rule from claiming absolute right or permanence. In the common memory over the course of time, there was the ploy to remember David as the ideal king and his time as that of the ideal theocracy. This permitted faithful followers of the covenant to look forward to an epoch when such a king would be restored to God's people, and all the nations of the earth would acknowledge the lordship of Yahweh and his servant.

Under this king the whole people would be filled with the spirit of God, with the law written in their hearts rather than on stone tablets.

The disciples of Jesus were taught to separate faith in the God of Jesus Christ from earthly rulerships, but early Christians used the image of kingdom to express his lordship. Whatever their situation in life, affirming the presence of God's kingdom was to show where true hope resided and how God's reign could endure within the vicissitudes of earthly dominion. Those who answer the call to be disciples have entered the kingdom, they are a new kingly and priestly people, and they witness to the kingdom, which is already at work in opening the world to a more perfect future.

Parables have a key part in proclaiming God's kingdom. Using the parable stories that illustrate the nearness of God's kingdom is provocative and enigmatic and causes a crisis of expectations and ethical standards. As in comments on the law, Jesus stretches the imagination and the behavioral demands he makes of his hearers to the limit. Naming one's neighbor, loving one's neighbor, forgiving those who offend, caring for the poor, suffering false accusation and persecution, and choosing God above all else are pushed to extremes and remain question marks that accompany the disciple and the community of disciples all along the road of life. By what horizon must disciples live, at any time, in any place, to allow this kingdom to come into being, to find its place in human enterprise.

God's reign involves an eschatological expectation since it must be fulfilled in God's time and will be complete only at the end of time, when God's judgment is revealed and the Son of Man returns in judgment. Without resorting to efforts to reconstruct the actual teaching and words of Jesus himself, we see in New Testament writings that advent and expectation are attached to the person of Jesus, who is revealed through his death and resurrection as the true and awaited Son of Man. This attenuates the hopes of a more apocalyptic expectation and accentuates his ethical teaching. For those who hear and believe, the advent of the kingdom, with its ethical and eschatological tones, means living as though in a new place, a new time, a new community.

Among other passages, the end of the narrative of Jesus' ministry in Galilee (Luke 9) gives a portrait of the community that Jesus wished to gather around him. He is an itinerant preacher, having some itinerant followers, women and men, surrounded by the sick and by children. His mission is revealed in his attention to the sick, in his compassion for the crowds who need spiritual and bodily nourishment, in his naming of the children as the greatest, the most important, in the kingdom. Any authority exercised in communities of the kingdom is the authority of the Christ who suffered and died as a servant and Son of God. It is properly exercised in his manner and under his lordship. It is located first and foremost in the preaching of the Word and then in forgiving sins, healing, and releasing from spirits. It may be claimed only by those who follow the way of the cross. In a time when the Church commits itself anew to the concerns of the poor and to seeking true justice and peace, this portrayal of the kingdom has an important role to play in describing mission and the kinds of ministry that serve it.

People of God

The Constitution on the Church (*Lumen gentium*, 1964) of the Second Vatican Council made foundational ecclesiological use of the image of "the people of God" to single out the call of the Church to witness to God's power and covenant and to portray the basic oneness and equality of all believers. The conciliar reference to 1 Peter has sometimes been criticized, so it is not out of place to ask what the use of this biblical imagery says to the Church's self-understanding.

The disciples are never formed into a people in the way in which the Israelites were God's people, a visible and self-governing entity with a sense of covenant and mission, ruled by God's law. However, there is a historical continuity between Israel and the Church, and this is brought out in 1 Pet 2. Most basic is the idea of God's covenant and call. In a number of texts, it is the prophetic writings and promises that are to the fore in referring to those called from among Jews and Gentiles to be God's people, or one may say, his eschatological people. This comes from Acts 3:23; 15:14; and 18:10, as well as Heb 8:10–13; 10:30; 13:12. In going to the roots of this calling, 1 Pet 2:4–10 is important, with its appeal to Exod 19:5–6. Because they were a people chosen by God, the Israelites were (among other things) called a royal priesthood, that is a people who have been given release from their enemies through God's power and who engage in true worship. The writer of 1 Peter applies this to disciples of Christ in a spiritual sense, to convey to those subjected to earthly domination and suffering the sense of their dignity. This dignity has been given to them because they were purchased through the price of the precious blood of Christ (1 Pet 1:18–19). They are now a spiritual household, a royal priesthood, a people who in Christ have dominion over the powers of the world, a people who endure suffering in the hope of the transformation of heaven and earth through the lordship of Christ. They are a people who by their works in Christ offer true worship. This is said of the people of the new covenant, without allusion to any distinction of offices among them such as there were among the people of Israel, with its rulers and its priestly caste. It is a reminder that under the covenant the people held primacy as God's elect, not any office or ruler. As a people, the followers of Christ may live in this new knowledge of God's love and election shown in him.

For this kingly and priestly people, worship is worship in spirit and in truth. It comes from the heart and is free of ritualistic attachment, whatever ritual actions may still be practiced in freedom and remembrance.[4] Acts of common worship, of which there is some evidence in the New Testament, include blessings, hymns, canticles, and table fellowship. If cultic and priestly terms are used, they are used of preaching the Word, of ethical behavior, of acts of charity, and of table remembrance. There is never any designation of a person or persons who have a priestly office or perform ritual priestly acts.

Reference to Rom 9–11 is, however, also important in understanding what it is to call the community of disciples who profess faith in Jesus Christ the people of God.[5] As James Dunn comments, what is at stake is not only the sort of the Jewish people but the self-identity of the Church of Christ. In comparing the place of the new community with Israel, Paul wants to affirm both a continuity and a future reconciliation. To Israel belong the "adoption, the glory, the covenants, the giving of the law, and the promises; to them belong the patriarchs, and from them according to the flesh, comes the Messiah" (Rom 9:4–5). The Gentiles who have believed in Christ by God's gracious mercy were grafted on to this olive tree (Rom 11:17) and cannot vaunt themselves.

Paul brings out several points pertinent to the call of the Church. There is a history to God's call and salvation that will be completed only at the end of time. The Church as well as Israel are to find their place within this history, whose complexities are in God's hands, a history still to be written. Within this plan Paul points to the divine initiative on which all depend and to the story of Israel as a story of election and mercy. As Israel was a nonpeople made into God's people, so it is with the Church of Jews and Gentiles. As with Israel, the Church is to carry out a mission to all peoples, though it is first and foremost to bear witness to the promises given to Israel and now made flesh in Christ. It is in Christ that reconciliation is effected, and in Christ, and only in him, that there is a divine answer to the unbelief and the disobedience of humanity. The sense of Rom 9–11 is linked with the comparison of the two Adams in Rom 5. The future of the people and of its mission is in the hands of God, as the clay is in the hands of the potter. For the community of believers in their mission, what is primary is witness to Christ, but they must also continue to consider the place of Israel and to recognize that their own call is one of mercy. Their own future belongs to a history written by God, a future therefore to which, in a faith like that of Abraham, they must look for the fulfillment of the promises. The Church is God's elect, sent to bring peace to the world. It is to learn the ways to attest to the presence of God's kingdom and to speak the word of love and reconciliation, which it knows from the gospel of Jesus Christ.

Discipleship and Authority

There is only one power or authority in the Church, and it is that of Jesus Christ. It belongs to him by the power of the resurrection in the Spirit, by reason of his lordship, a lordship by which he is one with the lordship of God over heaven and earth. When the Gospels give stories of his exercise of this power during his earthly sojourn, these have to do with teaching, forgiving sins, casting out demons, and healing. The nature and source of his authority are expressed in various ways: he is the one sent by God, he is the prophet of the last times, he is the Son of God, the Son of the Father, with whom he is one in the Spirit, he is the Son of Man, who is to come in judgment. Though the stories tell of his actions on earth, they make it clear that these can be understood only in the light of his resurrection and his coming in judgment.

Within the community of disciples after his resurrection, or within the Church, this authority resides first and foremost in the apostles and in their witness. This is a witness through word, through the life of discipleship, through deeds like unto his. This witness remains an authority in the Church for all time. The apostolic witness is transmitted to us in the forms in which it was received by early Christians and in ways that shaped their life in community. Even then it was diversely received and transmitted within communities that do not represent a highly organized Church but a collection of communities. The temptation to read later ecclesiastical organization back into New Testament texts has to be resisted. Nonetheless it is of some help to see how the rather diverse communities represented in the canon conceived of the exercise of authority as it related to their vision of life as followers of Christ.

Gospel of Mark

The eschatological or even apocalyptic physiognomy of the kingdom and so of the believing community is most clearly set forth in the Gospel of Mark.[6] Little is to be found there by way of development of structure and ministry. The word and witness of the disciples is associated with the ways in which they envisage the power or authority of Christ, the Son of Man. With other scholars, Edward Schillebeeckx looks for an initial christological faith in what are called the Q sources and in Mark's Gospel. This faith's characteristic is that it finds in Jesus the coming judge of the world, whose judgment will mean salvation for those who persevere in their evangelical way of life, and in their belief before the world, even when they are condemned. The renunciation of possessions, abstinence from worldly affairs, special concern for the poor and hungry, and unconditional trust in God are characteristic of such Christianity. There has to be a period of trial because of the world's opposition and persecution, but Jesus, Son of Man, who came among his own and accepted the cross, assures victory and reward. Power and authority belong to those who in preaching Christ endure suffering in Jesus' name. The principal ministry is to preach the word about the coming of divine rule and judgment, and to help the faithful to endure to the end, ready to face up to the reversal of worldly expectations that this entails.

To those sensitive to current cultural, economic, political, and indeed ecclesiastical ruptures, Mark's Gospel receives a special hearing. The Gospel speaks to those whom it exhorts to persevere in their testimony and way of life, with hope and expectation in view, even as their world of gospel adherence seems under threat. The figure of the Son of Man is an inspiring one, as it plays out the advent of God's messenger among his people, his embrace of the suffering necessary to his mission, and his promise to return at the end of time, bringing a judgment that will show forth the truth of his mission and his glory. As far as this Gospel is concerned, the community of Jesus' followers lives in unsettled circumstances but with hope that life is lived and mission undertaken. In a Markan perspective, there is good reason to couch the exercise of power in perseverance in face of hostility, in proclaiming repentance and the forgiveness of sins, in casting out demons, and in healing the sick. This Word and these works are the signs of authenticity in the Lord's service.

Gospel of Matthew

Matthew's Gospel offers many teachings about the advent and the presence of the kingdom of God and gives some idea of how early believers exercised authority among themselves.[7] It is often cited in magisterial or theological writings for the foundation of the authority of the see of Rome and of the bishops, on the basis of words that Jesus addressed to Peter or to the Twelve. However, the interpretation of these texts is not even or homogenous in the writings of the Church fathers, and before making any conclusions about Church ministry or Church authority, one has to take another look at this Gospel. The Church has to consider what it says of the kingdom and how it sees this focused in the person of Jesus. In this light it is possible to examine what it says of authority or power, the two words used in English to translate the Greek *exousia*.

The focus on Jesus, in keeping with Matthew's concern to show continuity with the covenant and with the Jewish people, consists often in portraying Jesus as the new Moses, in his teaching, in his feeding of the crowds, in his walking on the water —all summed up in the acclamation of the disciples, "Truly you are the Son of God" (Matt 14:33). What is hailed in this is that Jesus brings the unique power to release from sin, in the name of God's own forgiveness, and to cure the sick. The kind of authority or *exousia* exercised in the Church derives from this and testifies to it.

As Raymond Brown describes it, the community that emerges from a historical reconstruction of Matthew's Gospel is a Church learning to take a second breath, after a period marked by the Gospel of God's kingdom being proclaimed and extended to the Gentile peoples. As the Church expands, it is still anxious about its relation to the historic covenant with the people of Israel, for to them belong the promises. The evangelist helps the people to look back over the Church's development as a community of Jew and Gentile, to relate the Church to Jesus the Christ, and to find ways to ensure the exercise of Christ's own irreplaceable authority or power in the community. The power of the Word, the power to heal, the power to forgive, and the power to make judgments, which marked the work of Jesus himself has been in some way given to his followers, who live in the light of the resurrection. It may be exercised by persons sent or named by Jesus, and empowered in his name, but it is his power. In the exercise of power in the community, nothing is tolerated that departs from the source and criterion of Jesus himself.

The Twelve represent the original discipleship, the community that gives the covenant with the twelve tribes of Israel a place and a renewal in the following of Jesus and in proclaiming him as the Son of God, in whom the kingdom's final stage has come. The importance of their role emerges in the stories of their call, but most of all in the narrative of the Last Supper and in the mandate to keep memorial in bread and wine of what God has wrought in Christ. Besides being the primary disciples, they are also the first and commissioned witnesses to the resurrection of Christ. As for Peter, the authority and mission given to him as the foundation of the community of faith are based on his profession of Jesus as the Son of God and are given through him to the Twelve. But as Matt 16:21–24 shows, he cannot exercise it until he embraces the gospel of Jesus' suffering and death. As long as he opposes this, he is "Satan," not "Cephas."

Those who continue to preach the gospel continue to exercise the power to heal and to forgive and to lead the Church, which derives from the original Twelve and is always based on their profession of faith and on their witness. They do not replace the Twelve or their testimony, but whatever power resides in their word and actions also owes its origins to the power of Jesus and must be faithful to it. The story of the Last Supper, as sign of the covenant with its memorial mandate, is the focal point for the meaning of the Twelve and what is transmitted through their word to the Church. In the words attributed to Jesus, covenant and the forgiveness of sins are highlighted. There are only three other meals mentioned in Matthew's Gospel, and they all have to do with forgiving and healing and the care of the needy (8:14–17; 9:9–13; 14:14–21). They serve as a kind of commentary on what takes place in the Lord's Supper and what should be remembered by the Church in remembering Jesus. If the saying in Matt 5:23–24 about forgiving enemies as a condition for offering sacrifice is connected with this, or the procedures outlined in Matt 18, then the meal of the kingdom is one at which forgiveness is proclaimed, and the forgiveness of each other is both a condition and a description of the kind of community that assembles.

Matthew's Gospel anticipates the time after Christ's departure even as it narrates the events of his life and ministry and his dealings with his disciples. Apparently the author wished to bring to his reader's attention that the kingdom takes form in a definite place and group of people, in which the teaching of Jesus is taught and followed and Gentiles and Jews belong together. In other words, the teaching and the faith in the Gospel are not invisible matters of the spirit, but they find concrete existence in communities of people whose lives are lived by this faith and whose testimony is evident as a light on a lampstand and as salutary as salt of the earth.

The Gospel of Matthew has long been the one favored by those seeking scriptural sanctions for apostolic and episcopal authority. The texts most often cited are Matt 16:13–19; 18:18; and 28:18–20. Looking more closely at the Gospel as a whole, readers today realize that clearly defined positions and structures of authority in the Matthean community may not be assumed. With the reality of a community of disciples "drawing second breath" to the fore, the concern is rather that the exercise of authority should truly reflect that of the Master. From Christ comes the power to preach the gospel of God's reign and to forgive sins, and these are corroborated by the power to heal and drive out demons.

Matthew 28:18–20, the Great Commission, is a missionary mandate addressed to the disciples who witnessed the resurrection. It is a mandate to preach the good news, to teach and to forgive sins, and it derives from Jesus' own authority over heaven and earth. It has to do with apostolic ministry and not with ecclesial orga-nization. Matthew 16:13–19 is a word addressed to Peter and commits to him the power of the keys of the kingdom. Again it has to do with apostolic witness and not with community organization, though it does give Peter some special place among the Twelve. This may have to do with how communities who hear the apostolic word are to relate among themselves, and turns attention to the mother community of Jerusalem as a center, for there Peter belongs, among the Jewish converts. The concern may be less ecclesial organization than the place that Jerusalem keeps in the divine plan of salvation.

Matthew 18 is a chapter about how a community is to embody within itself the command to forgive and be reconciled. It reflects some form of community gath-ering and community organization, though its nature is not very clear. What is most important about the chapter as a whole is that it is about forgiving one another according to the pattern of divine mercy. What excludes somebody from the com-munity is the refusal to forgive or to accept forgiveness. The exclusion is pro-nounced in solemn form, through the appeal to the power to bind and lose, on earth as in heaven. In other words, the pronouncement has a divine sanction. There is certainly a community action involved, and the binding or losing is an action of the Church. It might be assumed that some Church official takes an initiative and draws a closure to the process, but who this might be or how it is done is not clarified.

In the end, therefore, what Matthew's Gospel presents is not so much the forms of authority as its nature. The exercise of authority or power (*exousia*) in the Church comes from the authority of Jesus, and like that of Jesus, it has to do with divine mercy, with preaching the Word, with forgiving, and with healing.

Luke-Acts

The picture of the Church, its mission, and its ministries that emerges from the two works attributed to Luke, the Gospel and the Acts of the Apostles, is dominated by four things.[8] First, there is the mission of Jesus himself as the servant and Son of God to bring good news to the poor, a mission continued in the apostolic church. Second, there is the centering of the story of the mission of Jesus, and of the Church, around Jerusalem. Third, there is the role of the Spirit which dominates in the story of Jesus himself and in the story of the Church. Fourth, there is the desire to show continuity between the story and vocation of the Jewish people and that of Jesus, as well as continuity between Jesus, the apostles, and the churches founded by them among the Gentiles, rich in the diversity already signaled in the phenomena of the Day of Pentecost.

At the very beginning of Jesus's public ministry, in the synagogue at Nazareth, Luke places the proclamation of the gospel to the poor through this prophet in a new time and a new location, or in a time and place transformed by this advent of God's power (Luke 4). The accustomed time of worship and the accustomed as-sembly to whom God's Word is addressed are changed by reason of the advent of Jesus in the power of the eschatological Spirit. The words of Isaiah are fulfilled. It is in the power of the Spirit that Jesus proclaims the word of freedom, the good news of liberation for those in many ways held in bondage. In saying that the word heard is fulfilled "this day," he is in fact declaring a new day, that of God's redemptive action. He disrupts the time of Sabbath observance by this gospel and also virtually gathers a new congregation, a people diversely formed, made up of the blind, the lame, the sinner, and the many women who were foremost in making the profession of faith that gives entry into the discipleship of the one who has come. The kingdom is made known not to those whom one would expect, but to persons comparable to the widow of Zarephath and Naaman the Syrian. When therefore the apostles and prophets brought the gospel outside Jerusalem and to the Gentiles, they continued to preach this new day and new gathering. Luke portrays it, they acted in continuity with the word of Jesus himself, and always with reference to Jerusalem as the place where God makes his word, his law, and his Son known to Jerusalem—which is the eschatological city and mountain of divine revelation. Luke shows that the mission given to the many called in the Spirit is in continuity with the mission given to the Twelve. There are two stories about persons sent out to preach the kingdom. Luke 9:1–6 tells of the sending of the Twelve. Luke 10:1–11 tells of the sending of another seventy-two in terms similar to the preceding story. The gospel must go beyond Galilee, even beyond Israel. Many laborers will be needed to bring the news of the kingdom, and God will provide.

According to the book of Acts, which is related to Luke's Gospel, some particular ecclesial ministries appear in the early life of the communities of disciples. Chief among them is the apostolic ministry of preaching the gospel, always accompanied by the power to work cures, that resembles the power and activity of Jesus himself. Though those given this apostolic ministry—whether this be the Twelve, Paul, Silas, Barnabas, or some others—belong in no particular community, they form and develop churches in particular places and equip them with their ministries. Of the apostolic ministry, it can be said that it always points to what took place in Jerusalem, testifying to the resurrection of Christ and the event of Pentecost. Rather than being attached to a particular church, the apostles by the gospel of Christ hold all the churches together in communion.

Luke's eucharistic teaching and the place that he shows it to have in the life of any local church is important to us. It is in the breaking of the bread that disciples know Jesus as the risen one, in whose teaching, death, and resurrection the Law and the Prophets are brought to fulfillment and the destiny of Jerusalem as center of God's rule is realized. It is also in the breaking of the bread that they truly know each other and bond together as the discipleship of Christ. The teaching of all those named apostles fits into this milieu, as does fidelity in prayer, the care of the needy, and all the elements of a common life. It is at this table that followers of Jesus find the image and assurance of the eternal eschatological banquet.

In connection with this liturgy, Luke's writings give a commentary on what leadership in the Church means and to what pattern it is to conform.[9] It is to be the kind of service that is exemplified in the service of Jesus himself. Indeed, Jesus as

God's servant is imaged not only in the apostles, who spare nothing in bringing the gospel to the Gentiles, but also in the service of those who wait at tables and care for the weary and forlorn. The authority of Jesus now given to those who share the table and who learn to serve is related to the presence and to the future coming of the kingdom. This is an authority to witness to the kingdom, but it is also a power of judgment in the light of the Lord's expected return. Luke seems to wish at this point to affirm the existence of authority among the disciples after the departure of Jesus, but also to make some comment on its nature.

With churches today (confessional and local), spelling out their missionary options in favor of service among and to the poor, Luke's Gospel exercises a particular attraction. Jesus' own mission as God's servant and beloved Son, anointed by the Spirit, is spelled out in terms of bringing the gospel to the poor and introducing a new day in God's work. As it was for the Son, so it must be for the disciples. In the midst of change, Luke's Gospel offers some reassuring factors. The Church continues to be guided by the Spirit in the face of new events and in God's work of salvation. There is continuity despite appearances, and this is symbolized by the centripetal placement of Jerusalem in the ongoing story, but there is also diversity.

The Johannine Corpus

John's lack of interest in any structures of authority has often been noted of late.[10] He is most concerned with the relationship of faith and love that the disciple has with Jesus and with the gift of the Spirit, which each believer receives to perfect this union. The community of disciples is the community of those loved by Jesus, Word made flesh and one in love and glory with the Father. It is the community of those to whom Father and Son give the gift of the Spirit that each one possesses. This call is personified in the figure of the well-beloved disciple, to which image even Simon Peter must conform if he is to exercise his mission of feeding the sheep. The disciple is one who is attached to Jesus, the Word made flesh, by faith and love and who is born of water and the Spirit, and who eats and drinks in faith of the body and blood of Christ. In the suffering of the Word, in his cross, the disciple sees his glory shine forth, for his glory is to do the will of the Father and always to remain in a communion of love with him. This means receiving the commandment of love exemplified in Christ's washing the feet of his disciples and made known in the love shown within the discipleship. The mission of giving apostolic word and testimony is shared by all, and in John's Gospel women are among those who testify in this way to the Lord, whether this is exemplified in Mary or in the Samaritan woman.

Conclusions on the Gospels

Of the place and meaning of authority in the Gospels, one has to conclude that they tell us little about early church order and indeed reflect a diversity of approaches. They are concerned with how the gospel is to be preached and with the veracity of witness to Jesus Christ. In this, they tell us much about the nature of authority or power, which is always a witness in truth and reflects or shows forth the authority that Jesus exercised in his own ministry and that as risen Lord he gives to his disciples. The concern of those who have authority is to make Christ known, to pass on his teaching about the kingdom of God, and to bring to all, Jew or Gentiles, the forgiveness of sins and a healing power, which come from God through Christ and the Spirit.

The Pauline Corpus

With the letters of Paul, we enter a world in which questions of ministry are more obviously taken into consideration.[11] Paul's own call and conversion were to the risen Christ, who identified himself with his disciples, whom Paul was persecuting. From the very outset it was a conversion to mission to the Gentiles and a mission of reconciliation, to bring together, by the blood of Christ and the promise of God's justice, those who were separated. If three things characterize Paul's apostolic endeavors, they are the absolute character of God's justifying grace in Christ given with the gift of the Spirit, a reconciliation that would eventually bring about the submission of all things in Christ to God, and the convening of the *ekklēsia*, or Church, as the people who live in eschatological hope and see the world already being transformed, awaiting the resurrection of the dead to complete this transformation.

Paul's missionary strategy was to go to centers of civilization, to the areopagus, to cities where the ways of the world were debated and determined, and there to convene communities of believers, who would be living witnesses in all their conduct to justification in Christ. What brought Christ's grace to the world were the apostolic word that testified to him and the accompanying witness of the apostles sent to preach, and of all who accepted this word. It is commonly thought that Paul and his contemporaries looked for a ready return of Christ, but this did not mean that he was not concerned with changing the order of things. Indeed, he saw the world as a place in which good and evil were in conflict, and a community of belief served to change the order by which evil prevailed. We cannot say that he undertook a vital change of the structures of society and of injustices, but what he wanted and expected would necessarily change the ways in which people lived and related to each other. Changing the order of worship, with emphasis not on ritual but on spiritual sacrifice and changing modes of behavior, or what today would be called the values to which Christ calls his followers, would have necessary social consequences, even if Paul never tried to spell these out. In his mission, as typified by his comparison of the two Adams, he was conscious of the solidarity of the whole human family. He was also conscious of the connection between human redemption and cosmic redemption, the same Spirit being at work in humankind and in the created universe. Paul uses the imagery of the kingdom to make the point that all powers in heaven and on earth are subject to Christ, that the faithful now share in the kingly heritage of the Son, who is seated at God's right hand, and that eschatological redemption comes definitively when all things are subjected to God in Christ.

The Pauline way of speaking of the Church and of its relation to Christ and Spirit is not perfectly harmonious and changes from one letter to another. In the Letters to the Corinthians, the Church is the body of Christ. This is presented in a way that underlines the identification of Christ with the disciples and the organic working of the Spirit through charismatic gifts within the Church. Paul puts the Lord's Supper at the heart of the life of the *ekklēsia*, serving as its memorial of Christ's death and the expectation of his coming, as it also serves the reconciliation of all into the one living reality. In the Letter to the Colossians, what is to the fore is the cosmic headship of Christ, in whom all things are created and redeemed and in whose lordship all will be perfected. Within this vision his headship of the Church converges with his headship of creation, and there is some distinction between Christ and members. This is complemented in Colossians and Ephesians by the imagery of the Bridegroom, which is another way of showing how Christ is one with the Church, his Bride, through complete and total self-giving love.

With regard to authority in the Church, it is always the authority of the risen Christ and his Spirit, and the authority of the apostolic word, complemented by apostolic witness. Paul did get into controversies about whom or what is to be obeyed and at times called for submission, but he was careful to relate the obedience asked to obedience to Christ and obedience to the gospel proclaimed. Even though Paul bears in his heart the concern for many churches, the exercise of authority is realized in particular churches, according to the situation and the need of each one.

First Letter of Peter

First Peter is basically a letter about the Church, its life, and its place in society.[12] It has in view a community that is living in a difficult situation, in a society in which its members suffer hardship and alienation, possibly because for the most part they are of the slave class. The writer wants to impress on them what they mean in God's plan of salvation, the dignity of their calling, how to endure suffering as disciples of Christ, and how to present an acceptable face to the world around them.

Redeemed by the precious gift of the blood of Christ, they are the people of God's covenant, who may be compared to the people of the covenant with Israel. They are a spiritual household, God's own people, a royal priesthood, in which all live as one. They have a call to make known the gospel of redemption. In the world of sin, they are saved through baptism and can look forward to a new heaven and a new earth. In the transfiguration of Christ, a perception of this glory has already been given, and in the sufferings of Christ, they find an example of how to endure suffering in trust and hope.

To describe the inner life of the community, the author makes an abundant use of the household codes of the time, mapping out a way in which as believers they may live by these codes and not present a scandalous image to those around them. Thus he spells out the duties of slaves, of husbands and wives, of children, of young and old. It is their motivation and their virtue, their way of seeing one another as members of the same royal priesthood, that changes their way of life, even while remaining within established codes.

It is most probably in line with this appeal to social codes that we ought to place the reference to presbyters or elders in 1 Pet 5:1–5. As elders, these persons have received the gospel message to pass on, and they have acquired a reputation by reason of their witness in suffering, in the same manner as the author of the epistle. Thus they are to act as shepherds in a way that commands ready obedience. Others can submit to them without feeling subjected purely to an exercise of authority, as they would in a pagan society. Whether these elders had received an official status or an office in a more formal sense is not perfectly clear from the letter, but since the writer is appealing to household codes as models, it is likely that they had. In any case, authority and office are placed in the context of a community that as a whole and as a body is called to covenant, called to be a royal priesthood, and all service or ministry serves this end.

Ecclesiologies

If there are differences in ways of perceiving the Church community or God's kingdom within the New Testament, this goes with differing ways of perceiving Christ himself. Edward Schillebeeckx says some important things about the Church and about its mediation of Christ through the power of the Spirit which it is well to remember.[13] As he puts it, there is no Christology and no pneumatology without an at least implicit ecclesiology. On the nature of the Church, he notes the two ways of speaking in the New Testament. First, it is a concrete, local reality: the church that is at Jerusalem, at Antioch, at Ephesus, and so forth. This is foundational to the second way of speaking, one that talks of the Church of Christ, of the body of Christ, bringing out a universal reality, a communion between all churches in the one Christ and Spirit, a fellowship that comes from God's eternal design to make of all one in Christ. But this can never come about without the mediation of local and regional communities, peoples living by faith in Christ and by the gifts of the Spirit, in the concrete circumstances and conditions of their environment and of their life together.

It is through these that faith in Christ is mediated to the world. As Schillebeeckx puts it, the historical Jesus is professed as the one whom God raised up in the Spirit, the one in whom is revealed the meaning of the kingdom, the one who through the work of the Spirit becomes the Christ of faith. That is to say that belief in what God has done through Jesus, the belief in who he was and what God has done in him, is mediated in concrete ways and with all the differences that show themselves from church to church and from one book of the New Testament to the other. While for all time the reference point is the apostolic witness, to which the Scriptures give testimony, the Christ shall always be mediated through the living witness of the Church, and through the very particular ways in which local and regional churches testify to Jesus Christ and to the power of the Spirit in their midst.

The Christ of faith, known only through the Church, is not an abstract reality. He is the Christ living in and lived by the community through the gift/s of the Spirit. As the Church through time lives by the life of the Spirit given to it through the risen Christ and carries out the mission it has received, these factors are blended in different ways. When reform and renewal, for the sake of salvation and of mission, are necessary, narrative recall generates fresh vision, allied with the kind of action that the intuitions of the Spirit in face of human reality suggest. How the mission is carried out, and how ministries take form to serve this mission, go hand in hand with the ways in which faith in Christ and in the divine Trinity are formulated, in relation to human destiny.

Inevitably this means a certain clash of symbols, as members of any church take their stance on human affairs. In gearing Church mission toward a broader sense of God's reign and especially toward the demands of human and ecological justice, the image of divine *kenōsis* (cf. Phil 2:6–7) before the powers of the world has a key role.[14] In African and Latin American churches, the image of a promise of liberation, of a new kind of exodus from slavery, can go hand in hand with the belief in the power of Christ's self-emptying. It is the radical way of life in communion with the poor and with the earth that goes with such belief, which is the true power of a freedom that promises justice to the poor. In African churches the relation of Christ and his Spirit to the spirit world is important, as Christ makes himself one with those who are deprived of all things, even their own cultural inheritance. In Europe and North America, there is no way of negotiating the presence of Christian communities in modern society without working through the letting go of the structures and impressions of a self-contained and self-reliant Church.

The Inner Service and Structuring of Local Churches

In the course of time, magisterial documents and theological treatises have all too often cited New Testament texts in support of the divine origin of certain forms of societal structure and ministerial order. It is even asserted, without more ado, that Jesus established the episcopacy as an office in the Church, either during his public life or after his resurrection. When exegesis became more circumspect, comparable citations were intended to show the legitimacy or even the necessity of developments that were not, it might be conceded, to be found in their exact form in New Testament times, but were in line with apostolic tradition.

In general it seems proper to say that there are few direct warrants of particular forms of ongoing ecclesial ministry in the New Testament, given the nature of the growth of this movement, as recalled above. The issue of congruence with the origins of the Church is to be argued in a more complex and less determinative way. The canon of the New Testament gives a narrative of tentative efforts to set up structure for local churches, which are interconnected by faith rather than by organization, so that what we see is not a plan that is fixed for all time. It is possible to read the narrative in such a way as to be inspired by the story and to pick up its questions or issues, without finding in it something determined once and for all.

From an open but solid reading and interpretation of the Scriptures, we may see to what origins, and to what characteristics of ministry and mission, the Church is to be obedient, with the guidance of the Spirit and through a constant process of discernment.

Apostolic Witness

The fundamental authority in the early Church is that of the witness of the apostles. As witnesses to the death and resurrection of Christ and in the story of ministries, the Twelve as a group and sometimes as individuals retain importance. This is for three reasons. The most basic is that it is on their original witness that the faith of the Church is founded. Second is their role as companions of Jesus, who as a community are forever the sign of the eschatological kingdom, indicating that through those who believe in Jesus and adhere to him in faith and hope, the kingdom of God is present in the world. Third is the commission that, in various ways, Jesus is recorded to have given the Twelve, the commission to teach what they have seen and heard, to make disciples and bring forgiveness of sins through Word and baptism, and to heal and cast out demons.

Their position is unique, and in this sense it is without succession. But it has succession through the communities and ministries that continue this mission and that always have the authority of Jesus and of the Twelve as their exemplar and point of origin. Some writers speak of the ministry of the Church as a "continuation" of the mission of Jesus and the Twelve, but this word needs the same qualifications as the word "succession." It is never a matter of doing the same thing but of finding services that look to the work of Jesus and to the community that he gathered around him as the truth and witness, to which all look back and seek to promulgate. That to which witness is borne is summed up in the few words of Paul in 1 Cor 15:3–5 and in the announcement of the gift of the Spirit poured forth upon those who believe, bringing them into communion with the God of Hebrew ancestors, whom they now know as "Abba."

Granted the abiding roles of the Twelve, the apostolic ministry at the origins of the Church is confided to others as well. What matters is not an exact count of apostolic witnesses but that the faith of the Church and the Church itself is built on the proclamation of Christ and God's kingdom and on the personal testimony of those who saw and believed. It is through this gospel that Christ and the Spirit are made present to the Church, and they become the Church's foundation and its inner breath. This always remains the foundation of ecclesial communities, an irrevocable witness that is given in the Scriptures and transmitted as a living communion with Christ and the Father, through a continued witness of discipleship, through worship, through prayer, through life in community. After the first generation, there is no further apostolic witness in the sense that it was given by the early apostles, but a life and a ministry that continues to live by this truth and transmit this truth. Every service and ministry of later times has to refer back to this apostolic witness, to be faithful to this, to transmit this in various forms, to renew itself in its light.

Ordering of Particular Communities

It is in the light of the apostolic witness and of the call to faithful discipleship to be lived out that we consider the nature of inner community services and of the inner ordering of communities. Nowadays scholars relate the ordering of communities to the surrounding social and religious milieu, suggesting on the one hand that churches were inspired by forms of order that they found around them, and on the other hand that in giving their witness they had to relate to differing cultural realities. As the issues to be faced differ, so also the inner needs of order adopted or fostered in the communities.[15]

Where local churches were mostly Jewish, they were more likely to be concerned about continuity with Israel and to take the synagogue as a model of order. The Pauline letters, and some passages of the Acts of the Apostles, favor an order that opens the way to inner diversity and plurality. They speak of a Church marked by its own distinctive practice of worship, which makes it stand apart from the common cultic character of Hellenic society. The communities certainly do not take the temple worship and priesthood of Hellenic culture as their model, but are probably influenced by what they learned from associations and household gatherings that favor the exchange of members in sharing wisdom and knowledge and mutual care. For its part, Johannine literature relates to a gnostic milieu, with its profusion of gnostic forms of wisdom and worship. In such a context the gospel is considered to be the one true Gnosticism or path to truth, and since the inner wisdom and love of each member is given primacy, the concern with structures of authority is much lower than in the other two forms of early Christian community.[16]

In looking at particulars and at specific texts, a useful insight with which to start is to take together two Pauline passages, 1 Cor 13 and Eph 4. In 1 Cor 13 we find the hymn to love, which follows Paul's discussion of the Eucharist and of the gifts and services given to the Church. The Eucharist is the celebration of one communion, and the gifts have their source in the one Lord and the one Spirit. After some guidelines for the discernment and ordering of gifts, Paul introduces the hymn to love, which is the most important gift and the binding force of unity and communion. In love, all serve each other and foster the life of the community. It is within the communion of love that gifts and services find their place, and it is for the good of this that they are given and are to be exercised.

In Eph 4, Paul distinguishes the founding ministries of apostle and prophet from all others. These belong to the past, to the initial foundation of the Church. All others are intended to continue this apostolic witness and to build up the body of the Church, the communion together in Christ, and his wisdom. Their purpose is then made clear, and their origin is in the Spirit, but there is no clear enunciation of any one pattern by which ministries are ordered. If there is a priority among services, it is lodged in the importance of word ministries and of the supreme gift to inform all services, which is that of charity.

There is some controversy associated with Eph 4:11 over what is meant by *diakonia*, or ministry, and who exercises it. This has practical present-day concerns in mind, with interpretations of the text supporting either a controlled and limited ministry or an all-inclusive one. In the New Testament the word *diakonia* itself is used in different ways. It designates acts of loving service toward a neighbor in a general way, or it designates the office of serving at tables given to the seven mentioned in Acts 6.

For some,[17] this generic meaning is also at work in Eph 4, where it is said that all work toward building up the body of the Lord through different gifts, all being equipped to serve growth to maturity by reason of the gifts each one receives. The text is then read to say that all are called to *diakonia*. Another reading[18] wishes to find a distinctive use of the term in this text, having to do with an exercise of a task in which one represents another. The term is said to apply only to those who are given the gift of being apostles, prophets, and evangelists, and then, when a local church has been formed, to pastors and teachers. When it is said that the service of these persons is to "equip the saints" for building up the body of Christ, what is meant is that this is done "by" ministry, not "for" ministry. In other words, all have gifts that serve to build up the body, but only some are charged with ministry. This reading resonates with the desire today, based on a reading of the use of the words *ministerium* and *munus* in the documents of Vatican II, to restrict the use of the term to those who are ordained or who have an official mandate to pastoral service, or what in the American context is called ecclesial lay ministry.

The second reading may be verbally correct, but to apply this to later structures is to go beyond what the text warrants. It is either an advocacy of clergy/lay distinctions or at least a residue of this. That is why other commentators prefer to point out more simply that this and other New Testament texts speak of a charismatic Church and mission, in which all share, each according to their particular gift and positions. Distinctions of offices and tasks there certainly are, and Paul does point to the importance of Word and pastoral ministries, but it is hardly justified to make much out of the terms used.

The reading of Eph 4:11 needs to be put in the context of the whole chapter. At the beginning of the chapter, Paul expresses his desire for what the local church should be. He wants a community in which there is one Spirit, one Lord, one Father, one faith, one baptism, all living together in peace and harmony. At the end of the chapter he states the aim of service, to build up the Church unto the stature of the fullness of Christ, through the exercise of the gifts given to each one. Among the gifts that contribute to the building of the body, he names those of apostle, prophet, evangelist, pastor, and teacher. These do indeed have their own particular role, but they belong within a Church in which each and all have a part to play in service to the body.

In the works of Luke, the ministries that foster the life of local churches remain somewhat indeterminate but are clearly existent, as is testified, for example, in Acts 13. The appointment of those designated to serve in Acts 6 and their subsequent ministry has always been hard for exegetes to decipher. It seems that a number of developments are made to converge in this story, but not too successfully. One thing is that Hebrews and Greeks are to belong equally to the Church of Christ, just as in the story of Acts 8 we see the Samaritans made one with the Jews who first received the gospel. Another thing is that the persons of Stephen and Philip embody the story of bringing the Word to those "outside the law," signaling a moment of change in the story of salvation. A third thing is that some diversification of services is emerging, though one has to be careful not to confuse the aim of the story with the constitution of the later order of deacons. From one point of view, the role of the apostles themselves is given a focus, that of prayer and that of preaching. Along with this, however, there has to be a ministry that tends more to the material needs and the cohesion of the disciples through care of the body.

As long as magisterial documents try to find the origin and meaning of the order of deacons in this text, they are in difficulties, since they seem to feel obliged to combine the mandate to preach and the mandate to serve tables in one ecclesial group. This does not seem to be verified by reference to Acts 6, which is dealing at once with a number of things that can evolve structurally and ministerially in quite different ways. It is to the guidance of the Spirit that this and other Lucan texts point. Hence one can say that within the diversity of ministerial growth, the continuity with Jesus and the apostolic church endures. Directions for discernment and blueprints of structure are quite different, one from the other. In view of the questions about the recognition of new ministries in churches today, one may certainly ask of Luke whether he sets any guidelines, at least by way of food for thought. Nevertheless, we must purge our minds of the tendency to connect the laying on of hands in these writings with the later sacrament of ordination. Some texts certainly connect the beginning or continuation of a ministry affirmed by the community through the Spirit with a laying on of hands, but there is something indubitably fluid about this gesture and community action that prevents a narrow and fixed sacramental interpretation. All we can say is that the mission of the Spirit, the life and prayer of the community, and the commissioning to service are brought together in an act of prayer and ritual action, but the types of service thus approved may be quite different.

The role of houses, or house churches, and of the women and men in whose houses people gathered, is well documented.[19] These are the first "churches" in the era after the break with the synagogue. All service and ministry is charismatic in origin and come as a gift of the Spirit, for the life and work of the Church. Whatever the texts say about local leadership has to be put within this horizon.

This said, we may note the mention of specific persons who exercise leadership in local communities, the titles used to apparently designate what we would call offices, and the apparent use of household models of governance. Among persons mentioned are Euodia, Syntyche, and Clement at Philippi (Phil 4:2–3), who at the time of Paul's writing seem to have become involved in rivalry and need to be reconciled. Elsewhere Paul refers to Priscilla and Aquila and to Phoebe. Among the titles of office are overseer/bishop, elder/presbyter and deacon, presider, pastor, teacher, but it is impossible to find exact descriptions of the functions intended. It is possible that in dealing with Jews in the cities he visited, Paul adopted something from synagogal models of organization, but in working with Gentile converts, he employed the model of the large household, giving rise then to the term "household churches." This model helped to pick out roles and also to give some authority, based on a comparison between the common household and the household of faith, or family of God. Whatever is entailed by way of teaching and leadership in these households, their charismatic purpose is always to build up the Church and to build it up on the foundation of the apostolic word.

The Pastoral Letters

The Pastoral Letters show a more advanced period in the life of the Church, one that is marked by the disappearance of the first-generation apostles and prophets. [20] The rules about the appointment and duties of leaders are clearly spelled out, though the exact meaning of terms like *bishop*, *presbyter*, and *deacon* is disputed. The writer of these letters is concerned with fidelity to the apostolic tradition, now that the apostles are no longer at hand, and with the good conduct of the community, which ought to witness to the truth.

It is in the Pastoral Epistles that we find first mention of the three ministries of bishop, presbyter, and deacon in the same context. There is no problem about seeing the deacons as a distinct group. There is, however, much difference of opinion as to the separate identity of bishop and presbyter. For some, 1 Tim 3:1–10 and Titus 1:5–7 seem to suggest that these are names referring to the same persons and the same position within the community. After telling Timothy to appoint presbyters or elders, the writer proceeds to enumerate the qualities required in a bishop. He then passes directly to the qualities required of deacons, making no further mention of the title of presbyter. If elders existed as a distinct group, one would expect some words on qualifications of those appointed.

Against this reading, the principal argument for distinguishing the bishop from the presbyters is that *episkopos* is always found in the singular, whereas the plural is used for the *presbyteroi*. Added to this is that the qualities asked of a bishop seem to apply to a single individual. According to 1 Tim 3:1–7, he must receive the faithful from other churches and must enjoy the good opinion of the heathen. This may indicate that for those not of his own community, whether Christian or pagan, the bishop stands as its representative. In Titus 1:7 the bishop is called God's steward: this may possibly be a development of an idea suggested by 1:6, which says that he ought to be an exemplary husband and father, ruling well over his own household. If so, his role as God's steward in the Church is compared to that of the father in the family or the head of the household.

If the arguments that favor a distinction between bishop and presbyters prevail, it must be accepted that, at the time of these epistles, the churches of Crete and Ephesus had only one bishop, who had authority perhaps over a number of communities, and that in particular bodies he was to work along with several elders. Even if this were the case, however, the bishop cannot be said to have had the same authority as bishops in a later period. He is in fact subordinate to Timothy and Titus, who have authority in a number of local communities rather as the apostle Paul had authority in the churches he had founded. The principal function attributed to the *elders* by the Pastoral Epistles is that of presiding (1 Tim 5:17). They are also called teachers (1 Tim 5:17; Titus 1:9). Similar functions are linked with the name of *bishop*, or overseer (Titus 1:9; 1 Tim 3:2, 5–6), as well as possibly some part in financial administration (cf. 1 Tim 3:1–7), since it is required that he should be a good manager and no lover of money. The appointment of a bishop is still expected to flow from a charism and a way of life, a charism and virtue discerned in the community and given formal recognition by a laying on of hands. Living as one of the community, he has to earn their respect by this life of faith and discipleship.

It also seems that in these churches leadership is assigned only to males, despite the apostolic, prophetic, or diaconal authority of the several women whom Paul regarded as companions in the ministry. Nonetheless, one must note that the image of the Church is that of the household of God, the Church of the living God, the sign and upholder of truth. It is in reference to this total reality that leadership is to be exercised. Appointed heads are to be judged in virtue of how they serve the Church. The Church is not judged in reference to them but by its obedience to truth and the apostolic word.

Summary on Church Structuring

Given the evidence, it is impossible to argue that all churches at this stage of dissemination of the gospel had the same structure. Much about the stages of this development and the geographical distribution of the different forms of community government is unclear, and it will probably always remain so. In other words, while there is plenty of evidence in the New Testament to show the existence of a pastoral ministry whose purpose is to maintain the fidelity of each community to the apostolic tradition, it is difficult to know what form this ministry took in each instance, although it seems that the forms were different.

Arguments are forwarded in favor of the influence of three models for internal ordering and leadership. These were the organization of the Jewish synagogue, with its elders, the household meetings and codes of Gentile peoples, and forms of voluntary association that brought together persons of common interest or purpose. Whatever the model, the story demands respect for the basic apostolic ministry of the Word, and the need to so order life as to be faithful to this, and the discernment of charismatic gifts of the Spirit.

Tracing the development of local church ministry in the New Testament era, James D. G. Dunn suggests the need to distinguish between sociological principles and theological principles when reading present situations against the background of New Testament writings.[21] The sociological and cultural principles have to do with how a community, in living from faith in Jesus Christ, adjusts to its surroundings and environment. The forms taken can be quite different from place to place, just as today we need to allow organization and ministries differ within the global Church. Among the theological principles that serve as criteria in assessing developments, Dunn mentions three. The first is fidelity to the challenge of Jesus' call to discipleship. There is no pretense that early communities lived this fidelity in an ideal way or had any ideal pattern of leadership to follow. The second is Paul's vision of a charismatic community, where services and ministries in their diversity come from gifts of the Spirit. This is a principle that imposes the need for discernment of spirits and for a say of the whole community in authenticating the call of its leaders. The third principle is eschatological. Christian communities always live in the light of the future, both the ultimate future, when God's kingdom will be universal, and the immediate future of the next generation to whom the gospel is to be confided. For Dunn, this openness to the future means that any generation that is too rigid in imposing structures or narrowly defining ministries, once and for all, may be handing on too heavy a burden and an impediment to those that come after it. In the light of present day needs and movements, these three principles or criteria of discernment seem quite pertinent.

Critical Contemporary Retrievals

The principles just enunciated allow a more open reading of the ministerial heritage of the apostolic era. Both historical critical method and sociological theories have contributed to an enlightened study of the making of the early Christian communities. Beyond these, we need ways to receive the gospel message with fresh inspiration in today's circumstances, so as to be open to the movements of the Spirit.

Often at stake is attention to approaches that have omitted or obscured some elements about life and ministry or that have distorted the reading of texts or bodies of texts. Hence, in reading New Testament texts on community, charism, ministry, and ordering, both feminist and postcolonial critical and reconstructive approaches are necessary. They both help to free the meaning and potential meaning of texts on kingdom, people, mission, authority, and order. It is possible to move from more-classical interpretations of texts to interpreting them in new contexts in creative ways.

Both approaches are sensitive to the restrictive ways in which passages have been used doctrinally, such as placing the origins of the episcopacy in Matt 18:18, and reading the household codes in the Pauline Letters to restrict the role of the woman in family and Church. Both approaches attend to factors of conflict or decoding procedures within the texts themselves. Examples are how the apostolic mission of the different women who go by the name of Mary is subordinated to an all-male apostolic group, how the Letter to Philemon seems to allow for the continuation of benign slavery among Christians and in society, despite all that is said of personal dignity in Christ, how some passages on charism and ministry, such as Eph 4 or the Pastoral Letters, can suggest tension between charisms and their subordination to office. Both approaches look for texts that in a forceful way show up the liberating power of the gospel of Jesus and the work of the Spirit, and when invoked allow for a transforming effect in Church and society.

Postcolonial Readings

Postcolonial interpretations are chiefly concerned with how the Bible and the Church may be received in a time and place that have been freed from foreign domination.[22] They attend to the fact that the Bible and Church traditions were transposed in European garb to other climes, with disastrous consequences for culture and for sowing the word of the gospel within cultures, as well as for the forms taken by ritual and ecclesiastical structure. In all of this, the power to receive the gospel creatively was suppressed. Sometimes it was released in part through syncretistic readings and popular religiosity, but these were never allowed into the mainstream of Church life and were viewed negatively by churchmen, missionaries, and scholars.

Postcolonial interpreters offer several ways for reading biblical texts that relate their transforming potential to new postcolonial contexts. For example, they attend to oppositional forces within the New Testament, as with the quarrels between Paul and Peter, and ask how this may be heard by those who know all about such exercises of compromise. Reading how Paul addresses Philemon on the lot of Onesimus, they ask what this sounds like to the ears of the slave who has accepted Christ as his liberator. The free person may be happy to adopt a new and fraternal attitude to his servant, but can the servant be satisfied with this? Even his voice is suppressed in the canonical text. The reader can ask how Jesus' gospel of love, forgiveness, and reconciliation, or 1 Peter's esteem of the price paid for true freedom by the blood of Christ may have more to say than Paul and the pseudo-Peter dared. Another example is the reading of the story of the Canaanite woman in Matt 15:21–28 as a story of power relations and how these are subverted by the teaching and example of Jesus, as well as how hard it was for the evangelists to make sense of this story.[23] How then may it be read today by a community that sees as its mission to serve the marginalized and to exercise authority within itself in true response to Jesus?

In the volume *Voices from the Margins*, there is a reading of the Exodus story in the light of African situations by Jean-Marc Ela that is pertinent to both ministry and the exercise of Church authority. In the essay Ela asks what a reading of this freedom story says to peoples who have suffered and now suffer the aftermath of colonial impositions and endure many economic and social oppressions. Ela asks how the Church fulfills its mission in this kind of situation. Towards the end of the essay, Ela shows the connection between the place of the Church in face of social developments and the exercise of leadership within the community. He writes:

"Will it be enough to run schools and hospitals, dispensaries and orphanages, all manner of charitable activities, or rather will it be in order to prioritize the assumption of the new aspirations of all the disinherited by bringing the problems of women and men crushed by injustice into religious education, religious formation, and prayer?"[24] An implied question is what this means in terms of life within communities and the exercise of a leadership that attends to and privileges these voices.

One tactic suggested is to visualize an event or the implications of some sayings, to imagine that as a scene and see how it opens itself to enactment among different peoples. Something like this was actually done among the Masai of Kenya, according to the account of Vincent O'Donovan.[25] First the people listened to the kingdom parables of Jesus and discussed what import these might have on their lives, including the stories about forgiveness, about neighbor, about the least and the greatest. Then they responded to the realization that accepting such teaching means accepting the person and what he suffered. Next they were invited to listen to the Supper Narratives in the Gospels and come up with ideas about how such a meal of fellowship, blessing, forgiveness, sacrifice, and reconciliation might be celebrated among them. The Catholic Church is quite timid about allowing for such responses, we know, but the invitation comes with the text.

One thing to which postcolonial criticism attends in Church life is also the nature of charism and types of ecclesial leadership. It is not possible to locate the particularities of a later theology and canonical regulation of order, or the sacrament of order, in the New Testament. The imposition on Southern continents of an ordered ministry that developed in Asia Minor and Europe is not justified by appeal to scriptural grounds. Indeed, the scriptures suggest the fact and the possibility of a wider divergence of charismatically grounded ministry and of Church order than has in effect been known since early centuries. Postcultural criticism helps to retrieve this possibility of diversity for churches of today.

Feminist Readings

Feminist interpretation[26] is obviously most concerned about the position of women in social and ecclesial life, but writers make the point that this has liberating consequences for all. Regrettably, one has to accept with them, or as one of them, that the New Testament is patriarchal through and through inasmuch as it favors masculine domination and gives a subordinate place to woman. To counteract this, a threefold procedure is followed. One is to trace the positions of women in communities since something can be known of this through relating Christian communities to the sociological models that apparently played a part in the way these communities were organized. A second approach is to be truly critical of specific texts, such as the use of household codes or stories from which women are omitted, such as in the story of the giving of gospel mandates to the Twelve, even though the voice of Mary can be heard, as it were, through the door or window. The third way is to pay much more attention to texts that have the power to set free and open up creative possibilities.

The use of sociological models by women writers asks whether we can have some insight into the place that women actually had in early communities.[27] This tells us two things. First, women were certainly not invisible, but some of them as householders exercised considerable power in household churches, such as was exercised in that time in the Greco-Roman cultural tradition. The second is that we cannot be idealistic in reconstruing woman's influence. The attitude of women who had authority was not necessarily egalitarian, but women could live with social distinctions just as readily as men. To be a community where there is neither Jew nor Greek, neither man nor woman, neither slave nor free might have been an ideal on the part of those reading Jesus' teaching, but it was not often readily realized. What Paul found wrong in the divisions of the Corinthian community was probably not all that exceptional. Even in early decades, Christians—men and women—quite easily accommodated belief and discipleship to current cultural and social trends.

Even with such insights, we know that New Testament writers often put a masculine spin on discipleship. A more constructive approach is to read texts for what they offer beyond what was ever realized in practice. A liberative approach of this sort, highlighting the power of texts, is found, for example, in a reading of the story of the Samaritan woman in John 4, or in a reading of the episode of Jesus' appearance in the synagogue of Nazareth in Luke 4. Other examples would be the stories of the presence of the women at the foot of the cross as true disciples when the men have fled, the account in Matt 18 of what goes on in an ecclesial assembly where the issue is about forgiveness and all have a voice, sayings about the greatest in the kingdom that point to the lowly and to children in particular, recommendations about the nature of true worship that are quite free of charges other than the general invitation to the community of disciples. The issue is not to be narrowed to the question of admission to order. It is more fundamentally an issue of who has authority in the Church in virtue of discipleship, and what kind of community is implied in accepting the gospel of the kingdom and the person of Jesus himself. To put it another way, it is a matter of a large view of the kind of Church within which charisms and ministries have to be ordered by the Spirit and in keeping with the gospel. Discernment is then called for, not simply protocol.

Two Examples: Luke 4 and John 4

As a general mode of interpretation, Rebecca Chopp's concern is through the scriptural word to listen to the Word who is Jesus, from whom we hear a new kind of God talk, and thereby can engage in a critique and exploration of the power of language and of speech. For her, a reading of the scene in the synagogue of Nazareth narrated in Luke 4 opens up the perspective for a hearing of the entire scriptural Word, in the life of living communities.[28] Jesus has been baptized and sent forth as a prophet in the power of the Spirit. In the synagogue in the power of this Spirit, he presents the text of Isaiah about the freedom of God's reign. In the power of Spirit and Word, he gives not only a promise of emancipation but a voice to those who are weak and poor in their societies.

When Jesus announces that "this day" the prophecy is fulfilled, he is not talking in calendar time, but invites his hearers (and readers) to step outside the usual mode of calculation and to be attentive to the time of God's action, which is free, unexpected, and liberating. The critique of would-be hearers is that Jesus is not heard among his own but is sent to speak to others, as Elijah was sent to the widow of Zarephath and as Elisha healed Naaman the Syrian. Though they are in the synagogue in the town of Nazareth, those assembled are invited to let themselves be set down in another place and another time, within a community of the misbegotten. To hear that word now, or in any time and place, is to be invited to be elsewhere than one's accustomed places, to live by a new measure of time, to live among an unwonted community of persons. For the Church, this means that the power of the Word of ministry is ordained to this, that the gifts of the Spirit move toward this eschatological horizon, that ministries that are true in God's sight are those that bring alive the teaching and witness of Jesus among the poor.

Often enough nowadays, the story of the Samaritan woman in John 4 is read as a text about the possible place of women in the Church. It certainly has that application, but its meaning is quite deep and concerns one and all. To begin with, Jesus embarks on an unusual and unapproved encounter by asking a service not only of a foreigner and alien but of a woman at that.[29] Surprisingly for those who hear the story, though the woman is a sinner, she is more ready to receive the prophetic word, to respond, and to proclaim than those who are considered just and observant of God's precepts. In conversation with her, Jesus teaches about the true nature of worship and about the expansive and all-embracing love of the God of the covenant, of the Father, with whom Jesus himself lives in communion. Not only does she become a believer and a disciple, but Jesus sends her as an apostle who announces the good news to her co-citizens. While this has much to say about the place of women in the work of Christ and so in the life of the Church, it speaks even more fully of the ways of God's dealings with the disciples. It is by breaking out of conventions, by being able to receive the liberating message of love, by knowing God through worship in spirit and in truth, by heeding all who speak and prophesy, whoever they be, that the Church lives by the gospel of Jesus Christ. Even within the necessary quest for structure, it asks for a constant openness to Word and Spirit, a readiness to see how and where and among whom they are at work, and so to accept the necessary changes to order.

These two examples illustrate the open and critical reading that church communities need to give to all scriptural texts about discipleship, mission, and ministry as they try to engage with the power of God's Word and Spirit in their own lives and in their milieu. They provide some living criteria for discerning spirits and for discerning a change of Church order that the mission of the community may exact.

Conclusion

The purpose of this chapter has been to recall elements from studies of the New Testament that are pertinent to present-day global discernment and reordering of ministries. As churches in various parts of the world seek to envision their mission and their service to God's reign, they revisit New Testament texts. First, we saw the part played in the development of the life of the Church through the retrieval of the images of kingdom of God and priestly people. Second, we looked at the different ways in which, according to the writings of different churches, communities saw themselves and their part in God's design, and thus how they saw the nature and foundation of authority. Third, we considered how leadership is viewed and how different communities encouraged and ordered their ministries in building up the body of disciples. Fourth, some ventures in critical retrievals of what has been omitted, obscured, or distorted were recalled for consideration, since they have an impact on how the future may be seen. Finding the origins of ministry in the evidence given in New Testament writings is surely a complex but hope-giving process, which inspires creativity. Taking all of these elements into account should bring us well beyond the intention of looking for institutions that are scripturally sanctioned.

6

Ordering of Ministries

The principles of interpretation enunciated at the beginning of this section are important in considering postapostolic developments in Church order and ministries. Speaking of orders and of ordained ministry in the Church—with the ministry of bishop, presbyter, and deacon specifically and almost exclusively in mind—makes the issue too narrow. Other services within communities were also ordered, as indeed were the rules, liturgies, and workings of specific groups, such as those of penitents and catechumens. Behind what we think we know about the past, we have to ask what was being ordered and why was it being ordered in some specific way. One looks for the spiritual and practical purposes that dictated choices made, as well as for the influences at work and the significance that rulings embody.

Recognizing the particular role of ministries conferred by the laying on of hands, the tripartite clerical order of bishop, presbyter, deacon is usually assumed as the proper tradition, even if it is acknowledged that this took a while to emerge. There are three cautions to keep in mind on this. First, since the settling of this pattern took time and did not develop in a uniform way in every church, the story of how churches were ministered and why they came to this pattern is important to our own epoch when ordering has to come out of new settings and new stories. Second, even when the three names or offices are mentioned globally, we should not think that exactly the same thing is always intended nor that the roles described function in homologous fashion. In our own day we might well think of the striking difference between a bishop in the northern islands of French Polynesia, working with five priests, and a metropolitan in New York, administering a heavily populated city church with the assistance of five auxiliary bishops. Third, this tripartite major ordering has to be seen within the context of the total ordering of gifts and roles that served the life and the mission of communities, which means getting behind and beyond the separation between clergy and laity that prevailed for many centuries.

An issue much discussed today is the emergence of a clear distinction between clergy and the rest of the baptized. Sometimes this is referred to in a general way as a distinction between clergy and laity. The term *laity* does not respond well to historical usages of the word. In early centuries *lay* did not usually refer to all the baptized who were not considered clerics. It had quite a diversity of meanings. It could designate a group of laymen who held esteem in a community and were considered eligible for inclusion among the clergy, or it could mean, as in Ireland, those who did not belong to the core of those who pursued Christian perfection, but remained attached to a monastery. In this chapter, some care will be taken in the use of the term *laity*, but it will be used in quoting authors who use it broadly in its contemporary meaning to refer to all the baptized as distinct from those ordained by a laying on of hands.

Within the first millennium of the history of Christianity, attention to diversity has to be key to the reading of history. Hence, in this chapter we will look at the way in which through that millennium different regions ordered Church ministry and Church life, looking as it were at the canonical dispositions rather than at more theological writings. In the next chapter, to gain more insight into the reasoning behind the factual, we will consider some significant bishops and ecclesiastical writers. Naturally there is overlapping in this approach, but it seems to be a suitable way to look at the material with some clarity.

A broad division of periods is adopted. First is the pre-Constantinian period, when Christians were a minority population. Second is the period of expansion, eastward and westward, with the recognition given by the Roman Empire to the Christian Church, while at the same time there was an expansion of Christian influence outside the empire in places such as Ethiopia and Armenia. Third is the Carolingian era, when Christianity encountered new populations and took shape accordingly, with the establishment of a Christianized universe in mind. While this chronology is followed in principle, geographical realities have to be taken into account. This means noting differences between East and West, as well as what is peculiar to Ethiopia and Armenia and in the Latin world to northward countries such as Gaul and the islands. Thus one can see what is common in developments of ministries and structures and what is particular to given places or local churches.

Early Beginnings

In surveying the early age, when Christian people were a minority, one can look at the emerging image of the local bishop, the continued exercise of several ministries, and the incipient distinction between laity and clergy. The place of the whole community in mission and ministry is basic. Hence it is after an introduction on the part played by all the baptized in a community that other developments are considered.

Role of All the Baptized in the Ancient Church

Church ordering deserves a context, difficult though it may be to describe. It occurred within communities that had a vision of discipleship lived in common but that, in the minds of its leaders, needed more order and clearer lines of authority, for the sake of fidelity to the apostolic tradition.

It is sometimes said that in the early centuries of Christianity, all the members of the Church were missionaries.[1] This is so to the extent that sincere and committed persons willingly testified to Christ by their way of living and even by suffering persecution and death rather than renounce their faith under coercion. It is also true that the expansion of the faith owed much to ordinary faithful rather than simply to its leaders or those who went out specifically to evangelize. It was the general body of the faithful who enticed converts. Within the domain of Roman rule, believing Christians appear to have made contact especially with the least fortunate members of society, giving them hope through their belief in what Christ had brought and promised. Besides these, there were merchants and travelers who brought knowledge of Christ with them as well as their merchandise. Apart from this, the more prominent exponents and defenders of the faith in these early times were what today would be called lay persons. One need think only of such as Justin and Origen, who lived in days before communal and episcopal ordering was well established. On the practical side, *diakonia*, or the care of the needy, was often the task of householders and richer members of the community, along with which necessarily went the exercise of some power in determining internal and external relations.

In a short essay from 1958 titled "The Role of the Layman in the Ancient Church,"[2] George Huntston Williams succinctly elaborates on the place of the baptized who did not hold office in the period before clearer Church ordering. He considers this under the headings of worship, instruction, and deliberation, and then asks what missionary influence Christians had when they were scattered around the world as small minorities. These are helpful headings under which to consider the matter. As far as worship is concerned, one could start by noting that Sunday worship and other major occasions such as baptism were actions and celebrations of the community, and that on weekdays also they came together for prayer, instruction, and evening meals as one body. Theologically, this fitted with the image of the Church as a royal priesthood, a living sacrifice, a holy covenant people, where it is the whole that is intended rather than individual members. On this foundation, all the baptized in Christ and the Spirit were said to offer spiritual sacrifices in which acts of worship and holy lives came together. This could mean that while it was the ordinary thing for a head of a community or a bishop to preside and say the prayers, as well as baptize, these things on occasion could be done by the people without a bishop, since the thing in itself was primary rather than the person of the one doing it.

In conjunction with this part in worship, Williams also points to what he calls the eleemosynary role of all the baptized and of the community as such. That is to say, it would not have been possible to worship in spirit and in truth if the poor and needy were not looked after. This indeed is something that carried over into later centuries and is the reason why the Sunday assembly was also the occasion to collect the gifts of the faithful for the needs of their sisters and brothers.

On instruction, Williams only has to point to the characteristic role of such as Justin, Tertullian, and Origen to show that distinction in office allowed for a broad participation in teaching the faith, this being a matter of gift and competence. Williams notes that in later centuries, when councils took up matters of doctrine, the contribution and agreement of the faithful were necessary for a teaching to take hold. He finds the roots of this understanding in the early years of the Church. To this, one has to add that the work in passing on the faith of mothers, fathers, and elders is rarely documented, but that without this, the faith would never have been transmitted or have endured.

This leads to the third heading, that of taking part in deliberations affecting the life of the Church. While this includes passing on and assenting to apostolic teaching, it stretches also to matters of Church discipline and organization. Even for centuries after incipient clericalization, for example, people were to have their say in the choice of bishops. The exact process differed and is hard to map with exactitude, but the admonition to the members of a church of the *Didache* may well be seen as an enduring rule: "Choose bishops and deacons for yourselves" (15.1).

For the influence of Christians in their milieu, one could combine what Williams says with the perspective of David Bosch in his writings on mission.[3] It was the responsibility of all to see that the gospel of Christ became known and that nonbelievers would be welcomed. In effect, this went with the testimony of Christian living. Pursuing the way of light rather than the way of darkness, Christian people were bound to be noticed even when they did not strive for attention. In some way they influenced those around them, even if they were also reviled. It was a way of life that first attracted others and drew people into the fold of Christ. When some then wished to become members of the community, it was the responsibility of the community as a whole to welcome and prepare them. Gifts of the Spirit fitted some members to take on a greater role in this regard, but this did not take away from what we would now see as the missionary consciousness and responsibility of all. It was when the sense of Christian community and commitment began to weaken, or when inner coherence in matters of faith, worship, and *diakonia* was at stake, that the way appears to have been paved for a greater concern for ordering and appointing, and that is the story that needs to be followed.

It is also possible to take up positions of advocacy in reading historical evidence. Edoardo Hoornaert, who writes from the perspectives of the Brazilian church,[4] considers early church history as the story of communities of the poor and the socially marginalized, a kind of early church counterpart to today's base Christian communities. He contends that in its authenticity, the gospel of Jesus Christ appealed to those living at the margins of society, giving them a sense of what they become through the grace of Christ and feelings of hope. They formed communities that were truly communities of the people, having their own ministries among their own members. One might call this the story of the poor, whom the gospel privileged in the proclamation of the good news, the Lord's triumph over sin and death, and a discipleship that is for and of the people. A different view of the composition of early communities is, however, put forward by some social historians who think that Christianity attracted the upwardly mobile more readily than the poor.[5] Even if this is so, what remains is the picture of a community where all share responsibilities.

From these perspectives on the early centuries of Christianity, we can turn to the story of the ordering of ministry and try to understand it, both positively and critically, as Christian communities take their place within a historically and culturally developing world.

Early Church Orders

Paul Bradshaw refers to the documents called church orders as a continuing enigma,[6] which indeed they are in terms of origin and actual pertinence to the way communities lived and celebrated. However, they serve to give us some map of how people went about ordering offices and ministries in local churches. They place provisions for ministry within the total context of ordering life, prayers, rites, practices, and groups within a community, even as they give us what were the prevailing perspectives on a moral and Christian way of life. This total context allows us to grasp the purpose and significance of ministries. The orders also show us how the distinction between clergy and the rest of the faithful was codified, with some glimpse into the reasons for this. The three collections that are of most interest here are the Syrian documents called the *Didache* and the *Didascalia*, and the text commonly known as *The Apostolic Tradition*.

Didache

The first known Church order is particularly pertinent to the vision that inspires order, namely the *Didache* from East Syria, because it starts with moral teaching and ends with an eschatological admonition. The moral teaching is based on the distinction between two ways of comporting oneself, the way of life and the way of death. On this basis, the collection proceeds to give instructions about baptism, fasting and daily prayer, the common meal or agape (possibly the Eucharist), the treatment of prophets, the importance of gathering on the Lord's Day, and the appointment of bishops and deacons. The final admonition on vigilance gives the horizon within which the Christian community lives its days in expectation of the Lord's coming. In other words, fidelity to the Lord's teaching and the hope of his coming give the framework within which all ordering occurs. This tells us what is being served by all rulings about common life, including the naming of bishops and deacons.

Though it is difficult to date it with precision, the *Didache* represents an early community in which the leaders were householders and communities could be visited by apostles, teachers, and prophets, persons known for their gifts and the authenticity of their testimony to Christ. Toward the end of the document, the writer recommends the appointment of bishops and deacons, apparently sensing the need in the postapostolic generation of a more stable form of governance and of appointment of leaders. There is no very precise indication about the kind of government envisaged, but it may be surmised that the bishops were plural, something like a body of presbyters or elders who held responsibility. This conforms to another early text, *1 Clement*, which seems to support the view that this mode of rule prevails in the Church in Rome, still divided up into household communities.

Hard conclusions cannot be drawn from the *Didache* about the role of bishops. Some commentators assume that they were to be the heads of household churches and that they would preside at the Lord's Supper. Recently, however, Aaron Milavec has called this into question precisely because of the household structure that is assumed.[7] He believes that in this setting the man or woman, or couple, who managed the household would say the blessing prayer, unless this was ceded to an apostle or a prophet who enjoyed gifts of word and speech. In the injunction to appoint bishops and deacons, he sees the need to have persons who would be able to manage the growing requirements of a common life. Hence, in face of different opinions about these bishops, it would be wrong to read too much into the text of the *Didache*.

Other texts

In later church orders the figure of the bishop becomes clearer. Bishops were to take over from the apostles and prophets in teaching. They also preside at the Sunday gathering. A bishop is like a "householder" who administers the life of the Church. Deacons are to assist bishops, particularly in caring for the needy. For this reason they also assisted them at the agape and eucharistic gathering.

A number of Syrian collections belong to the third and fourth centuries. Turning to them, we find these listings or rankings. The *Didascalia* (*Teaching of the Twelve Apostles*), the *Apostolic Constitutions*, and the *Testament of the Lord* are documents variously modeled on the *Didache* but drawing on other sources as well and belonging to later periods. They include more ministries, offices, and orders than the *Didache* does and represent a clear distinction between clergy and people, even though they do not agree on which offices bring one into the ranks of the clergy. However, only bishops, presbyters, deacons, and in one case deaconesses receive the laying on of hands. Purported to be an order governing the life of the church in Rome, the document known as the *Apostolic Tradition* achieved lasting significance in the influence it exercised in the East and is important for today because of the uses made of it in forging some communality within ecumenical dialogue.

From a study of these Church orders a number of things stand out in the development of ministries and their organization and the ways in which persons are inducted into them. Detailed and minute studies have been done on these texts so that what is given here is a summary of important facts and factors.

First, it is always a matter of ordering the entire life of a community and the place of persons and groups within it, but there is a perceptible move to a growing distinction between the clergy and the rest of the faithful. The matter has to do primarily with the role and ministry of bishop, presbyters, and deacons in individual churches, but others might also be ranked among the clergy.

Second, there is evidence in these documents of the change from a more presbyteral and synodal form of government to a monoepiscopal rule. This comes out especially in the ordination prayers of the *Apostolic Tradition*. Third, we see how the figure of the bishop takes shape and some of the practical reasons for this. Fourth, individuals or groups not ranked among the clergy contribute to the community's life and mission. Fifth, we can see what happened to the place of women in Christian communities and some of the practical reasons for this. These matters will be looked at under the appropriate headings.

Orders

The lists of groups or orders in a church varies somewhat, but on a whole there is convergence. The *Didascalia*, modeled on the *Didache*, lists bishop, presbyter, deacon, reader, and widow, and augurs the institution of deaconess. Other texts include deaconesses and subdeacons. Not particularly associated with official service, there is mention of widows, virgins, and confessors who continue to leave some imprint on their communities. Charismatics too have their place in these lists. We learn of the inclusion of healing, knowledge, and tongues as charisms given to persons to be honored alongside those installed in office (*Testament of the Lord*). The *Apostolic Constitutions* explicitly state that the exorcist is not a member of the clergy nor an office. It is rather a gift that has to be put to the test by its fruits.

Clergy/Faithful

A differentiation between clergy and those whom we now broadly call laity is prominent in these documents, beginning with naming as clergy bishops, presbyters, and deacons, but then extending beyond them to include readers and subdeacons (*Testament of the Lord*, *Apostolic Constitutions*) and deaconesses (*Apostolic Constitutions*). The extension of the name of clergy to include all those who perform any sort of liturgical service, however minor, goes still further in Syria about 380 according to the *Canones apostolorum*, where the persons just mentioned and the psalmist are considered clerics. It did not take long before the doorkeeper was added to their ranks.

There are two characteristics that together distinguish the clergy from other members of the Church. Those distinguished are those giving liturgical service, of whatever sort, and those who, holding office, receive sustenance from the community chest. Others, like widows, receive sustenance and support, but since they have no liturgical function, they are not clerics. The extension of the name *cleric* to include all manner of liturgical ministers indicates how much liturgy has been subjected to careful control. There are no longer roles for both the ordained and the laity in the liturgical ministry, but all liturgical ministry is clerical.

The *Apostolic Tradition* shows how, in the mind of the compiler, members acquired their positions in the community. Bishops, presbyters, and deacons receive the laying on of hands. Fellow bishops are to lay on hands at episcopal ordination. When presbyters are ordained, fellow presbyters impose hands along with the bishop. The deacon receives laying on of hands from the bishop alone. He is presented as an assistant to the bishop, in the liturgy and in the works of charity demanded in serving the congregation of the faithful. A number of other offices belong within the community, to serve it in one way or another. In these cases, laying on of hands is excluded, but the word is of forms of installation and appointment, indicating a stable and approved place in the life of the Church. Widows are installed, not for a liturgical function but to serve the Church through their prayer. As well as the widow, another member of the community is said to be installed. This is the reader, who is appointed but does not receive the laying on of hands. A subdeacon is simply said to be named, and he is ranked after the reader. Perhaps this shows even a third type of appointment, but it is not possible to be sure that installation and naming mean two different things. In any case, here it is not clear what is meant by "subdeacon." Three other persons are given special status in the document, but in each case it is pointed out that no official appointment is involved since the foundation for this status is either charism, personal honor, or free choice. These three are the confessor, the virgin, and the one who has received the gift of healing. The confessor has gained personal honor by open and persevering profession of the faith, and has a dignity equal to that of the presbyters, and apparently takes his place among them. The virgin acquires her place in the Church order through personal choice as a way of following Christ, and healing is a charism given by the Spirit.

The presence of an order of virgins among the orders of the Church is important because of its eschatological significance. This does not mean simply living as though anticipating eternal life. In its social setting, it points to the liberating force of the eschatological Spirit and to a vitality present in the community. Women were wont to be the property of their fathers or their husbands, who had to conform to the social demands of familial arrangements. From the Acts of Martyrs we know how many of those who embraced virginity in the name of Christ were abjured for this reason: their readiness to renounce the usual marriage arrangements and expectations of the time showed that through faith in Christ they were given a gift of freedom in regard to these matters. The fact that the Christian community had a special place for them certainly expresses a readiness to respect and protect their choice. More important, it means that their witness to Christ and the freedom that he gave was a factor in animating the life of the Church.

The relation between ordination, installation, and charism is of interest. The confessor and healer probably represent an earlier stage of Church life, when personal witness and charismatic gift could be grounds enough for holding authority, or when the Church's intervention consisted mainly of recognizing gifts of the Spirit and channeling their exercise. Now, while this recognition of gifts still plays its part, there is established the constant necessity of ordination for higher office. Ordination, not charismatic gift, becomes the definitive distinguishing mark in the Church and the stamp of authority, even though the gifts of the Spirit are still considered necessary to the exercise of the office, as the ordination prayers show. Not only is order more highly structured, but as the case of the reader shows, the tendency is to submit even other services to tighter control and modes of appointment.

Presbyteral/Episcopal Government

While the *Apostolic Tradition* is usually taken as evidence of a high episcopal profile and ministry, it is also evidence of the movement from a presbyteral to a monoepiscopal form of government.[8] This comes from a careful study of the prayers for ordination.[9] One of the most fascinating things about the document is that while its compiler intended it for the Roman Church, its influence in later times is found chiefly in Syria and Egypt. Dispute about its authorship and dating will probably never end, but it is safe to take it as a document of the early third century that had considerable influence on Church life. It sets out to give clear instructions on living together in community, with the avowed purpose of adhering to the apostolic tradition, even while in fact giving the force of "canonicity" to what seem to be some new Church structures. What it in effect portrays is a Church developing an ordered way of life, where functions, liturgies, services, and ranks can proceed according to more or less stable regulations.

The section on the ordination of the bishop and of presbyters is one of the most strongly disputed parts of this treatise. Given what is known of ministry and its organization in the early days of the Roman Church, the prayers for bishop and for presbyters are not likely to come from the same source nor to represent a long-standing tradition. The rite for presbyters is probably older, and was used for ordination when various house churches had their respective ministers, who worked together to supervise the more collective church life connecting city and suburbs as a whole. What the Church order is trying to do is to impose the rule of a single bishop for Rome and to place the college of presbyters in relation to his office.

The prayer for the ordination of a presbyter is of historical importance because it probably represents an earlier order of Church life, when households were still the primary gathering place for the assembly. The ordination of a presbyter marks his incorporation into the presbytery, or body of presbyters. His ministry is exercised in conjunction with the other members of the order. The grace sought for him is that "of the presbytery" and shows the corporate and collegiate nature of the ministry. It is further described as the "spirit[10] of grace and of counsel," which enables the recipient to "help and govern God's people with a pure heart" and "to serve God in simplicity of heart." The text of the *Apostolic Constitutions* that incorporates items from the *Apostolic Tradition* indicates that the original Greek word, translated here as "to serve," was *douleuō*. This verb is used together with the words "in simplicity of heart" in Eph 6:5 and Col 3:22 to designate the attitude a slave ought to have in regard to his master.

The nature of the grace received is further specified in the prayer as the "spirit of counsel [*pneuma symboulias*]": this expression helps us to determine for what kind of ministry it is intended. In this prayer some authors have understood the expression to mean that the role of the presbyters is to give advice or counsel to the bishop, so that in the local church they form his senate of advisers or counselors. However, such a hypothesis supposes the existence of the monoepiscopate. There is nothing in the immediate context of the prayer to support this interpretation. The sentence does not directly designate any person or persons as the subject to whom advice is to be given. It says, rather, that this spirit permits the recipient to "help and govern the people." This implies that the grace of his order concerns the presbyter's relations with the people, and if there is any question of giving advice or counsel, it would be to the people rather than to the bishop. This in itself is a form of government, for it means that the pastor or counselor indicates a mode of behavior to the faithful, who in turn practice a form of obedience by adhering to this advice. This interpretation is confirmed by the rubric preceding the ordination of a deacon, where it is said that the presbyters do not lay hands on the deacon, because he "has no part in the council of the clergy." The words "to help and to govern" further describe the nature of the presbyterium's ministry. The combination of these two words recalls two of the charisms mentioned by Paul in 1 Cor 12:28: government and assistance of the weak. This is likewise mentioned by Paul in his address to the elders at Miletus as one of their duties toward the faithful (Acts 20:35).

The petition for grace appeals to a typology taken from the Old Testament, asking that God may now act in his Church as he acted when he "looked upon the chosen people and commanded Moses to choose elders whom He filled with the spirit which he granted to His servant." Some authors have argued that this part of the prayer places the origin of the presbytery's spirit in the bishop's spirit, and by implication asserts the derivation of their charge from that of the bishop. According to these authors, this is implied because the presbytery of the Church is placed in the same relation to the bishop as the elders of Israel were to Moses: as the Jewish elders received a share in the spirit of Moses in order to rule with him over the people of Israel, so the presbyters receive a share in the spirit of the bishop, which gives them a part in his priesthood and leadership.

Such reasoning supposes the existence of a community order over which there is a single bishop. There is no cogent argument, however, to show that the prayer does intend this parallel. It is not made explicit, and there is no good reason to believe that it is implied. Since this type of figure is found generally in the tradition of the Eastern churches, which is usually supposed to depend in this matter on the *Apostolic Tradition*, what it brings out is the sending of the spirit to the presbyters for governing the people, a task similar to that for which the elders of Israel were chosen. There is no great emphasis on the fact that the spirit given to the elders was originally the spirit of Moses other than to suggest continuity and divine intervention.

When it is prescribed that the presbyters lay on hands for the ordination of one of their fellows, but not for the ordination of a deacon, we see how the compiler of the work is trying to relate the three orders. The explanation given is that the deacon is not ordained for a priesthood, which implies that the presbyters are so ordained. In other words, a priestly role is attributed to the presbytery of the church. This is the sole explicit mention of the priesthood of the presbytery in the *Apostolic Tradition* and belongs to the compiler's reasoning rather than to the tradition itself. This compiler wished to affirm the bishop's role and to place the *presbyterium* in a subordinate role to his ministry, as a kind of participation in it. Since he has attributed the spirit of high priesthood to the bishop, the reference to priesthood of presbyters is quite coherent. In the context of the text that we have in hand, it goes with the part of the presbyters in the liturgy of the Eucharist, where they are said to extend hands over the gifts along with the bishop, while the deacon serves the bishop. The ordination prayer itself predates the association of cultic priesthood with presbyteral ministry.

The Bishop

In putting these ordination prayers alongside each other, the *Apostolic Tradition* presents a figure of the bishop that fits the idea of monoepiscopal government. The prayer for the bishop states that he is to possess the spirit of headship and high priesthood. His office is described by the pastoral metaphor of feeding the flock and as the exercise of the high priesthood. By reason of the spirit of priesthood, he offers the gifts of the faithful in the Eucharist and has the authority to forgive sins, to choose and ordain the clergy of his church, and to bind and loose. He is to receive the same spirit, that of Christ himself, which was given to the apostles. By virtue of this spirit, he can exercise functions originally committed to them. The power to forgive sins, mentioned here, recalls John 20:23, that to bind and loose Matt 18:18, and that to ordain Acts 1:26. The spirit of headship and the spirit of high priesthood are one and the same. In other words, it is by virtue of the spirit of Christ, given to the apostles and then to the bishops, that these latter exercise both headship and high priesthood in the Church. This description of the bishop makes him a figure of prime importance and gives him preeminence over the other clergy.

For the emergence of an episcopacy that is not only a monoepiscopacy but a monarchical one, the high point of these Church orders is indeed the *Didascalia Apostolorum*,[11] with its exceptionally monarchical vision of the bishop, ruling like a king and a high priest in his church. The context is that of a household church,[12] presided over by a patriarchal figure who is likened to God the Father, over whose household he rules, with mercy, compassion, and humility.

The bishop is the *oikonomos*, or steward, of God in leading the Church. This image is taken from household society, where the chief steward ruled in the place of the patriarch or owner of the house and head of the family. The bishop is put in an analogous relation to God, who is the true Father and the Lord of the household. In this vein, the bishop is also called priest and king. Putting penitential discipline under the bishop's control contributed to the power he exercised. He was the only one with the power to judge sinners and their place in the community, or, in other words, he exclusively exercised the power to bind and loose, though the consent of the faithful would still be necessary.

Roles for Women

Mention has already been made of the presence of orders of widows and virgins. If this is historically accurate, it is through the order of deaconess that women have access to the ranks of the clergy and that their office in the liturgy is established. According to the *Didascalia* and the *Constitutions*, the deaconess is entrusted with many of the duties that the *Testament of the Lord* assigns to widows, but she is considered a member of the clergy since she receives the laying on of hands on account of her liturgical functions. These functions are the duty to assist women at baptism when they go down into the pool and to keep order in the assembly, particularly among the women.

According to the *Ordinato sacerdotalis*, the deaconess, the subdeacon, and the reader are to receive a laying on of hands, and installation into these offices has many other features of an ordination. In all three ceremonies, the presider prays for the gift of the Spirit to be given to the candidate. The three prayers of blessing invoke Old Testament paradigms for the ministry bestowed. In the case of the deaconess, these are holy women endowed with the gift of God's Spirit—namely Miriam, Deborah, Hannah, and Huldah—and the "guardians of the gates of the temple." In the case of the subdeacon, the keepers of the ark of the covenant and the guardians of the sacred vessels serve as paradigm, and in the case of the reader, it is Esdras proclaiming the law to the people. As a further parallel with ordination, these three offices involve a liturgical service, intimated by the Old Testament paradigms. The deaconess has something to do with keeping the holy place, the subdeacon with keeping vessels used in worship, and the reader with proclaiming the Scriptures to the assembled people.

The compiler of the collection may inflate these functions somewhat by paralleling the installation into office with ordination. His reasoning appears to be that a service to the community, and especially to its worship, requires the gift of the Spirit, and since these offices imply such service, they are to be in some way compared with the offices of bishop, presbyter, and deacon. However, the book remains an isolated witness to this form of blessing, and therefore also to the concept of office or ministry involved.

Ironically, writers appeal to *Apostolic Constitutions* both as evidence of the inclusion of women in sacred order in the past and as evidence of the inferiority of women's roles, the deaconess not being on a par with those in the order of deacon. Authors still argue over the exact status of the deaconesses and whether their ordination put them on a level with male deacons or not. It is obvious enough that their ministry is to be among women, but then one could also argue that the ministry of deacons is primarily among men, such was the division of the sexes in those times. What seems to make male deacons stand out is their role as servants of the bishop in financial matters, and especially in the distribution of alms to the needy, the traditional *diakonia* of early church communities. Indeed, the effort to make sure that control of finances is placed under the bishop explains much in this Church order and even contributes to the high and lofty image given to the head of the local church. The ordination of deaconesses belongs within the steps taken to control and minimize the role and activity of widows, who apparently had attained a place of influence.

This goes back to ideas about the care of widows, noted as early as in the Pastoral Letters of the pseudo-Paul. Being against second marriage, churches took on themselves the care of widows, some of whom would have been quite young. They were even called the "altar" on which Christian sacrifice was to be made. What apparently happened is that the duty of almsgiving took on new shapes as time progressed. Instead of being arranged through the community collection, individuals began to take their own initiatives, which could mean preferment of some of the poor over others. In such a situation, widows had to look after themselves, and sought access to the richer folk, and could thus exercise an influence in community life. In the service of the community, they also took on some ministerial roles, including liturgical ones. In short, in the ways of dealing with monies and in the ways of exercising influence in community life, both the rich and widows caused problems for community leaders.

The *Didascalia* says some nasty things about widows and about their ways of seeking their own gain and disturbing the life of the community. Some of these remonstrations may have been justified, some no doubt were exaggerated. All in all, to have them exercise influence was not pleasing to those who wanted a hierarchical form of Church order, with males dominating. Putting all care of funding and of looking after the poor under the control of the bishop, with the assistance of male deacons, was a way for the bishop to have greater control. In that context, ordaining women as deaconesses for some well-specified duties was an ordered alternative to the roles exercised by widows under a system of Church life that was more fluid and flexible. This fits with the fact that the *Didascalia* gives us a good sense of how transition was made from the early communities that were more communal and more withdrawn from society, to the more ordered life of a hierarchical and monarchical Church.

Remarks

Taken on their own, these stories of ordering the life and service of a local church do not give us a full picture of Church life and the development of ministries and services. They do give a framework for a fuller interpretation, so it is worth drawing some conclusions about patterns that emerge from Church ordering as we know it from these texts.

The Church orders show us how the total life of a church is ordered and how ministry and worship fit within a larger pattern of Christian community and relationship. The communities in question are still quite small, though the treatise on the *Apostolic Tradition* probably represents the effort to bring a number of communities together under one bishop. If the document is to be situated within the city of Rome, not as a description but as an aspiration of the compiler, this fits with what is otherwise known about Christian communities in Rome in early Christian times. The Syrian documents belong to churches that always remained quite small and whose membership remained a minority in their cultural setting.

The distinction between the ministries requiring a laying on of hands and other ministries is formulated to show the difference between clergy and the rest of the faithful. With this, the figure of the bishop is put into high relief. He is to devote himself totally to the service of the church, and his livelihood is to be provided by the faithful. His relation to the apostles is put to the fore in order to provide theological basis to his ministry, power, and status. His responsibility for financial administration, as this affects the needs of the poor in the community, is important in delineating his role and authority in the Church. Those associated with the bishop as presbyters and deacons share in the status and respect afforded him.

With regard to the place of women, we have seen that some internal struggle was involved and that compromises were sought, such as the ordination of women as deaconesses or the assignment of services to some widows. By and large, however, we see that the importance given to determining the locus of power in the Church and the felt need to diminish the factual influence of widows affected the exclusion of women from positions of authority. This was supported by odd ideas about how men and women relate by nature, as we are able to see from other texts, which will be mentioned later.

Early patterns of order are more comprehensible when they are related to what we can know about the use of the model of household fellowship in early church communities. The chapter on ministry according to the New Testament showed that early Christian communities adapted forms of government from other religious and social institutions. Among these was the household of the times, with its complex network of relations and services. This adaptation may be usefully revisited in looking at how Church life evolved in postapostolic times.

In these centuries cities were in a process of development, with people of diverse ethnic or geographical origins moving to urban areas. Socially, the household in its purest form consisted of all who in one way or another belonged to it, as kin, as subordinate, or as servant. Some houses, belonging to wealthier families, were larger and could provide accommodation and sustenance to others who gravitated toward them because of ethnic or cultural relations. Commodious and comfortable households became a focal point for common life and for gatherings, including gatherings for worship.

Christian households, however, had the particular perspectives that emerged from faith in Christ and from living as his disciples. The fact of wanting to join with other followers of Jesus was motivation enough for coming together in a suitable household dwelling and structure. Although closeness or difference in social class and wealth had some impact, common life and gathering were more fundamentally grounded in the principle of being a discipleship of equals. In the house of God built on Christ as cornerstone, all were of equal dignity, and none was to lord it over others. Though the formation of communities was influenced by how common origin and ethnic identity draw people together, they had porous boundaries and welcomed members of other ethnic or social realities. The ideal was the Pauline one, that in Christ there is neither Jew nor Greek, male nor female, slave nor free. A practical *diakonia* of care for the needy left an important imprint on common priorities, on how people related to each other, and on how the Christian family was organized. In understanding the nature of Church, we can never sufficiently estimate the fact that the deaconate of service is integral to a fellowship in Christ and has an impact on its whole being and ordering.

Given the expansiveness of the gospel vision of human reality, which excluded boundaries set by particular identity, bringing these diverse households together as one was an important ministry and affected the modes and structures of Church leadership. In Rome, anyway, organizing the care of the needy or of those falling on bad times had a key role to play. The members of single households or communities appear to have been inclined to share the responsibility with each other. The role of deacons, deaconesses, and faithful widows serving wider areas as well as individual communities developed along these lines.

On the other hand, this also affected the episcopal office since oversight of community need and of the work of those designated for it was considered an integral part of Church leadership. One might say that the needs of service to the poor brought communities together as one. Though it was not their direct concern, this affected the role of presbyteral government since presbyters needed to confer across boundaries. In turn, when the monoepiscopate emerged, this had to absorb responsibility for the common *diakonia* as well as for teaching and worship. It is quite in keeping with this early development that later we will see how much persons such as Cyprian of Carthage or Ambrose of Milan or Basil of Caesarea found that the oversight of Church possessions and their use for the needy was a part of their episcopacy. It is also unsurprising that in Rome, deacons were often ready choices for election to episcopacy, given the prominence that they had in the life of communities and cities.

Though social and culturing settings influenced the role of bishops, with presbyters and deacons sharing a common ministry, we ought not to lose sight of the role that smaller units continued to play in fostering Christian identity, a common faith, and a shared discipleship. In these smaller units, presbyters, teachers, deacons, widows, and charismatics played their part, not precisely as representatives of the bishop but as his collaborators or colleagues/college. The place and influence of virgins is likewise not to be neglected.

For the most part, one would have to say that this early history of induction into lesser church offices reflects the difference between charges given through the laying on of hands and other forms of commissioning to specific functions. Despite the occasional presentation of a candidate to an assembly, or the use of a prayer of blessing, or an appeal to a biblical paradigm—these offices do not share in the understanding of ministry in and to the Church associated with ordination. Induction is by assignation to a task, rather than by an invocation of the grace of the Spirit, and for the most part the tasks concern the performance of cult rather than the service of the people.

The Church at Rome

We can pass on from these documents to what is otherwise known about the ordering of life and ministry in local churches or regions.[13] As mentioned, deciphering the early history of church ordering in the city and environs of Rome is problematic for early Christian centuries. It is hard to fit the evidence with the ecclesiastical or hierarchical reading often given to early Christian literature.[14]

For the early postapostolic days of this church, the letter of Clement to Corinth has often been cited in favor of the monepiscopacy and of the Roman primacy among the churches. In fact, the diffusion and practice of the Christian faith in Rome in apostolic and subapostolic times seems to have given rise to a number of culturally and ethnically diverse communities scattered around the city. The old *tituli*, or churches later dedicated to the cult of martyrs, probably represent the location of communities each ordered in its own way, though not without connection with other titles.

In some cases the life of these communities could be ordered on the model of household family codes or that of schools of philosophy that involved sharing some kind of common life as well as education. Some think that these communities of faithful were led by groups of presbyters or elders, with possibly the aid of deacons and other ministers. There are no clear prescriptions for the presidency of liturgical actions, but the description of liturgies given by Justin,[15] who gives no title to the one who presides, is read against this background, with the hypothesis that one or other of the presbyters would have taken this role. It is also surmised that the task of certain elders was to keep communion with other households, with one possibly serving as what might now be called "general secretary" (which would explain Clement's letter), from which emerged in time the role of bishop serving the whole city and its diverse communities. If this hypothesis is correct, it gives a new reading, as has been said, to the ordination rites of the *Apostolic Tradition*.

An early piece of evidence showing authority exercised by one person is the demand of Victor (189–199?) that all the city churches who wish to be in communion should observe the annual Pasch on Sunday and not on the day observed by Jewish communities. In a letter of one who is named and cited by Eusebius in his *Ecclesiastical History* (6.43)[16] as Cornelius Bishop of Rome writing to Bishop Fabius of Antioch in 251 CE, it appears that the Roman Church at that time had forty-six presbyters, seven deacons, seven subdeacons, forty-two acolytes, fifty-two exorcists and readers and doorkeepers, and fifteen hundred widows and indigent. Given that the era of persecutions is not quite over, this is quite an imposing list, and how accurate Eusebius was is open to discussion.

The letter of Cornelius predates the better-known papal decretals of the fourth and fifth centuries. Some development could take place because the Church was becoming a more visible society. Though persecutions had not come to a close, the Church from a community of worship and fraternal charity had begun to assume a position in the world, that of a more-visible and authoritative body, which needed the kind of structure that would uphold its place and influence. In the case of Rome, full commitment to the Church's administration is as much a reason why someone belongs to the clergy as is liturgical ministry or service of the altar.

In the post-Constantinian age, the position and rankings of the clergy developed into a system of ecclesiastical administration and a way of life.[17] The vision of the sacrament of order and of the ordered clergy as a hierarchy of office is clearly proclaimed in the writings of Leo I, who will be studied later, and in the ordination prayers of the collection called the *Leonine Sacramentary*, or the *Sacramentary of Verona*.[18] In the ordination prayer for the blessing and installation of a bishop, words that figure prominently are *cathedra episcopalis, auctoritas, potestas, firmitas,* and *dignitas sacerdotalis.* The very prominence of the cathedra, or episcopal chair, in the church building reflects the importance of his teaching office, something that, in the church of Rome, Leo associates with his succession to the office of Peter.[19] The words *auctoritas* and *potestas* were introduced into Christian vocabulary by Tertullian and Cyprian and became popular with bishops of Rome from Siricius onward. A distinction of meaning between the two words is not clearly definable, though the latter leans toward a more juridical conception of office and headship. Juridical power carried little weight if the officeholder did not possess moral influence and moral authority, an authority that might be enhanced by suffering in the name of Christ and in the service of the Church. When exercised in this fashion, and when the bishop is chosen or received by all the people, his teaching has *firmitas,* that is stability, efficacy, and endurance. This way of looking at the episcopal ministry retains a sense of its spiritual and charismatic origins or grounding. On the other hand, however, the juridical perspective of the office comes to the fore when its authority or power is compared to that of the emperor or his magistrates in the provinces. The authority to which Leo the Great lays claim, as we shall see, is primarily pastoral, not juridical, but elements of this are included. The bishop has to be conformed to the Good Shepherd, Christ, and must above all be a shepherd to his people who gives his life for them.

The hierarchical, or ranked, vision of the Church and of ministry appears in the ordination prayers for installation of candidates as presbyters and as deacons. The disposition of ministries and distribution of offices by ranking is praised as a work of divine providence, brought about through the wisdom, power, and word of Christ and foreshadowed in the types of the Old Testament. The presbyterate belongs in the second place after the bishop. Using the Latin terms *munus, gradus, dignitas, meritum,* presbyters were called *secundi sacerdotes* and cooperators in the ministry of the bishop, or were said to hold the *secundi meriti munus.*[20] The terminology used was taken from civic arrangements but adapted to signify a spiritual hierarchy. The scriptural types invoked are those of Moses and the elders, of Aaron, his sons, and the Levites, and the addition of other disciples to help the apostles in preaching the gospel. The choice of candidates is consistently presented as a choice made by God, though various rituals over time show that the consent of the people was asked in one form or another.

After the peace of Constantine, the role of bishop in creating a sense of community in one faith and one Eucharist was prominent. The actions for which he was responsible were the teaching of the gospel and of sound doctrine, the preparation of catechumens, care of neophytes, and reconciliation of penitents. To keep in communication with all the communities under their care, popes made use of stational liturgies, especially during the seasons of Lent and Christmas. By this time, most of the household churches had gone from being households to being titular churches, with Roman style basilicas as gathering places, over the tombs of its heroic martyrs. This cult of martyrs was something that helped unity since members of the faithful from other titles were drawn to the cult, especially of the best known such as Praxedes, Perpetua, Lawrence, and Sebastian, and of course of the church's founders, Peter and Paul.

Communion did not mean strict conformity since even festal liturgies like those of the Pasch and ceremonies of initiation had to be celebrated in presbyteral titles, not all following exactly the same order of celebration. More problematic was what to do with outlying communities, in rural areas. This vexed the mind of Leo, who did not favor the ordination of bishops for hamlets and villages since it would be contrary to the dignity that he thought a bishop should have, both for the sake of the faithful and for the sake of dealings with secular authorities.[21] When in time the rural areas around Rome were given their bishops, these were called suburbicarian churches, and the bishops were subject to the authority of the Pontifex, the Bishop of Rome. To our own day, some members of the college of cardinals are given the titles, if not the administration, of the suburbicarian churches.

All of this is evidence of a structuring and a restructuring, of an ordering and reordering, of the church of Rome, in the service of the one communion in faith and the one eucharistic communion. The concept of authority had to develop in the service of these needs, and the structures of authority made to minister to the royal priesthood of the Church. Within the structuring of the household of the faith, Rome like other churches attached importance to the household of the clergy as an ideal communion. Though this had its merits in assuring quality, as elsewhere it was a wedge between priests and people. With Leo the Great and those who come after him, and in the ordering of the *cursus honorum*, we see the tension between the primacy of the community of faith and worship and the hierarchical conceptualization of ministry. On the one hand, the fundamental image of the Church as one body and one royal priesthood, enriched by the gifts and ministries given to it, remains. On the other hand, the hierarchical ordering of ministry is seen as a measure of divine ordinance, whose meaning is embodied in scriptural types of Old and New Testament.

The name of *cleric*, earlier a generic name for everyone holding ecclesial or liturgical office in a community, became a word to designate a state in itself. In Rome, this state was acquired by anyone who was accepted into the papal service, provided that he in turn accepted the duties of the office and its way of life. From being tonsured, which became the normal process for becoming a cleric, one could hope to ascend along the scale of honors to the higher rungs. The *cursus honorum* of clerical service assumed a physiognomy quite similar to that of the civil service. Finally, it became practice, and even law, that anyone in the service of the papal household and the administration of the Church should be a cleric rather than a layman.

Judging from the medieval *Ordines Romani* on papal ceremonial, however, it appears that the odd layman remained around the papal household as a servant in less intimate relation to the papal person, or perhaps working in the notary office or the treasury. Since in time most of these functions were taken over by clerics, the lay incumbent became a rather rare breed. The majordomo, officials in the treasury, notaries, and defenders of the papal person—these being officers whose services were required by the expanding business of papal administration—did not have to be clerics by nature of their offices, though they seem to have often been clerics from the time of Gregory onward, thus from quite early in the history of such offices.

The reasons why at first conjugal abstinence and later celibacy were imposed on those in major orders were related to the need for their freedom in serving the church to which they belonged, to their sacramental ministry, and to the expectation of a congruent life of prayer. It was the hope that only those would be ordained to these offices who fitted the high expectations that required that men be put to the test in lower ranks before acceding to the higher.

As far as the place of women in order is concerned, a letter of Gelasius I is cited as evidence that some exercised the priesthood. While it seems to indicate that diverse opinions and practices existed on this matter even at this date, it is also evidence that the church of Rome entertained the common prejudices of the era, and this practice was not deemed acceptable. The reasons given may appeal to biblical traditions which show a divine ordering of both covenants that gives leadership to men, but more fundamental is a generally negative attitude toward women. In 494, writing to the bishops of southern Italy, Gelasius professes himself chagrined to learn that "women are encouraged to officiate at the sacred altars," thus usurping a role which is that of males.[22]

Considering the place of the body of the Christian faithful, we see that their lives were ordered according to the liturgical and temporal seasons of the year, with a growing stress on all doing penance, so that this is not simply a matter for penitents seeking reconciliation. To be engaged in penance by prayer, fasting, and almsgiving is a collective work, an act of common worship to be offered in the Eucharist, with the gifts of bread and wine and with praise. This is given a place in the liturgical cycle, first for Lent but also for the Quarter Tense observances of June, September, and December. The kingship and priesthood of the baptized, which gives them their organic and sacramental role in the Eucharist, works itself out in life in doing constant acts of penance, striving to do all year what they do more intensely in Lent. This helps to define the relation between pastors and faithful since the bishop as pastor supervised the discipline of penance.

Ministry in National Churches: Armenia and Ethiopia

Well before Charlemagne established a Christendom in which there was a convergence of civil and ecclesiastical rule to create one cohesive society, something of this nature existed in Armenia[23] and Ethiopia,[24] with implications for the forms of ministry and ecclesiastical institution. Both churches were founded by married lay persons who, while working as officials of royal regimes, spread the Christian faith, first by their witness and then by their preaching. The church owes its origins in Armenia to the Cappadocian Gregory, whose name is known to posterity as Gregory the Illuminator or Enlightener, and in Ethiopia in the kingdom of Aksum to Frumentius, native of Syria and known to posterity as St. Abuna Salama, meaning Father of Salvation. In both cases, their wives were partners in their ministry. Some Christian communities existed before these two apostles, but it was due to their influence that the Christian faith was more widely acknowledged. In both cases, their work resulted in the establishment of Christianity as the official religion. In 301, Tiridates III of Armenia was the first ruler to make the Christian faith the national religion. Somewhat later in the century, having long resisted Christian missionaries, King Ezana of Aksum embraced the faith as the religious practice for his whole domain.

In these two churches, the testimony of martyrs or confession under suffering was vital for the acceptance of the faith by royal personages. In both cases, mass conversions were the order of the day, sometimes a matter of people following their leaders, sometimes one of forced conversions. As a result, the work of evangelization of the already baptized had to be undertaken by means suited to that end. Since both men wanted their work consolidated in communion with other churches, they were ordained bishops, Gregory in Cappadocia and Frumentius in Alexandria, and sent back to Armenia and Ethiopia respectively. Other bishops (auxiliaries, or chorbishops) were appointed to work with them to continue the work of evangelization. Evangelization could be undertaken by lay persons, but ecclesial communion required having bishops.

The style of episcopacy that Gregory and Frumentius and their companions embodied was modeled on the activity of the apostles in the book of Acts. They were sent to preach the gospel and establish eucharistic communities. To better serve this purpose, presbyters and deacons were ordained to work with the bishops in serving local bodies of faithful. However, the witness and influence of monks (men and women) and holy men did much in the subsequent rooting and inculturation of the faith. The recognition of their place in the Church may be considered part of the ordering of ministry.

In grounding the Christian creed among the people, some of the elements of pre-Christian religions were incorporated into Christian practice.[25] On certain occasions priests offered animal sacrifices, and this was considered part of their official duties. Such sacrifice preceded the eucharistic offering and was done outside the church building. Such sacrifice seems to have had a relationship to the Eucharist, which is akin to domestic meals of fellowship or to the offering of fruits, olives, cheese, wine, and bread in Western and Eastern communities. What animal sacrifice signified was a relation to the past, to a spirit world, and to the earth, which gave of its fruits and flocks. At least in Ethiopia, the Judaic doctrine of creation may have served to integrate such elements into Jewish and then into Christian religious observance.[26]

Another practice inherited from cultural tradition was that priesthood was passed on from father to son for some time. An outcome of this was that the ordained lacked the kind of education that came from schooling. Hence, in the service of the Church, educated laypersons were essential to the ministry of Word, and religious services were not conducted without them. In Ethiopia, these lay persons bore the title of Debtera.

To see how these churches were served and ordered, it is not enough to note that they had bishops, presbyters, and deacons. There was also the more varied ministry provided by holy persons, by monks, and by educated laity. One has to note how all ministry was affected by the political and religious situation of the societies that were evangelized and converted to Christianity. Frumentius and Gregory, together with the kings whom they served, saw their mission as one not only of converting people but of transforming the whole social and religious fabric, and this affected their views of ministry and the kinds of ministry introduced or adopted.

Church of Gaul

That the church of Gaul[27] at that time was still figuring out the exact roles of its ordained members, or clergy, comes across in reading the canons of the Council of Arles, held in 314.[28] Though this council was convened to deal with the Donatian controversies in North Africa, it made some rulings for the clergy in Gaul. The distinction between clergy and the rest of the baptized seems well established, but the exact place of the orders is not so clear, and there may have been differences over questions of status. Deacons are told not to "offer the sacrifice," which some of them must have been doing, and not to claim superiority over the presbyters (canons 15, 18). Presbyters are admonished to remain in the churches for which they were ordained and not to seek other incumbencies (canons 2, 17, 21). Bishops are told not to interfere with the rule of their neighboring bishops, though visiting bishops were to be treated with courtesy and even allowed say the thanksgiving at the Eucharist.

Once the era of persecutions was over, the ideal bishops proposed to following generations were Martin of Tours and Gregory of Tours. Martin was considered an ideal for a number of reasons. He was made bishop by the choice of the Holy Spirit, the precise method used being that of casting biblical lots (a random choice of a biblical text, which is read as a sign) and the voice of the people. Martin was a monastic founder who supported this ideal style of Christian living. He was an apostolic preacher who spread the gospel throughout the territory confided to him, giving authenticity to his teaching by working miracles. He played a large part in overthrowing pagan cults, destroying pagan sanctuaries, replacing them with Christian churches, and fostering the cult of saints in places of worship that had been dedicated to pagan gods.

During the period between Martin and Gregory, the link between city and countryside and between bishop and presbyters took on a specific pattern. There was the cathedral church in the city, where the bishop lived with his household of clergy. The bishops set up village churches, which were staffed by priests, deacons, and other clergy, all under the supervision of an archpriest (or chorbishop?). Practicing a common life in their own households, the bishops themselves went out around the territory that they served, to preach and teach, to visit the sick, to give the sacraments and perform other required rituals.

Church buildings and sanctuaries were also established on large estates and administered by landowners. In principle, these did not have resident clergy but were to be served from the village church. In practice, landowners over time liked to have their own priests ordained to work under them on their estate. These were poorly educated, often lived with female consorts, and had sons and daughters. They were looked upon quite often with a certain amount of opprobrium, giving rise to the derogatory term *homiunculus* (weakly man), used in the eighth century by Agobard of Lyons. Many times church synods and councils were intent on reining in these ministers and monitoring their way of life, but it was hard to countermand the landowners' claims to resident priests and other clergy since they controlled the wealth of the rural regions.

Four principles seem to be at work in this ordering of churches or dioceses. First was the constant need to spread the gospel and then make it take firm root by sound teaching. Second was to look to a distribution of places of worship and of clergy that would best serve the needs of the faithful. Third was the establishment of households that image the ideal Christian life, this being either monastery or clerical chapter. Fourth was the desired connection between being a minister or pastor and living the ideal life, so that the principle of common life for the clergy was affirmed.

The old Gallican ordination rites that we know from the *Missale Francorum* and the *Statuta ecclesiae antiqua*[29] of fifth-century Gaul reflect the pastoral arrangement of churches. In the two books the lists of offices differ somewhat but for the most part are similar. Besides the ordination rites for bishop, presbyters, and deacons, among offices for which there is an installation ritual are acolytes, porters, and exorcists. The subdeacon makes his appearance in the Missal as an office of transition whereby one moves from the lesser orders to the higher, since those ordained as such were apparently candidates for higher orders. Other services mentioned, but for which there is no installation rite, are those of the psalmist and of the widows and holy women who assist with the baptism of women.

Frankish Kingdom

One cannot finish with developments in the first millennium north of the Alps without taking note of developments in the Christian Empire from Charlemagne onward and the attempts at the Romanization of the new converts to Christianity.[30] The mission undertaken was to convert a whole populace and a whole civilization to Christianity, using even coercion to this purpose. In what happened, we can identify the confluence of several forces.

As frequently noted in history, Charlemagne desired to establish a unified rule among a variety of peoples and to assume an imperial role under the title of Holy Roman Emperor, at the service of the spread of Christianity. He was probably influenced by the part played by religion in the success of the Islamic Empire, whose advance northward had been arrested by Charles Martel at Poitiers in 732. One of his notable actions was taking the first step in bringing the Roman liturgy to all areas of his rule. Once the Roman books were available, he did not take a direct part in the formation of ritual, but the clerics of his empire served his purpose of finding common ritual activity to undergird a cultural, social, and religious unity.

In the cultures of Nordic peoples, it was almost a given that when a leader converted to the Christian faith, all his followers would do likewise. This changed the format and purpose of pastoral ministry: in earlier times it would have been taken for granted that conversion in faith and morals had taken place before baptism, but now this was no longer the case. As a result, much energy and strategy had to be put into devising appropriate forms of ministry. This is where, for example, the use of frequent penance and of penitential books has to be placed: penance was put at the service of a deeper conversion of those who had been baptized without much preparation or any clear change in moral behavior.

Cultural ways of viewing world and human society and of self-expression left a mark on ministry and order. The religious outlook and wants of the Germanic peoples had to be satisfied, and in their own way the common people foisted these upon their civil and religious leaders, who felt it needful to accommodate them if they were to be truly won to Christianity. Socially, the mass of peoples were accustomed to a life within a system of vassalage, and this influenced their attitude to both priest and ruler. Religiously, they had a strong sense of communion with the dead and of dependence on nature. They wanted to satisfy the need to render these forces beneficent through ritual practices. Though an approach to liturgy as drama had already made its appearance, both East and West, this was heightened by the sense of the dramatic, which had a big part in influencing how these peoples new to Christianity saw ritual activity and on how it was interpreted for them by some clerics. Devotion to the saints found a ground in their sense of communion with the dead, in a process of mutual benefit. In the saints, of whom there were abundant legends, they found intermediaries, and this brought relation to them far beyond the early Roman cult of martyrs and relics.

These peoples had confidence in the power of sacrificial mediation, and this contributed to the way of conceiving Christian priesthood. Clerics accommodated themselves to this vision, especially to the prevalence of the notion of sacrificial and mediating priesthood. Divines made more frequent appeal to the imagery of the priesthood of Aaron to explain their role, and this enhanced the vision of the Eucharist as a cultic offering more than a thanksgiving memorial. In practice, this meant an increase in Masses for the dead, beginning with the stipends that lay persons gave to monasteries to have their dead commemorated in conventual offices and Masses, or eventually in Masses privately celebrated. What started in monastic communities affected the attitudes and actions of regular clergy and enhanced their function as sacrificial priesthood.

In accommodating the devotional attitudes of the people, those responsible for liturgy added texts and rites to the Roman books, additions corresponding to their mentality. This cannot be called inculturation in any exact sense of the term, but at best one may speak of accommodation. There was no revision of the liturgy as such but simply the adjunction of new texts and gestures, composed in a more florid style. These include formulas for Requiem Masses or for the commemoration of saints and elaborate rites for the dedication of church buildings. The rites for Holy Week were given a more dramatic flow, and this too was in great part an accommodation to popular piety. Since accommodating cultural perception meant incorporating a strong desire for sacrifice and mediation, all of this accentuated the distinction between clergy and people. So too did the fact that it was the clergy who had access to books and who knew Latin, which was looked upon as the sacred language of ritual.

Overall we may remark on a new kind of collaboration between *imperium* and *sacerdotium*, between ruler and priest, in the service of Christianity's spread. With Charlemagne and his sons, the respective roles seem to have been clearly enough delimited, but with the breakdown of the empire and the succession of petty kings, lords, and landowners, lay persons of substantial standing encroached on the work of the clergy. This gave rise to a rather disastrous situation, of which even schoolboys learn when they hear of the controversies surrounding lay investiture.

Spain

A word about Spain may be added to these considerations on the church in Gaul, since in Spain rather similar positions are found in the development of Christianity that supported a particular way of relating spiritual rule and temporal rule.[31] The kind of Christian belief that took hold in the Iberian peninsula among the Visigoths was Arian, and this was supported by an assortment of temporal rulers. Spain was unified as one kingdom under Leovigild (570–585) but still held to Arianism. In unifying his kingdom, Leovigild evoked old Roman traditions of rule and located a permanent central government in Toledo, where he built a church to which central ecclesiastical authority was confided. Under his successor, Reccared, Spain converted to orthodox Christianity, espousing the Creed and authority of the Councils of Nicaea, Constantinople, and Chalcedon. The influence of Isidore will be seen later, but as of this time, there was need for an educated clergy. This was not always assured, but its promotion is what separates the clergy from the rest of the populace and fits their role of serving religious uniformity within the unity of the one kingdom, under a king whom Isidore described as the Lord's Anointed.

Ireland and England

Celtic peoples today often bemoan the abandonment of early Celtic forms of Church order and piety.[32] No doubt a big change was made in Church life and piety when a Roman type of religious practice and organization was imposed, with the coming of the Normans and through the efforts of Rome's emissaries, such as Malachy, who though born in Ireland sought authorization for monastic and episcopal rule from the Bishop of Rome. Historically and in light of the possibilities of ecclesial diversity, this background needs examination.

After the evangelization of Ireland by Saint Patrick, probably in the wake of less successful forerunners, the principle of episcopal governance was established. The ideal of monasticism, however, was quickly taken up, for both women and men, with a quite wide foundation of monasteries under the patronage of local kings and Celtic holy persons, male and female, belonging to their lineage. Rather than a radical departure from Patrick's establishment of the church throughout the country, this development seems to have had its roots in his way of evangelizing and in its successful accommodation to Irish custom and culture. Social roles and exchange between communities among the Celtic peoples were regulated to a great extent by the exchange of gifts, which could include property, vassals, and land. Patrick apparently was able to fit his proclamation of the gospel into this manner of life: in exchange for the gift he brought of faith and teachings, he was given patronage and land. This gave the church ties to the social order. In return for the church's ministry and spiritual patronage, it received tenure, land, and gifts of various kinds. When there was a massive foundation of monastic establishments, male and female, this was put under the patronage of royal families, inclusive of the protection of saints who belonged to royal lineage, as hagiographies were at pains to depict. In return, the local kings and their people were clients of the monastery, seeking spiritual benefits.

Since monasteries were endowed by kings and princes with abundant land, this meant that many of the baptized were under the pastoral care and jurisdiction of abbots and abbesses. They were even called *manaigh*, which is the Gaelic rendering of *monks*, if they lived and worked on the land of the monastic foundation. A monastic form of ecclesiastical government thus prevailed over the episcopal, and the bishops and priests who served places of worship on their lands were members of the monastery. They lived and worked under the jurisdiction of its head, be this man or woman, lay or cleric.[33] The relation between the monastery and its clients, and so between church and its clients, was not so much one of subordination as of reciprocity, according to the custom of gift exchange. The dark side of this arrangement was that the conversion of some of the Irish to Christian life was not very deep. Especially the warrior classes and princely leaders continued a way of life that did not conform well to the gospel, but they were considered members of the church and in some way its partners. Maybe this is what led Bernard of Clairvaux in his life of Malachy to refer to the native Irish as *"magis bestiae quam homines* [more beasts than humans]." With the affiliation to Roman ways, little space was left for the earlier form of pastoral leadership and government, and for all the forms of spirituality and piety that went with it.

Among the Anglo-Saxons of the greater island of Britain, episcopal government was also established with the first preaching of the gospel, but there too much of the pastoral work gradually fell upon the shoulders of monastic foundations. However, the exact process of development is unclear, due to uncertain vocabulary. It appears that two kinds of household or ecclesiastical family were set up to promote the vital place of communal life in Christian perspective. There were monasteries of women and men following a rule of life, within which there eventually were some priests and clergy, and these households took on pastoral ministry in their surroundings. There were also clerical households after the manner of Augustine's foundation at Hippo, following out the principle that pastoral ministry needed to find its source in common life, prayer, and contemplation.

The writings of the Venerable Bede serve as some mirror to the Christian ideal. For all believers he wished some combination of prayer and the practice of virtue, and he talked as though all belonged to a household of some sort, be this the family, the monastery, or the clerical conclave. Preaching the gospel and teaching were foremost in his idea of what constitutes Christian ministry. It is teaching that earns a person the title of pastor, and in fact this pastoring role could be extended to lay persons. He says in one of his homilies: "As pastors are understood not only bishops, priests and deacons but also rulers of monasteries, also all the faithful who take charge even of small households should rightly be called pastors."[34]

Celtic Missions

When missionary monks from the islands went to the European continent, the Celtic way of disciplining a people through penance and spreading the practice of Christian life proved to be of importance in the work of the church on the continental landmass. Although the Irish monks have been sometimes credited with bringing private penance into the Church, this picture is more nuanced in recent studies. Other pastoral leaders also developed a more private penitential discipline in conjunction with spiritual guidance or direction, even before the arrival of these wandering monks. In assessing the influence of the Celtic monks, it is of note that the Celtic practice had a serious social and public dimension. To have sins shriven by a monk rather than by a bishop and to receive penance more than once in a lifetime did not mean easy absolution. The rituals that have come down to us were quite elaborate, and the penances were long and severe, so that there was no cheap grace involved. The aim within the Irish church and then within Europe was twofold. First, this discipline could guide some to a more perfect way of life and so constitute a spiritual elite, which lived at the very heart of all Church order, be they cleric or otherwise. Second, in dealing with the less worthy, it set boundaries to an otherwise undisciplined way of life.[35] Sins like murder and physical cruelty, or the abuse of women, married and otherwise, or physical relations with beasts were in some measure controlled in this way among peoples whose conversion to Christian life was always tenuous. Even less grave matters such as poor and disagreeable hygiene could be in some way disciplined by the imposition of less severe penance, such as some time of fast for eating scabs off one's own body or for gluttonous eating and drinking. All of this had something to do with fostering a way of life more appropriate to the gospel than the forms of Christian observance that followed from simple obedience to the will of temporal kings and lords. In organizing ministry, there is need to consider to whom it is directed and what are the suitable ways of fostering obedience to the gospel.

Conclusion

This overview of the formation of Church order brings several things to our attention. First, there are many different roles and offices in a community, and ordering has to do with them all, not only with the clergy. Second, there is diversity in the way matters worked out from region to region, and the material gives some insight into reasons behind particular options or developments. Third, given the fundamental reality of the community as a whole, some understanding is found as to how and why the division between clergy and laity came about. As mentioned in the introduction to part 2 of this book, one has to be circumspect in appealing to divine origin or institution. The ideal was a perfect community of discipleship, serving its membership and allowing for a Christian witness suitable to each locality. But there also were power struggles and rather human motivations at work. Ordering lent itself at times to compromise, inasmuch as there was a strong alliance between religious discipline and political or cultural ideals. Discernment as to whether the patterns that evolved best suited fidelity to the apostolic witness and tradition is necessary. As ministries and orderings in the first millennium were configured to cultural and regional diversities, so one would expect patterns today to be adjusted diversely across the globe, while taking care to avoid the less acceptable currents noted.

7

Significant Figures and Writers

To complement the overview of how churches were ordered, the purpose of this chapter is to focus on some significant bishops and writers to get at the meaning of what was done. In their words is a mixture of the practical and the theological, which helps us to get beyond the institutional development of order to the reasons that underlie it and to a broader picture of ministry. A generally chronological order is tempered by attention to regional differences, especially those between East and West.

Letters of Ignatius of Antioch

The story of Ignatius of Antioch and his letters is one that fits into the story of a small church living amid a plurality of religious cults and always at risk of persecution and martyrdom.[1] Though their authenticity has of late been called into question, it is possible to take the seven letters attributed to Ignatius of Antioch as a body of texts that show the development of Christian teaching and organization in Asia Minor in the early second century. They are usually dated between 105 and 115 C.E.

In Catholic teaching of yore, it was wont to point to these letters as evidence of an early monoepiscopate and even of the primacy of the Roman Church, given the salutation to her "who presides in the place of charity." However, the ecclesial developments in question are somewhat more complex and should in all likelihood be associated with the early existence of some form of house church. It is within the communion of the house church that ministry and office developed. This is natural enough, given that such a type of gathering, with its elements of common life, would readily support a style of leadership that allowed one leader to stand out in prominence among others.

All of the Ignatian letters, save that addressed to Rome, support the authority of one bishop in a given area, who governs along with the elders or presbyters and the deacons of the community. It is not to be supposed that this type of ecclesial leadership was taken for granted at the time of Ignatius. It seems rather that, given the existence of more than one house church in a locality, the letters give support and legitimation to having but one bishop whom all acknowledge, lest there be division on matters essential to faith and tradition. Since Ignatius appears to allow for more than one eucharistic assembly in the churches of Asia Minor whom he addresses, his accentuation of the authority of a single bishop does not mean that all the faithful gathered of a Sunday in one household. If there were more than one gathering, this accounts for his ruling that others may preside at the Eucharist but that no Eucharist should be held without the authorization of the bishop. In the exercise of his authority, it is quite clear that this bishop needs to rule together with the presbyters and deacons, who should also have the reverence of the faithful.

The personal charismatic authority of Ignatius, be he the author of the letters or not, has a large part to play in advancing this style of ministry. Those who receive the letters appear to have welcomed him in person and his correspondence with considerable piety and zeal, on account of his personal holiness, teaching ability, desire for martyrdom, and presumed link with John, apostle and evangelist. His concern to have but one church in an area and so but one bishop was moved by his wish to assure the purity of faith in following the one apostolic tradition. It seems probable that, in this era of persecution and of still unsettled doctrine about Christ, the different households and their leaders varied in their teaching. Ignatius suspected some of them of what is now called Docetism, a teaching that in its formulation put the veritable flesh of the Son of God into question. The insistence on one Church, one Eucharist, and one bishop is all in support of unity in faith and of harmony in the common life.

The Ignatian letters use several strategies to promote episcopal rule. These include an appeal to Ignatius's own witness, to that of the elders (in the Johannine tradition), and to a theological model on which to base the legitimacy of the bishop, presbyters, and deacons. This incipient theology compares the authority of the bishop to that of the Father, of the presbyters to that of the Twelve, and of the deacon to that of Christ the servant, about whom the Johannine communities would have known the story of footwashing. In sum, in these letters we can recognize the priority of the one communion of all believers in the faith of the one apostolic tradition about Jesus Christ. This entailed respect for the oneness of rule and the oneness of the eucharistic assembly, at which the faithful are fed of the very flesh of Christ, about which dissenters of other gatherings were ready to doubt.

In a recent article, Allen Brent offers an interpretation of Ignatius on bishops, their presbyters, and their deacons that places the imagery of his letters in the context of pagan cultic processions.[2] Brent agrees with the opinion that Ignatius does not offer a theology of apostolic succession as that has come to be understood. What he does do is give symbolic character and force to the place of the bishop, and with him the presbyters and deacons, in the celebration and communion of the eucharistic liturgy, and thus in the whole life of the Church. All the members of the gathered community are meant to image together the reality of participation in the mystery. The ordained ministers, however, have a special symbolic role that assures this participation for those who remain in communion with them. As it were, they in a particular way represent what all are meant to participate, that is, communion with the Father, Jesus Christ, and the apostles, who gave the original testimony to Jesus Christ. This interpretation would show a theology that is supportive of a distinction between clergy and laity but one that depends totally for its meaning and effectiveness on their presence within the one fundamental reality, that of the communion of all in the mystery of Jesus Christ, which has a sacramental basis in the celebration of the one Eucharist.

Irenaeus of Lyons

The city of Lyons was an important Roman city in the second century of the common era, ethnically and culturally diverse because of the confluence of various peoples.[3] It is said religious cults there are indications of the observance of Asian, Celtic, and Roman rituals. In the midst of this, the Christians were a small population, rather unique in their domestic and nonsacrificial style of worship.

When Irenaeus became bishop, there were several issues to be addressed in his leadership of this church. He and his fellow Christians lived in a time of intermittent persecution, and he held up the martyrs who were remembered in the community as models of fidelity to Christ. He was also ready to give recognition to various spiritual gifts among the people and allow them expression as signs of the Spirit's presence in the Church. In doing this, however, he had to face the fact that among Christians there were gnostic influences. Some gatherings that he saw as gnostic followed their own manner of worshipping Christ based on the persuasion that material creation comes from an evil principle and that the Old Testament is to be repudiated by true believers.[4] In facing what he saw as error, Irenaeus sought ways to guarantee fidelity to the apostolic tradition, which comes from the disciples of Christ. In his time this was in part realized through reverence for some of the immediate followers of these early disciples, who were recognized as elders in the Church.

In keeping with reverence for the martyrs, among living leaders Irenaeus includes confessors, that is people who had suffered for the faith, even if not to the point of death. The offices to which males alone were appointed were those of the bishop, who had to be chosen by all the faithful, presbyters, and the deacons. There is no indication in his writings of a paradigmatic distinction in status between clergy and the rest of the faithful.

In teaching and writing, Irenaeus's main concern was to keep alive the apostolic tradition, or the true faith and creed and practice of worship among the people. For this reason he gives importance to the churches of reputed apostolic foundation and most of all to Rome, founded by Peter and Paul. In doing this, he guarantees the communion of the church of Lyons with other churches, since all wish to hold to this one faith. His listing of the leaders of the Roman church is always a bit puzzling to scholars, first as to its accuracy and second as to its meaning. However, it clearly is not some special personal or official authority of these men that is the issue but their handing on of the faith and of the tradition that comes from apostolic times. The Roman Catholic Church and its theologians have tended to find early origins of a later idea of the apostolic succession of bishops in this text, forcing it somewhat. It is what is handed down that matters, but one expects fidelity in this from the revered leaders of so great a church.

In his book against the heretics, there is strong teaching on the place of the Eucharist in the Church.[5] It is an act of true worship, which Christ himself gave to his apostles, the only act of sacrifice to be celebrated by his followers and contrasting with the rituals of other cults. Irenaeus affirms that bread and wine, fruits of the earth, are offered to God in Christ's name, through proclaiming the prayer of thanksgiving over them: as he puts it, they are offered "with thanksgiving." The sacrament of Christ's body and blood, sanctified by the thanksgiving, is received in hope of the remission of sins, and in the eschatological hope of the resurrection of the dead, a belief fostered by the cult of martyrs. It is nourishment for mind and body, the gift of immortality and the forgiveness of sins. Made of a spiritual and material element, it is a sign and confirmation of the goodness and restoration of creation. It is also the guarantee of the communion and unity of the community. An important part of the bishop's role is to offer this sacrifice and nourishment within the community gathering. It is clear that the role of the bishop is taking shape, but in service to maintaining the apostolic tradition as the community's faith and in service to the sacrament of unity celebrated in their midst, which is the Eucharist.

Cyprian of Carthage

In North Africa, Tertullian (ca. 160–235) enunciated the idea of apostolic tradition in a way rather similar to that of Irenaeus.[6] Arguing against some heretics,[7] he says that an appeal to Scripture is never in itself sufficient, for it has to be asked to whom the Scriptures belong. The true knowledge of these writings is to be gained from the apostolic teaching or tradition. The original apostles, the Twelve, were sent by Christ to bring the gospel to the whole world, Jew and Gentile. They were sent as Christ himself had been sent by the Father. In spreading the gospel, they founded churches, and from these in turn came other churches. Into each new foundation there is made a transplant of faith, a sowing of doctrine. All genuine apostolic churches are then bonded together as one fellowship, in peace and mutual hospitality, through the one sacrament (or mystery or deposit, as Tertullian writes) of the apostolic tradition. In this work Tertullian says nothing of the teaching authority of bishops or other ministers but accentuates the faith in the one apostolic teaching that all churches hold together as apostolic foundation.

This is an interesting background to Cyprian's development of ideas of episcopal authority. Churches were considered apostolic because as communities they held to the apostolic tradition, reading the word of the Scriptures as passed on through apostolic preaching. The veracity of faith had to be tested by comparing that of each church with that of other apostolic churches. It was this need for an authentication of the faith of a church that eventually gave importance to the role of the bishop in teaching, since it was largely through their bishops that local communities could keep in touch with each other and discuss matters of faith.

Even before the time of Cyprian, whose death is estimated to have taken place in 258, Carthage was a wealthy North African city and a center of trading. As a result of this, it had a culturally diverse population. Even before persecution ceased, the Church had acquired a certain prestige, and its public appearance changed with the transition from using the house church as a place of gathering to making a Roman style basilica the place for worship. The shape of such a building and its interior disposition reflected the ideal of being a people of importance among other peoples, and it also served to separate clergy and the rest of the faithful.

However, the Church had not yet been assured tranquillity, and a major concern of Cyprian in his ministry was to be shepherd to a people facing the threat of persecution and the sufferings of martyrdom. Internally there were divisions, and Cyprian had to withstand the schismatic tendencies of the Novatians. His pastoral leadership was complicated by the fact that some saved their lives by a formal renunciation of the faith and yet in the aftermath wished to remain Christian disciples. The Church was divided over this question and the appeal to ideals which it aroused. In the wake of the rigorism espoused by Tertullian, some wished to see the Church as a communion that is pure in spirit and devoid of worldly ambitions. Even the confessors, those who had suffered for the faith but not unto death, had differing views. Some wanted to reconcile the lapsed through penance, others opposed this. Cyprian apparently tried to steer a middle course, taking the Church to be indeed a spiritual brotherhood but one ruled externally and strongly by a bishop and able to make room within itself for penitent sinners. The need to resolve the question of the lapsed in the interests of Church unity was an important factor in contributing to the authority of the bishop in the local church and in the communion of churches.[8]

From his correspondence, it seems that Cyprian was trying to do several things. He wanted first and foremost to help people face the perils of martyrdom, holding up for their example those who had suffered and died, preaching the resurrection of the dead, and offering the Eucharist as the food and drink that would sustain them in their hour of peril. He defended both orthodoxy and right practice. He had several quarrels over the latter with other bishops, but in the long run the Church's need for the bishops to mediate the position in the community of those reputed to have abjured the faith enhanced their standing.

One issue seems trivial, which is whether or not water is to be put into the wine for the Eucharist. It took on importance because of the attitude of some purists who thought sobriety a major virtue of the holy. These were the kind of people who believed in the small remnant of the truly holy. More important were the problems Cyprian had over baptism, the rite of incorporation into the Church, and over the reconciliation of the lapsed. In the first case, it was a matter of whether or not to accept the baptism given in schismatic gatherings, on which point he quarreled with Stephen of Rome. In the second case the issue was whether there was any hope of reconciliation for those who, out of fear, had renounced faith in Christ. Scholars have written the story of these disputes at length, but what is of note here is that Cyprian's concerns as bishop had to do with membership in the Church and the rites of annexation to it. If the Church is to be the community that is faithful in its following of Christ according to right doctrine and practice, how are its boundaries to be kept? How are the demands of fidelity and of compassion to be reconciled? What is the role of the bishop as pastor in these situations?

To help those held in prison, Cyprian allowed presbyters to celebrate the Eucharist outside the common assembly in order to guarantee them the nourishment of this sacrament when they most needed it. In his work as shepherd of the flock, he put much energy and time into the care of widows and orphans and the support of those who had suffered loss of property or wealth in times of persecution. In connection with the issues of faith, practice, and care of the people, Cyprian gave a strong profile to the role of bishop and contributed much to the emerging authority and doctrine of the episcopacy.

It is pertinent to see within what ways and in what set of relationship Cyprian exercised his ministry. His relation with other bishops is important. It is shown in his consultation with them and in the role he felt councils or meetings of bishops had to play to keep unity. Within his own local church, he believed the bishop to be supreme (he is described as an autocrat), yet the practical definitions given to the place of the presbyters and clergy are noteworthy, showing that he did not break entirely with a more collegiate style of government. While they helped him in ministry, they most of all needed to be consulted on several matters important to the ecclesiastical life. His consultations extended beyond the ranks of the clergy, for the people also were to be given their say, as in the choice of a bishop and on the reconciliation of some accused of having lapsed from fear. Even with this, the needs of some synodality in the life of the Church were satisfied above all through the body of the clergy.

In this way Cyprian fostered a growing distinction between clergy and people (*clerus* and *plebs*), but never a separation since all lived and worshipped together as one. He was very demanding of the clergy. If they were to exercise a spiritual leadership, they needed to give an example of what it means to be a follower of Christ. It is not rank that counts but the need for the small few in the midst of all the faithful, the few who could stand out as true followers and be capable of ministering to others. The few were to show forth in their lives what is expected of all, and their call to special ministry is attached to this role of being an example. One who himself is holy can be a leader among the holy people. When any presbyter deflected from this, Cyprian no longer wanted him in the number of the clergy.

Cyprian asserted that it is the right of a bishop to decide on the reconciliation of the lapsed. In this he set aside the influence of charismatic prophets and confessors in the life of the Church. Arguing for agreement between bishops on matters of doctrine and favoring councils, he made it clear that in what concerns the life of communities, the final appeal is to what is decided by the episcopacy. Though current argument for episcopal collegiality appeals to Cyprian, his position on the relation between the authority of individual bishops and the collective authority of councils is not too clear, but he did favor this way of all acting together in the interests of unity.

Alongside these positions on the rule of bishops, Cyprian gave them a higher and scripturally founded profile. This he did through his description of their liturgical role, for all authority is centered in the Eucharist. Using Old Testament imagery, like the author of *1 Clement*, he found that the ordinances for the priesthood of the Old Testament found fulfillment in the New. Within a social and cultural milieu where sacrifice and priesthood were important to Jewish and pagan religion, Cyprian gave a clear priestly and sacrificial understanding to the bishop's presidency of the Eucharist. There is, however, considerable nuance in this. There can be no question of a sacrifice to replace that of Christ or in the sense of repeated sacrifices. What the bishop offers are the thanksgiving and intercession of the eucharistic prayer, which claims the assent of all and the gifts of the people. In this he acts *vice Christi*, offering in submission to God's will as Christ offered himself at the Last Supper. It is thus within the celebration of the Eucharist, and especially in the thanksgiving prayer over the offerings, that the bishop acquires a symbolic role that accords him in a particular way the title of *sacerdos*, or priest.

For Cyprian, the spiritual qualities of a bishop were necessary to his sacrifice and to his leadership. If a bishop were to prove unworthy, he should be set aside. Though he supported two Spanish bishops whose case was placed before him when they were threatened with deposition, it is clear that for him it was indeed their spiritual worthiness and not some other issue of authoritative position that was at stake. Cyprian does not touch on the theological and canonical questions about ordination that surfaced in later centuries, but it is of note even for today how much authority and spiritual gift were inseparable in his eyes.

In establishing the foundations for the authority of the bishop Cyprian referred to Matt 16:18.[9] Drawing on concepts of Roman law, and by analogy with the Torah, he saw this text as a divine foundation for the episcopal office, which made of bishops successors of the apostles, with special authority in the teaching of true doctrine.[10] His right to the provision of sustenance by the community is integral to his authority and its legal provisions. In all of these positions, Cyprian in later centuries became an important figure to consider in establishing the foundations in tradition for the office and ministry of bishops. Paradoxically, because of his quarrels with schismatics and his differences with Rome, he is cited as one who favored a broad Catholic communion. Whatever differences Cyprian experienced with other bishops, he eschewed any notion of separation and schism from Catholic communion.

Lessons from Origen of Alexandria (ca. 185–254)

History and patristic studies recount the problems that Origen had as a lay teacher with Bishop Demetrius of Alexandria, but often enough the matter is treated with certain assumptions about how churches were ordered and about the authority of bishops.[11] One may learn from his story useful lessons about the slow procedure of ordering a church and about how charismatic and institutional leadership had to be coordinated. By assuming too much clarity on the role of bishops in his time, the tendency may be either to dismiss Origen as a difficult person of somewhat obscure doctrine or to rehabilitate him, as did Hans Urs von Balthasar.[12] The issues at stake have to be put into a historical context in which relations between persons in the Church were still being worked out.

First to be taken into account is Origen's teaching on gnostic wisdom, then his thoughts on the spiritual priesthood, and finally what he says about penitential discipline. In the light of this, one can grasp the sense of his criticism of episcopal leadership and the genuine issues that were at stake and in some sense recur even in our time.

His ideas of gnostic wisdom are found within what he says of the interpretation of the Scriptures and of the eating of the Word in the Eucharist. Origen is rightly seen as someone who was careful about the literal or exegetical meaning of the Scriptures but who also indulged in considerable allegorical interpretation. This latter is one with what he sees as the spiritual meaning of the Scriptures, and for him this has to do with the ability to comprehend revelation as a whole and thus the interrelationship of the parts. Only those gifted with spiritual insight could comprehend this full meaning, and these were the true gnostics or truly wise. Origen was concerned about what he saw as the general lack of spiritual perfection or commitment to the gospel among the general run of Christians, and so he intended much of his teaching for those who could and did aspire to spiritual perfection. He was also disturbed by an absence of spiritual leadership in men who, when appointed to office, relied on their authority and did not ground their service in true spiritual wisdom in guiding the faithful.[13]

In the Church, priority needed to be given to the spiritual priesthood and not to any vestige of cultic priesthood. The priests of the covenant of Sinai and all that is said of them in the Pentateuch were of interest to Origen inasmuch as he saw in them and their consecration and function a typology of the priesthood of the New Testament. This was not because they served as models for the leaders of the Church but because in the interpretation of their choice and service of the sanctuary, in the light of Christ or the fullness of revelation, one found that to which all followers of Christ are called. The priests of the order of Aaron were chosen by God and were totally dedicated to God's service. Anyone who is spiritually minded accedes to this priesthood and to the true sacrifice of an entire life that is made possible for all through the priesthood and sacrifice of Jesus Christ. In writing of celebrating the Eucharist, Origen gives parallel importance to the hearing of the Word and the communion in the body and blood of Christ. The ultimate call is to communion with Christ, which is symbolized in the eating and drinking of his flesh and blood. Without the spiritual understanding of the Word, this sacramental communion becomes a mere ritual.

It is only if they themselves live the spiritual priesthood and sacrifice that bishops are able to lead the faithful along this road. This has a particular application in what Origen wrote of penitential discipline, a role that he believed to be of great importance in the ministry of a bishop. The bishop has to be able to "eat the sins" of the penitent as Jesus did and has to be able to lead sinners on the way of reconciliation. Peter, he says in his commentary on Matt 16:13–20, is one of the spiritual elite who know the Son by the revelation of the Father, and that is why he is given the power to bind and loose. Any spiritual person can have a part in this ministry, but the spiritual quality spoken of is a prerequisite in the bishop, who exercises the public function of guiding penitential discipline and reconciling sinners. Origen did not question the need for order in the Church and for the ministry of the bishop. But he could not place confidence in bishops who lacked true wisdom, and he granted a role in leading others to anyone gifted with spiritual wisdom.

For much of his life, Origen was not appointed to office but exercised his call to teach as one of the faithful. He himself is thus an example of the leadership role that could be exercised on the basis of gift and competency, which in itself was not found problematic in the Church at the time. In his writings, he developed the teaching that all believers are equally called to New Testament priesthood and sacrifice. When it came to the call to office or leadership, he held that the one called needed to combine the exercise of office with spiritual wisdom, which was necessary to exercise leadership. On this basis he queried the exercise of authority by some bishops. Whenever ecclesiastical authority or the faithful rely simply on office and a call to obedience, the Church loses its moorings. That is as true today as at any time in the life of the Church. Seeing things through the lens of Origen is hard and difficult in practice, but it is something that the Church needs to learn and meditate.

Ambrose and the Church of Milan (ca. 339–397)

The service of Ambrose as bishop in the cathedral seat of Milan was confided to him by popular acclaim at a time when the position of the Church in society was changing.[14] The age of the martyrs had passed, though Ambrose employed a certain dexterity in keeping their memory alive through excavating the remains of Gervase and Protasius and building the cathedral church of the city over them. The Church now, and especially its leader, had to exercise a strong role in society in face of secular leaders, in order to safeguard orthodoxy against the visible intrusions of heresy and to promote good Christian morals among the populace. A strong pastoral leader was needed, and Ambrose's past experience in secular administration fitted him for the task, as well as his considerable erudition.

Ambrose portrayed the Church as the mystery of communion in Christ and in God. Structural and jurisdictional issues were secondary to this.[15] In his pastoral government, we are well acquainted with how he strengthened the catechumenate as the road to true Christian life and with his care for the newly baptized. The order of catechumens in the body of the Church was a sure sign of the need for authentic preparation. Incorporating them into the life of the Church through the liturgical cycle gave them visible presence.

It was clear that not all Christians lived the evangelical ideal of Christian community, so it was necessary that some groups in the Church provide this example. Ambrose was careful to keep to the fore the presence of the order of virgins and the order of widows, and he strongly advocated the practice of charity toward the poor. Working in this direction, he built a strong clerical body around himself, sharing his household and life of prayer. This was not primarily a matter of ranking or distinction in ethical demands and spirituality. It was, as with Cyprian, a way of assuring that the true form of Christ's following be kept alive in an exemplary body of young men, who would in time grow old in spiritual wisdom and be capable of exercising pastoral leadership. For this group, he offered his Christian ethical vision in the work *De officiis*.[16] This treatise was a series of instructions for all, but from its pages emerge the particular demands that Ambrose made on the clergy. From them, he wanted not only personal and individual honesty of life but also the example of true community, after the manner of the primitive Jerusalem household of the faith, in which they would be held together by the bonds of affection and mutual respect. Using his own Latin terms, one could say that they have to represent *amicitia* and the *forma iustitiae*, that is friendship in Christ and the very form of true Christian righteousness. One of the advantages of the episcopal household was that the existence of the holy few, offering an example of true Christian life, would not be located in some maverick and independent group but would be clearly contained within ecclesiastical order.

Although Ambrose wrote on virginity and valued the place of virgins in the Church very highly because of their realization of the ideal of Christian holiness, he totally excluded women from ordination by the laying on of hands. This was apparently because he subscribed to an idea of the weakness of woman's nature. Among other texts, we find this curious reading in his commentary on Luke when he refers to John 20:14 to speak of Mary Magdalene. When she is sent, he says, to bring the message of the resurrection to the Twelve, she is "elevated to male completeness." This was a common way for writers to show what baptism did for women, who by nature are inferior but are made equal to men by faith and baptism. However, even if Mary is thus elevated, as are all women by baptism, the order of nature must prevail in the distribution of offices. Having given her message, Mary has to yield to the apostles, who as men will more perfectly grasp the meaning of her proclamation, and this remains the proper order of things in the Church.[17] In this one sees the difficulty that ecclesiastical bishops and writers had in reconciling what they read in the Scriptures and what they believed to be the effects of grace with what they took from common learning and opinion about the human personal and social condition. Baptism would of its nature appear to posit the equality in Christ of all, without distinction, but ideas about the comparative nature of man and woman exclude the latter from apostolic ministry and from ecclesiastical office.

In the relation of the Church to society, there is a clear distinction in Ambrose's mind between the *ecclesia* and the *saeculum*, the Church and the secular world. Those who were of the Church were not to be preoccupied with the things of the world. However, the distinction is not watertight, and Christians were to mirror the ideals and forms of behavior that those in the world were to pursue. Ambrose played his own part in the politics of emperor and kings for the sake of the Church, but even if his flock and his clergy were not to take part in political and secular life, they were to exemplify the virtue that is the oil of a well-working state. In today's terms, one might say they were to give Christian witness in the midst of the world and secular occupations.

What we see in Ambrose is the ideal of a Church in which all the members are holy and live the life of the gospel. This not being the case in practice, procedures had to be adopted that would give a framework within which all might aspire to the ideal. In the course of setting this in place, Ambrose furthered the contribution of virgins and widows, but he likewise bolstered the distinction in ministry and the way of communal life between the ordained and the rest of the baptized, not in the name of a distinct spirituality but with the purpose of keeping the common ideal alive and visible to all.

Augustine of Hippo

Augustine exercised his ministry as bishop at Hippo, to which he was appointed in 396, at a critical juncture in the life of the North African church.[18] The time of persecution from Rome was at an end, and the threats of the barbarian hordes were still in the future. The church was emerging from its condition as a small and often tormented community and learning to take its place as an important institution in public as well as private life.

In this new situation, Augustine pondered the nature of the Church and the role of the Church in society, and this naturally affected his views on pastoral ministry.[19] By way of contrast with the Old Testament dispensation, which saw Jerusalem as an earthly city that was a sign of the city of God, the Church was to drop all civic aspects to its existence on earth. It is a community of sojourners, of those who belong to the city of God, looking to heaven as its goal. Nonetheless, the Church was to exercise an influence in society and seek the welfare of any earthly city of which its members were a part. It had a mission to all humankind, the concern for its spiritual well-being, and hence its pastors and its people have a part in temporal affairs, not for their own sake, but for the sake of building the spiritual reality of the city of God.

When Augustine was appointed bishop, the makeup of communities in North Africa was by no means clearly settled. Bishops were numerous and often jealous of their own place and people, though it is also on African soil that there is witness to the effort to settle relations and opinions through conciliar assembly. As living communities with their bishops in charge, churches often overlapped in territory as people belonged to bodies that followed diverse directions in living Christian lives in common. The way in which during or after persecution bishops were appointed and deposed, or in which rival bishops were set up in rival communities, reflects the rather varied way in which bishops were appointed and the part that the general populace had in naming them.

Donatist communities were probably in the majority among the Christians of the region.[20] They included their share of the rich and learned but exercised a particular attraction for the poor and for the Berber population. Their members, like those of the more Catholic community, had lived through the time of trial and wished to remain a company of recluses, as it were, who distanced themselves from society in the pursuit of holiness. They were still dealing with what they saw as the defection of some of their members who had failed the test of persecution and abjured the faith, offered sacrifice or handed over the Scriptures to officials as a sign of disavowal, yet wanted to be excused their failings or even reconciled to the community.

Donatus and his followers thought the only remedy to be rebaptism. Some wished to withdraw from the ministry of a bishop whom they found had at least compromised himself under questioning. In this they were not alone; even Cyprian had doubted the efficacy of sacraments celebrated by the unworthy. Historians still discuss why the Donatists eventually constituted a separate communion of churches while in previous quarrels among bishops and communities, reconciliation had eventually proved possible. It may have had to do with the continued opposition to the Roman Empire, the draw that attracted poorer inhabitants, the appeal to Berbers, the undoubted vision of a Church secluded from society, which they espoused, and the existence among them of social revolutionaries or fanatical groups. Most of all, it seems to have been because they refused reconciliation with the churches whom they considered to have betrayed the faith.

The Donatists felt affronted by a number of things in Augustine's teaching and practice. While preaching his own doctrine of withdrawal from the world, Augustine wanted to make the Church quite visible and important in civil society. Seeing the body of Christ made up in this world of saints and sinners, he reconciled the lapsed through a long period of penance but without rebaptism. He judged the Donatists to be outside the communion of charity and the communion of the Spirit because of their continued opposition to Catholic bishops, crystallized in their positions on reconciliation of penitents and their refusal to accept the sacraments of those who were not one with them and whom they judged to be unworthy.

As bishop, Augustine himself was troubled by the unworthy lives of some of the ordained, as we see from his sermon on pastors.[21] He likens them to shepherds who feed and clothe themselves from the sheep but do little to protect them or go after them when they stray. He asks himself what the people may expect from such pastors and offers the consolation that Christ is at work, whoever be the minister of word or sacrament. Augustine's theological solution to the question of baptism and rebaptism was to recognize the celebration of the sacraments by anyone rightly ordained, whatever his moral standing. This was because those rites expressed true belief in the mystery of the Trinity and invoked the name of Christ, which was thus imprinted upon candidates through baptism, though to enjoy the life of the Spirit, they needed to be reconciled with the Catholic communion of churches. He formulated his own policies and his vision of the Church, which in its visible structure could include sinners, not presuming to anticipate God's judgment in separating the saved and the unsaved. He worked out practical and theoretical issues of sacramental celebration and ecclesial belonging, and his resolutions had a lasting and powerful influence on Western theology and polity, though unfortunately in the course of the Middle Ages, his theories were transmitted in truncated and excessively juridical form.

Augustine's own experience helps us to understand how he wished to order the life of the church at Hippo. He himself knew the experience of conversion and its maturation through the process of the catechumenate. He was accustomed to life in community, according to the ideal of the early church of Jerusalem, as presented in Acts 2. Even during his catechumenate, he lived a common life with others, and then he was part of a garden monastery, which he left on being ordained bishop. He had learned to know and admire Ambrose of Milan and was attracted not only by his holiness and rhetoric, but also by his willingness to confront rulers and influence civil polity, if the interests of the Church required it.

Throughout the history of the Western church, Augustine was famed for his solution to the issue of upholding that baptism is given only once and for his teaching on the visible/invisible character of the city of God. Ecclesiastical politics were involved in the struggle between different communities in the one city seeking the allegiance of the faithful, and Augustine was not reluctant to plead his cause with vigor and even invective: was the Church to remain a withdrawn ascetical group, or was it to augment its numbers, be prominent in public life, and be the home of both sinner and saint?[22]

Some historians believe that the Donatist Church was closer to the people. Though it drew its membership from the rich as well as from the poor, its sights were set on the poor, to evangelize them and to assist them. Its leaders seem to have made considerable use of the Berber language in their preaching and even in the liturgy, though they often needed interpreters to bridge the gap in communication. Before Augustine, this was a strong influence on the fortunes of the gospel in North Africa, but the Donatists' incessant quarrels and their tendency to isolate themselves through such conflicts as that over rebaptism led to their communities losing influence so that gradually they dwindled in numbers. Nonetheless, historically one has to see that their way of being Church was a viable and alternative option to that of Augustine—if they had not been so fanatical and exclusive in their attitudes to others. Frend encapsulates the alternatives quite succinctly, seeing the Donatists and the way of the Catholics as two ways of being Church, two societies, two ways of relating to the present world:

> Donatism and Catholicism represented opposite tendencies in early Christian thought. . . . Did "Catholic" refer to the purity of sacraments, or to the extent of the Church over the inhabited world? Was the Church "within the Roman Empire," sustaining and sustained by the Christian Emperors, or was the Empire the representative of the outer "world," whence the Christian must separate himself in order to progress in the faith? Were social evils and injustices to be

fought in the name of Christ, or were they to be tolerated for the sake of Christian unity? To all these questions Donatists and Catholics gave different answers.[23]

Not harboring the ideals of the Donatists, Augustine was anxious to find a place within the larger empire for the Church and remained less culturally attuned to the Berbers. Nonetheless, in his own way he sought to remain close to all the people, as is often pointed out in citing the well-known quotation "I am a Christian with you, a bishop for you."[24] The vivacity of his pastoral supervision of the catechumenate and celebration of the sacraments of initiation appears in his sermons to neophytes. Repenting of their sins, they have entered a life of good faith and morals through the exercises of this ecclesial venture. They like flour have been moistened by the waters of baptism, baked with the fire of the Spirit, and laid upon the altar as a single loaf of bread.[25] When their offering has been consecrated by the thanksgiving of all the Church, they receive in communion that which they already are, the body of Christ. All through his episcopate, initiating newcomers into the body of Christ by these steps was a priority of his pastoral ministry.

Both through the ministry to his people and through his disputes with the Donatists, Augustine developed a theology of Church as a communion,[26] which focuses on the importance of those sacramental rites performed in the name of the Trinity, through which Christ himself acts, and on the animating fire of the life and love of the Spirit. To be in communion is to profess together the faith to which the ritual gives expression, to belong to Christ, and to live together in the communion of the Holy Spirit.

Augustine spoke as a leader who was one with the people through baptism, but who was appointed to lead them as bishop. He believed that bishop and presbyters needed to model the ideal Christian life for those whom they served. He expected all the clergy to live a communal life in the bishop's house and to follow the rule of life that he wrote for them.[27] This was the ideal basis and center for pastoral ministry.

What he intended is found in two sermons to the people of Hippo on the life of the clergy, occasioned by the scandal of a priest who made a will before he died, disposing of properties to which he claimed title.[28] In Augustine's mind, this was opposed to all that he held dear. A life of poverty, where none had any personal possessions, was the very ground of the kind of apostolic community that he wished the clergy to mirror to the faithful. Along with monks, they are the *militia* of the Church and ought to be to the fore in showing forth the true holiness of the Church.

In some of his sermons or catechesis on the sacraments, we also see how the symbolic role of the bishop develops in the course of sacramental celebration. Augustine gives a special role to the bishop in the "offering of the sacrifice" at the Eucharist. The sacrifice is the sacrifice of all, the sacrifice of the whole Christ, Head and members, as is said in the *City of God*.[29] Because he is the one who leads the people in the great eucharistic prayer and invites their participation, the bishop is said, in this particular way, to be the one who is offering the sacrifice. It is not only priesthood that is represented but also the bishop's presence among the people as the good shepherd, the one who makes Christ known in all respects. The people too are given their own sacramental representation in the bread and wine offered when they are brought to the altar and when they have been sanctified through the great thanksgiving prayer, and in their responses to the eucharistic prayer.

Though Augustine strengthened the role of clergy and their ideal form of life in the Church, he kept to the fore the image of the body of Christ as the whole community of the faithful. One example comes from his comments on the power of the keys given to Peter (Matt 16:18) as to what this means for the lay faithful.[30] They too share in the power to bind and loose, by their actions and by their prayers. In their actions they help to loose sinners from their burden and reconcile them to the Church, simply by how they relate to them; and in the liturgy they bring their needs into the prayer of the Church, so that the bishop does not act alone in the prayers and actions of forgiveness and reconciliation. What Augustine seeks of the laity in this aspect of Church life fits well with his eucharistic vision of the whole Christ, the *totus Christus*.

In his teaching on God's kingdom, Augustine was realistic about the composition of the Church if it were to embrace the masses of the population. Its visibility is necessary and is assured by a common faith, communal celebration, and the manifest holiness of its members. It is a family in which life is nurtured and sinners can find the way to progress in virtue. Using the image of the kingdom, to which the Church is witness, and of the body of Christ, Augustine allowed for three kinds of person in its organic communion. These are typified in the Old Testament figures of Noah, Daniel, and Job. Noah signifies Church leaders, Daniel represents contemplatives who are monks or hermits, and Job stands for those who labor in temporal things and are married.[31] From the point of view of the spiritual life and closeness to Christ, the life of contemplation is the ideal. Church pastors, though caught in the activities of serving the faithful, should strive through a rule of life to approximate the contemplative life. For the group of those who live in the world like Job, it is necessary to do everything for the reign of God, to contribute to the Church, and to await in hope the advent of the kingdom.

With his ambivalent relation to temporal realities, Augustine did not pursue the implications of using the image of Job to develop a spirituality for persons who engage in the affairs of this world. In his theology of history as spelled out in *The City of God*, there is a sense of divine providence that guides the story of humanity and protects the ecclesial community, but one cannot say that history is the work of God, since there are so many factors at work in mapping historical events. In any case, the body of Christ lives in the hope of the final resurrection and so need not be unduly concerned about the affairs of this world, except insofar as they guarantee the Church freedom of congregation and worship.

In the course of his controversies with the Donatists and the Pelagians, Augustine came to ruminate more and more on the human condition of sin and to defend his grasp of the sin in which all are born, and so of the constant sinfulness of human nature. To his flock therefore he preached on the need to be prepared for death and on the need for daily penance.[32] True, the catechumenate and canonical penance for those seeking reconciliation with the Church were still practiced at Hippo, but Augustine's theology and preaching led more and more to a vision of Christian life for all as a constant daily penance. His discourses on daily penance are many. Under that rubric he includes the recitation of the *Pater*, the giving of alms, the performance of works of mercy, fasting, and even the lifting up of hearts in penance in the Canon of the Mass. A leitmotiv of his pastoral leadership was to encourage people to this kind of penance, within the conception of life as a guard against sin and a preparation for death. Through their rule of life, monks and clergy practiced such penance and achieved other ideals of Christian virtue within the ideal Christian fellowship. The lay faithful, falling short of this ideal, needed to be led along the way of daily penance, even helping one another in this.

Augustine's ideas about clerical life and pastoral ministry had a profound impact on later Western order and thought. His rule was the model for the canons regular in the medieval church, who lived communal life precisely in service of good pastoral ministry. Some, such as Anselm of Havelburg, spelled this out in terms of the ideal conjunction between contemplation and action.[33] He located the origin of this in Christ himself as teacher, through a rather unusual exegesis of the texts about his visit to the home of Martha and Mary, or in his exegesis of the relation between Peter and the beloved disciple who rests on Jesus' breast at the supper and is the first to arrive at the tomb when hearing from the holy women. It is not John or Mary who model the true teacher, and not even Peter. It is Christ himself who finds room among his disciples for both the active and the contemplative, but also presents some ideal connection between the two. Anselm digresses somewhat from Augustine in all of this, but he keeps the same model pattern for the clergy, that is, to join together common life, contemplation of the mystery of Christ, and active ministry, especially that of teaching.

Several factors in Augustine's positions on the Church, its presence in the world, and its ministry continue even today to have their influence. There is his teaching on the body of Christ and the sacrifice of all the members together with their Head, a sacrifice that is the offering of the whole self and of every deed of mercy that leads to God. On the other hand, there is his fostering of a particular clerical culture and the separation of the clergy from the people, in an ideal community of sharing and penance. There is his preaching on the presence of Christ in the heart and mind of the baptized, the desire for God and eternity that is within the person, and the joy that he can put into the singing of an Alleluia in Paschaltide, but on the other hand, he exhorts to penance and stresses the need to do daily penance. There is his desire to serve the presence of God's kingdom in this world, but on the other hand he thinks that a believer should be fully caught up in the expectation of the kingdom that is yet to be revealed. How all this is to be sorted out in fostering a life in Christ of the whole body is, with all due temporal and social differences, an issue today as it was then.

Jerome and the Parity of Ministers (ca. 340–420)

It is not possible to turn from Latin Christianity without giving thought to how some worked out the differences between bishops and presbyters in a more egalitarian fashion. Given the transition from presbyteral rule to episcopal, it is not surprising that there were both practical and theoretical difficulties in working this out, and historians have found what is known in more recent writing as the Doctrine of the Parity of Ministers.[34] This doctrine or opinion was generated in an atmosphere of polemics. Substantially, it affirmed that episcopacy and presbyterate were originally the same order and that as far as the priesthood is concerned, they remain equal. The distinction between them is on the basis of authority, not on that of any difference in sacerdotal status, and is a matter of Church custom rather than of divine institution. The principal objective of the writers to whom this position is attributed was to defend the dignity and rights of presbyters, whether against the pretensions of deacons or the autocracy of bishops.

While the idea is most commonly associated with St. Jerome, he was preceded by an unknown writer, usually referred to as Ambrosiaster. This person wished to defend the Roman presbyters against the twelve deacons of that church, who apparently sought to exalt themselves above the presbyters. He proves the superiority of presbyters to deacons by showing that presbyters are equal to bishops insofar as the priesthood is concerned. In Paul, he argues, the names *presbyter* and *bishop* apply to the same persons, because there is only one order of priests. Not all presbyters, however, are bishops, because the bishop is the first of the presbyters and the high priest. The consequence of this is that though there are some functions, such as confirmation, normally reserved to the bishop, this is not of necessity, and when occasion demands any presbyter can perform them.

Jerome, too, was opposed to the pretensions of the Roman deacons, and most probably made use of Ambrosiaster in forging his arguments against them. Although he had a great influence over later theological developments, his own personal position is not without its inconsistencies and has been much disputed. In affirming the dignity and rights of presbyters, he starts from the fact that both presbyters and bishops can consecrate the body and blood of Christ, for this clearly shows that they are the same as far as priesthood is concerned. Because of this equality in the power to celebrate the Eucharist, he can only conclude that the presbyter can perform all the functions of a bishop, though he excludes ordination without giving any precise reason for this. Jerome also claims for them the right to preach and finds it autocratic of a bishop to deny this right.

His two principal arguments in support of the equality of bishop and presbyter are the way in which the names are used in the New Testament and the practice of the church of Alexandria, where the presbyters chose and installed one of their own number as bishop. This shows that there is no need of a new ordination when a presbyter is made bishop. The distinction, therefore, between bishop and presbyter is found in the order of authority and dignity, and Jerome sees the fear of schism and disunity as the reason why, at an early stage of the Church's history, one of the presbyters was elected to head the government of the Church. His practical conclusion was that bishops should closely associate the presbytery with themselves in the exercise of the priesthood, like Aaron and his sons, as well as in the exercise of government, following in this the example of Moses and the elders of Israel.

Whatever he may say about its origins as an office in the Church, Jerome refers to bishops several times as successors of the apostles. He also lays great stress on the role of bishops in keeping unity in the Church, and he never seems to question that only the bishop should ordain. In this, Jerome is a witness to the association between the episcopacy and the apostolic succession, and between the episcopacy and Church unity.

The fifth-century author of the treatise *De septem ordinibus ecclesiae*, which came down to posterity among the writings of Jerome, is even more explicit in affirming the rights of the presbyter to perform the same functions as the bishop. This treatise asserts that it is purely for reasons of the need for a clear authority that such functions as ordination of clerics and the consecration of virgins are reserved to the bishop. The reservation of such functions to the bishop is purely a matter of Church law and custom and not at all a matter of divine right.

Writers of the Church of Alexandria

Leaving developments in Latin Christianity aside, it is appropriate to follow up on the earlier considerations about Origen with a further consideration of ecclesiastical authority in Alexandria.[35] The historical accuracy of Jerome's claim about church government in Alexandria has never been fully verified, but it has a certain likelihood about it. By the fourth century, however, the choice of the bishop of Alexandria followed the more-common norm of nomination by the clergy, approval by acclamation of the people, and consecration by the bishops of the province.

It is said that until the time of the appointment of Demetrius, known because of the difficulties encountered between him and Origen, there were no bishops other than the bishop in the region of Alexandria, and that those who exercised pastoral care in the rural areas were only chorepiscopi to the bishop of Alexandria. Be this as it may, the bishop of Alexandria continued to exercise a controlling power in the ecclesiastical province, which also developed its own Coptic liturgy, built on the liturgical foundation known as the Liturgy of Mark.

We know quite a lot about the part played by some bishops of Alexandria as defenders and promoters of the orthodox faith. These are Athanasius, who waged battle against the Arians, and Cyril, who took on Nestorius and was an important figure at the Council of Ephesus (431). They were also important figures in the history of the church of Alexandria itself. In supporting the Nicene and the Ephesian formulations of the Creed for the entire apostolic catholic communion, they contributed to the importance of the Alexandrian patriarchate and the influence it would wield in the universal Church. Of Athanasius, it is also pointed out that in his own person and in his *Life of Anthony* he exemplified the importance for Egypt of an ascetic form of monasticism, which played a role in determining the forms that Christian community took in that region and even beyond its boundaries. At Nicaea, the rights of the bishop of the see of Mark over the bishops of Egypt, Libya, and Pentapolis were recognized. Athanasius's successors did not hesitate to pass judgment on the great see of Constantinople, as we know from the story of John Chrysostom. At Ephesus, Cyril's voice prevailed in formulating orthodox christological faith. Somewhat later, in 455, Proterius was able to resist Leo the Great's effort to establish a common date for the observance of Easter.

There is something ironic about Cyril's dominance at Ephesus because much of the later resistance to the Chalcedonian formula in support of what is called Monophysitism came from Alexandria. In the developing political context in which the Christian emperor was trying to subordinate the provinces to Roman rule and uniformity in all matters, civil and religious, this is comprehensible not only as a doctrinal matter but as a question of political and ecclesiastical autonomy. The church of Alexandria in effect gave support to the ideal of national and cultural autonomy and is an illustration of how, in times of conflict, the Church may support a people's proper autonomy. As E. Hardy puts it, the story of the church of Alexandria up to the time of Muslim invasions is "on the whole a glorious story of resistance to either pagan or officially Christian imperialism, and a valuable exhibition of the strength and limitations of a predominantly national form of Christianity."[36] Not only in its history but even today, the patriarchate of Alexandria is a monument to the reality of a church province with its own local center, within Catholic communion but able to make its own decisions in matters of doctrine, government, and worship. Recent accords between Rome and Monophysite Churches show some slow realization of the possibility of diversity within a universal communion.

Cappadocia and Basil of Caesarea (ca. 330–379)

Basil of Caesarea presents a follow-up on the positions of Ignatius of Antioch in a very different religious and social setting. His story shows what became of the ideal of a single bishop in a single church.[37] Ignatius was striving for the recognition of this model while Basil could take it for granted, and take for granted indeed that a bishop carried considerable prestige in society as well as in the Church. Those passing on the faith, and especially bishops, could no longer have their teaching and authority related to their personal witness under persecution or in death as sign of its authentication. The demands of spiritual wisdom put forward by Origen still needed to be satisfied if their authority were to stand test.

On how Basil lived, how he ruled his church, and how he was regarded by the faithful, we have much information from the funeral oration of Gregory of Nazianzen, even after making allowance for the rhetoric of piety.[38] In the first place, Basil's family standing and lineage was not lacking in importance, showing us that social prestige was not without significance in the exercise of ecclesiastical authority. It is apparent that he was a very busy man, ruling his flock in every matter of moment, from good liturgy to sound and impressive teaching to oversight of the works of charity, as these exhibited Christian concern for the poor and needy. Gregory makes evident the primordial role of Basil's personal holiness, of which there is evidence both before and after his election to the episcopacy. The new witness that took the place of fidelity in suffering under persecution is a way of life that has its ideal in monasticism.

Gregory's own ideal of episcopacy is known to us from his apologies. Gregory himself had resigned his bishopric, experiencing great difficulties in its exercise and finding himself in danger of being cut off from a life of contemplation due to the demands of his office.[39] As far as he was concerned, spiritual purification and contemplation of divine mysteries had to be the ground for a bishop's ministry; if this was impossible to him, he could not be a pastor. Pursuing the idea of a spiritual sacrifice and priesthood that we have found in Origen, Gregory saw the bishop as a priest, a teacher, and a leader of the community of faithful. The ideal of spiritual perfection was one to which all ought to aspire, but only one who did indeed pursue it could be a leader of a truly spiritual communion.

From the apologies of Gregory, it appears that at that time clericalism in its worst forms was rife. For their standing in the Church, some relied simply on their office and led lives quite unbecoming the role of shepherd. Against that kind of clericalism, Gregory and Basil brought the influence of monasticism into the forging of a clerical lifestyle: rather than office or status, holiness and erudition should distinguish the pastor from the flock, the clergy from the people.

There is evidence enough in his personal writings and correspondence that Basil himself saw matters this way. The monastic life already flourished, and he himself contributed a monastic rule. Monks, though unordained, exercised considerable influence among the people. In choosing clergy from monastic communities and being persuaded that only good monks make good bishops, Basil was not without political astuteness since he co-opted the influence of the monastery into episcopal and clerical government. His principal reason for this approach to ecclesiastical rule, however, was that he was truly persuaded that in his own time the Spirit had provided this kind of holiness, witness, and authority, whereby to guide and direct the church of Christ through its shepherds.

As one author says of Gregory's eulogy of Basil all roles in the Christian community "were projected onto the bishop of the day—that he was to be lawgiver, politician and statesman, popular leader, educator, monk and ascetic, example to contemplatives, pastor and comforter, support to the aged, guide to the simple and the young, reliever of poverty and steward of abundance, protector of widows and father of orphans, friend of the poor, entertainer of strangers, physician to the sick, brother to all, and all things to all men."[40] While in its own way this approach was meant as a corrective to a more vile clericalism, it could also accentuate the separation of pastors and baptized unless it were apparent that all followed a like ideal and that other gifts were respected.

There is no doubt but that Basil viewed the ascetic and monastic vocations as the ideal of baptismal perfection.[41] The Church by its nature is a communion of all the members of Christ's body in the gift of the one Spirit, who makes of them a new creation. Basil saw a tension between the charismatic principle, which allows for the special gifts of the Spirit and the need for Church order. He was more comfortable with the use of these gifts in the brotherhood that followed his Rule of Life than with their use in the body of the Church as a whole. The mortified life of the monks and obedience to elders and to leaders assured a right discernment of gifts, which could not it seems be guaranteed among the lay faithful, as Basil saw them. While therefore the primary gifts in the community are those of the ordained, in principle the Spirit may give special gifts to others. These need to be exercised with discipline and disinterest, as Paul had already said to the Corinthians, and it was in monastic communities that this was best assured.

The development of an ideal and image of the Church through the ministry of Basil is not unlike that of Ambrose. There is a comparable desire to bring all the members to holiness and a comparable desire to have all the baptized active in the life of the Church. However, in the very pursuit of this ideal, there is also a practical difference between the clergy and the common Mass of the faithful.

John Chrysostom (349–ca. 407)

Even after the advent of Christian peace, bishops could suffer for the faith, as we see well in the story of John Chrysostom. In an age that saw considerable doctrinal disputes and evolution of dogmatic formulation, especially through councils and the communion between bishops, the emperor and his magistrates had their own ideas of what constituted good teaching and its contribution to the unity of imperial rule. Any bishop who fell afoul of political authority bore the consequences, and John was exiled for a while from the Church for which he had been chosen bishop.

It is of no little import that in his treatise on priesthood,[42] which is a treatise on the episcopate, the image that dominates is that of shepherd. John gives attention to the bishop's holiness of life, his teaching function, and his exercise of the keys in bringing penance and pardon to sinners and indeed to all the faithful, something that demands a penitential life on the part of the bishop himself.[43] Though his role in celebrating the Eucharist is given prestigious treatment, the priesthood of the new covenant is first of all a priesthood of the Word and of being a shepherd of the people, linked inextricably with the ideal of the spiritual sacrifice of a life lived according to the gospel of Jesus Christ. Though John conceives of a tradition handed on from the time of the apostles, he does not build his sense of the ministry on an official transmission. His idea is that, like the apostles, the bishop receives a call from God, to which he is to respond. Like them, he receives a grace to preach the Word and to witness to Christ as they did.[44]

In John Chrysostom's mind, since the figure of the bishop demands much respect and conveys a position of authority, three further things need to be noted. First, there are his protests of equality among all Christians and of the humility required of bishops, as well as his view of the eucharistic liturgy as the work of all the people and the common sacrificial offering, through which they contemplate the mystery of the Trinity of divine persons, who grant and bring salvation and a divine image to the world. Second, this is no simple official authority. The holiness of the bishop and his imitation of Christ are necessary to the exercise of his ministry. Third, we see how it is John's sense of the prestige of the bishop that means the exclusion of women from this office. On this he says: "When one is required to preside over the Church and to be entrusted with the care of so many souls, the whole female sex must retire before the magnitude of the task, and the majority of men also, and we must bring forward those who to a large extent surpass all others and soar as much above them in excellence of spirit as Saul overtopped the whole Hebrew nation in bodily stature."[45] In this quote, there is both the sense of a difference between the general run of the baptized and bishops and the common persuasion of the social and human inferiority of women. If the bishop is to lead others to perfection, then he himself needs to be one who soars above all "in excellence of Spirit." If he is to "adorn the Bride of Christ," he must be like Christ.

Both Basil and John Chrysostom provide a fundamental vision of the Church as a eucharistic communion, united at the eucharistic table in the mystery of Christ, through the gift of the Holy Spirit. In the communion of the Spirit, the Church as a people constantly offers a sacrifice of praise to the Father through Christ and in the Spirit. In the communion in the body and blood of Christ, the fundamental baptismal equality of all is made visible, as well as in the offering of sacrifice of praise and thanksgiving that the bishop proclaims. This is eloquently expressed by Chrysostom:

> There are occasions when there is no difference at all between the priest and those under him; for instance when we are to partake of the awful mysteries; for we are all alike counted worthy of the same things. . . . Before all one body is set and one cup. . . . The offering of thanksgiving again is common: for neither doth the priest give thanks alone, but also with the people. . . . Now I have said all this in order that each of the laity also may keep their attention awake, that we may understand that we are all one body, having such difference among ourselves, as members with members, and may not throw the whole upon the priests; but ourselves also so care for the whole Church, as for a body common to us.[46]

It is, however, in this communion at the one table and in the liturgical action that surrounds it that the bishop's role takes on symbolic and priestly characteristics. Not only is he the Head and the Shepherd, but within the sacramental action what he does represents and symbolizes the presence of Christ, his mysteries, and particularly his sacrifice. While Chrysostom himself is quite sober in what he says on this point, his teaching was the foundation for much allegorical interpretation in later Orthodox writers.[47]

While there is not much in Chrysostom about the special gifts of the Spirit or charisms given to others, there are two areas in which he sees practical ways in which the lay faithful work for the body and bring into the whole of life what they celebrate in the Eucharist. The first is by the public witness of their lives, somewhat moralistically portrayed in his instructions on baptism and in some of his homilies, but nonetheless important to what the Church signifies for the world. The second area is in the care for the poor, a task that he places alongside eucharistic participation: there is no point in reverencing the body of Christ on the altar if this same body is not revered in the poor who are its members. Though naturally it is not mentioned in his discourses, there was a third way in which lay persons played an important role, in conjunction with the bishop, and that was through patronage. Without the assistance of more wealthy persons, or of the elite, the bishop could not have done his work, since their help was necessary to enable him to perform his duties. This was true not only for John in Antioch and in Constantinople, but it was true for all churches at that time. Surrounding every strong bishop was a group of lay persons, women and men, without whose assistance he could not have done all that was expected of him.

One could also say that there is a foundation to the presence and action of Christians in the world and within the community in the way in which Chrysostom and later Eastern writers include creation in what is represented and celebrated in the Eucharist. While the Eucharist is the memorial of the Lord's death and resurrection, with his victory over sin and death, it has its beginning in the mystery of the Incarnation, when in taking flesh the Word became one with created reality and transformed not only humanity but the entire creation. After his death, when Christ is raised up in the Spirit, this transforming work of the Incarnation is perfected and awaits its consummation at the *eschaton*. Christians praising God for the presence of Word and Spirit in the universe, and being made one with the Word made flesh through the power of the Spirit in communion, could only see themselves as bringing this divine life into society and into the whole of created reality.

Given this kind of christological, pneumatological, and eucharistic foundation, one might well ask of Chrysostom as of Basil or Augustine what prompted him to lead the Church in such a way as to make the life and work of the ordained and the call to the monastic life stand out in such contrast to that of the rest of the baptized. The ecclesiological principle is that of the Church as body of Christ in the Spirit, and hence of a fundamental equality of all Christians, in which each or any may receive special gifts of the Spirit that distinguish them from each other and create an organic order. While all at the eucharistic table are equal in that Christ's gift is for all without exception and all are children of God, in living the life of the body there are differences. There are differences of class, of wealth, of education, as well as of charismatic gifts, and it is in this diversity that the body promotes its life and shows itself to the world. The ideal would be for all to live the height of Christian perfection. Failing this, it was in a monastic or a clerical brotherhood that the ideal of the Church was best realized.

Writing of the strong role exercised by bishops such as we have considered, East and West, Michel-Yves Perrin observes that authority is always exercised and accepted within the context of interchange between bishop and people.[48] As in any human community, various pressures could be at work, and the more affluent may have had too much influence on the choice and pastoral agency of bishops, but over all there was no concept of authority that did not include qualities that evoke trust and dependence. The sources show the variety in this process rather than giving one unique model. Perrin ends his article with a certain apposite rhetorical flourish:

> The strength of the links that could be tied between the faithful and a bishop were always special. Was it his power of oratory, a quality increasingly required of bishops, that had magnetised his audience? Was it his qualities of *pater pauperum* that gave him the recognition of a numerous clientele enrolled on the church register? Was it his ascetical way of life that aroused ardent fascination? Or was it the fruits patiently cultivated through a unanimous election? The sources only let us know in rare cases.[49]

Leo the Great (d. 461) and the Church at Rome

As noticed, deciphering the early history of church ordering in Rome and its environs is problematic.[50] It is hard to fit the evidence with the ecclesiastical or hierarchical reading often given to early Christian literature.[51] Leo's way of speaking and exercising his episcopal and priestly authority is better understood in light of what was said in chapter 6 about the transition in how the Church of Rome was ordered. He belonged to an epoch when the distinctive Roman liturgy was taking shape and when the communities of the households or *tituli* in and around Rome were being brought into stronger communion, in a special way through the one presiding bishop's exercise of authority and his city liturgy.

While the bishop was expected to conform to the model of Christ as Good Shepherd, Leo gives his role greater juridical weight. The juridical is inherent to the sacramental rather than added to it, and the juridical cannot be conceived without its moorings in the sacramental and its relation to pastoral ministry. Leo often appeals to the presence of Peter in the midst of this church, and indeed the presence of Peter's tomb is not to be dismissed as a merely factual or theological nicety. There is a symbolism in this of public moment on which Leo is ready to seize when he says that he acts *vice Petri*. The claim to succession is made in mindfulness of the presence of Peter symbolized by the tomb. A metaphor that goes well with the symbolism of the tomb is that of possessing a heritage, a *hereditas*: Leo is the heir to Peter and so now receives the inheritance that Christ gave to his august forebear. As Peter, Leo too gives his apostolic witness.

The *dignitas* of the episcopal office is of importance, since it gives him status not only in the Church but in the society whose life and mores he is to influence. Words like *honor, gradus,* and *meritum* paralleled official state terms in describing office and service, underlining the intrinsic worthiness of the office itself, to which the officeholder is expected to measure up. When we read Leo's homilies for the anniversary of his own ordination,[52] we see how he relates this ministry to the royal priesthood of the whole body. Episcopal authority and priesthood are exercised in service of the common royal priesthood. Leo adopted the terms that were then being used of bishops, calling them *sacerdotes* and referring to the laying on of hands as an *unctio sacerdotalis*. In these sermons, Leo presented a spiritual, sacramental, and organic vision of how all in the body of Christ are constituted as a royal and kingly priesthood and as such offer together the memorial of Christ's sacrifice. The church of the city of Rome is fundamentally a society or community in which all share the dignity of their calling, in virtue of the unity of faith and unity of baptism. As the holy priesthood proclaimed by the apostle Peter (1 Pet 2:4–10), all are to offer spiritual offerings acceptable to God because offered through Jesus Christ. All have been regenerated in Christ, all have been made kings by the sign of the cross, all have been consecrated priests by the anointing of the Holy Spirit. The priestly action of offering spiritual gifts goes with the kingly domination, which brings the body into conformity with mind and spirit. Although by reason of his special ministry, the bishop receives more copious blessings, even the least of the community is not left untouched. The priestly service of the bishop is to act as agent of the priesthood of Christ within the one royal priesthood of the Church, to assure the faith in the passion of Christ on which it is founded. The bishop's ministry is to exercise his authority in teaching so that faith may be always at the heart of the life of the body of Christ and of the royal priesthood.

In several sermons on the passion of Christ, Leo teaches the people of the unique mediation and sacrifice of Christ, on which the priestly and kingly people is founded. Of this, the Eucharist is the visible sacrament, in which is united the devotion of all peoples in many places—in a sacrament made perfect and visible, fulfilling what was offered under obscure foreshadowings in the one temple of Jerusalem.[53] Through bodily and vocal action, the people offer their gifts, their devotion, and their prayer as they join with the bishop. They join together as one in the singing of the sacrifice of praise, in memorial of what God has wrought through Christ, and in communion with the choirs of angels and those who have preceded the living in faith and now enjoy glory. Because of his presidency over the celebration, the title *sacerdos* accrues in a special way to the bishop, but he acts only in communion with the whole gathering of the faithful. The way of associating the presbyters who served the titles with the bishop was to call them members *secundi ordinis* and *secundae dignitatis*.

With Leo and those who come after him, and in the ordering of the *cursus honorum*, we see the tension between the primacy of the community of faith and worship on one hand, and the hierarchical conceptualization of ministry on the other hand. The fundamental image of the Church as one body and one royal priesthood remains. But the hierarchical ordering of ministry is seen as a measure of divine ordinance, whose meaning is embodied in scriptural types of Old and New Testament.

Gregory the Great (d. 604)

In the West, before the works of the Pseudo-Dionysius (of which more later) became well known through Latin translation, Gregory the Great was the primary proponent of a hierarchical view of world and Church.[54] It is respect for hierarchical order that keeps tranquillity in the workings of the material universe and in the regulation of secular realities. The same principle of hierarchical order, the lesser being ruled by the greater, is to prevail by God's design within the Church. This vision is not simply a matter of power and jurisdiction. It is first and foremost a spiritual principle and the bishop, with his clerical subordinates, is to rule in virtue of his greater spiritual closeness to God and his greater spiritual discernment and authority. The structured order of Church life comes from God, but it would simply fall apart if the clergy did not live up to their spiritual ideal—if bad shepherds, as he puts it in some of his homilies, were more numerous than good shepherds. Within this picture, Gregory subscribes to the importance of daily penance for bishops and clergy, motivated in his case by what seems to have been his constant fear of falling short of the high ideals that a bishop should follow in order to be a good bishop.

At times there is something startling about Gregory's reactions to what he sees as a lack of clerical or monastic perfection. On his ordination he was shocked to be served in the papal chamber by nonclerics and decreed that thenceforth such an office be assigned only to clerics. In the *Dialogues*, we are also familiar with the story of what was later seen as the beginning of the custom of saying Gregorian Masses for the dead, that is thirty Masses on thirty consecutive days. What strikes a reader in this story is the severe judgment pronounced on the deceased monk who was found on his death to have a coin in his pocket. It took a vision to persuade Gregory to even allow his community to pray for this man's eternal rest.

On the other hand, his work on pastoral rule, *Regula pastoralis*, puts clerical supremacy in context.[55] In this treatise, Gregory wished to show that it is holiness of life that commands respect and fits a person to guide others in the spiritual life. Though in common with others he saw this as something needed in anyone being ordained bishop, priest, or deacon, he also saw that it could be exercised by others, particularly monks and the devout among the baptized. While clerical organization gave the Church its public profile and provided for the care of communities, anyone who followed the way of perfection could be a guide to others in other ways. This poses an oft-repeated question throughout the history of the Church: How much obedience may a bishop command if he is not truly holy? What respect is due him simply in virtue of his office, and what obedience is to be given to others who earn it by reason of their lives and spiritual wisdom?

Isidore of Seville (d. 636) and the Church of Spain

Two things are usually mentioned in textbook theology about Isidore of Seville's contribution to the theology of priesthood.[56] First is that in his work on ecclesiastical office, he treats of both bishop and presbyter under the heading "*De sacerdotio*" and then outlines the functions of bishop and presbyter respectively.[57] The second thing is that he defines the New Testament priesthood by taking the priesthood of Aaron as model because of the importance given to cult, but in the New Testament priesthood he includes the distinctive role of preaching and the exercise of the power of the keys, relying on Matt 16:18 and the mandate given to all priests in the person of Peter.

In chapter 6 we noted that under Reccared, Spain converted to orthodox Christianity, espousing the Creed and authority of the Councils of Nicaea, Constantinople, and Chalcedon. In support of this orthodox Christianity, Isidore espoused an ideal of Christian monarchy. He believed Christendom to be the sixth and final age of the world's history and wished to make of the Visigoths a "most Christian people." Monarch and Church needed to work together to achieve and maintain this ideal. Isidore had two dominant ideals in mind in his service of a Christian rule, one cultural and the other religious. Being pastor to an unruly barbarian people, Isidore revived the cultural traditions of ancient Rome in a rather encyclopedic display of learning and sought to make this heritage the foundation of a Christian kingdom. His religious intent was to support and divulgate an orthodox belief that would go hand in hand with cultural traditions, to solidify a people in a way of faith and a way of living.

In achieving this purpose, the clergy were to have a dominant role. They were to be educated in both doctrine and the chosen cultural heritage. Thus Isidore fostered the foundation of diocesan schools in which both the humanities, as he expounded them, and doctrine were taught. Furthermore, a uniform celebration of sacraments across the peninsula could help in unifying the kingdom, worship thus serving both civil and religious purposes together. His etymologies distill his knowledge of classical learning, and in defining priesthood he followed what he believed to be the linguistic model of clear definition. In his treatise on ecclesiastical offices, his chapter on the clergy probably served as description and prescription for parish work and for liturgical celebration, being functional rather than profoundly theological. They are to instruct, to teach, to baptize, to celebrate the Eucharist. An educated clergy in the Church of Spain would serve not only the Church but the realm.

Pseudo-Dionysius the Aeropagite

No consideration of order is complete without attention to the works and influence in both East and West of the person called the Pseudo-Dionysius.[58] Although practice and a sense of mission influenced the development of ministries in various ways, a mentality was also taking shape that was given clear expression in the theological writings of the Pseudo-Dionysius, now assumed to have been a Syrian monk. The work of this fifth-century writer which gives the best picture of the mentality that shaped ideals of Christian perfection and Church order, since his ideas are set out in systematic fashion, giving a vision of the Church that fits with a vision of the whole universe.

The writer has a hierarchical vision of all creation. The word *hierarchia* is a common cultic word among Greek-speaking peoples, meaning "sacred source or principle," so that the one who presides at sacred rites is a hierarch or indeed even a high priest, being in touch with the sources of life and knowledge. For the Syrian monk, God created the world as a hierarchy in which from the greater flows the lesser, positing every thing and every person in their proper place. It is only by keeping this arrangement intact that it is possible for things and persons to attain perfection.

In his work entitled *The Ecclesiastical Hierarchy*, this writer introduces a hierarchical conception into the discussion of ministry when he calls the bishop a *hierarch*. In the Christian usage that the Pseudo-Dionysius makes of this word, it is defined in another of his works, *The Celestial Hierarchy*, as a "sacred order, knowledge, and activity" that assimilates one to likeness to God, and from which graces flow to others. In other words, the likeness to God is the reason why graces may be mediated to others. In the bishop, holiness of life or divine perfection and the call to govern the Church are as one gift. He is the font or source of wisdom that brings others into communion with God.

In describing the divine liturgy or sacred mysteries in *The Ecclesiastical Hierarchy*, it is clear that teaching, praying the common prayer, and sanctifying the gifts for the communion of the faithful go together and are bound up with the bishop's spiritual gifts. Presbyters and deacons, each according to their holiness and ministry, also have a part in leading the faithful to God, but in a lesser way. Presbyters are charged with illuminating or teaching the divine mysteries as expressed in rites or symbols, while deacons may lead catechumens and sinners along the path of purification. The writer even looks for a parallel between the ecclesiastical hierarchy and the heavenly hierarchy of angels that belongs within his conception of the universe. The order of heaven is, as it were, participated in ecclesiastical hierarchy to the glory of God. The clerical order of lesser ministries, through which a candidate ascends, is a preparation. It is meant to gradually purify and perfect him so that he may become worthy to enter the earthly sanctuary that reflects the heavenly and enter into the enlightenment of the priestly liturgy, contemplating divine mysteries, revealing them in symbol and prayer to the faithful, and inviting their participation through partaking of the body and blood of the Word made flesh.

If the Syrian monk, as it is proposed he was, espouses a high ideal of holiness for the bishop and other clergy, he does this because he knows no distinction between ecclesiastical office or task and dignity on the one hand, and likeness to Christ or holiness in the Spirit on the other. He is so severe about this that he thinks an unworthy presbyter should not be accorded Christian burial, being in effect denied in death the place in the Church assembly that he would normally occupy.

The Church and the Temporal Order

A significant factor in the development of ministry is the way in which the Church's relation to the secular, or temporal, order was perceived, so an excursus on this is warranted. In his book *Ministry*, Ken Osborne holds that after Constantine the churches adopted three forms of relationship to the empire and secular authority, with the third option prevailing. What Osborne says is worth rehearsing.[59]

The first attitude was that of the church now called the Donatist. To begin with, the members of this church or of communities similar to it held a very high and ascetical ideal of Christian life and Christian community and could not tolerate members who failed this ideal. Concretely, their dilemma was how to relate to imperial authority and what to do with those of their leaders or members who seemed to support it. They had suffered persecution at the hands of Rome, and remembered this only too well, so that they were not inclined to work as partners in any way with imperial powers. When Cecilian and others accepted imperial decisions about the appointment of bishops, this seemed to be a betrayal, something that classed them with the *traditores* who in time of persecution offered sacrifice to pagan cults. Hence these leaders were refused, and the option was to take a hostile attitude to secular government in order to maintain purity of membership.

The second option taken was that which we know best from Augustine but which was shared by such as Gregory the Great. This was to live as an ecclesial community in the world, more or less side by side with secular powers, but staying aloof from temporal affairs. Within this option it was chosen to foster monasticism and to give the clergy, as we have seen, a quasi-monastic profile, since they were to live the ideal Christian life in community and in worldly detachment. This played, and continues to play even today, a great part in the distinction between clergy/monks and lay. This may be persuasive enough if Christians are seen to be people who detach themselves from concerns with temporal affairs and live always in the expectation of the death, which will open the door to eternal life, or indeed in a more or less apocalyptic awaiting of the final judgment. This sense of the coming end, which is found in Gregory the Great and assumes greater proportions in the later Middle Ages, is not to be discounted as a factor in shaping the portrait of the ideal Christian.

The third option, to which Osborne attributes greatest weight, was that embodied in the political theology of the imperial historian Eusebius (ca. 263–339). This option was to see the emperor and secular power as in its own way divinely established, within a hierarchically ordered view of created reality. In this view, Church and empire share responsibility for the order of the world, the secular and the spiritual converging and completing one another. Within that perception, the lay persons who truly counted were those who held power and authority or who exercised an influence on public order or contributed to the security and dignity of the Church, and especially of its bishops. While some of the theology that spoke of the three orders of Noah, Daniel, and Job embraced quite an array of workers and artisans, around the turn of the millennium the order of knights took on great importance. These were those who even fought for the protection of the Church and devoted themselves ideally to the service of the widow, the orphan, the poor, these still being considered privileged members of a community that awaits the end, when justice shall prevail and the poor will be blessed. To these ways of being Church identified by Osborne, we could add the ideal Christian order embraced by Charlemagne, Isidore, and the national Churches of Armenia and Ethiopia.

Concluding Reflections

In reflecting on what has been presented in the last two chapters, a number of factors capture attention. To begin with, the fundamental concern of ministry and order is to serve communion in the mystery of Christ. This is a unity in the faith of the apostolic tradition, sharing together in the celebration of the Eucharist at the one table, and the harmony of charity in life together. These were the concerns of everyone and were assured by different gifts and ministries, but they were also the concerns prominent in the development of the episcopacy.

The developing role and image of the bishop seemed to meet the needs of growing communities most fully, especially when the *cathedra* was occupied by a strong person. The complexity of the bishop's ministry is noteworthy. To be head of a community who satisfied both the inner needs of a church and its relation to society or its dealings with other churches, many things had to be done. First and foremost were the importance of episcopal teaching authority, the guidance of sinners and penitents, and the presidency of the eucharistic gathering, which brought all into one communion of faith and worship. This latter at times meant being able to hold in communion in one region a number of different assemblies, and different strategies were adapted to this purpose, and it also meant the extended role of presbyters in presiding at the Eucharist. As well as exercising these roles, the bishop attended to the common need and to the needs of the poor, often with the assistance of deacons. A church that did not live in charity toward its weak members could not be a true discipleship, and no leader could be a stranger to this need. In today's world, meeting the needs of the poor and underprivileged has quite different demands and requires a more varied and public action, but a *diakonia* of service to the poor is essential to a genuine eucharistic fellowship.

Particularly but not exclusively within the assembly for worship, the figure of the bishop assumed the role of symbolic representation, related to his total action and to the action of the whole assembly. The people gathered regularly for the enactment of the sacramental mystery of Christ's Pasch. Though they rejected pagan and Jewish forms of sacrifice, their worship was for them a spiritual sacrifice, one which developed its own array of sacramental symbolism. They expressed their participation in many outward prayers and actions, and with the assistance of different ministries, but all led to the communion in the body and blood of Christ at the one table of those who were one in faith and charity. Within the sacramental action and fundamental equality of this spiritual and royal priesthood, the bishop, and often his assistant presbyters and deacons, had a specific sacramental role to exercise. To this was attached the symbolism of showing to the people the presence of the Good Shepherd, the Priest and the Victim of the new covenant, so that through communion with him all might be one as offerings and as priests in the one mediator. From within such a setting, bishops were more and more spoken of as priests and as representatives of Christ. This representative role is one that needs more reflection in our day, but it is one that can be accommodated to a fuller active role in Church and liturgy of all the faithful and can lead to different forms of exercising episcopal ministry.

While the purpose of the gospel and of all ministry or service was to make of all a living sacrifice unto God, living in holiness of life, in practice some persons were set apart as exemplifying the holiness to which all were called. In this regard, from early days, the importance given to virgins and widows in any church is significant. In time it was monks, male and female, who embodied the ideal of Christian holiness. So as to assure good spiritual leadership in communities under their care, bishops drew on this ideal for their clergy or for all called to public ministry in its more important services. The distinction and even separation between clergy and the rest of the faithful was not meant to suggest a special call to holiness. Rather, insisting on the clergy's practice of what was the common calling meant that a church would have its model of Christian discipleship, and that those placed in leadership would live the ideal and thus be able to lead. This allowed for a growing separation between clergy and faithful, especially where cultic ideals of priesthood took prevalence. Today this relationship between people and ordained ministers needs a different configuration.

Whatever the distinctions within it, all members of the body of Christ were thought to contribute in some way to building it up and to its witness in the world, but too often an ideal of withdrawal from the world determined the lives of even the laity. How the relation of the Church or of the kingdom of God to the world was seen exercised a great influence on the lives of the Christian faithful. That women were given lower positions in the Church or barred from ordination was thought over time to be within the order of things, but this was not by any appeal to what it means to represent Christ. As we have seen, it was thought to be determined by the order of creation.

With regard to the idea of divine institution, we find in this history a confirmation of what was recalled about this concept earlier on. Rather than speak of the history of an institution, we would have to speak of the history of a community pursuing an ideal and finding the institutions that meet its need. In seeing the role of bishops, we are reminded that the purposes they served still need to be served, and hence we find good historical argument that some form of episcopacy is necessary to the Church. On the other hand, we would expect an evolution that allows for its exercise in different circumstances and with institutional flexibility.

Looked at from the point of view of the gospel and the gift of the Spirit, it can be said that Word and Spirit guided churches in this process and in discernment. However, since the Church also is affected by more human spirits, this does not mean that decisions were always the best possible ones. The past as well as the present requires a discerning eye, and we do well to look for possibilities of change in institutional forms. We may well think that the Church needs to look again at the procedures and institutions put in place to make one eucharistic communion truly possible, following a process of spiritual discernment that has this goal in mind.

We noted the desire to keep alive models for the call to holiness in fostering a distinction between laity and clergy. The life shared by bishops and all ministers with communities was affected by developments that privileged their distinction and separation. It is helpful to realize that this had to do with an ideal of common holiness and of the skills and sanctity of life needed for leadership. Today we are in a better position to see that leadership is exercised in different ways by different people, and that there is a diversity of models of holiness around, so that having a distinctive model of clerical community is not important. Indeed, by being more intimately a part of the community of the faithful, someone called to ministry may well find the holiness of life and the skills appropriate to ordained ministry as community service and not as office. On the other hand, moving beyond centuries of clerical/lay and male/female polarities is not easy.

8

Second Millennium

In looking at the progress of churches in the first millennium, it was noted how ministries evolved in specific contexts, how meaning was given to them, and what reasons led to the strong distinction between clergy and laity. It was seen that the ordering of bishop, presbyter, and deacon was not perfectly homogenous but allowed for differentiation in the way each was exercised or in the way the three were related. The place of laity and lay services to the life of the Church was also noted in conjunction with attitudes to temporal matters. It is now time to turn to what happened in the course of the second millennium of the life of the Church.

Split between East and West: Eastern Orthodoxy Perspectives

The split between churches of the East and of the West in the early years of the second millennium is of paramount importance to the history of order.[1] In disputes and disagreements, the East retained its focus on the local church and the eucharistic mystery, whereas the West adopted more legal and jurisdictional approaches in resolving issues about order, ministry, and sacrament and tended to centralize power and authority, with growing importance given to the role of the papacy.

The definitive split between East and West is dated to the mutual excommunications of 1054. The later attempts at Florence to bring the two together only seem to have exacerbated the grievances of both sides. Theological concerns were the procession of the Holy Spirit and the primacy claimed by the Bishop of Rome. While Rome centralized all ecclesial rule in the Pope, the Orthodox took the local eucharistic church as primary ecclesial reality.

For Orthodoxy, the processions and missions of Son and Spirit must be seen together as coming from the Father, and there must be no suggestion of subordination, either in the work of salvation or within the communion of the Three. The view of the relationship is intimately linked with the work of the Holy Spirit in the Church and in bringing humanity and indeed all of creation into a participation in the mystery of the Trinity. Through the Word and the Spirit, Christians receive the mission to bring all things into this mystery of divine glory, something that is expressed most truly in eucharistic communion.

For the Orthodox, the Church is the living temple of the Spirit, the spiritual sacrifice acceptable to God in Christ. While the Church is hierarchical, it is the local church that is given most attention, and the hierarchy is to be viewed within the perspective of the body of Christ, replete with all its gifts and services. There may be no suggestion of subservience. Though patriarchates have an important role in serving a communion of churches in a region, this cannot mean a jurisdiction over bishops of other churches. Institutional aspects and organization are but expressions of the deeper nature of the Church, or in other words, they are in the service of the eucharistic communion, whose principal symbol is the invitation of all to the one eucharistic table.

What emerged in the division between East and West was a profound difference in views of the Church and thus of its ordering, particularly with regard to the ecumenical communion of all churches. Up to the present time, this dilemma has not been resolved, despite Catholic efforts to place the Eucharist at the center of its ecclesiology and the good results of the proposals made by the International Theological Commission set up by Rome and the Orthodox.

The West

This said, one can look at developments in Western churches and communities. In dealing with mission, ministry, and order in the second millennium in the West, one may roughly divide the period into that of the pre-Reformation, the Reformation, and the post-Reformation/Tridentine centuries.

The early centuries of the second millennium of Christianity were a time when the Church had to sort out its relation to society in a new way and discover how in a new setting it was to live by the gospel. In the course of this development, the relation between clergy and laity was in constant flux, as one group or the other was to the fore in efforts to control ecclesial life. At first it was a matter of Pope and bishops wresting control over ecclesiastical affairs from lay princes, but later the struggle was with another class of lay person, those who wished to return the Church to a more evangelical way of life.

The Frankish heritage, dating back to the conversion of Clovis (496), was a Christian faith that clung to the belief that the "God of Christians procured for them victory over their adversaries."[2] This belief, accepted by laity and propagated by clergy, drew liberally on the Old Testament narratives and legal codes. Abandoning the attempts at forced conversion, Church leaders at the turn of the millennium thought to build up what we call Christendom through ecclesiastical influence on secular society and on the morality of the powerful and the weak, the rich and the poor alike, rather than by coercion. Even the location of its buildings in city and in country signified its prominence in public life. Sadly, joined to the influence of the clergy was the decadent life of all too many bishops and priests. It has been remarked that the reform associated with the name of Gregory VII was at first supported by influential lay persons and influential clergy alike, all of whom saw hope for the struggle against princes and for attempts directed against ecclesiastical laxity in a strong and controlling papacy.

At the same time, among educated and more wealthy classes, there was a new appreciation for secular learning and secular arts, which gave them some freedom from the grip of the kind of religious outlook and piety mentioned above. Some now refer to this as a form of secularization, but it is more the issue of the proper balance between faith and reason, between the capacities of human artifice and belief in God. In this positive sense, secularization was given impetus by the efforts of universities and Schoolmen and found its way into the greater achievements of Scholastic theology.

Against this secularization, monasteries—made up of choir and penitent members—wanted to provide a stimulus to a revival of faith and piety, which would be center of the true religion. The Franciscan movement and Franciscan theologians were also hesitant about the relation of reason and secular pursuits to faith and revelation. In practical terms, this allowed room for a more affective piety and provided for an outlook on life that continued to place the value of the temporal within the higher esteem of the eternal, known only through faith and the Scriptures.

Many of the laity, however, lived their lives outside both learned circles and monasteries and looked for reform through a return to a more evangelical way of life in following Jesus as he was known to them through the reading and hearing of the Gospels. Critical of the clergy, they refused the intermediary power of those whom they found to be dissolute men and formed their own communities, living on the fringe of society and Church, seeking a worship "in spirit and in truth" rather than in ritual ceremonial. Though not all such groups are to be dismissed as heretical and schismatic, among them there were some who were distrustful of all material reality and of the fleshly side of the mysteries of the Incarnation and of grace. Despite the rough treatment of such as the Cathars and the odd ideas of some about the dual force of good and evil in creation, it cannot be forgotten that once again we witness in history the difference between two ways of being Christian in society. One looked for a way of influencing society by remaining at its heart, and the other for a way of life suited to the small remnant, the more truly evangelical. The efforts of ecclesiastical authority and clergy to foster and control penitential discipline was a key way of keeping such lay inclinations in check, submitting action and conscience to the judgment of the priest. Within this context we can place the prescription of the Fourth Lateran Council that all the baptized should present themselves at Paschaltide to their pastors and the emergence of a type of literature that we know as manuals for confessors.[3]

Outside of these more or less dissident or contestatory groups, the laity found a role in the life of the Church along various paths. One was through what is called the peace movement. In a time of inner strife and struggle against enemies, God was looked to as giver of peace, reconciler, and upholder of a just and peaceful social order. Monasteries were often the center of pilgrimages and of action for peace, but all the faithful found a role in this activity. André Vauchez remarks that this gave a place to the lesser laity in the Church and its mission, as it also fostered an eschatological piety that even looked ahead to an apocalyptic triumph of Christ and an eclipse of all things temporal. In this climate, pilgrimages to sanctuaries and devotion to hermits and errant preachers flourished. The spread of divine peace and the defense of Christianity found its high point in the "ordering" of the laity through the Crusade movement. This included the founding of military orders and hospitalers to serve the purposes of the Church and its place at the heart of the civilized world.

Contemporaneous to this ordering, and serving another idea of the Church's mission, were groups of lay preachers who combined evangelical poverty, penance, and preaching in their way of life. Some of these fell afoul of Church authorities, such as the followers of Pierre de Vaudois (Waldensians). Others received approval with inbuilt restrictions, provided they submitted a rule of life for papal approval. Well known among such movements are the *Humiliati*, who included both women and men in their membership.[4]

A grassroots lay movement, a search for new forms of common evangelical life, attuned to the times, attentiveness to the lot of the poor, and new forms of popular devotion seem to have been the characteristics of the religious renewal movement of the twelfth and thirteenth centuries, exemplified in the above-mentioned *Humiliati*, or Humble Ones. They were mostly lay persons, some married, who continued to live at home with their families, or else unmarried or formerly married, who chose to live a common life in the religious manner. Calling for all to do penance, these Humble Ones imitated the church of early days in living the ideal of apostolic life in common and in engaging in the apostolic preaching of the gospel.

With them as with others, clergy, bishops, and popes had misgivings about their preaching, since preaching was an episcopal responsibility and not a lay one. In 1201, they received official recognition from Innocent III, giving them both a rule of life and the conditions under which they were allowed to preach. By this rule, they were recognized as an officially sanctioned order of the Church, allowing for three variants in their form of life, namely canonical or clerical, monastic, and lay association. In their communal life, coming to the assistance of the needy was considered important, as was the duty of praying for the dead. All extended their charity in a particular way to embrace the poor and downtrodden, with special attention to lepers, and sought to live by the work of their own hands. They also had their own way of participating in the regular prayer of the Church. Those who could recited the canonical hours and those who were not literate recited the Lord's Prayer a certain number of times a day instead. Innocent allowed them to preach penance but not to expound on the gospel, thus distinguishing between the preaching done by the clergy and lay preaching.

Other changes in the life of the Church and in the spirituality of the laity began to come about in the twelfth century on account of new forms of economy and the status that many began to enjoy in society. Agricultural workers experienced a new freedom from overlords, and in cities a merchant economy came into being. This "new economy" enticed people to an enjoyment of temporal realities that earlier Christian visions of flight from the world often forbade them. As it happens, some lay persons and some clergy saw this negatively. Others found in it a fresh appreciation of secular realities and secular culture that could be accommodated to the faith and a Christian way of living.

At the beginning of the millennium, the reform of the clergy was a great concern. It is associated with the name of Gregory VII, but it was a concern shared by many. The emergence of the canons regular, or of cathedral chapters living the common life, is an important consequence of this desire for reform. As in the rule of Augustine, it was thought that priests and other clergy would live up to the ideals of their calling if they lived a common life, practicing the evangelical counsels and in the process offering the faithful an ideal of the Christian life.

In such a context, the mendicant movement, whether in its clerical form in the Dominicans or in the lay form espoused by Francis and his followers, had considerable significance. Especially in Francis we see an identification with the new poor of the new economy or with those left behind by progress. With his followers, through voluntary poverty, he pressed for a more radical following of Jesus Christ and a return to ideals of the renunciation of the temporal.

Not to be neglected is the missionary vision of Francis and his followers. The Church for the most part renounced the attempt at forced conversion and accentuated the need to base teaching of the faith on Christian witness.[5] At first, Dominicans and Franciscans alike aspired to go to the lands of "heathens" and suffer martyrdom. The encounter of Francis with the Sultan of Babylon in Egypt seems to have inspired a new attitude. Refusing the ordeal by fire proposed by Francis, Malik al-Kamil returned this peaceable man, in whom he could find no hostility, to the Christian camp. Hence Francis in his rule recommended that the friars sent among the Saracens begin by showing submission to every human creature and to profess their faith as Christians. If the situation then seemed opportune, they should proclaim the Word of God and baptize those who wished to adhere to the Christian Creed.[6]

The history of the Franciscans shows how the role of the laity was co-opted into clerical forms of life. From the beginning there appear to have been problems with the idea that Francis in preaching had expounded on the gospel, as the story of his creation of a nativity scene on Christmas night testifies. His hagiographers turned him into a deacon to justify this kind of preaching, though it seems rather doubtful that he was in fact ordained to this order. In any case, under the generalship of Bonaventure, the Franciscans became primarily a clerical group of mendicant preachers living a common life, and in that guise they could exercise without hindrance the dual ministry of preaching and of administering penance in sacramental form.

As is well known, Francis and his first followers did not see themselves as a community of priests, but while practicing poverty among the poor, they did engage in preaching and in bringing people to penance and conversion. In approving their way of life, Pope Innocent III had given some authority to their preaching by allowing them the small tonsure. Rather than a clerical tonsure, this seems to have been a kind of *ad hoc* solution adopted by Innocent to save them from the suspicions often directed against lay preachers at the time. Despite this approval of preaching by the early Franciscans, Church authority over time put more and more restrictions on lay preaching and frowned on the hearing of confessions by lay persons as a nonsacramental ministry, under whatever circumstances. As a result, it was felt that the ministries of preaching, teaching, and confessing practiced by friars required ordination, and this gradually changed the major composition of the order of Friars Minor.

Laity

While Bonaventure promoted the clericalization of the Friars, he also provided a way of dealing with the upsurge of lay involvement in the ministry of the Church by constituting a "third order," whose members were subjected to the authority of clerical members. The total order then included priests and brothers living in community, and lay members who could practice some form of common life but not within the houses of the order. The Dominicans likewise promoted the existence of third orders attached to the friars.

Apart from this direct association with vowed communities, there were other kinds of life lived by laity that contributed to the work of the Church and its place in society. Worthy of special mention are lay confraternities, which were often associated with parish or cathedral churches. Somewhat like the *Humiliati*, these adopted penitential, devout, and charitable practices that constituted a way of life for their members. Though they fostered many devotions among themselves, they should not be thought of as withdrawn from life since they helped their members to develop a spirituality suited to the new economy. Not only did they promote penance, but they were also concerned with such matters as exacting restitution for unjust acts and fostering reconciliation among those at enmity with each other. Confraternities continued to flourish, right through and even beyond the termination of the Council of Trent.[7] The trend toward works of charity and service of the poor increased, balancing well with devotional goals. The confraternities had a part to play in breaking down social barriers since they attracted membership from various walks of life. Preachers seeking the reform of the Church found suitable allies in these bodies, even when ecclesiastical authorities were ambivalent and wanted to place them under tighter control.

Other lay inspirations and activities were not as readily accommodated to the clerical dispensation, even though they did not directly challenge it. This includes the spirituality and way of life of many devout women. Some lived in abbeys, such as Hildegard of Bingen (1098–1179) and Gertrude of Helfta (1256–ca. 1301). Some such as the Beguines formed secluded lay communities, and others belonged to third orders, as did Catherine of Siena (1347–1380). Others like Angela Merici

(1476–1540) gathered companions together for the service of the poor under a rule of life.

A more or less common factor among these women was their devotion to the humanity of Christ and an aspiration to mystical communion with him. A eucharistic dimension to their lives was manifested through piety toward the reserved sacrament or through communion under unusual circumstances, which released them in part from dependence on priests but did not deter reverence for the celebration of the Mass. There were quite a number who seemed to live only from the food that they received in sacramental communion. Some who could not receive communion at Mass, such as Gertrude of Helfta over a period of her life when her convent was under interdict, witnessed the Lord himself celebrating Mass and in visions received communion directly from him. This meant not only communion in the form of bread but also communion in the chalice at a time when this was prohibited to the laity.

Among these women were several who claimed and were recognized to have a prophetic and teaching ministry. These include Hildegard of Bingen, Catherine of Siena, Margarite Porete (d. 1310), and Gertrude of Helfta, and in their way they served the purpose of ecclesiastical reform. Like the followers of Francis under Clare of Assisi, these women developed their own forms of communal living and of piety, forms that had their own symbolic structure. They could live their lives in a more independent way and, in the case of those who did not enter cloistered convents, engage together in works of education, charity, and the care of the sick. But given clerical control and the generally negative attitudes toward sexuality and toward women, their activity and possible contribution could not be fully assimilated into the life of the Church, still less into its governing and pastoral structures.

From their writings the women themselves appear to have been ambivalent about their position and about themselves. Gertrude had no doubts about her call to a teaching and prophetic ministry, but she continued to see womankind, herself included, as weak and inferior beings. Hildegard traces ideals of gender complementarity between man and woman and was able to have close friendships with men. But she too accepted woman's inferiority in the social order, and maybe even in the spiritual, and was uncomfortable about sex and sexual relations.

As for the men, scholars included, they could account for the high level of spiritual life among some women, and for their capacity as heads of flourishing communities, as guides or as teachers, only by seeing this as an extraordinary grace, lifting them above their own nature. Having lauded the achievements of Hildegard, her male biographer, Guibert of Gembloux, could only say, "She has transcended female subjection by a lofty height and is equal to the eminence, not just of any men, but of the very highest."[8] Here is combined both a recognition of who she was and a principle of female subjection. With such a perspective, how could it have been possible to think in more general terms of according women an equal role in the spiritual and pastoral leadership of the Church?

In contemporary parlance, we would say that these roles of women were given no place in the public symbolic order of the Church, either in sacrament, in governance, or in public devotion. This meant that their work could not be appropriated in such a way as to make a structural difference in ecclesiastical ordering. Consequently, even when their words were addressed to hierarchy, they did not challenge their ecclesiastical position. Nonetheless, we can ask now whether a clearer and ordered recognition of the roles of women would not have changed the ordering of ecclesial communities, were it not for the prevailing conceptions of the relations between men and women and of the place of women in the abiding social order.

Popular Devotion

Besides all that has been said of the laity, there was the way of popular devotion, centered to a great extent around devotion to Mary and the saints, often localized and at times inclusive of seasonal celebrations such as Rogation Days. In the promotion of these devotions, there was a delicate and changing balance between clerical supervision and lay initiative. On a whole, one might say that in popular devotions the mass of laity got what they wanted, a beneficent presence in their harsh lives, some sense of a power that assisted them. They did not upset the supremacy of the clergy in the life of the Church since generally the clergy knew how to adapt themselves to popular demand.

What is missing in the forms of spirituality that emerged during these centuries is a good conjugal spirituality, due in large part to prevailing ideas about women. Marriage was indeed recognized as a sacrament, and the place of the married in the life of the Church through childbearing and education was affirmed. Conjugal spirituality, however—in a new cultural climate that in tales, art, and poetry lauded the erotic—was closely allied to the ideals of virginity. The normality of the erotic in marriage was not well integrated, but married couples were sometimes taught to use marital relations to subdue passions or to attend to higher stages of the spiritual life through forms of abstinence, even ranging to the ideal of virginal companionship exemplified in Mary and Joseph.[9]

Theology

To this survey of practical Church ordering, in all its variety and even newness, we can append how ecclesiastical writers and theologians developed views of sacramental order. The division of Christian society into three classes of people at the beginning of the millennium is often cited,[10] though it is not as neat as it may seem at first sight. It was an adoption of the Augustinian distinction of human beings according to the typology of Noah, Job, and Daniel. Now the division was between those who prayed, those who fought (*bellatores*), and those who worked, and it was justified by appeal to Paul's discussion of the many members who go to make up the body of Christ. The first group included monks and clergy. The second was applicable primarily to the nobility, among whom many took up the sword in defense of the Church and in defense of the poor and needy. The third group was more fluid in description. To begin with, it meant mostly peasants who worked the land, but with time it expanded to include artisans, bakers, vintners, and all those whose labor in one way or another contributed to building up Christendom, a society impregnated with Christian values and the acknowledgment of the reign of Christ. The stained-glass windows of the Cathedral of Chartres are a monument to the way in which these various groups saw themselves as part of the body of the Church, since they are often depicted at the bottom of windows of which they were the donors.

Scholastic Theology

While monastic schools stuck more or less to the patristic method of the spiritual reading of the Scriptures, Scholastic theology offered a more systematic treatment of doctrine, offering reasons for how God has ordered the universe and the Church.
[11] On the sacrament of order the Master, Peter Lombard (d. 1160), opted for a sevenfold division of order in the ecclesiastical hierarchy, corresponding to the seven gifts of the Holy Spirit. In this he was followed by the majority of commentators on the *Sentences*. Other writers in opposition to this division invoked the authority of Dionysius the Areopagite, who had affirmed nine orders, to correspond to the nine choirs of angels. Guy of Orchellis (ca. 1215) citing this authority simply stated that the reason given by Dionysius for nine orders was as good as that given by Peter Lombard for seven. He gave the reasons why the episcopate could be seen as an order distinct from the priesthood. In the consecration of a bishop, he argued, the candidate's head is anointed with oil, and such anointing, as in baptism and confirmation, imprints a character. Along with some others, Guy considered the archiepiscopate as the ninth order, and the reason usually given for this was that the metropolitan had greater power, and it was he who on principle consecrated other bishops.

Philip the Chancellor (ca. 1236) tried to reconcile the two authorities, Peter Lombard and Dionysius, by offering two alternate grounds for calculating the number of orders. It could be said that there are nine orders *secundum officia et potestates*, but that in the strict sense, *secundum potestates et characteres*, there are only seven. Apparently he separated what is given by jurisdiction from what is given through ordination.

Alexander of Hales (ca. 1223–27) was the first to give an explicit definition of order in terms of the Eucharist and at the same time to elaborate a theology of the sacramental character that explained this connection. He did not fully agree with Peter Lombard's definition of order because according to it the episcopate would have to be considered as a sacrament, while even the Master himself denied this. Alexander therefore gives his own definition: order is a sacrament of spiritual power for some office that is directed in the Church to the sacrament of communion. Since the episcopate is not directed to the Eucharist, it is not a sacramental order. The sacramental character is a mystical configuration to Christ, who offered himself on the cross through his priestly character as Son of God and mediator. It follows that the priest who consecrates the bread and wine in commemoration of the cross must be distinguished by a sacerdotal character, which is a configuration to Christ's reception of the character of being mediator between God and humanity. This connection between priesthood and Eucharist is what ultimately led the majority of theologians to see the episcopate as neither a sacrament nor an order.

Some said, as did William of Auvergne (ca. 1228), that even the power to consecrate a bishop or ordain a priest is given in ordination to the presbyter or priest, but that it can be exercised by the bishop alone *ex officio*, that is in virtue of his higher administrative power. To this he added that the power of jurisdiction of a bishop given to him for his pastoral role in the Church requires a higher degree of spiritual perfection even if it is not a sacrament and imprints no character.

With the development of Scholastic theology, both Bonaventure and Thomas Aquinas placed their ideas about order within the overarching vision of an order of spiritual perfection. Some elaboration on both of these follows.

Bonaventure (1221–1274)

As Master General, Bonaventure favored the clerical nature of the order of mendicant friars and preachers. He gave his decisions a theological foundation that associated ordination with a profession of obedience to the Pope and with the evangelical way of life. Direct obedience to the Pope freed the friars from any restrictions that local bishops might put on their preaching and their hearing of confessions.[12] In explaining why Francis himself had revised the original rule,[13] Bonaventure gave three reasons: to imitate the virtues of Christ as do the cenobites, to contemplate Christ as do the hermits, and to imitate Christ in saving souls as do those who exercise priestly ministry. According to Bonaventure, the ministry of preaching and of hearing confessions becomes a task of the order through religious profession. This is a community goal and purpose, which of its nature requires both ordination and learning. The relation of the friars to the Holy See was a big factor in Bonaventure's practical and theological response to the quarrel over the rights of mendicants to exercise the ministry of Word and penance. The claim to have immediate jurisdiction from the Pope, supreme head of the Church, outweighed any episcopal prescriptions.

Bonaventure's vision of order comes to the fore in his theological compendium, the *Breviloquium*.[14] In his treatment of the sacrament of order, he related it to the work of the divine Word. As the divine principle, bringing redemption and restoration to a fallen world, the Word Incarnate instituted the sacraments as remedies for sin. Since creation and redemption are brought about through the Word according to the order of divine wisdom, this order is to be reflected in the dispensation of the sacraments.

The power of order exercised in sacramental dispensation fits into a higher spiritual order. Tonsure serves as the sign that sets off a candidate from the rest of the people. It represents a total dedication to the love and service of God, cutting off temporal appetites and elevating the mind to God. Together, the seven orders combine the powers that lead to the priesthood, which is the power to confect the sacrament of the altar. Passing through them brought both purgation and illumination, leading to the perfection of charity. The perfection of charity and a vision of the spiritual order provide the context for visible hierarchical order. Situating the priesthood in the Church in this way subjects the exercise of the power of order to the regulation of the power of jurisdiction, while both are placed within an overarching spiritual vision. Order and jurisdiction ought to be exercised only by those in whom the spiritual hierarchy of perfection parallels the ecclesiastical hierarchy.

Bonaventure was able to harmonize the spiritual understanding that he gave to the exercise of ministry with the Franciscan ideal of following Christ. As a follower of Francis, Bonaventure found poverty in the discipleship of Christ as the key to the evangelical way of life. To be poor was to be poor in the following of the poor Christ and to love the poor with the compassion of Christ. It was to have no possessions, to work with one's hands, to beg, and to count oneself as nothing in relations with others.

All of this comes out in Bonaventure's writings on the way of the friars and on Francis. In the *Itinerarium mentis in Deum*, the completion of this life in contemplation becomes clear. It is exemplified in Francis's reception of the stigmata on Mount Alverna, which showed his complete oneness with the crucified Christ. What is also shown there is the way to contemplation and union with the crucified Christ along the sixfold way of purification and illumination. The relation to creatures is that of forgoing attachment to them in order to find in them the revelation of the divinity. Poverty is the very foundation of the following of Christ and so also for preaching Christ. The perfection of charity and poverty are combined in communion with Christ crucified.

Thomas Aquinas (ca. 1225–1274)

Thomas Aquinas, like Albert the Great and Bonaventure, opted for seven orders and for the opinion that the episcopate is neither a sacrament nor a distinct order. The reason for this was the connection between order and Eucharist. However, when it came to spiritual perfection and pastoral rule, Aquinas fitted the episcopacy into the hierarchy of the Pseudo-Dionysius.

Before going into the theology of Aquinas on the sacrament of order, we must first see how his conceptions of episcopacy related to the hierarchy of spiritual life that he adopted from the Pseudo-Dionysius. In this way he incorporated his view of ministry into a conception of order that exceeds but includes the sacramental. This is most evident when he compares religious life and the episcopacy on the basis of the pursuit of perfection, which is measured by the degree of one's charity.[15] Religious life is directed to the pursuit of perfection for the sake of one's own salvation, whereas the ministry of the bishop is dedicated to the salvation of others. Religious are committed by vow to a lifelong pursuit of the perfection of charity and are taken up with observances, prayer, study, and discipline that lead to their own holiness. Episcopal ministry is destined to the service of others and requires that one be able to lead others on the way of charity. Since a bishop is called to a full and lifelong engagement in this ministry, the candidate for this order has to be one who has already attained a higher or perfect degree of love of God and neighbor. If a candidate for episcopacy is a religious, he is well served by this in his ministry for he will be able to combine the observance of religious life with his duties, ordering the pursuit of charity to the service of charity. But one who is a bishop should not abandon this ministry in order to join a religious order.

Aquinas obviously had some difficulty in reconciling the authority of the Pseudo-Dionysius with the tradition that there is no difference in order between episcopate and presbyterate but only a difference in rank and office. Because he chose to define the sacrament of order in terms of the Eucharist, as did Alexander of Hales, he denied that the episcopate is a sacramental order, since it gives no new power over the real body of Christ but only over the mystical body. Elsewhere, in keeping with the authority of the Areopagite, he calls the episcopate an order, precisely because it gives power over the mystical body. This is not a mere matter of jurisdiction but is a spiritual power, and the power given in episcopal consecration can be likened to the sacramental character.

Although Aquinas does not call the episcopate a sacramental order, he insists strongly on the distinction between the episcopate and the presbyterate from the very beginning of the life of the Church; it is a division that goes back to our Lord himself, who named twelve apostles and seventy-two disciples, and is prefigured in the distinction between Aaron and his sons in the Old Testament. In this we can see how Thomas dealt with the twofold tradition that we noticed in the medieval authors. He accepts the opinion that originated with Ambrosiaster and has Jerome as its principal authority in affirming that presbyter and bishop are equal in the power to consecrate the body and blood of Christ. But he shows no signs of following Jerome when it comes to the origin of the distinction between presbyter and bishop, for this can be traced to the Lord himself. He even gives a benign interpretation of Jerome, saying that he did not wish to deny the distinction between the orders but only to affirm that the names of presbyter and bishop were not distinguished in New Testament times.

Thomas Aquinas affirms the bishop's duty to preach to be one of his principal obligations since this is a task to which the apostles gave great importance, and the bishop is their successor. The power of the bishop is superior to that of the presbyter in all that concerns the faithful. As ruler of the mystical body, he acts in the person of Christ, and he appoints its members officially to the different functions that exist in the body; thus, the sacrament of confirmation and the sacrament of order are administered by the bishop. To presbyters, however, he delegates powers for the personal sanctification of the faithful, since it is only right that the head should concern himself with the officers but delegate care for the lesser members to his collaborators. Since by reason of their nature, women cannot represent eminence, they cannot be bishops.

Aquinas considers presbyters and deacons as persons committed to a lesser ministry than that of bishop, for they hold their ministry in dependency on him. Being less engaged in ministry, they have a lesser obligation to perfection. This indeed reflects a historical situation in which priests engaged in pursuits other than ministry. While holiness of life befits a priest's sacramental task, which is to be undertaken in service to the people, it is not exacted of him to the same extent as of the bishop.

In examining the thirteenth-century quarrel between secular clergy and mendicants over the right of the mendicants to preach and hear confessions, one is struck by the practical side of the reasoning of Thomas. He allows a place in ministry for mendicants because they are in a position to bring greater holiness to the task. Thomas clearly addresses the pastoral need for preachers and confessors who live holy lives and who are well versed in doctrine and the Scriptures, in a way that many parochial clergy were not. The mendicant therefore is not attached to a local church but rather, with the proper jurisdiction, he can come as needed to the aid of local priests.

As for the life of the friar, the main relation between his religious life and his activity as preacher or as teacher lay in what Aquinas said about the comparison between contemplative and active life. The essence of the active life is service in charity to one's neighbor, but the finest form of charity lies in contributing to another's spiritual welfare. The highest form of religious life is found in institutes founded to teach and to preach. There the contemplative and active lives converge in one, in a way that is closest to the perfection of bishops. One teaches best who passes on what he contemplates in prayer. On the other hand, it is not religious life itself that gives the right to teach and to preach, but that is authorized by the reception of order and the proper jurisdiction from higher prelates. Given the pastoral need of the era, an ideal solution was the foundation of mendicant orders, who followed Christ as his disciples in search of holiness and who preached and led people to penance. While any friar could preach and preach penance, only the ordained could give the sacrament of penance and offer the sacrifice of Christ for the people and give them communion.

In the *Summa theologiae*, where Aquinas develops a theology of sacrament, one of the foundational articles is his treatment of the sacramental character, which he relates to the priesthood of Christ. The background to this is his treatment of Christ's priesthood and of the mediation of what he calls the *gratia Capitis*; this grace comes from Christ to his body and makes of him and the Church *quasi una persona*.[16] In the mediation of Christ, he distinguishes a downward and an upward movement. The first brings healing and mediates grace to humanity through the power of the cross. The second is the worship of God, offered by Christ principally on the cross, and with which the Church is associated, principally in liturgy. The perfection of the Church in its communion with Christ is found in its public worship, where it benefits from the twofold movement of Christ's mediation. There it receives the grace that heals and sanctifies, and there it is one with Christ in his worship of the Father. The sacramental character is a participation in this priest-hood or mediation of Christ. In receiving the character of baptism, the Christian is given the passive power to receive the sacraments and to take part in the Church's worship. In receiving the sacrament of order, the priest is made an instrument of Christ's sanctifying power. He is one with Christ, the principal instrument of God's grace in both the downward and the upward movement of grace and worship. This character is therefore called an active power.

When the character of baptism is dubbed a passive power, Aquinas is making use of the Aristotelian enumeration of the powers of the soul. This is not meant to suggest passivity, even if it indicates that the human person to be sanctified has to be totally receptive. It requires an act of faith and an intention to be one with Christ and the Church in divine worship. It asks of the faithful that they join not only their hearts but their voices and bodies with the act of worship in its sacramental and bodily form. It is a true participation in the one priesthood of Jesus Christ.

As well as the participation in the priesthood of Christ in the sacraments, Aquinas exacts a public profession of faith, a public testimony, from the Christian who receives the character of the sacrament of confirmation. Explaining the rites for the celebration of confirmation, he says that the confirmed are made soldiers of Christ, persons who must defend the true faith in public, not by taking up arms but by taking up the spiritual struggle against the forces of evil. It is in his treatment of confirmation that Thomas seems to abandon the comparison with Christ's priesthood in order to allow for those activities on behalf of the Church that, we have seen, were in fact followed by lay persons at that time.

On the other hand, this theology does sharply distinguish the action of the priest from that of the faithful in the Church's public worship. He alone consecrates, he alone offers the sacramental sacrifice. The part of the baptized in the Mass is to be united in mind and heart with the action performed by the priest in the person of Christ. Another consequence of Thomistic theology of the priesthood is that the sacramental ministry of the priest is distinguished from all that he receives through jurisdiction and pastoral charge. The powers are connected in practice, but they have distinct sources. In the practical order, room is left for the priest who has no pastoral role but is ordained solely to offer the eucharistic sacrifice, in the person of Christ.

By way of summation, it can be said that the theology of order in these early centuries of the second millennium was in touch with practice even as it attempted a systematic explanation of the order of grace. In its own way it accounted for the part of the laity in the Church. It was dominantly spiritual in tone and in purpose, seeing life in general in terms of spiritual hierarchy. As new ways of life emerged, whether those of lay persons seeking perfection or those of mendicant friars, it incorporated them into a theological vision of the Church. In all of this, however, it operated within what had become the established distinction between clergy and laity, between priest and people, and gave it a firm theological basis.

Pre-Reformation Reform Movements

After Thomas Aquinas and Bonaventure, much of the treatment of priesthood was devoted to his power to offer the sacrifice of the Mass, for the living and the dead. In practice, what has been said of lay activities remained true. Ways developed in which laity claimed a certain independence and distinctive Christian spirituality, as exemplified in the practice of the *devotio moderna*. Groups that were looked upon as dissident are also found right up to the eve of the Reformation. Notable are John Hus and the Hussites, who were influenced in their thought and practice by the ecclesiology of the Englishman John Wyclif.

What is called the *devotio moderna* is associated with Geert de Groote (1240–84) and the Brethren of the Common Life. This was a lay movement of reform that found some institutional structures in this brotherhood, though it also spun off into a monastic movement. Giving importance to the reading of the Bible, de Groote and others emphasized the sinfulness of the human person and the need for conversion and repentance, while accentuating an interior life of intense communion with Christ. The devotees called for a reform of the Church and the return to the evangelical life. Though they called for reform, they did not challenge the work and order of the clergy but showed that lay people claimed a voice in bringing the Church back to the Bible and to the simplicity of the gospel. While in some ways they anticipated the spirituality of the Reformation era, they did not look for any radical reform of Church structures.

John Wyclif is sometimes called "the morning star of the Reformation," since he thought in terms of changing ecclesiastical structures as well as looking for an evangelical reform of life and custom. Two things in his teaching had to do more directly with the ordering of the Church. One is the appeal to the Bible, Word of God, as criterion for judging the Church, its officials, and its members. The other is the connection he made between spiritual witness and sacramental ministry. This is in one way quite traditional, but Wyclif sided with those of earlier times who questioned the validity of sacraments celebrated by the unworthy. The way to reform lay in great part with the laity, who could underline the role of faith in all things, including sacraments, and who could press reform on the clergy, who were supposed to serve them. It is often judged that he went too far in what he expected of the reform of structures, in his pointing to the Bible as criterion of truth without seeing its link with tradition, and in his rejection of eucharistic transubstantiation. However, what he pointed to by way of the place that the Bible should have in the life of the Church and of the Christian and his desire for more evangelical simplicity in the Church, top and bottom, are always factors to which the Church needs to attend in its self-ordering.

Jan Hus and those who remained his disciples even after his execution at the stake, now called Hussites, were influenced by the teaching of Wyclif, so much so indeed that a posthumous condemnation of Wyclif was seen to be condemnation of the Hussite movement. Hus, a reformer to the core in his concern with moral probity, showed his own genius in how he wrote of the headship of Christ over the

Church. His desire for moral evangelical reform and his theology of the Church converged in the call to return to the form and ideals of the primitive church of the New Testament period. Insisting on the unique headship of Christ, he questioned how the Pope could call himself head of the Church. That there was some form of Petrine ministry, he did not question, but it could not be exercised in such a way as to appear as a dignity and a status or be an interference with the legitimate freedom of particular churches.[17]

Hus encouraged lay preaching, being himself a preacher and a lay person. He like Wyclif wanted to restore the Bible to a proper place in ritual and in the life of the faithful. In the celebration of the Eucharist, he espoused greater simplicity and the right of all to communion from the chalice. All of this was seen as a questioning of Church authority and doctrine and earned him condemnation.[18] At the time it seemed impossible for ecclesiastical authorities to integrate the elements of reform espoused by this essentially lay movement; they were unable to grant audience to what lay people were saying when they criticized the clergy.

If we were to summarize how clergy and laity influenced the exercise of the Christian life in the centuries prior to the Reformation, we would have to work with a rather broad understanding of order, of how activities were ordered. There was a predominating ecclesiastical and clerical perspective that appealed to divine power as justification for a pastoral rule over the body of the Church. Lay persons, women and men, however, ordered their lives of prayer, preaching, teaching, and ministering to others in their own distinctive ways, without for the most part directly challenging clerical dominance. One cannot write of the significance of Christian faith for society, nor of ministry, nor of how lives and communities may be ordered, without taking all this into account and so stretching the boundaries of canonical and theological discussion on Church order, on the power to sanctify and the power to teach and rule. Stretched it has to be, however, and when it is stretched, we are faced with the question as to whether contemporary churches, universal and local, can do better at integrating all service and all ordering into a common model.

Sixteenth-Century Reformation

In a kind of rehabilitation of Catholic Reformation—or Counter-Reformation, as in an earlier more-common expression—it has become customary to say that the old devotion worked or that people were well served by the ordering of life and worship that prevailed. That may be true as long as we are talking only about what worked in fostering devotion among the faithful. It leaves open the question of fidelity to the gospel and to nature of the Church as known from Scripture and tradition.

Clearly the Reformers did not always think that things worked well. There was a practical dissatisfaction with the ideals pursued by clergy and monks and promoted among the laity. This extended to practices such as indulgences and stipendiary systems and the manner of administering auricular confession, which seemed to run contrary to the gospel and reliance on God's Word and grace. Fundamental was the dissatisfaction with the fact that people were being diverted from the true forms of worship in hearing the Word and participating in the Lord's Supper to subsidiary devotions—and that the promotion of auricular confession kept people from the table. The appeal to justification by Word and faith rather than by works leading to righteousness was not just a theoretical matter.

In presenting a theological ideal for how they thought the Christian order should be regulated, the Reformers of the sixteenth century were intent to overcome the distinction between the baptized and ordained ministers associated with the doctrine of the sacramental character and priestly anointing. As christological foundation, they applied Christ's titles of *king* and *priest* to spiritual things and not to the temporal. They saw in this the foundation for the participation of all in the life of the Church and its worship, as well as for the exercise and ordering of ministry. Though they saw appointment of pastors to the preaching of the Word and the administration of the Lord's Supper as a matter of divine ordinance, the Reformers did not think that this justified the distinction of priestly character advocated by Scholastic theology, which supported a dignity that separated ordained and baptized faithful.

Martin Luther

In Martin Luther,[19] the primacy of the Word of God over structures and ministry was clearly affirmed, as was the basic ecclesial doctrine of the royal priesthood of all believers. While he found grounds for ministerial order in the New Testament and upheld as gospel ordinance the call of the candidate by God, and not by the congregation, to the pastoral ministry of Word and Sacrament, his teaching on the royal priesthood influenced his ideas of ordering the ministry.

The call to ministry is to serve the royal priesthood and is a call to the preaching of the Word and the right administration of the sacraments of baptism and the Lord's Supper. It is a divine call but confers no special status or permanent mark, and it is not to be defined in terms of priestly sacrifice. In the normal way, this is handed on through ordination within a line of succession going back to apostolic times, but to safeguard the primacy of the priesthood of all believers, endowed by faith with the grace of justification and the Spirit, and with the dignity and freedom of being believers, this strict temporal succession in ordering may have to be broken in times of crisis. This is precisely to safeguard the Word and the equal dignity of all believers, for which the service of pastoral ministry is ordained, and hence by implication to safeguard the fidelity of the ministry itself.

In his writings on the role of Christ in human salvation, as well as in what he says of the baptized, Martin Luther joins the function of king with that of priest.[20] In several of his biblical commentaries, he elaborates on the sacrifice of Christ in terms that often sound similar to those found in patristic writers, but with his own particular view of the imputation of Christ's righteousness to sinners and of justification by faith. By his anointing, Christ like Melchizedek is both king and priest, and he enters into these offices through the sacrifice of his death. None can properly share in this priesthood and kingship, but baptism nonetheless can be said to confer a royal priesthood, the benefit of what Christ has won for his people.[21]

Luther resolved the conflict between *regnum* and *sacerdotium* in his own unique way, for example, in the work *Secular Authority: To What Extent It Should Be Obeyed*.[22] He believes in Christendom, that is, that society should be organized and ruled to serve the kingdom of God and the mission of the Church. Secular authority is willed and ordained by God in the interests of the gospel. Its role is to protect the followers of the kingdom and to punish the wicked. However, it is not said to be in any way a participation in Christ's kingly powers. Luther's fundamental principle is that through baptism, all are of the royal priesthood, all are priests and kings without distinction. Within this priesthood or kingship, each must serve according to the position that one holds. Some are called to ministry, some to rule, others to do more ordinary tasks. By meeting these duties, one lives out the common priesthood or kingship that comes from Christ, through baptism and the Spirit.

For the government of the Church, the Germanic and Scandinavian countries kept an episcopal system in place. The bishops retained the control of pastoral appointments and supervision. At the same time, a synodal body was constructed to have its part in Church government and pastoral nomination, though its functioning differed from place to place. The rights of civil authorities were respected in all that had to do with the Church and God's law.

John Calvin

In John Calvin's writings,[23] the term "priesthood of all Christians" prevails over that of "priesthood of all believers." While it belongs to those who are members of the body of Christ, and its meaning is seen in terms of the service of the kingdom of God in the world. The purpose of the Church is to allow Christ's exercise of authority through Christian living and through the Church's ministry for the "establishment and extension of his kingdom." This is done primarily through the action of all Christians, who offer to God all that they have and are, joining their lives to Christ and his once and for all sacrifice. It is the liberating salvation enables them to do this that confers on them the role of "priest" in accordance with its New Testament foundations.

Calvin generally limited the use of the term *ministry* to the offices that he believed were given by Christ for the proclamation of the gospel, the celebration of the sacraments, and the ordering or governance of the life of faith. The context for Calvin's reference to "the priesthood of all Christians" is his comparison of governance by presbyters and elders with the ecclesiastical orders of the Roman Church, particularly its office of "priest." Calvin argued that Christ, our high priest, has already made the single, necessary sacrifice for our salvation, and therefore any priest offering the sacrifice of the Mass was contradicting Christ's effective work. He concludes, "In him we are all priests [Rev 1:6; cf. 1 Pet 2:9], but to offer praises and thanksgiving—in short, to offer ourselves and ours to God." With this there goes the duty to live out the faith in daily practice and even the duty to admonish each other for mutual edification, or to aid each other in the understanding of the Scriptures. Those called by God and elected to particular offices in the community of faith share in the priesthood of all Christians. As officers and ministers, they have particular responsibilities within the dispensation of the variety of gifts given by the Spirit.

Serving the kingdom of God means proclaiming the gospel, safeguarding its truth, forming community through the sacraments of the Lord's Supper and baptism, and ordering its institutional and communal life so as to grow toward sanctification. To attain this purpose, there is need for Church governance through properly appointed pastors and teachers and through the diaconal ministry of care for the poor. The foundation of this teaching is to be found in the Scriptures. Calvin appealed especially to Eph 4:11—16, where he found the distinction between the offices that served the founding of the Church and those that endure as permanent offices, namely pastors and teachers. To these he added the ministry of government by elders as ordained by Rom 12:7–8 and the ministry of the deaconate in caring for the poor, especially as evidenced in Acts 6.

For Church government, Calvinists modeled a synodal type of government. There were the general synod, provincial synods, and local consistories. The consistory was presided over by the chief pastor and was comprised of pastors, elders, and deacons. The pastors were responsible for the ministry of the Word and sacraments; the deacons for the care of the sick, the poor, and prisoners, and also for family catechesis. The elders were thought to continue the role of elders in the New Testament and were charged with the supervision of morals and conduct. Calvin espoused a return to the ministries of the New Testament, with primacy given to Word. He kept the titles of pastor, elder, and deacon, believing that the terms *bishop* and *elder* were used of the same men.

Anabaptists

The call for a return to the evangelical simplicity and reliance on the Word of God and on the Spirit of the early church is never silenced in the history of the Church. At the time of the Reformation, the Anabaptists[24] continued the agelong aspiration to a more radical evangelical simplicity and an even greater dependence on the Word of God alone. They contested the Reformers as much as they did the Roman Church. They upheld the ideal of the Church as a sectarian body, that is, one that could never be identified with the social order but that was called to give a witness of a holy and evangelical life. They held to the principle of a community life in which all things were held in common and were in line with those of the earlier Middle Ages who had a definitely eschatological outlook and awaited the advent of the kingdom of God. This meant that those who live by the Word and by faith paid little heed to an elaborate system of ecclesiastical government. Nonetheless, some Anabaptist communities spoke in terms of different ministries: these were the tasks of itinerant apostles, who had to be "found faithful" in their own lives, and prophets, who were charismatics and heads of local communities that were close to the early ideal of the household church.

In written history the Anabaptists often appear to be marginal. Their presence nonetheless is a keen reminder that no age has been without those who aspire to a more evangelical style of community life and who represent an alternate way for the followers of Christ to relate to temporal society. It is an aspect of its own being that a church neglects at the cost of the truth of the gospel.

Council of Trent

While there is much to the history of early dealings with Luther and others, the Council of Trent (1545–63) is taken as the final response of the Roman Church to the Reformers.[25] At the same time, in these days when we argue over the interpretation of the Second Vatican Council, it is well to remember that at the convocation of the Council of Trent, not all were clear on the agenda to be followed, and that on its close it went through a period of reception that determined the way in which its decrees were thenceforth to be understood.

The bull of convocation, *Laetare Jerusalem*, presented a threefold purpose: to eradicate religious schism, to restore peace among Christians, and to reclaim the holy places in Palestine and Jerusalem. The emperor was mostly concerned with healing schism since it was tearing the empire apart in bloody fashion. Others thought that the reform of the Church from top to bottom should be the major topic. Pope Paul III and the Roman Curia wanted to make dogmatic definitions that would eradicate the ideas of the Reformers among faithful Catholics the priority. In the end, at the early sessions of the Council, those present voted for a dual procedure of reform and of dogmatic definition.

While the reform agenda had much to say about pastoral priorities and clerical mores and about abuses in the celebration of the Mass, it was the doctrinal teaching that had long standing consequences for relations between Christian bodies. The decrees on the Eucharist were key to ecclesiology since they affirmed the place and sacramental authority of ordained ministers, always keeping a clear difference between ordained and baptized. The decree on the sacrifice of the Mass is the most crucial in defining differences on ministry between the Reformers and the upholders of what was believed to be Catholic tradition. Trent affirmed the power of the priest to offer the memorial and sacramental sacrifice. It upheld the legitimacy of the Latin Mass and the right of priests to celebrate without congregations. Though it encouraged all to take communion at Mass, it did not consider this necessary to the Mass itself. In a separate decree, it deemed mandating communion under both kinds inexpedient for the time being, given what was going on in doctrinal and practical conflicts with the Reformers. Though in other decrees of reform the Council stressed the importance of preaching, it did not introduce the vernacular reading of the Bible into the Mass, and in this way it continued to withhold familiarity with the Word of God from the people.

The teaching on the sacrament of order is of more direct interest to how ministries are ordered, and its main points have already been recalled as the prelude to the theologies written prior to the Second Vatican Council. A study of history shows that the issues appearing in the conciliar debates were quite broad, but that the doctrinal decree was preoccupied with the relation between bishops and priests. The essence of priesthood is to offer the sacrifice of the Mass, but the origin and authority of the bishop has its foundations in the New Testament and the apostolic tradition.

In the rift between Rome and the Reformers, one might say that the node of dispute was whether to define ministry in the Church in terms of the Word of God or in terms of a sacrificing priesthood. The principal Reformers kept an important place in Church discipline and doctrine for the celebration of the Lord's Supper, but they related this to the proclamation of the Word and to faith so that the Word had first place in the understanding of ministry. Catholics wished for better preaching and a reformed and better-educated clergy, but they held to the definition of ministry in terms of priesthood and sacrifice. In ecclesiology, the Reformers brought the priesthood of all believers to the fore, while Catholics looked at the Church as a divinely instituted hierarchical body. For centuries this key difference in conceiving and ordering ministry endured, and even today, despite agreed statements, it is hardly possible to say that the difference has been resolved.

The reception of Trent into the life of the Church is marked by a centralization of power in Rome and by actions that were geared toward greater uniformity of liturgical practice and teaching of doctrine among Latin Christians. The Roman Missal of 1570 and the Roman Ritual of 1614 demanded a conformity in liturgical practice that was unknown before the Council. While the divulgation of the Roman Liturgy had gone ahead since the days of Charlemagne, it allowed for much regional and local diversity, a diversity that was now excluded. The Catechism of the Council of Trent in turn established one model for teaching the truths of faith, a model of doctrinal proposition that attended little to the reading of the Scriptures. Points to which the conciliar fathers gave only temporary resolution, seeing them as matters for further scrutiny, were left untouched. Excluding the vernacular from the proclamation of the Scriptures in the liturgy and refusing the chalice to the laity became permanent rules in a way not intended in the decisions of the Council. The need for clergy reform and preparation was channeled through the institution of seminaries, which for centuries determined the mindset and the lifestyle of ordained ministers in the Catholic tradition. At its twenty-third session the Council laid down norms for the choice and education of candidates for the priesthood, and implementing this decree led to the diffusion of the seminary system, with its minor and major components, that is institutions for lower and higher education and formation.[26] As far as the implementation of the Council is concerned, Kenan Osborne puts it succinctly:

> Circumstances after the council either officially moved the effects of the council in a direction not advocated by the council, e.g., the focus on the universal

church rather than on the local church, or placed some of these directions virtually on hold, e.g., the role of the Scripture in the life of the individual Christian. . . . Tridentinism moved the effects of the council into a clerical and Roman conformism.[27]

Catholic Order after the Council of Trent

In its focus on reform within the Church, the Council of Trent attended to bishops and diocesan clergy. It had little to say of priests who belonged to religious orders, though several newly founded ones had a large part in working toward reforms in the domain of pastoral care and in addressing ministry to new needs, such as that of the education of the clergy. Nor did it attend to lay Christians other than to see them as subjects of pastoral care.

In studying the history of Trent, if one were to take this as the whole history of the time, one would miss out on the missionary expansion that had begun even before Luther pinned his theses on the door of the church at Wittenberg. With the discovery of a new world, canons regular and mendicants had gone to preach the gospel among the *indos* of the Americas and the Philippines. In those areas, their pastoral work was not subject in any way to the regime of bishop or diocese, but they exercised an independent missionary task. Unfortunately, their attitudes toward indigenous peoples and traditional religions were extremely negative, but what is of interest here is to note how this work brought a new kind of Church order into being, one that confided whole territories to the care of religious priests and then bishops who were not ordained for any diocese but specifically for missionary work.

Likewise to be noted is that during and after the period of the Council of Trent, priests took on new kinds of work, independent of close diocesan authority.[28] The work of the newly founded Jesuits in the education of youth may stand for this new trend. While they showed allegiance to the Pope, and in some way to local bishops, their work as such fell under the special jurisdictional authority of the order and constituted their own special mission.

When one pursues this further in the developments of following centuries, the work of women religious has to be taken into account, both in Old Europe and on the new missionary continents. Without their work the mission and ministry of the Church would simply have faded away. On a whole the women accepted the authority of priests and were subject to them, but there are quite a few stories of how foundations and their work went forward only because some women wrangled with bishops over the divine inspiration and thrust of their work and of the kinds of religious life that they adopted. Some who founded religious communities for works of service, such as Anne Jahouvey and Mary MacKillop, endured long periods of ecclesiastical censure before their work prevailed.

The vast missionary work of women's and men's congregations between the sixteenth century and the twentieth hardly needs to be recorded. While they are to be lauded for bringing the gospel across the world, it also has to be said that they looked unkindly on non-European cultures and indigenous religions. The effort was to implant the Church, with its elaborate organization of church, hospital, school, catechetics, as it was known in Europe. In this atmosphere, there was little possibility of a growth of ministries or ecclesial structures that fitted with the cultural heritage or way of life of the many peoples whom they evangelized.

Between Trent and Vatican II, in summary, one could point to three defects in the ordering of ministry in the Church. The first is the split between ordained and faithful, so that whatever service lay persons actively rendered the Church and its mission had inadequate institutional and theological place in the ordering of ecclesial life. Second is the dominance of a male hierarchical priesthood. This meant that while women rendered more service to the Church in health care and teaching and did more to pass on the faith, it was not possible to give this work its due place in Church order and government. The third defect is the implantation of the Church outside Europe according to the model of a late medieval and post-Tridentine ecclesiology, and the total shunning of any recognition of the cultural and religious traditions of the peoples evangelized. In a way, one could say that the story of Church order during this period is one of no growth and no change, though this would do vast injustice to the work of congregations of women and men who devoted themselves to the poor, to teaching, and to missionary work. Overcoming the defects inherent in an ecclesiastical system is necessary so that the effective work of preaching the Gospel that was done is being revised and reordered in such a way as to move beyond this ecclesiastical paralysis. How this began before Vatican II and continued under its impulse has already been considered at the opening of this work. Taking this movement into account has allowed a more critical and, it is hoped, constructive way of looking at traditions, reading in the margins and out of the mainstream as much as possible.

Mission and Ministry in Post-Reformation Churches

The exercise of ministry in missionary work was not confined to Catholics. One should take account as well of those who subscribed to the basic principles of the Reformation. What follows is meant to be broad in scope.

John Wesley

From among those who continued ministry in the spirit of the Protestant Reformation, attention could be given to quite a number. Since he left a strong mark on Christianity and preached the gospel under new circumstances, it seems worthwhile to single out John Wesley and his particular significance for the understanding of mission and ministry. He believed strongly in the personal experience of Christ but also in the social mission of believers. The normal means of grace, to use his own phrase, are searching the Scriptures (which means hearing them and meditating on them) and receiving the Lord's Supper in remembrance of Christ. The inner working of these means of grace cannot be separated from the work of the Spirit within the believer.[29] Since all believers are filled with the Holy Spirit, all who are disciples have the duty to spread this knowledge and to live in society in such a way that it be transformed and won from its sinful ways. This is "scriptural Christianity."[30] Holiness of life is demanded of all, but in a special way it is incumbent on the one who preaches. At first Wesley was slow to admit lay preachers, but as his work of "revitalization" of Christianity developed, he came to consider the work of lay preaching to be vital.

On the ministerial office, Wesley needed to provide from Scripture the roots of both its ordinary and its extraordinary transmission.[31] In the New Testament he found evidence for the offices of deacon, elder, and bishop, or superintendent. Elders are ordained by the laying on of hands and have what he called an ambassadorial role, preferring not to speak of mediatorial, which savored of Catholic principles and a reliance on human mediators. They are representatives of God's kingdom, and their office is to preach and administer the sacraments as pastors of their congregations. In keeping with the traditions of the Anglican Church, from which Wesley never wished to be separated, he saw ordination by a bishop as the normal way of transmitting the ministerial charge. However, in extraordinary circumstances, to assure the means of grace to the faithful and provide them with pastors, an elder may receive the extraordinary call of the Spirit to act as a superintendent or bishop. This too he believed to have a scriptural warrant.

In this understanding of ministry and its transmission, Wesley is true to the primacy of the priesthood of all believers and to the priority of the end over the means. One must first see what ministry serves according to God's ordinances and then consider the means in relation to the end, allowing for what is ordinary but also for the extraordinary.

The Protestant Sense of Mission

In their works, David Bosch[32] and Andrew Walls[33] allow us to appreciate the sense of mission that arose and guided the evolution of ministry and then flourished in churches other than the Catholic in the centuries after the Reformation. The great Reformers did their work at a time when the discovery of other continents was only at its beginning. Both Luther and Calvin believed in the importance of the Great Commission to bring the gospel to all peoples, but they did not think much beyond their efforts to establish the Reformed view of Christianity in European countries. When more came to be known about peoples in other parts of the world, there seemed to be too many insurmountable obstacles to contact, civilization, and conversion. Some theologians held the view that the Great Commission had already been implemented and that in the time of the apostles, the whole world had heard the gospel. If more was to be done, this should be left to clear indications of God's initiative, who alone can give the gift of faith and salvation.[34] While at first some Protestants were inclined to see Catholic missionary efforts favorably, for the most part they were seen as a human work, an effort to spread Catholic and even papal control to all parts of the world.

Thus in the early Reformation period, not much was done to spread the gospel among new peoples. The Pietism of the eighteenth century (and we have already written of John Wesley), however, changed that. Having themselves a warm and devout union with Christ and putting the stress on personal experience in salvation, the Pietists thought to bring this faith experience to other peoples. Their sense of communion with Christ and their missionary impulse allowed them to be more independent of colonial powers than were the initial Catholic missions. They went abroad simply thinking to bring Christ as Savior to all who would hear them.

They could not, however, separate themselves so readily from reliance on the secular powers from various European countries—whether they be Spain, Portugal, England, or the Netherlands—whose envoys had conquered vast territories across the globe. The Enlightenment, for all that it wanted to free society from dependence on religion, had an influence on the thought and action of missionaries. Those leaving England to bring the gospel to others were convinced enough of the achievements of "civilization" to wish to bring its benefits to those whom they evangelized, as also did Catholic missionaries in their own mission fields. Catholics thought to implant the Church, that Church known to them from its past history, and Protestants thought to bring the message of personal salvation. They were alike in that they wanted to bring not only faith but also what they saw as their superior civilization and mode of life. Thinking quite poorly of other cultures and religions, which we know they would have seen neither as true culture nor true religion, they worked with colonial powers in imposing a European way of life on those whom they evangelized.

Given their different ideals of faith, there were inevitable frictions between Catholic and Protestant missionaries.[35] Catholics gave pride of place to sacraments and to the teaching of doctrine and so to formal catechesis. Protestants gave first place to the Book and to preaching and to the personal experience of Christ. Though they too put much work into schools and health care, as far as the divinely transmitted reality of the Church is concerned, they set less store by hierarchies and institutions.

There were also significant differences in their recruitment of personnel. As far as ministry and order are concerned, the work of Catholic missions was done mostly by ordained priests, usually belonging to religious orders, and by women religious or religious brothers, whatever use they made of local lay persons as catechists or interpreters. Together they planted the Church, with its places of worship, its schools, and its health facilities. On the other hand, Protestants to a great extent relied on lay missionaries who went out as single men or women or indeed as families. From England alone, the stories of the Christian Mission Society and the London Mission Society is the story of how whatever ordained or commissioned preachers there were relied on the lay persons who volunteered to do the work of mission in foreign fields.[36]

As Walls points out, whether the mission was Catholic or Protestant, its success depended on a combination of three factors.[37] These were reliance on a substantial corps of competent and willing persons, promoting good organization, and having access to new territories. For Catholics, the first two factors were provided by the religious orders, old and new, that flourished across Europe. For Protestants, they were provided by lay volunteers and the missionary organizations that sponsored them. In that sense, Protestant mission showed in a unique way the missionary and ministerial capacities of the baptized faithful while Catholic mission continued its work according to the old clerical paradigm.

What we generally look upon as the weak side, or in some respects the failure, of missionary movements is their reluctance to relate to the cultures of those to whom they preached, or at least their inability to take them seriously. On the one hand, missionaries of different churches did pioneer work in studying languages and in giving them written form, as some also did important work in the field of cultural anthropology. They did not take these cultures or the religions of peoples into account in the way of formulating the gospel or implanting the Church or calling persons to ministry.

For this reason, Andrew Walls has an important section in one of his books on the challenge of African Independent Churches, to whom he refers as the Anabaptists of Africa.[38] Their importance in missionary history and in offering a new paradigm for ministry is that they result from the work of African peoples themselves. Having received the gospel from foreigners, they took it over in their own way and gave it its African expression and organization. They have their origin in the gospel and in personal religious experience, embodied in persons whom they consider to be prophets, who they believe to have been in their own time vessels of divine revelation, endowed with gifts and charisms. While being so personal, they are also well organized; to some Europeans, they might even appear to be autocratic, with so much power invested in their prophets, preachers, and individual leaders. Walls points out the peculiarly African pattern of common life found in these churches, where there is such a unique blend of the hierarchical and the ritual on the one hand, with the charismatic and the spontaneous on the other.[39] For inculturating mission and ministry, the established churches need to look to these bodies for inspiration and to take them as dialogue partners within the ecumenical movement.

Concluding Observations

In what we have surveyed, on the one hand we may note a constant interchange between the work of the ordained and the work of the laity, while on the other it is only of ordained office that there is a developed theology.[40] While at times it is said that the faithful were passive within a Church dominated by the clergy, we should be aware that this is not completely true. More than their absence from ecclesial activity is their absence from canonical and theological provisions of Church order, except in the case of those following a vowed life. This fixed their status in the Church but did not abolish their contribution by works of service to the Church's life and mission. In some sense herein lies the challenge of the moment: not so much to call the laity into service as to promote their part in mission and ministry by means of an appropriate theology and just canonical provisions. Theology and Canon Law have not quite caught up with reality even yet and still work with a clerical/lay dualism instead of with a focus on community as an organic unit.

Looking at history, we are also indebted to reformers, at whose apex stand the great Reformers of the sixteenth century, for a retrieval of the scriptural idiom and theology of the royal priesthood of all the faithful. Theologies of mission and ministry have to be built on this. In the work of mission after the discovery of new continents, we are also indebted to many in the Protestant tradition for including the lay faithful in this work. As the Catholic Church looks ahead, it needs to think of this past as part of a common heritage. We need to acknowledge that neither Catholic nor Protestant came to firm grips with the relation of the Church to society and peoples, so that missionaries could easily become tools for spreading a civilization dubbed necessary by secular powers. Caring for the needs of the poor remained a core part of the mission of the Church, and many women and men dedicated their lives to this, but it is impossible to claim that Christians had worked out a social doctrine that gave priority to an order of justice that would address the plight of the poor.[41]

The Protestant tradition challenges the understanding of ministry and its transmission in serious ways. While continuing to look to scriptural ordinances for its foundation and generally to uphold ordination within the established ecclesiastical order, it puts the purpose and not the institution of ordered ministry to the fore. It calls into question the equation of ordained ministry with office and status and keeps alive the need to invoke the power of the Spirit to provide for extraordinary situations. While Catholic tradition will continue to draw on the resources of its own theological and canonical resources and espouse some distinctive positions, it needs to be more alive to the challenge that comes to it from these Protestant questions.

Looking back even further in history to the split between East and West, what is more striking is how Catholicism, in becoming more ritualistic and more Rome-centered, in many ways became less eucharistic. The tradition of the Eucharist is not kept alive simply by ordaining men to consecrate the body and blood of Christ, to offer sacrifice and forgive sins, by observing rituals. It is kept alive by attending to local churches and to the celebration of the Eucharist as the work of a believing community, served by its ministers. Retrieving this kind of centrality of the Eucharist for the life and mission of the Church may be the key challenge to the Church today. This does not mean abandoning traditional institutions but putting them to the service of the royal priesthood in a truly evangelical fashion.

PART 3

Contemporary Theological Reflections on Ministry and Mission

Introduction

A suitable theological perspective on ministry today must take account of the contemporary global situation in all its diversity as well as of efforts to bind together the human race as one family. Theology develops in the light of tradition but in such a way as to answer to current realities, inspirations, and needs. Some key issues recur and are important to consider in a new light. These are the royal priesthood of the Church, what it means to represent Christ, and what is to be expected of effective leadership in a Church that acknowledges many gifts, services, and ministries. This part of the present work is meant to offer reflections on how these issues might be seen in the light of developments presented in the first parts of the book, which show how over time churches have engaged with tradition and with contemporary situations, in the light of tradition.

The first chapter is addressed to an understanding of the royal priesthood of the Church, which is participated in several ways. The second is about what it means to represent Christ in the Church, with particular attention to how the understanding of the vicarious role of the ordained took shape. The third is a reflection on leadership, taking into consideration requirements of a current ordering of ministries and services that relates to how churches across the world are developing a sense of their mission. Some points included in the historical part of the book will have to be recalled, without, it is hoped, too much repetition. It does seem necessary for present needs to give the theologies of priesthood and representation specific treatment by attending to their historical development as well as to current magisterial teaching and ecumenical interchange.

9

Royal Priesthood

Images, ideas, and theologies of priesthood have played a big part in questions about order and ministry and still do today.[1] Images of priesthood have also been consistently associated with those of kingship. This is retained most clearly in speaking of the royal priesthood of the baptized. To facilitate new developments in ministry, we need a good understanding of this theological foundation. Despite an apparent initial clarity on what is meant by priesthood, it has been a very fluid concept. To sort out the matter, we need to relate the kingly priesthood of Jesus Christ, the reality of the Church as a royal priesthood, and what this means for its members as individuals or as groups. To see where we now stand, we begin with a presentation of the current teaching of the magisterium and then turn to tradition in order to better look at the question in its contemporary context.

Magisterium

Following *Sacrosanctum concilium* 14, *Lumen gentium* 9 talks of the Church, among other things, as a priestly people and a royal priesthood. This expresses the communal and collective nature of the Church and the idea that the Church in itself is the true worship of God, or the living sacrifice worthy of God's name. The difference between the two texts is that *SC* 14 takes this designation (priestly, priesthood) as the foundation for full and active participation in the liturgy, whereas *LG* 9 offers it as a designation of the Church in its entire corporate reality as sacrament of Christ in the world.

Thus *LG* 11 says that it is "Through the sacraments and the exercise of the virtues, . . . that the sacred nature and organic structure of the priestly community is brought into operation." It concludes from this that the faithful share the worship of the Church by reason of the baptismal character but are also expected to profess their faith openly before the world. Practicing the Christian life, offering spiritual sacrifices, openly professing the faith by word and deed, and taking part in sacramental worship all in some way or another are brought under the umbrella of the baptismal priesthood. What the Church is as a body in its royal priesthood and what individual members are or do by reason of a share in Christ's priesthood are evidently connected, but how this is so is not clearly explained.

241

To enter into the particulars of how different members participate in the life of the Church, *LG* 10ff. resorts to the theology of the threefold office of Christ as priest, prophet, and king. This meant distinguishing the kingly from the priestly, as well as adding the prophetic. In chapter 2, *LG* attends in a very particular way to the respective participations of baptized and ordained in the priesthood of Christ as it is distinguished from the other two offices attributed to him.

If one is to judge from the synodal acts of Vatican II, the distinction between the threefold office of Christ and its application to the Church seems to have been adopted without much discussion.[2] Though it has been recognized that this was not a common way of writing about Christ in the patristic Church, it is justified by an appeal to Eusebius of Caesarea. However, not much can be made of the one passage cited from his *Ecclesiastical History* (1.3). Eusebius affirms that in Christ all Old Testament anointings are brought to fulfillment, whether these be of priests, kings, or prophets. The distinction between the three anointings is not developed, and nothing is said of any implications for the life of the Church. The plan followed at the Vatican Council, maybe unwittingly on the part of most of the bishops present, is that of John Calvin in the *Institutes of the Christian Religion*.[3] In adopting the schema, the Council members and their theological advisers seem to have found it a useful plan to follow in sorting out offices and ministries in the Church, and its practicality may have prevented any investigation of its origin or of its exact meaning in Calvin's work.

As mentioned before, in *LG* 10 very precise attention is given to the distinction in priesthood between the ordained and the other baptized, since this apparently was a preoccupation for many members of the Council. Associating priesthood with worship and sacrament, the document said that the difference in the two participations in the one priesthood of Christ is one in kind and not only in degree: *essentia non solum gradu.* To some this seems rather ambiguous, but to others it was a useful way to get over the idea of distinctions in state implied by the language of degree, or *gradus.*[4] In other words, it is possible to say that there is a distinction in essence without implying a difference in state or rank.[5] However, one is still left to wonder why the Council embraced a difference between what is called the spiritual offering of all the baptized and the sacramental offering of the ordained priest. Is it possible to make a spiritual offering in worship without external sacramental sign of some sort to indicate this inner attitude?

In chapter 4, *LG* 31 again addresses the question of differences or distinctions among the members of the Church in a way that has implications for the understanding of priesthood. As mentioned earlier, it assigns different fields of responsibility to the laity, distinguishing the realms of the secular and of the sacred. Because of their ministry of Word and sacrament, the ordained foster the Church's relation to the sacred, while the lay are charged with promoting the kingdom of God in the realm of the secular. *LG* 34 follows up on this by associating the exercise of the priesthood of the faithful with offering spiritual sacrifices, particularly in the celebration of the Eucharist. It is indeed brought out that all these ways of sharing in the life and mission of the Church are interrelated or ordained to each other. The image of communion in the one people and one royal priesthood is played down in a way that makes the distinction in priesthood, or between the sacred and the secular, fundamental to different roles in the life and mission of the Church.

Since the Council, the magisterium has continued to employ these distinctions in talking of ministry in general or of the sacrifice of the Eucharist and the priesthood in particular. As illustration, we can cite John Paul II, the *Catechism of the Catholic Church*, some texts of Pope Benedict XVI, and the *General Instruction on the Roman Missal*.

John Paul II

In his letter *Ecclesia de eucharistia* (2003),[6] apparently reacting to those who seem to emphasize too much that the Eucharist is given in the sign of a meal, John Paul II states that the Eucharist is a "sacrifice in the strict sense." (§13). In this he relates his teaching to that of the Council of Trent when it says that the Mass is a "true and proper sacrifice."[7] At Trent, this was itself a problematic statement, chosen amid controversies over the Mass, whose exact meaning was not clarified. Whatever about its original intent, in giving an explanation of what he means by the phrase, the Pope affirms that it is because the Eucharist is related to the "sacrifice of Golgotha" that it is said to be a true and proper sacrifice. Of Christ's sacrifice, he highlights the love of the Son for the Father, to the point of giving his life in obedience as gift. Christ does not simply offer himself as spiritual good to the faithful but in love and obedience makes "in the first place a gift to his Father." The Pope then goes on to explain that this is "a sacrifice that the Father accepted, giving, in return for this total self-giving by his Son, who 'became obedient unto death' (Phil 2:8), his own paternal gift, that is to say, the grant of new immortal life in the resurrection." In giving his memorial sacrifice to the Church, Christ "has also made his own the spiritual sacrifice of the Church, which is called to offer herself in union with the sacrifice of Christ." At this point the letter quotes the Vatican Council on the Eucharist, where it says: "Taking part in the Eucharistic Sacrifice, which is the source and summit of the whole Christian life, they [the faithful] offer the divine victim to God, and offer themselves along with it."

John Paul explains the role of the ordained minister by speaking of his "specific sacramental identification with the eternal High Priest" (§29), which allows him to effect the sacramental "representation" of Christ's sacrifice (§15). The pope relates the participation of the faithful in this sacrifice primarily to sacramental communion, where the "saving efficacy of the sacrifice is fully realized" and the communion of the Church as a body is perfected through "the inward union of the faithful with Christ," which can be compared to the life of the Trinity (§16).

In short, John Paul locates the priestly act of the Church in the sacramental representation of the sacrifice of the cross through the ordained minister, with which the faithful are joined as beneficiaries principally through communion. It is to this communion in the body and blood of Christ that the papal insistence on eucharistic adoration, both here and in *Mane nobiscum Domine* (2004), is related: receiving the gift that brings them into the communion of Christ's self-gift to the Father draws them to contemplation of the mystery, a contemplation that can be fostered by eucharistic adoration.

Catechism

The *Catechism of the Catholic Church*[8] (§782) includes the title *People of God* among those to be given to the Church as a body. To this title it attaches the images of chosen race, royal priesthood, holy nation. It is true to the biblical origins of these titles in Exod 19 and 1 Pet 2:4–10, where what is to the fore is indeed the divine choice and initiative. On the priestly vocation of the baptized in particular (§§748, 901), it is content to repeat *LG* 34.

The Catechism offers its own explanation of the way in which the death of Christ is a sacrifice and of how the Eucharist is a memorial sacrifice and so a priestly act. Pointing out that the Father gave his Son to the world, it explains the whole life and mission of Jesus as an act of loving obedience and communion with the Father: "The Son of God, who came down 'from heaven, not to do [his] own will, but the will of him who sent [him],' said on coming into the world, 'Lo, I have come to do your will, O God'" (§606). In suffering and death, his humanity became the free and perfect instrument of his divine love, which desires the salvation of all people. The Catechism goes on to explain that Jesus is the true Lamb of God, the Paschal Lamb, who takes away the sins of the world, and that he is at the same time the Suffering Servant, who is led like a sheep to the slaughter (§608). Here it shows that to know what is meant by sacrifice, several Old Testament images have to be brought into play.

The Eucharist is connected to this sacrifice through the deeds and words of Jesus at the Last Supper. There he anticipated the free offering of his life, so that the Eucharist became the memorial of his voluntary offering to the Father (§610). It adds that Christ "includes the apostles in his own offering and bids them perpetuate it" and by so doing "institutes his apostles as priests of the New Covenant" (§610).

In its section on the Eucharist, the Catechism is more specific about the nature of eucharistic sacrifice: "We carry out [the memorial] command of the Lord by celebrating the memorial of his sacrifice. In so doing, we offer to the Father what he has himself given us: the gifts of his creation, bread and wine which, by the power of the Holy Spirit and by the words of Christ, have become the body and blood of Christ" (§ 1357). It goes on to explain that this sacrifice is one of thanksgiving and praise, and because it "represents" (§ 1366), makes sacramentally present, the sacrifice of Christ himself, it is also an offering by the Church of the divine victim, truly and really present. Because the sacrifice of Christ and the eucharistic sacrifice are one single sacrifice, "the Eucharist is also the sacrifice of the Church, which is the Body of Christ," and the Church participates in the offering of her Head, for "with him, she herself is offered whole and entire" (§ 1368). (The English translation introduced the ambiguous element into the doctrine by translating *representat* as "re-present.") In short, "Christ's sacrifice present on the altar makes it possible for all generations of Christians to be united with his offering." Later, in the chapter on the sacrament of order, the Catechism reiterates the teaching on the essential difference between the two participations in Christ's one priesthood and speaks of the ministerial priesthood as a means by which Christ leads and builds up his body (§1547).

Benedict XVI

Pope Benedict XVI prefers to speak of the Church as a mystery of communion, with less stress on its being called People of God. In the postsynodal exhortation *Sacramentum caritatis* (2007),[9] he associates the understanding of priesthood with the eucharistic sacrifice, careful to emphasize the distinction between the role of the baptized and the proper function of the ordained priest to represent Christ and make the Eucharist possible (§53). The active participation of the faithful is realized most of all in a greater consciousness of the mystery celebrated (§52). They are joined with it in communion but should also join with Christ in his offering. Through and with the priest, they offer the immaculate Victim and should also offer themselves so that they may be one with Christ the Mediator (§52).

Pope Benedict turns to the theme of love to explain the meaning of Christ's death and of its memorial:

> The mission for which Jesus came among us was accomplished in the Paschal Mystery. On the Cross, from which he draws all people to himself (cf. Jn 12:32), just before "giving up the Spirit," he utters the words: "it is finished" (Jn 19:30). In the mystery of Christ's obedience unto death, even death on a Cross (cf. Phil 2:8), the new and eternal covenant was brought about. (Ibid.)

Benedict speaks of the act of the cross as the moment when "God's freedom and our human freedom met definitively in an inviolable, eternally valid pact." This, he declares, is love in its most radical form: "Christ's death on the Cross is the culmination of that turning of God against himself in which he gives himself in order to raise man up and save him. This is love in its most radical form."

The exhortation then turns to the meaning of the Eucharist as the celebration of the paschal mystery and refers to John 1:29, where John the Baptist points to Jesus as the Lamb of God, recalling how these same words "are repeated at every celebration of Holy Mass, when the priest invites us to approach the altar: "This is the Lamb of God who takes away the sins of the world. Happy are those who are called to his supper." Jesus is the *true* Paschal Lamb who freely gave himself in sacrifice for us, and thus brought about the new and eternal covenant" (*Sacramentum caritatis* 9).

These documents show quite well that the contemporary magisterium associates the priesthood of the Church with the eucharistic sacrifice, and that what is to the fore in much of the teaching is the distinction between the two ways of participating in the one priesthood of Christ. At the same time it is clear enough that it is one thing to affirm that the death of Christ and the Eucharist in turn are a "true and proper sacrifice" or a sacrifice "in the strict sense," and another thing to explain what exactly that means. These documents themselves show that there is much to be taken into account from scriptural texts in order to get some sense of how Christ's death is a sacrifice and how the Eucharist is its memorial in which all partake.

GIRM

The *General Instruction on the Roman Missal* (revised and reissued in 2002)[10] highlights all that is problematic in the distinction between the two ways of sharing in the priesthood. It gives the basic theological principle that "as often as commemoration is kept of Christ's sacrifice, our redemption is renewed" (*GIRM* 2) and explains that it is inasmuch as it is memorial that the Eucharist is a sacrifice. The instruction locates the offering in the eucharistic prayer as proclaimed by the ordained priest, though it gives special importance to the epiclesis as well as to the words of Jesus in the Supper Narrative (*GIRM* 79). It repeats several times (§§2, 5, 16) that the eucharistic action and eucharistic offering is the work of the whole Church. It explains that the offering is achieved in virtue of the Church's hierarchical ordering as it is brought to play in worship (§16), since it depends on the exercise of the ministerial priesthood. It is much less at ease with the inclusion of the people in the sacrifice (§§5, 79): their role is to offer their spiritual sacrifice, to offer not only Christ but themselves. This is their exercise of their royal priesthood, as distinct from the ministerial priesthood. The presentation suggests that in the Eucharist the ordained minister has a sacramental role in offering while the people have a spiritual one. Since the action is entirely sacramental by nature, this is not a very satisfactory distinction.

Kingship

Following the principle that all share in the threefold office of Christ, the Constitution on the Church associated the bishop's participation in Christ's kingship principally with his governance of the Church, which is closely related to the prophetic office of teaching For the laity, the participation in kingship is connected with their responsibility for the presence of God's reign in secular matters (*LG* 36). Their main task is to witness to God's lordship and the kingdom brought about through Christ and to show that here on earth we live in the hope of that kingdom, whose fullness is yet to come. This does not mean detaching themselves from earthly concerns, for they must help to imbue all things with true values, show care for the needy, and exemplify proper respect for human creativity and for creation itself. It is this concern for dialogue with human affairs and a concern for justice that is spelled out in the constitution *Gaudium et spes.*

John Paul II

In his 1990 encyclical *Redemptoris missio* (2.12–20),[11] John Paul II identifies the kingdom of God in this world primarily with the recognition of the lordship of God over all things spiritual and material. For Christians, it means that they live in hope of the final realization of the kingdom, and that they live in this world inspired by eschatological hope. The freedom they enjoy is the freedom won by the sacrifice of Christ, in which they have their part through right worship. At the same time, if the members of the Church live by "gospel values," they will have an influence on secular realities and the way in which they are conducted. In their works, Christians will be most concerned about the poor, caring for them, offering them the consolation of God's love, and endeavoring to improve their lives. When the Pope says that the Church is at the service of the world, he emphasizes that this means establishing churches and particular communities that make God's lordship known to all, and that also teach their members the proper respect for human values and institutions. It spreads respect for gospel values and so helps to change this world as it "strains toward eschatological fullness" (§20). It is for the sake of inspiring others with spiritual values and true hope that Christians should strive to be present at the *areopagi*, where the future of the world in this global time is discussed and planned (§72).

In his two letters on the Eucharist in the closing years of his papacy,[12] Pope John Paul II brought priesthood and kingship together through putting the inner eschatological tension of eucharistic celebration to the fore. In *Mane nobiscum Domine* (*MN*, 2004) he quoted *Gaudium et spes* on the place of Christ in history, when he is proclaimed Lord of history, the focal point of the desires of history and civilization (*MN* 15). This meaning is to be reclaimed by the Church through eucharistic celebration, the memorial of His Pasch and the anticipation of the fullness of his lordship. This is a follow-up on what he had written in *Ecclesia de eucharistia* (*EE*) on eucharistic eschatology. For the Pope, this means an inherent tension between looking to the future in the hope of God's final advent in Christ and contributing to the building of a "more human world" in harmony with God's plan. The eucharistic memorial, for those who celebrate it, must lead to commitment to work for peace and to solidarity in seeking a justice that shows a true respect for human life, from start to finish (*EE* 20). One might say that by their own witness and work, Christians who are imbued with the true spirit of their priesthood will let the light of Christ's hope shine forth and so fulfill their participation in his kingship.

Catechism

When the Catechism of the Catholic Church treats of the participation of the laity in Christ's kingly office (§§908–913), it speaks first of "the gift of royal freedom," which allows them to overcome the reign of sin in themselves. As far as their part in the affairs of the world are concerned, the Catechism chooses to note their influence in remedying those institutions and conditions that lead to sin and in impregnating culture and human works with moral values. It says nothing about their part in building a society that promotes greater justice, and in this fails to incorporate the perspectives of the Vatican Council.

With relation to the inner life of the Church, the Catechism quotes the Code of Canon Law (CIC) on the part that the laity may have in Church governance by reason of their kingship (CIC 129.2). This means their part in synods, pastoral councils, diocesan and parish works of different sorts. It apparently suggests that if a bishop delegates a lay person to be in charge of a parish lacking a resident pastor, the lay person has a part in Christ's kingship through a particular share in that of the bishop.

If we return now to the teaching of the Vatican II on the priesthood of Christ and the Church, we can say that it indubitably gave impetus to the participation of the laity in the liturgy and in all activities of the Church, while keeping a clear distinction between ordained and baptized. This needs to be connected with the action of the Church as a people, as a body, as a communion. All sacramental action and all ministry and service belong within the life of the people as a people, the body as a body. Participation in the kingly priesthood of Christ is first and foremost that of the one body, of the Church as a communion of all the baptized. It is only when the Church's nature as sacrament of Christ in its corporate being and action is kept to the fore that we may meaningfully treat of distinct roles and see their relation to one another, in sacramental worship as in the rest of the life of Christ's body.

From this summation of teaching, we see that several things need further investigation. What is the reason for the scriptural designation of the Church as a royal priesthood? In what sense is Christ's death called a sacrifice? What is the meaning of Christ's own royal priesthood? How are the Church and its members said to participate in this? The issue of sacramental representation is intermingled with these questions, but chapter 10 will treat this as a specific item. One thing that makes it hard to sort out the issues is that the original denomination of the Church as a priestly and kingly people does not derive from participation in Christ's kingship or priesthood. It has a distinct rationale in its original usage, but in the course of tradition, it is connected with participation in Christ's priesthood and kingship. These questions are pursued here by looking at Scripture and tradition because they are raised as much as they are answered by Vatican II and its follow-up. Clarifying them may contribute to understanding the relation between mission and ministry and the existence of different orders in one body and people of the Church.

Biblical Foundations

Considering biblical foundations, four things are in order. The first thing to clarify is the sense in which some New Testament texts call the Church of Christ a priestly and a kingly people. Then it may be seen how Christ's death is presented as a sacrifice. Third, the connection between priesthood, kingship, and sacrifice in the Letter to the Hebrews is explored. Finally, a word may be said about the sacrifice of Christians and of the Christian community.

The Royal and Priestly People

The key text to which appeal is made in speaking of the Church as a royal priesthood or as a living sacrifice is that of 1 Pet 2:4–10.[13] Though linked with it in later tradition, this passage has no direct or intended connection with the Letter to the Hebrews on Christ's priesthood. The passage in 1 Peter calls upon Old Testament texts and settings different from those of Hebrews and has nothing to do with prayer in the assembly of the disciples. The author is concerned with the dispensation inaugurated in Christ and in the shedding of his blood. He writes of the people themselves in pointing to a new dispensation of worship, one that is not founded in ritual but in the sanctification of the people, in their lives and their ways of being and doing. However poor and lacking in esteem they may be in the eyes of others, they are themselves a sacrifice, a temple, a priesthood. Whatever their position in the world of which they are a part, they have their dignity and the freedom given to them through the price of Christ's death, and they witness to the works of God.

The letter evokes Exod 19, where the words of God spoken at the striking of the covenant of Sinai call the people of Israel a people set apart, a kingly people, a royal priesthood. These same words may be used of those who have been bought through the precious blood of Christ and in this way made a people. It is by faith in Christ, by living lives worthy of the price at which they were bought, even by letting their sufferings be sanctified by his sufferings, that they exercise this kingly priesthood. The transformation of a life into a spiritual offering worthy of God and the dignity given to believers are at issue, not any act of public worship. This is indeed the sense in which the text is taken in *LG* 10, but then it slips over into a discussion of sacramental worship and there distinguishes between ordained and faithful, saying that the sacramental or ministerial priesthood is ordained to the service of the spiritual priesthood common to all the faithful. It might be more correct to say that the people of the covenant in Christ's blood live out in him and in the Spirit the sacrifice of obedience that he showed in his filial obedience to the Father, and that communion with Christ in this obedience is given sacramental expression and vitality in the memorial of his death and passing over into life. It is impossible to understand the meaning of sacramental memorial and communion without saying that this is built upon a teaching of communion in Spirit and in obedience to the gospel. What distinctive roles are to be played within it is another matter, but the spiritual and sacramental sacrifice is that of the people as such.

Christ's Sacrifice

In the two papal documents reviewed, we have seen the twist given to the meaning of Christ's sacrifice by placing an emphasis on love and self-gift. This is not to deny that it is an act of expiation for sin, but if so, it is as an act of self-giving love. Rather than looking for this in any single text of the New Testament, one has to see it as a collation of images and ideas found in texts that interpret the death of Christ.

As has often been noted, a number of texts in New Testament writings refer to Christ's obedience and death as a sacrifice, or as the paschal sacrifice of Christians, to whom it is given to keep its memorial. All these texts are of the same tenor: by doing God's will and because he is sent by God, Christ makes reconciliation and offers the acceptable sacrifice that undoes the powers of sin and death. It is disputed whether the Supper Narrative of the Synoptic Gospels may be quoted in favor of a precise sacrificial interpretation of Christ's death. What is clear is that Jesus is shown to submit to the will of the Father in order to fulfill the Passover and its promise, and that he gives his body and blood to his disciples as a gift, with the command to keep memorial of him.

Beginning with the Supper Narrative in the Synoptic Gospels, we see that Jesus offers himself "for the many," explaining the meaning of his death by drawing on the practices and conceptions of sacrificial ritual and prophetic interpretation in the Law and the Prophets. Beginning the Passion Narrative with the story of the Supper, the meaning of Christ's willing death is related to the Jewish Passover and to the covenant of Sinai. His own Passover through death to the Father is related to these two events, and to the Lamb and to the covenant sacrifice, which seal their meaning. The implied reference to the Paschal Lamb of itself cannot be seen in the stark terms of sacrifice, since, strictly speaking, the ritual celebrated in sprinkling its blood and eating its flesh, is not a sacrifice but a sign of God's expiation and redemption of the chosen people. At the same time, the annual celebration of the Pasch did include temple sacrifice. The words of Jesus in the narrative suggest sacrificial offering when he speaks of his body given and his blood shed and poured out for the forgiveness of sin, but this is in the order of a truth expressed through metaphorical language.

If Christ's disciples eat and drink of his body and blood, which he offers them, they are faithful to his command to keep remembrance, and they enter into a new age of salvation. The memorial act involves coming together to eat and drink, with thanksgiving, of the one loaf and the one cup. This is to be one with Christ in his death, or in his sacrificial self-offering, and in what it inaugurates. To say that at this meal, Jesus "instituted his apostles as priests," as the magisterium says, is obviously a gloss on the text, reading back into it a meaning added later. Nowhere in the New Testament is there any indication that Paul or others of the apostles (the Twelve plus) see themselves as priests or locate an exercise of priesthood in the memorial action. The community shares in Christ's death and his self-offering, but the language of priesthood is remarkably absent from eucharistic discourse when it comes to the breaking of the bread or the Lord's Supper.

Paul on the Death of Christ

If the Eucharist of the Church is done in memory of Christ's death, how is that death to be understood?[14] Paul's whole theology of salvation hinges on the cross of Christ: it is there that the story of Jesus comes to its full significance. In what can be seen as a foundational principle, this is illustrated through the comparison between the first and second Adam (Rom 5:12–17): as through one there came sin and death, so through the other comes justification and life. Only through the death of Christ is there a way out of the abyss in which sin and death hold humanity.

To explain the significance of this, Paul resorts to sacrificial analogies and most of all, it seems, to the ritual of the Day of Atonement. However terrible it may seem, in God's love salvation must come through bloody suffering and death. In Rom 3:21–26, Paul says that God in his justice/righteousness presents in Jesus "an expiation by his blood" (NRSV). The word *expiation* (*hilastērion*) carries a sacrificial meaning because it alludes to the mercy seat on which blood was poured out. There is some discussion as to whether the Greek is to be translated as "propitiation" or as "expiation." Dunn[15] opts for expiation because it is God's own act that is in question, and in Israelite cult God is not said to be propitiated or appeased. The atoning act, that which restores to oneness with God, is God's own act, for it is God who removes the sin. Paul here attributes the atoning and expiating power of God to the death of Jesus, saying that with the expiation given in the shedding of this blood, God no longer acts through the ritual offerings of the temple.

Elsewhere Paul says, "Our Paschal Lamb, Christ, has been sacrificed" (1 Cor 5 7 NRSV). It is not said that Christ sacrifices himself but that he has been sacrificed. To the meaning of shedding the blood of the Lamb in expiation and redemption, he clearly adds that of a sacrifice offered. The Pauline theology of Christ's death is even more stark when he says, "For our sake [God] made him to be sin who knew no sin" (2 Cor 5:21). This appears to recall the rule that only unblemished animals were to be offered, but it also alludes to the ritual of sending the scapegoat out into the desert, bearing the sins of the people.

From the above passages, it is evident enough that Paul applies images of substitution for sinners to the death of Christ. In suffering death, the second Adam fulfills a substitutionary role. Nonsacrificial images make the same meaning come out, as where it is said that Christ became a curse on humanity's behalf (Gal 3:13). Elsewhere Paul calls the blood of Christ the price of redemption (Rom 3:24). A summing up of these images and ideas can be found in 2 Cor 5:18–20, where Paul says that through Christ, God reconciled the world to himself, not counting human transgressions against offenders. To this Paul adds that God conquered the powers that held humanity captive in a world of sin (Rom 8:31–39; 1 Cor 15:24–28; Col 2:15).

From all of these passages, it appears that if anyone offers sacrifice, it is God, for God is the one who gives his own beloved Son, Jesus. As Abraham did not spare his son (Gen 22:1–19), so "God did not spare his own son" (Rom 8:32). In other words, God remained faithful to his covenant with Israel and so gave forgiveness of sin and reconciliation through handing over his Son in sacrifice and as the price of redemption. It is by his willing obedience that the Son is one with the Father's design and allows himself be handed over willingly to death, victim, as it were, of the sacrifice offered for humanity.

Dunn concludes his examination of these texts by saying: "Paul uses a rich and varied range of metaphors in his attempt to spell out the significance of Christ's death."[16] He points out, however, that a special place has to be given to the metaphor or image of sacrifice. While this means Christ's obedience unto death and the giving up of his life for others, the sacrifice is first and foremost the act of God's love, of the love of the Father for the world with which the Son has been made one, or in whom the world is again made one despite sin and death. With this divine expiation is given the power by which believers have dominion over sin and death and engage with all things in a new freedom.

The Gospel according to John

The connections made between the death of Jesus and sacrifice in John's Gospel are more vague although they do appear. The tenor of this Gospel is to emphasize that Jesus is the one whom the Father sent into the world for the salvation of sinners, so that the Father's glory and his own glory are made manifest on the cross. In John 1:29, 36, John the Baptist hails Jesus as "the Lamb of God who takes away the sin of the world." He is the Lamb of God in the sense that he is God's Lamb, the one whom the Father gives to the world for the expiation of sin. Exegetes discuss at length what references to Jewish sacrificial practice lie behind this. Apart from a general impression that there is reference to the Paschal Lamb, making a connection with John 19:36, it seems to be agreed that while a sacrificial meaning underlies the expression, there is no particular ritual or scriptural passage to which the writer wants to allude.[17]

The other Johannine passage that might imply sacrificial meaning is John 17: 19, where Jesus declares that he sanctifies himself, consecrates himself, makes himself holy, for the sake of the disciples. Jesus may be saying that he sets himself apart for service, as the temple priests had to sanctify themselves if they were to officiate at sacrifice, or that he sets himself apart as unblemished animals were set apart to be offered. However, it seems more likely that Jesus refers to the power of his Word and of his love to make holy. If he, the one sent by the Father, is holy, it is thus that he may make others holy. Throughout the farewell discourse, what is suggested is not that Jesus offers himself to the Father but that he is one with the Father in love for the disciples and for the world, into which he sends them and on account of which he gives up his life, embraces the cross. It is the love that makes him servant and the truth to which he testifies that bring remission of sins and holiness to others. If there is a reference to the Hebrew Scriptures, it is not to any cultic setting but to the power of the Torah to make holy: here Jesus' word and love make holy.

With these Pauline and Johannine texts in mind, to say then that Christ's death is in the first place his gift to the Father, as we have seen in magisterial texts, is a gloss on the New Testament. If one word is to be used of his relation to the Father, it is that of filial obedience, the obedience of love that allows himself to be handed over, to be given in sacrifice. What is at stake in the scriptural texts is an initiative of God, a divine act of mercy and love, which gives the Son to the world for the forgiveness of sins and for atonement. Jesus acts in perfect accordance with this; because of his communion with the Father in love for the world, he hands himself over and endures the cross. No doubt the papal texts wish to move away from any idea that God is being appeased by Jesus' death, and so in the first instance they appeal to God's love and initiative, and on the other hand to Jesus' self-gift to the Father. The impression is given that if doctrine is to uphold a sacrifice "in the strict sense," this has to mean an offering made *to* God. These scriptural texts on the other hand speak of an offering made *by* God, of a sacrifice of the Son given by God, for the sake of the world. The significance of Christ's death is his perfect communion with the Father in his love for the world and his obedient submission to the Father's will in the act of self-gift and self-abasement. The banishment of sin and death and the generation of new life result from this divine love.

Kingly Priesthood of Christ

It is the Letter to the Hebrews[18] that casts the mediation of Christ, the Son sent by the Father, in priestly and kingly terms. An active role is assigned to Christ as priest as well as victim. This has exercised a large influence in theologies of priesthood throughout the centuries.

The letter was probably written to a congregation of Jews that had come to regret their separation from temple worship. This explains why it elaborates on cultic sacrifice to explain what Christ has done for them. The word *priest* refers to the mediation of Christ in the sacrificial shedding of his blood. The word *king* refers to the dominion given to him over sin and the world of sin, and thus his establishment of a regime of holiness and access to God.

All that is recalled of Christ's mediation takes place in "the fullness of time," when cult is perfected. His sacrifice of the new covenant may be compared to the priesthood of Aaron, the worship familiar to the readers, which he perfects, but it evokes a different priesthood, that of one who is priest and king, Melchizedek. Of his kingly priesthood, several characteristics are to be noted. First, Jesus is said to be anointed as priest by the Father because he is the Son, sent into the world to be the mediator of a new and lasting covenant. Second, by evoking the person of Melchizedek, the contrast with the temple priesthood is highlighted even as what that priesthood sought can be said to have been fulfilled. Christ is priest, not by any human and ritual anointing, not by reason of the transmission of office, but because he is anointed from eternity, the only Son of God. Third, Son though he is, he can act for humanity because he has assumed human flesh and calls all human persons his "brothers and sisters." In contrasting the priesthoods, the image of the covenant is to the fore. The priests of the temple offered sacrifice according to the covenant but had to do so repeatedly. Christ the priest offers according to the covenant, but this is a new covenant sanctioned by a sacrifice made once and for all, and which introduces the worship of the heavenly sanctuary with which all may join by learning obedience from him who learned obedience by suffering.

By obedience to the Father, by reason of his perfect communion with the Father's will, the Son makes his death, the shedding of his blood, an acceptable and once and for all sacrifice in atonement for sin. It is a sacrifice of perfect obedience that he "learns through suffering" (cf. 5:8). The sacrifice is perfected or consummated when he pierces through the veil of the flesh and is placed at the Father's right hand, to make priestly intercession for those who believe. The twofold moment of the shedding of the blood on the altar and of the entrance beyond the veil is by way of comparison with the annually repeated rites of Yom Kippur in the temple of Jerusalem.[19] Through Christ and because of his once and for all sacrifice, believers have access to the Father and to his mercy. It is totally outside the order of ritual and cultic worship that the mediation is effected and that sacrifice is offered, for this sacrifice is one of a perfect obedience, of a perfect communion of the will of the Son with the will of the Father. The symbols of worship are used to signify that the true sacrifice and worship are in heaven, where Christ dwells with the Father, and those on earth worship now inasmuch as they are one with him and have access through him, following the example of his loving obedience. It is to participation in the heavenly sanctuary, in the heavenly worship of Christ, that the readers are invited while being reminded that they too must pass through suffering.

By appealing to the figure of Melchizedek, king of Salem and priest, to whom Abraham makes obeisance, the priesthood and kingship of Christ are joined together in the act of mediating the new covenant. The two titles jointly bring out the characteristics of this mediation: it is an offering through obedience, an act of priesthood, and it is the establishment of a new divine reign of peace in a world undone by the reign of sin.

Unlike Paul and John, who highlight Jesus' role as the one offered, this letter pinpoints his role as the priest who offers sacrifice; in this case his own self. It is not a sacrifice made to the Father in appeasement. Rather, it is the Father who anoints the Son as priest, who gives him to the world so that through his suffering and offering he may make a new and better covenant. In other words, it is God's initiative in remitting sin and in making a covenant that is constantly to the fore. Jesus' offering is one of obedience to this will. Coming into the world to do the Father's will, he acts as priest and victim to wipe away sin and to fulfill the covenant that God makes with his people. Being sanctified through the shedding of his blood, he pierces through the veil of the flesh into the heavenly sanctuary. It is there that he offers something to the Father, the heavenly intercession through which all have access to God.

It is because of his sacrifice and his access to the Father in passing through the veil of the flesh that Jesus, Son of God, has dominion over sin and death. Those who have faith in him share in this dominion and freedom as they share in his worship and have access to the Father. Though powerless in the world, they have the ability through Christ's grace to live "outside the camp," and among themselves to live as a community that practices charity. They are relieved from the kind of dominion that would deprive them of the grace and freedom given them through their oneness with the one who was not ashamed to call them sisters and brothers.

The theme of Christ's kingship occurs in other texts as well, indicating that through his death he has been given a kingship. In the Letter to the Colossians, God is said to have transferred the inhabitants of Colossae who have embraced Christ in faith from the reign of darkness, in which they once lived, into the kingdom of God's beloved Son (Col 1:13). No longer subject to their passions and to sin, they have been rescued from the powers of darkness and enjoy a new freedom. It is this grace that constitutes the exercise of Christ's kingship. At the same time, the writer of the letter distinguishes Christ's kingdom, which belongs to the present time, from God's own kingdom (Col 4:11), which will come at the end, when all hostile forces will be subjugated to divine rule. The letter thus points to a present kingship, when people may live in the midst of sinful forces with freedom by the grace of Christ, but look forward in eschatological anticipation of God's glory (Col 3, 4).

The most spectacular presentation of God's kingship and of Christ's kingship is given in the book of Revelation and is clearly associated with the Lamb's sacrifice, the shedding of his blood. At the end of time, when victory is won, the Lamb will be seated on the throne in the midst of the new Jerusalem. In the present time, Christ works in the world to subject his enemies and has his witnesses in those who testify. Indeed, as the rider of the white horse, Christ seems to be credited with inaugurating the final victory in the upheavals of the end of the world. This vision of Christ's reign brings together a past, a present, and a future. He has come into the world at the Father's bidding as the Alpha and the Omega. He is now to reign by giving victory over sin and death to those who live by the freedom of the Spirit in the midst of many tribulations. This, however, is but an anticipation of a final end, a final realization of kingship, which is imaged in the visions of the heavenly Jerusalem.[20]

The Sacrifice of Christians

On particular ministries and ministers in the New Testament books, it is enough to recall what is now commonplace, that terms used of those who exercise any form of governance are secular, not cultic, and that nowhere is there any discussion of eucharistic presidency. This is part of the general intention to distinguish between the Church and the people of Israel on the basis of cult and organizational structure. A temple priesthood designated to offer sacrifices has no place in the Christian community, even though this is a community that in obedience to the gospel, in its prayer, in its acts of service, in its spiritual and moral conduct, "offers sacrifice." Though its life has its center in the Sunday gathering for worship and for keeping memorial, its leaders or officers do not make claim to priesthood.

On what is meant by the sacrifice of believers, or what is meant by their spiritual sacrifice, a good place to begin is with Paul's word about his preaching in Rom 15:15–16. To be a minister of Christ in bringing the gospel to the Gentiles is in Paul's eyes to exercise "a priestly service." Earlier in the letter, when he had written of how the gospel is given to the Gentiles and passes to them from the Jews, Paul exhorted his readers/hearers to present their bodies as a "living sacrifice," this being their "spiritual worship" (Rom 12:1). In both passages, Paul is quite deliberately using the vocabulary of temple worship to write not of a new cult but of obedience to the gospel, of a life lived in conformity to what believers have heard in faith of Jesus Christ. After asking for this service of obedience to the gospel, Paul immediately goes on to speak of living together as a community, as the body of Christ, in which there are many members. The faithful are to serve each other in love and by the gifts of service they have variously received, being "members one of another" (Rom 12:3–9).

As James Dunn puts it, this is a "community without cult."[21] There are no cultic sacrifices among Christ's followers, but their dedication to God's service is to be transferred into the everyday relationships empowered by love and by the gifts of the Spirit. From this there follows, throughout the New Testament, the vocabulary that speaks of disciples as God's temple, as temples of the Spirit, as a living sacrifice, or as a royal and priestly people. This does not mean that there are no assemblies. Indeed, the word itself for assembly, *ekklēsia*, gives a name to the community of each place where Christians live in common. But the assembly, founded on the apostolic word, is to bring together the hearing of the Word, practical charity "in the body," and worship offered to God in hymns and canticles. That is how the community finds its life-giving center in the gathering of the Lord's Supper, or in the breaking of the bread. A reading of Acts and of Paul indicates that the assembly convoked for the first day of the week of its nature included care of the poor and sharing a common meal. This meal was to be an act of fellowship, which Paul wanted to be simple rather than an elaborate repast intended to satisfy hunger and express a more boisterous conviviality. It was in such a gathering, marked by obedience to the gospel, indicative of a harmony of relations, animated by an exercise of the gifts of the Spirit, that the Lord was remembered when all partook with blessing of the one loaf and the one cup.

As explained in an earlier chapter, there appears to have been no clear line of official authority in these early Christian gatherings of household churches. Authority indeed there was, but it was that of the Word spoken by apostle or prophet or teacher, that of the gifts of the Spirit exercised with discernment, and that of the householder who arranged the place and what was needed for the gathering. It seems useless to ask who said the blessing prayer over loaf and cup, for we can go no further than surmise that it may have been one who had the authority of the Word, overflowing into prayer, or perhaps even the heads of the household, in virtue of their place in the assembly.

Any ordering that was done was in channeling gifts into the service of all. Over time, this might turn quarrelsome, as we know from the Pastoral Letters, from the *Didache*, and from *1 Clement*. Hence we appreciate why there was a need to make rules of order and succession in office, especially in teaching. However, this cannot suppress the charismatic foundation of authority exercised in the name of Christ or as his minister.

Nor does it mean that the disciples were indifferent to the world around them and the social constrictions they suffer. Since they were powerless to change things, they sought to live among themselves as true children of God. As Edward

Schillebeeckx has expressed it, early Christians formed society among themselves, a society representing the freedom of grace and not dominated by divisions, unjust power structures, or predominantly worldly concerns. "They could realize this renewal of the person and the structures only within the Church and on the periphery of society."[22]

The foregoing on the sacrifice of early Christians might be summarized as follows, with the magisterial teaching earlier recalled in mind and recognizing the change of terms taking place. In what is now common language, we would say that the spiritual worship of the body of the faithful is its faith in the Word preached and a life lived in obedience and thanksgiving and mutual service. This life lived out in daily exchange is expressed in gatherings in a varied but harmonious form. There is the gathering together as a people, one in all things, with its care for the need and its shared meal. Within this *ekklēsia* is the eating and drinking of the memorial food and drink, the one loaf and the one cup, Christ's body and blood, which is the very ground of their unity. In other words, spiritual worship, corporeal service in charity, and memorial action are such that none exists without the others.

We end this study of the Scriptures with a number of disparate elements, all pertinent to the mystery of the Church but awaiting to be interconnected by spiritual and theological reflection. It remains to be seen how in the course of tradition the kingly priesthood of Christ, his death as the ultimate act of worship, the royal priesthood of the Church, and the Church's memorial participation in Christ's mystery were joined.

Patristic Teaching

To follow this scriptural foundation, we will see how some patristic writings joined these themes together as they elaborated on Christ's mediation as a priestly and kingly act and related the life and actions of the Church to this. What is recalled here is not meant to be a survey but a selective presentation. An attempt is made to point to some salient features in what Eastern and Latin traditions say of priesthood and kingship when they treat Christ's mediation and the Church's relation to this mediation. The kingly priesthood of Christ, the nature of the Church as royal priesthood, and the priesthood of bishops are all worked out together, in relation to each other, not by an exercise in logic but by the power of often rhetorical and spiritual discourse. The themes are seldom systematically treated, but the connections can be perceived.

To develop this with some clarity, four things may prove useful. First, an early text is cited to show the true meaning of comparisons with the Old Testament priesthood when these are introduced into Christian literature. Second, some writings of the fathers of the Church of Alexandria are called upon for their understanding of the spiritual priesthood of the New Testament and its sacramental expression. Third, John Chrysostom's work is examined to show how the priesthood of the bishop fits into that context. Fourth, from the liturgy of the church of

Rome, it will be seen how the notion if sacrament embraces the total view of the royal priesthood of the Church in all its parts.

The New Priesthood of the New Testament

From the ordination rites of the Roman liturgy and from such writers as Isidore of Seville, we are familiar with how analogies with the Levitical priesthood are in time used to explain order in the Church. Whatever its later elaborations, a look at the letter called *1 Clement* gives the true sense of this comparison when it was first adopted.

This is the earliest nonscriptural document in which a reading of biblical texts to elaborate on the Church and on its ministry occurs. It has to be situated in the church of Rome at a time when a system of household churches appears to have been the common arrangement, so it is too early to speak of a single bishop over the whole community of the city. However, some concerned with the liaison between these communities wished to make contact with the church of Corinth, where there was a feud between leaders and members of the community. The writer of the letter, who speaks for others as well as for himself, wants to settle this by way of an appeal to the place of the Old Testament priesthood within the people. The controlling idea is that by divine dispensation, an ordering of offices was established under the old dispensation, and that we should expect divine providence to regulate the ordering of offices in the new community. By comparison with the priesthood of the temple, the author teaches that the Church too has a divine ordering, and to rebel against this is to rebel against divine ordinance. This is not to compare priesthood to priesthood but order to order. If the notion of priesthood is used to speak of the leaders of the Christian fellowship, it is in an analogous way.

The point of the reference to the priesthood of the leaders (bishops or presbyters) is first to insist on the need to respect the divine dispensation in the new order of things as much as in the old. What this new priesthood means is shown in its relationship to how the author sees the worship of the Church as a whole, within which a place is given to the appointed leaders. The author appeals to the Corinthians to think upon their justification in Christ: "This is the way in which we found our salvation, Jesus Christ, the High Priest of our offerings, the defender and helper of our weakness, . . . who being the brightness of his majesty, is as much greater than the angels as the more glorious name which he has inherited" (36.1). In associating priesthood and kingship in Christ's mediation of the covenant, the allusion to Hebrews is evident. The people are justified through Christ and are to act and worship accordingly.

The difference of New Testament worship from that of the temple comes from the fact that it has its origins in Christ and his sacrifice. While it is centered in the assembly for Eucharist, it brings to this formal act of worship all that belongs to the life of the community, all that fits into spiritual sacrifice. In an important way, this includes the service of the poor. The role of the bishop/presbyter in the eucharistic gathering is one with his responsibility over the life of the Church. As Stuart Hall puts it: "If the sacrifice of the Christian were thought of in terms of giving one's goods into the central pool, to be offered with the thanksgiving of Christ, the bishop is the 'inspector' who makes sure that the sacrifice offered is acceptable to God."[23] Deciding who belonged, who was to offer, who professed the right faith, what was to be given—all fit with the role of the leader in the eucharistic gathering. Hence the priesthood and offering of the appointed leader as such is grounded in the very nature of the Church's worship as a spiritual offering made tangible in the assembly's action, or in other words, in its priesthood, which is to be one with Christ in his sacrifice.[24]

Spiritual Priesthood

Writers of the Church of Alexandria, and especially Origen, explain the spiritual priesthood and sacrifice of the New Testament. It is commonplace to note that the ideas of Philo of Alexandria influenced Origen and Clement. In the temple priesthood and in the figure of Melchizedek, Philo found images of the divine Word. Remaining within a Jewish perspective, he gave a spiritual meaning to the act of sacrifice. He connected priesthood and Passover, and in his allegorical commentary on the vestments of the high priest, he indicated the universal character of the new spiritual priesthood.

For Origen,[25] the mediation of the Logos originates and indeed is continually exercised within the communion of the Trinity, and it is made manifest in the Incarnation. The Word made flesh, Christ the Son of God, is eternal high priest according to the order of Melchizedek. On the one hand his work is done on earth, but on the other, since he is the eternal Word, he never left the sanctuary of heaven, where he dwells in light inaccessible. Christ exercised both priesthood and kingship, winning dominion over principalities and powers, "making a show of them openly" when nailed to the cross. The eternal and the earthly are not so much two stages of the one priesthood as two complementary offerings.

In several places Origen relates the royal priesthood of the Church to the priesthood and kingship of Christ. The true Jerusalem is the Church, built of living stones, a royal priesthood in which spiritual sacrifices are offered. Martyrdom is the most perfect form of this spiritual worship, but it is exercised by all who live according to the law of the Spirit. It is given a sacramental or symbolic character in the Eucharist, for by drinking the blood of Christ the people are initiated into the mystery of the flesh and blood of the Word, who rendered God propitious to sinners so that they might become one with the risen Christ in his eternal offering. Contemplation of the Word in the Scriptures and communion with the Word made flesh in the Eucharist go together. Within this eucharistic setting, the bishop exercises a priestly and kingly role by reason of his teaching, his supervision of penance, and his presidency at the Eucharist. Like Christ, bishops must eat the sins of the people "in a high place," which is that of perfect faith and charity, teaching them sound doctrine and purifying their consciences. They exercise their priestly role by becoming themselves victims of the Word of God and in this way lead the people in turn to offer spiritual sacrifices.

In Origen, then, four aspects of the priesthood of the new dispensation are related to each other. The foundation is the priesthood of Christ, the Word made flesh, which is both heavenly and earthly. From this arises the royal priesthood of the Church, which is the people saved and sanctified by his blood and his obedience to the Father, and with which it is particularly associated in the Eucharist. Priesthood is exercised by each and all of the faithful in offering spiritual sacrifices, in their daily lives, and in the sacrament of the Eucharist. Into this fits the priesthood of bishops, who are in an exemplary way configured to the priesthood of Christ in their ministry and thus are able to sanctify the people by their teaching and spiritual guidance.

In Athanasius and Cyril,[26] the theme of mediation is even more highly developed through the imagery of sacrifice, priesthood, and kingship. The Word of God, divine in nature, took on human nature and human flesh to be the mediator between God and a fallen humanity. Athanasius and Cyril use various biblical metaphors to describe this mediation. Enlarging upon the language of painful but victorious conflict, they speak of paying a debt, occasionally of paying a debt to the devil, but most of all to death itself. They also speak of Christ's death as a sacrifice, depending primarily on Paul and the harshness of what he says about the victim's identification with sin (2 Cor 5:21). They call the mediator "King" because he was victorious over sin and death and now reigns over the faithful, who have been redeemed and who dominate these enemies in their own flesh, in the hope of being with Christ in eternity. Drawing especially on Hebrews, they call him "Priest" because he offered himself as sacrifice in the once and for all offering of his death and his entry into the heavenly sanctuary. His is called a priesthood according to the order of Melchizedek and not of Aaron, because it had no origin in this world but comes from the eternity of the Word's communion with the Father. Being exercised once and for all in his transition through death to heaven, it is an eternal priesthood, whose act of sacrifice need never be repeated but is forever efficacious.

By the sacrifice of his own body, Christ put an end to the law of death, which barred humanity's way to God, and he made a new beginning of life for those who obtained the hope of the resurrection. The images of priest and king are together related to anointing. The Son of God was anointed for the apostolate in coming into the world, joining the created thing in union with himself and anointing humanity with his deity, making one out of the two. This is the basis for the power of his sacrifice and for the royal priesthood of the Church. Having acted as high priest in the sacrifice of his death, the Son entered through his death into the heavenly sanctuary. From there he now acts as high priest in the Church by sanctifying it through communion with his life-giving flesh, bringing believers near to God and offering to the Father those who in faith approach him. Through the gift of the Spirit, this mediation of Christ gives the members of the Church the participation in the mystery of the Trinity that the Greeks call *theōsis*, or deification, and whereby in the love of the Spirit they are related to the Father as is the Son, Christ.

This is efficacious for those who belong to the Church because the baptized eat of the body given in sacrifice. They are joined with Christ in the Eucharist, at the table at which they make, through the minister, a sacrifice of memorial thanksgiving. This is illustrated by Cyril when, in commenting on John's Gospel, he appeals to one of the types of Levitical sacrifice. It is the one in which what was sacrificed was considered to be made holy. Whereas in the Law it was forbidden to anyone but the anointed priest to touch the holy, in Christ the holy body is given to all. Cyril writes:[27]

> He said, "I make myself holy," meaning, "I consecrate and offer myself as a spotless victim with a sweet savor." For what was offered on the altar was made holy or called holy according to the law. Therefore Christ gave his body for all, and through his body planted life among us again. . . . Thus the body of Christ gives life to those who share with him.

The members of the Church made holy by Christ's body make spiritual offerings in union with its Head, who offers in the heavenly sanctuary. They are brought into communion with Christ in grace and so are his body, one with him in his communion with God in the Spirit. The royal priesthood mentioned in 1 Pet 2:4–10 is exercised by drawing near to God with Christ through faith. The people are made holy through communion in the Word made flesh. They offer prayers of thanksgiving and praise, drawing near to the eucharistic table, from which they receive the Word made flesh, receiving life and blessing both spiritually and corporeally.

In this same commentary on John's Gospel,[28] Cyril writes of ordination to the episcopacy as a transmutation, just as Gregory of Nyssa had called it a transfiguration (or metamorphosis). The reason why the apostles share in the mediation of Christ is because they have received the same transforming Spirit who descended at the Incarnation on his humanity. This is true also of those whom Cyril likens to the apostles, such as bishops and dispensers of the mysteries in the time of the Church. He is here pursuing the teaching on *theōsis*, or deification, of the human creature as a transformation that does not change nature but lifts it to a participation in the communion of the Trinity. Through the gift of the Spirit, the baptized and in a particular way the apostles and the ordained share in the relationship of the Son to the Father. Ordination gives the minister the Spirit as a gift of service, that special entry into the communion of the Trinity that makes him within the communion of the Church share in the mediatory work of Christ, the Son and *Logos*.

Episcopal Priesthood

At first sight these two words do not fit together. As is known, the choice of secular terms such as *bishop* to designate leaders was a deliberate eschewal of priestly ones. How the two come together is here illustrated from looking at the writings of John Chrysostom, where the priesthood of the bishop is located within the exercise of the priesthood by all and within the eucharistic celebration. It is because of his role in the Eucharist, not otherwise, that the bishop may be called a priest.[29] As we have seen, for John the ministry of bishops includes eucharistic ministry, teaching ministry, and guidance of the faithful along the way of penance. Setting this within the Eucharist, he shows the particular sacramental expression of this ministry as a priestly action.[30]

The Eucharist is the sacrament and representation of Christ's mysteries. It is here that in a special way the faithful exercise the royal priesthood, which originates in baptism, where John points to the anointings found in this rite. Given the victory over sin, the people immolate their bodies in offering themselves as a sacrifice to God and in offering a sacrifice of thanksgiving. Their royal priesthood is founded in the communion with Christ, priest, and victim, given through the eating and drinking of his sacramental body and blood. The hymns sung and the rites performed in the sacraments, whether this be the Eucharist or the act of binding and loosing in rites of penance, are done in concert with the heavenly choirs. This is to partake of a new and better covenant, whose sacrifice is that of Christ, never repeated but accessible to all in its eucharistic memorial.

The role of bishop as priest relates to this by reason of his teaching of the Word and of the guidance he gives in leading people to penance, and because of his proclamation of the prayer of memorial thanksgiving, in which the people are one with him. In a particular and even dramatic way in the Eucharist, the Bishop represents in his actions the work of Christ the High Priest. To represent the mysteries of Christ before the eyes of the people is to exercise a particular symbolic or representative role. Chrysostom calls the bishop in his sacramental action an ambassador of Christ. This is not a juridical delegation but rather means participation in the mystery of Christ. As John Zizioulas puts it, it is representation by participation. Within the eucharistic participation in the mystery of the Christ of all the baptized, the royal priesthood, and only with this priesthood, the bishop has a particular sacramental role. Without communion as one body in the Spirit, which makes the people one with and in Christ, this participation could not be conceived.

Priestly and Sacramental Worship

In the Western tradition it is frequently noted that in North Africa, Cyprian of Carthage opted for a sacerdotal vocabulary in writing of the naming and role of the bishop. While giving strong importance to the teaching and governing powers of the episcopal order, Cyprian places his exercise of priesthood in his action, *vice Christi*, in offering, with the people, the eucharistic sacrifice. In a somewhat different way, Augustine is well remembered for his words on the one true sacrifice and on the mediation of Christ in *The City of God* (10.6:19–20, 29:32). Through the mediation of Christ, through his descent and ascent, there results the one sacrifice of Head and members in the Eucharist, where they are together offered as the *totus Christus*, represented in the loaf and the cup, over which thanksgiving has been made. The people are to join with the bishop in the sacrifice in which Christ is commemorated and show their assent through their loud "Amen" to the prayer and all that it says.

In looking to the Latin tradition for further insight into the exercise of priesthood, rather than say more of Cyprian and Augustine, it serves a purpose to focus on what is done in liturgy. Hence a closer look is taken at the development of liturgy and its theological perception in the period when the Roman liturgy as the liturgy of the city church of Rome was taking shape. Coming out of an epoch when it was a minority religious group into a time when it could see itself as the people of God, comparing itself to the ancient people of Rome, the Church gave greater solemnity to its public worship and afforded greater dignity to its bishop and indeed to all its clergy. This provided a new setting in which to develop the idea of priesthood. Leo the Great, to quote one of the most authoritative sources on the Roman tradition, in his sermons on the passion of Christ points to the one unique mediation and sacrifice of Christ, on which the existence of the priestly and kingly people of the Church is founded. The Lord, who drew all things to himself in his sacrifice, makes it possible that in the Eucharist " the devotion of all peoples everywhere might celebrate, in a sacrament made perfect and visible, what was carried out in the one temple of Judea under obscure foreshadowings."[31]

In several of his sermons, Leo explains that the mediation of Christ comes about through the assumption of human nature into union with the divine, for it is by this exchange that all humanity is made a new creation and a temple of the Holy Spirit.[32] Assuming human nature, Christ became the peerless victim, the spotless priest who pierces the veil of the flesh.[33] In the Church, which lives by this sacrifice, the royal priesthood of the community of all believers is fundamental, but it needs the priesthood of the bishop. He too is chosen as priest according to the order of Melchizedek, by divine beneficence and not by any merit or human lineage.[34] On the foundation of this metaphor, Leo associates the authority he has as a teacher with the action the bishop performs in offering the sacrifice of praise in the Eucharist.

The priestly role of the Church, people, and ministers, is given expression in a singular way in the Roman Church's liturgical understanding of the Eucharist as the sacrament of the sacrifice of Christ. The Roman Canon highlights the sacrificial understanding of Christ's redemption in a way not found in other prayers apart from the Liturgy of Mark. The Canon appeals to biblical types of sacrifice and employs a strongly sacrificial vocabulary that is related to three moments in the unfolding of Christ's sacrifice: his action at the Supper, the shedding of his blood upon the cross, and his glorification through his resurrection and ascension, which leads to the offering of his heavenly intercession.

The sacrament of this sacrifice in the liturgy of Rome is comprehensive of a diversity of actions on the part of its priestly people and its priestly ministers. The people are to offer their bread and wine, their gifts, their penance, their very selves. The sacrificial terms *hostia* and *munus* are predicated of the hymn of praise, which is the name given to the Canon of the Mass, the praise being communally voiced in a special way in the singing of the Sanctus. They apply also to the gifts the people bring, their fasts, all their acts of devotion, which come to a head in the Eucharist. It is through this sacrifice of praise, as it is called, that the Church is most of all one with Christ in his sacrifice. After the recital of the Supper Narrative and memorial command, the Church offers the pure, holy, and immaculate sacrifice (*hostia*), and then in the following prayer appeals to the memory of the sacrifices of Abel, Abraham, and Melchizedek, which God saw fit to accept.

An early Christmas preface, found in both the Veronense and the Gelasianum, or Verona and Gelasian sacramentaries,[35] includes all sacrifices in the sacrifice of praise offered in the Eucharist. The Church unceasingly immolates the sacrifice of praise (*tuae laudis hostiam iugiter immolantes*) that was prefigured in the offering of Abel, celebrated by Abraham and Melchizedek, instituted by the Lamb, pre-scribed by the Law, and fulfilled this day (in the sacramental mysteries) in the true Lamb and eternal high priest. To this praise, which is a celebration of what prefig-ured it, are joined all the other gifts that are brought forward and that express the assembly's communion with Christ in his priestly intercession, while the Church prays as he did at the Last Supper. In short, in Roman terms, the sacrifice of Christ, and the sacrifice of the Church in communion with Christ, is sacramentally ex-pressed in the bringing of gifts, the prayer of praise that is the Canon, the prayer prayed by the bishop with and for the people, the petition that is integral to the Canon, and the Holy communion in Christ's body and blood. Though the role of the priest is clearly set forth, the sacrificial celebration is inclusive of the entire action, culminating in sacramental communion, and the offering is made by all.

From the foregoing points, it is clear that the priesthood of the people and the priesthood of the ordained are intimately linked, not only spiritually but in sacra-mental expression. No discourse on the priesthood of the ordained is possible without taking into account the priesthood of the people, and there is no sacra-mental exercise of it except within the sacramental action of the assembly of all.

Priesthood in the Carolingian Church

To see how the notion and exercise of priesthood developed with the dissemination of the Roman liturgy throughout the north of Europe is an exercise in contrast with what went before.[36] The ceremonial of eucharistic sacrifice was enacted in a new cultural, social, and political setting, with the result that the role of the ordained was given a rather different priestly interpretation, which set him apart from the people as a mediator rather than placing him in their midst. The more restrictive, if not exclusive, focus on the priesthood of the ordained, to which Catholics were later long accustomed, has to be located in the developments of Church life, min-istry, and thought that began within the Carolingian reign.

With the rather precarious or incomplete conversion of barbarian peoples, who followed their kings and chiefs into the Church, penance took on a new tenor and dispensation, as has been previously explained. The devotion of peoples into which this practice fitted was developed in a context where culturally multiple mediation was a constant and where sacrifices of various sorts were important, involving the living and the dead. A religion that professed but one mediator and one sacrifice had to somehow integrate other forms of mediation, and this provided a setting for understanding the mediation of the priest, who offered sacrifice for sins, of the living and of the dead. Separating this out from the action of all the people was supported by the continued use of the language of the educated, Latin, and the appeal to the authority of books, which only clergy or monks could read.

The practices and writing of the time bolstered multiple offerings of the Mass, with or without congregation, by explaining the priesthood of the ordained through an appeal to the prototype of the Aaronic priesthood and the cult of the temple. This allowed for a practical and theoretical description of the priest as one ordained to offer sacrifice and even justified Masses celebrated without congregation but offered for the intentions of those who by gift and stipend sought mediation. While the prescribed Mass ritual of the Roman Liturgy went relatively unchanged, apart from a multitude of accretions, the practice and place of the Mass in life changed considerably.

Changes in theology were gradual. After Isidore of Seville, ecclesiastical writers often maintained his broad understanding of the nature and functions of the *ordo sacerdotalis*, which by definition includes teaching as well as liturgical action. More and more, however, they focused on the priestly power exercised in the act of consecration in the Mass, which was also viewed as the act of eucharistic sacrifice. Authors made a distinction between the action of the priest in consecrating and that of the people in offering, distinguishing in sacrifice between *offerre* and *immolare*. The people offered, the priest immolated, immolation of the victim being the consummation of offering. In the Mass, immolation is located in the consecration when something is done to the bread and wine offered; by being changed into the body and blood of Christ, they are immolated, as it were, and this immolation represents the immolation of Christ. All offer themselves, bread and wine, even Christ, but only the ordained priest can consummate the sacrifice and represent the immolation of Christ's death.[37] The various parts of the prayer of the Canon were increasingly explained as prayers that come before and after the sacrifice, which is immolated and represented in the consecration of the Mass.

A treatise on the Canon of the Mass from the eleventh century shows how this came to be done. Odo of Cambrai, in his work *Expositio in canonem missae*,[38] locates the sacrifice of praise, sung by all the people, in the Sanctus of the Mass, the consecration of the body and blood of Christ and the true sacrifice in the repetition of his words by the priest, and the daily offering of this sacramental sacrifice of the whole Church (both present and absent) in the prayers of offering that follow the consecration, when the body and blood of Christ are present on the altar. The people are thus able to join their sacrifice of praise and their offering with the real sacrifice, which is that of Christ now sacramentally represented through the words of the priest. This makes a very straightforward distinction between the action of the priest and that of the congregation, and in Odo's eyes it allowed for the celebration of a priest-monk in his private cell since even there he was united as a priest with the whole Church and could offer for it. This fitted into a new priestly spirituality that saw in the offering of the Mass the culmination of a life of contemplation.[39] Allowing contemplative monks to be ordained let them enter into this contemplation in the quiet of their cells and at the same time exercise mediation on behalf of the Church.

Sacerdotium et Regnum

Since this is how priesthood was conceived, one rightly asks what happened to kingship and its association with priesthood in the days of the Carolingians and beyond. The exercise of Christ's kingship was distinguished from the exercise of his priesthood to cover his rule over temporal realities. Rulers were to help establish the kingdom of God on earth by configuring their fiefdoms to an image of Christ's reign, which absorbed the temporal as well as the spiritual. As emperors and kings justified their rule by appeal to God's and Christ's kingship, this redefined the mission of the Church and the nature of its position in society. Popes and bishops reacted when rulers encroached on the Church's freedom, but they too shared the ideal of Christendom.

The idea and pursuit of a single *societas christiana* took shape. The divine commissioning of temporal rulers gave them a sacred role bound by divine law to establish a society built on what were conceived as Christian principles. Rulers used this to enhance their own power, aided by ceremonies of crowning and anointing, of which bishops were the functionaries. Appealing to the kingship of Christ, now clearly distinguished from his priesthood, the norm was that the role of the prince was to defend the Church and uphold a Christian society against its enemies. This claim allowed some princes to claim power over the Church when it came to the ordering of society, and it was this to which Popes and bishops objected, not to the general notion of a Christian society.

In liturgical books[40] the model for kingly anointing was taken from the Old Testament, according to which kings, priests, and prophets were all anointed, to fulfill diverse functions within the one divine order. The divine origin of temporal power, whether through natural law or by special ordinance, was confirmed by jurists, canonists, and even theologians. It was justified by an appeal to God's lordship established in creation and exercised in his name by divinely consecrated rulers. At times the emperor or kings were even called "vicars of Christ" in the exercise of their rule.

This league between spiritual power and temporal power in effect changed the Church's sense of its mission. Rather than giving witness to Christ amid nonbelievers, or within a larger Christian society creating select groups such as monks and clergy to witness to an ideal form of evangelical life, the mission of the Church's ministers was to establish a society in which all things are ruled by Christ. The performance of worship with solemnity and in the presence of rulers represented the total political and social reality participating in a worship established by his priesthood but acknowledging his kingship. This unfortunately sometimes sanctioned a use of power and even violent repression of dissenters in the name of Christ. Temporal punishment, forceful suppression, negation of the rights of Jews and Muslims, and even war, could all be justified in the name of the mission to totally Christianize society and public, as well as private life.

Not all were content to accept the constant warfare between kings and lords over the domain to which they laid claim nor the violence they used in oppressing enemies. They saw the kingship of Christ as one of peace. In the eleventh century there was a movement for peace that was a popular reaction against the constancy of wars. History refers to this movement as the *Pax Dei* and associates it with attempts to allow God's and Christ's peace to rule in the world.[41] The thrust of this movement, which included clergy and people, was to find peaceful ways to settle disputes rather than engaging in constant and repeated warfare. Christian hope was behind this quest, and it had some but not lasting results. Some historians indeed find beginnings of later apocalyptic expectations of a rather extravagant sort in this movement. People began to search in the persons and events of the time for signs of the forthcoming end of the world. This raises the question as to whether it is possible to hope for some present realization of a divine rule of peace and order, or whether all hope of this has to be associated with a coming judgment at the end of time.

Around the cusp of the millennium, episcopal authorities found the encroachment on ecclesiastical affairs by princes impossible to concede and responded by asserting their supremacy over principalities in both religious and temporal matters, though without claiming direct temporal rule for themselves. They could be seen to exercise the priesthood of Christ in spiritual matters and his kingship in the power they had over the temporal, which was needed to protect the spiritual, thus taking back to themselves something of the kingship yielded to princes.

The claim to some authority in temporal matters is exemplified in the words and deeds of strong popes like Gregory VII and Innocent III. Innocent was ready to admit that temporal rule came to lords of the realm from God, whatever be that process, but he asserted some control over the temporal in virtue of his spiritual authority. This was because of the ultimate subordination of the temporal to the spiritual. Temporal rulers needed to acknowledge papal superiority over the *regnum* in virtue of the higher order of *sacerdotium*.[42] Between the two luminaries set by God in the universe, the *pontificia auctoritas* and the *regalis potestas*, the first to rule over souls and the second to rule over bodies, the greater dignity is that of the pontifical. From it, as the moon from the sun, the regal receives its dignity and splendor.

At this point, it is worth mentioning that these attitudes were later clarified by Thomas Aquinas in his work on the rule of princes.[43] Kings, he taught, hold their authority from God both by reason of the very nature of rule and by reason of the ordinances of divine providence. Earthly rule, however, is to be clearly distinguished from the kingship of Christ since Christ's power has to do with the spiritual realm, the kingdom of God (chap. 14). The regimen of this kingdom, in which all the faithful are kings and priests, is not given to earthly princes but to priests, especially to the high priest, who is the successor of Peter and the vicar of Christ, the Roman Pontiff. Since this is the highest kingdom, the one that is the end of all earthly administration, earthly kings are subject to this high priest. This does not mean that the Pope in virtue of his kingly priesthood as vicar of Christ exercises temporal power as a matter of course. It only means that kings and rulers have to acknowledge his ultimate supremacy and that he may intervene in temporal affairs when this seems to serve the spiritual end of the rule and priesthood that he holds from Christ. This reasoning placed the kingship of Christ clearly in the spiritual order and related it to his priesthood, but the theory of the subjection of the temporal to the spiritual provided popes and bishops a say in temporal affairs when they felt this was needed.

Seeing how Aquinas accounted for the kingship of Christ and for the Church's royal priesthood, we can recall the theological positions on priesthood within the explanations of order given previously, leaving further treatment until chapter 10, which deals with representations of Christ. Aquinas, as we know, related the tradition of priesthood to worship, a worship offered in communion with Christ the priest and the Head, from whom all grace flows and brings humans into communion with him. He explained both the priesthood of all the baptized and the priesthood of the ordained within one comprehensive vision of worship and priesthood. However, the baptized laity were ascribed what he called a passive power, to indicate that by faith they were recipients of the sacraments. To the ordained he ascribed an active part, to show that they acted as ministers of Christ and the Church. The terms were not meant to regulate the external modes of participation in the liturgy, which Aquinas saw as active on the part of all, but they belonged to his theological synthesis about participation in the one priesthood and worship of Christ. What was affirmed, however, is that in the core act of the Mass and of sacramental ministry, the priest acted alone in the person of Christ, and the people had no part in this. His understanding of liturgical structures explains this at least in part. Aquinas thought that the ministerial role was affirmative and declarative and divorced the instrumental acts of sacramental "confection" (his word) from the prayers in which they belonged or with which they were associated. He understood the Canon of the Mass in the way explained above, prayers coming before and after the declarative words of consecration by the priest. Unlike the Orthodox, Aquinas did not have the vision of the Church's relation to Christ, which allowed them to see Christ and Spirit acting together through the prayer of the Church, the body of Christ.

More will be said in the next chapter about the relation of the priest to Christ in the sacraments. Here it may be recalled that Thomas refined a theory of instrumental causality in the exercise of Christ's priesthood in the Church through his ministers. Though in the aftermath this could be given a quite mechanical interpretation, some things have to be noted about the context into which it fits in Aquinas. The entire treatment of the sacraments is a discussion of participation in Christ's priesthood and in the grace of his headship given to his members. His theology of causality is related to what is more fundamental for him, a theology of signs. What is mediated is what is caused, and what is caused is what is signified, and this is participation in the priesthood and grace of Christ. The theorem that the sacraments work *ex opere operato* was meant to safeguard the freedom and gratuity of God's action, for it is not by any human work but by the free grace given through Christ and through faith in him that human beings are sanctified. In hindsight, it can be said that what was absent in the sacramental theology of Aquinas was a theology of the Holy Spirit, which alone could fully explain the communion in which sacraments and ordained priesthood operate.

Royal Priesthood and Ministry in the Reformers

We have seen the rather passive role in which the baptized were placed by medieval piety and sacramental performance, both spiritually and liturgically. It is to the writings of the Reformers that we have to turn to see efforts to take account of biblical and patristic teaching on the priesthood and kingship of Christ and on the royal priesthood of the baptized. They worked with an idea of the divinely given right of princes to rule and with a distinction between the first table of the Law on service to God and the second on matters of right conduct. But it was to the spiritual realm that they turned to write of priesthood even as they saw repercussions of this on the temporal order.

Catholics need to begin a study of the sixteenth-century Reformation, acknowledging that it offered a new way of thinking about the human-divine relationship and that in face of late medieval misdirections, it was necessary. The failure of all participants in controversy to integrate the needs voiced and to find a way of speaking about them in a common language led to a split within the Church along the lines of different confessions. Even the Second Vatican Council, in speaking of all the baptized as one royal priesthood, whether wittingly or unwittingly, was developing a theme of the Reformers.

To speak of misdirections is to highlight the hiatus between clergy and laity, which could all too readily mean various abuses of clerical power, as well as the proposal to the laity of monastic forms of spirituality. The unholy alliance between the spiritual and the temporal, governance and ecclesiastical office, the maintenance of a harsh penitential discipline and the cruel treatment meted out to dissenters, were made to fit within the purview of a hierarchical vision of Church and society. Over against this, humanist thinking and discourse, with the importance it gave to the human person and human creativity, provided a way of thinking about faith that could serve to free the Church and most of all the laity from the oppressive weight of order. Admiration for the Scholastic synthesis that sometimes takes over in current theological writing, at academic and popular levels, often seems oblivious of how imperious was the ordering built on this synthesis. Such is the necessary background to considering what the Reformers still contribute to an understanding of the priesthood whereby the Church shares in the one priesthood of Christ.

Martin Luther

Special note has to be taken of the teaching of Martin Luther on the priesthood.[44] In his writings on the role of Christ in human salvation, as well as in what he says of the baptized, Martin Luther joins the function of king with that of priest in a way close to that of early church writers. In several of his biblical commentaries, he elaborates on the sacrifice of Christ in terms similar to those found in patristic writers, fitting it with his own particular view of the imputation of Christ's righteousness to sinners and of justification by faith. In his Incarnation, Christ took on the effects of Adam's sin, indeed took on his sin, in order to endure suffering and death on behalf of sinners. Thus he earned the right to have his righteousness imputed to them. It is by the death and the blood of Christ that the baptized are cleansed and sanctified. Taking on the form of a servant and offering himself in the flesh, Christ is the true Aaron, or fulfills the type of the Aaronic priesthood. None can share in this priesthood, because his sacrifice is unique, once and for all, and does away with all sacrifices. His anointing as priest according to the order of Melchizedek is associated more readily with his present role in heaven and his present relation to the Church. By his anointing, like Melchizedek, Christ is both king and priest, and he enters into these offices through the sacrifice of his death.

Though it is mentioned in several places in Luther's writings, a convenient and short presentation of his view of the priesthood and kingship that Christ now exercises and in which the faithful participate is found in the 1520 treatise on *The Freedom of a Christian*.[45] He starts with the affirmation that under the Old Testament the birthright of the firstborn male was that of priesthood and kingship, but that this is only a type of the priesthood and kingship of Christ, who is the firstborn of the Father. Of his kingship, Luther says, "He reigns in heavenly and spiritual things" that pertain to the righteousness by which God makes us righteous and rules over believers, protecting them against evil onslaughts. While his priesthood and kingship are exercised through his heavenly intercession, he exercises them on earth through the living instruction of the Holy Spirit, who guides those who believe in his word and receive his righteousness.

All faithful Christians have a share in this kingship and priesthood because of the freedom they have been given through Christ and their faith in him. In virtue of a spiritual power, Christians are kings and lords of all things spiritual and cannot be harmed by evil, even though they are subject to suffering and the onslaught of the devil. As priests, Christians are able to appear before God and pray for others, as well as to teach one another spiritual things. In *The Prelude to the Babylonian Captivity of the Church*,[46] Luther elaborates on the many spiritual offerings that the baptized can make because of their life in Christ. These include prayer and almsgiving and the self-offering by which they cast themselves upon Christ. In later years, Luther evolved his teaching on ministry, but while he recognized the need and gospel mandate for ordained ministers of Word and sacrament, he did not acknowledge any participation in Christ's kingship and priesthood other than that of baptism. To preach the Word and duly administer the sacraments, as ministers are called to do, is to exercise their baptismal priesthood. A part in society is also an exercise of priesthood since secular power serves the kingdom of God and the mission of the Church.[47]

Many other texts could be quoted from the works of the Reformer, but one quotation sums up well all that he said on the matter. In *On Christian Freedom*, Luther remarked: "Not only are we the freest of kings, we are also priests forever, which is far more excellent than being kings, because as priests we are worthy to appear before God to pray for others and to teach one another the things of God." He goes on to say that "Christ has obtained for us, if we believe on him, that we are not only his brethren, coheirs and fellow kings with him, but also fellow priests with him, who may boldly come into the presence of God in the spirit of faith." For these reasons he affirms that injustice is done the words *priest* or *ecclesiastic* or *cleric* (meaning set apart) "when they are transferred from all other Christians to those few who are now by a mischievous usage called 'ecclesiastics.'" Nonetheless, there is a difference in roles "for although we are all equally priests, yet we cannot all publicly minister and teach, nor ought we if we could."

It is clear enough in this that in the ordering of the Church, Luther kept a distinction between the role of pastors and their ministry of Word and sacrament, and the works and roles of the baptized in general. Indeed he taught that the constitution of the ministry was of divine ordinance and that the call to it comes from God. What he objected to was to single these men out as priests while denying the term to the faithful in general and making of the ministry a clerical status or a priestly caste. Because of the central role of Word and sacrament in the life of the Church, he made allowance for the exceptional case in which the faithful might choose one among themselves for this ministry. Unfortunately, it is this which captured, and still captures, attention when Catholics look to Luther's teaching on ministry. In ecumenical dialogues it is still a question, and a proper question, as to whether in an era of crisis such exception to the general procedures of ordination to ministry might not be necessary. Allowing for the exception is not the essence of Luther's teaching on people and ministry.

John Calvin

John Calvin formally distinguished the three offices of Christ as priest, king, and prophet.[48] Starting with the word *Messiah*, or "anointed," he elaborated on how the Old Testament anointings are fulfilled in Christ. It is uniquely to priesthood that he attaches Christ's mediation, by reason of his propitiatory sacrifice. His kingship means dominion in spiritual things, which he exercises in defending the Church and its service to God's kingdom on earth. This is done in expectation of the end of time, when the kingdom will be handed over to the Father. Since he sees sacrifice as the act of priesthood, when he introduces the idea of the priesthood of all believers, it is to say that they too in dependence on Christ can offer the sacrifice of their lives. He rejects the idea of the priestly anointing of those ordained to ministry as firmly as Luther. On the other hand, he held to the ideal of a Christian regime and tried to implement this in the city of Geneva. Temporal rulers enjoy their independence and are governed by the second table of the law, but their service in the order of God is a service to the spiritual.

Catholic Priesthood after Trent and the Reformation

It has already been seen that the Council of Trent defined the sacrament of order in terms of sacrifice and that it affirmed a clear distinction between ordained and baptized in virtue of the sacramental character, even as it refrained from any explanation of this character. There is no doubt that in later Catholic thought and practice, such importance was given to the bishop and priest and to a theology of ordained priesthood that little room was left for the priesthood of the baptized. In practical activity, however, there was a diversification in the ministry of priests ordained for a diocese and priests ordained as members of religious communities, a diversification that was not integrated into theological works. Differences in titles to ministry began already before Trent with the mission to "Indians" in Mexico, Southern America, and the Philippines, mostly on the part of canonical, mendicant, and new religious orders. In Old Europe it meant that religious priests took up quite a diversity of works, such as education and the care of the sick.

As centuries progressed, the greatest influence on the spirituality of diocesan priests came from the French School of Spirituality, associated with Saint-Sulpice in Paris. The thought of Cardinal Bérulle[49] represents the dilemma facing the organization of ministry and its theology. Bérulle held to a high ideal of ministerial priesthood, and so did the School of Saint-Sulpice, which owes much to his influence. In his whole *persona*, the priest is united with Christ in his sacrifice. This is understood to cover his entire life and work, not just sacraments and explicit ministry. To foster a fitting discipline and spirituality, Bérulle valued the practice of the evangelical counsels and the discipline of vowed religious life and could see how this had helped to form clergy, especially in canonical chapters and orders of canons regular and monasteries. However, he also held to the ideal of a diocesan, parish clergy and did not believe it necessary for them to make vows or enter religious communities to follow Christ and conform their lives to his following and to communion with him. While manual theology explained the nature of the Church as a perfect society, in which the due powers of sacrament and governance are given to the ordained, this school kept to the fore the close relation between ministry and spirituality.

A further note to be added is that the writers of the French School never completely lost sight of the royal priesthood of all the baptized. The writings of Saint John Eudes exemplify this.[50] He taught that all are configured to Christ as priest through baptism and that this royal priesthood marks the whole of Christian life. In words reminiscent of the teaching of the Second Vatican Council, he explains that it is to serve this priesthood that some are ordained by sacrament to the ministerial priesthood. Because of this mission and ministry, the image of Christ the Priest should be conspicuous in the lives of those called to serve the royal priesthood of Christ in all his members.

These historical observations show us that development of the themes of Christ's kingship and priesthood, and of the royal priesthood of the Church, have not been uniform throughout history but have been much influenced by social and ecclesiastical context. They have suffered most on three counts. In the first place, at times the kingship and priesthood of Christ himself have been well nigh separated and seen to apply to different realities. In the second place, the attention given to the priesthood of the ordained has obscured the more basic corporate metaphor of kingly and priestly people of God and given rise to too great a separation between the ordained and the rest of the baptized. In the third place, a theology of Spirit has been lacking in Western theologies of priesthood after Augustine. These are therefore themes that need to be reconsidered.

Contemporary Considerations

We have seen how *Lumen gentium* first uses the image of royal priesthood to speak of the Church as a people, which is the sacrament of human reconciliation in the world. Moving away from this, without adverting to the change, it goes on to speak of priesthood and kingship as two distinctive offices of Christ and so of two distinctive ways for the members of the Church to participate in Christ's mystery and mission. When that is done, more is made of the distinction in the Church between the ordained and the rest of the baptized than of the corporate reality.

In light of this, to discuss priesthood in a contemporary setting, we can start with the relationship between priesthood and kingship. Participation in the kingly priesthood of Jesus Christ does not in the first place designate a variety of activities. It means the reality and truth of the one community, the one body, which lives by his grace of redemption, manifests it in the world, and celebrates it in sacrament. The Eucharist is central to the existence of the Church because it is there that the body is ever drawn into the communion of the Spirit with its Head, Lord and Savior. If we follow the indications of the Scriptures and of patristic writings, we see that kingship is founded in sacrifice, for both Christ and his Church. The love, the act of grace and freedom, the obedience to the Father, and the hope of the kingdom are expressed in the Eucharist and are translated into witness and work for the kingdom in the life of ecclesial communities.

Christ's Sacrifice

To understand the royal priesthood, we need to base it on the meaning given to Christ's death and to the ways in which it is seen as a sacrifice. The contemporary emphasis in magisterial teaching that the Eucharist is a true and proper sacrifice or one in the strict sense, or that the death of Christ is similarly to be regarded as a true and proper sacrifice, can be understood only in the light of the history of dogma. The term was used at the Council of Trent to affirm the efficacious nature of the eucharistic memorial and to exclude the idea that it is simply a pious and devout recall of the death of Jesus to nourish piety. Sacrifice as such was not given any further explanation, and a study of sacrificial language in New Testament sources shows that it would be impossible to tie the word down to narrowly definable meaning.

When it is taught that the death of Christ was a true and proper sacrifice, what appears to be at issue is the relationship between God and sinful humanity, and the mediating role of Christ. Jesus Christ is not merely a teacher and an example for the life of his disciples; his death was an act of reconciliation, according to the Father's design and purpose, that brought forgiveness of sins. Papal teaching today, in accentuating the gift of self in love that is embodied on the cross, gives it a meaning that has not been the one highlighted through the whole course of tradition. This is not without importance in determining what is commemorated and how the Pasch is represented. It teaches that the whole economy of redemption and of the Church's relation to the world is one of love, a love originating in the Father in the eternal communion with the Son in the Spirit and expressed by Christ in an act of perfect obedience to the Father's will. What this teaching retrieves is the Adamic paradigm, the truth that by the obedience of the second Adam sent into the world by the Father, the sin of the first Adam is overcome. Where sin abounds, grace does more abound. It is in this confidence that Christians live and give themselves to the service of the Gospel and of the world. To this, one can readily relate the priesthood and kingship of Christ, Mediator of a new covenant. Hebrews explains his death as an act of obedience, and for those who live by this covenant, access to the Father through Christ is had through obedience. By that same token of loving obedience, of communion with the will of the Father, it is an act of kingship that gives dominion over evil and restores peace.

Royal Priesthood of the Church

The Church's part in Christ's kingly priesthood is in the first place that of the royal priesthood of the community of the faithful, organically complete in all its members. As body and sacrament it participates as community in the one kingly priesthood of Jesus Christ through faith and the Spirit. Sacramental celebration and representation embraces all that the worshipping community does in the name of Christ and the power of his Spirit, and then the whole life of witness given to Christ in a diversity of services. Within this one sacramental priesthood of the Church as a body, there are a variety of sacramental activities and a variety of ministries. Every action of the community and every ministry has sacramental significance when it is seen in relation to the whole, which is the action of the body as such. They all relate to the one act of spiritual and sacramental worship. To focus too strongly on the distinction between ordained and lay, or to speak in terms of differences in essence and degree, is not helpful when it makes the action of the priest the action in which the faithful join rather than an action for and together with the community. The action of the ordained minister does not simply serve but depends for its existence and meaning on the action of the community.

The convergence we find in tradition between spirituality on the one hand and pastoral and sacramental ministry on the other needs to be recaptured in a way that does not separate the ordained and the baptized. As has been seen, in the past the spirituality of the baptized and the spirituality of the ordained were not distinct spiritualities. All are called to live by the gospel and the law of the Spirit, but only persons advanced along this path were considered suitable to be appointed and ordained as pastors, in and for the community. A sacrament that does not bring a living faith and a living communion to expression is empty ritual, and a minister who does not find a place in this communion is misplaced.

Church and Christ's Kingship

The Church's service of the kingship of Christ through its witness and through the different activities of its members is rooted in its participation in the mystery of Christ through the Eucharist and through the other liturgical activities that relate members to it. To be anointed kings in Christ is first to enjoy freedom from the domination of sin and freedom of the Spirit in face of the powers of this world, which inflict war and injustice upon peoples and nations. It means working for a better humanity, inspired by Christ and his Spirit and nourished by reading and meditating the Scriptures, the Word of God. All are one in this pursuit of the kingdom of God and pursue it as a body. The bishops and priests cannot presume, in virtue of their office, to teach the laity what the kingdom values are or what their tasks in secular matters ought to be. If they have a leadership, it is to engage all in prayer, in reflecting on the Word, and in deliberating the appropriate course of action in obedience and witness to Christ. In many areas of Christian witness and action, lay persons will be more knowledgeable than the ordained because they are immersed in the world. Bishops and priests have to learn to see the contributions of the Church to the world as a joint and collaborative activity, not only in implementation but in the phase of deliberation, believing in truth that the Spirit inspires and guides one and all.

Facing the call of the day to gospel witness and to participation in the royal priesthood of Christ means, as we know, taking stock of what it means to serve the kingdom of justice and peace and reconciliation. That is the particular aspect of kingly service that is asked of the Church today. If it is to take shape, it has to be related to community worship, and there have to be ways of bringing common reflection on the Word of God into the celebration of the liturgy. There is much yet to be done by way of renewing the liturgy of churches as the action of communities, where gifts and voices come together in harmony, to reflect on the Word and celebrate the Eucharist.

In his writings on the Eucharist, Pope John Paul II followed a line of thought that shows how the priesthood and kingship of Christ and so of the Church belong together. In the invitation to a special year of Eucharist in the very year he died, he spoke of it as a celebration of Christ the Lord of history, the one in whom all human history finds its pivotal point.[51] In his encyclical *Ecclesia de eucharistia*, he had written of the eschatological tension of eucharistic memorial in a way that relates it to the place of the Church in serving worldly realities within the human family: "A significant consequence of the eschatological tension inherent in the Eucharist is the fact that it spurs us on our journey through history and plants a seed of living hope in our daily commitment to the work before us."[52] This work, he went on to explain, is the service of justice, of peace and human solidarity, and the defense of human life at all its stages. In all of this, the Church lives out its particular option for the service of the poor of the world. In this sense, the priestly worship of the Eucharist is the ground and motivation for the service of God's kingdom in the world. Christ's kingship and Christ's priesthood are aspects of the same reality of redemptive work.

Though it is difficult to situate the restoration of the permanent diaconate in the present life of the Church, and not much success in this reform can be marked, this intertwining between kingship and priesthood may offer some opportunities. In earliest tradition, as has been seen, the role of the deacon in serving in liturgy derived from his role in caring for the community's needs, the spiritual as it were being grounded in the material. Over the centuries, the service of the Church to the needy of society has gone far beyond care for the immediate members of the community of faith. It has extended to the poor of society and to those who suffer injustice. In our day it is said that service of the kingdom of God means solidarity with those who suffer injustice and persecution, those whose situation cries out for respect for human rights and dignity. Perhaps deacons might in new ways serve as liaison between the act of worship and the act of service of the poor. To be attentive to the Word, to be attentive to worship, to be attentive to the service of the poor— all come together in the ideal for ministry of the deacon in serving the Church's mission.

Word, Kingship, Worship

It is in relationship to the royal priesthood that the actualization of the Word of God in the lives of Christian communities can be understood. Three steps in this process are outlined in a document of the Pontifical Biblical Commission.[53] First is to hear and ponder the Word of God together from within concrete situations. Second is to attend to what in these situations is put into question by the biblical text. Third is to draw from this exercise that perspective and those values that may advance the reign of God in the world of which the community is a part. It should be added that this kind of reflection on the Scriptures cannot be done without the Holy Spirit. This is not only because of the gifts that the Spirit brings. More basically, it is because the Spirit brings freedom, the love of God as Father, the ability to pray along with the Son, the readiness to suffer in Christ's name, and compassion in travail not only with humans but with creation itself (Rom 8:22–23). Only with such a heart can Christians serve the reign of God in this world.

In another section of the document, the commission states that the most perfect actualization of the Word of God occurs within the liturgy.[54] Though the document does not explain it this way, one can give two reasons for this that relate it to a community's study and discussion of the Scriptures. First, it is within the liturgy that the members of the community together submit their thoughts and wills in obedience to the Father, together with Christ. Second, it is from the liturgy that they are given the perspective on history within which they place their reading of the Word.

It is here that Christ is proclaimed as the pivotal point and goal of history, the one in whom all things and all events are subjected to the judgment and to the rule of the Father. Sacramental memorial brings together in a moment of gratitude and hope past, present, and future. How faith in the Christ event gives a meaning and an eschatological tension to the understanding of the Scriptures and to their relation to present reality is brought to light in this memorial. The members of the royal priesthood together ponder their service of God's kingdom in the world, in the light of the Scriptures and by the inspiration of the Spirit. They bring this to the worship, where they keep memory of Christ and join in communion with him in the communion of the one Spirit, in love submitting their service, their projects, their hopes, and their aspirations to God's will and purpose. The one who presides cannot serve the people in this exercise of their royal priesthood unless he is one with them in pondering the Word of God and relating this to human events and history as they are currently lived.

Relationship within the One Body

Placing ordained ministry within the communion of the whole Church, living it in relationship, is offered as a paradigm in *Pastores dabo vobis* (1992).[55] This is exercised in a relationship to the Father and Christ, in the Spirit. It is a relationship lived in the Church as a communion of persons, and thus also to the world, according to one's place in the human and social network of relationships. Sacramentality has to give an ordered form to this being in relationship, and it signifies what is the nature of the relationship of the Church to Christ as Mediator, Priest, Shepherd, Head, and Spouse. It expresses unity of being in the Spirit of a communion of Love, coming from the Father and going to the Father as Christ came forth, lived, and ascended. The language used to speak of sacramental structures is sometimes that of institution, but we have to see it more as an expression of being that is essential to participation in Christ. This is why what is "instituted," what comes from God, shows some fluidity in form, for it is worked out in relationship with communities, with peoples, with cultures, and with the needs of the times. The Church is truly the sacrament of God's being in the world, and so the sacrament of communion and reconciliation, that which draws the diversity of humanity, the wonderfully differentiated humanity, into a communion of being and acting through self-gift. This is not an abstract truth, but it is located within a community that in diverse ways lives of this kind of communion. We saw how in the Roman liturgy the people were thought to bring their prayer, their devotion, their fasting, their gifts to the Eucharist, and that this was considered integral to the offering of the memorial sacrifice of praise. Today we would say that people bring their total engagement with temporal realities in the service of a reign of justice and peace to eucharistic expression, that full sacramental meaning occurs when the symbols, prayers, and rituals include such self-gift and commitment.

Eastern thought has always looked to the eucharistic communion of each local church to find the reality of Church, whereas Western thought highlights the communion of churches through a communion of bishops, centered in their relationship to the Bishop of Rome. Fifty years ago Edward Schillebeeckx already wrote of the communion of ordained and baptized as relationship. Today, however, Western writers who prefer the eucharistic rather than the institutional paradigm are inspired by the work of the Greek theologian John Zizioulas, of the Orthodox Church, in which he is now a bishop.[56] Zizioulas defines person in relational terms, believing that this is an understanding promoted by reflection on the mystery of communion between the divine persons. All thought on order begins with the assembly of the local church, where the memorial and mystery of Christ are represented in their fullness and all participate in divine communion.

For Zizioulas, the terms *ordination* and *order* may first be used of the baptized (and chrismated, chrismation never being separated from water baptism in the Orthodox Church), and this supports the idea that order and ordering involves the entire Church and not only those inducted into pastoral office through the laying on of hands. Being brought into the communion of the body of Christ through the gift of the Spirit and being one with Christ in his mystery and receiving gifts of service go together. To ordain a person to the specific ministry of bishop or presbyter is to build on this basic relationship and to reconfigure the relationship by assigning the person to a place and a role within the assembly and its one eucharistic action. The Spirit at work in the body is at work in the commissioning of its ministers. It is within this theology of communion that we may speak of diverse ministries and relationships within the one priesthood of Christ, in its kingly as well as in its sacerdotal aspects. Since action within the assembly corresponds with pastoral responsibilities, the participation in Christ's royal priesthood, which has its utmost expression in the Eucharist, is complemented by the evangelical life of his followers, as people in their time, bring this to fulfillment in the pursuit of God's reign in the world. Thinking of priesthood in this way situates the ordained within the community, which is one royal priesthood, sharing the mission and life of the community, rather than in a distinctive clerical body that has a separate vocation and spirituality. Rather than say that ordained ministers are called to a special kind of spirituality, we have to say that a condition for ordaining someone is to expect that this person has advanced in the Christian way of life and has the appropriate relationship skills to exercise leadership. It is by participation in the communion of the Son with the Father in the Spirit that the work of mediation continues to be done in the Church and in the world. Separating the domains of sacred and the secular is in the long run unhelpful. It is the one living communion of Christ's body that lives by Word and Spirit in the midst of human realities. It is the engagement of the whole that is discerned in reflection and prayer, and finds in the Eucharist "its source and its summit."

Conclusion and Nexus

The discussion of priesthood in the Church has been looked at in the light of Scripture and tradition and put into a contemporary setting, showing how closely kingship and priesthood are intertwined in describing the work of Christ and in describing the participation of the Church in his mystery. It is important to retrieve the corporate metaphor of royal priesthood as basis for all discussion of mission and ministry. Discussions of representation and of priesthood mesh. However, to take account of tradition, it has seemed helpful to distinguish the two themes. They belong together and need to be situated within the prevailing vision of the royal priesthood of the Church, in the communion of its members with Christ. With what then has been said about royal priesthood, it is now possible to turn to the issue of how Christ is represented in the Church and in its liturgical actions.

10

Presence and Representation

While acknowledging the one priesthood of Jesus Christ and the one royal priest-hood of the Church, doctrine and teaching often focus on the priesthood of the ordained and on their particular relation to Christ. They are said to represent him in their actions, especially in the sacraments, and to act *in persona Christi*. Explaining this without derogating from the common priesthood of the body is also a particular contemporary question. If the Church assembly of all the faithful is a sacramental representation of Christ, how does the symbolic role of the ordained minister fit into this mystery? In this chapter we will first review current magisterial teaching and matters that have emerged in ecumenical dialogue. We will then look at the historical background to the question and offer some contemporary theo-logical reflections pertinent to the development of the Church's mission and ministry and to the meaning of the sacrament of order.

Current Magisterial Teaching

The question of how ordained ministers, bishops, and priests act in the person of Christ or represent him has been addressed in several recent magisterial documents. These include the texts of the Second Vatican Council and teachings of both Pope John Paul II and Pope Benedict XVI.

Vatican Council

The idea of representation was used at the Second Vatican Council in the decrees on bishops and on presbyters. *Christus Dominus* (*CD*, 1965) on bishops is mostly about their pastoral role. In their lives and in their ministry, they are to give witness to Christ, the Prince of Pastors (*CD* 11), and in the exercise of their office, they continue the work of Christ the Good Shepherd (*CD* 2). More pertinent to the issue at hand is the decree on the ministry and life of presbyters, *Presbyterorum ordinis* (*PO*, 1965). In this decree the choice of terms used is itself of note. First of all, the title given to the decree speaks of presbyters and not of priests (*presbyteri*, not *sacerdotes*) and was intended to treat of the entire ministry and life of those ordained to this position.[1] The decree began by specifically relating the role of the priest to his own baptismal anointing. Then in place of the medieval phrase *in persona Christi* to speak of his action, it adopted the phrase *in persona Christi Capitis* (*PO* 2). While this is traced to a special configuration to Christ the Priest, the reference is not only to sacramental action but also to preaching of the Word. In evoking the scriptural image of Christ as the Head of the Church, as used in the Letters to the Ephesians and to the Colossians, the decree signifies that what the priest is and does in the Church relates to the total action of Christ as Head, through the gifts of the Holy Spirit. Since the priest is configured to Christ as Priest some reference to sacramental action is clearly intended, but to represent Christ as Head goes beyond the original limited sacramental use of the term *in persona Christi* in medieval theology and takes in the entire pastoral ministry. In referring to the preaching of the minister, the decree shows its priestly nature by referring to Rom 15:16 and 12:1. The role of preaching is to invite the faithful to make a spiritual offering of themselves, and preaching relates intimately to Eucharist, wherein the presbyter offers in communion with Christ's offering the spiritual sacrifice of all the members.

What this decree says of the representation of Christ by the ordained minister has to be collated with *Sacrosanctum concilium* 7, where the Council speaks of the many modes of Christ's presence in the liturgy. These include his presence in the assembly and in their prayer, his presence in the Word, his presence in the ordained minister, and finally his presence in the eucharistic species, which are to be given in communion. It is not possible to speak of the sacramental or symbolic representation of Christ through the ordained without relating this to his presence and representation through these other ways.

John Paul II

In several places Popes John Paul II and Benedict XVI relate the role of bishops and of presbyters to Christ. For John Paul, the discussion cannot be limited to the sacraments. It has to do with how bishops and priests, by all their activities and by their manner of life, bring Christ to the people. Drawing on *Lumen gentium* 8, the postsynodal apostolic exhortation on the ministry and life of bishops, *Pastores gregis*[2] is insistent on the need for personal holiness and a poverty that imitates that of the self-emptying of Christ if a bishop is to exercise his ministry. This is the necessary foundation to any powers or authority that he invokes.

The bishop's role indeed relates to the communion of the Trinity. Writing of what the bishop represents, the document refers to the ancient "tradition which sees the Bishop as an image of God the Father," who is "like an invisible Bishop, the Bishop of all."[3] The primary symbolism of this role is the "Bishop's chair, which especially in the tradition of the Eastern Churches evokes God's paternal authority," as it invites each bishop to be a devoted father and guide to the people.

With the bishop's relationship to the Father established, the Pope in fidelity to the synodal propositions voted at the synod goes on to show how the bishop relates to Christ, who is himself the "primordial icon of the Father and the manifestation of his merciful presence among men and women." Acting in the person and in the name of Christ, the bishop becomes "a living sign of the Lord Jesus, Shepherd and Spouse, Teacher and High Priest of the Church." To be for the people a shepherd means imitating Christ the Good Shepherd in "the three functions of teaching, sanctifying, and governing the People of God." To complete the trinitarian imagery, the next paragraph of the document speaks of the anointing with the Spirit, which enables the bishop to exercise the above-described ministry of good shepherd.

In the passages quoted, it is clear that the Pope points to a symbolic or sacramental role of the bishop in his whole ministry but is spelling out its spiritual implications. In the opening part of the letter (*PG*), the Pope relates the ministry of the bishop to his following of Christ in poverty and in readiness to suffer even persecution.[4] It is in the holy exercise of the ministry of shepherd that the bishop represents the Father and Christ. The papal teaching shows how intimately one are the sacramental role, the full ministry, and the personal holiness of the bishop. In a wholesome perspective on ministry, it is not really possible to separate juridical provisions affirming authority from this full treatment of office. In other words, representation and acting in the person of Christ are not to be related only to liturgical acts or official words but designate the entire life and service of a bishop.

As already noted, the exhortation *Pastores dabo vobis* (1992), on the formation of candidates for ordination, speaks of priests in similar terms. This apostolic exhortation develops a doctrinal approach to ministerial priesthood in chapter 2 that gives it a relational meaning. First, it is a relation to the mystery and communion of the Trinity, from which the Word and the Spirit are sent into the world. Then it is explained as a relation to Christ, to the Spirit, to the Church as itself a communion, and to the royal priesthood of all the faithful, to which it is a service. When the document speaks of the relation to Christ, it locates this in all the works of presbyteral ministry, inclusive of the ministry of the Word, sacramental ministry, and pastoral action.

In representing Christ, the priests relates to him as Mediator, as Priest, as Head, as Shepherd, and as Spouse. Furthermore, it is Christ's presence in the Church under all these titles that the ordained signify and bring to life. Ministerial service to Christ's presence in the Church is done within a communion of all its members: "Priests are called to prolong the presence of Christ, the one high priest, embodying his way of life and making him visible in the midst of the flock entrusted to their care." The Pope quotes the First Letter of Peter: "As an elder myself and a witness of the sufferings of Christ, as well as one who shares in the glory to be revealed, I exhort the elders among you to tend the flock of God that is in your charge, exercising the oversight, not under compulsion but willingly, as God would have you do it. . . . Do not lord it over those in your charge, but be examples to the flock. . . ." (5:1–2 NRSV).

Other texts from the papacy of John Paul are written in the same vein. The postsynodal exhortation *Ecclesia in America* (1999),[5] in speaking of the priesthood as a sign of unity (§39), uses the idea of configuration to Christ as Head and Shepherd, quoting the document of Vatican II on presbyters. Being bearers of grace, priests need to let themselves "be configured to Christ the Head and Shepherd, the source of all pastoral charity, offering themselves each day with Christ in the Eucharist, in order to help the faithful both personally and communally to experience the living Jesus Christ."[6] Because they are witnesses and disciples "of the merciful Christ, they are called to be instruments of forgiveness and reconciliation."

The immediate context for this teaching is the synodal and papal concern with building up ecclesial communion so that the Church may be truly the sign of reconciliation and unity in the world. At the heart of this communion is the Eucharist, the sacrament of love and of a living encounter with Christ, in which all the faithful actively participate (§35). It is the peculiar responsibility of each bishop and of all bishops to build this unity, which is formed at the table of the Word and of the Eucharist (§36). Bishops and their collaborators have to promote communion within the diocesan church and communion between particular churches, beginning with those in their own region. It is to this end that the priesthood is a sign of unity and priests, in their service to the Church, are called upon to configure themselves to Christ, Head and Shepherd.

Another postsynodal exhortation, *Ecclesia in Europa* (2003),[7] uses similar imagery and relates the priest's work to the visible presence of Christ and his mystery in the community of the faithful: "They are called to prolong the presence of Christ, the One High Priest, embodying his way of life and making him visible in the midst of the flock entrusted to their care" (§34). In identifying the distinctive responsibility of the ordained, the document echoes the distinction made in *Lumen gentium* between the responsibilities of the laity and those of the priest: "As persons who are "in" the world yet not "of" the world (cf. John 17:15–16), priests are called in Europe's present cultural and spiritual situation to be a sign of contradiction and of hope for a society suffering from "horizontalism" and in need of openness to the "Transcendent."

In all of these texts, while there is a specific application to sacrament and Eucharist, it is apparent that the relation of the priest to Christ regards the whole pastoral office, to be exercised within the communion of the Church and to promote this communion as steward and shepherd. In the Church and on behalf of the Church, priests are said to be a sacramental representation of Jesus Christ, who is Head and Shepherd. Hence they authoritatively proclaim his word, repeat his acts of forgiveness and his offer of salvation, particularly in baptism, penance, and the Eucharist. In this ministry in their own attitudes they are to show his loving concern to the point of a total gift of self for the flock, which they gather into unity and lead to the Father through Christ and in the Spirit. In a word, priests exist and act in order to proclaim the gospel to the world and to build up the Church in the name and person of Christ, the Head and Shepherd. In the sacramental anointing of holy orders, the Holy Spirit configures them in a new and special way to Jesus Christ, the Head and Shepherd. The priest forms and strengthens the people with his pastoral charity and helps them to exhibit the fullness of Christ to the world. In relation to the whole of their ministry, bishops and priests are given a specific sacramental and eucharistic ministry, which is efficacious because symbolic in nature. By it the action of Christ on the cross and his action in his body of the Church is represented.

The apostolic exhortation on the laity, *Christifideles laici* (1988), requires special attention because of the teaching it gives on the relation of the ordained to Christ and to the Church respectively and because of the questions it raises. In this post-synodal exhortation, Pope John Paul II uses the phrase of Vatican II, *in persona Christi Capitis*, to describe the work of the ordained as that of "gathering" all together, for Word and sacrament. Later, in talking of the sacraments and specifically of the Eucharist, the same document reverts to the older phrase *in persona Christi*, and on this basis excludes women from the possibility of ordination to presbyteral and episcopal ministry. To act in the person of Christ in a true and symbolic way, a candidate has to be a male. The Pope affirms this to be the case even though he insists on the equal dignity of woman and man and on the placement of women in all other ministries and institutions of Church teaching and government. He affirms that the ruling that only men may be included among the ordained is in the first place a practice that the Church has found in what she knows of the express will of Christ. As is known, this is repeated in the later statement *Ordinatio sacerdotalis* (1994).

Pope John Paul goes on to give some symbolic reasons for this ordinance. The practice, he says, can be understood from the rapport between Christ the Spouse and his Bride, the Church. Here it is the imaging of Christ as Spouse or Bridegroom and of the Church as Bride that is to the fore, but it is associated with identification with Christ the Priest. We are, the Pope asserts, "in the area of function, not of dignity and holiness [*in ambitu functionis, non dignitatis et sanctitatis versamur*]," and indeed even this male structuring must be seen as totally ordered to the holiness of all Christ's members. The reference to function is hard to understand since the text is about the symbolism of priestly person and action.

This reasoning is complemented in the papal letter on the Eucharist, *Ecclesia de eucharistia*,[8] which offers the climax of Pope John Paul's teaching on Church, on Eucharist, and on ordained ministry. In the celebration of the Eucharist, to act *in persona Christi* "means a specific sacramental identification with the eternal High Priest who is the author and principal subject of this sacrifice of his" (§29). Nobody can replace the priest, because he does something which "radically transcends the power of the assembly." This is to affirm the traditional connection between the power by which the priest acts and the power given by Christ through ordination, but John Paul adds the specific note of relation to a transcendent power.

The Pope is concerned with the communion of the Church, which is built up around the celebration of the Eucharistic mystery, in ways continued and deepened by the encounter with Christ in the reserved sacrament. When he writes of the communion signified in the Eucharist and the invisible bond that is Christ working through the Spirit, he turns to the visible bond, which entails "communion in the teaching of the apostles, in the sacraments, and in the Church's hierarchical order" (§35). The letter speaks of the particular relation of acting *in persona Christi* in the chapter that treats of the apostolicity of the Eucharist and of the Church. By doing this, the Pope relates the Church in the person of the minister both to communion in the apostolic tradition of the one faith and to the origins of the Eucharist in Christ's commandment to the apostles to offer the sacramental sacrifice in memory of him.

Benedict XVI

Benedict XVI has addressed the role of the ordained, bishop and priest, in the postsynodal exhortation of 2007, *Sacramentum caritatis*.[9] It is to the title *in persona Christi Capitis* that he has resort, but to the title of Head given to Christ, he adds others familiar also from the teachings of John Paul II: "in the ecclesial service of the ordained minister, it is Christ himself who is present to his Church as Head of his body, Shepherd of his flock, High Priest of the redemptive sacrifice."[10] The priest is a sign pointing to Christ and a docile instrument in his hands. Benedict adds that "the ordained minister also acts in the name of the whole Church, when presenting to God the prayer of the Church, and above all when offering the Eucharistic sacrifice."

Though the Eucharist cannot be celebrated without an ordained minister, Christ himself, the *totus Christus* of Head and members in one communion, is the subject of the celebration (§36). Hence it is for the whole community to learn and practice the right *ars celebrandi*, but bishops, priests, and deacons have a special duty in this regard (§39). Here Benedict refers to the role of the bishop as "chief steward of the mysteries."

The teaching on bishops and priests is grounded in the document's teaching on the Eucharist as sacrament and heart of ecclesial communion (§15). To the Eucharist, the Pope attributes a "causal" connection that makes of it the source of a communion in love working in the Church's life when all the faithful are gathered into the common celebration of the mystery as one body. It is this that makes of the Church a sacrament of trinitarian communion, which is the ultimate source and image of the communion of the Church (§16). In the celebration of the sacraments, all of which are related to the Eucharist, the Church expresses what she is by the gift of Christ's love. Since the gift of Christ's self in love is the meaning of the sacrificial character of eucharistic memorial, the priest who acts in his person must relate to this in a particular way. The spiritual and moral implications of this teaching are that the priest should, in celebrating and in his life, be and act as the servant of others. Benedict quotes the words of Augustine that speak of ministry as *amoris officium*, "the office of the good shepherd, who offers his life for his sheep (cf. Jn 10:14–15)."

For Pope Benedict, it is the gift of Christ himself to the Church as represented in the eucharistic sacrifice that makes the Church his Body and brings each local church into ecclesial communion. The office of the ordained minister represents this gift of Christ, to the Father and to his people, and thus is related to the reality of the communion of the body. As Pope Benedict puts it, "For all eternity he remains the one who loves us first" so that the "the unity of ecclesial communion is concretely manifested in Christian communities and is renewed at the celebration of the Eucharist, which unites them and differentiates them in the particular Churches" in which and from which the one Catholic Church exists. This means that the priest's or bishop's representative ministry in the sacraments has to be one with their presentation of Christ to the Church in their entire pastoral ministry. The accent on communion, complementing what tradition teaches about the need for ordained ministry, opens the way for further dialogue with the Orthodox Churches, with whom the Catholic Church already has an effective sacramental bond. At the same time "emphasis on the ecclesial character of the Eucharist can become an important element of the dialogue with the Communities of the Reformed tradition."[11] In these considerations the role of the ordained in acting in the person of Christ is placed in a truly congregational and ecclesial context and is at root related to Christ's own self-gift.

On another and less formal occasion, Benedict used the shorter expression *in persona Christi*. This was in his homily for the Chrism Mass on Holy Thursday, 2007.[12] He first recalls the sacramental sense of this term, saying that "in the sacred mysteries, [the priest] does not represent himself and does not speak expressing himself, but speaks for the Other, for Christ." He derives a priestly spirituality from this, illustrating it through the vestments by which at ordination "he put on Christ." Here he seems to be inspired by the allegories of medieval treatises on priestly vestments and by the prayers provided on charts in the sacristy that priests used to say as they donned them. The fundamental sense of all this is that in virtue of his call, the priest is to put himself totally at Christ's disposal, to be with Christ "for all," as Christ is "for all." The principal characteristic of this configuration to Christ is love, to love as Christ loves, to practice the ministry of love.

To sum up recent magisterial teaching on representation of Christ by the ordained, it seems right to place it in the context of concern with ecclesial communion and with the transcendent. It is as a communion of love that the Church is the sacrament of Christ and of the human community to which she aspires in eschatological expectation. The Vatican Council and the Popes were therefore particular in relating the role of bishop and priest to the communion and to the action of the whole body of the Church and all its members. Their representation of Christ fits into this setting.

There is first a general sense in which the ordained represent Christ, which is summed up by speaking of their relation to the Good Shepherd. In their entire pastoral ministry, they are to be configured to the one who gave his life in love for the flock and who is ever present in its midst by reason of this self-giving love. This is the image that they should constantly show to the people, in a relationship of communion with them that has its origin in the communion of the Trinity of Father, Son, and Spirit.

There is a second or particular sense in which they represent Christ in sacramental activity and most of all in the Eucharist. This can be expressed through the term *in persona Christi Capitis*, to indicate that the minister is acting with the whole body in an action, which is that of the Church as a community and in a communion in Word and sacrament, in which all are one with Christ and Christ is present in all. Acting in Christ's service, they are in a special way responsible for the sacramental communion within apostolic tradition and hierarchical order that is constitutive of the nature of the Church as visible sacrament of an invisible communion. Within this sacramental representation, there is an even more specific sense for which the term *in persona Christi* is retained in papal teaching. This term is employed to express the relation of the Church to the transcendent, which breaks in upon it and is not any human or worldly reality. Or the term expresses the relation of Christ to the Church as his Spouse. This suggests some particular love of Christ for his body and some action upon the body that somehow transcends its activity and its communion; while it is for the body, it is situated within the Church's total dependence on Christ, who remains in some manner distinct from it, though totally united with it. In liturgical action this relation is best expressed in the words which signify that the priest is performing an action or speaking words that are Christ's own and indeed uniquely his. This is another way of relating to the Scholastic dictum the sacraments cause what they signify. Rather than limit the sign to confection or consecration in some narrow sense, it can be seen to represent love and communion in love. What is made present to the Church is Christ's loving self-gift and his invitation to his members to be one with him as his body and as a royal priesthood, sacrament to the world of God's saving and reconciling action.

Ecumenical Convergence and Questions

Teaching on the ordained ministry in the Catholic Church is today influenced by relations with other Churches and in particular by the results of ecumenical dialogue. What this implies can be filled out by looking at some agreed or joint statements of the past few decades.

Orthodox–Roman Catholic

In the ongoing dialogue between Orthodox and Catholics, the relation of the ordained to Christ is placed firmly within the context of their relation to the Church as body and as a communion, with specific attention to the action of the Holy Spirit. In a statement on the sacrament of order (1988),[13] the joint international commission states that "episcopal ordination confers on the one who receives it by the gift of the Spirit, the fullness of the priesthood" (§28), relating this to the unity and apostolicity of the Church. Indeed it states that "the gift conferred consecrates the recipient once and for all to the service of the Church" (§30). The role of the bishop (and presbyter) in the eucharistic celebration is given a nuanced expression that needs to be quoted in full:

> In the Eucharistic celebration believers offer themselves with Christ as a royal priesthood. They do so thanks to the ministerial action which makes present in their midst Christ himself who proclaims the word, makes the bread and cup through the Spirit his body and blood, incorporating them in himself, giving

them his life. Moreover, the prayer and the offering of the people incorporated in Christ are, so to speak, recapitulated in the thanksgiving prayer of the bishop and his offering of the gifts. (§35)

With the entire ministry of the bishop in mind, inclusive of the sacramental, this statement explains his relation to Christ in this way: "He is the icon of Christ the servant among his brethren" (§33).

Faith and Order Commission of the World Council of Churches

On a larger front, in the dialogue between diverse Churches about ministry, some points of convergence and indeed of reconciliation have emerged in new forms of ecumenical communion. A broad perception of how the presence of Christ is symbolized in the mission and life of the Church, and of how communities are diversely ordered, provides a context within which to assimilate these tentative steps toward agreement. At the same time, it needs to be acknowledged that the special relation to Christ and the doctrine of the distinctive sacramental character in Catholic theology continues to raise questions for further ecumenical convergence.

Efforts to come to understanding bear some fruits. The Baptism, Eucharist, and Ministry (BEM) document (1982) of the Faith and Order Commission related ordained ministry to the presence of Christ in paragraph 26:

> The ordained ministry should be exercised in a personal, collegial and communal way. It should be *personal* because the presence of Christ among his people can most effectively be pointed to by the person ordained to proclaim the Gospel and to call the community to serve the Lord in unity of life and witness. It should also be *collegial*, for there is need for a college of ordained ministers sharing in the common task of representing the concerns of the community. Finally, the intimate relationship between the ordained ministry and the community should find expression in a *communal* dimension where the exercise of the ordained ministry is rooted in the life of the community and requires the community's effective participation in the discovery of God's will and the guidance of the Spirit.

The statement places the exercise of ordained ministry in the context of the community and asks for its collegial, not purely individual, exercise. The presence of Christ, to which the ordained point (a term that the statement prefers to *represent*), is the presence of Christ in the community and is located in the first place in the preaching of the gospel. This has similarities with the Catholic statements that speak of ordained ministry as the exercise of Christ's headship in teaching the gospel and in calling the members of the Church together. On the subject of a collegial exercise of ordained ministry, this same documents suggests that there may be different modes in which *episcopē* (or pastoral oversight) is exercised, and this is indeed more easily seen if, from early tradition, we remember that in a local church the bishop was expected to work with the college of presbyters. Indeed, with more fluidity in applying the notion of divine institution, as earlier suggested, it is possible to see how ministry takes diverse ministerial and sacramental forms across the centuries and from place to place.

The Faith and Order document of 2005, *The Nature and Mission of the Church*, offers some important elements of convergence on ordained ministry when spoken of in its total complexity and in relation to the ministry of all members gifted with special charisms. It recalls the service of the Church to the world, through promoting God's reign. It recalls that the place of Word and of sacrament are inseparable in the life of believing communities, as it also relates these to the indwelling and the life-giving powers of the Spirit. In treating of ministry in particular, it relates the ministry of the ordained to the ministry of all the faithful.

While the document gives proper place to a discussion of the episcopacy, it is apparent that looking for convergence in visions of the Church and ministry by placing the focus on structures or indeed on the episcopacy is thought to limit the discussion. This has at times appeared to be the main concern of ecumenical dialogue and agreement, but the issue belongs in a broader context. Though at a certain point, the US Lutheran–Roman Catholic dialogue in its recent statement specifically addresses the link between episcopacy and apostolic succession, it does so within the theology of *koinōnia*, with which it opens, as is also the case with *The Nature and Mission of the Church*. If it is in the communion of the Church in visible form that the apostolic tradition is handed on, where does the tradition and office of episcopacy belong within this? The WCC document places it within the context of a number of other "visible and tangible" signs of communion: these include the transmission of the faith of the apostles, sharing the eucharistic bread, prayer together, serving one another in love, giving material aid, working together for justice and peace (§32). If sacramental representation, and in particular the sacramental action of the ordained, do not relate to these other visible signs, they have lost their meaning. In this document, however, discussion of the role of the ordained minister in the Eucharist is avoided. "Eucharistic Presidency" is simply listed among "issues to be explored further" (§89). So is "the restriction of ordination to the ministry of Word and Sacrament to men only" (§89).

The context for these questions is provided in the documents in which representation of Christ in the Eucharist is related first and foremost to the representation of his Pasch, or of his death and resurrection. This is sometimes spelled out as "re-presentation," or presenting anew.[14] It is to this that the role of all ministers needs to be related. One of the first things that dialogues observe is that for the Catholic Church the Vatican Council reinstated, as it were, the importance of the ministry of the Word and related all sacramental presence to a presence of Christ through the proclamation of the Word as well as in the action in the bread and wine. The celebration is an action of the Church community gathered in assembly. Not only the action of the ordained minister but the action of the assembly, inclusive of all its ministries, belongs within sacramental celebration. Some form of ordained ministry is generally accepted as necessary to complete the sacramental character of what is done and signified, but this may not derogate from the representative character of the action of the whole.

To express the sacramentality of the assembly itself, different statements refer to the text of Matt 18:20, "Where two or three are gathered in my name, I am there among them." Apart from affirming the significance of assembly, there is also some retrieval, after the manner of Augustine, of the symbolism of the loaf and the cup, the bread and the wine. In these signs the members who gather are represented as members of Christ, so that indeed the bread and wine, when they are offered and when they have been sanctified, signify the one Christ, the whole Christ, Head and members joined in unity. The representation of Christ's Pasch and his presence through Word and symbol are unthinkable without the relation of his presence to and in the baptized. More recently some have noted the ecological import of this symbolism or the way in which the bread and wine represent the communion of humanity with earth so that the sanctification of the gifts of and for the faithful includes creation in the mystery of salvation. It is in pursuing this ecclesial symbolism and relating it to diverse activities and ministries in the Church and assembly that ecumenical statements put an increasing accent on the mystery of *koinōnia* or communion, taking 1 Cor 11 on the Corinthian Supper as their cue.[15]

Eucharist and Holy Spirit

Increasingly, mostly due to increased dialogue between East and West, many churches and agreed statements note that sacramental action is a work of the Spirit, from which the action and presence of Christ may not be divorced. This is to add the pneumatological foundation of sacramental representation to the christological and ecclesial. Finally, what is commonly noted is that the sacrament of the Eucharist is the sacrament of Christ's presence, in his love and obedience to the Father, in and to the community through self-gift. This means that the focal point of all eucharistic doctrine and theology, and indeed of all liturgical or sacramental theology, has to be the common table, where all receive as one the gifts of Christ's body and blood, sanctified by proclamation of Word and thanksgiving in the power of the Spirit. This is where and when the representation of his Pasch is given the fullness of its meaning.

Not all Churches or communities give the same weight to eucharistic celebration. Some, especially the more evangelical, emphasize the role of the Word and of their personal encounter with Christ in the whole life of Christians. Some also point to the continued presence of charismatic ministries of a prophetic character. These may be ministries of Word, ministries such as that of healing, or simply a continued witness to Jesus Christ in the way of living in the world. Such congregations do not want to see an emphasis on sacrament that would diminish the importance of the Word and of these ministries.

No Catholic theology of ministry, of ordained ministry in particular, or of sacramental representation, can go ahead without taking all these points into account, whether in particular matters or in attempting to offer an organic synthesis of thought and action on the relation of ecclesial ministry to mission.

Historical Perspectives

The teaching of Council and Popes and the results of ecumenical dialogue are to be placed within the heritage of past teaching and theology. In chapter 9 we surveyed tradition on priesthood. Here the specific question has to do with what was said at different times about the role of the ordained minister. Account is taken here of patristic teaching, of medieval teaching, and of the Reformation era.

Patristic Teaching

It seems helpful to summarize the apposite patristic teaching under three headings: (1) the relation of bishops (and by derivation, priests) to Christ as Good Shepherd; (2) the relation of the ordained to Christ in the enactment of the sacramental mysteries; (3) the specific sense in which in the sacraments Christ acts through any ordained priest of the Church, whatever his worthiness, or conversely, how the minister acts by the power of Christ and not his own.

Shepherd

The idea that bishops represent Christ the Good Shepherd is often stated in the nature of an admonition. It fits with what has already been seen about the exemplary holiness required of bishops if they are to exercise the spiritual authority granted them in virtue of their ordination to guide the faithful.

Augustine's *Sermon 46: De pastoribus*[16] and *Sermon 47: De ovibus*[17] are typical of this kind of discourse. Speaking to the faithful, who are the sheep of Christ's flock, he alludes to what is expected of those who are appointed shepherds for the community. In these sermons we find an oft-quoted phrase locating bishops first within the flock, Christians with the people, but then as ones who are placed over them, to be in charge.[18] If they do not heed the voice of the Good Shepherd and are not obedient to him, they cannot be good shepherds but will be wicked shepherds, who feed themselves and not the flock. The ideal is that all the baptized imitate Christ and become a light to the world, but the bishop is to lead the people on this way. The people, Augustine says, should be assured that if they imitate the bishop, they will imitate Christ himself.

Bridal imagery turns up in two ways in Augustine in association with the role of bishops as shepherds. As he puts it in his sermon on shepherds, Christ feeds the flock because he is one in them and they are one in him. Commenting on the communion between Christ and Peter, who stands for all shepherds, Augustine compares this to the union between bridegroom and bride. Peter is the figure of the Church and its shepherds, and so is as the Bride, who is one with Christ the Bridegroom.[19]

In another place, while arguing for the good of a lasting marital fidelity, he refers to the fact that the bishop, "a man of one wife," "signifies the unity of all nations subject to one man Christ."[20] This relates to the usual patristic opinion that the relation of a bishop to his church is similar to the kind of man-woman relationship lauded in Eph 5 as the image of the relationship between Christ and his Church.

Sacramental Representation

Patristic teaching frequently refers to the bishop or priest as one who takes the place of Christ in the sacramental liturgy, for it is in liturgy that one finds the deeper sense of representation. The context for this is provided by what was said in chapter 9 of the royal priesthood.

Earlier in this work we pointed out that already in Ignatius of Antioch, a symbolic significance of episcopal ministry is located within the Eucharist. The reference to Christ, however, is made more specific after Ignatius. Though in its earliest use, as in *Letter 63* of Cyprian, the idea is that the bishop acts in the place of Christ (*vices gerere Christi*), this develops into speaking of the celebrant as acting in the person of Christ. The meaning Cyprian gives to the act of the one saying the blessing prayer is in line with what was seen about Ignatius of Antioch's imagery of the bishop being the figure of the Father, or the figure of Christ, the icon of the Father, when he celebrates the Eucharist in the communion of the faithful.

Cyprian wanted to resolve what may seem a peculiar question, put to him by a fellow bishop, that is, whether to fill the cup with wine, with water alone, or with wine mixed with water. His answer comes both from tradition and from symbolism. The answer from tradition is that what the bishop does in mixing and blessing the cup must "correspond to the Passion," as this is known from apostolic tradition. We should do as the Lord did and commended, he says: celebrate with wine but mixing some water in it (§10). The bishop, whom Cyprian calls priest (*sacerdos*), in praying over the bread and cup offers the true and full sacrifice in the Church, imitating what Christ did at the Supper when he anticipated his immolation on the cross: "If he offers according to what he sees Christ himself to have offered, he truly acts in the place of Christ" (§14).

The symbolism inherent in the action shows what Cyprian believes to be done in the Lord's Supper. It is the offering of the whole Church, the offering in prayer of Christ and of all those who are one with him as his body. As he puts it, there must be water mixed in the wine so that all the baptized may be mixed with Christ in the cup and thus offered with Christ (§9). In other words, the bishop's action in sacramentally representing the action of Christ is done in, with, and for the Church and has its location and meaning within the sacrament of the Eucharist, which is the sacrament of the Church.

The mystagogical catechesis and the homiletics of the fourth and fifth centuries treat of the role of the bishop in similar fashion. For example, according to Chrysostom, when in baptism the faithful see the priest touch the head of the candidate, "our spiritual eyes see the great High Priest as he stretches forth his invisible hand to touch the head of the candidate." This is linked with the action of the Spirit of the risen Christ, for elsewhere Chrysostom says, "It is not a man who does what is done, but it is the grace of the Spirit that sanctifies the nature of the water and touches your head together with the hand of the priest." In such passages, what is being explained is that in the sacraments of the Church, as performed by bishops and presbyters, who are called priests, it is Christ and the Spirit of Christ who are at work. Because the role of the Spirit is kept to the fore, it is clear that Christ's sanctifying action belongs within the communion of the Church, Christ's body. Chrysostom's treatise on the priesthood also gives an awesome description of the priest's prayer in the liturgy for the sending of the Spirit upon the sacrifice (*thysia*) and upon the people.[21]

To see it in practice, as it were, these considerations may be related to what Augustine has to say of the bishop (priest) praying the eucharistic prayer and inviting the people to join with him, lifting up their hearts to their Head, who is Christ. In an Easter sermon,[22] Augustine assures the neophytes that they have been symbolically placed on the altar in the loaf of bread, dough moistened with water and baked by fire, as they were wetted with the waters of baptism and baked by the fire of the Spirit. The prayer for all and in the name of all and with all is proclaimed by the bishop, who "offers the sacrifice" and "sanctifies the offering." When it has been sanctified, the baptized represented in the offering are themselves sanctified as Christ was sanctified in his self-offering. The sanctified offering is the sacrament of the reality that is the body of Christ, the whole Christ, Head and members. In short, according to his place in the Church and in its sacramental action, what the priest does in the blessing is to express how Christ and Church are together united as the new creation, and it is as one body that in communion all are sanctified and are one with Christ in his sacrifice.

In the Person of Christ

This vision of the sacramental role of the bishop within the sacrament of the Church[23] has some roots in the Latin translation of the Bible and in dramatic enactments or allegorical interpretations. It was thought that in the Scriptures some things are said *ex persona* (or Greek *apo prosōpou*), where the person concerned may be Christ, the Church, the apostle, the sufferer, and so forth. The particular purpose was to attribute specific words to a given person in interpreting a biblical text. Thus, in the exegesis of Ps 2, certain words are attributed to Christ; others to God the Father, who anoints Jesus as his Son, others to the apostles, and others to the psalmist, who admires the mystery of Christ's defeat of the nations, who battle against God's reign. It is more specifically in the exegesis of 2 Cor 2:10, according to the version of the Latin Vulgate, that the foundation is laid for the sacramental use of the term *in persona Christi*. Translated into English, the Vulgate reads: "What I have pardoned, if I pardoned anything, for your sakes have I done it in the person of Christ." The phrase in the original Greek text is more properly translated "in the presence of Christ" than "in the person of Christ."[24] Church writers, however, went by the words *in persona Christi* of the Vulgate and read the text as an official pardon of sins by Paul, in virtue of the power given him by Christ (e.g., Thomas Aquinas). There is some justification for the Vulgate reading in that Paul pronounces forgiveness by appealing to his apostolic authority. Paul asks the Church to join with him in this, as one sent from God and standing in the presence of God and of Christ's final eschatological judgment God (2 Cor 2:17).

In this way of interpreting psalms and other texts, there is a tendency to dramatize the scene and the action of prayer, to make it more appealing to the senses. With regard to sacramental liturgy, this kind of dramatization occurs in mystagogical catechesis. In the course of following centuries, this took strong hold in both East and West and had an influence on the way in which the priest and his actions were seen and understood. Though other liturgical actors played their part, the priest was the one in whose words and actions the mysteries of Christ were made tangible and visible. It was in great part the need to make liturgy accessible to the people that occasioned its dramatic representation and gave a high profile to the celebrant, making him a visible actor to be watched and removing him more and more from his place within the assembly of all the baptized.[25] He was seen to take the part of Christ in the drama that unfolded before the eyes of the people.

Transcending the Human Action of the Minister

In the course of time, the sharp attribution of core sacramental actions to Christ rather than to the person of the minister had to do with situations in which its efficacy could be put in doubt. Due to his refutation in *De baptismo* of the Donatist contestation that only the sacraments of holy people and holy ministers are true sacraments—Augustine is cited as the fountainhead of this terminology and its theology. His aphorism "whether Peter baptizes or Judas baptizes, Christ baptizes" is most often quoted.

Augustine upheld the truth and reality of sacramental action within a Church that mixes saints and sinners. From this, he proceeds to say that Christ acts even within schismatic groups, though they need to enter into the communion of the Spirit in the one true Church to benefit from this action. Augustine is talking of the total sacramental ritual, which conforms to the tradition of the apostles, and includes the profession of faith in the Trinity and the blessing prayer invoking Christ and the action of the Spirit, and uses the correct ritual actions. The lack of true faith on the part of the community or of its bishop cannot negate the work of the Church, which passes on this ritual tradition, nor the action of Christ himself, who operates through his Church. To explain this respect for and this ecclesial nature of sacraments, Augustine used the metaphors of character and consecration but insisted on the need to be within the communion of the Church to live by the mark that Christ places through baptism on those who are of his fold and to receive his Spirit. In brief, then, in holding for the action of Christ in any sacramental celebration properly performed, Augustine is treating of the ecclesial nature of what is done; it is within this context that he holds to the truth of the action of Christ himself, whoever the minister may be.

When Augustine introduced this imagery into his debate with the Donatists, the principal point was that those who received baptism, even in heresy or in bad faith, were marked with the seal of Christ upon them, indicating his claim on them as his members. By right they belonged within the body of the Church. His belief was rooted in what he saw as the implications of having the name of the Trinity,

Father, Son, and Spirit, invoked upon one, according to the rites of the one, catholic, and apostolic Church. His thought on the imprint of the sacrament is totally within his thinking on the sacramental action of the Church and on what it visibly signifies about the mysteries of salvation.

In the thick of controversy, what Augustine said of the baptismal character was applied to the sacrament of order. However unworthy a person, a minister does not lose the sacrament of order any more than one can lose the sacrament of baptism. Once ordained, he belongs within the sacramental order of the Church: what he does are acts of the Church and so of Christ, with whom it is one body. At one point, writing on marriage, Augustine compares the sacrament of order to the bond of marriage, showing how he conceived the relationship of the ordained to Christ. Marriage and order are irrevocable bonds, intended for the good but remaining to one's judgment if fidelity is lacking.[26]

Postpatristic Theology and Canon Law

As noted, historical origins for the use of the image of *imprint* or *character* are found in the writings of Augustine against the Donatists, where it occurs as a striking metaphor. It was the theology of the late millennium and of the Scholastic period that complicated the matter by appealing to the doctrine of the sacramental character in trying to resolve the issue of an unworthy minister's power in celebrating sacraments. However miscreant a priest might be, when he performed the rite of baptism, it was Christ who baptized; or when he said the words of consecration, it was Christ who consecrated. No appeals to the unworthiness of the minister would allow dissidents to disassociate themselves from the Church to have their own Mass and communion, since in the actions of the priest they were to see the actions of Christ. Seeing the ordinand consecrated, sealed with the sign or character of Christ, was the way to affirm his distinctive role.

When therefore the term *in persona Christi* was adopted in Western theology, from the beginning of the second millennium it was given a specific application to sacramental rites in order to underline specific actions or words, indicating that these are the precise words or actions in which, in the assembly, Christ acts through the ordained minister. The reference, however, was narrowed down to a few specific words and actions, considered to constitute what was essential. Priests were already in the habit of celebrating without a congregation, or before and in front of the people rather than with the people. The theology of sacramental character applied to priests therefore focused on their specific actions and was developed outside the context of ecclesial communion, where it belonged in Augustine's thought.

Appeal was made to the official position of the ordained within the society of the Church, which held its mandates from Christ. Saying that a minister acts *in persona Christi*, as a minister of the Church, to whose officers Christ gave his powers, brought the assurance that Christ acted in the sacraments through his sanctifying action. In a similar way, the phrase was employed to give a guarantee that Christ's power was extended to those teachings that were offered, in virtue of episcopal authority, as the authentic word of Jesus Christ. In either case, we see that it is the formal act or word of the ordained minister that is intended, those moments when in the Church he performs those central acts of the Church's worship that are sanctifying, or those wherein he formulates the apostolic witness and the Church's belief. Sometimes, too, the phrase was extended to include all those official acts whereby the bishop acted as head of the Church, emphasizing the point that such authority is a power given by Christ and not a human authority earned by the bishop in his own person. A term that had parallel or similar meaning was *gerere vicem Christi*, which has its antecedents, as we have seen, as far back as Cyprian of Carthage.

A reversal of expectations was involved in this approach. In early centuries it was supposed that candidates for ordination practiced holiness of life and enjoyed the esteem and spiritual authority that fitted them for ministry. Now the call to ordination and its ministry became the foundation for a spirituality, for a call to be holy. In other words, if one is called to orders, one is to become holy. This was admirably expressed in the Pontifical of William of Durand in the admonition to candidates for the presbyterate. This admonition was retained in later editions of the Roman Pontifical: *agere quod agitis, imitamini quod tractatis* (act according to what you do in the Mass, imitate the mystery which you treat or enact).[27]

Thomas Aquinas

In the theology of Thomas Aquinas, the sacramental character and the action of the priest *in persona Christi* were treated in a more systematic way and integrated into a fuller sacramental synthesis, which derived from the doctrines of communion in the grace of Christ as Head (*gratia Capitis*) and in his priesthood.

In the question on the headship of Christ in the *Summa theologiae* (*STh* III, q. 8, art. 6, c.), Aquinas treated of the ways in which ministers are instruments of Christ and share as such in his headship. Christ, he says, is the Head of the Church by his own power and authority, but others may be called heads "as taking Christ's place." In support of this, he quotes 2 Cor 2:10: "For what I have pardoned, if I have pardoned anything, for your sakes I have done it in the person of Christ"; and also 2 Cor 5:20, where Paul says, "For Christ therefore we are ambassadors, God, as it were, exhorting by us." In the same article, in reply to an objection, he cites Augustine in words we have already seen: "If the rulers of the Church are Shepherds, how is there one Shepherd, except that all these are members of one Shepherd?"

In treating later of the minister of the sacraments (*STh* III.82.1), he explained that one could act *in persona Christi* in pastoral ministry and in sacramental ministry. The bishop as chief pastor in the Church has power over the mystical body and in the exercise of this office acts in place of and with the authority of Christ. In sacramental actions the priest acts in the person of Christ and by his power or authority when he speaks in the first-person singular. This was particularly important in the eucharistic consecration, when Christ's own words are pronounced, words that Aquinas took to be the form of the sacrament. He attached an analogous importance to the words said by the priest in the first-person singular in giving absolution or conferring baptism. Though these are not directly Christ's words, they express what the priest does precisely as Christ's instrument, in virtue of the power of the sacramental character. Thus, for Thomas Aquinas, the phrase means to have power from Christ to act in such a way that one's acts are the acts of Christ.

To give fuller expression to the action of the ordained minister in the liturgy, he allies the action in the person of Christ with the priest's action *in persona Ecclesiae*. To act *in persona Ecclesiae* can mean two things. The first is to make a public profession of faith, precisely as expressing the faith of the Church, which comes from the apostles and is contained in the Creed. All acts of worship for Thomas are by their nature protestations or professions of faith. When faith is lacking in the recipient, as in the case of an infant candidate for baptism, the profession of the faith into which it is received is expressed by the sponsors, but when they fail to do so, the minister of the sacrament supplies this faith in the threefold invocation of Father, Son, and Spirit. Elsewhere, in a way not fully integrated into his theology, Aquinas describes the purpose of the sacrament of confirmation as a deputation or designation to make public profession of faith, to speak or act in the name of the Church in such a way as to make the faith of the Church known before all. Not only the ordained act or speak in the person of the Church. All the baptized and confirmed also speak in public life or in some sense in the liturgy in the person of Christ.

The second case in which the minister acts in the person of the Church has to do with his duty to express the devotion and worship of the Church as a body, especially in the offering of its spiritual sacrifice. Besides professing ecclesial faith, worship is intended to unite the Church with Christ in devotion and reverence toward God. This is expressed by the ordained minister when he offers prayers of homage and intercession to God. Hence his action *in persona Ecclesiae* is a cultic action wherein the Church's devotion and spiritual sacrifice is expressed.

All of this may be related to what Aquinas gives as the profound reason for the unity of the Church with Christ. By the grace of the Head, the Church is one with Christ as though together they were one person. In other words, it is the communion in grace between Christ and the Church that constitutes the basis for understanding ecclesial worship. It is thus that in writing of Christ's sacrifice, Aquinas follows the definition of Christian sacrifice given by Augustine in *The City of God* 10.6: The purpose of sacrifice is to bring persons together into one communion in God, to take up into itself all the deeds of mercy and love performed in the grace of Christ the Head (*STh* III, q. 48, art. 3,c).

Despite the dramatization of liturgical interpretation, to which some commentators were given, the Eastern churches arrived at a more felicitous expression of the mystery of the body and its prayer because of their use of the epiclesis to ask for the sending of the Spirit on the assembly and on their gifts, whether these be bread and wine, or oil and water. It is the transforming power of the Spirit that weds Christ and faithful together into one body, as it is the Spirit who turns the prayer and ritual of the body into a life-giving action. After Augustine, whose sacrament theology includes the role of the Spirit, the West was unable to find as clear a way of expressing the unity of Christ with the Church, and of his action in the Church. The preference was for more institutional and juridical formulas, but Saint Thomas's attempt to place the meaning of such formulas in the context of the exercise of Christ's priesthood and of the profession of ecclesial faith should not be forgotten.

Ordination and Women

The exclusion of women from ordination refers to the capacity to exercise authority in a human society, ecclesial or otherwise.[28] It depends on how relations between male and female were seen in Church and society. For Aquinas, the significance and beauty of the sacrament of order lies in the fact that it meshes with the way in which God influences and directs all his works. As in all things according to the law of nature, God orders his dispensations by having some creatures influence others, so in the Church he exercises the power of sanctification on all through the ministry of some. Those who are ordained to confer the sacraments, or in the case of the bishop to govern the Church, by their actions express God's eminence and influence (*STh, Supplementum* q. 34, art. 1). On these grounds Thomas excludes women from ordination. Because of the natural and social relations between male and female, Thomas does not find it fitting to ordain women. It is not in the nature of things that they should exercise public office or leadership: "cum in sexu femineo non possit significari aliqua eminentia gradus, quia mulier statum subiectionis habet" (*STh, Supplementum* 39, 1, c).[29]

He knows that women can be more gifted and more virtuous than men, but in that case the order of nature, rather than anything specific to the Christian order, requires that they exercise their influence over others in a private, not in a public, setting. Aquinas says this despite the fact that in his own time some women held regal sway over kingdoms and principalities. He appears to think that what might by exception be acceptable in the temporal order is in no way acceptable in the spiritual, where the hierarchy of nature and of divine order is to be constantly respected. It is clearly a specific notion of gender differences that determines the case of women's ordination for Aquinas, and it goes with his specific notion that the ordained minister is vicar and representative of Christ's power or headship over the Church. For him, it is not a mere historical fact that ordination requires masculine sex, but a historical fact that is itself in keeping with the order of nature, whereby the male exercises leadership and the woman practices subjection.

This last point was made much more specifically by Bonaventure when he ruled out the ordination of women (*Commentarium in sententias* IV, d. 25, a. 2, q. 1), with important reference to an understanding of God's relation to creation and to the Church. He sees this as a masculine-feminine relation, basing his notion on a gender differentiation that sees the masculine as active and the feminine as passive (*Sent* II, d. 18, a. 1, q. 1). Since the ordained minister must represent God's action in the Church, it is necessary that the minister be male. The relation for Bonaventure is not directly to the incarnate Word but to the nature of God and of God's creative relation to the world, though this no doubt has implications for the vision of Christ as medium of creation and redemption.

Given his more legal and moral approach to the sacrament of order, Duns Scotus could bypass the question of fittingness or symbolism and simply appeal to the positive fact of God's ordinance that the Word take on flesh in masculine form, and to Christ's ordinance that males exercise the priesthood in the Church. Even to this day, this remains the first reason given for not ordaining women, even when some symbolic meaning is added. While Aquinas always looked for the "necessity" or fittingness of divine ordinances, in the Scotist tradition what counts is the positive divine will and divine freedom. Though the terms are legal and moral, the setting is not purely institutional for it is a matter of Divine Covenant, of the promises attached by God to certain institutionally determined ecclesiastical forms.

The position of Duns Scotus contrasts with that of Thomas.[30] Within what may be called his covenantal theology, Scotus does not find that the character and what it empowers has anything to do with a quality of the soul. It is rather to be explained by moral and legal analogies as a relationship assumed by one who has an obligation to another. By divine ordinance the priest is given the relationship to Christ within the Church that gives him the duty, which he freely accepts, to perform certain sacramental actions, in particular those of consecrating the elements and of absolving from sin.

In 1980, Aimé Martimort surveyed medieval legislation (from the fifth century onward) on the exclusion of women from any supposed intrusion on the sacred. [31] They were not to enter the sanctuary, not to touch the sacred vessels, not to handle priestly vessels. In other words, they were to stay completely outside the space of the sacred reserved to the clergy. Martimort speculates that this was because normally assisting at the altar and taking care of all that belonged to the ministry of the altar belonged to the responsibilities of those in minor orders, and that minor orders were seen in that period of Church history as an extension of the order of deacons. If women therefore were to be excluded from ordination by a laying on of hands, even from the deaconate, they were to be excluded from any role that touched on the responsibilities of deacons.

Given the different opinions of Schoolmen, it is not surprising that the Council of Trent took no refined position on the theology of the sacramental character. When Trent used this doctrine, it was to support the distinction between the ordained and the baptized and thereby the power of priestly action, without specifying further what it means. The existence of sacramental character was affirmed in quite vague terms in order to counter what the Council members saw to be a Protestant unwillingness to distinguish between the ordained and the baptized faithful. Apart from the fact that the now expected failures to understand opponents were at work, it has to be said that appeal to the doctrine was intended to affirm a distinction. In what the distinguishing mark consists, the Council members were unwilling to say.

Church Sacrament and Sacramental Representation: A Contemporary Reflection

From the above survey of doctrinal and theological tradition, what is clearest is that ordination was considered necessary for someone to be the pastor of a church and to celebrate the sacramental actions that guaranteed the action and presence of Christ in the worship and sanctifying actions of his body. As Pastors, bishops, and presbyters were considered one with Christ as Shepherd and represented him to the community as the Good Shepherd. Their actions in liturgy had a more precise symbolic meaning related to the celebration of Christ's mysteries. Patristic teaching is firm on the fact that liturgical action belongs within the assembly of the faithful and that it draws its symbolism from the assembly. Latin medieval theology unfortunately allowed for celebrations without congregations, and even in the case of public celebration it weakened the relation between the action of the minister and the action of the whole. If there is to be some better understanding of the part of the ordained in the sacramental representation of Christ and his mysteries, it has to be related to the fundamental sacramental signification of the whole body as the sacrament of communion in Christ, in the power of the Spirit and of the Eucharist as representation of the mystery of the Pasch.

Drawing on contemporary teaching and on theological writings, the best way to approach a theology of representation is with the affirmation that the Church itself, as body of Christ made one in the Spirit, is the sacrament of reconciliation and of humanity's destiny to be one. The community as such shares with Christ in his kingly priesthood, giving glory to God and mediating grace and reconciliation to the world. In view of its mission to make the reconciliation of Christ stand forth before all, with its message of God's unifying love, the Church is to be bound together in the communion of the Spirit, but it is also to be bound together in its prayer as the body of Christ and in giving the witness of humankind's reconciliation to the world (*Lumen gentium* 1).

Of this, the primary symbol is the communion of all the baptized at the one eucharistic table, sharing in the one loaf and the one cup, the one body and blood of Christ. The whole action of the Mass itself, and the placement of all other sacraments, leads to the common sacramental table. It is there that Christ makes all one with himself as one body, it is there that the sacrifice of Christ is most truly renewed in his members. It is there that the communion in the Spirit, in the one love of God given as gift, is made manifest. To be a eucharistic community, or eucharistic communion, the Church must live from the gift and from the truth of this table. Ministry, of whatever kind, serves this communion; it finds its origins and its summit in this communion. It is not enough to say that the priest makes the spiritual offering of the faithful possible and unites it with that of Christ. It needs to be said that the communion in the Spirit with Christ is represented in the gathering of the assembly and in the common table. The action of the ordained contributes to this sacramental representation of the whole by symbolizing its relation to the communion of all churches and to the apostolic tradition whereof it lives. If there is to be no eucharistic celebration without the presidency of an ordained minister, this is because the mystery of Christ cannot be fully represented outside ecclesial and apostolic communion. To overcome claims to represent Christ that foster juridical attitudes or narrow sacramental claims of a rather personal sort, it is necessary to keep this vision of the sacramental communion of the body in mind. The representative role of the ordained belongs within a corpus of signifiers from which it cannot be separated.

In the book *The Eucharist in the Reformation: Incarnation and Liturgy*,[32] Lee Palmer Wandel has noted that in the sixteenth century there was considerable practical and devotional difference between Reformers and Catholics on the meaning of the words of the Supper Narrative: "Take and eat: this is my body" and "Take and drink: this is my blood. Do this in memorial of me." If Christ's sacrifice was offered once and for all on the cross, it was asked how it could still be present to the Church or the Church be present to it. Protestant Reformers exhorted believers to live by faith in this event of the past, whose effects endured. Catholics thought of a sacramental presence, but to the eyes of Protestants the importance given to the words and actions of the priest obscured the sufficiency of the cross. To assure that the Mass and the graces received through it relied upon this sufficiency, the Council of Trent spoke of it as a memorial and sacramental sacrifice. However, it still asserted a priestly role that could be exercised even outside a community celebration on the plea that the minister performed a ritual of the Church and acted in Christ's name.[33] Though Catholic and Protestant communities alike celebrated the memorial of the cross, differences in perception affected the mode of celebration and in particular the action of the ordained minister. For the Protestant communities, it was faith in the once and for all sacrifice of the past that was to be highlighted. Catholic communities looked to an enduring presence of this sacrifice in sacramental form. The difference was reflected in the ritual, especially in the importance given or not given to the proclamation of the Word as an integral part of the action.

As churches have begun to engage in ecumenical dialogue, it becomes clearer that these perceptions are not in diametrical opposition and that some differences within the one apostolic tradition are acceptable. Nonetheless, they have to persevere in seeking agreements that may lead to communion. In a very particular way, they have to address what may be meant by presence in sacrament and by sacramental representation of the Pasch of Christ. As we said above, some weight has been given to the idea of representation of a past event, but this needs deeper probing to make sense, lest it remain at the level of rhetoric.

To say that the risen Christ is present in his Church is to say that he is present through the power of the Spirit and through remembrance of a past event, to wit, the event of his death and resurrection. No discourse on representing Christ can be divorced from this, and this has particular importance when we turn to sacramental representation and the place of the ordained minister within this.

If we look to the gains from ecumenical dialogue, we may summarize them by saying that Christ is represented through proclamation, through anamnesis, through epiclesis, and always in expectation of the *eschaton*, of the coming judgment of God, which is also the fulfillment of all that has been given and promised. This is to say that the entire liturgical form has to be taken into consideration in talking of sacramental representation since this shows the relation to time that is integral to it. Sacramental representation is enacted through the entire action and includes diverse modes of presenting the mystery of the Pasch and Christ's presence within the act of commemoration. What is done in Eucharist or sacrament has to be related to the other ways in which Christ and Spirit are present in the life and community of the Church. Christ is present to the life of the Church in many gifts and forms, and in an important way through the Word proclaimed and meditated and through the gift of the Spirit ever at work among the faithful. However, the reality of that total presence is expressed in its inmost truth through sacramental commemoration. It is as remembered in a way thtat assures that Christ is one with the body of the Church in this world and indeed inseparable from it. Presence is affirmed only through a recognition of how the present time is held in tension between past and future, between the enactment of the Pasch and the future coming of the Lord. Christ's salvation and lordship are rendered actual to a gathered congregation that is sensitive to its own being, suffering, and action amid all that constitutes living in the simultaneous threat and hope of the surrounding world. To be present to Christ as Christ is present to them, Christians live the present time in eschatological hope and commitment, as we have seen John Paul II say. Every present action and moment is incomplete in itself because it depends totally on its past origin and its future fulfillment.

Symbolic Exchange

Issues of Eucharist and of ministry have now been set in the context of communion, or *koinōnia*,[34] because indeed sacramental representation makes sense only within communion. To take account of the total action of eucharistic or sacramental celebration with due respect for all its component parts, it is possible to talk of symbolic exchange. Some time ago, to explain the mystery of eucharistic presence and the tradition that speaks of substantial conversion, Edward Schillebeeckx modified the language of causality and substance in order to present the mystery in terms of the symbolic exchange between Christ and the Church in the memorial of his passion.[35] Symbolic exchange highlights the relation between persons, even the gift of self by one person to the other, in the giving of something tangible that carries the weight of this giving. Though priority is on the side of the initial giver, the giving demands reciprocity, a reciprocity expressed through the actions that show the openness to receive. When Christ is present to his people through the sacramental gift of his body and blood, the sacramental representation of this gift is the offer to a community, and includes the response to invitation, which is the the communal eating and drinking at the one table, of the one loaf and the one cup.

Problems arise in Catholic teaching when the action of the priest in representing the sacrifice of Christ as minister of the Church is afforded a sufficiency within itself, distinct from the action of the community as a community. This still happens when the representation of the sacrifice is located in the words of the priest and the communion is said to be a participation in the sacrifice thus offered. It is difficult to see how it may be said that the priest "performs the commemoration" or that he brings the spiritual sacrifice of the faithful to "completeness" by putting it into communion with the sacrifice of Christ.[36] This is to take an action within an action as the moment of sacramental representation and to obscure the fact that this is enacted within the entire celebration and through the action of all, acting according to the proper distribution of roles and ministries. Communion in Christ at the one table, where the many share, is what constitutes the representative action as this is done through proclamation of the Word, through thanksgiving over the gifts, and through communion in the gifts that are thus sanctified. To attribute a representative role to the ordained minister is to relate it to this total and communal representation. However necessary it may be to have an ordained minister to place the Eucharist within a fuller ecclesial communion, his actions take meaning from the symbolic exchange of and within the body. Learning the symbols of this communion is a task still to be engaged, one that affects the placement of the role of all ministers, including the ordained, within the action and consequently within the life of the Church. The whole essence of the mystery stands out at the common table, the sharing of all in the one loaf and the one cup. This is where Christ is most fully present and one with his Church, through the gift of himself, a gift that is known and believed in the power of the Spirit, a gift that through the very simplicity of the symbols and symbolic action makes participants look forward to the fullness of the kingdom.

To represent this communion, to bring about this presence of the sacrifice remembered and of the living Lord, many ministries of the Spirit are needed, not only that of the ordained. When John Paul II says that the priest is to gather all through Word and sacrament, we have to ask what else and who else is needed for a gathering in truth. Though they profess to have a stronger faith in Christ's real presence, Catholics still have to learn more from Protestant tradition about the importance of the Word and of the role of the signs of shared loaf and shared cup. It is ironic that focus on real presence and on the ordained priest obscures the true signs of bread and wine, of what they are, of whence they come, and of what they signify.

Churches that celebrate in the Roman tradition have, in these last decades, come to highlight the role of the Word and the role of memorial thanksgiving. This helps to give us a better sense of a plurality of ministries that converge in collaboration and of how the Sunday Eucharist fits into the entire life of a community of faith. To create the exchange of all as members, one in dignity and in the call to holiness, diverse services and ministries are needed. These belong not only in the assembly. In the entire life of the church, they create the possibility of gathering, of bringing people to the memorial table, and of bringing to the table that which is laid out upon it to be blessed and shared. The role of families and of small communities, which was highlighted in postconciliar statements of episcopal conferences in the global South, needs to be seen as finding its purpose and its center in the one eucharistic gathering. Without these, there may be no Eucharist in truth. What is done in these communities—the *diakonia* they practice, the love by which they build up communion, the food and drink they lay out and share—is the necessary provision for a true symbolic action of sharing in Christ and in the Spirit. This we might learn from the history of eucharistic celebration that tells us that at one time eucharistic gathering and communal *diakonia* were thought to be inseparable, just as charity and charism of the Spirit had to be the ground for an induction to ministry of any sort. The fact too that people bring of their produce, fruits of their life lived in struggle and in plenitude, in communion with earth and living creatures, belongs to the nature of the symbolic action. The hearing and sharing of the Word that takes place in the Sunday gathering begins among the people when they read the Scriptures and pray about it together. It is such a sharing in the Word that gives life to the proclamation and actualization of the Word in the Sunday assembly and to participation in the paschal mystery.

We then can say that the sacramental representation of the mystery of Christ is made possible by a variety of actions and that in its symbolism it integrates them all into a communion or symbolic exchange of *koinōnia*. As mentioned earlier in commenting on the origins of the liturgy of the church of Rome, the sacramental action, which is presided by the bishop, included all that was done in the life and liturgical participation of the community. Word, gift, and prayer do not accompany the action of the minister but under his presidency constitute the sacramental representation of the Pasch.

Living by an economy of symbolic exchange means living by a different order than that which attaches commercial value to things and productive efficacy to actions. It is to live a life marked by the relational, by what brings people into an exchange of shared life and mutuality, where even the things held in common are valued for what they mean for living by community and in harmony with nature. There is a danger that an order of symbolic exchange can lead to rivalry, or to efforts to dominate by reason of the strength of the gifts one has to give, or by forcing others into the subordination of gifts returned. This may even lead to violence, in efforts to substitute one order of gift-giving by another, by bringing into commerce what can be called countergifts. These are the gifts that replace the original and point to an alternate source of life and power in the relational exchange of persons. When therefore Christian liturgy is put at the heart of a whole order of things, the exchange between members is related to its origins in God. The mystery of the Word springing forth from the heart of the Trinity is proclaimed a wondrous exchange, a sacramental commerce. The accent is on the gift that God gives out of pure love and on the gift that Christ makes of himself on the cross and continues to make of himself in the Eucharist, where his communion with the Father in the Spirit is put forward as the source of exchange and of gift. To appreciate this, and its impact on the very meaning of ministry, we have to relearn the language of symbolic exchange in faith, just as we have had to relearn the language of sacrifice.

While knowing that with the sacrifice of Christ on the cross, an order of living by repeated rituals of sacrifice was replaced, Christian believers did not abandon the language of sacrifice but changed its meaning, or, as some say, subverted it. When Eucharist was spoken of as sacrifice, to make sure that the once for all sacrifice would be respected, what was intended was a sacrifice of thanksgiving made in memorial of God's creative and saving deeds. To honor God, only thanksgiving is to be made, and to live by the sacrifice of Christ is to live in communion with his love, with his self-emptying, with his life in the Spirit, with his obedience to the Father. Giving back could not be part of this dispensation, built totally on receiving, on receiving what God gives by loving mercy through Jesus Christ. As Irenaeus already saw, and as Luther later saw, this included bringing the fruits of creation and shared life and the offerings of *diakonia* to the table, not to be offered in any ritual sense, but to be "lifted up," to be presented before the Lord, in order to be filled in their sharing with the life-giving power of the Word and of the Spirit. The symbolic action of the eucharist makes its divine mark on economies of symbolic exchange. It breeds a willingness to love totally by the gift given, to let oneself and the community be transformed into a living testimony to this gift, to live as gift for one another by the life of the Spirit. There can be no violent competition in efforts to dominate the economy of gift, for it is only by grace and by faith that we share a common life and that we live in hope.

The Second Vatican Council gave a refreshed importance to the transmission of the apostolic tradition through Word and sacrament. It related episcopal succession to the succession in faith and witness of the local church. It was thus able to give some recognition to the authenticity and evangelical meaning of ministries of Word and sacrament exercised in Western churches that have emerged on the scene since the Reformation divisions. What is at issue is first and foremost fidelity of the entire community to apostolic foundations in Word and sacrament. The episcopal succession has its sacramentality and its authority through its relation to the entire body of the faithful, and so to Christ, who is Head of the body, and to the Spirit, who guides the Church in its witness to Christ. Rather than remaining content to say that Christ and Spirit "are active" in the celebration of Holy communion or Lord's Supper in the assemblies of other churches, it is time to boldly say "present." This does not resolve the issue of a shared communion table, but it does allow it to be discussed with greater mutual respect.

When we relate this understanding of sacramental representation to the traditional terminology that affirms that the action of the priest is done *in persona Christi*, we may see that it is necessary to place it alongside the phrase *in persona ecclesiae* in a more integral way. The minister does not act in the person of Christ and in the person of the Church in two distinct ways or by two distinct sets of actions and words. The one act of presiding, proclaiming, and praying is an action of the *totus Christus*, of Christ present and acting within his body, the Church. If it does not include the Church in what it represents, neither does it present the truth of Christ's presence and of the presence of his Pasch. In short, what has to be seen is that it is the community of faith that acts and prays and in this represents Christ and his mysteries. It is within this and only within this that it is possible to give a representative character to what the ordained priest does.

Along the lines of the Orthodox-Catholic dialogues, it is by situating the ordained within the community and by seeing the relation of their ministry to ecclesial communion that we can see its relation to Christ. Along the lines of dialogue between Protestant and Catholic communities, we can say that even when Churches are not in communion and do not fully accept one another's ministries, it can be acknowledged that Christ's mystery is sacramentally represented by the other Church. What is lacking is the fullness of communion between Churches that responds to the mystery represented and to the gift given. The Catholic Church might still deny the fullness of the sacrament in other communities because of a deficiency in order, meaning the order that expresses full apostolic communion and brings diverse eucharistic communities together as one. It does not need to demur over what their celebrations represent when they keep memorial through the power of the Spirit in Word and sacrament of the cross of Christ. Nor should it fail to acknowledge its own lack of full communion as long as some members of the people of God are unable to share the table with its own members.

Bridegroom-Bride Imagery

In looking at papal teaching, we saw the significance given to the imagery of communion between Christ as Bridegroom and his Church as Bride, as well as the practical consequences of this imagery. Discussion of sacramental representation would therefore be incomplete without probing what this means.

Bridegroom or spousal imagery was at times used in patristic and liturgical traditions, though not in only one sense.[37] In some cases the bishop is called the bridegroom of the Church, the *vir unius uxoris*, to whom he must always remain faithful. This appears to be the meaning of giving him a ring in the rite of ordination. In other cases he is said to be the friend of the Bridegroom, the one who mediates the espousals between Christ and the Church. Added to this, we have seen how Augustine saw pastors as images of the Bride in their communion with the Bridegroom Christ.

Taken in its traditional sense, this imagery explains the bishop's (or presbyter's) role of teacher and pastor as much as it does his role in the liturgy. Pope John Paul II, however, in explaining why only males may be ordained to the priesthood, attaches the image of the ordained as representative of Christ the Bridegroom to the eucharistic liturgy. When used in this way, the priest's representation of Christ the Bridegroom supports the exclusion of women from candidacy, and this is the precise point that the pope makes in *Christifideles laici*. This has not put an end to discussion nor removed the bitterness that is at times felt. Sadly too, the practice of ordaining women in some confessions seems to be taken as a matter that divides churches more severely, internally and externally. It is an issue that requires frank discussion about how apposite this imagery is in explaining the relation of Christ to the Church and of the ordained to Christ. Since there are many facets to this question—sociological, cultural, and psychological as well as theological—it would be brash to claim to have a working answer to whether women should be admitted to the sacrament of order, but an open ecumenism requires that it be an integral part of true dialogue, not seen a priori as an obstacle to it.

Generally for the Orthodox Church as for Pope John Paul II in his letter *Ordinatio sacerdotalis*, it is taken as a given that the Church has no authority to ordain women because of Christ's exclusive choice of men to make up the college of the Twelve. From a strictly scriptural point of view, this argument is dismissed even by a goodly number of Catholic and Orthodox scholars and believers. It is the claim to be the authentic interpreter of how Scriptures are transmitted through tradition that clinches the argument. In *Ordinatio sacerdotalis* the Pope offers no theological rationale, but this is found in the letter on the lay faithful, *Christifideles laici*. He is at pains to avoid arguments drawn from the inferiority of woman's nature, which we have found invoked in the course of history, and so he offers this biblical symbolism to explain the matter.

In contemporary Orthodox theology, the discussion is given some attention,[38] usually in favor of the traditional ruling, but in some cases with more questions asked. Quite interestingly, the location of the imagery in eucharistic action is not taken as decisive, and it is more the pastoral role of the bishop (and presbyter) that is said to support the representation of Christ through male activity. At the beginning of every discussion on this point, the long-standing Orthodox theology of creation and salvation is invoked. Every baptized person, male or female, has put on the form of Christ and is an image of the divine Trinity. This makes of the baptized the primary icon of Christ and of God, and in this all are equal. As far as being male is concerned, this is not specifically related to finding in the bishop the icon of Christ in the enactment of the mysteries. There he also represents the work of the Spirit and the Church, the Spouse, who is one with the Bridegroom in eucharistic prayer and communion.

What is said of how Christ is represented by ordained ministers is said of their role as pastors of the Church. There they are thought to be icons of Christ, Shepherd and Bridegroom who loves his Church and gives himself for it. It is thought that some gender differentiation, though not one of subordination or inequality, is at work here and has to be kept. If it is hard to describe what this differentiation is or how it is now to be explained, for the Orthodox this is not a reason for putting aside this aspect of salvation through Christ and of the pastor's role. It is seen rather as a call to look for fuller understanding.

When one or the other writer[39] asks that the matter be more fully discussed among the Orthodox, it is on the basis of the nonconclusiveness of liturgical imagery and on the experiential reality of the leadership given by many women in the life of churches. Because of belief in the gifts of the Spirit working within the Church, what may be required on the foundation of experience is the discernment of spirits. Such discernment might reveal that a woman may show pastoral concern as fully as a man and serve the Church through effective leadership in its fidelity to apostolic faith, unity, and universal communion. This has to be taken into account in ongoing discussion.

A test of what women contribute to leadership in the Church would be made fully possible by following the counsels of John Paul II in *Christifideles laici*, which he attaches to his reaffirmation of the exclusion of women from ordination. He says of the place of women in the Church: "Above all the acknowledgment in theory of the active and responsible presence of woman in the Church must be realized in practice." The exhortation recalls that the revised Code of Canon Law contains many provisions on the participation of women in the Church's life and mission that need to be realized according to various cultural situations "with greater timeliness and determination." What was said in the Synod on the lay faithful about the participation of women in the life and mission of the Church should lead to their role without discrimination even in the process of decision-making. Beyond this, "women, who already hold places of great importance in transmitting the faith and offering every kind of service in the life of the Church, ought to be associated in the preparation of pastoral and missionary documents and ought to be recognized as cooperators in the mission of the church in the family, in professional life and in the civil community".[40] If such provisions were implemented one could have a better perception of the symbolism that ordination is supposed to maintain and what it says of the relations between men and women. Given the tradition and current practice of male hierarchical superiority the Church lacks the experience of living and working together in community whereby to test the implications of the teaching of the magisterium.

However the discussion of spousal imagery is pursued a return is needed to its scriptural roots. The text usually invoked is Ephes 5, 25-32 where Paul presents a new ideal for husband and wife relationships based in Christ's love for the Church. He is talking about how all relations change when lived in Christ, and his introduction to this passage places the appeal for woman's obedience within the general admonition that all members of the community are to be obedient in love to each other (5:21). Having compared Christ and Church with husband and wife, he goes to customary household codes or rules for applications. Despite his logic of love, it appears that he is not prepared to take strong issue with what was expected in the cultural and social context of the time and place. This makes it necessary to think further about the meaning and implications of the Bride/Bridegroom imagery in other settings.

The imagery of bridegroom and bride is already found in the Old Testament, as is the imagery of shepherd and flock, where both illustrate God's relations with Israel. They affirm God's covenant fidelity, a fidelity that endures even when Israel strays from the law or from the acknowledgment of the one true God. In Old Testament texts, the cultural background is that of patriarchal marriage and a man's dominion over his wife. The comparison made to speak of God's covenant and fidelity is one of contrast. Though a Semitic patriarch might well within his rights abandon his wife or repudiate her when she is unfaithful, God by contrast remains faithful. This has much the same meaning as saying that though a mother might abandon her child, for whatever reason, God will never abandon his people. The imagery does not put a stamp on gender relations but simply looks to what is found in the social ways of dealing with gender and familial relations in order to offer images of divine covenant fidelity to his people.

In the New Testament the metaphor of bridegroom is found in the parables of the kingdom in Matthew's Gospel that have to do with eschatological expectation (Matt 22:2–13; 25:1–13). They are about the wedding feast to which people are invited and express the privilege and joy of being in the kingdom as well as the need for constant vigilance. The book of Revelation mentions the marriage feast of the Lamb, which is still in the future (Rev 19:9). In both cases the setting is not of marital union but of the wedding feast.

Paul gives the image a slant in Ephesians, which is more directly related to the experience of marriage. Instead of evoking only Jewish custom, he has also in mind that of Gentile households. Christ is faithful and even tender beyond what was common. In his fidelity he gives up his life, to cleanse his bride with his blood. Used to express the extent of Christ's love for the Church, the comparison has virtually the same meaning as depicting Christ as a shepherd who gives up his life to save the sheep from marauders and wolves. What is brought to the fore in using the comparison with marriage is the union as two in one flesh, male and female, as described in the story of creation in Genesis. The union between Christ and the Church is compared to this, and it may be restored by Christ's generous self-gift.

The comparison fits into the concern of the epistle as a whole when it speaks of the power of the risen Christ, foreseen from all eternity, and of the one communion to which all those made children in him are destined. He has dominion over all the powers that seek to subject the Church, he is the source of all the gifts that serve its growth to the plenitude of Christ, he is the one in whom all are heirs. The unity of his disciples is described rather graphically in Eph 4:4–6: "There is one body and one Spirit, just as you were called to the one hope of your calling, one Lord, one faith, one baptism, one God and Father of all, who is above all and through all and in all." The Church "is his body, the fullness of him who fills all in all" (1:23). In such a context, the imagery in Eph 5 does not highlight the distinction between Christ and his Church but the intensity of communion whereby the Church as his body is his fullness. The rather strong eschatological accent given to the Church's nature in this letter makes unnecessary and even undesirable any development of the theme of communion that would disrupt standard social codes.[41] That reticence, however, is not normative for today.

Hans Urs von Balthasar

In Catholic circles today the argument for male ordination often means an appeal to the authority of Hans Urs von Balthasar, who reads a fundamental anthropology into the comparison with the relation between bride and bridegroom. Beginning with his early work *Love Alone*,[42] he claims that the story of creation, the Old Testament texts about God's fidelity, and the scriptural imagery of Christ as Bridegroom, reveal the fundamental differentiation of male/female relations within the one human nature. It is to keep this in place that reserving sacramental and pastoral roles to men is intended. Even if we affirm the fundamental equality of man and woman in creation and salvation, the distinctive complementarity of man and woman has to be preserved and indeed kept sacramentally intact. The argument is based on what is highlighted as the receptive character of woman, not a passive receptivity but an active capacity to be open to what is offered to her, to receive and embrace gift. The exemplar of this is Mary, and it is in her rather than in the office of Peter that the most basic image of the Church's relation to Christ is to be found. Christ, for his part, the Son sent by the Father, is the one who gives and who is to be received in a communion of love.

There are a number of essays in which one may trace von Balthasar's reasoning on how the priest or officeholder represents Christ and what male and female complementarity say to this.[43] Late in his life, in an essay supporting the position of the magisterium that males alone can be ordained and represent Christ, he made a rather crass statement that is startling though it is in line with his consistent argumentation. In giving what he calls reserved approval to the position of Louis Bouyer, he writes: "While man, as a sexual being, only represents what he is not and transmits what he does not actually possess, and so is, as described, at the same time more and less than himself, woman rests on herself, she is fully what she is, that is, the whole reality of a created being that faces God as a partner, receives his seed and spirit, and preserves them, brings them to maturity, educates them."[44]

Whatever his stated reservations on Bouyer's reasoning, he has for long supported a theory of gender differentiation in what he says about sacramental ordination. He places this alongside his appeal to the self-emptying of Christ in explaining office in the Church. The bishop (and priest) is an ambassador of Christ, one who may be compared to the apostles, who in the succession of the apostles is a person sent to teach and to represent Christ in the community.[45] It is not simply by reason of his office but by his testimony, by his configuration to Christ in his humiliation, in his self-emptying, that the bishop or priest represents Christ. This is given sacramental and institutional form through the laying on of hands, but the bearer of office owes it to his ministry to be configured to Christ by the "essential condition that it presupposes."

While the image of self-emptying love appeals to Christ himself, it is developed through a comparison between Peter, John, and Mary. Like John, Peter and all who after him are given pastoral charge have to develop attitudes of faith, humility, and receptivity. These are exemplified in Mary, whom the beloved disciple took as his mother, for what is asked of the officeholder belongs more typically and by nature to woman than to man. By assimilating these feminine characteristics, one is worthy of office and more configured to Christ. As a man he has to overcome the limitations of his male nature by taking on feminine qualities and attitudes.

When he treats of the sacramental form of the Church's life, von Balthasar holds that this expresses a distinction between Christ and Church, and so between masculine and feminine. He makes it clear that he is not thinking in terms of woman being subordinate to man, but rather in terms of a sexual complementarity that is confirmed and sanctified in the mystery of the Incarnation. Woman, typified in Mary, expresses the femininity of the Church, while the ordained male expresses the masculinity of Christ, Word and Son of God made flesh. He can thus write of "the masculine mission of the Son of God"[46] and relate it to the self-emptying of the Son in the Incarnation and in his death on the cross. Commenting on Eph 5, he interprets Paul's words to mean that in his communion of self-giving love with the Church, Christ "discovers himself in the Church," which he loves, just as a man discovers himself in the bride whom he loves as one with him in the unity of the flesh.

This makes sense only if in his sacrifice and in his self-emptying it is inherent in Christ's redemption that he overcomes in his own being the limits and hubris of the male, which are so apparent in male-female relations in the order where sin dominates. Within the order of redemption, the man-woman relationship is restored, and Christ himself in his masculinity learns to be receptive by a receptivity typically feminine and in the order of redemption typified in his mother and Bride, Mary. He learns to be perfectly open himself to God's gift and so to be truly obedient, to yield himself as the Son to the Father. For von Balthasar, this is sacramentally shown at the Last Supper when "Christ himself consumed the sacred species, . . . above all because he is able to be the perfect giver and the perfect receiver."[47] Those who are ambassadors of Christ, those who represent him, have to live not simply by configuration to Christ in his sacrifice and self-gift but by the self-emptying through which he learned of woman and restored the right way of male relationship to the female. This is inherent to the work of redemption since it is a restoration of the order of creation.

Those who wish to appeal to von Balthasar as an authority on the theology of the sacrament of order and to his reasons for affirming a hierarchy that is "entirely male" need to reflect on its implications. It would certainly mean an episcopacy that is humble in face of woman and that does all it can to acknowledge the very active role in society and in Church that comes from woman's perfect receptivity and her superiority over man in the capacity for a more perfect faith. This would mean considerable ecclesiastical reform.

Apart from appeals to experience, there are questions to be put to von Balthasar's reasoning. Its biblical basis is insecure, and so is the anthropology that lies behind his exaltation of Mary's role. It seems without foundation and indeed somewhat bizarre to say that the Word of God took on male flesh precisely in order to humble man before woman. In the total context of von Balthasar's theology, this sits poorly with what he says of the Incarnation and of how the event of the Word made flesh gives us the perfect form of the human response to the Father's love and of this love's image in human freedom and event. His argument about the masculine character of the mission of the Son would mean that his learning obedience by the surrender of masculine hubris, and by implication his learning from Mary, would be an inherent part of this free obedience and free self-gift. The role given to Mary in this interpretation of the event also sits poorly with the claim that in Mary's "*Ecce ancilla*" (Luke 1:38 Vulgate), "the Christ form attains the greatest splendour within the greatest simplicity and hiddenness."[48] In other words, Mary is the figure of the Church because she is the ideal realization of the reception of the Christ form, though Christ has in fact learned from her.

Critique

An Anglican scholar and pastor, Sarah Coakley, has offered a telling critique of this position in an essay in which she significantly details how eucharistic celebration and communion reverse accepted gender differentiation.[49] She suggests that in his theory about the feminine and the representation of the Bridegroom-Bride relationship in the liturgy, von Balthasar is influenced by a prevailing binary conception of relations between man and woman and by the desire to hold to a prevailing symbolic order. Though in general she shows great respect for von Balthasar, she argues the counterposition that the Eucharist can prolong and represent in the life of the Church the sort of attitude to differentiation that Paul exhibits in his Letter to the Galatians (granted not in all that he writes) when he writes of making naught of generally accepted differences and classifications within communion in Christ (Gal 3:28).

Coakley does not overlook differences between male and female. She takes her cue on feminist issues from the French scholar Julia Kristeva, and in this she subscribes to the theory that there is a particular feminine way of knowing. In cultural history, this has been relegated to what Kristeva calls the semiotic, to the sphere that is of language and expression which is not granted place in the approved and prevailing symbolic order. Arguing from the nuptial symbolism inherent in the Eucharist, Coakley contends that the feminine should be given its place even in presiding. The Eucharist is the action in which Bridegroom and Bride are one, where there is a fusion between the divine and the human. The one who presides is to express this union or communion, and it is necessary to express the voice of the Bride as well as of the Bridegroom in the key words and actions of sacramental celebration. This is the place where testimony to the resurrection and its transforming power is given in memorial parlance, and this requires the complementarity of male and female voices. Rather than put the bishop or priest on the side of representing Christ, one can say that the power of Christ is given to the Bride to let her speak, to give her testimony. The role of the bishop or priest within the community of disciples is to open them to the voice and the Spirit of the Bridegroom among them and thus to let both find voice together. If women preside as well as men, this subverts prevailing symbolic orders of male and female roles and allows male and female to testify together to the power of Christ's *kenosis* and resurrection, and to the communion in one body of the male and the female, the divine and the human.

For many, Coakley's distinction between woman's and man's kind of knowing and speaking would not be acceptable since it too may suppose too much that is unproven about gender differentiation. Whatever about this, we see how the ordained minister may be resituated, not putting the one who presides on the side of Christ over against the Church. The power of Christ and of his Spirit is a power that resides within the Church, allows it to share Christ's *kenōsis* and to give witness in proclamation and prayer to memorial thanksgiving and testimony, to offer the one sacrifice of the royal priesthood, "through him, in him, with him." It is this power of Christ residing in his body the Church through the Spirit, making it one with him as two in one flesh, that the bishop or priest represents, not a power from above or outside that risks separating Christ and Church once again after they have been made one in the power of Christ's passion and resurrection, but his solidarity in this with the whole human race.

The Vatican has argued that the act of Jesus in choosing to have women in his immediate community even while choosing males to number among the Twelve shows that he did not want women ordained. But in truth the inclusion of women as companions and witnesses is striking, not their exclusion from among the Twelve, whom the Church later saw as primary witnesses to his death and resurrection and who do not account for the various ministries and ordering of local churches during the apostolic age. It takes a quite institutionally oriented mind-set to see Jesus make a once and for all decision about the future rather than remarking on how much he did, within the circumstances of the time, to give a new place to women in the community of disciples and in the witness to the gospel of his burial and resurrection. Avoiding an unwarranted leap from the situation of the Twelve to the form of order in the Church and so to the episcopacy, it might well be asked what inspiration for current change comes from a reading of the New Testament on this point. If we cannot yet clearly see what the New Testament asks of us, we have to openly and evenly consider the entire presentation of the place of women in the life and ministry of Jesus and of the early church's witness to him.

This helps us to see the implication of the spousal imagery of Eph 5. It belongs with the image of the one body, according to the Genesis image of Adam as one person, male and female, no longer two but one. As the letter puts it, "Christ loved the Church and gave himself up for her, in order to make her holy by cleansing her with the washing of water by the word, so as to present the Church to himself in splendor" (5:25–27, NRSV). This imagery accentuates unity more than it does the male-female distinction. Christ is the recapitulation of the renewed human, in which male and female together constitute the one. Through the Spirit, Christ is in the whole Church as a body without distinction, and the whole Church without distinction is in Christ. In other words, Jesus Christ through the metamorphosis of his death, descent into Hades, and resurrection represents redeemed humanity in its solidarity. Though in his historical existence Jesus Christ was indeed a male, this was the submission of the divine Word and Wisdom to the limiting conditions of human enfleshment. By his very surrender to these limiting conditions, culminating in a death that gave divine testimony against all evil and negative limitation, Jesus established his total solidarity with the whole human race. When raised up from the dead and made Lord, Jesus Christ was transformed by the Spirit in such a way that he takes body in the Church, in the communion where there is neither male nor female, Jew nor Greek, slave nor free. While the outflow of grace is the exercise of his headship, it is expressed in the Church in the unity of Christ with his members as one body, the whole Christ. The actions of Christ in the Church are the actions of the body: there is only one action, which is that of the body, Head, and members, as though one person.

One need not expect churches in every part of the world to look in identical ways at gender relations. In pastoral developments, bishops and pastors have to be more closely allied with the communities that they serve. This affects not only gender differentiation but also all cultural expressions of a common life. Within cultural diversity, local churches can give expression to their own particular identity within the symbolic and sacramental representation of Christ, the *Christus totus*, which they inherit from tradition. This is a challenge to consider the role of the ordained and the presence of Christ in his Church and sacraments in forms of thought and speech that come from other than Greco-Roman culture or from Greek thought. Chapter 1 reported how churches of both Africa and Asia see life in the extended family as core to the life of the Church and the place from which ministries and ministers will emerge.[50] A communal and cosmic vision of reality and of the human person is inherent to African and Asian tradition and reality. As other members of the community, the ordained minister finds his place in relation to Christ and Church within family-like communities, with their relation to ancestors and to the living sense of being one with all creation. Within this universe, portrayal of the role of bishop takes another shape, and the presence of Christ, or any capacity to present Christ to others, has to be located within such a perception of life.

Conclusion

The conclusion to all of this is that, when related to history, the language of representation is subject to multiple qualification. It must start with the fact that the primary act of representation in the life of the Church is that of the memorial of Christ's Pasch celebrated by the *totus Christus*. Any other acts of representation have to fit into this setting. The pastoral role of bishop and priest is indeed an important one, to be exercised collaboratively with community and other ministers, in the assembly as elsewhere. The best account is given of it through a grasp of symbolic exchange and by positing it within a theology of relationships within the one Body. In this regard, there is no adequate basis for employing anthropological notions about the distinction between male and female.

Sign of God's kingdom, the Church is a community of reconciliation, one that is the chosen of God and lives by God's justifying grace given in Christ. Anyone who claims to represent Christ, to speak or act in his name or person, is a minister of this communion and has a representative role only in relation to the representative character of the body in its total membership. What is represented through memorial is the presence of Christ and his Spirit in the body within time, its communion with Christ in the Spirit, which anticipates its consummation. Poised between past and present and in constant anticipation of the future, all representation is linked to commemoration and expectation, harking back to the Christ event and looking forward to eschatological fulfillment. Any representation attributed to particular acts of persons has to be in harmony with the truth that the most essential presence and representation of Christ, in the power of Word and Spirit, is that of the community of believers, which lives by his paschal mystery. They are one with him in their whole life of faith as a community, and this is symbolized in sacramental form around the table of the one loaf and the one cup.

When the ordained minister is said to represent Christ, this is in relation to his presence and representation in the body of all believers, and to the presence of this body in the world, at the service of God's rule, in particular times and places. Though it is given institutional form, the service of the ordained is charismatic in origin. They are one with Christ in virtue of the charisms they receive from the Spirit and by reason of the office whereby they serve and represent his headship over the Church, that headship in virtue of which Christ is present and active in all his members and through all his members. To exercise this service becomingly and effectively, they have to put on the form of Christ and live their service in a relationship to him in the total being of his life, death, and resurrection. Throughout history and in current teaching, this is expressed by relating the service of bishops and priests to Christ through the varied images of Head, Priest, Shepherd, Lamb, and Bridegroom.

When the service of bishop or priest to the Church is given sacramental form in their actions as liturgical ministers, this makes it clear that it belongs within an action of memorial and is therefore related to all the components of memorial action. A specific concern of Pope John Paul and Pope Benedict appears to be the tensive relation of the ordained to Christ, which shows that as sent by God, Lord, and the One to come, he is not to be confused with any moment of the Church's life or any particular realization of communion within time. For this reason they opt on occasion for the simple expression *in persona Christi*. The meaning of this, however, depends on locating such significance within the reality of the people of God and body of Christ as sacrament of Christ and sacrament of reconciliation, and within a sacramental action that is of the whole community.

Mission, Ministry, Leadership, Order

In the theologically oriented survey of historical realities in this work, we showed the influence of different understandings of mission and ministry in determining ecclesiastical structures and the variant relation to social and cultural contexts. Chapters 9–10 were about the understanding of priesthood and representation of Christ and his mystery. In the light of these reflections and of what was said earlier about developments around the globe, we can further explore how the mission and ministry are developing and are being reordered in our own time.

The chapter begins with some words about the critical reappraisal of ministry and order needed in the light of how mission is developing. This is then related to the missionary character of the Church as it is being worked out across the world in the wake of the Second Vatican Council. Church ordering is next considered against this background. The fourth section of the chapter is about the sacramental expression of the Church as a eucharistic community of the baptized, within which ministries are exercised and ordered. Some reflections are then offered on the power of being Christian. On this basis an understanding of order is presented as a process of the canonization of power, and this leads to a consideration of cultural models of power and authority, past and present. The chapter closes with some words on the powers of the weak apposite to the call to be the Church of the Poor.

The Present Moment of Critical Reappraisal

The Church is at a point where the significance and impact of the Second Vatican Council and the manner of its reception into the life of local churches is still an issue. We may wonder what has become of the hope of a new Pentecost, voiced by Pope John XXIII in convoking the Council. For him, the gathering of the Council was the opportunity to learn to speak again the word of the gospel and to find Christian meaning and presence in the broad realities of human life and whatever forces and aspirations moved peoples. He also held out the hope of moving significantly toward communion between separated churches, both East and West.

For us today to receive the Council in Christian hope is not only a matter of reading texts but one of trying to find and to grasp the meaning of an event in the history of the Church, not as a once and for all occurrence but as one that continues to happen in a diversity of ways around the globe. The Councils of Trent and Vatican I were also key events marking moments of challenge to the Church, but they were quickly solidified, made rigid, turned into texts on a page, canonical provisions, catechisms, and authoritative liturgical books, all considered normative, *semper, ubique, et pro omnibus* (always, everywhere, and for all). Forty odd years beyond Vatican II, there seems to be a similar move in the direction of rigidity in canonical provisions, liturgical forms, and doctrinal interpretations, but true freedom, which casts out fear, is still an option.

Particular disappointments that affect ministry can be specified. It is tragic that the genuine prospects of ecumenism, being one Church and people of Christ, sensitive to a common mission, have become "mired in a profusion of doctrinal conferences" that end up in the form of statements, while actual communion in Word, worship, and apostolate lags behind.[1] What is also tragic is that what was spoken of as "the moment of the laity" has been subjected to an ordering that supports the distinction between clergy and laity rather than promoting a genuine coresponsibility for mission and ministry. Those who prefer retrenchment and a separation between religious life and temporal affairs, or who are hesitant about ecumenical openness and about lay ministries, have to be allowed their voice, but the impetus toward a reordering comes from the impulse of the Council to look outward, to find Christian identity in a way of relating to multiple others, or as it might be put through living faith in dialogue. Sharing coresponsibility for the Church's life and mission, an interest in the name of faith in contributing to temporal affairs, and a willingness to be involved with others are marks of the kind of community in which roles and activities need to be ordered. Though failures of various sorts are to be regretted, saddest of all is that the rigidity of structures and canonical expectations prevents many communities from having a weekly celebration of the Eucharist that relates well to their common life.

Although ecclesiastical and sacramental order is always needed, the urgency of the moment is that of naming leaders with the right charisms, the right human gifts, the right skills of leadership. Such leadership does not necessarily in the first place emanate from the episcopacy, though one hopes indeed that episcopal appointments are given to those who can be true leaders and shepherds. Given the collaborative necessity of mission, what is needed is a diversity of leadership and a diversity of forms of recognizing and ordering ecclesial life. Possession of charism and relationality within the one communion and mission are the foundation of good order, even as it is clear that people of different cultures and churches can see mission and relationality from different angles and locate the charismatic in various positions, powers, and actions within their own households.

In the last forty years, it has been difficult to break in practice with the understanding of the Church as a hierarchical institution, whether hierarchy be understood in terms of juridical supremacy or of a higher spirituality. To speak first and foremost of institution, however, is to speak the wrong language and to forget the question to which this idea was an answer. In history behind the recognition of episcopacy as an institution was the question whether as structures and institutional forms developed, they could be said to be true to the gospel. In short, it was queried whether they could be seen as of "divine origin," or as coming from God, a providential result of gospel, tradition, and Spirit working together within the communion of churches faithful to the one apostolic tradition. If the emergence of episcopacy, presbyterate, and deaconate were deemed to be of divine origin, this was because they seemed to serve apostolic truth and continuity, one eucharistic communion, a communion between churches, and a pledge of *diakonia*. As any church orders its ministries, it can still be asked whether it is true to the fundamental apostolic witness, adhering in truth to what was revealed and given to the world in the death and resurrection of the One who is confessed as Lord. These are still vital questions, to be answered in practice through regional sensitivity to the place of the Church in cultural traditions and in a developing social forum.

The Church Missionary

Instead of seeing missionary work as a distinct activity in the Church's life undertaken by some among them, churches around the world have learned to see being on mission as integral to their very existence. Since new challenges were highlighted by the Second Vatican Council, in the decree *Ad gentes* and the constitution *Gaudium et spes*, this has prompted communities to rethink the nature of mission and of ecclesial existence. With an articulation that often came from theologians like Chenu, Congar, and Rahner, such missionary consciousness had begun with lay movements in the decades preceding the Council. These theologians and what they stood for were at first rejected by Rome's central authority, but through the Council their voice was integrated into the life, work, and mission of churches.

While peoples in some parts of the world remain deeply spiritual, the civilizations of Europe and North America are increasingly de-Christianized, and the influence of churches in the public forum has decreased considerably. This move from Christian religious affiliation is not simply something negative, but it emerged and emerges in many respects by way of disaffection with the negative side of religious belonging and ambition and in a genuine quest for what is truly human. As even Pope Benedict has remarked, without the Enlightenment and its social consequences, there would not today be a concern for human rights and for shared responsibility within the ordering of the human community. Christians have to continue to work with insights from various cultures as well as philosophies that are offered to the Church for its consideration. The realization that it is not for the Church to control the temporal order means working in collaboration with all who see the human good as something higher than the pursuit of material prosperity.

We are in an age when those of Christian faith and persuasion can indeed commit themselves to action in the world rather than withdraw from it, working for the betterment of humanity in the realization of a greater human solidarity. It is the "age of the laity," or in better terms, an age when local churches are taking account of their identities as communities of all the baptized and of their mission within the world around them. This is true not only in the sense that lay persons have become more active in the Church's life and in the ministries of the Church than they had been. It is true more profoundly in the sense that lay persons are at the forefront of the Church's presence in the social order, and in building the reign of God in the world, in fulfillment of an ecclesial mandate. For this to come to maturity, several things are required. First, the full meaning of being Church, being the sign of God's presence in the world in and by dialogue, has to be explored and discovered. The need for the acts of confession and pleas for forgiveness evoked during the jubilee of 2000 has to sink into the heart of Christianity. The Church has been at fault in the way that its order and teaching have provoked insult and injury toward others inside and outside its communion or have failed to build an organism that is open to other bodies and persons and cultures. Not only must it now reform itself internally, but it has to listen and learn through the ears of all the faithful. There are various other paths to the truth and to the pursuit of the good of humanity available to people in most contemporary cultures and societies of which the baptized are cognizant. The Church can learn from those who pursue these paths, and with them she can converse and work without losing her own fidelity to Jesus Christ.

The word *secular* is much used and abused in talking of our present age, but it can be employed to suggest that this is not a time in which any particular religious body or religious belief determines the ordering of human relations or the pursuit of justice and peace. We can learn from Benedict XVI when he says that a point of convergence between religions may be respect for reason. However, this cannot be reduced to the kind of reason that Christianity espoused when it gave special credit to Greek thought. This helped the Church providentially in the past to formulate its thought and aspirations, but now it is time to engage with other cultural and philosophical traditions, East and West. What is at stake is a use of reason and discernment that comes to light in various forms of humanism, that in solidarity allows an encounter of persons and bodies who are not committed to self-interest but to a great and common human good, and are ready to give of themselves, for the good of others. In his encyclical on Faith and Reason (*Fides et ratio*, 1998), Pope John Paul II invited Catholics (and others) into a conversation with a variety of reasonable and cultural pursuits, both to deepen the faith and to deepen a solidarity through which the many might work together as the one.

To serve that movement of the Spirit, which goes by the shorthand of "the emerging age of the laity," whereby a new presence in the world is realized, many things have to happen within the Church itself. As Christians we are called upon to overcome polarizations of the past that have cut deeply into the life of Catholic culture and identity. Such polarizations are those of clergy/laity, sacred/secular, lay/religious, women/men. The polarizations between Catholic/Protestant and East/West among Christian communities also need to be set aside.

When it comes to Church ordering, we have no need today for bodies of clergy or monks who present a model for holiness and a Christian way of life. Religious communities living a vowed life will probably always have some place, but not in the ways of the past, when they seemed the only avenue to advance holiness or forms of apostolic work and presence in society. Various movements among the baptized, whether in the form of new global organisms or more especially in the shape of small local communities, themselves model Christian holiness and initiate persons into it. Whatever hierarchy of the spiritual may exist, it does not have to be identified with specific bodies or with any particular status in the Church. The call of all to holiness propounded in chapter 4 of *Lumen gentium*, when taken seriously, allows varieties of Christian groups to come together in commitment to the gospel, within churches and across ecumenical boundaries. This kind of personal and communal charism is the proper foundation for developments in the ministry of the ordained. A new discernment of the call to order and new ways for the ordained to be of significance and help to congregations are in the process of being discovered. Though this causes some tremors of change and fear, they are to be surmounted or banished only by trust in the name of Christ and in the gift of the Spirit.

Within this process of change, churches in Europe and North America have to find their new place and their new ways of being. On other continents the broad but deeply rooted sense of mission has developed with the call to be a Church of the impoverished, seeking to be a truly localized communion of communities that brings flesh to the gospel in totally new circumstances. Believers struggle to over-come in Christ's name and Spirit the many forms of slavery and loss that impede authentic human development.[2] Churches are also learning to live as people in dialogue, in dialogue within their own membership, in dialogue between Christian communities, and in dialogue with religions and with cultural traditions. Trans-porting the privileged status of Greek thought together with the gospel seems questionable in face of the vast richness of the cultural contribution and the thought of other peoples and of living faiths.

When more focus is put on the evangelical option for the poor and on being a Church of the Poor, being a communion of discipleship means communities living the Beatitudes and the wisdom of the cross, in hope. Christian witness is grounded in this, and the first evangelization is to confess before the world in life and word that the God known to us through revelation is the God of love, the communion of Father, Son, and Spirit at work in the human community and in the universe.[3] From this, too, emerges an ecumenical aspiration, an anxiety to realize the unity of the dispersed body of Christ, to be truly the one people of all the baptized. Without such communion, there is a false note to the claim to be the sacrament of the reconciliation and unity of all peoples.[4]

Entering willingly into exchange with peoples of other living faiths, churches have spelled out their sense of mission in terms of dialogue. In contact and con-versation with others, Christians seek to know, to evoke, and to bind together the spiritual instincts and aspirations of all peoples and religions. Doing so, they seek to be present at what John Paul II called the *areopagi* of human development as a global community of peoples, religions, cultures, and languages. In this multiple relationality, Christians have focused on their desire for God's reign, seeking and aiding the integral development of all, a dispensation of justice, peace, ecological awareness, and reconciliation. They themselves relate such aspirations to profession of faith in Jesus Christ and in his place in human history, with more and more attention to the active presence of Word and Spirit in human actions and in creation. Appreciating how peoples of other religions see the same realities and how they engender respect for the holy is integral to a dialogue of genuine reciprocity.

The dialogue with others espoused by the Second Vatican Council cannot be undertaken from some standpoint of doctrinal purity nor with the conviction that Christians are gifted with an enlightened reason that allows them to judge all things. It is possible to invoke reason without much reasoning, and two approaches have emerged that seem to hinder engagement.

There is a move away from the kind of commitment to dialogue espoused in the encyclical of Paul VI, *Populorum progressio* (1967). Although its listing of social issues is somewhat outdated, it cannot be forgotten that in promoting just human development, this encyclical was ready to take on a conversation with all members of the Church and then with all those who by their own insights pursued the good of society and of a global humanity. The Bishop of Rome seemed ready to reason things out, to argue, and discuss in the hope that Christians themselves might be enlightened while speaking with the world. Now the laity are told more and more insistently that they need to give their witness in the secular field and to enter the world of politics, economics, education, and so forth. But then they are instructed about doctrines and social positions that they must uphold, even under pain of being excluded from participation at the communion table. Papal encyclicals, too, while affirming the concerns for peace and justice and reconciliation, which the Church has come to associate with the kingdom of God in the world, have become more doctrinal. Instead of guiding an open dialogue with others, they inform Catholics (and the world) of the premises on which they are prepared to work with others. It is as though there were clear doctrines on practical affairs rather than the need to work from a historically conditioned tradition in openness to the light that others may bring to an understanding of human affairs and what it is to be human. As a result of excessive clerical domination and censure, many in the Church are deeply involved in promoting the social good and caring for the underprivileged within Church institutions, but the involvement in broader social realities seems too perilous to undertake.[5]

The second approach that stands in the way of full engagement with others comes from something that ironically is advanced as a new foundation for interreligious dialogue. Appeal is made to the common readiness of all religious persons to listen to reason, to be guided by the light of reason. This was, for example, the gist of Pope Benedict's academic discourse at Regensburg (2006). The difficulty is that what is promoted in the name of reason owes much to Greek philosophy, and among Church writers to Augustine and Bonaventure. Gone is the mention of the philosophies and the hermeneutical twists to which the Church and faith need to be open and which were worked into the encyclical *Fides et ratio* of John Paul II. Absent also is the mention of what is contributed by philosophies of Africa and Asia.

Apart from these problems with ideas of dialogue, becoming more open to others has to be a process that engages the entire ecclesial membership. A fuller and more sincere engagement with the world in all the fields mentioned is impossible without greater trust in the laity and indeed dependence on them on the part of ecclesiastical authority. They are the ones directly involved in these matters and who understand their motivations, their workings, and their goals. From them, the Church as a community has to learn the practical meaning of commitment to the poor. It is they who will often be best able to see what are biblically called the signs of the times, that is, the prophetic challenges of this commitment. It is they who live side by side and pursue common goals with persons of other religious traditions or nonreligious persuasions about the common good.

In pursuing dialogue and engagement toward a global human good, the Church is faced more and more with the challenge to be the Church of the Poor, not only committed to the poor but seeing them as having a privileged place in the kingdom of God. All are invited to follow the ideal proposed by some who saw the mission among the poor, the service of justice to be rendered to them, as an evangelical imperative. Those who thought themselves rich are conscious of becoming poor in the sense of losing influence, of being left with nothing to speak but the Word of Jesus Christ, of suffering a critical moment of *kenōsis*, of being as nothing before the world. It is possible to fight against this, but it is more desirable to embrace it, like Christ, in a spirit of obedience and self-emptying, as beloved children of the Father, who trust in the pledge of hope offered in the gift of the Spirit. It is against the background of this developing sense of what it is to be a Christian community, and what it is to give witness to Jesus Christ and to the Father of Jesus Christ, and what it is to redefine mission in this dynamic context, that questions of leadership and Church order today take on a new urgency and a new shape.

Church Ordering

The responsibility of local churches, and by implication the principles of episcopal collegiality and subsidiarity, cannot be set aside or diminished in favor of greater centralization, though there has been a move in this direction since the Second Vatican Council. One of the great failures in the reception of the Council has indeed been the refusal to implement, pastorally and canonically, the theological principle of episcopal collegiality set down in *Lumen gentium* and voted on early in the days of the gathering in St. Peter's Basilica.[6] Local churches have largely failed to give due weight to those pastoral and diocesan councils that include lay membership, and give them not only consultative but deliberative voice. To become a truly global Church, there has to be greater diversity and the fostering of communion through means other than a central bureaucracy and a forcefully canonical papal supremacy.

Eucharist is central to the very nature of ecclesial communion. In ordering the life and ministries of a local church, the priority has to be to assure that those who live a common life in faith may be a eucharistic community, one where the people may gather regularly at the eucharistic table as the body of Christ.[7] It is in fact quite some time since the Roman Catholic Church was truly a eucharistic community in the more traditional sense of the term, however much it may be known for the regularity of its eucharistic ritual. Being a eucharistic Church is not to be confused with having the ritual available nor with the frequency of its celebration by ordained priests. It is to have the eucharistic celebration at the heart of the life of a community of people. The model for this is always that of the description of the Jerusalem community in Acts 2:42. A community that lives together, that shares life in common, that cares for the poor, and that prays together regularly comes together for the eucharistic breaking of the bread as the true center of its being and its communion. In other words, eucharistic communion find its place within a life of discipleship shared in its fullness, and the life of discipleship has the common Eucharist as its axis. Today, small communities permitted the ritual rather rarely actually contribute much to the recreation of the Church as a eucharistic community. Whatever kind of Eucharist they have, be this the irregular visit of an ordained minister or regular Sunday communion services, is intimately inserted into their common life and apostolic witness.

In canonical discipline about orders, surely this has to be the key factor. In an otherwise helpful catechesis on the Sacrament of Love in the postsynodal apostolic exhortation of 2007, it is disconcerting to read the advice to people in places where priests are not available, to go to some location in the diocese where full eucharistic participation is possible because of the presence of a priest.[8] There is a strong emphasis on the difference between communion services and Mass, bringing out the point that a full celebration requires the presence of an ordained minister. People are encouraged to have their services, under the proper supervision of the bishop, when nothing else is possible, but the exhortation is at pains to bring home to them how incomplete they are. One would expect some words that recognize that these are the regular liturgies for many congregations, and that bring out their significance and their importance in creating the life of a Christian community. Giving precedence to the priestly ritual rather than to enabling the people to be a eucharistic community responds poorly to the situation of so many persons. Encouraging them in their present endeavors and in the long run allowing for change in discipline might well belong to the order of the day. Since ordination is necessary to a fully adequate eucharistic celebration, one would expect attention to be given to the necessary changes in canonical provisions and in the choice and preparation of candidates for ordination within living communities of faith.

In allowing for a true eucharistic communion, Church ordering has to do with integrating gifts and ministries into the life of a community. This is where the focus on small communities found in documents of churches in Africa, Asia, and Latin America comes into play. These are the units in which people at the grass roots are involved and where interrelationship and communal action fosters Christian life and Christian responsibility in society. The integration of gifts and ministries has a double purpose. The first is to help its members through their gifts to animate their common life, serving the flow of the Spirit and fidelity to the gospel that comes from the apostles and that has been kept alive through apostolic tradition, whatever the changes and varieties of expression of faith. The second purpose is to enable the community and all its members to serve their mission to make God known and bring about God's reign in the world, involving themselves first of all in their own locality and from there extending their influence beyond it.

For the sake of mission and ministry, it is time to eschew the strong distinction between clergy and laity, the ordained and other members of the baptized. This dates back a long time but is not of the original apostolic tradition. History tells us that ordering the life and activity of a Church community has been a complex matter, setting out the relations between different bodies in its membership and providing for the coordination of their activities. Besides providing for liturgical presidency and governance, in the early centuries this meant making provisions that envisaged a role for widows, virgins, confessors, and healers, all of which orders or services remained in place even as the clericalization of liturgical ministries took on preponderant importance for reasons examined in earlier chapters of this book. Through the Middle Ages, order provided for lay movements and confraternities, for the emergence of new communities of sisters and brothers, and in time for the vast role played by women, both contemplative and apostolically active. The fact that the canonical provisions and some of the theological reasoning set bishops, priests, and deacons apart cannot obscure the fact that these groups were incorporated into the ordering of the life of the Church and that ecclesial communities would not have existed without them. Today we ask whether the provisions that subjected others to clerical domination and privilege were the necessary and only possible ways of integrating what was new.

Today there are many and diverse realities of service to be acknowledged and ordered into a well-coordinated congregation. There is the strong role of the witness and apostolic activity of lay persons, without whom the Church would simply have no part in society at a time when it redefines its mission so as to relate to all human enterprises, in the service on the one hand of a common human good and on the other of the reign of God in the whole of creation. There are those who live new forms of community within what are called lay movements, and across the world there is the vital role played in life and in evangelization by what are dubbed base Christian communities or small faith communities. There are the new ways in which communities of women religious carry on their traditional services in ways of acting within Church and society. There is the rather poorly guided emergence of the permanent diaconate, sometimes however turned into leadership of communities with all responsibilities other than that of presiding at the eucharistic table, when this is in fact what is most cogently needed. Finally, in every church there are new kinds or groups of members resulting from globalization, groups such as legal immigrants, illegal immigrants, and refugees. Not only must these be served by the local church, but their contribution to its life is to its enrichment.

None of this is well provided for by an undue accent on the distinction between ordained and baptized in essence and not only in degree,[9] nor by the division of labor into the areas of the sacred and of the secular. This verges on considering the Church as a collection of individuals with different roles rather than seeing it as a community of common concern and mission, enlivened by a common Spirit and a collective hearing of the gospel of Jesus Christ.[10] Within a communal responsibility, there is room for diversification, but not for a diversification that precedes all communal engagement and is canonically superimposed on the lives of people. What is needed is an integrated community of the whole, which has its clear cultural, social, and geographical grounding. This total and collaborative view of Church membership is more suited to order than jurisdictional distinctions that are then theologically justified. It in no way jeopardizes the place and sacramental significance of bishops, priests, and deacons as servants with, in, and for particular communities. The unquestioned, and apparently deemed unquestionable, exclusion of woman from the sacrament of order and by implication from leadership positions is also a practical dismissal of the work of the Spirit, when it is clear that their service to the Church and their capacity to lead are no less than those of any male. The situation is all the odder when it is justified by a symbolism that at its most curious expresses the sin-tainted and biologically constrained inferiority of the male, even as it gives him unquestioned authority, with rather dreadful implications for the understanding of the mediation of Christ.

Sacramental Expressions of Communion in Christ

Without the gifts of the Spirit and without a leadership that is modeled on the authority of Christ, ordering and ordination are barren. In practical terms, churches across the ages and throughout the world have to ponder and discern what the most effective leadership may be. Without more ado, they have to refuse to identify it with office or the holders of office. Leadership is not confined to the ordained or to officially installed officeholders but is shown in a variety of ways by the members of the Church. Those officially designated in any way are there to serve the royal priesthood of the Church as a body, not as a passive entity but as an active one.

For a complete and comprehensive theology of ministry, one may start by situating the site of Christ's and Spirit's presence and power in the life of a community. In trinitarian terms, the locus of God's power is the community itself, for the reality of power is the Spirit of Christ poured forth into our hearts, enabling us to keep memory of Christ and to be configured to him and to be one with him as a body, sacrament of God's reign in the world. In this, all members of the Church are active and all mediate the life of the Spirit to each other, according to the services and ministries exercised.

No spiritual or human reality is complete without its symbolic expression and cannot be shared and exchanged among many without this. This is what gives it form and presence in time and space. The symbols that signify the presence of Christ and of the Spirit belong to the interaction between the members in mutual charity and service, and to their witness to Christ in the world around them to the justice of God's reign. From New Testament times onward, different churches have been inspired to express their identity as followers of Christ, as a community of the called and saved, through appropriate symbolic images, such as eschatological people of God, living temple of the Spirit or living sacrifice, kingly priesthood, body of Christ with its twofold NT variant that points to the risen Christ as Lord and to the Church living in communion with him.

Since liturgical action or sacramental action is the primary form of Christian symbolic expression, it is there that the action of the Word and the Spirit are represented. Even the outreach beyond the boundaries of any particular community is sacramentally expressed. Without questioning the true place of the sacrament of order in the Church, in speaking of the action of the Spirit that keeps the Church in communion with Christ and with the Father, it is necessary to first recall that the liturgy is the gathering and action of the baptized in their diversity of personal identities, roles, and ministries. In acts of worship, the Church expresses its sense of being called by a loving divine initiative and of being sent out to make known this good news. It is significant and needs to be signified that Jesus is present to his community in every action of word, prayer, and mutual charity, and in every exercise of the gifts of the Spirit. The ultimate symbolic expression of ecclesial being, before which all else fades into the background, is the reality of the body of the Lord around the communion table. There the people, without differentiation or discrimination, break the bread and drink the cup. There it should be most obvious that there is neither male nor female, slave nor free, Jew nor Gentile. This is not meant to say that these differences vanish but that the different are integrated as one, without privilege and precedent. The call and gift to preside is to lead people to this oneness and to gather in the service of each and all. To affirm that the one who presides is as the one who serves is not merely rhetoric or an exhortation to leaders to be humble. It expresses the fact that the leader is not above the community, that to function this person has to be acknowledged and integrated into the community and is not to replace or suppress the gifts of others. At the communion table the Lord himself is host, gift, and guest.

Communities that try to be faithful to the gospel are conscious of the gifts of the Spirit in their own midst. They trust in the Lord and hope that they will be provided with the ministries that they need. Free of stereotypes, they are free to discern the gifts of word, of service, of prayer, of presidency that are most suited to their prophetic and evangelical presence in society. In their community gatherings, they are drawn to the simplicity of a place that accommodates a table of bread and wine and the flow of oil and water. Chosen in the Spirit as the symbols of Christian faith and mediation, these bespeak the beauty as well as the tragedy of the lives of those who gather and of the lives of those whom they remember. It is as expressions of human communion in its openness and in its vulnerability that these materials of an earthy communion are made the sacramental symbols of the self-gift of Christ and of the gift of the Spirit of love. Pointing to this does not mean a literal return to the most historically primitive rituals. Faith in Christ's fidelity to his people, who live in remembrance of him amid the world, requires that the recipes for making bread, wine, oil, and living water may be different from those used for the preparation of the Upper Room. The basic principle of acclimating gospel and apostolic witness to culture is shown in the relation to cultural constructs of these fundamental symbols and in incorporating the memories and lives of those who congregate.

It is in being most local that the Church in the power of the Spirit is most catholic. In responding to the mission given by Christ, the life of community in its indigenous expression is enhanced by the challenge to barriers and divisions that is enunciated in the story and remembrance of Jesus Christ. Church order as the ordering of a local church is called upon to make room for the foreigner and the socially or ethnically alien. If the local church does not reflect on the cultural matrix of common expressions of identity, there can be no conscious breaking of boundaries in the name of Christ, no genuine efforts at inclusion. There is a natural tendency to render holy one's own kith and kin, one's ethnic group, one's social class, without giving much thought to the matter, and this shows up often enough in ecclesiastical gatherings and configurations. The challenge of the memory of Christ present amid his disciples is to respect and reverence the things of common life in cultural settings, to stand in awe before the holy that is therein revealed as the very holiness of God among us. With this, discriminations and divisions are willingly banished. Making room for the alien is to open the heart to her or his suffering and to accept oneself to suffer. This means recognizing a vulnerability of life that is healed only through compassion. If Church order and ministry do not give high priority to suffering, and to the suffering, and to the compassion of sufferers with each other, they are not of Christ.

In provisions about candidacy for ordination to the threefold ministry of bishop, presbyter, and deacon, we may learn from the history of these orders in the Church rather than be misled by a given fixed definition. In early centuries it was a matter of providing communities with the ministers they needed in response to the conditions of their existence. Various models served this purpose, and there was no question of elevating a person to a status, with powers to be used anywhere or at any time. There is still some justice to the comment of Saint Jerome that the names found in the New Testament remain in use, but the offices change. Adaptation of the office to what any given set of circumstances required was the norm. There could be considerable difference between the exercise and form of any of these offices from one place to another. The episcopacy of Leo the Great in Rome was quite different from that of Martin of Tours in Gaul or Patrick in Ireland. The presbyters in the city church of Rome had a different role and a different life from that of presbyters in isolated rural communities. If today it is necessary to differentiate roles within the order of presbyters in order to assure the proper celebration of the sacrament of the Eucharist in every community of living faith, so be it. There could be a variety of forms of choice of candidate, of preparation, and of canonical mission among ministers ordained to care for a community and provide it with sacramental celebration. Given the priority of constituting communities as true eucharistic communities, this is the way to move, and it is in true continuity with tradition. It would allow for ordination of those who, by reason of their charisms and their recognition by communities, in fact exercise leadership in their households of faith.

Considered in the light of history, the sacrament of order is best understood when it is seen as an expression of Church and located within the Church as a eucharistic community. As episcopacy and presbyterate developed, this was in service to the life of the Church as a communion in particular localities. First, they served unity within the community in either immediate place or region. Second, one of their major responsibilities was to keep fidelity to serve the community's fidelity to the apostolic faith and tradition, again at local and regional levels. In the third place, the episcopacy in particular was a service and a sacramental expression of the communion of all eucharistic communities within the one communion in Christ and Spirit, the presence in the world of the *Perichoresis* (communion) of Father, Son, and Spirit. It was as services to the Church and within the Church that sacramental ordination was considered to express the relation of its recipients to Christ and to the Spirit. No authentic leadership could be exercised except through the gift of the Spirit and except participating in the authority of Christ himself. This perspective is somewhat captured today in the use of the expression *in persona Christi Capitis*, an expression that could be complemented by another, *in persona ecclesiae corporis Christi*. If the expression is to be used at all, it would be better formulated in this way. On the other hand, the meaning of the sacrament of order might be better presented as a ministry of the Spirit, in service to the body of Christ in its communion with him.

Ecclesial tradition is continually reinterpreted in the light of new experience, and new experience is interpreted in the light of ecclesial tradition. Within this interplay, the realities of power and order in the Church are in a constant process of change. The Second Vatican Council brought with it a fresh experience of Christian community in its interaction on the horizontal as well as the vertical axis, and a new sense of openness to the power of God's Word and the presence of the Spirit of the risen Lord. With change in the Church's experience of its own being and mission, there has to be some change in how ecclesial reality is articulated. It always remains true that as a society the Church embraces members of varying commitment, not all of whom are inspired by an evangelical way of life and many of whom need pastoral assistance in coping with life and with God's commandments. It is also true, however, that the Church has many resources that risk going unattended or insufficiently integrated if they are not given doctrinal and canonical formulation.

The Church needs structures and paradigms of divine power that are comprehensive. The ordained belong within a body of organic and charismatic fellowship that at heart is eucharistic. As essential to its reality and well-being, this fellowship integrates the ministry and responsibility of Christians who remain in secular occupations just as much as it integrates persons engaged in what is called "ecclesial lay ministry." While official recognition of this latter is a step in the right direction, the voice of all the baptized needs to be given a formally recognized place in the process of articulating and enacting mission. Though ordination is thought of as the primary liturgy of empowerment in the Church, and in a secondary way the commissioning of lay persons, sight can be lost of the radical mutual empowerment of members that is the more basic expression and reality of baptismal and eucharistic belonging. This is the setting within which official forms of leadership are situated.

The ordering of communal life starts with local communities. In the evangelical sense, a sign of the times is the widespread move to small or basic communities. The extent to which these may be allowed to be fully responsible eucharistic communities has to be explored more in the Catholic Church. In face of reality, especially in Africa, Asia, and Latin America, the Church has to dare to open the question of the ordination of married men as well as of the ordination of women, instead of constantly closing these issues to any pastoral and theological debate. It is distinctly odd that Church government of late seems more anxious to preserve historical structures in place and the distinction between clergy and laity than to do its utmost to assure that every community, large or small, be assured of a Sunday Eucharist.

All development of leadership and structure needs to be at root related to the Word, even as it is charismatic and guided by the Spirit. There is no unavoidable or desirable conflict between charismatic gifts and institutional structures, provided the institutional is subordinated to and grounded in the charismatic. It is by reason of the gifts of the Spirit in communities and the guidance of communities by the Spirit that institutions and rituals can develop and find their place. In face of new and rather diverse needs on all continents in these times, institutional development has to change, grow, and take root in different cultures and different social situations. This can happen only if churches are open to those gifts of the Spirit that help ecclesial life to adjust well to the environment of the people and to their developing mission. They have to engage in a process of discernment, not primarily by an appeal to past structures and offices, but rather by attending to how communities are helped to grow in the faith and how the mission exercised in the name of Christ is best served. For this to happen, we have to remember the nuances of Karl Rahner's explanation of what is of divine law, as noted in the introduction to part 2 (above).

In responding to the call of the Spirit manifesting itself in such a variety of ways, we see that it is time to pursue the inspiration to think anew of the relationship within order between episcopacy, presbyterium, and diaconate. From history we know that the role of presbyters has changed considerably over time in accommodation to regional needs. The bishop was originally the head of a particular eucharistic fellowship, yet this role soon changed to that of presiding over a number of eucharistic communities in a given region. Presbyters accordingly became those who presided in liturgical gatherings. They also assumed responsibility for preaching the Word.

It is not helpful to say that presbyters (or priests) share in the fullness of the priesthood given to the bishop. The expression is more juridical than it is sacramental. We can better grasp what presbyters are called to be when they are ordained within the communities they are called to serve. Their first relation is to specific communities. There they are called by the Spirit to be pastors, teachers, and presiders in the service of eucharistic fellowship. Their relation to the bishop has to be defined as one of communion within a communion of communities. Nowadays it is sometimes said that a diocese was and is structured as a communion of communities, once the bishop lost his place as the one who presides over the Eucharist where all the faithful gather. The presbyterium is thus the body responsible for apostolic communion within a diocese, and some current canonical arrangements allow it to recapture the synodal role that it had in the beginning. In appointing presbyters as pastors, stricter attention has to be given to the conditions and needs of local communities, and this requires flexibility in the choice of candidates. If it is to be said that there is to be no Eucharist without the bishop, this simply means that each celebration properly takes place within a fuller communion, which cannot be rejected. With the recognition that those ordained presbyters are the local pastors with responsibility for their communities and for the region, the role of the bishop is twofold. The first is to serve communion in all its forms within his own diocese. The second is to serve the full catholic communion of all churches across the world.

The order of presbyters is open to even further developments within our time. The history of the ministries of bishop, presbyter, and deacon cannot be looked at as the history of an institution as such, whatever the institutional elements at play. It is possible to find room for different ways of appointing persons to presidency of a community and to distinguish different kinds of selection and preparation. It should not be unusual to find some ordained to this ministry in and for a particular community, without thought of transfer to other places. This can be done on the basis of experience, community acceptance, and discernment of a *de facto* leadership.[11] This offers a new mission to those who would still go through a more lengthy theological and spiritual preparation in seminaries and theological schools. These have to be open to a variety of appointments that would give them the ability to engage in a special kind of service to communities, in a way that assures communion between communities. Saying that this is the episcopal role or complaining that what is proposed would introduce a ranking within the one sacramental order is to give priority to homogeneity. It would mistake the theology of priesthood for one of investigating linear institutional growth, not taking the narrative of past diversity and the call to serve present needs into account.

The place of the diaconate within the sacrament of order is more ambivalent. If retrieving the permanent diaconate is to help the growth and mission of the Church, the place to start is with the responsibility for community sharing and the care of the needy, which it originally expressed. Having persons responsible for this within the sacrament of order could help us see how *diakonia* is integral to the life of any Christian community and to its sacramental worship. It might also help to put this concern and its organization on a diocesan level. So far, the restoration of the permanent diaconate in the Catholic Church has not done much to serve this purpose.

We are obliged to keep on thinking further about the sacrament of order and the distinctions within it. The fundamental perception is that it is a sacramental, canonical, and institutional expression of that ordering within the Church that serves the charismatic life and mission of communities. The shape it takes at any time and in any region has to be a response to how eucharistic fellowship in one apostolic faith and a communion without boundaries is best served. One might use the insights of Karl Rahner to say that we may still have to learn all that divine origin or divine initiative offers us, this being the true meaning of the term "divine institution."

Ecumenical Implications

In ecumenical dialogue and interaction, it seems time for churches to act as eucharistic communities in conversation with eucharistic communities. Subtle though the statements are, there appears to be a recognition in magisterial teaching that the true eucharistic nature of many Protestant celebrations of the Lord's Supper or Holy communion is not in question. It is rather whether they are celebrated within the full ecclesial communion that is determined by episcopal communion with the Bishop of Rome. Eventual reconciliation would mean several churches of different traditions living and celebrating within the same place. In other words, the notion of one place, one Eucharist has to be modified, as it was in earlier times when presbyters began to preside over individual communities within a region whose chief pastor was the bishop.

Here and there, some thought has already been given to how bishops of different traditions would work together in the event of arriving at full communion. It could, for example, be asked how, in the city of Belfast, the Anglican bishop, the moderator of the Presbyterian Church, and the Roman Catholic bishop would work together as leaders of communities that keep their own traditions but share in the one catholic communion and espouse the practice of an open communion table. The supposition is that these would remain distinct communities living side by side, modifying therefore the older supposition of one Church to one place. Not only goodwill but some synodal structure would have to be part of the common life and order of such churches.

The question is not simply one to be reasoned out for some future eventuality. In the present situation of Christianity in the world, there is an ecumenical imperative that requires churches to work together in the service of the kingdom of God, making Christ known and ministering to peace, justice, and ecological care. Every church already needs to include dialogue with others in its internal ordering. There is indeed a multiplicity of offices for ecumenical dialogue, for the dialogue with all responsible for the global community, for dialogue with other religions. This readiness for dialogue has to be inserted into the life of every community and into the communion between communities. It requires a new attitude on the part of Christian churches, an attitude that affects how all lead lives of discipleship, witness, and service. Openness to dialogue within each church goes necessarily with mission and with redressing wrongs, and this has to lead to structural change. While churches have to begin with Christian conversation, they have to stretch the capacity for dialogue with persons of other living faiths.

Several elements of dialogue are at work in different sectors and are worth recalling.[12] These include an effective and practical understanding of human being as interrelational, being with and through others. Dialogue is promoted by a common sense of solidarity in addressing issues vital to the survival and destiny of the human race and of the planet Earth. Since much in the past has made relationships difficult or impossible, there has to be a collective and prophetic examination of conscience, with regard to a collective past and an admission of fault, together with a petition to be pardoned. From such repentance may follow a conversion in the way of relating to others that holds promise for the future. Bodies that wish to relate will engage in whatever actions and symbolic expressions of exchange are seen to be currently possible.

The exchange that goes on between members of different ecclesial affiliations is empowering and in some respects structured into life. It begins with the readiness to share the Word of God together and moves into a readiness to take on ministry to the needs of a shared neighborhood. For the prayer of the week for Church Unity in 2007, those appointed by the World Council of Churches and the Vatican Secretariat for Promoting Christian Unity looked for inspiration to the people of the township of Umlazi, outside the city of Durban, in South Africa.[13] Having lived through the harsh days of apartheid together, the citizens of that township continue to pray and work together in struggling against crime, AIDS, abuse of women and children, and the like. Prayer and work together in such circumstances demands leadership and management. It might not be *called* ordering life and ministry, but that is in fact what it is. If ecumenical exchange is to be promoted, this requires leadership and ordering, beginning at the local level. How the bishops and moderators of churches are going to pray and work together so that they may help all the baptized to do so is a challenge to our ideas about Church order at a time when ecumenical communion is a source of power for the mission of the whole people of God.

Ecumenically, one area that has to be included in conversation is the presence and activity of women in ordering Church life and in its mission. When it is said that ordering has to be nonpatriarchal, this means that authentic order is not rooted in systems of domination, or superiority, whereby certain groups are thought to be naturally, culturally, or spiritually superior to others. In the present time, this means taking a critical look at the history of order. In a special way, it means finding real, canonical, and symbolic ways of including women in the fundamental natural and baptismal equality of all. From one country or continent to another, this has to mean overcoming the persuasions of cultural superiority and inferiority that were too often inherent in the process of evangelization or in the conviction that ranking among professions and social classes is culturally imperative. It is hardly possible to continue this process without talking of women's access to the sacrament of order, but one at least has to start with giving them factual and canonical responsibility for ecclesial life and making their presence in liturgy symbolically visible.

The Power of Being Christian
If ordering the Church's life is to give priority to the reality of communal life, one has to understanding what it is to be a baptized member of Christ's body. When the royal priesthood of the Church is expressed in appropriate sacramental form, it is apparent that service, leadership, and the exercise of being a channel of God's saving power belong within the broader network of relations within the ecclesial and social body as a community of the baptized. Sacramentally affirmed leadership relates to the various ways in which individuals and select groups affect one another and in which they affect the corporate reality. The principal images of power in the Christian kerygma are the power of God's Word, the cross of Jesus Christ, the lordship of the Risen One, and the Spirit who indwells. These images speak not merely of a power to which Christians are subject, but of a power that is given to them. The ability to be free of dependence upon intrusive powers is expressed in the image of Christ's lordship and in the image of the indwelling Spirit. The power granted by the Spirit over human suffering is signified in the cross, on which humanity is redeemed and refashioned. Compassionate power is proclaimed in the images of the Father's prevenient love for sinners and sufferers shown on the cross. This is a new wisdom, a power that is hidden in powerlessness, the strength and testimony of suffering undertaken for others. By the same token, it is the power of judgment pronounced against other wisdoms and powers, not in pronouncing sentence but through the testimony of a life lived where life given by Christ abounds.

The Symbols of the presence of the Spirit are those that signify interaction between the members in mutual charity and service. The liturgy is the gathering and action of the baptized, enlivened by a communion of love and by the many services of the Spirit that shape the reality of apostolic and evangelical life. The ultimate reality of communion in Christ and Spirit, before which all else fades into the background, is the reality of the body of the Lord, and the ultimate ground of the Lord's presence is the community of faith that breaks the bread of the Word and the bread of his self-gift.

A radical sharing in mission and power is given through the sacraments of initiation by which people enter the community and are covenanted with Christ. In the last few decades, with some early initiatives in African countries,[14] the vigor and power of the order and ritual of Christian initiation has been rediscovered. In the process, the contribution of many different services and ministries has come to the fore, along with the realization that receiving new members into the Church is the work of the whole congregation. As far as other sacraments are concerned, we need to recognize what part the baptized have in the sacrament of marriage and in the anointing of the sick. In some meager way, if communal celebrations are well done, it may also come to light how repentance and reconciliation require the encouragement, guidance, and service of others besides the ordained priest. The liturgical symbolism of a manifold participation of community members in sacraments comes to life in mutual service and a common engagement to living and making known the gospel.

Happily, with the renewal of liturgy and catechesis, the Catholic Church was able to bring the Scriptures back into the life of the faithful, though making this a reality still requires attention. The Word of God, along with the charisms of the Spirit, is the foundation of Christian living. This does not simply mean that people are instructed by the Scriptures: they are empowered by the Word of God thus communicated. From the *ars celebrandi*, we learn that liturgy is a reality to the extent that it represents the life of a people that live together by the Word of God and serve its power in different ways, thus bringing one another to its knowledge. One of the contributions made to the Church through small Christian communities is the significance that they gave to reflecting on the Scriptures and living by their light. Through their hearing, discernment, and prayer, the liturgy of the Sunday is prepared, provided that what they contribute is integrated into the service in music and song, in the reflections offered by lectors, in the homily, in commemorations made, and in the common prayer of the faithful gathered.

Being aware of one another at the common table of the covenant people is integral to the strength and power and mission of being one by the grace of Christ's self-gift. It is a power that reconciles, makes one, and allows the Spirit-filled community to witness in hope to Christ's unique lordship. The inclusion of the foreigner and the alien, or today of the migrant and the refugee, is integral to this common table. This is what makes us conscious that there is no common table at the Eucharist, however meticulous ritual observance may be, if there is no common table among the people who prepare it. Life together as body of Christ gives truth to the sacrament.

In brief, all canonical provision for order is rooted in the life of the baptized people, empowered by Word and Spirit. The question of power, its symbolic expression, and its canonical forms cannot be properly addressed unless communities become increasingly aware that it is through the share of all in Christ's lordship and Spirit that the life and mission of the Church as Christ's body and God's people is engendered and enlivened. Since the Church's place in society and culture is diverse and yet caught up in a global network, a theology and ordering of ministry and leadership is important for pointing to the power of God residing in communities that gather in God's name. Ministry and leadership are shared among them and are more fundamental than the official forms of power that come with organization and office. Only through retrieving this mutual empowering can new structures of officially recognized authority be developed, whether these touch on ordination to eucharistic presidency and service or on other kinds of structural leadership. The ultimate ground of acceptance as a leader, in whatever post or ministry, lies not in official recognition or appointment but in the integration of one's witness and service into the life of the community, which as an entity lives the call to discipleship. A rediscovery of the significance of ordination and other forms of social appointment to ministry depends on this integration. This is a process that has to overcome multiple discriminations in the life of the Church as in the life of society, beginning with discriminations against women and whole cultural groups, and more fundamentally touching on the discrimination inherent to a distinction between clergy and laity.

Since life changes over time, the service of needs in the Church changes, and these have a human face. In the early church, orders were set up for the care of such as catechumens and penitents. From its beginnings, the Church took it as the Lord's command to care for those in need. This was expressed quite concretely, for example, in care for widows, but over time the poor of various sorts have commanded the Church's attention. We know that looking after the common chest was one of the causes of strife and rift, and the control of subsidies to the poor was one of the things that contributed to the unique power of bishops. Whatever the problems, however, this remains a necessary and vitally evangelical part of being a Christian communion. In the Middle Ages, lay confraternities looked in special ways to the care of the indigent, while organized groups of women took care of education and the needs of the sick. The revival of the deaconate augured by the Second Vatican Council ought to serve to highlight this aspect of the common life, though so far it has not often met such expectations. Some churches have revived their diaconal energies in other ways through the activities of lay members in a more broadly based service. If the order of deacons is to be restored, it has to be on this basis and within this kind of shared responsibility. Its true necessity is not yet clear.

With economic and global migration being so prevalent, new groups emerge that need the Church's service and the growth of new ministries, for which the Spirit gives charisms. Refugees, newcomers to a country, illegal immigrants, the unemployed, people suffering from AIDS and its indirect consequences for family and neighborhood life, and those who suffer debilitating infirmity have to be integrated into the life of diocesan and parish communities so that these communities may serve them. In the process, the communities will be enriched by the new potential for life that they bring.

Instead of drawing uniquely on paradigms of order from the past, with its wonted listings, we need to attend to the historical flexibility and historically conditioned character of Church ordering. An awareness of new situations, new needs, and new resources can motivate the Church to tackle the question in spiritually creative ways and to learn what structural changes have to follow in the wake of Spirit-filled multiple activity and new theological insight.

Canonization of Power

Theological insight may derive from attention to the process of canonizing power. To talk of the canonization, or the fixing of a canon, of power is to recognize that for the good of the Church, the exercise of ministry, power, and leadership is given canonical forms and a duly approved status, but these forms have a historical conditioning and are not to be confused with the reality itself. Nor is this simply a matter of legislation. It is connected with symbols and ideas of how power is imaged and seen. All power in the Church is a participation in the power of the Word, in the lordship of Jesus Christ, and in the gift of the Spirit, and belongs within the life of the baptized community as God's people.

Canonical forms serve to set some needed boundaries but have no precedence over the power of Word and Spirit. There are points of reference in the history of the Church, things that we learn through a discriminating reading of history in the light of the Scriptures. What is served is fidelity to the apostolic tradition, building the unity of each church as the one body of Christ, and the catholic communion of all churches that profess faith in Christ's lordship. Rules have to be fixed that will guarantee, at least in some measure, the authentic nature of acts of power, as well as ways of supervising the various acts of the communion of those who lay claim to be led by the Word and by the Spirit.

The most fundamental canonization of power in the Church's history is actually the determination of the scriptural canon. Deciding which books are to be taken as the embodiment of God's Word and of the apostolic tradition is to give a point of reference for all life and teaching and to fix the boundaries within which power is to be exercised.[15] Claims to holiness, to authoritative teaching, to sacramental action, and to pastoral evangelical leadership have to offer guarantees that refer to the scriptural canon and can be subjected to judgment on this basis. This is not a simple and straightforward process, and the laws of interpretation require refinement. In the life of the Church, nonetheless, the ultimate appeal that authenticates the presence of power is to the revelation made known through the Scriptures. This was something brought to attention by the constitution *Dei Verbum* of the Second Vatican Council, and it has had great influence in ongoing ecumenical dialogue.

The power given with the sacrament of order as it relates to the power of the Word has been expressed through history in ordination rites. This may be by the transmission of the Book to the ordained or by laying the Book of the Gospels over the head of the bishop elect. What these rites signify is that the canonical form given to ministry in the Church goes necessarily with recognizing the canon of the Scriptures and the power of God invested in them.

Unfortunately, the power of order, in the course of time, was understood to be the power to confect the Lord's presence by changing the bread and wine into Christ's body and blood, to the neglect of the ministry of the Word, which has to go with sacramental ministry. This obscured the service to the twofold table of Word and sacrament, where the Lord is present among his followers through the power of the life-giving Spirit. The clearer it becomes that all the people share in the proclaiming of the Lord's Word and in the breaking of the bread and in the gifts of the Spirit, the clearer the nature of the power of order will also become, for it will be related to its authentic living context.

The Spirit works in the Church together with the Word, but its gifts can never be given canonical shape in the same way since it is always the Spirit of newness and of eschatological expectation. Likewise, even in the ordination of ministers through the laying on of hands, there belongs a recognition of the freedom of Spirit, who resides in all the members of the one body. The choice, consent, or approval of the people is at bottom a recognition of the Spirit's charism bestowed on the candidate and their part in the candidate's preparation is a fine-honing of that gift. An active assembly in the ordination rite can make it clear that the Church that lives under the power of the Word also lives by the gifts of the Spirit. While recognizing the Spirit's presence and gifts in the persons of the ordained, the community continues to exercise the many other gifts that are bestowed by this same Spirit. The giving of the Spirit to the ordained does not stifle the other gifts. The prayer of ordination, since it is an invocation of the Spirit over the candidate not only for the present but for the future, makes it clear that the candidate can exercise ministry only in dependence on a continuing renewal of that gift. Difficult situations, especially those that arise from the presence of unfit priests in the Church, have led both theology and canon law to spell out the nature of the priestly office in the rather narrow terms of sacramental and jurisdictional power. The traditional ordination ceremony belies those definitions. It invokes the Spirit as a gift to be continuously renewed, and it invokes the Spirit as one that gives together holiness of life, a spirit of true service, and the gifts necessary to serve the community in the office bestowed. Canonical procedures for the removal of pastors have taken on a sharp edge due to recent sad misadventures.

The permanence of ordination became an acute question when spiritual authority waned and again at the time of the Reformation, when possession of priestly status was often divorced from pastoral ministry. As the question is revisited, permanence in order cannot be expressed in terms of a state or status that remains unchanged. If there is legitimacy in the concept of permanence, it has to be expressed in terms of a call, where the relationship between the particular gift and the community served by it appears to have an irrevocable quality. Only when an ordination is done outside of relation to a community to be served can it appear to be something that concerns the person of the candidate in some abstract way, allowing him to lay claim to powers defined in terms other than that of service to a community.[16] An officeholder without a ministry of service is an anomaly. There may be a hundred different ways in which this relationship of service to a community of believers is exercised, but it is an essential part of the office and its power. Fidelity to the Church's liturgical tradition, which means not only the service but all that leads up to it, can keep this before our eyes. Living testimony, choice, appointment, approval, acceptance by a community, and the laying on of hands coalesce in showing what ordination means and how it serves the people of God.

A priest ordained for the cult of the divine and as an oracular intermediary can claim powers and status that do not depend on the community's consent and acceptance. Such a sacral figure takes on an independent status, one that makes him the bridge between the sacred and the profane, with an attunement to the sacred that earns him special respect and reverence. There is no doubt that the priesthood has often been spoken of in this way in the Catholic Church, though the very titles given to officeholders in the New Testament indicate how inappropriate this way of thinking is. The only special attunement to the holy that the New Testament allows is that of configuration to the cross of Christ and of obedience to the gospel in a way of life, and of a deep-felt communion with all called by God as a covenant people. It is thus to resituate order within community that in chapter 10 we examined what is meant by representing Christ.

Cultural Models for Ministry and Power

Although the primary images of power, those that pertain both to the baptized and to the ordained, have to come from the biblical tradition, they have been complemented over time by images taken from the contemporary culture, and their use has been affected by cultural perceptions of society and of authority. The Church community visualizes and names its power in relation to the ways in which power is envisaged and exercised in the social sphere and in other contemporary bodies. It is always part of grasping the particular quality of one thing to see how it relates to and is distinct from others. For the Church, it is inevitable that its members share in the common cultural grasp of what constitutes power and its exercise. The Church may then proceed in one or other of two ways. (1) It may define its own nature and purpose, particularly its sense of power, by way of contrast with current models, not conforming to the ways of this world. (2) It can for good policy adopt these models, modifying them by relating them to the biblical images and remembrances.

Power and Sacrifice

The power that shapes a community may not be immediately associated in contemporary Western society with the practice or notion of sacrifice, though the language persists in ways of speaking of war or of good citizenship or of valorous deeds performed for others. In the history of cultures and religions, the offering of sacrifice is one of the primary images and exercises of power or of the recognition of power. In the Jewish and Hellenistic societies of early Christian beginnings, sacrifices of various kinds were important social rituals and an outstanding ritual way whereby to denote the presence of a numinous power in the world. Because of the redemption in the blood of Jesus Christ, early Christians saw themselves cut off by their beliefs from any sacrificial practice. They took account of this practice and its imagery in meeting the accusation of being irreligious and in relating their own sense of the holy to cultural models. The initial appropriation of sacrificial imagery was done by way of relating it to ethics and an interior life of faith and evangelical obedience. This was quite a startling procedure, because it implied that divine power was primarily an internal gift, and it manifested itself most of all in a community's way of living and, hence, not in sacred rituals of the numinous. Since sacrifice was a ritual confided to a priesthood, within a practice of sacrifice, priests or priestesses were persons who shared in the power of the numinous manifested in the ritual that they had to perform. When the power of sacrifice was located by Christian belief in the community's interior faith and ethical behavior, all the people and not only some of the community's leaders were enriched with the imagery of the priestly.

Such beliefs about the holy naturally found their way into the Christian community's acts of worship. Since these were the daily round of prayer, modeled on Jewish practices and the sacraments of baptism and Eucharist, these activities were enriched by the imagery of sacrifice and priestliness. Part of the general persuasion about the holy meant that no one member of the community could be thought to exercise a priestly power in community worship, since such metaphor could be applied only to the corporate reality and to the life of interior faith, expressed ritually and in prayer. Leaders of Christian communities, whether apostles or local ministers, were careful to divest themselves of any claim to power and authority other than what they possessed by reason of the Word that they preached, of their participation in the cross of Christ, and the gifts of the Spirit that they received. Any suggestion of participating in a numinous sacerdotal and sacrificial power would have been found in flagrant contradiction of the gospel's teaching on the sacrifice of Christ.

This is a good example of how Christians conceived power and holiness in relation to cultural models, not by way of assimilation but by way of contrast and metaphor. It is an example that remains of vital moment to the Church in all ages, because it is one that belongs within the very shaping of the apostolic tradition and kerygma. The challenge to the idea of sacrificial priesthood has been revived and renewed at various times in the history of the Church. It is always there to modify other models and to challenge some directions of institutional development. In early centuries its presence in the Church's tradition meant that power was granted in particular ways to martyrs and confessors of the faith, by reason of their witness to the death and resurrection of Jesus Christ. At times this was an embarrassment to those whose power had been given more official forms, but their own power was also subject to the evangelical norms, at least in the sense that their candidacy was thought to rest on a common acknowledgement of their evangelical way of life. From time to time in later centuries, various movements have associated a restructuring of power in the Church with a renewal of the apostolic or evangelical life. They have expressed the fundamental persuasion that the primary way in which

God's power is present in the Church has to do with fidelity to the gospel and its ethic, and not with priestly offices or structures.

Sacerdotal designations of the bishop at first fitted into what was seen to be the sacrifice of the Church and the celebration of worship by the body of faithful. Later this took hold by way of an Old Testament typology that looked at Christian sacrifice in its ritual form as a perfection of the temple sacrifice. A stronger sacrificial understanding of the Lord's Supper, or Mass, itself confirmed and bolstered the sacerdotal imagery applied to any who celebrated it or presided at it.[17] In the West, with the transmission of the gospel to northern climes and to suit the mentality of peoples converted to the Christian religion under the influence of their kings and chieftains, sacrificial imagery was readily available, but it bore more resemblance to the dispensation of the law than to the New Testament. This tendency has to be considered critically in today's renewal of worship and ministry.

Hierarchy

In its origins this is a spiritual concept and not a social or juridical one. In the course of the first millennium and well beyond, various forms of Neoplatonism combined with legal ideals of social order borrowed from the temporal order to give Christian communities the cultural models to which they related their understanding and assimilation of biblical images and memories. The carefully ordered society of ancient Rome gave an institutional model of juridical foundation and good functioning. The Neoplatonism of the Pseudo-Dionysius supplied the philosophical and spiritual ideals that gave power a cosmic grounding. The Church community then related to cultural models of power much more by way of assimilation than by way of contrast, as had been the case in early Christianity. A hierarchical vision of cosmic order served as a model for internal ecclesiastical structures. This meant that the concept of power was developed more strongly in the development and justification of Church office than in the theology of the Christian life and ethical observance. Even as images and attributions of power continued to be associated with holiness, this itself was placed in a hierarchical order affecting spirituality and a reputed closeness to the divine. When bishops were able to appeal to miraculous powers in healing the sick or controlling devils, this suited a common expectation of the way in which the holy should manifest itself and helped to foster the sense that they were attuned to higher powers. Today it might well be acknowledged that the hierarchy of spiritual power is not confined to the ordained but is exercised more broadly. Though the ordained continue to have their role, it has to be exercised within the community and with greater reciprocity with other members. Synodal participation in government is not merely a useful tool. It expresses the reality of ecclesial communion and of where the power of the Spirit resides.

Cosmic Power and the Holy

In diverse cultures the more spiritual or the more juridical concepts of power fitted into more cosmic perceptions of holiness and divine power. The images of priestly power were thought to harmonize with hierarchically conceived cosmologies. Current renewal of liturgy and of office is marked by some effort to return to more evangelical perceptions of both. This, however, has brought some disarray and some criticism. For example, critics of recent reforms in Western liturgies complain that they have lost the sense of the holy or the numinous. In common parlance it is often said that the liturgy fails to give the sense of the holy and that priests and religious have become too mundane and democratic. In more sophisticated language, the criticism is that liturgy has lost its reverence for cosmic forces and that these are taking their revenge on those who do not know how to relate to them as holy and as signs of the divine ordering of the universe. Ecological and sexual issues are related to a more radical disrespect for life and to a sense of human autonomy that permits total control of the body and of nature. A reaction to change is therefore marked by an effort to bring back the priestly sense of worship and the priestly and sacred images of Church office that are linked to cosmic order and hierarchy.

The apostolic and evangelical renewal of the Church is not well served by a revival of images of the sacred that sharpen distinctions between members of the community or that negate the sense of the power that all Christians share by attributing a greater and more holy power to officeholders. The fundamental challenge to Christians is to discover how the Spirit that enlivens each and all of the members brings them into communion with the source of all life in the universe, and how it is the same Spirit who animates cosmic forces, history, and the witness of Christian communities. Inasmuch as the numinous expresses a power that the human community has not fully appropriated, one that is beyond human comprehension and is the ultimate force at work in the world, it is essential to all worship, including Christian.

Christianity has its own take on this when Christians locate the presence of numinous mystery, of the awesomeness of God, in the sharing of daily bread and in its ritualization, and not in bloody sacrifices or in things kept apart and made accessible only to the few. The power of God is experienced in the welcoming forgiveness of a community of love and at its common table. It is as much in mutual forgiveness that Christians extend daily to one another as it is in the rituals of absolution that reconciliation with what is most holy in life is affected. The dialectic of power in the Church is such that, although office is respected for what it signifies and for the unity that it brings to the Church, it is recognized that the holy person who lives by the gospel has greater potential in mediating God's love and life than the unholy officeholder. If this is ignored, office and officeholder are invested with an aura of the sacred that is fearful and overpowering. While all cosmic, ancestral, and natural forces are to be respected and praised, testimony to the Word and to the Spirit and conformity with Christ in his loving service can be the only criteria for the exercise of any service or appointment to authority within the community.

In our times, concern with the Church's relation to the cosmos has entered the picture in a new way. Attention to the environment and to ecological issues is a common call. Humans are not simply masters or protectors of earth and cosmos.

They live in communion with all created things. Hence Christians are moved by a concern for the integrity of creation and the call on humanity to live in relationship with all creatures in the service of a peaceful and just relationship. This includes all human peoples but also all that God has brought into being by one and the same creative act.[18] The simplicity of Christian ritual expressions of the love of the whole universe and admiration for the presence of God in creation is located in the things used in ritual, namely bread, wine, oil, and water. All the baptized bring the wonder of these elements to sacramental celebration. Parsimony in their use or an excess of law in governing what may be used is a sin against God and creation and a disavowal of the Incarnation.

New Cultural Models for Ministry

Fresh insight into mission, ministry, and order is emerging on the Latin American, African, and Asian continents. For the sake of all churches, some features of their ways of relating ministry to mission are here mentioned, not in the hope of being comprehensive but simply to highlight some outstanding aspects of global development.

From Latin America we learn more of the relation of the Church's mission to the kingdom of God as it augurs justice for the oppressed and the strategy of what Leonardo Boff dubs *ecclesiogenesis*, that is to say, the growth of appropriate ecclesial structures from within the life of communities, especially the alternative communities of the base. A reader is struck by how deeply and authentically sacramental are such ecclesiologies. In a book titled *The Principle of Mercy*,[19] Jon Sobrino spells out the mission of the Church in terms of bringing mercy and the hope of freedom from the travail of injustice and poverty, working together in solidarity with the people who suffer. He offers fresh considerations on priesthood, which have deep roots in biblical and ecclesial tradition. True participation in the royal priesthood of Christ belongs to the community of the baptized and is exercised in their whole lives, with the Eucharist taking its meaning therefrom. Going back to Hebrews, he draws out the meaning of Christ's own royal and priestly service, and so of the Church's, as servitude to human beings in their fleshly existence, in the reality of lives lived in struggle and in the hope that comes from Christ's sacrifice. Though Sobrino does not spell this out, it is clear that this is the context for ordering ministries and for a profound grasp of the meaning of pastoral leadership. The experience of base church communities is not over and is not to be overshadowed, as some current trends would seem to want. It has to be revived and instated at the heart of the Church's work for the kingdom of God and for the development of forms of ministry suited to mission and presence in a society still redolent of injustice.[20]

In African and Asian Churches, the holy is expressed in unique symbolic ways that often derive from a more cosmic vision of life than what is found in the West: the person is seen within the community or family, the human within the cosmic, all aspects of life pervaded by a sense of the sacred and the holy. To integrate this in such a way as to allow the gospel to transform the culture and the culture to inform the gospel requires time and thought. Without a relation to ancestors and without a relation to the spirit of life inherent in all things, there is no true holiness. Symbols of sacred place, sacred person, and sacred action speak of a power that precedes any specific expression of meaning. It is a numinous force that influences human life and cosmic movements, a force that the human needs to acknowledge, for the integrity of both the human and the cosmic order. The good of the human community seems to depend on respect for this power and on attuning human life rhythms to the cosmic and to the life that is in the bowels of the earth. Connecting this with Christ's Word, and Christ's Word to this, is a task that is being undertaken in close affinity with the religious sentiment of the peoples concerned. These churches of Africa and Asia are thus today shaping ecclesiologies that are more pertinent to their cultural patterns of life and cultural histories. What is said of ministry or leadership in the Church develops in tandem with culturally rooted ways of speaking of Christ.

Africa

Among African peoples, the image of tradition and the image of minister are related to an inbuilt respect for ancestors. Christ himself is known in some Christologies as Proto-ancestor. From him who comes from the Father and is sent by the Father, all wisdom about life and the holy comes. Leaders in the community are expected to transmit together the wisdom that comes from Christ and the wisdom about life and the world that peoples see as peculiar to their own ancestral heritage. Christ becomes incarnate in African ancestry, expressing that wisdom and respect that is freeing rather than what can enslave peoples or families to the hold that ancestral spirits and customs may have on them. The respect for ancestors as guardians of the moral fiber of the community will have importance, as this imagery is used of Christ or of saints and respected ancestors. Bénézet Bujo offers a model of African ecclesiology[21] that has its grounding in the Eucharist when this is considered as the proto-ancestral meal, where all life converges and from which the life force emanates. In such a proto-ancestral ecclesiology, bishops and priests are seen to be at the service of the life force that flows through the whole community.

When it is said in Africa that family provides an image of the Church that serves as model for the origin and structuring of ministries, family is understood in terms of African culture and the extended family. This is inclusive of the communal responsibility for passing on life and nurturing and respecting it, and inclusive also of the relation in the lifeline to ancestors who remain bonded to the community in a sharing of life. To give the gospel grounding in this cultural perception, life may be seen as the common appropriation of the life of Christ, Proto-ancestor, and of the Spirit. Christ is the one who liberates life from its various forms of bondage. He is the one in whom all life finds its present center and its future hope, as well as the one in whom there is a binding and healing relation with ancestors.

In relation to such an understanding of Church as family within its social context, Bujo comments, "The bishop should not behave as if he were the central figure of the Eucharistic celebration,"[22] for this can be said only of Christ. All ministers serve the life force within the community. They need to be particularly sensitive to those whose participation is weakened, who are impoverished and suffering travail. As genuine servants of Christ, they need to identify with these, his suffering members. Bujo does not pursue his own insights to the point of situating the origins of ministry within such a family environment, but as we have seen earlier (chap. 1), some episcopal documents from Africa suggest this orientation.

For bishops and priests to take their role in ecclesial communities according to this model, some desacralization of power, ecclesiastical and spiritual, is needed. In writing of using African models of consensus building in politics, Kwame Bediako has observed that an African exercise of authority can be quite oppressive because it is based on a sacral vision of power and authority.[23] For a true democracy in which all enjoy freedom and have a part in political change, there is a need, as he puts it, to make room for the "way of Jesus," that is, for the exercise of a nondominating and nonpaternalistic use of power. Something similar has to be said of the exercise of episcopal power in the Church. Episcopal power has to leave room for the power of the Spirit at work more broadly and for building a community life that is served in a variety of ways. Discernment rather than executive power has to become a much more common word and a process in the life of ecclesial communities. Power is not located outside the people. By the grace of Christ, it is located within and among them.

In a recent survey of African ecclesiologies, by one himself an African theologian, it is striking to note how some writings are faulted for their failure to relate to a social context in a way that sees cultural issues and issues of justice, sickness, and reconciliation interwoven.[24] As African writers themselves affirm, the model of African family cannot be taken for the Church without some critique of family issues that remain matters of concern in Africa. Such are patriarchy, the limited role allowed women in some places, the need for more openness to outsiders, and the at times superstitious fear of the power of ancestors in causing illness or misfortune.

Using the model in a constructive way, the above cited writer, orobator, associates the Church's mission with advocacy for the ill and especially for those subject to the HIV-AIDS crisis. The role of healing thus takes on dimensions in Africa not known to the West, and the Church in its ministries is trying to find the place of such service and power within its family boundaries.[25] Indeed, it is suggested that healing is not just another ministry, but that the power to heal is at the heart of the inculturation of ministry, given that in essence to heal is to restore life and life connections with others.

The Church's own healing tradition is to relate all power over sickness, bodily and spiritual, as over life and death, to Christ and the Spirit. There is within that tradition a plea for bodily healing that was over time obscured and is now being retrieved as integral to the needs and hopes that people have when faced with very grave bodily disease and hunger, from which they seek release. Basically, what has to be integrated into the life force is the freeing power of Christ and the Spirit, with its capacity to free both mind and body from slavery to malign forces.

In Africa, when Jesus is venerated as healer or is given the messianic title of Healer, this is connected to the role of the healer in traditional society. Some bishops or theologians are concerned about transposing to Jesus or to saints the elements of fear of ancestors or of superstition connected with resort to healers and diviners. However, this is a good example of how the gospel may take root in culture and at the same time bring resolution to some issues connected with healing in the history of cultural transmission. In essence, to heal is to restore vitality to life and right relations to other living persons and to ancestors or forebears, as indeed to the world to which one belongs in and through the body. It includes the capacity to discern the source of suffering and malaise that permits bodily need to harm persons, families, and communities.

Naming Jesus Healer derives from the Gospel stories of cure and exorcism and relates closely to African experience and tradition. The Gospel stories are about faith and have to do with faith in him as the Savior, who in his own poverty reached down to the roots of suffering and evil and offers the promise of the life that comes from God and the Spirit. For ministers of the Church, and in a special way for Church leaders, this means that they are called and sent to heal and restore life in its fullness in the name of Christ. Their charism is one of compassion and of an ability to bring people to know the true source of a life that does not end with death. It means addressing injustices, for much human hunger and suffering stems from the injustice and violence that violate the relationships among people, not only in the local but in the global community. Today, to be a true healer in Africa has to mean a ministry that speaks to the fundamental issues of life and of the restoration of a place within the human community, whether persons be well or sick, young or old. As Cécé Kolié puts it, "The principal task of Christianity in black Africa is not so much to heal illness as it is to exorcise it, demystify it."[26] In other words, it is to reveal illness as a human reality, on the one hand a necessary passage to the fullness of life, and on the other something to which people may surrender because of the failure to deal with the all-too-human roots of much inordinate sickness and suffering. If the healing powers of Christ, and of the power that he gives to his disciples to cure and to exorcise the demonic, are put within the setting of the full story of his redemptive action and of his being as the fullness of life, they address precisely what is sinful and unbalanced in human life and the ways in which it is shared.

Asia

Given the long-standing religious pluralism peculiar to Asian countries, it is from Asian Christians that we may learn to see how relation to other religions affects the origin, nature, and diversification of mission, ministry, and order. The church in

Asia has begun to attend to the ancient spiritualities of Eastern religious traditions. It is forging a vision of Church and mission that, in the very hope of Christ and Spirit, makes working with people of other religions possible and imperative, searching with them for the meaning of the work of justice and reconciliation. As cited earlier, the mission of the Church is not simply *ad gentes* but *inter gentes* (see n. 47 in chap. 1).

Developing Catholic ecclesiologies seem to be linked closely with the work of the Federation of Asian Bishops' Conferences (FABC). This is possible because the positions taken in FABC documents emerged from a process of dialogue in which many churches took part and which included the input of their grassroots membership. Fundamental to this ecclesiology and to the growth of ministries within Asian churches is a redefinition of the Church's mission. Christian people find themselves amid other ancient and still vibrant religious traditions that have helped to shape the life of Asians in different ways. They are enriched through dialogue with these traditions and feel called to work with their followers toward defining and achieving a common good. The impulse toward serving communities in a quest for justice, peace, and reconciliation, prompted for Catholics by Vatican II and its aftermath, is shared by Asian Christians with other religious bodies. Reading the gospel provides an inspiration for reconciliation and reappraisal and for the growth and diversification of ministries accordingly. In this, Asian theologies in their own way point to the (Asian) family as the place where life sharing, service, and ministry have their well-spring.

We may recall how a common theology for Asia, and a particular theology for each church, takes into account those who have remained marginal and inferior for long centuries within their own cultures (see chap. 5). Such are the *dalit* in India, the *minjung* in Korea, and women and girls almost everywhere. Christians are asking how these poor may be served within the horizons of the gospel and interreligious dialogue. They also ask what it means for a Church to hear their voices and profit from what they bring to the common life. Their reading of the Bible, the values they hold dear, and their work belong within a Church that seeks to promote that justice that belongs within the service of the reign of God, affecting not only ecclesial life but society as a whole.

Power/s of the Weak

The service of justice and peace as an integral part of the Church's mission is expressed by the phrase "the fundamental option for the poor." There is by no means a common understanding of what this means. From the notification of the Congregation for the Doctrine of the Faith on the works of Jon Sobrino in 2007,[27] it appears that the relation to the poor in the preaching of the gospel and in the ministry of the Church is still an issue. The notification states that the Congregation's concerns are with Sobrino's Christology, but the introduction shows that it is also discontent with how his ecclesiology relates to the position of the poor and with the description of the Church as the Church of the Poor. What is taken as a given is the special commitment of the Church to the aid of the poor and to the promotion of their human development. What is denied is that any special understanding of the gospel and of Christ's mission "to evangelize the poor" comes from the poor themselves or from solidarity with them in working for the promotion of their interests.

The notification quotes Sobrino where he says that "the poor in the community question Christological faith and give it its fundamental direction" and that "the Church of the Poor . . . is the ecclesial setting of Christology because it is a world shaped by the poor." It lauds Sobrino's preoccupation with the poor and oppressed but affirms that this setting is of no special epistemological importance in knowing Christ and the meaning of the gospel. The ecclesial foundation of Christology, it says, "is found rather in the apostolic faith transmitted through the Church for all generations." This is to beg the question as to what constitutes the apostolic faith and its modes of transmission, for Sobrino after all is anxious to interpret precisely this. Granted this demurral of the Congregation, then, it does seem that here is here a matter to be continually pursued.

The foregoing excursus on the inculturation of ecclesial ministry in Africa and Asia prompts a final consideration on the power of the weak. In a number of countries, the most vibrant Christian communities exist among those who are materially and socially weak or marginal. This has been articulated in liberation theologies of different sorts, or in such forms as the theology of the *dalit* in India. For Africa and Asia, and the same is true for Latin America, the formation of small communities among the poor is one of the principal ways for living amid society as a people that looks forward in Christ and the Spirit to the hope of a reign of justice and peace. Some of the documents from these regions have made the point, as we have seen earlier, that ordained members, especially priests, have to situate themselves within these communities and that their formation also should be located within them. How all of these communities and populations are to be given the possibility of regularly celebrating the Eucharist remains a crucial question. Some bishops spoke rather tentatively of this at the recent Synod on the eucharist. Only then is the option for the poor realized in its fullness. Structures and clerical cultures are so ingrained that even though some recognition is given to the power and mission of poor or marginal communities, this is not allowed its ultimate articulation, which is the regular celebration of the Eucharist as a community.

In other parts of the world, where the basic Christian community and social marginalization are not so prominent, there is a comparable awareness of the power that actually exists among those who have always been socially inferior in Church structures, as well as in other social structures. We are helped in seeing what this means for ministry in the Church by a number of the perceptions that we owe to the social sciences and in a particular way to the observations of Elizabeth Janeway. [28] She has pointed to the participation in the dynamics of social power that belongs to the socially subordinate and to the importance of giving this expression. This is a matter of discovering where the forces that can change the life of a society are located and the attitudes toward their own weakness and suffering that can enable persons to become transforming agents.

While there are passages in the New Testament that retain the sacral name of priest for Jesus Christ, the principal images of his mediation are *kenosis*, or taking on the form of servant or slave, becoming victim, giving up his body, pouring out his blood, offering himself in ransom and exchange, and the foolishness of the cross. These are all images of poverty. It is in poverty and weakness that God's power is made present and transforms the life of the world. Because of his love, Christ is reduced to being one without power, to being the plaything of the powerful. This is in Christ the revelation of God's very being, not something accidental to the divine presence in the world. This self-emptying becomes a power for believers in its celebration. It is then appropriated by them as an act that frees, whose power is in the endowment of freedom. It frees from self-interest as it frees from subordination to the powers of the world and to the principalities and powers that thwart the coming of the reign of God. The Church in its celebration of faith can take hold of the power given to it only by participating in the commemoration of Christ and the commemoration of others who by his grace enjoy similar power.

Gathering under the presidency of its ordained ministers, and maintaining its communion in respecting their authority, a Christian people finds and locates the power of the Spirit in the act of commemorating the Christ who was poor so that humankind might be saved. The power of order and jurisdiction that rightly belongs to the ordained is not to be confused with the freeing power that lives in the body. It is rather at the service of this life-giving power. The early church showed a realization that its power against evil and its power in the world came from those who, in testifying to Christ's name, opposed other powers of secular and religious domination. The powerful ones in the eucharistic assembly of early centuries are the martyrs of both genders, whose memory was kept and whose passion narratives were read. Sometimes a certain power of this sort fell to the confessors who had survived persecution. If the power of the martyrs were to be recognized, power could not be denied to confessors, even when it left difficult administrative issues to be solved. Power was also present in the community of virgins, who showed how freedom from cultural domination may be won. It was present in widows, who were free to be independent from the social norms governing the future of their like. What was being recognized was the force of liberation that comes in the cross of Christ and in the hope of the resurrection. This was not kept as an abstract idea but was given flesh in the death or testimony of all those who testified in Christ's name against opposing dominations.

If each particular church today were to recognize something comparable in the dynamics of its own life and witness, it would be easier to find ways by which to locate the power of ordained ministers within a power that is more fundamental and that has to do with being free from fear and free to testify in word and act. The commemoration of those who in the recent past have given their lives in love and witness, who have in word and deed testified in suffering against cruelty and the forces of annihilation and oppression, is more basic to an understanding of God's power in the Church than is ordination.

The cultural models that over time have affected the Church's own conception and exercise of authority have usually prevented it from giving much recognition to the socially weak in governance or in the symbolic order. The socially weak in society turn out to be the ecclesiastically weak as well. The unlettered, women, children, the handicapped, and the sick have had little to do in determining the flow of Church life, even when, as in the case of women, the Church has relied on them for multiple services to itself and to humanity. What remained historically and theologically unexamined until quite recently is the actual impact of women on the life of the Church, or the power that the poor have exercised, for example, in the domain dubbed that of popular religion. The clergy has often been compelled to work with these forces, even to compromise with them, but this has nearly always been in the interest of keeping their own official authority and position.

As has been noted, the churches on several continents have engaged themselves in living out the "preferential option of the poor," even making this the criterion of deep evangelization.[29] Like Jon Sobrino, the Nigerian theologian Agbonkhian-meghe E. Orobator has proposed that a contemporary theology of the Church has to be developed from the site, as it were, where the church is the Church of the Poor, in all of the present-day agonies of impoverishment and suffering.[30] In doing this, he believes that he is pursuing the theological hermeneutical key of incarnation, proposed by the Vatican II document on mission, *Ad gentes*.[31]

Given the principle that the Church of disciples is a eucharistic community, gathered as one at the Lord's table, within liturgical celebration, the power of the socially weak in the Church and in society can be recognized and expressed and thus given its place in a meaningful search for the good of order. As Elizabeth Janeway says in *Powers of the Weak*, no good is achieved by romanticizing the virtues of the poor or socially weak. What is to be sought is public recognition of their place in the social order and an articulation of how their presence and activity affects the goals and aims and achievements of society. Such recognition affects these goals and aims since it removes the notion of privilege and disrupts some assumptions of hierarchical ordering. It goes along with the theological principle of different kinds of liberation theology that the voice of the poor is key to hearing Christ's message in truth and in love.

Today we see a close connection between recognizing the weak in the Church and recognizing the weak in the social order. Believing Christians look to their faith in Christ and in God's kingdom to find ways in which to affirm their place in building human society. It is often the case that the same people find themselves in a position of inferiority in both churches and society because of the way in which churches share the common cultural assumptions. When liturgical celebration allows for a shared activity based on the assumption of basic equality in the community, this leads to recognizing the powers of the weak. Not only is this true when ministries and mutual services in greater variety are given place in liturgy, but some of the liturgy's most basic symbols relate much more to the socially weak than to the socially powerful.

One good example of this is eucharistic bread. As a church, Catholics are slow to recognize this since they prefer to camouflage the bread and wine in more sacral forms. However, true eucharistic bread is real bread produced by real people. It is made from wheat sown and grown in the fields, gathered by laborers, milled to flour, baked, and set upon the table. This is why the offering of the people's gifts was such an integral part of the commemorative sacrifice of praise offered by the Church in memorial of Christ. Even the early days of the Roman liturgy gave verbal and ritual expression to this. In due time, the preparation of eucharistic hosts and the way in which they appear on the altar have camouflaged this fact so that even the recently revised General Instruction on the Roman Rite finds no place for the faithful to offer their own bread but rather perversely tries to attribute a symbolic meaning to the current rite of the preparation of the gifts. In reality, these gifts turn up in such a way that they seem to have no connection with the people.

When the bread blessed at the Eucharist is actually produced and provided by the people, when it is spoken of in ways that recognize its provenance, then it becomes clear that there can he no Eucharist without the people who provide bread and wine, not only for the Eucharist but for the poor of the community, and indeed bread often coming from the poor themselves for common sharing. It is bread and work that become the shared property, concern, and communion of the people called together in Christ. The ordained minister is minister to this sharing. The exercise of the ministry is dependent on the bread given by the people and on their willingness to share it, whatever the struggles and sufferings of making a livelihood. When the communion of the Christian people is recognized in such a fundamental act as the producing, giving, blessing, and sharing of eucharistic bread and cup, then the eucharistic symbolism also speaks to the place that the socially weak have in the ordering of society and of public life. It affects the way in which people make conscious the real, if unrecognized, role that they play in public life, and it influences the manner of their further participation. If the people do not bring bread, the priest does not celebrate.

From the African, Asian, and Latin American continents we see what happens in the rooting of the gospel when the poor themselves develop community and in Christ's name take on the work of living from and making known the gospel. It stands to reason that the way in which the past is remembered by the Church affects the power of the weak in both Church and society. Women are telling tales and writing books about the past that reclaim the role that other women have had in the past but that has often gone unnamed and unrecognized. In so many parts of the world, the poor and deprived read the Gospels with fresh insights into the blessings of the kingdom preached by Christ. His healing and compassion were so integral to his ministry and message that in his lordship, the poor find a symbol of the power of the weak triumphing over the powers that crush and oppress. They have found their own hope and strength in a fresh reading of the story of the liberation of the Hebrew slaves from Egypt. Their veneration of Mary, who sang the song of the blessings of the weak, takes on new forms that reinforce their hope, as in the devotion to our Lady of Guadalupe. They institute their own feasts and find their own saints and heroes in people who, outside the official structures of Church and state, brought the poor to an awareness of their dignity and their strength. They give their own testimony in a struggle for freedom that does not yield before apparently superior forces.

Along with this sensitivity to the powers of the weak, there has to go an innate sense of human vulnerability. Without this, we lack true awareness of what is shared in human life. Moments of weakness, such as the birth of a newborn child, sickness, imminent death, grief over the departed, are privileged moments of liturgical celebration. Recognition of human dependency and inner personal fragility is essential to such acts as giving and taking in marriage, assuming ministry in a community, sponsoring others in the way of prayer, offering God's forgiveness, consoling in grief, and the like. Liturgical celebration can place such experiences of dependency and fragility at the heart of the celebration of grace. The witness of the oppressed, the vulnerable, and the wounded can be accepted as an expression of power within the Christian gathering because daily, in joy and hope, it keeps memory of the self-emptying of Christ and of the manifestation of God's power in the cross.

What is implied in hearing their voices and in giving expression to the powers of the weak is far from being worked out as yet in the life of the Church. Taking this into account has to be related to the confidence in base Christian communities expressed in Latin America, or the trust in small faith communities exhibited in statements of African and Asian episcopacies. If charisms, gifts, ministries, and leadership appropriate to the missionary objectives of those churches do indeed originate and find support in communities of the weak, it will have unforeseen consequences for the ordering of the Church.

A happy outcome is by no means assured. Indeed, the continued defense and fostering of the hierarchical and clerical models, and of hierarchical and clerical subcultures, is all too obvious. This may teach us to recognize that the work of the Spirit is to be found in many ways of witness, life, and ministry not officially integrated into Church structures and doctrines. On the cross, Christ gave witness to the poor of the earth and to God's, not simply the Church's, preferential option. Whatever the vagaries of the preaching of the Gospel and of ecclesiastical ministry in the past and in the present, Christ takes flesh among them, and they witness to him, as he witnessed to them. The rehabilitation of ministry and order is a work in progress. It requires both a good interpretation of the past, a constant retrieval of the memory of Christ, and a keen attention to the work of the Spirit in the present, as well as a living sense of mission.

Divergence over the way in which the poor and the weak are integrated into the life-giving reality of Church community causes problems and even divisions in the ordering of Churches today. It appears to be a given that the Church makes an option for the poor and that small communities have a role in animating the life of the Christian faithful. Not all see this in the same way. As spelled out in the decade or so following the Second Vatican Council, this frequently meant taking an evangelical option to give voice to the poor and the weak of society, making them agents of their own history, agents too in the hearing and interpretation of the Scriptures, and agents in shaping the life of the Church. It also means attending to the voices of those Christians engaged in the public sphere in one way or another, taking it that their own grasp of the Christian faith had much to say to the Church's presence and witness in the world. Rome and some episcopacies now seem to fear that such listening to the laity, whether poor or active in the public sphere, has led to misunderstanding and even error. While still giving support to constituting small communities, they see these more as a way to educate the laity than as a way to the growth of these communities as agents for understanding and exercising the mission of the Church. In conclusion to this study, we might say that it is the fate of small communities, and especially of communities of the weak and the poor, that will determine how mission and ministry take shape in the coming years.

In the introduction to the book, some words of the philosopher Gadamer were quoted, inviting his readers to be open to those solidarities to which, in a time of uncertainty and change, they should be faithful. By solidarity with those who seek a more just human community, by solidarity with those who suffer want and injustice, by solidarity with those who treasure rather than exploit the earth it is possible to find responses to many queries as to what is right and wrong. The thoughts offered here on the powers of the weak, on the power given to the weak by the justice of God, indicate the solidarity by which the Church of Christ will be renewed in its mission and in its very flesh. As to what is right or wrong in the exercise of ministry, as to what is right or wrong in the ways of ordering and structuring ecclesial life, the criterion is whether this solidarity at the heart of the kingdom of God is served.

Conclusion

This chapter has been written to take account in our time of all that has been written in the rest of the book. It was meant to highlight the implications of defining the Church and local communities as a eucharistic communion even as we are attentive to how mission and ministries are taking shape across the world. The power of being through Word and sacrament a community of persons who follow Christ on the way of the gospel was considered to be the foundation for coresponsibility in the service of life and mission, as well as the inspiration for developing ministry and order. This cannot be done globally without seeing how different orderings are related to different, culturally determined, senses of the holy and of community and hence of power. Orientations on mission, Church, and ministry in Latin America, Africa, and Asia were given particular importance. Finally, taking all these into consideration, something was said of the new foundational reality of the powers of the weak. This is an appropriate note on which to end the book.

Notes

Introduction

1. Fritz Lobinger, *Like His Brothers and Sisters: Ordaining Community Leaders* (Quezon City, Philippines: Claretian Publications, 1998; New York: Crossroad, 2002).
2. David N. Power, *Gifts That Differ: Lay Ministries Established and Unestablished*, 2nd ed. (New York: Pueblo, 1985), 120.
3. Ibid., 118.
4. This is one of the mistakes sometimes made in arguing the possibility of ordaining women to episcopacy and other offices. Even if there were no past instances of women in important ministries, the question is still a necessary one for the present and has to be thought about along different lines.
5. Hans Georg Gadamer, *Reason in the Age of Science* (Cambridge, MA: MIT Press, 1981), 86.
6. Some of this is a reprisal of matters that I have treated over the years. Nothing previously written, however, is simply repeated in this work, though clearly much of it works its way into the treatment of the subject.

1. Mission and Ministry since Vatican II (A)

1. Giuseppe Alberigo, "Fedeltà a creatività nella recezione del Concilio Vaticano II: Criteri ermeneutici," *Cristianesimo nella storia* 21 (2000): 383–402.
2. For example, Hervé Legrand, "Forty Years Later: What Has Become of the Ecclesiological Reforms Envisaged by Vatican II?" *Concilium* 2005, no. 4:57–72.
3. This attention to local churches is what Karl Rahner meant when he spoke of the global Church coming into being: "Das neue Bild der Kirche," in *Schriften zur Theologie*, vol. 8 (Einsiedeln: Benzinger, 1967), 329–54; English translation [ET], "The New Image of the Church," in Rahner, *Theological Investigations*, vol. 10 (London: Darton, Longman & Todd, 1973), 3–29, esp. see 7–12.
4. Regretfully, nothing is included about churches in Oceania/Australia, which like other continents were convoked for a Synod in Rome. For this, see the Apostolic Postsynodal Exhortation, *Ecclesia in Oceania* (Washington, DC: United States Conference of Catholic Bishops [USCCB], 2005).
5. English Translation, International Commission on English in the Liturgy, ed., *Documents of the Liturgy, 1963–1979: Conciliar, Papal, and Curial Texts* (Collegeville, MN: Liturgical Press, 1982), 908–11, §§2922–38.
6. Ibid., 798–803, §§2576–91.
7. Ibid. 650–54, §§2073–88.
8. Ibid., 641–43, §§2043–53.
9. Paul VI, *On Evangelization in the Modern World* (Washington, DC: United States Catholic Conference [USCC], 1976).
10. Code of Canon Law = Codex Iuris Canonici [CIC], canon 230, §3.
11. CELAM = Conference of Latin American Bishops.

12. John Eagleson and Philip Scharper, eds., *Puebla and Beyond: Documentation and Commentary* (Maryknoll, NY: Orbis Books, 1979).
13. Ibid., 177.
14. Ibid., 210–14.
15. For an evaluation of Pueblo, see Jon Sobrino, "The Significance of Puebla for the Catholic Church in Latin America," in *Puebla and Beyond*, 289–309.
16. Alfred T. Hennelly, ed., *Santo Domingo and Beyond: Documents and Commentaries* (Maryknoll, NY: Orbis Books, 1993); for an evaluation, see Jon Sobrino, "The Winds in Santo Domingo and the Evangelization of Culture," in ibid., 167–83.
17. Almost as a footnote, but one implying great consequences, it has to be remarked that in a recent Latin American missionary congress in Guatemala in 2003, there was no mention of basic Christian communities, while the discussion centered on the renewal of parish and local church. The report in Spanish, French, and English is published in *Mission: Journal of Mission Studies / Revue des sciences de la mission* 11 (2004): 157–204.
18. "Disciples and Missionaries of Jesus Christ so That Our Peoples May Find Life in Him." For text, *V Conferencia General del Episcopado Latino Americano y del Caribe, Aparecida, Brasil 2007: Documento de participatión y fichas de trabajo* (Bogotá, Colombia: Centro de Publicaciones CELAM, 2006).
19. See Agenor Brighenti, "El documento de participación de la Quinta Conferencia," *Christus: Revista de teología y ciencias humanas* 71, no. 755 (July/August 2006): 25–32.
20. See http://www.vatican.va/roman_curia/congregations/cfaith/documents/rc_con_cfaith_doc_20061126_notification-sobrino_en.html and http://www.vatican.va/roman_curia/congregations/cfaith/documents/rc_con_cfaith_doc_2 0061126_nota-sobrino_en.html.
21. "Esto significa que los pobres son el principio inspirador de la Iglesia, no sólo los beneficiarios de su opción"; http://www.cpalsj.org/publique/cgi/cgilua.exe/sys/start.htm?infoid=1558&sid=25 (accessed March 7, 2007).
22. CELAM, V Conferencia, *Documento Conclusivo*, www.celam.info/download/Documento_Conclusivo_Aparecida.pdf (accessed August 5, 2007).
23. Benedict XVI, "Address to CELAM," *Origins* 37, no. 2 (May 24, 2007): 17–24. Already in June 2007, helpful comment may be found in articles published in Italian by Latin American writers. See João Batista Libânio, "La scelta dottrinale: Benedetto XVI e la conferenza di Aparecida," *Il Regno/Attualità* 52 (June 15, 2007): 366–71; Mario de França Miranda, "Conversione e Missione; Aparecida: note sul documento finale," in ibid., 371–73.
24. For a study of the developing role and ministries of the baptized in another particular church, see William Antonio Correa Pareja, *Los laicos en Colombia después del Concilio Vaticano II al la luz de los documentos de la conferencia episcopal* (Rome: Pontificia Università Lateranense, 2000).
25. Conselho Permanente de CNBB, "Comunidades Eclesiais de Base," *Comunicado Mensil: Conferência Nacional dos Bispos de Brasil*, no. 362 (November 1982): 1180–95.
26. See http://www.cnbb.org.br/documento_geral/LIVRO%2062-LEIGOS%20E%20LEIGAS.pdf (accessed December 22, 2007).
27. For a current view of the place of the basic ecclesial communities, see Celso Pinto Carias, "De Volta às comunidades eclesiais de base—una alternative para a evangelização atual," *Revista eclesiástica Brasileira* 64 (2004): 802–21. Some sociologists have expressed the view that base communities of the poor are nothing but a figment of the imagination of middle-class revolutionaries who exploited the idea of the Church of the Poor for their own purposes. See Malik Tahar Chauch, "La théologie de la liberation en Amérique Latine: Approche sociologique," *Archives des sciences sociales des religions* 52, no. 138 (April–June 2007): 9–28. But sociology is not a neutral science.
28. On these directives, see Odilo Pedro Scherer, "A Eclesiologia des diretrizes gerais de ação evangelizadora da Igreja no Brasil (CNBB)," *Rivista di cultura* 12 (January/March 2004): 121–41.
29. "Conferência Nacional dos Bispos do Brasil, Síntesis das contribuições de Igreja no Brasil à Conferência de Aparecida" www.cnnb.org (accessed March 9, 2007). This is no longer on the website.

30. It is noteworthy that in his address to youth on the occasion of his visit to Brazil, Benedict XVI made mention of the various types of communities in which these youth lead their Christian lives, talking of "the Christian life you lead in numerous parishes and small ecclesial communities, in universities, colleges, and schools, and . . . in places of work both in the city and in the countryside"; http://frtodd.blogspot.com/2007/05/pope-benedict-to-youth-of-brazil.html (accessed May 12, 2007). This recognition did not recur in his other addresses during this visit.

31. See note 7, above.

32. John Paul II, *The Church in America, Ecclesia in America: Postsynodal Apostolic Exhortation* (Washington, DC: USCC, 1999).

33. Ibid.

34. Clodovis Boff, "The Catholic Church and the New Churches in Latin America," http://www.sedos.org/english/boff_1.html (accessed December 22, 2007). A perceptive comment on the Latin American situation written in 1988 still has considerable validity: Madeleine Adriance, "Brazil and Chile: Seeds of Change in the Latin American Church," in *World Catholicism in Transition*, ed. Thomas M. Gannon (New York: Macmillan, 1988), 283–96.

35. For a helpful survey of the story of Asian Churches before, during, and since the Council, see Peter C. Phan, "'Reception' or 'Subversion' of Vatican II by the Asian Churches? A New Way of Being Church in Asia," in *Vatican II: Forty Years Later*, ed. William Madges (Maryknoll, NY: Orbis Books, 2006), 26–54.

36. There is ample documentation in *For All the Peoples of Asia: Federation of Asian Bishops' Conference Documents*, vol. 1, *From 1970–1991*, ed. Gaudenco B. Rosaes and C. G. Arévelo (Maryknoll, NY: Orbis Books, 1992); vol. 2, *Documents from 1992–1996*, and 3, *Documents from 1997–2001*, ed. Franz Jozef Eilers (Quezon City: Claretian Publications, 1997–2002). For a brief survey, see James H. Kroeger, "Theology of Local Church: FABC perspectives," in J. H. Kroeger, *Becoming Local Church* (Quezon City: Claretian Publications, 2003), 31–54.

37. *For All the Peoples of Asia*, 1:9.

38. Ibid., 14.

39. Ibid., 60.

40. Ibid.

41. Ibid., 63.

42. Ibid., 193.

43. Ibid., 109–13.

44. Ibid., 126–34.

45. Ibid., 252–53.

46. Peter C. Phan, ed. and compiler, *The Asian Synod: Texts and Commentaries* (Maryknoll, NY: Orbis Books, 2002).

47. Texts found at http://www.fabc.org/.

48. See Jonathan Y. Tan, "From 'Missio ad gentes' to 'Missio inter gentes': Shaping a New Paradigm for Doing Christian Mission in Asia," *Vidyajoti Journal of Theological Reflection* 69 (2005): 27–41; idem, *Theologizing at the Service of Life: The Contextual Theological Methodology of the Federation of Asian Bishops' Conferences (FABC)*, FABC Papers no. 108 (Hong Kong: FABC, 2003), http://www.ucanews.com/html/fabc-papers/fabc-108.htm.

49. *For All the Peoples of Asia*, 1:67–92.

50. Ibid., 125–64.

51. Ibid., 149.

52. Luis Antonio G. Tagle, "Mission in Asia: Telling the Story of Jesus," *Omnis Terra* 40, no. 371 (2006): 368–75.

53. Catholic Bishops of Thailand (CBCT), "Master Plan for the Years 2000–2010 of the Catholic Church of Thailand," *East Asian Pastoral Review* 40 (2003): 186–202.

54. National Conference of the Philippines, "Pastoral Letter," *Weltkirche* 2 (1999): 43–54.

55. For a survey, see David W. Antonio, *An Inculturation Model of the Catholic Marriage Ritual* (Collegeville, MN: Liturgical Press, 2002), 93–103.

56. On the at-times contentious story of the Mindanao-Sulu Pastoral Conference in the 1970s, see Power, *Gifts That Differ*, 32–36.

57. See Karl M. Gaspar, "Localization Resisting Globalization: Basic Ecclesial Communities in the Postmodern Era," *East Asian Pastoral Review* 38 (2001): 316–50.

58. This includes the churches of the Sudan, Ethiopia, Kenya, Uganda, Tanzania, Malawi, and Zambia.

59. Documents are available at www.amecea.org.

60. For a report on the 1973 plenary assembly, see *African Ecclesiastical Review* [*AER*] 16, no. 1 (1974), with study guidelines on 9–10. For a report on the 1976 assembly, see *AER* 18, no. 5 (1976): 249–311.

61. Bishop John N. Jenga, "Christian Community in Life Situations," *AER* 18 (1976): 301–11.

62. Report in *AER* 21, no. 5 (1979): 258–316.

63. For a report of this assembly, its resolutions, and its mandates, see *AER* 44, nos. 5–6 (2002): 263–85.

64. Ibid., 267.

65. See http://www.amecea.org/vision.htm (accessed March 1, 2007).

66. On this African family model, see Theological Institutes for the African Synod, "Lay People Must Be Empowered," in *African Synod: Documents, Reflections, Perspectives*, compiled and edited by Africa Faith and Justice Network under the direction of Maura Browne, SND (Maryknoll, NY: Orbis Books, 1996), 56–58; Bénézet Bujo, "On the Road towards an African Ecclesiology," in ibid., 139–51; idem, *African Theology in Its Social Context* (Maryknoll, NY: Orbis Books, 1999); Agbonkhianmeghe E. Orobator, *The Church as Family: African Ecclesiology in Its Social Context* (Nairobi: Paulines Publications Africa, 2000).

67. This includes the conferences of Angola, Botswana, Lesotho, Mozambique, Namibia, São Tome and Principe, South Africa, Swaziland, and Zimbabwe.

68. See http://www.imbisa.org.zw/html/plenary.html (accessed March 1, 2007); the site gives plans, not papers or conclusions, and only one statement of objectives and procedures, on "Poverty and Economic Justice in Southern Africa," for 2001.

69. For an elaborate treatment, historical, theological, and canonical, see Richard Kulimushi Mutarushwa, *La charge pastorale: Droit universel et droit local* (Paris: Éd. du Cerf, 1999).

70. Ibid., 517.

71. Ibid., 511–64.

72. See a communiqué of 2002 and one of January 2007, both available at www.sceam-secam.org (accessed February 25, 2007).

73. See the English translation in *African Synod*, 233–83.

74. "Synod of Bishops: Second Special Assembly for Africa; The Church in Africa in Service to Reconciliation, Justice and Peace (*Lineamenta*)," *L'Osservatore Romano*, Weekly Edition in English, no. 29 (1,953), July 19, 2006, 3–14.

75. See, for example, Emmanuel Bueya Makaya, "Ecclesia in Africa: Ultime étape vers un concile africain?" *Telema*, nos. 125–26 (September 2006): 5–10; Josée Ngalula, "Le problématique des sacrements dans un Afrique des guerres et des conflits après Ecclesia in Africa," ibid., 59–72.

76. For a rather pessimistic assessment written in 1988, see Adrian Hastings, "East, Central, and Southern Africa," in Gannon, *World Catholicism in Transition*, 308–19. For a study on how these communities developed and functioned in one particular church, see Krzysztof Cieslikiewicz, *Small Christian Communities: Pastoral Priority and a Vital Force for Evangelization in the Archdiocese of Dar Es Salaam (Tanzania); An Evaluation and New Perspectives* (Rome: Pontificia Università Lateranense, 2004). The SACBC (Southern African Catholic Bishops' Conference) also published a document on the vocation and mission of the laity in preparation for the Synod on the Laity, but it focuses on the secular status of the laity and says little of parish ministries or of community. See Synod of Bishops, *Vocation and Mission of the Laity in the Church and in the World Twenty Years after the Second Vatican Council* (Pretoria: SACBC, 1985). Given the situation of the people and the Church under apartheid, the accent on transforming the secular was pertinent.

77. Magloire Somé, "Christian Base Communities in Burkina Faso: Between Church and Politics," *Journal of Religion in Africa* 31, no. 1 (2001): 275–304. Burkina Faso is not an AMECEA member, but what is said in this article seems to fit the situation of a number of African Churches that tried the pastoral policy of small Christian communities.

78. For descriptions, see John Baur, *2000 Years of Christianity in Africa: An African History, 62–1992* (Nairobi: Pauline Publications Africa, 1993), 318–21; Joseph Healey and Donald Sybertz, *Towards an African Narrative Theology* (Nairobi: Pauline Publications Africa, 1996), 137–67.

79. See, e.g., Baur, *2000 Years,* 352–59.

2. Mission and Ministry since Vatican II (B)

1. On the evolution over decades of the position of the Catholic Church in face of *laïcité,* see Philippe Portier, "L'Église Catholique face au modèle français de laïcité," *Archives des sciences sociales des religions* 129 (2005): 117–34.

2. *Documentation Catholique* 67 (1970): 311–17.

3. Robert Coffy and Robert Varro, *Église signe de salut au milieu des hommes* (Paris: Le Centurion, 1972), containing *Église-sacrement* by Coffy and *Vie apostolique et langage culturel.*

4. Msgr. François Frétellière, *Préparation au ministère presbyteral: Rapports presentées à l'Assemblée plénière de l'episcopat français, Lourdes, 1972* (Paris: le Centurion, 1972).

5. Ibid., 61.

6. Assemblée plénière de l'Episcopat français, *Tous responsables dans l'église? Le ministère presbytéral dans l'église toute entière "ministèrielle"* (Paris: Le Centurion, 1973).

7. Hervé Legrand, "Le role des communautés locales," *La Maison-Dieu* 215, no. 3 (1998): 9–32. On the issue of the baptized in pastoral ministry, see Alphonse Borras, *Des laïcs en responsabilité pastorale? Accueillir de nouveaux ministères* (Paris: Éd. du Cerf, 1998); Joseph Doré and Maurice Vidal, eds., *Des ministres pour l'église* (Paris: Éd. du Cerf, 2000). For an assessment of the gains and risks of this situation, see Monique Brulin, "La prise en compte de l'histoire dans le domaine des pratiques sacramentelles," in *La théologie dans l'histoire,* ed. Joseph Doré et François Bousquet (Paris: Beauchesne, 1997), 169–99.

8. "La collaboration entre ministres ordonnés et laïcs en pastorale liturgique et sacramentelle," *Documentation Catholique,* no. 2149, vol. 93 (1996): 1011.

9. Ibid., 1012–13.

10. "Proposer la foi dans la société actuelle: Lettre aux Catholiques de France," ibid., 1016–49.

11. Ibid., 1035–36.

12. Conferenza Episcopale Italiana [CEI], "Evangelizzazione e Sacramenti: Documento pastorale dei vescovi Italiani," *Il Regno-documenti* [*Regno-doc*] 18 (1973): 396–405.

13. CEI, "Evangelizzazione e promozione umana," *Regno-doc* 20 (1975).

14. CEI, "Verifica degli orientamenti pastorali," *Regno-doc* 46 (1998): 512–17.

15. "Comunicare il Vangelo in un Mondo che Cambia: Orientamenti pastorali per il primo decennio del 2000," *Regno-doc* 50 (2001): 441–56. Also at www.chiesacattolica.it.

16. "Un discernimento comunitario"; ibid., 456.

17. "Fare di Cristo il cuore del mondo," *Regno-doc* 11 (2005): 305–12.

18. "I laici nella chiesa," *Orientamenti pastorali,* nos. 1–2 (2000): 92–94.

19. "Atti del congresso," *Regno-doc* 9 (2001): 279.

20. One thinks here of movements such as the Focolarini, Comunione e Liberazione, the Community of Sant'Egidio, the Neocatechumenal Movement—all of which left their imprint on the Italian Church. There was also an agglomeration of base Christian communities, though they were rather marginal: see Fausto Perrencho, *Bibbia e comunità di base in Italia: Analisi valutativa di un'esperienza ecclesiale* (Rome: Libreria Ateneo Salesiano, 1988).

21. In the number of *Orientamenti pastorali* in which this statement is published, there are a number of theological and canonical articles on the place of the laity in the Church. Giorgio Campanini, "Speranza e disincanto nel cammino dei laici nella chiesa" (ibid., 7–20), writes

of the meaning and modes of ecclesial synodality; and Agostino Montan supplies a canonical study of pastoral councils: "I consigli pastorali" (ibid., 29–57).

22. A good review of these perspectives as they are reflected in Italian theology is given by Tommaso Turi, "L'identità dei fedeli laici nella 'Pastores Gregis,'" *Rassegna di teologia* 46 (2005): 405–20.

23. All three documents may be found on the conference's Web site, www.conferencia episcopal.es/.

24. For a summary and citation of documents of the conference, see Zeni Fox, "Laity, Ministry, and Secular Character," in *Ordering the Baptismal Priesthood: Theologies of Lay and Ordained Ministry*, ed. Susan K. Wood (Collegeville, MN: Liturgical Press, 2003), 121–51.

25. The most noteworthy document to date is that of the National Conference of Catholic Bishops, *Called and Gifted: The American Laity* (Washington, DC: USCCB, 1980). More recently, idem, *Co-Workers in the Vineyard of the Lord: A Resource for Guiding the Development of Lay Ecclesial Ministry* (Washington, DC: USCCB, 2005).

26. See "US Bishops' Pastoral Letter on Hispanic Ministry," *Origins* 13 (1984): 529–41.

27. See Bernard Lee and Michael Cowan, eds., *Gathered and Sent: The Mission of Small Church Communities Today* (Mahwah, NJ: Paulist Press, 2003).

28. For some of the canonical implications of a more-formal recognition of the rights and duties of all the baptized, see Elissa Rinere, "Canon Law and the Emerging Understandings of Ministry," in Wood, *Ordering the Baptismal Priesthood*, 68–84.

29. In 1997 a colloquium on ecclesial lay ministry was organized that brought together some bishops, pastors, theologians, and canonists. The published papers are of interest enough but do not echo much grassroots activity nor the option for the poor: National Conference of Catholic Bishops, *Together in God's Service: Toward a Theology of Ecclesial Lay Ministry* (Washington, DC: USCC, 1998). For a description of how a typical middle-class community promotes common responsibility at a communal and structural level, see Robert Duggan, "Opportunity Knocks: A Parish Leadership Development Model," *Origins* 37, no. 5 (June 14, 2007): 75–79.

30. Fritz Lobinger, *Priests for Tomorrow: A Plea for Teams of "Corinthian" Priests in the Parishes* (Quezon City: Claretian Publications, 2004).

31. Prelude to what follows is what I have written on the mission of the Church in *Love without Calculation: A Reflection on Divine Kenosis* (New York: Crossroad, 2005), 63–116.

3. Events and Theologies before Vatican II

1. For an overview, see E. Fouilloux, "Mouvements théologico-spirituels et concile (1959–1962)," in *A la veille du Concile Vatican II: Vota et réactions en Europe et dans le Catholicisme oriental*, ed. M. Lamberigts and Cl. Soetens (Leuven: Bibliotheek van de Faculteit der Godgeleerheid, 1992), 185–99.

2. É. Mersch, *The Theology of the Mystical Body*, trans. C. Vollert (St. Louis: Herder, 1951); the French edition originally appeared in 1933.

3. *Summa theologiae* III, Q. 72, art. 5, c. and ad 2m.

4. Pius XII, "Litterae encyclicae 'Mediator Dei et hominum,'" *Acta apostolicae sedis* 39 (1947): 521–95.

5. Lambert Beauduin, *La piété de l'église* (Louvain: Mont César, 1914).

6. Yves de Montcheuil, *Aspects of the Church*, trans. A. LaMotte [from French] (Chicago: Fides, 1955).

7. Yves Congar, *Lay People in the Church*, trans. D. Attwater [from French], rev. ed. (Westminster, MD: Newman, 1965).

8. See Karl Rahner, "Notes on the Lay Apostolate," in *Theological Investigations*, vol. 2 (Baltimore: Helicon, 1963), 319–52.

9. See Jacques Gadille, "Fondement spirituel d'une théologie du laïcat, selon Jacques Maritain," *Revue des sciences religieuses* 81, no. 3 (2007): 323–40. The influence of Maritain on Giovanni Batista Montini, later Paul VI, is well known.

10. See the preconciliar articles, dating from a 1961 collection in German but published in English only in 1991: Hans Urs von Balthasar, "The Layman in the Church" and "Toward a Theology of the Secular Institutes," in *Explorations in Theology*, vol. 2, *Sponsa Verbi* (San Francisco: Ignatius, 1991), 315–32, 421–57.

11. Bernard Minvielle, *L'apostolat des laïcs à la veille du Concile (1949–1959): Histoires des congrès mondiaux de 1951 et 1957* (Fribourg: Éditions Universitaires, 2001).

12. Pius XII, "Six ans se sont écoulés," *Acta apostolicae sedis* 49 (1957): 922–39. On the history of this distinction between order and jurisdiction, see Laurent Villemin, *Pouvoir d'order et pouvoir de jurisdiction: Histoire théologique de leur distinction* (Paris: Éd. du Cerf, 2003).

13. For bibliography, see Yves Congar, "Faits, problèmes et réflexions à propos du pouvoir d'ordre et des rapports entre le presbytérat et l'épiscopat," *La Maison-Dieu* 14 (1948): 107–28; E. Hocedez, "Une découverte théologique," *Nouvelle revue théologique* 51 (1924): 332–40; Michel Andrieu, "La carrière ecclésiastique des papes et les documents liturgiques du moyen âge," *Revue des sciences religieuses* 21 (1947): 90–120; Bernard Botte, "Holy Orders in the Ordination Prayers," in *The Sacrament of Order* (Collegeville, MN: Liturgical Press, 1962), 5–23. Trends are well represented in the book, which appeared toward the beginning of the Second Vatican Council, edited by Bernard Dupuy and Yves Congar, *L'Episcopat et l'église universelle* (Paris: Éd du Cerf, 1962).

14. Jacques Lécuyer, *Prêtres du Christ: Le sacrement de l'ordre* (Paris: Fayard, 1957).

15. Pius XII, "Litterae encyclicae 'Mystici Corporis Christi,'" *Acta apostolicae sedis* 35 (1943): 193–248.

16. On the Council of Trent, see A. Duval, "The Council of Trent and Holy Orders," in *The Sacrament of Order* (Collegeville, MN: Liturgical Press,1962), 219–58; A. Duval, "Les données dogmatiques du Concile de Trente sur le sacerdoce," *Bulletin du comité des études* 38/39 (1962): 451–72.

17. Decree on the Sacrifice of the Eucharist, DS 1739; Decree on the Sacrament of Order, DS 1764.

18. For easy reference in the English language, see Karl Rahner, *The Church and the Sacraments* (New York: Herder, 1963); and Edward Schillebeeckx, *Christ: The Sacrament of Encounter with God* (London: Sheed & Ward, 1963).

19. Giuseppe Battelli, "Daniel Comboni et son 'image' de l'Afrique," in *Église et histoire de l'église en Afrique*, ed. Giuseppe Ruggieri (Paris: Beauchesne, 1988), 63–88.

20. A. Abble et al., *Des prêtres noirs s'interrogent* (Paris: Éd. du Cerf, 1956).

21. Karl Adam, T*he Christ of Faith: The Christology of the Church* (New York: Pantheon Books, 1957).

4. Remarks on the Vatican Council and Its Reception

1. For the study of the Vatican Council, inclusive of its Acta, a most useful tool is the five-volume history edited by Giuseppe Alberigo and Joseph Komonchak, *History of Vatican II* (Maryknoll, NY: Orbis; Leuven: Peeters, 1995–2005). A summary is given in Giuseppe Alberigo, *A Brief History of Vatican II* (Maryknoll, NY: Orbis Books, 2006). There is a vast literature in a variety of languages and genres.

2. Benedict XVI, "Address to Roman Curia, December 2005," English text in *Origins* 35, no. 32 (January 26, 2006): 534–39.

3. In the text quoted by Benedict, Basil speaks of "raucous shouting, . . . incomprehensible chatter . . . confused din of uninterrupted clamouring."

4. See *Concilium* 2005, no. 4, *Vatican II: A Forgotten Future*, ed. Alberto Melloni and Christoph Theobald (London: SCM, 2005); Christoph Theobald, ed., *Vatican II sous le regard des historiens: Colloque du 23 septembre, 2005*, Centre Sèvres (Paris: MédiaSèvres, 2006); Philippe Bordeyne and Laurent Villemin, ed., *Vatican II et la théologie* (Paris: Éd. du Cerf, 2006); John O'Malley, "Vatican II: Did Anything Happen?" *Theological Studies* 67, no. 1 (2006): 3–33.

5. Paul Gauthier, *Christ, the Church and the Poor* (Westminster, MD: Newman, 1965); the book includes interventions in the aula by members of this group.

6. Christoph Theobald, "The Theological Options of Vatican II: Seeking an 'Internal' Principle of Interpretation," *Concilium* 2005, no. 4:87–107.

7. Peter Hünermann, "The Ignored 'Text': On the Hermeneutics of the Second Vatican Council," *Concilium* 2005, no. 4:118–36.

8. On these implications, see Mauro Velati, "The Others: Ecumenism and Religions," *Concilium* 2005, no. 4:35–47.

9. On the reception of *Dei Verbum*, see Christoph Theobald, "La transmission de la révélation divine: À propos de la réception du chaptre II de 'Dei Verbum,'" Bordeyne and Villemin, *Vatican II et la théologie*, 107–26.

10. The Pontifical Biblical Commission, *The Interpretation of the Bible in the Church* (Vatican City: Libreria Editrice Vaticana, 1994).

11. The Pontifical Biblical Commission, *The Jewish People and Their Sacred Scriptures in the Christian Bible* (Boston: Pauline Books & Media, 2003).

12. Peter Hünermann, "Kirche als Volk Gottes," in *Theologischer Kommentar zur dogmatischen Konstitution über die Kirche*, vol. 2 of *Herders theologischer Kommentar zum Zweiten Vatikanischen Konzil*, ed. Peter Hünermann and Jochen Hilberath (Freiburg: Herder, 2004), 371–404.

13. See Hervé Legrand, "Forty Years Later: What Has Become of the Ecclesiological Reforms Envisaged by Vatican II," *Concilium* 2005, no. 4:57–72.

14. Noteworthy in this regard is the message *motu proprio* (in virtue of his authority as Pope) of John Paul, *Apostolos suos*, found in English in *Origins* 28 (July 30, 1998): 152–58.

15. Edward Schillebeeckx, *The Definition of the Christian Layman* (Chicago: Franciscan Herald Press, 1979).

16. Émile Marcus, "Où en sommes-nous dans la réception du décret de Vatican II sur le ministère et la vie des prêtres?" *Esprit et vie*, no. 174 (June 2007): 1–11.

17. John Paul II, *Postsynodal Apostolic Exhortation Christifideles Laici* (Vatican City: Libreria Editrice Vaticana, 1988).

18. The understanding of priesthood in terms of relationships in the postsynodal exhortation *Pastores dabo vobis* will be considered in chap. 9 (below).

19. International Theological Commission, *From the Diakonia of Christ to the Diakonia of the Apostles* (Chicago: Hillenbrand Books, 2004). Three recent articles illustrate the impasse: A. Borros, "Le diaconat exercé en permanence: Restauration ou rétablissement?" *Nouvelle revue théologique* 118, no. 6 (1996): 817–38; Paul De Clerck, "Note sur l'expression non ad sacerdotium sed ad ministerium (episcopi)," *La Maison-Dieu* 249, no. 1 (2007); Richard Gaillardetz, "Towards a Contemporary Theology of the Diaconate," *Worship* 79, no. 5 (2005): 419–38.

20. Address of His Holiness Benedict XVI, Hall of Blessings, Thursday, March 2, 2006: www.vatican.va/holy_father/benedict_xvi/speeches/2006/march (accessed November 22, 2006).

21. Author's own translation from the Italian on the Vatican Web site.

22. These have been presented in chap. 1 (above).

23. Claude Prudhomme, "Les évêques d'Afrique noire anciennement française et le Concile," in *Vatican II commence . . . approches Francophones*, ed. E. Fouilloux (Louvain: Bibliotheek van de Faculteit der Godgeleerdheid, 1993), 163–88; Adrian Hastings, "East, Central and Southern Africa," in *World Catholicism in Transition*, ed. Thomas M. Gannon (New York: Macmillan, 1988), 308–17; L. J. Baraúna, "Alguns aspectos de participação brasileira no Concilio Vaticano II," in *Experience, Organisations and Bodies at Vatican II*, ed. M. T. Fattori and A. Melloni (Leuven:Bibliotheek van de Faculteit der Godgeleerdheid, 1999), 1–23; P. Pulikkan, "Indian Bishops in the First Session: From a Slow Start to an Emerging Conciliar Ethos," in ibid., 87–122.

24. A conference on this had been held in Nijmegen before the Council.

25. John Paul II, "Slavorum apostoli," *Acta apostolicae sedis (AAS)* 77 (1985): 802–3.

26. This is enshrined in the instruction of 1994, "Legitimate Differences," *Origins* 23(1994): 745–56.

27. See the study by Giovanni Turbanti, *Un Concilio per il mondo moderno: La redazione della costituzione pastorale "Gaudium et Spes" del Vaticano II* (Bologna: Società editrice il Mulino, 2000).

28. Eric Borgman, "Gaudium et Spes: The Forgotten Future of a Revolutionary Document," *Concilium* 2005, no. 4:48–56.

29. For a recent study of the thought of Chenu, see Christophe F. Potworowski, *Contemplation and Incarnation: The Theology of Marie-Dominique Chenu* (Montreal and Kingston: McGill-Queen's University Press, 2001).

30. For the critique of Schema 13 by the German theologians and bishops, led by Karl Rahner, and implicitly of Chenu's approaches, see Hans-Joachim Sander, *Theologischer Kommentar zur Pastoralkonstitution über die Kirche in der Welt von Heute*, vol. 4 of *Herders theologischer Kommentar zum Zweiten Vatikanischen Konzil*, ed. Peter Hünermann and Bernd Jochen Hilberath (Freiburg: Herder, 2004), 650–63.

31. English translation in *The Encyclicals of John Paul II*, edited with introductions by J. Michael Miller (Huntington, IN: Our Sunday Visitor, 1996), 426–77.

32. Lukas Vischer, "Humanity—Centre and Summit of the Earth," *Concilium* 2005, no. 4: 148–52.

33. Alberigo and Komonchak, *History of Vatican II*, 4 (2003): 271–74, 281.

34. "Schema bene dignoscit illa elementa per quae Deus homines fortiter suaviterque ad se attrahit," in *Acta Synodalia Concilii Vaticani II* (Vatican City: Typis Polyglottis Vaticanis, 1960–), 4:376, in *Periodus Quarta*, Pars II.

35. Denis Hurley, *Vatican II: Keeping the Dream Alive* (Pietermaritzburg: Cluster Publications, 2005), 104.

36. Joseph Ratzinger, "Commentary on Chapter One," in H. Vorgrimler, ed., *Commentary on the Documents of Vatican II*, vol. 5 (New York: Herder & Herder; London: Burns & Oates, 1969), 93–102. See also Charles Moeller, "Preface and Introductory Statements" (ibid., 99): "the expression *signa temporum* is used here (art. 4), the only time it is, and bears John XXIII's sense of the main facts which characterize an age."

37. Paul VI, *Ecclesiam suam*, ET (Washington, DC: NCWC, 1964).

38. John Paul II, *Encyclical Letter: Ut unum sint* [1965] (Boston: Pauline Books & Media, 1995), §34.

39. José Comblin, "The Signs of the Times," *Concilium* 2005, no. 4:73–86. For a proposal for a fuller theology of the signs of the times, see Rino Fisichella, "Signs of the Times," in *Dictionary of Fundamental Theology*, ed. René Latourelle and Rino Fisichella (New York: Crossroad, 1994), 995–1006. Likewise, Juan Alfaro, "Reflections on the Eschatology of Vatican II," in *Vatican II: Assessment and Perspectives Twenty-Five Years After (1962–1987)*, ed. René Latourelle (New York: Paulist Press, 1988), 501–3. Alfaro calls for a concrete, historical form to eschatological hope, especially in acting against injustice.

40. This is why some commentators think it legitimate to speak of a needed rupture in the life of the Church, without putting into question the truth of continuity.

41. See what has already been said about the life of the Church on these continents.

42. Pope Paul VI, "*Adhortatio apostolica quinque iam anni*," *Acta apostolicae sedis* (*AAS*) 63 (1971): 102–105.

43. John Paul II, *Encyclical Letter Laborem exercens* (Vatican City: Libreria Editrice Vaticana, 1981).

44. John Paul II, *Encyclical Letter Sollicitudo rei socialis* (Vatican City: Libreria Editrice Vaticana, 1987).

45. See www.vatican.va//212.77.1.245/news_services/press/vis/dnamiche/aO_en.htm (accessed September 9, 2007).

46. The translation is the writer's own, made from the Italian on www.vatican.va/holy_father/ benedict-xvi/speeches/ (accessed March 11, 2006).

47. See the text of this discourse in *The Tablet*, September 23, 2006, 10–12.

48. See www.vatican.va/holy_father/benedict_xvi_spe_20070513_conference-aparecida_en.html.

49. "The Utopia of going back to breathe life into the pre-Columbian religions, separating them from Christ and from the universal Church, would not be a step forward: indeed, it would be a step back. In reality, it would be a retreat towards a stage in history anchored in the past."

50. Pope Benedict XVI, *Encyclical Letter on Hope, Spe salvi* (Vatican City: Libreria Editrice Vaticana, 2007).

51. For a statement of Cardinal Ratzinger, expressing a recognition of Lutheran ministry and Lord's Supper, in which he affirms the "salvation-bringing" presence of Christ, see the citation in *Koinonia*, 49, note 106. The source of the quotation is *Una Sancta* 48 (1993): 348.

52. "Report of the Joint Lutheran–Roman Catholic Study Commission on 'The Gospel and the Church,' 1972," in *Growth in Agreement: Reports and Agreed Statements of Ecumenical Conversations on a World Level*, ed. Harding Meyer and Lukas Vischer (Geneva: WCC; New York: Paulist Press, 1984), 183.

53. Ibid., 271.

54. Ibid., 259.

55. John Paul II, *Ut unum sint* (1965), §67.

56. Apparently Cardinal Kasper thinks that, in a matter of such consequence, the Anglican Church ought to have worked it out in discussion with Rome before proceeding to act, but this is a delicate matter touching on questions internal to churches.

57. "Report of the Joint Lutheran–Roman Catholic Study Commission on The Eucharist," in *Growth in Agreement*, 192–203.

58. John Borelli and John H. Erickson, eds., *The Quest for Unity: Orthodox and Catholics in Dialogue* (Crestwood, NY: St. Vladimir's Seminary Press; Washington, DC: USCC, 1996), 131–42.

59. The difficulty associated with the office of the Bishop of Rome in Catholic-Orthodox dialogue was duly noted by Pope John Paul II in his encyclical on ecumenism, *Ut unum sint*, §§86–95.

60. Commission on Faith and Order, "Lima Report: Baptism, Eucharist and Ministry, 1982," in *Growth in Agreement*, 482–95.

61. *Nature and Mission of the Church: A Stage on the Way to a Common Statement*, Faith and Order Paper No. 198 (Geneva: WCC Publications, 2005).

62. See Nicholas Lossky, *Dictionary of the Ecumenical Movement* (Grand Rapids: Eerdmans, 2002), s.v. "Orthodoxy"; J. Meyendorff, *The Orthodox Church: Its Past and Its Role in the World Today*, revised and expanded by N. Lossky (Crestwood, NY: St. Vladimir's Seminary Press, 1996).

63. John Meyendorff, *Byzantine Theology: Historical Trends and Doctrinal Themes* (New York: Fordham University Press, 1979), 209.

64. For an account of worldwide and North American dialogues between the Roman Catholic and Orthodox Churches, see Borelli and Erickson, *Quest for Unity*.

65. Walter Kasper, *That All May Be One: The Call to Unity Today* (London: Burns & Oates, 2004), 27.

66. Benedict XVI, "To Papal Nuncios Serving in Latin America," *L'Osservatore Romano*, Weekly Edition in English, February 28, 2007, 3.

67. Working together on prayers for the Week of Church Unity in January 2007, the joint commission mandated by Rome and the WCC looked to the ecumenical fellowship of the township of Umtata, outside Durban, South Africa. In the life of the people of this township, there is a striking convergence between working together for the healing of social ills and listening together in prayer to the Word of God. It would take another book to gather together all such testimonies from around the world.

68. Randall Lee and Jeffrey Gros, ed., *The Church as Koinonia of Salvation: Its Structure and Ministries*, Lutherans and Catholics in Dialogue 10 (Washington, DC: USCCB, 2005).

69. See the collection of statements up to 1992 in James A. Scherer and Stephen Bevans, ed., *New Directions in Mission and Evangelization*, vol. 1, *Basic Statements* (Maryland, NY: Orbis Books, 1992).

Introduction to Part 2

1. Margaret O'Gara, "A Roman Catholic Perspective on *ius divinum*," *The Church as Koinonia of Salvation: Its Structure and Ministries*, ed. Randall Lee and Jeffrey Gros, Lutherans and Catholics in Dialogue 10 (Washington, DC: USCCB, 2005), 226–46.
2. Karl Rahner, "Reflection on the Concept of *ius divinum* in Catholic Thought," in *Theological Investigations*, vol. V (Baltimore: Helicon, 1966), 219–43; idem, "Aspects of the Episcopal Office," in *Theological Investigations*, vol. 14 (New York: Seabury, 1976), 185–201. Rahner presents his position clearly and briefly in a 1982 essay, one of his last: "Authority," in *Theological Investigations*, vol. 23 (New York: Crossroad, 1992), 80–82.
3. How this worked out in practice will be seen later.
4. Francis A. Sullivan, *From Apostles to Bishops: The Development of the Episcopacy in the Early Church* (New York: Newman; Mahwah, NJ: Paulist Press, 2001).
5. Hans Urs von Balthasar, "Office in the Church," in *Explorations in Theology*, vol. 2, *Spouse of the Word* (San Francisco: Ignatius, 1991), 81–142.
6. The approach to history offered is influenced by many, but in a particular way I would like to mention Nicholas M. Healy, *Church, World and the Christian Life: Practical-Prophetic Ecclesiology* (Cambridge: Cambridge University Press, 2000); and Lewis S. Mudge, *Rethinking the Beloved Community: Ecclesiology, Hermeneutics, Social Theory* (Geneva: WCC Publications; Lanham, MD: University Press of America, 2001). Both deal in a measured way with theoretical underpinnings to historical interpretation.
7. Bernard Cooke, *Ministry to Word and Sacrament: History and Theology* (Philadelphia: Fortress, 1976); Alexandre Faivre, *Emergence of the Laity in the Early Church* (Mahwah, NJ: Paulist, 1990); Kenan Osborne, *Ministry: Lay Ministry in the Roman Catholic Church* (Mahwah, NJ: Paulist 1993); idem, *Priesthood: A History of the Ordained Ministry in the Roman Catholic Church* (Mahwah, NJ: Paulist 1990); idem, *The Permanent Diaconate: Its History and Place in the Sacrament of Order* (Mahwah, NJ: Paulist, 2007).
8. Edward Schillebeeckx, *The Church with a Human Face: A New and Expanded Theology of Ministry* (New York: Crossroad, 1985); idem, *Church: The Human Story of God* (New York: Crossroad, 1990).
9. In literature and secular history, some writers talk of this as looking for the plot, or in French *la mise en intrigue*.

5. The Scripture

1. Oft-cited works available in English are Rudolf Schnackenburg, *God's Rule and Kingdom*, trans. John Murray, 2nd ed. (New York: Herder & Herder, 1968); Norman Perrin, *Jesus and the Language of the Kingdom* (Philadelphia: Fortress, 1976); Jack Kingsbury, *Matthew: Structure, Christology, Kingdom* (Philadelphia: Fortress, 1975). For a summary of positions, see Brevard S. Childs, *Biblical Theology of the Old and New Testaments: Theological Reflection on the Christian Bible* (Minneapolis: Fortress, 1993), 636–46. On the way in which the metaphor of the kingdom is integrated into how the evangelists present the preaching of Jesus, see Donald Senior, "The Foundation for Mission in the New Testament," *The Biblical Foundation for Mission*, by Donald Senior and Carroll Stuhlmueller (Maryknoll, NY: Orbis Books, 1983), 141–312.
2. For example, Orlando E. Costas, "Christian Mission in the Americas," in *New Directions in Mission and Evangelization*, ed. James A. Scherer and Stephen B. Bevans, vol. 2 (Maryknoll, NY: Orbis Books, 1994), 9–10.
3. Though it is an important study in its own right, there is no attempt here to go into the efforts to reconstruct the historical words of Jesus from the New Testament data.
4. This is further developed in chapter 9, "Royal Priesthood."

5. Peter Hünermann indicates that *Lumen gentium* (1964) did not attend to this text; "Kirche als Volk Gottes," in *Theologischer Kommentar zur dogmatischen Konstitution über die Kirche*, vol. 2 of *Herders theologischer Kommentar zum Zweiten Vatikanischen Konzil*, ed. Peter Hünermann and Jochen Hilberath (Freiburg: Herder, 2004), 373. Yet it is mentioned in *Nostra aetate* (1965) and in subsequent work of the special Commission for Religious Relations with the Jews. On the meaning of Rom 9, see James G. D. Dunn, *The Theology of Paul the Apostle* (Grand Rapids, MI, and Cambridge, UK: Eerdmans, 1998), 499–532; Markus Barth, *The People of God*, Journal for the Study of the New Testament Supplement Series 5 (Sheffield: JSOT Press, 1983), esp. 29–50.

6. Edward Schillebeeckx, *Jesus: An Experiment in Christology* (New York: Seabury, 1979), 179–227; Perrin, *Jesus and the Language of the Kingdom*.

7. For a reading of Matthew's Gospel, I refer primarily to Raymond Brown, *The Churches the Apostles Left Behind* (New York: Paulist Press, 1984); Daniel J. Harrington, *The Gospel of Saint Matthew*, Sacra pagina 1 (Collegeville, MN: Liturgical Press, 1991); and the works cited above in note 1. For exegetical commentary, see M. Eugene Boring, *The New Interpreter's Bible*, vol. 8 (Nashville: Abingdon, 1995).

8. Luke Timothy Johnson, *The Gospel of Luke*, Sacra pagina 3 (Collegeville, MN: Liturgical Press, 1991), esp. 144–60, 386–406.

9. Ibid., 343–49.

10. Raymond E. Brown, *The Community of the Beloved Disciple* (New York: Paulist Press, 1979).

11. On Paul's missionary paradigm, see David J. Bosch, *Transforming Mission: Paradigm Shifts in Theology of Mission* (Maryknoll, NY: Orbis Books, 1991), 123–78.

12. Paul J. Achtemeier, *1 Peter: A Commentary on First Peter* (Minneapolis: Augsburg, 1996); John H. Elliott, *A Home for the Homeless: A Social-Scientific Criticism of I Peter, Its Situation and Strategy* (Minneapolis: Fortress, 1981).

13. Edward Schillebeeckx, *Church: The Human Story of God* (New York: Crossroad, 1990), 144–59.

14. David N. Power, *Love without Calculation: A Theological Reflection on Divine Kenosis* (New York: Crossroad, 2005).

15. See, e.g., Gerd Theissen, "Kirche oder Sekte? Über Einheit und Konflikt im frühen Urchristentum," *Theologie der Gegenwart* 48 (2005): 162–75.

16. The fact that in developing a canon of Scriptures, the Church of early centuries embraced all three kinds of literature is implicitly an acknowledgement that Christianity can allow for different kinds of local Church order.

17. Marcus Barth, *Ephesians: Translation and Commentary on Chapters 4–6*, Anchor Bible Commentary (Garden City, NY: Doubleday, 1974). For a presentation of opinions, see Margaret Y. MacDonald, *Colossians and Ephesians*, Sacra pagina 17 (Collegeville, MN: Liturgical Press, 2000), 291–93. For a good commentary that somehow rises above this argument, see Pheme Perkins, *Letter to the Ephesians: Introduction, Commentary, and Reflections*, New Interpreter's Bible 11 (Nashville: Abingdon Press, 2000), 359–60, 422–24.

18. Principally John N. Collins, *Diakonia: Re-interpreting the Ancient Sources* (Oxford and New York: Oxford University Press, 1990), 232–34. He is supported in this reading by Jean-Marie Tillard, *L'église locale: Ecclésiologie de communion et catholicité* (Paris: Éd. du Cerf, 1990), 308–9.

19. For an overview of the topic, see Roger Gehring, *House Church and Mission: The Importance of Household Structures in Early Christianity* (Peabody, MA: Hendrickson, 2004). See Benedict XVI's view of these communities in early times in a recent midweek audience, February 14, 2007, www.vatican.va/holy_father/benedict_xvi/audiences/2007/documents/hf_ben-xvi_aud_2007021_em.html (accessed March 4, 2007).

20. Among other studies, see Jacques Schossler, "Le ministère de l'episcopé d'aprés les épitres pastorales," in *À la recherché de la Parole: Études d'éxègese et de théologie biblique* (Paris: Éd. du Cerf, 2006), 561–96.

21. James D. G. Dunn, "Models of Christian Community in the New Testament," in *The Christ and the Spirit*, vol. 2, *Pneumatology* (Grand Rapids, MI, and Cambridge, UK: Eerdmans, 1998), 245–59.

22. An example of postcolonial readings from around the world may be found in a collection edited by R. S. Sugirtharajah, *Voices from the Margin: Interpreting the Bible in the Third World* (Maryknoll, NY: Orbis Books, 1997). As the editor says, what is envisaged are "flesh-and-bone readers—*minjung, dalits*, indigenous people, male and female, professional and lay, standing within their own social location" (3). A book that combines feminist and postcolonial reading is by the Botswanan writer Musa W. Dube, *Postcolonial Feminist Interpretation of the Bible* (St. Louis: Chalice, 2000).

23. Ibid., 157–96.

24. Jean-Marc Ela, "A Black African Perspective: An African Reading of Exodus," in Sugirtharajah, *Voices from the Margins*, 253.

25. Vincent O'Donovan, *Christianity Rediscovered* (Maryknoll, NY: Orbis, 2002).

26. Elisabeth Schüssler Fiorenza, *In Memory of Her: A Feminist Theological Reconstruction of Christian Origins* (New York: Crossroad, 1984), and the works of Rebecca Chopp and Sandra Schneiders quoted below, stand out in the increasingly abundant literature.

27. Carolyn Osiek and Margaret MacDonald, with Janet H. Tulloch, *A Woman's Place: House Churches in Earliest Christianity* (Minneapolis: Fortress, 2006). This approach can readily be compared with Dunn's above mentioned criteria.

28. As presented by Rebecca Chopp, *The Power to Speak: Feminism, Language, God* (New York: Crossroad, 1991), 99–128.

29. As presented by Sandra Schneiders, *The Revelatory Text: Interpreting the New Testament as Sacred Scripture* (Collegeville, MN: Liturgical Press, 1999), 180–99.

6. Ordering of Ministries

1. See W. H. C. Frend, "The Missions of the Early Church, 180–700 A.D.," reprinted in *Missions and Regional Characteristics of the Early Church*, edited with introduction by Everett Ferguson (New York & London: Garland Publishing, 1993), 1–22. In the same volume, see Einar Molland, "L'antiquité chrétienne a-t-elle eu un programme et des methodes missionaires," 23–36.

2. George Huntston Williams, "The Role of the Layman in the Ancient Church," *Ecumenical Review* 10 (1958): 225–48.

3. David Bosch, *Transforming Mission: Paradigm Shifts in Theology of Mission* (Maryknoll, NY: Orbis Books, 1991), 123–78.

4. Eduardo Hoornaert, *The Memory of the Christian People*, trans. Robert R. Barr [from Portuguese] (Maryknoll, NY: Orbis Books, 1988).

5. Abraham Malherbe, *Social Aspects of Early Christianity*, 2nd ed. (Philadelphia: Fortress, 1983).

6. Paul F. Bradshaw, *The Search for the Origins of Christian Worship: Sources and Methods for the Study of Liturgy* 2nd ed. (Oxford: Oxford University Press, 2002), 73–97. Bibliographical details for each of these compilations are given by Bradshaw and will not be repeated in what follows. English translation of the texts pertaining to Order and Ordination are given by Paul Bradshaw, *Ordination Rites of the Ancient Church of East and West* (Collegeville, MN: Liturgical Press, 1990). This writer has previously studied some of these texts in David N. Power, *Ministers of Christ and His Church* (London: Geoffrey Chapman, 1969); and idem, *Gifts That Differ: Lay Ministries Established and Unestablished*, 2nd ed. (New York: Pueblo, 1985).

7. Aaron Milavec, *The Didache: Text, Translation, Analysis, and Commentary* (Collegeville, MN: Liturgical Press, 2003), 67–68, 78–80.

8. A survey with bibliography of some of the positions on this development may be found in Anthony Barratt, "What Is Ordination? A Roman Catholic Perspective," *Ecclesiology* 3 (2006): 57–80.

9. James Puglisi, *The Process of Admission to Ordained Ministry*, vol. 1, *Epistemological Principles and Roman Catholic Rites* (Collegeville, MN: Liturgical Press, 1996), 10–46.

10. In writing of this text, "spirit" is not capitalized because at this stage of history the doctrine of the Holy Spirit had not been clearly worked out.

11. A close analysis of the *Didascalia* is given by Georg Schöllgen, *Die Anfänge der Professionalisierung des Klerus und das kirchliche Amt in der Syrischen Didaskalie*, published as *Jahrbuch für Antike und Christentum*, Ergänzungsband 26 (Münster: Aschendorf, 1998). Also see Cécile et Alexandre Faivre, "Mis en place et déplacement de frontières dans la Didascalie," *Revue des sciences religieuses* 81, no. 1 (2007): 49–68.

12. On house churches, we can recall what was already said in chapter 6 on life and ministries of the Church in the New Testament evidence.

13. W. H. C. Frend, *The Rise of Christianity* (Philadelphia: Fortress, 1984); Karl P. Donfried and Peter Richardson, eds., *Judaism and Christianity in First-Century Rome* (Grand Rapids: Eerdmans, 1998); Wayne A. Meeks, *The First Urban Christians: The Social World of the Apostle Paul* (New Haven: Yale University Press, 1983); Rodney Stark, *The Rise of Christianity: A Sociologist Reconsiders History* (Princeton, NJ: Princeton University Press, 1996).

14. P. Lampe, *Die stadtrömischen Christen in den ersten beiden Jahrhunderten*, 2nd ed. (Tübingen: J. C. B. Mohr, 1989); Allen Brent, *Hippolytus and the Roman Church in the Third Century* (Leiden: Brill, 1995), 368–457; J. F. McCue, " The Roman Primacy in the Second Century," *Theological Studies* 25 (1964): 161–96; Alan L. Hayes, "Christian Ministry in Three Cities of the Western Empire," *Community Formation in the Early Church and in the Church Today*, ed. Richard N. Longenecker (Peabody, MA: Hendrickson, 2002), 142–48.

15. Justin Martyr, *First Apology* 65, in *Early Christian Fathers*, Library of Christian Classics 1 (New York: Simon & Schuster, Touchstone, 1995), 285–86.

16. Eusebius, *The Ecclesiastical History of Eusebius Pamphilus*, trans. Christian Frederick Cruse (Grand Rapids, MI: Baker House Books, 1977), 265.

17. Karl Baus, "The Clergy of the Church of the Empire," in *History of the Church*, ed. Hubert Jedin, vol. 2 (New York: Seabury, 1980), 269–89.

18. L. C. Mohlberg, ed., *Sacramentarium Veronense* (Rome: Herder, 1956).

19. On the juridical aspects of this, see W. Ullmann, "Leo I and the Theme of Papal Primacy," *Journal of Theological Studies* 11 (1960): 25–51.

20. A study of ordination rites is found in Puglisi, *Process of Admission.*

21. Leo the Great, *Epistulae* 12.10, in *Patrologia latina* [PL] 54:654.

22. Gelasius I, Letter to the Bishops of Lucania, Southern Italy; Latin text in J. D. Mansi, ed., *Sacrorum conciliorum nova et amplissima collectio*, vol. 8 [for 492–536 CE] (1901; repr., Paris: Welter, 1960).

23. For an overview, see Jean Mégéian, H*istoire et institutions de l'église Armenienne: Evolution nationale et doctrinale* (Beyrouth: Imprimerie Catholique, 1965).

24. A short survey with further bibliography may be found in John Baur, *2000 Years of Christianity in Africa: An African Church History*, 2nd ed. (Nairobi: Paulines Publications Africa, 1998), 34–39.

25. In the case of Ethiopia, there was also a strong Judaic influence The Ethiopians believed that the ark of the covenant had been transported to their country. What is believed to be the ark is still preserved in the Church of Saint Mary of Zion, and every church building has a sanctuary where a replica of the ark is kept. On this and other practices, see Marilyn E. Heldman, "Architectural Symbolism, Sacred Geography and the Ethiopian Church," *Journal of Religion in Africa* 22, no. 3 (1992): 222–41; J. T. Pawlikoski, "The Judaic Spirit of the Ethiopian Orthodox Church [EOC]," *Journal of Religion in Africa* 4, no. 3 (1972): 179–99; Getnet Tamene, "Features of the Ethiopian Orthodox Church and the Clergy," *Asian and African Studies* 7 (1998): 87–104.

26. See Pawlikoski, "Judaic Spirit of the EOC"; and Tamene, "Features of the EOC."

27. Raymond van Dam, *Leadership and Community in Late Antique Gaul* (Berkeley: University of California Press, 1992).

28. Charles Joseph Hefele, *A History of the Christian Councils*, vol. 1 (Edinburgh: T&T Clark, 1894), 184–95.

29. Charles Munier, ed., *Les statuta ecclesiae antiqua* (Paris: Éditions-Études Critiques, 1960); L. C. Mohlberg, ed., *Missale Francorum (Cod. Vat. Reg. lat. 257)* (Rome: Herder, 1957).

30. Rosamond McKitterick, *The Frankish Church and the Carolingian Reforms* (London: Royal Historical Society, 1977), 789–895.

31. Eugen Ewig, *History of the Church*, ed. Jedin, 2:558–73; Judith Herrin, *The Formation of Christendom* (Princeton, NJ: Princeton University Press, 1987), 220–49.

32. For recent study, see R. Sharpe, *Medieval Irish Saints' Lives: An Introduction to Vitae sanctorum Hiberniae* (Oxford and New York: Oxford University Press, 1991).

33. This fits into the social and cultural expectations of the Celtic people. While it shows that, given the right circumstances, women could take on considerable ecclesiastical responsibility, they did not received ordination. Bishops might serve under women, but women were not made bishops.

34. Bedae Venerabilis, *Opera homiletica*, in Corpus Christianorum: Series latina [CCSL] (Turnhout: Brepols, 1953–), 122:49.

35. To a great extent this discipline is known through penitential books, but the books are not to be taken outside their social and missionary context.

7. Significant Figures and Writers

1. On Ignatius, see William R. Schoedel, *Ignatius of Antioch: A Commentary on the Letters of Ignatius of Antioch* (Philadelphia: Fortress, 1985); Christine Trevett, *A Study of Ignatius of Antioch in Syria and Asia*, Studies in the Bible and Early Christianity 29 (Lewiston, NY: Edwin Mellen, 1992). Schoedel's view of ministry in Ignatius is summarized in *Ignatius of Antioch*, 21–23, and 112–15, where he comments on *To the Magnesians* 6.1–2. For a study of the episcopacy in Ignatius, Irenaeus, and Cyprian, see Odd Magne Bakke, "The Episcopal Ministry from the Apostolic Fathers to Cyprian," in *The Formation of the Early Church*, ed. Jostein Ådna (Tübingen: Mohr Siebeck, 2005), 379–408. For some apposite insights, see Edward Schillebeeckx, *The Church with a Human Face: A New and Expanded Theology of Ministry* (New York: Crossroad, 1985), 70–73.

2. Allen Brent, "Ignatius' Pagan Background in Second Century Asia Minor," *Zeitschrift für antikes Christentum / Journal of Ancient Christianity* 10, no. 2 (2006): 207–32.

3. See Alan L. Hayes, "Christian Ministry in Three Cities in Western Europe," in *Community Formation in the Early Church and in the Church Today*, ed. Richard N. Longenecker (Peabody, MA: Hendrickson, 2002), 129–56.

4. Nowadays it is asked how faithfully Irenaeus reflects the positions of those whom he considered to be gnostics, but in any case we are clear enough about what he wanted to contend for in his own community.

5. For an examination of texts, see David N. Power, *Irenaeus of Lyons: Baptismal and Eucharistic Texts; Selected Texts with Introduction, Translation and Annotation*, Alcuin/GROW Liturgical Study 18 (Bramcote, Nottingham: Grove Books Ltd., 1991).

6. W. H. C. Frend, "The African Church in the time of Cyprian," in *The Donatist Church: A Movement of Protest in Roman North Africa* (Oxford: Clarendon, 1952; repr., 1985), 124–40; Stuart G. Hall, *Doctrine and Practice in the Early Church* (Grand Rapids: Eerdmans, 1991), 85–94.

7. Tertullian, *De praescriptione haereticorum*, 20–21, in Corpus Christianorum: Series latina [CCSL] (Turnhout: Brepols, 1953–), 1:201–3; English translation, in *Ante-Nicene Fathers* 3:252–53.

8. Vittorino Grossi, " Episcopus in Ecclesia: The Importance of an Ecclesiological Principle in Cyprian of Carthage," *The Jurist* 66 (2006): 8–29.

9. Cyprian, *Epistulae* 33.1; 43.5.

10. See Andreas Hoffmann, *Kirchliche Strukturen und römisches Recht bei Cyprian von Karthago* (Paderborn: Ferdinand Schöningh, 2000).

11. On Origen, see Théo Hermans, *Origène, Théologie sacrificielle du sacerdoce des chrétiens* (Paris: Beauchesne, 1996); Hermann Josef Vogt, *Das Kirchenverständnis des Origenes* (Cologne-Vienna: Böhlau, 1974). A helpful article is that of Joseph W. Trigg, "The Charismatic Intellectual: Origen's Understanding of Religious Leadership," *Church History* 50 (1981): 5–19. Though the consideration of Origen might seem more suitable among non-Latin writers, it is put here because of what it says about early questions on the authority of bishops.

12. Hans Urs von Balthasar, "Le mystérion d'Origène," *Recherches de science religieuse* 26 (1936): 513–62; 27 (1937): 38–64.

13. Fred Ledegang, "Origen's View of Apostolic Tradition," *The Apostolic Age in Patristic Thought*, ed. A. Hilhorst (Leiden and Boston: Brill, 2004), 130–38.

14. I. J. Davidson, "Ambrose," *The Early Christian World*, ed. P. F. Esler (London and New York: Routledge,1999); Neil B. McLynn, *Ambrose of Milan: Church and Court in a Christian Capital* (Berkeley: University of California Press, 1994).

15. Andrew Lenox-Conyngham, "The Church in St. Ambrose of Milan," *International Journal for the Study of the Christian Church* 5, no. 3 (2005): 211–25.

16. Ambrose, *De officiis*, edited with an introduction, translation and commentary by Ivor J. Davidson (New York and Oxford: Oxford University Press, 2001).

17. Ambrose, *Expositio in Lucam*, in CCSL 14:390.

18. On his ecclesiology, see P. Borgomeo, *L'église de ce temps dans la prédication de Saint Augustin* (Paris: Études Augustiniennes, 1972); Joseph Ratzinger, *Called to Communion: Understanding the Church Today* (San Francisco: Ignatius, 1987).

19. Eugene TeSelle, *Living in Two Cities: Augustinian Trajectories in Political Thought* (Scranton, PA: University of Scranton Press, 1998), 39–42.

20. On the Donatist church and schism, see Frend, *Donatist Church*.

21. Augustine, *Sermones* 26, in CCSL 41:529–57.

22. On this, as well as Frend, *Donatist Church*, see James O'Donnell, *Augustine: A New Biography* (New York: HarperCollins, 2005), 209–26.

23. Frend, *Donatist Church*, 332.

24. In his sermons, Augustine referred to the bishop as *episcopus, pastor*, or *praepositus*.

25. Augustine, *Sermo 227, Concerning the Sacraments*, delivered on the holy day of Pascha; English translation is given in *The Eucharist*, ed. Daniel J. Sheerin (Wilmington, DE: Michael Glazier, 1986), 96–99.

26. This is one of the major inspirations for Joseph Ratzinger's theology of ecclesial communion. As well as the above-cited works, see Joseph Ratzinger, *The Meaning of Christian Brotherhood*, 2nd ed. (San Francisco: Ignatius, 1992); Aidan Nichols, *The Thought of Benedict: An Introduction to the Theology of Joseph Ratzinger* (London: Burns & Oates, 1996; repr., 2005), 66–75, 133–54.

27. See Adolar Zumkeller, *Augustine's Ideal of the Religious Life*, trans. Edmund Colledge [from German] (New York: Fordham University Press, 1986).

28. Augustine, *Sermones* 355–356, in Patrologia latina [PL] 32:33–36.

29. Augustine, *The City of God*, 10.6. On the offering made by the bishop, see *Sermones* 7 (Codex Wolfenbüttel); English translation in Sheerin, *The Eucharist*, 99–102.

30. Joseph Carola, "Augustine's View of Lay Participation in Ecclesial Reconciliation," *Augustinian Studies* 35 (2004): 73–93.

31. Augustine, *Quaestionum evangelicarum* 1.12 and 2.44, in PL 35:1326, 1357.

32. See Eric Rebillard, *In hora mortis: Evolution de la pastoral chrétienne de la mort aux IVe et Ve siècles* (Rome: École Française, 1994).

33. Anselm of Havelberg, *Epistola apologetica professionis canonicis regularibus*, in PL 188: 1113–16.

34. See T. G. Jalland, "The Doctrine of the Parity of Ministers," *The Apostolic Ministry: Essays on the History and Theology of Episcopacy*, ed. K. Kirk (London: Hodder & Stoughton, 1947), 305–50; Joseph Lécuyer, "Aux origines de la théologie thomiste de l'épiscopat," *Gregorianum* 35 (1954): 56–89.

35. E. R. Hardy, "The Patriarchate of Alexandria: A Study in National Christianity," *Church History* 15 (1946): 81–100.
36. Ibid., 100.
37. For useful comment and bibliography, see P. J. Fedwick, *The Church and the Charisms of Leadership in Basil of Caesarea* (Toronto: Pontifical Institute of Medieval Studies, 1979); Frances Young, "Ministerial Forms and Functions in the Church Communities of the Greek Fathers," in Longenecker, *Community Formation*, 161–80. For the stress on the pastoral role of the bishop as conformed to the Good Shepherd and on his holy life in Basil and others, see Lewis J. Patsavos, "The Image of the Priest according to the Three Hierarchs," *Greek Orthodox Theological Review* 21 (1976): 41–52. On Basil's work in serving the communion of churches after the fractions caused by the Council of Nicaea, using a strong collegial exercise of his episcopal role, see Françoise Vinel, "Basile de Césarée face aux divisions de l'église d'après sa correspondence," *Revue des sciences religieuses* 81, no. 1 (2007): 79–93.
38. Gregory of Nazianzus, *Oration 43*, in Nicene and Post-Nicene Fathers, Series 2 (NPNF²), vol. 7.
39. On Gregory, see Francis Gautier, *La retraite et le sacerdoce chez Grégoire de Nazianze* (Turnhout: Brepols, 2002). For a summary and critique, see George Demacopoulos, "Leadership in the Post-Constantinian Church according to St. Gregory Nazianzen," *Louvain Studies* 30, no. 3 (2005): 214–28.
40. Young, "Ministerial Forms and Functions," 160.
41. See A. Faivre, *Naissance d'une hiérarchie: Les premières étapes du cursus clerical* (Paris: Beauchesne, 1977), 223–28; Fedwick, *Church and the Charisms*.
42. See John Chrysostom's tract in ET, *On the Priesthood* (Crestwood, NY: St. Vladimir's Seminary Press, 2006); critical edition: *Jean Chrysostome sur le sacerdoce*, introduction, critical text, translation, and notes by Anne Maris-Malingrey, Sources chrétiennes 272 (Paris: Éd. du Cerf, 1980).
43. For Chrysostom's description of the episcopal ministry and office, see esp. *On the Priesthood* 3.3–7.
44. On the harmful effects of choosing bishops badly, see ibid., 3.10, 22–30.
45. Ibid., 2.2.
46. Chrysostom, *Hom. 18 in 2 Cor.*, in PG 61:381–610.
47. For an overview of this development see Hugh Wybrew, *The Orthodox Liturgy: The Development of the Eucharistic Liturgy in the Byzantine Rite* (Crestwood, NY: St. Vladimir's Seminary Press, 1990).
48. Michel-Yves Perrin, "The Relationship between Bishops, the Church and Christian Communities in the Roman Empire of the IV Century," *Centro pro Unione: Semi-annual Bulletin* 71 (Spring 2007): 3–13.
49. Ibid., 13.
50. W. H. C. Frend, *The Rise of Christianity* (Philadelphia: Fortress, 1984); Karl P. Donfried and Peter Richardson, ed., *Judaism and Christianity in First-Century Rome* (Grand Rapids: Eerdmans, 1998); Wayne A. Meeks, *The First Urban Christians: The Social World of the Apostle Paul* (New Haven: Yale University Press, 1983); Rodney Stark, *The Rise of Christianity: A Sociologist Reconsiders History* (Princeton, NJ: Princeton University Press, 1996).
51. P. Lampe, *Die stadtrömischen Christen in den ersten beiden Jahrhunderten*, 2nd ed. (Tübingen: J. C. B. Mohr, 1989); Allen Brent, *Hippolytus and the Roman Church in the Third Century* (Leiden: Brill, 1995), 368–457; J. F. McCue, "The Roman Primacy in the Second Century," *Theological Studies* 25 (1964): 161–96; Hayes, "Christian Ministry in Three Cities," 142–48.
52. See Leo the Great, *Sermo 4: De natali ipsius* 1, in *Léon le Grand, Sermons*, translation and notes by Dom René Dolle, vol. 4, Sources chrétiennes [SC] 200 (Paris: Éd. du Cerf, 1973), 264–66; also in PL 54:143–48.

53. On the one priesthood of Christ, in which all Christians share by participation in its blessings and its offering, see Leo, *Sermones* 8.6–8, on the passion of Christ, in PL 54:159–60. Though the term is not frequent, the image of the Church as body of Christ exists in the sermons of Leo alongside that of royal priesthood.

54. On Gregory the Great, see Claude Dagens, *Saint Grégoire le Grand: Culture et expérience chrétienne* (Paris: Études augustiniennes, 1977); Jeffrey Richards, *Consul of God: The Life and Times of Gregory the Great* (London and Boston: Routledge & Kegan Paul, 1980); Carole Straw, *Gregory the Great: Perfection in Imperfection* (Berkeley: University of California Press, 1988).

55. See Peter Brown, *The Rise of Western Christendom*, 2nd ed. (Oxford: Blackwell, 2003), 207–212.

56. Pierre Cazier, *Isidore de Séville et la naissance de l'Espagne catholique*, Théologie historique 96 (Paris: Éd. du Cerf, 1994).

57. Isidore of Seville, *De ecclesiasticis officiis* 2.5–7, in PL 83:780–88.

58. René Roques, *L'univers Dionysien: Structure hiérarchique du monde selon le Pseudo-Dionysius* (Paris: Aubier, 1954).

59. See Kenan B. Osborne's treatment, *Ministry: Lay Ministry in the Roman Catholic Church, Its History and Theology* (Mahwah, NJ: Paulist Press, 1993), 163–232.

8. Second Millennium

1. Specifically on the Council of Florence, see Giuseppe Alberigo, ed., *Christian Unity: The Council of Ferrara-Florence 1438/39–1989* (Louvain: Leuven University Press, 1991).

2. André Vauchez, *The Laity in the Middle Ages: Religious Beliefs and Devotional Practices*, ed. Daniel E. Bornstein, trans. Margery J. Schneider (Notre Dame, IN, and London: University of Notre Dame Press, 1993), 5. Much of what follows is indebted to this book. See also Marie-Dominique Chenu, *Nature, Man, and Society in the Twelfth Century* (Chicago: University of Chicago Press, 1968); Yves Congar, "Laïcat au moyen âge," *Dictionnaire de spiritualité*, 17 vols. in 38 (Paris: Beauchesne, 1937–95), vol. 9, cols. 79–83.

3. On these manuals, see Jacques Le Goff, *Pour un autre Moyen Age* (Paris: Gallimard, 1977), 162–80.

4. Gérard Meersseman, *Ordo Fraternitatis: Confraternite e pietà dei laici nel medievo* (Rome: Herder, 1977).

5. André Vauchez, "L'évolution de l'idée de mission et de la pratique missionaire en occident à l'époque médiévale," in *Église et histoire de l'église en Afrique*, ed. Giuseppe Ruggieri (Paris: Beauchesne, 1988), 13–27.

6. Francis, *Regula prima* 16.6–10.

7. Robert Bireley, *The Refashioning of Catholicism, 1450–1700: A Reassessment of the Counter Reformation* (Washington, DC: Catholic University of America Press, 1999), 115–18.

8. Quoted from Mary T. Malone, *Women and Christianity*, vol. 2, *From 1000 to the Reformation* (Maryknoll, NY: Orbis Books, 2002), 118.

9. On women, their place in the Church, and their spirituality, see ibid., vol. 2; as well as Vauchez, *Laity in the Middle Ages*, 171–229.

10. See David N. Power, s.v. "Church Order," *The New Dictionary of Sacramental Worship*, ed. Peter Fink (Collegeville, MN: Liturgical Press, 1990), 212–33, with bibliography. For a description of how three important writers treat the topic of laity, see Michel Grandjean, *Laïcs dans l'église: Regards de Pierre Damien, Anselme de Cantorbéry, Yves de Chartres*, Théologie historique 97 (Paris: Beauchesne, 1994).

11. R. Didier, "L'élaboration scolastique de la théologie de l'ordre," *Bulletin du comité des études* 38/39 (1962): 423–47; A. McDevitt, "The Episcopate as Order and Sacrament on the Eve of the High Scholastic Period," *Franciscan Studies* 20 (1960): 96–148. See David N. Power, *Ministers of Christ and His Church* (London: Geoffrey Chapman, 1969), 113–24.

12. Some of this material on Bonaventure and Thomas Aquinas already appeared in David N. Power, "Theologies of Religious Life and Priesthood," in *A Concert of Charisms: Ordained Ministry in Religious Life*, ed. Paul K. Hennessy (Mahwah, NJ: Paulist Press, 1997), 71–76.

13. Bonaventure, "Opusculum XIII: Cur sanctus Franciscus novam regulam instituit," in *Opera omnia* (Quarrachi edition), 8:338.

14. Bonaventure, *Breviloquium*, Pars VI, cap. XII.

15. Thomas Aquinas, *Summa theologiae* Iia–IIae, Q. 185.

16. In the following, the principal questions considered are from *Summa theologiae* III, qq. 8 (on the grace of Christ's headship), 22 (on Christ's priesthood), 26 (on Christ's mediation), 63 (on the sacramental character), 75 (on the sacrament of confirmation).

17. For an interesting contemporary reflection on Jan Hus, see Daniel Di Domizio, "Jan Hus's *De ecclesia*, Precursor of Vatican II?" *Theological Studies* 60 (1999): 247–60.

18. On a recent visit to Prague, John Paul II sought pardon for the execution of this preacher and holy man.

19. His works on ministry are collected in *Luther's Works*, ed. Jaroslav Pelikan and Helmut Lehmann (Philadelphia: Fortress; St. Louis: Concordia, 1955–1986), vols. 39–41. For a study, see Ralph E. Smith, *Luther, Ministry, and Ordination Rites in the Early Reformation Church* (New York: Peter Lang, 1996).

20. Karin Bornkamm, *Christus-König und Priester: Das Amt Christ bei Luther im Verhältnis zur Vor- und Nachgeschichte* (Tübingen: Mohr Siebeck, 1998).

21. Chapter 9 will say more of Luther's teaching on priesthood.

22. *Luther's Works*, 45:75–129.

23. On the threefold office of Christ, see John Calvin, *Institutes* 2.15, in *Institutes of the Christian Religion*, trans. Henry Beveridge, 2 vols. (Grand Rapids: Eerdmans, 1975), 1:425–32. On the priesthood of all Christians, see *Institutes* 2.15.6 (ibid., 1:432). On ordering the ministry, see 4.2–5 (ibid., 2:315–52). A good survey of Calvin on the Church may be found in Alister McGrath, *Reformation Thought: An Introduction*, 2nd ed. (Oxford: Blackwell, 1993), 194–200.

24. For a brief consideration of the Anabaptists' place in the Reformation, see McGrath, *Reformation Thought*, 202–5.

25. The principal recognized authority today is Hubert Jedin, *Geschichte des Konzils von Trient*, 4 vols. (Freiburg: Herder, 1949).

26. Kathleen M. Comerford, "Italian Tridentine Diocesan Seminaries," *Sixteenth Century Journal* 29, no. 4 (1998): 999–1022.

27. Kenan B. Osborne, *Ministry: Lay Ministry in the Roman Catholic Church* (Mahwah, NJ: Paulist Press, 1993), 443.

28. See John W. O'Malley, "Priesthood, Ministry, and Religious Life: Some Historical and Historiographical Considerations," *Theological Studies* 49 (1988): 223–57.

29. John Wesley, Sermon 16, "The Means of Grace." The sermons were edited and published in 1872 by Thomas Jackson. They are posted by the Wesley Center Online, http://wesley.nnu.edu/John_wesley/sermons.

30. Sermon 4, "Scriptural Christianity."

31. Sermon 115, "The Ministerial Office." For a presentation of Wesley's thought on ministry, see William R. Cannon, "The Meaning of Ministry in Methodism," *Methodist History* 8, no. 1 (1969): 3–19; Linda M. Durbin, "The Nature of Ordination in Wesley's View of Ministry," *Methodist History* 9, no. 3 (1971): 3–21.

32. David J. Bosch, *Transforming Mission: Paradigm Shifts in Theology of Mission* (Maryknoll, NY: Orbis Books, 1991).

33. Andrew F. Walls, *The Missionary Movement in Christian History: Studies in the Transmission of Faith* (Edinburgh: T&T Clark; Maryknoll, NY: Orbis Books, 1996); idem, *The Cross-Cultural Process in Christian History* (Edinburgh: T&T Clark; Maryknoll, NY: Orbis Books, 2002).

34. On the theology of Philip Nicolai, see Bosch, *Transforming Mission*, 249–52.

35. For an interesting story of friction and even abiding hostility in one place, see Claire Laux, *Les théocraties missionaires en Polynésie au XIXe siècle* (Paris: L'Harmattan, 2000).

36. Walls, *Cross-Cultural Process*, 215–35.

37. Ibid., 200–201.

38. Walls, *Missionary Movement*, 111–18.

39. Ibid., 118.

40. One may not discount the instructions to the laity living amid society, from such as Francis de Salles, nor the *ars moriendi* (art of dying); but while important, this belongs to spiritual writing and not to formal theology.

41. Full consideration of this would, however, require study of the nineteenth-century social mission of Protestant churches, and on the Catholic side would require study of papal social pronouncements, taking this study too far afield.

9. Royal Priesthood

1. This author has treated this topic in David N. Power, "Priesthood in the Christian Tradition," *New Catholic Encyclopedia*, 2nd ed., 15 vols. (Washington, DC: Catholic University of America, 2003), 11:690–707.

2. Neither the Vorgrimler commentary on the documents that appeared shortly after the Council nor the history edited by Alberigo and Komonchak reflect any discussion over this distinction: Herbert Vorgrimler, ed., *Commentary on the Documents of Vatican II*, 5 vols. (New York: Herder & Herder; London: Burns & Oates, 1967–69); Giuseppe Alberigo and Joseph Komonchak, eds., *History of Vatican II*, 5 vols. (Maryknoll, NY: Orbis; Louvain: Peeters, 1995–2005).

3. John Calvin, *Institutes* 2.15, in *Institutes of the Christian Religion*, trans. Henry Beveridge, 2 vols. (Grand Rapids: Eerdmans, 1975), 1: 425–32.

4. Otto Hermann Pesch, *Das Zweite Vatikanische Konzil: Vorgeschichte—Verlauf—Ergebnisse—Nachgeschichte* (Würzburg: Echter, 1993), 180–82.

5. We find the same concern to avoid distinctions in rank or status in John Paul II when he teaches that women are to be excluded from ordination to the priesthood but that they are not lower in dignity.

6. *Encyclical Letter of John Paul II, Ecclesia de eucharistia* (Boston: Pauline Books & Media, 2003).

7. This was to exclude from true doctrine what the Council Fathers understood the Reformers to say, namely, that the Mass is only a sacrifice of praise, not one by which sins are taken away. It teaches, however, that there is no question of the Church's appeasing divine anger with sinners and leaves further explanation of sacrificial efficacy open to theological discussion. For a study of the Tridentine decree on the sacrifice of the Mass, see David N. Power, *The Sacrifice We Offer: Reinterpretation of Trent* (Edinburgh: T&T Clark, 1987), esp. 50–135.

8. Catholic Church, *Catechism of the Catholic Church* (Vatican City: Libreria Editrice Vaticana, and Mahwah, NJ: Paulist Press, 1994).

9. Benedict XVI, *Post-synodal Apostolic Exhortation Sacramentum caritatis*, official English translation (Vatican City: Libreria Editrice Vaticana, 2007).

10. United States Conference of Catholic Bishops, *General Instruction of the Roman Missal* (Washington, DC: USCCB, 2003).

11. John Paul II, *Encyclical Letter Redemptoris missio* (Boston: Pauline Books & Media, 1990), chap. 2, §§12–20.

12. John Paul II, *Ecclesia de eucharistia*; idem, *Apostolic Letter mane nobiscum Domine* (Boston: Pauline Books & Media, 2004).

13. Something has been said about this text in chapter 1 of part 3.

14. Here I follow James G. Dunn, *The Theology of Paul the Apostle* (Grand Rapids, MI, and Cambridge, UK: Eerdmans, 1998), 207–35.

15. Ibid., 214.

16. Ibid., 231.

17. Leon Morris, *The Gospel according to John* (Grand Rapids: Eerdmans, 1995), 125–30.

18. Though they speak of the new covenant, neither the conciliar document *Nostra aetate* (1965), nor the Guidelines on relations with Jews of the Vatican Commission on Relations with the Jews mentions the Letter to the Hebrews. The omission may be explained

because of the intent of both texts to accentuate the continuity of the Church with the Jewish people rather than a break.

19. Georg Gäbel, *Die Kulttheologie des Hebräerbrief: Eine exegetisch-religionsgeschichtliche Studie* (Tübingen: Mohr Siebeck, 2006), esp. 236–54.

20. We will see that, in the course of history, this vision of Christ's kingly priesthood was very much alive in patristic writings, that it was lost to view in favor of a narrower view of sacrifice and priesthood in the Middle Ages, and that it was revived in the teaching of the Reformers, especially Martin Luther.

21. Dunn, *Theology of Paul*, 543.

22. Edward Schillebeeckx, *Christ: The Experience of Jesus as Lord* (New York: Crossroad, 1980), 362.

23. Stuart G. Hall, *Doctrine and Practice in the Early Church* (Grand Rapids: Eerdmans, 1991), 32.

24. This fits with what has been shown in chapter 6 (above) about the prayer for episcopal ordination in the *Apostolic Tradition*.

25. Some pertinent texts are Origen's commentary on John's Gospel and homilies on the book of Numbers. See Origen, *Commentaires sur Saint Jean*, ed. Cécile Blanc, 5 vols., Sources chrétiennes 120 (Paris: Éd. du Cerf, 1966); idem, *Homélies sur les Nombres*, introduction and translation by André Mehat, Sources chrétiennes 29 (Paris: Éd. du Cerf, 1951).

26. As in Athanasius, *Oratio secunda contra Arianos*, in Patrologia graeca [PG], 26:146–322; and Cyril of Alexandria, *In epistolam ad Hebraeos*, in PG 74:967.

27. Cyril of Alexandria, *In Ioannis evangelium* 12.20.22–23, in PG 74:710–711.

28. Ibid.: "Postquam magna dignitate apostolatus claros effecit, divinorumque altarium . . . dispensatores ac sacerdotes constituit, statim eos sanctificat, manifesto insufflato Spiritu eis largiens . . . veluti refingiens naturam hominis ad supernaturalem vim atque gloriam." See also Cyril, *In ep. ii ad Corinthios* 1.21–22, in PG 74:922–23; idem, *In ep. ad Hebraeos* 3.1, in PG 74:970–71.

29. On Chrysostom, see John Zizioulas, "Ministry and Communion," *Being as Communion* (Crestwood, NY: St. Vladimir's Seminary Press, 1985), 230–31.

30. E.g., John Chrysostom, *Homily XIV in ep. ad Hebraeos*, in PG 63:329–36; idem, *Hom. IV in ep. ii ad Corinthios*, in PG 61:417–28.

31. On the one priesthood of Christ in which all Christians share by participation in its blessings and its offering, see Leo the Great, *Sermones* 8.6–8, on the passion of Christ, in Patrologia latina [PL] 54:340–42. Though the term is not frequent, the image of the Church as body of Christ exists in the sermons of Leo alongside that of royal priesthood.

32. Leo the Great, *Sermo 21*, on the nativity.

33. Leo the Great, *Sermo 58*, on the passion of Christ.

34. Leo the Great, *Sermo 3*, on the anniversary of his ordination as Bishop of Rome.

35. Veronense liturgy, 1250; see L. C. Mohlberg, ed., *Sacramentarium Veronense* (Rome: Herder, 1956).

36. For the historical development, see Marcel Metzger, *History of the Liturgy: The Major Stages* (Collegeville, MN: Liturgical Press, 1997), 113–21.

37. On this, for example, see Amalar of Metz, *Liber officialis*, in *Amalarii episcopi opera liturgica omnia*, ed. Jean-Michel Hanssens, 3 vols. (Vatican City: Bibliotheca Apostolica Vaticana, 1948–50), 2:106, 108; and Paschasius Radbertus, *De corpore et sanguine Domini*, in Corpus Christianorurn: Continuatio mediaevalis 16 (Turnhout: Brepols, 1969).

38. Odo of Cambrai, *Expositio in Canonem Missae*, in PL 160:1053–70.

39. Jean Leclerq, "The Monastic Priesthood according to the Ancient Medieval tradition," *Studia monastica* 3 (1961): 137–55; idem, "The Priesthood for Monks," *Monastic Studies* 3 (1965): 53–85.

40. See, e.g., *Ordines Romani XLV, XLVI, XLVII*, in Michel Andrieu, *Les ordines Romani du haut moyen âge*, vol. 4 (Louvain: Spicilegium Lovaniense, 1965).

41. H. E. J. Cowdrey, "The Peace and the Truce of God in the Eleventh Century," *Past and Present* 46 (1970): 42–67.

42. See the letter of October 30, 1198, *Epistula ad Acerbum consulem Florentinum,* in PL 216:1186.

43. Thomas Aquinas, *De regimine principum ad regem Cypri,* ed. Joseph Mathis (Turin and Rome: Marietti, 1948).

44. See the study by Karin Bornkamm, *Christus-König und Priester: Das Amt Christ bei Luther in Verhältnis zur Vor- und Nachgeschichte* (Tübingen: Mohr Siebeck, 1998).

45. Martin Luther, *Luther's Works,* ed. Jaroslav Pelikan and Helmut Lehmann (Philadelphia: Fortress; St. Louis: Concordia, 1955–1986), 31:327–78.

46. Ibid., 36:11–26.

47. We have already mentioned (in chap. 8) how Luther resolved the relation between *sacerdotium* and *imperium.*

48. Calvin, *Institutes* 2.15.

49. For this school, see the texts collected in ET, William H. Thompson, ed., *Bérulle and the French School: Selected Writings,* trans. Lowell M. Glendon (New York: Paulist Press, 1989); esp. see Pierre de Bérulle, "A Letter on the Priesthood," in ibid., 183–85.

50. Saint John Eudes, *The Priest: His Dignity and Obligations,* trans. William Leo Murphy (New York: Kennedy, 1947), 8.

51. John Paul II, *Mane nobiscum Domine* §15.

52. John Paul II, *Ecclesia de eucharistia* §20.

53. Pontifical Biblical Commission, *The Interpretation of the Bible in the Church* (Vatican City: Libreria Editrice Vaticana, 1994), IV.A.2.

54. Ibid., IV.C.1.

55. John Paul II, "Post-synodal Apostolic Exhortation *Pastores dabo vobis,*" *Origins* 21 (1992): 717–59; chap. 2 is pertinent here.

56. See the collection of essays, John Zizioulas, *Being as Communion* (Crestwood, NY: St Vladimir's Seminary Press, 1985), esp. "Ministry and Communion," 209–46. Even before the influence of Zizioulas, writers such as Edward Schillebeeckx used the language of relationship to appropriate the tradition of the sacramental character, as in his book *Christ: The Sacrament of Encounter with God* [first Dutch ed., 1959], trans. from 3rd, rev. Dutch ed. (London: Sheed & Ward, 1963).

10. Presence and Representation

1. Vatican II, Decree on the Ministry and Life of Presbyters (*Presbyterium ordinis* 1965, http://www.vatican.va/archive/hist_councils/ii_vatican_council/documents/vat-ii_decree_19651207_presbyterorum-ordinis_en.html).

2. John Paul II, "Apostolic Exhortation *Pastores Gregis,*" *Origins* 33, no. 22 (2003): 353–92.

3. Ignatius of Antioch and the Syrian document the *Didaskalia* are noted for their presentation of the bishop as head of the family household and thus as image of the Father.

4. Quoting *Lumen gentium* (*LG,* 1964) §8, Pope John Paul spoke of the almost tangible presence of Christ in the Synod of Bishops as one who lived in poverty and suffered persecution. This leads him to say that a bishop has to be a *vir pauper,* who spends his life in the service of the poor.

5. John Paul II, *The Church in America, Ecclesia in America: Post-synodal Apostolic Exhortation* (Washington, DC: USCCB, 1999).

6. The preparatory document for the CELAM meeting in Aparecida, mentioned earlier, refers to this passage and says: "In the life of communion with the Lord and with his Church, the presbyter signifies in the midst of the community the presence of Jesus, who gathers his people together." The original reads (§74), "En esta vida de comunión con el Señor y con la Iglesia, el presbitero significa en el seno de su comunidad la presencia de Jesús que congrega a su pueblo."

7. http://www.vatican.va/ (accessed December 24, 2007).

8. John Paul II, *Encyclical Letter Ecclesia de eucharistia* (Boston: Pauline Books & Media, 2003).

9. Benedict XVI, *Postsynodal Apostolic Exhortation Sacramentum Caritatis* (Vatican City: Libreria Editrice Vaticana, 2007).

10. The words are from the *Catechism of the Catholic Church* (Vatican City: Libreria Editrice Vaticana, and Mahwah, NJ: Paulist Press, 1994), §1548.

11. As we know, this ecclesial character of the Eucharist has been an important consideration in bilateral and multilateral confessional dialogues. Given the negative approach to other Western churches in the questions attached to the *lineamenta* for synodal discussion, it is heartening to find this concern with dialogue and communion in the postsynodal exhortation.

12. Benedict XVI, "Homily at Chrism Mass," *L'Osservatore Romano*, weekly edition in English, April 2007, 2–3. Also *Notitiae* 487–88 (March–April 2007): 160–71.

13. "The Sacrament of Order in the Sacramental Structure of the Church with Particular Reference to the Importance of the Apostolic Succession for the Sanctification and Unity of the People of God," in *The Quest for Unity*, ed. John Borelli and John H. Erickson (Crestwood, NY: St Vladimir's Seminary Press, 1996), 131–55.

14. Documents from the Anglican–Roman Catholic dialogue, Lutheran–Roman Catholic dialogue, and the Faith and Order Paper on Baptism, Eucharist, and Ministry (BEM) of the Faith and Order Commission of the World Council of Churches may be found in *Growth in Agreement: Reports and Agreed Statements of Ecumenical Conversations on a World Level*, ed. Harding Meyer and Lukas Vischer (Geneva: WCC; New York: Paulist Press, 1984), 78–87, 190–214, 248–74, 465–503.

15. *The Nature and Mission of the Church: A Stage on the Way to a Common Statement*, Faith and Order Paper 198 (Geneva: WCC, 2005), §§24–33.

16. Augustine, *Sermo 46*, in Corpus Christianorum: Series Latina [CCSL] (Turnhout: Brepols, 1953–), 41:529–70.

17. Augustine, *Sermo 47*, in CCSL 41:572–604.

18. Augustine, *Sermo 46*, in CCSL 41:529–30: "Unum quod christiani sumus, alterum quod praepositi sumus. Illud quod christiani sumus, propter nos est; quod praepositi sumus, propter vos est." Also, *Sermo 47*, CCSL 41:573.

19. Augustine, *Sermo 46*, in CCSL:555: "Ego pasco, quia cui commendabat oves suas quasi alter alteri, unum secum facere volebat, et sic ei oves commendare, ut esset ille caput, ille figuram corporis portaret, id est, ecclesiae, et tamquam sponsus et sponsa essent duo in carne una." Here we see how the bride-bridegroom imagery is used to express the union between Christ and the shepherds of the Church, who represent the Church itself.

20. Augustine, "The Good of Marriage," chap. 18 in *The Fathers of the Church*, vol. 15 (New York: Fathers of the Church, 1955), 36. Original text in *PL* 46, 375.

21. John Chrysostom, *On the Priesthood* 3.4.35–45.

22. Augustine, *Sermo 227*, in Sources chrétiennes 116 (Paris: Éd. du Cerf, 1966), 234–42; English translation in *The Eucharist*, ed. Daniel J. Sheerin (Wilmington, DE: Michael Glazier, 1986), 96–99.

23. For what follows, see David N. Power, "Representing Christ in Community and Sacrament," in *Being a Priest Today*, ed. Donald J. Goergen (Collegeville, MN: Liturgical Press, 1992), 97–123.

24. As will be seen later, 2 Cor 5:20 is more important on representing Christ.

25. For the increasing dramatization of the eucharistic liturgy in Byzantine commentary from Germanus of Constantinople onward, see Hugh Wybrew, *The Orthodox Liturgy* (Crestwood, NY: St Vladimir's Seminary Press, 1990), 103–44, with a comparative table on 182–83. In the West, allegorization is associated chiefly with Honorius of Autun, Rupert of Deutz, Johannes Beleth, Sicard of Cremona and William Durand. For a summary of what this meant in practice, see Lee Palmer Wandel, *The Eucharist in the Reformation: Incarnation and Liturgy* (New York: Cambridge University Press, 2006), 14–45.

26. Augustine, "Good of Marriage," chap. 24 in *Fathers of the Church*, 15:47–48.

27. M. Andrieu, *Le Pontifical Romain du haut moyen-âge*, vol. 3, Studi e Testi 88 (Vatican City: Vatican Polyglot Press, 1940), 339.

28. A survey of the post-Vatican II state of the question is given by George H. Tavard, "Ordination of Women," *The New Dictionary of Sacramental Worship*, ed. Peter E. Fink (Collegeville, MN: Liturgical Press, 1990), 911–15.

29. Thomas Aquinas: "It is not possible for eminent status to be signified in the female sex, because a woman has the status of subjection."

30. See Richard Cross, "On the Polity of God: The Ecclesiology of Duns Scotus," *International Journal for the Study of the Christian Church* 7, no. 1 (2007): 29–45.

31. Aimé Martimort, "La question du service des femmes à l'autel," *Notitiae* 16 (1980): 8–16.

32. Wandel, *Eucharist in the Reformation.*

33. Though liturgical renewal in the Catholic Church has done much to restore communal celebration and to place the actions of the ordained minister in this context, it still upholds the right to celebrate without the presence of the faithful, since even then it is an act of Christ and of the Church (Code of Canon Law = Codex Iuris Canonici [CIC], canon 904).

34. In the Faith and Order Paper 198, *koinonia* has been accentuated: *The Nature and Mission of the Church: A Stage on the Way to a Common Statement* (Geneva: WCC, 2005), §§24–33.

35. Edward Schillebeeckx, *The Eucharist* (London: Burns & Oates, 1968; repr., 2005), esp. 122–52.

36. These terms are used in the 2003 revision of the General Instruction of the Roman Missal, §§2 and 5.

37. Laurent Touze, *Célibat sacerdotal et théologie nuptiale de l'ordre* (Rome: Edizioni Università della Santa Croce, 2002), 119–84.

38. Thomas Hopko, "Presbyter/Bishop: A Masculine Ministry," in *Women and the Priesthood*, ed. Thomas Hopko (Crestwood, NY: St. Vladimir's Seminary Press, 1999), 139–64; Nonna Verna Harrison, "Orthodox Arguments against the Ordination of Women as Priests," in ibid., 165–88.

39. Élisabeth Behr-Sigel, *Le ministère des femmes dans l'église* (Paris: Éd. du Cerf, 1987).

40. At a general audience on February 14, 2007, Benedict XVI spoke of the collaboration between women and men in the life and mission of the Church, mentioning the women who belonged in the circle of Jesus, Mary "apostle to the apostles," those who were house leaders or prophets in the early Church, and those whom Paul calls collaborators in the work of the gospel; www.vatican.va/holy_father/benedict_xvi/audiences/2007/documents/hf_ben-xvi_aud_2007021_en.html (accessed March 4, 2007).

41. On the use of household codes in the setting of the letter, see Margaret Y. MacDonald, *Colossians and Ephesians*, Sacra pagina 17 (Collegeville, MN: Liturgical Press, 2000), 324–42.

42. This has only recently been translated into English: Hans Urs von Balthasar, *Love Alone Is Credible* (San Francisco: Ignatius, 2005).

43. Hans Urs von Balthasar, "The Uninterrupted Tradition of the Church," in a publication of the Congregation for the Doctrine of the Faith, *From "Inter Insigniores" to "Ordinatio Sacerdotalis": Documents and Commentaries* (Washington, DC: USCC, 1996), 99–106; ibid., "Office in the Church," in *Explorations in Theology*, vol. 2, *Spouse of the Word* (San Francisco: Ignatius, 1991), 81–142; idem, "Priestly Existence," in ibid., 373–420; idem, "The Mass, a Sacrifice of the Church?" in *Explorations in Theology*, vol. 3, *Creator Spirit* (San Francisco: Ignatius, 1993), 185–244.

44. Von Balthasar, "Uninterrupted Tradition," 104.

45. Von Balthasar, "Office in the Church," 117.

46. Von Balthasar, "The Mass," 225.

47. Ibid., 239.

48. Hans Urs von Balthasar, *The Glory of the Lord*, vol. 1 (San Francisco: Ignatius, 1982), 485–86.

49. Sarah Coakley, "Woman at the Altar: Cosmological Disturbance or Gender Subversion?" *Anglican Theological Review* 86 (Winter 2004): 75–93.

50. More is said of this in the final chapter (chap. 11).

11. Mission, Ministry, Leadership, Order

1. Giuseppe Alberigo, *A Brief History of Vatican II* (Maryknoll, NY: Orbis Books, 2006), 128.
2. This is indeed a topic of magisterial teaching that continues to be articulated, as in John Paul II, *Sollicitudo rei socialis* (1987), §§27–33. It has also been a concern of different special synods, e.g., for Africa, Asia, Oceania, the Americas.
3. Paul VI, *Evangelii nuntiandi* (1975), §§21–23.
4. The matter is put very aptly by Douglas John Hall: "Perhaps if ecumenism were less concerned about the union of tired, old institutions and more concerned about the calling of the Christian movement in the world as a whole, ecumenicity itself would be more vital to all who take this faith with some degree of seriousness"; Douglas John Hall, "Finding Our Way into the Future," in *The Princeton Lectures on Youth, Church, and Culture 2006* (Princeton, NJ: Institute for Youth Ministry, Princeton Theological Seminary, 2006), 27, http://www.ptsem.edu/iym/lectures/2006/Hall-Finding.pdf.
5. René Rémond, "L'évolution de l'engagment politique des chrétiens," *Lumière et vie* 273 (January–March 2007): 19–30; Pierre-Yves Materne et Serge Maveq, "La question du politique depuis Vatican II," in ibid., 31–46.
6. Hervé Legrand, "Forty Years Later: What Has Become of Our Ecclesiological Reforms Envisaged by Vatican II?" *Concilium* 2005, no. 4:57–72. Some who knew the Council have been heard to remark that in hindsight the bishops might have done better to focus attention on the principle of subsidiarity, since this is what in effect has been denied in recent decades.
7. In conversation, Orthodox Churches make the point that all structure should facilitate and grow from the reality of a eucharistic community.
8. Benedict XVI, *Apostolic Exhortation Sacramentum Caritatis* (Washington, DC: USCCB, 2007), §75.
9. While one may not quarrel with this doctrine (of distinction in essence) when situated in a fuller context of ecclesial understanding, it is not appropriate to make it the code word for all ministerial ordering.
10. It is true that when this distinction is pursued, the element of community is upheld by placing the accent on communion: the communion in faith and mission of all with and under a presbyter, with and under the diocesan bishop, and finally with and under the Bishop of Rome. However, the sense of working together in discerning and enacting what is a common and communal mission is overshadowed.
11. These insights are largely due to the writings of, and conversation with, Bishop Fritz Lobinger of Aliwali in South Africa.
12. Some principles enumerated by Pope John Paul II, *Ut unum sint*, have already been mentioned.
13. See www.vatican.va/roman_curia/pontifical_councils/christuni/weeks-prayer-doc/rc_doc_christuni_doc20060703_week-prayer-2007.en.html (accessed September 1, 2007).
14. The influence of bishops and theologians from mission countries at the Council on the section dealing with this is recognized by Josef Jungmann, "Commentary on the Constitution on the Liturgy," in *Commentary on the Documents of Vatican II*, ed. Herbert Vorgrimler, vol. 1 (New York: Herder & Herder; London: Burns & Oates, 1967), 49–50.
15. The writer is perfectly aware of the challenge to the scriptural canon by certain Protestant, feminist, and postcolonial readings and that these have to be given attention, but this is not the place for that exercise.
16. There seems to be a strong temptation, especially in religious orders and communities, to have ordinations that show no reference to the particular service to be asked of the candidate nor even to a community of baptized that is sending them for a mission. It seems to be a time to give scope to family piety when in truth family piety cannot give ordination its due context.
17. As mentioned earlier, in both Armenia and Ethiopia, when Christianity was made the national religion, some priestly practices of cultural and religious heritage were retained,

but with an effort to harmonize these practices with the proclamation of the primary place of the eucharistic sacrifice.

18. See David N. Power, *Love without Calculation: A Reflection on Divine Kenosis* (New York: Crossroad, 2005), 167–72.

19. Jon Sobrino, *The Principle of Mercy: Taking the Crucified People from the Cross* (Maryknoll, NY: Orbis Books, 1994).

20. This was written before the notification on some of the works of Sobrino by the Congregation of the Doctrine of the Faith in March 2007. There is no need to change anything of what is said here.

21. Bénézet Bujo, *African Theology in Its Social Context* (Nairobi: St. Paul Publications Africa, 1992), 92–114. See also A. Ramazani Bishiwende, *Église-famille-de-Dieu: Esquisse d'écclésiologie Africaine* (Paris: L'Harmattan, 2001); Charles Nyamiti, "The Eucharist as Mystical Affinal Encounter in God's Family: The Church," *African Christian Studies* 16, no. 4 (2000): 44–60; 17, no. 1 (2001): 87–117; 18, no. 2 (2002): 5–56.

22. Bujo, *African Theology*, 97.

23. Kwame Bediako, *Christianity in Africa: The Renewal of a Non-Western Religion* (Edinburgh: Edinburgh University Press, 1995), 234–51.

24. Agbonkhianmeghe E. Orobator, *From Crisis to Kairos: The Mission of the Church in the Time of HIV/AIDS, Refugees, and Poverty* (Nairobi: Pauline Publications Africa, 2005). Orobator is himself author of *The Church as Family: African Ecclesiology in Its Social Context* (Nairobi: Pauline Publications Africa, 2000).

25. See Buti Tlhagale, "God, Ancestors, 'Izangoma' [medicine men/women], and the Eucharist," in *Inculturation in the South African Context*, by various authors (Nairobi: Pauline Publications Africa, 2000), 38–53; idem, "The Gospel Seed on African Soil," *Worldwide* 16/2 (February/March 2006): 13–18; Meinrad Hebga, *Sorcellerie et prière de délivrance* (Paris: Présence Africaine, 1992); F. Kabasele Lumbala, "Celebrating the Solace of the Sick," in *Celebrating Jesus Christ in Africa. Liturgy and Inculturation* (Maryknoll, NY: Orbis Books, 1998), 76–85.

26. Cécé Kolié, "Jesus Healer?" in *Faces of Jesus in Africa*, ed. Robert Schreiter (Maryknoll, NY: Orbis Books, 1991), 148.

27. As already cited.

28. Elizabeth Janeway, *Powers of the Weak* (New York: Knopf, 1981).

29. See chap. 1 of this work.

30. Orobator, *From Crisis to Kairos*.

31. *Ad gentes* (1965) §10: "If the Church is to be in a position to offer all people the mystery of salvation and the life brought by God, then it must implant itself among these groups in the same way that Christ by his incarnation committed himself to the particular social and cultural circumstances of those people among whom he lived."

INDEX

Scripture Index